OUR CONTEMPORARY CIVILIZATION

A STUDY OF THE
TWENTIETH CENTURY RENAISSANCE

BY

ROSCOE LEWIS ASHLEY
Author of *The American Federal State*, etc.

NEW YORK
HENRY HOLT AND COMPANY

Printed in the United States of America

To

M. P. A.

PREFACE

A changing civilization is intriguing because it is dynamic. Its transitions, which are making many things new, are not easily traced or analyzed. Static life can be classified and catalogued; dynamic defies diagnosis. In a study of the past, trends and tendencies are discoverable, because we know results as well as causes. An attempted analysis of the present gives us partial views of existing conditions and problems; but the picture as a whole lacks depth and perspective. Too often we have a single image when we need a view both stereoscopic and comprehensive. Even better would be a composite from several angles, taken at many times.

The twentieth century offers a series of kaleidoscopic changes following one another with bewildering rapidity. Compared with the late nineteenth century, the present often gives us more contrasts than similarities. Not only business and science are diverging far from accepted norms but religion and democracy are breaking new paths. Social habits are being re-molded on models at variance with sanctioned social patterns. Many centrifugal forces are at work, sweeping mankind from its accustomed orbit.

The challenge of the new age calls us to seek knowledge of the conditions and problems of this new renaissance and the dilemma of America, one chiefly of industrialism and of capitalism. Because our civilization is not an integrated product, for no one principle underlies it all, it may be easy to make any necessary reorganization. The great variety of American institutions and systems may include ideas and principles out of which we may possibly build a new social order. In this book a few American experiences have been selected, a few problems cited, a few suggestions offered. Inevitably the analysis is limited to materials organized to explain the American problem rather than to cover western civilization. Intentionally industrial capitalism and democracy are over-stressed. Of our outstanding institutions, these are primary, the one economic, the other political. Out of them in a real degree any new social order probably must be reconstructed. Yet each is in a critical condition. For democracy a severe series of treatments may be adequate. In the case of industrial capitalism nothing short of several major operations will probably suffice.

With hesitation, after many years of serious study in which his indebtedness has constantly mounted, the writer offers these analyses and comments. There cannot be full agreement on the character of changes or the evaluation of new conditions. This volume represents an honest attempt to diagnose a momentous reorganization that affects us all and will be redirected somewhat according to our courage, understanding and foresight.

The synthesis is necessarily inadequate, for none can discover the character of any new order that may emerge from the old. Yet even here the study attempts a real integration. Each part is considered, selectively and carefully, by itself and for itself; but the selection of materials and the treatment are decided less by the needs and conditions in that field than by the fundamental changes in the whole contemporary scene. Is it not possible, even if not probable, that out of dilemma, depression, and disaster may come a new America, reborn from the best of the old, a Twentieth-Century Renaissance? The opportunity and the obligation are ours. Will we let them go by default?

The author has received aid and suggestions from many friends and sources. He wishes particularly to acknowledge his appreciation to Dr. Walter S. Adams of the Mt. Wilson Observatory, Professor Edward McChesney Sait of Pomona College, Dr. George H. Ashley of Harrisburg, Pennsylvania, and Dr. W. H. Kimmel, Editor of *The Social Studies*. He is especially indebted to his wife, whose help and cooperation have been constant.

Pasadena, California,   R. L. A.
August, 1935.

CONTENTS

                        vii

PART II

THE DILEMMA OF INDUSTRIAL CAPITALISM

PART III

PUBLIC REORGANIZATION IN A NEW AGE

CONTENTS

CONTENTS

INTRODUCTION

Is man civilized? In what respects is civilization in mod- ern times similar to that of past ages, different from any previous type of human development? Is civilization a matter of changed human nature, of conquest over nature, of products or by-products of something which man has acquired or invented? Are we civilized to the degree to which we have become dependent upon the things which we call our civilization? Are we superior to our predecessors because of abundance of the things which we have or because of the quality of our possessions, because of the difference of the level at which we live or in the capacity to think out our problems more satisfactorily than did our ancestors?

What is civilization? Does it consist of machines and of power, of skyscrapers and of railroads, of homes and of apartments, of electricity and of radios, of libraries and public schools, of alternating work and play periods, of music, art, literature? Is it chiefly an affair of bigger and better groups, the nation instead of the tribe, the billion-dollar corporation instead of the shop; or is civilization primarily a matter of culture?

Many definitions of civilization have been offered by various writers or thinkers. Many of these stress the fact that civilization is the attainment of material achievement, perfected group organization, high cultural levels. But civilization is far more than that. It represents a balance between its three most important elements: material, organization, and culture. If these are perfectly balanced, we get a well-rounded type. But they never are. In successive periods and places first one then another element comes to dominate the others. The Greeks were far ahead of any other ancient people; some think ahead of any other race that has ever

1

lived. But their material civilization was in no wise comparable with ours. The Hebrews achieved little except in the field of high religious and moral stature; but their contribution to the race is wonderful and lasting. In the development of civilization leadership may count more than public coöperation. Shall we then measure civilization by the mountain peaks of the few or by the high plateaus of general living and accomplishment? Is not universality of standards more important than the attainments of the few? How can we call a people civilized unless the civilization is of the whole people?

What of values and standards? How do they enter in? Certainly no people who overvalue physical comforts and the material things of the world can hope to be rated high in an appraisement of their civilization. Will the money-madness of modern America condemn us to a low place in the galaxy of civilized nations? Because many of us have no other deity than the almighty dollar, shall our standards and our high regard for material things place us low when civilizations are judged? If the standards of the group do not measure up to those of the individual; if the corporation which has blessed us with its multifold products leaves us a curse because it has no soul; if our nations practice trickery and dishonesty and have no moral standards of what is right or wrong in gaining unfair advantage and in taking human life, can we count modern civilization a real success?

Shall we say that the savage, who is indifferent to creature comforts, and is appreciative of the beauty of nature, is uncivilized, and that the over-fed plutocrat, dependent upon comforts and luxuries, indifferent to the needs of neighbors and the cry of the submerged, represents the best of twentieth-century civilization? How much sacrifice and service must be made part of the new life and culture? If religion plays a smaller part in modern life than in ancient, shall we pretend that we really have risen above religious needs? Shall we not ask of ourselves genuine spiritual triumphs over self? Shall we not demand of the group an understanding, an appreciation and an apprehension of spiritual values before we call ourselves civilized?

It is sometimes useful to analyze a subject like civilization into its elements, even though we cannot synthesize them into that complexity which we call civilization. For practical purposes it may be useful to group elements under first, material and economic; second, group organization, development and interrelations; and third, cultural elements.

Elements of civilization

Two reasons explain why we give first consideration to MATERIAL AND ECONOMIC ELEMENTS. In the history of the race *material "culture"* [1] *preceded the development by human beings of any other form of civilization.* Man may have lived in groups before he had tools, because his pre-human ancestors were so grouped, but no animal or group of animals was ever a tool maker, or a tool user. Secondly, a study of the conditions out of which a new civilization or culture develops shows that occupation is likely to predetermine the type of group organization that is developed and possibly the nature of the culture achieved by that people.

To what extent does material and economic civilization determine what kind of organization and culture we shall have? Was the use of the small flint knife a reason for the vast superiority of Mousterian "culture" over that of Chellean and pre-Chellean times? Had Magdalenian man climbed still higher because bone gave him a material more delicate and more adaptable than flint to a much greater variety of needs? Did the Babylonians and the Egyptians start the world on its first historical civilization because metal replaced stone in tool making? Now that tools could be made quickly and successfully, with a capacity for work impossible in prehistoric times, was the result huge pyramids, fine art, a really spiritual religion? Will new sources of modern power pave the way for living in better as well as larger groups; will the leisure made possible or enforced by the productivity of

---

[1] In this book "culture" is little used in the sociological sense of a group of social "complexes," those in turn being sets of group habits or action patterns. Outside of certain chapters, especially IV and X, it is contrasted with materialism.

the Machine Age show itself in better preparation to understand as well as to live, and give us better music, finer literature, and higher ethical standards than were the possessions
of Roman or Babylonian?[2]

GROUP ORGANIZATION, a second set of elements of civilization, is older than man's first material achievements. In the
upward struggle of humanity the general tendency has been
for small groups to become larger, families to become clans,
clans tribes, tribes nations. Will the race for size end where
we find it today, or will each continent become a huge nation?
Or will world organization of a political type be the ultimate product? Comparing political groups with economic
and social we find many similar characteristics. The day of
the tribe could not give us big business. Practically all ancient peoples had social solidity because of the great importance attached to the group, little to the individual. This
was probably a protective device—internal to make all persons conform to the standards of that society, external to

[2] The following chart may be useful for reference.

HISTORIC PERIODS

Recent and Modern	A. D. 1453 (1600, 1715, 1789)—
(Renaissance and Reformation)	
Medieval	A. D. 376 (476, 800)—1300 (1453 etc.)
Ancient	B. C. 3400—A. D. 376 (476, 800)

PREHISTORIC EPOCHS

Period	Culture or Race	Tools or Techniques
NEOLITHIC	Semi-modern	Pottery, weaving, agri-culture, grazing, etc.
PALEOLITHIC		
LATER OR UPPER		
Magdalenian	Art, etc.	Fine bone tools, etc.
Solutrean ⎫	Earliest men of Homo Sapiens	Improved tools, etc.
Aurignacian ⎭	species	
EARLIER		
Mousterian	Neanderthal race	Small flint tools, burials
Acheulean	Unknown race	Good, large flint tools, fire
Chellean	Unknown race	Fair, large flint tools
PRE-PALEOLITHIC		
Pre-Chellean	Unknown race	Poor, large flint tools
Earlier but very long epochs	Unknown race	Beginnings of tools

give a more solid front against enemies. Modern unity and solidarity is not achieved so easily. *Interrelationships must be established* not only between a local government with the state and the state with the nation, or between the manufacturer, the wholesaler and the retailer, but between industry and railroads, between government and big business, between the public and those who create its wealth or who decide its policies. Nations formerly claimed absolute sovereignty; but Belgium had no choice of peace or war on the 4th of August, 1914; nor could the United States very well keep out of the international military struggle in 1917.

In estimating elements of civilization what types of CULTURE are to be considered most important for mankind? What shall be the standard of measurement by which we determine degrees of civilization beyond one that is chiefly a material success? By what rule shall we try to ascertain our cultural stature? The hallmark of the dollar cannot possibly help us here. If our ideal were size, we should probably glorify huge group organization as more important than economic achievement or any kind of music or religion. If it were speed, we should necessarily sacrifice art and literature, which require time and thought.

Culture has not been acquired by main strength, as material civilization may have been, or by virtue of numbers, as group organization may have developed. Like industry, it has had its techniques, such as the use of group institutions. Cultural heritage has been acquired in each generation by imitation. The arts are cultural; but the acquisition of culture has been an art not found by indifference but often secured at great pains by careful labor, aroused imagination, and vigorous thought. It capitalizes human emotions other than the instinct of acquisitiveness, and starts with human association, seizes or creates life interests and aspirations and values that cannot be measured by commercial or conventional yardsticks.

Concentration upon general material advance or upon group development has tended to prevent *intensive* improvement of any other element of civilization or any special type of culture. More often the reverse has been true; and concentration on some limited phase of one element of civilization has dominated the civilization of that period or people. Few historic civilizations have been well balanced. Yet it is probable that the few which have made real contributions to the upward struggle of humanity would have contributed less than they did, had they been better rounded and less specialized. The religion of the Hebrews was a contribution scarcely equaled by that of any other ancient people, and yet we would not rate high their civilization as one of the world's greatest civilizations. The Arabian attention to certain forms of science and mathematics leaves us their debtors, although it is rather doubtful whether their cultural success in those lines placed them in the van of their age or gave them a worthwhile civilization.

The Greeks made many contributions in the fields of science, of art, of literature, of government, and of many other cultural fields. But their advance in science never raised them above the low comfort level of their contemporaries nor did their skill in government enable them to form political groups large enough to influence world civilization. It was the *character* of their *ideas* and the *quality* of their *thought* which piled so high our indebtedness to them.

Shall we accept the thesis of Spengler that civilization is on the decline? If we do, shall we follow his idea that the decline consists largely in worshiping economic success, and subordinating to that not the society which creates it or benefits by it, but the *autocratic state* or political organization which business has thrust out of the limelight? Shall we agree with the pessimist philosophers who think that we have sold a spiritual birthright for a materialist inheritance? Or are we optimistic, believing that God is in His Heaven because all is right with our machine world? Shall we agree with those critics of present culture who believe we are just at the threshold of a new and better era, with a newer and finer civilization than anything the world has known? Whatever theory we accept, or use without accepting, what are the backgrounds of Americans in general? With what ideas, attitudes, and complexes do they plunge into the maelstrom of a changing world with its special problems brought into high relief by a prolonged world-wide depression?

America has the heritage of the race, remolded in a plastic environment, and redirected by a spirit of aggressive enterprise. Whatever we have borrowed from the past has been chiefly unconscious. New things appeal to us as to the Athenians. Our standards may stress difference rather than improvement, our aim size rather than quality. Our frontier forefathers exercised independence and a rather ruthless disregard of the rights of others, because they were not closely associated with others. Some of these traits have come down to us as precious heritage, and we, in a totally different environment, demand independence as our right. On a geographical frontier they claimed the right to take what they found. We, on the *frontier of civilization*, at least until the present, have been dynamic and aggressive. In our internal affairs the fate of the unfortunate and the "hindmost" has not seemed to concern us. In the twentieth century as in the eighteenth, individualism has seemed an American birthright.

America's problem in a dynamic world

Times have changed more than our attitudes. "Splendid isolation" was the American motto or ideal within the memory of many still living; but *"splendid isolation" is a trapper concept of national self-sufficiency.* Such a frontier ideal was possible in the America of the last century. But *in this twentieth-century world it will probably yield to international coöperation and world-mindedness.* In a real sense the day of isolation, personal and regional, may be past. But the fact that our fathers, long after the trapper stage of American experience, believed in isolation and used it, has left us with age-long social habits and ideals which have not always been remodelled in any real twentieth-century American style, whether the latest or the most honored.

America is a strange mixture of age and youth, of radical and Tory ideas, of selfishness and altruism. Our boasts to the contrary, we love tradition as it was beloved by our British ancestors. We are not abandoning it as readily as England has been doing. Direct thinking and straight speaking are our ideals. Yet it does not seem strange that the land of liberty and democracy should have the greatest inequalities and one of the most powerful aristocracies in human experience. The paradox of poverty in plenty is not more a paradox than many others we have, some economic, but often political or social. If we saw some of these more clearly than we do, we should no doubt be more ready to remove them; but the American problem is a different one. Living in a changing world, we expect to discover inconsistencies and encounter dilemmas. We should wish to unearth lags that make transitions in civilization incomplete and unsatisfactory. Dynamic societies must grow, and the unevenness of growth demands study and intelligent experimentation toward the solution.

A changing civilization awakens the interest and calls to the deepest interests of the true American. As our forefathers met the risks and dangers of the frontier, we look eagerly to a future that brings change and opportunities. If a crisis presses on us, we may not ask, "Do we know what it is, what it portends?" but "what shall we do?" If necessary, will we sacrifice old systems to meet new needs? That may not be enough. Have we the courage to do what it may be necessary for us to attempt? How well are we fitted by experience and by national character to face the future and its possibilities? The faith that conquered the wilderness need not falter before economic and social mountains. "I will" is not the monopoly of our greatest inland city, alone. Fear of the future, or of what the future may bring, should not make failure probable.

If our problem were simply to escape from older American types of thought, we should eventually slough off those ideas. This would naturally be so because old and new do not work very well together, and the new always must sooner or later be made to fit into the social environment, as well as the physical environment, in which it exists. For example, we have lost equality because equality is not possible in a highly developed society. Frequently we seem to have lost liberty also, although we have tried to keep liberty without realizing that what we wanted to keep was destroying equality.

A reason for these changes and difficulties has been the shift from country to city, which came inevitably as the society grew larger, but to which new impetus has been given by the creation of a new world of machines, power, and trade. These new interests of society can be carried on only in industrial or commercial centers. Even now we have only part of the story, for the shift from rural to urban life might have changed only our occupations and our habits. Instead it *has been changing our civilization* because all the old civilization, with its ideas and ideals and institutions was a product of agricultural life.

PART I

HISTORICAL TRANSFORMATION

I

ESSENTIALS IN OUR SOCIAL HERITAGE BEFORE INDUSTRIAL REVOLUTION

TOOLS AND MACHINES

The marvels of the modern world frequently blind us to the debt we owe past ages. We think in terms of machines, of conveniences, of food unknown to most civilized people three or four centuries ago. Our standard of living is separated by a large gulf from that of the medieval city dweller or peasant; by an abyss from that of prehistoric man. Why bother then to examine elements of civilization besides those of recent origin?

Make a list of essentials of civilization, those dealing with food, clothing, or shelter, with family or group organization, or with different types of culture. What do we find regarding the *time of their origin?* Note those which have had their beginnings in the present or the near-past, those which date from classical antiquity, and those which started in still more remote ages. Almost nothing exists today that really makes for civilization which cannot be found in essence before the world became acquainted with records, that is, before the dawn of history. Machines we have, but what are machines except tools made effective by indirect hand use, made efficient by power! The savage of the Old Stone Age [1] had tools that were used indirectly because attached to handles, as axes or spears, or used with other tools, such as darts, or involving interesting mechanisms and combinations, as the bow and arrow. The Neolithic miner with his pick of reindeer horn had mastered the technic of mining in its essentials. Neolithic engineers with the crudest of equipment at their

[1] Consult table, p. 4.

13

command built fairly substantial villages on platforms resting upon tens of thousands of piles.

Metal gave man a material far superior to stone and with metal came engineering projects impossible to prehistoric man. The Pyramids could not have been constructed by those who worked solely with flint; yet the technic of the prehistoric stone worker gave the huge, finely cut, beautifully placed blocks in a proximity not exceeding a thousandth of an inch at any point. With the pillar and the arch prehistoric man might have anticipated Roman architecture, and, had he known the use of steel, structural building and bridge-work. The superiority of modern man is rather in his knowledge of the forces of nature and his power to apply those forces. Steam and electricity, the transformers, rather than machines, the producers, are the modern addition to age-old forms of material civilization.

Modern industry and transportation would be negligible without the humble wheel. In all seriousness, the wheel has revolutionized modern life. Its beginnings are unknown, but in all probability represent a long story in human experience. It is not improbable that from rolling logs to wheeled ox-cart represented a span half as long as that from the two-wheeled cart to the eight-cylinder automobile. Used at first in or near Babylonia, chiefly for transportation, it found its way almost from the beginning into the arts. With a wheelbase at his command, the potter no longer circumnavigated his clay, but whirled it before him into far more symmetrical forms. Multiform as have been the uses of the wheel, chiefly in recent times, the idea and the first applications are very ancient.

FOOD AND CLOTHING

When human wants are considered, man's stomach claims first place. Present-day foods exceed in variety and in quality anything found in even the most luxurious of historic periods. Despots, oriental or enlightened, did not have on their tables the variety of attractive foods served daily before the average American. *The men of the rough Stone Age were food gather-*

ers, not producers. Their successors, some time before the dawn of history, had found most of the foods and had developed most of the technics of food raising which we have today. Grazing, it was formerly thought, antedated agriculture. This is at least doubtful; but *grazing and agriculture together are found not simply as means of producing food but as the basis of a social organization, of personal relationships, and of cultural achievements, many of which have been changed little from the Neolithic period to the Machine Age.*

In a single group of the prehistoric settlements, those of the Lake Dwellers of Switzerland, 170 varieties of plants were known, a fair percentage of which were cultivated by these primitive folk. Grains of barley have been found in the stomachs of Egyptian mummies antedating the First Dynasty. Probably the most civilized of prehistoric peoples were acquainted with wheat and most of the other cereals. American archaeologists give a list of nearly 100 food products, including white and sweet potatoes and Indian corn, which were grown by the much despised Indians and developed in times which were truly prehistoric. A careful student of life among primitive races, Robert H. Lowie, makes the following statement: "With all our vaunted science, our soil chemistry and animal husbandry, we have not succeeded in adding one solitary species of importance to the stock handed down by earlier cultures." [2]

Wherewith shall ye be clothed? Modern dress, such as it is, has changed within the memory of the youngest inhabitant; but the change simply carries us back to models and types of long ago. A very ancient painting, one of the oldest that humanity possesses, is of a group, chiefly women, in dresses of one piece, not radically different from those of 1930. Even in the Old Stone Age, men wore skins, probably for personal adornment—an idea earlier than covering—but chiefly as protection against the intense cold of the last glacial epoch. Our debt to the Neolithic includes many arts besides those of pottery and domestication of plants and animals. Among these are the combined technics of spinning and weav-

[2] Lowie, *Are We Civilized?* p. 45.

ing and basketry. Crude as was the procedure from the beginning, from early historic times spinning wheels changed but little. The old machines may have been clumsy, but the skill of the artists was unexcelled. The choice linens of Egypt are too well known for comment. Less is understood of the marvelous Peruvian cloth and tapestry, prehistoric material with texture so unusual that the threads cannot be separated. Not by us but by them was the perfect thread found. Their tapestries are compared with the famous Gobelin drapes, the world's most famous tapestries dating from the fifteenth century, and the Peruvian product was superior.

Social Organization

Of the family life in the Old Stone Age we know nothing. Possibly Westermarck is right in thinking that a true family is the oldest of all social groups. Certainly the family of the Neolithic period was probably not radically different from our own. The patriarchal concept both of family organization and of group life dates from this prehistoric time, if it cannot be traced earlier. The patriarch of pastoral life and the father as the head of the family in the prehistoric agricultural village have more than a strong family resemblance to the Roman *pater* and to the head of the family in nineteenth-century England or eighteenth-century America. The continental family still retains rather fully those characteristics of family solidarity and of interfamily alliances which previous ages bequeathed.

Modern life has lost the close-knit clan and tribal organization of primitive races and of very ancient times. Group needs are different, but if we believe James Harvey Robinson in *The Mind in the Making,* tribal or clan ideas still persist to our misfortune.

In the larger forms of group life the change from times prehistoric to times recent has not been so great as we would like to believe. Bismarck, Hitler, and Mussolini would have been much at home running a monarchy in the pre-Grecian period. Menes (3400 B.C.),[3] first of the world's historic

[3] Use is made of the "short" chronology.

kings, probably did little more than combine his own kingdom with another, making a complete *Egypt*.   In its essentials his kingdom was not very different from that found in the nineteenth century, especially in the former European monarchies. The *Assyrians* developed the art of government to include subject peoples.   The *Athenians* created a small democracy which they enlarged under the personal leadership of Pericles. *Rome* borrowed the imperial idea of Assyria and the personal leadership of Pericles.   It combined them when it organized the Principate, the world's largest and best empire before that of Great Britain.   *For all succeeding ages, the Roman Empire has been both a model and a type.*   The feudal kingdoms of medieval Europe departed in fact but not in form from this classical model.   The modern kingdom revived the imperial status as well as continued the imperial idea.   Note the modern use of "Caesar" in "Kaiser" and "Tsar."   Not until the Industrial Revolution and the frontier of America did there come into existence new types of political grouping and organization.

Codes of law may seem to many the achievements of modern America.   But law codes were found before the dawn of history among the Sumerians of the Euphrates valley.   Hammurabi[4] and Justinian[5] added and developed, they did not create, the idea and this form of legal summaries.

CULTURE

When we make an analysis of contemporaneous civilization, we find the cultural elements seem least dominant at present.   Is this to be explained on the ground that we have returned to nature and made nature serve us as never before? Again we learn our indebtedness to the distant past.   We are the heir of all the ages, but more the heir of prehistoric peoples than of those in later times.   This is not strange if we realize that history covers a span of barely fifty centuries, whereas prehistory had possibly fifty times that length.

Early culture

[4] The code of Hammurabi (Babylon, about 2000 B.C.) is the oldest complete code in existence.

[5] The latest, and greatest, of the Roman Codes was completed under the Emperor Justinian, A.D. 527–565.

The oldest known skull, human or near-human, that of *Pithecanthropus erectus,* is counted as more human than simian. Its skull capacity equals that of low human races; but the characteristic which counts most is the *probable capacity of its owner for speech.* Yet *Pithecanthropus erectus* is not even homo; it is simply homonid. When we come to a species distinctively human, like Neanderthal, which has disappeared, or Sapiens, which now occupies the earth, we find the capacity for speech universal. Language, a common language understood by all members of a group, must have been a prerequisite for the transitory *community life* of the Kitchen Middens, the earliest type of Neolithic settlements, the permanent village life of the Lake Dwellers, and the first kingdoms of prehistoric Egypt. When oral language was reduced to writing, man reached the artificial distinction of written records. We speak of all later development of humanity as history.

Early writing was probably in all cases pictorial. Later it became, but not with all races, symbolic. The *cuneiform script* of Babylonia was adopted at one time as an almost universal written language. Not from Babylon but from Egypt probably came the characters which were the bases of the invention of the *alphabet,* which probably occurred at the southwestern horn of the Fertile Crescent, south of Syria. This score of letters made possible the simple and successful recording of western language, literature, and thought.

Psychologically and socially man has always been a religious animal. We have few evidences of man in relation to human artifacts much earlier than the Neanderthal [6] burials. In one of these graves we find the skeleton of a chief laid away in a trough in the rock, accompanied by choice tools of his period, and, we can imagine, with food and more perishable commodities at his command. No interpretation of these remains seems to fit the facts so well as the one that, to this cave people, man was more than flesh and that some part of him lived on. We do not know the dates of these

---

[6] This great people flourished before our species, Homo Sapiens, appears. The race is called Neanderthal, the culture Mousterian.

early burials, but they may easily have been five or six times as far away from us, chronologically speaking, as are those huge mausoleums, the great pyramids of Egypt.

A study of primitive races and of Neolithic peoples gives us the clew to ideas which underlie much modern religion. There is close connection between the fear which probably led to interment of an ancestor or leader in Mousterian times and the fear which dominated the revivals that were characteristic of the eighteenth and nineteenth centuries. Primitive man lived closer to religious experience and to his deities than do most of us, for religion was a very real part of his every-day life. But a large number of our religious ideas and some of our religious practices can unquestionably be traced from prehistoric times. James Henry Breasted, in *The Dawn of Conscience* continually stresses our recently acquired knowledge on the great antiquity of moral standards of conduct. This debt to remote antiquity does not overlook our obligation to the Hebrews, who revolutionized early religious ideas and transformed religion first into a social and then into an individual plan which capitalized the best in human nature.

If we are art collectors, we will spend larger sums for a Renaissance canvas by an old master than for a painting by any other brush. What would not the world give for an original statue by Phidias, the greatest of the Athenian sculptors? Think how highly we prize a Winged Victory or a Venus de Milo, although the Greeks made no mention of them in their writings! The "Elgin" Marbles [7] still stand in their original form, but without colors; but most of our knowledge of Greek sculpture comes from replicas or records. If we go one step farther back, we are impressed with the naturalness and the artistry of Cretan painting. Far more impressive, however, are those marvels of the Magdalenian caves. For naturalness, for a wonderful technique, these paintings of cave man excel almost all others. Without hesitation we can pick out bison, deer, boar, and horse. Naturalists tell us that we

---

[7] These frescoes from the beautiful Athenian Parthenon were taken to England under the Earl of Elgin and are now on exhibition in the British Museum. They were designed by Phidias.

can distinguish the species and the season. Observation shows us whether an animal is stationary, is feeding, or is in motion. This art was a product of the Ice Age; and glaciers are far away in time.

Ancient
bases of
modern
culture

Modern science is to that of pre-industrial revolutionary times as a giant is to a pigmy. Yet modern science, like all other elements of modern civilization, owes a great debt to classical and prehistoric peoples. At least twenty-five centuries have elapsed since eclipses were predicted. The Greeks measured the size of the earth with fair accuracy. Our knowledge of Mayan science, especially astronomy, is still in its infancy; but we know that the observations of these Indians were keen, as were the observations of the Egyptians and Babylonians. Lacking telescopes and mathematical technology, these ancient peoples could not penetrate very far into the heavens nor understand very well the relationship of one body to another, yet Babylonian science has given us our present divisions of time. Unscientific as those may be, nevertheless they were a tremendous contribution and are a significant element of present-day civilization. Methods of counting, relatively speaking, are recent, because the *digits* could not be pyramided until they had *zeros* upon which to rest. The Indians, Arabs, and Europeans worked out their plan on the decimal scheme, whereas the Maya peoples made use of twenty characters because they used shoes less commonly. But both depended for their larger if not higher mathematics upon the use of the zero.

If we tend to despise the superstitions of early religions and the crudities of primitive science, let us remember the practical development of ancient peoples in Egypt, Babylonia, and Yucatan. In each case a *calendar* was worked out which was remarkable in its accuracy if not in its simplicity. At least eight centuries before Menes and the time of written records, the Egyptians had a calendar of 365 days, with an allowance made for the extra quarter day in each solar year. The Maya Indians went one step farther. Their calendar provided a correction for the inaccuracy which the Egyptians overlooked or disregarded. By a rather complicated procedure, the

Mayas developed a calendar almost as accurate as that which we now possess.

From so brief but comprehensive a survey several things stand out. The roots of modern civilization are very deep. Scarcely an element is found in which our prehistoric ancestors did not make some vital achievement and progress. Our problems are not their problems, yet human nature must have changed little in the long intervals, and human advance has been far more on the surface than in the fundamentals. Greek philosophy is undoubtedly the basis of philosophy in modern times. But how do we know that it was radically different from that of the thinker of an age very much earlier? The printing press has revolutionized our acquaintance with the writings of mankind, with the doings and the thought of the present day. Without it democratic education and large-scale democratic government would be impossible. Copernicus, Galileo, and Newton did not seem to go very far in creating modern science, but without their ground-breaking work the marvelous advances of the nineteenth and twentieth centuries might not have taken place. In a study of modern civilization it would not be fair, and probably it would be unwise, to lose sight of the heritage coming to us from past ages and of the debt we owe to humanity in its earlier years.

THE WORLD FOUND BY THE INDUSTRIAL REVOLUTION

Forty centuries before the Industrial Revolution have been surpassed by the two or three since its advent. The ox-cart of Queen Anne's time was not greatly changed from that before the days of Alexander the Great; but it has little place in an age of autos and airplanes. After the spinning wheel was attached to hundreds of companions whirling on the same shaft, factories, cities, and trusts followed swiftly. Formerly hand labor supplied almost everything, aided by the foot and helped by animals; now steam, gasoline and electricity work their magic by the button and lever which have replaced Aladdin's lamp.

A few centuries ago *small-scale agriculture prevailed*. The field system of cultivation in common [8] was in use on the continent of Europe as it had been for centuries. England and eastern Europe boasted huge estates similar to those of the later Roman Empire and possibly of the very ancient kingdoms. As always, the method of landholding was closely interrelated with the system of social organization and of wealth concentration or the reverse. Land and other forms of wealth were usually in the possession of an aristocracy, landed, social and political. Cultivation in common, however, was crude, being carried on in some instances in small plats, partly by individuals held responsible for the product of their tiny subdivisions. Crops were not diversified; there was little intensive agriculture. Strange as it may seem, in thirty centuries there had been little change in the plow and in methods of plowing. Farmers still depended upon cattle or possibly horses, several of which were necessary to draw a plow through fairly undisturbed turf. Seldom did the crop equal five times the amount of seed, and a triple return was typical.

In the field of industry there had been scarcely more change. Slave labor disappeared with the conquests by the old world empires, and with it went also the fairly large shops of ancient times. Labor had not yet become respectable. The *gild system*, vital in the Middle Ages, had disappeared in England by the time of Elizabeth. Throughout the Continent it was still maintained in something like its ancient vigor, although gradually yielding to the new demand for a more flexible system of production and a more effective use of capital. *Government paternalism* tended to discourage gild production and to promote home industry on a larger scale. There existed, however, a rather personal and intimate and fairly cordial relation between master and men working together. In wealth, but not necessarily in training, the master was different from his journeymen. In those "good old days" industrial problems as well as industrial products of later years do not appear.

Trade and commerce had always been transacted in fairly

---

[8] See any text on medieval history *e.g.,* R. L. Ashley, *Early European Civilization,* pp. 395–401.

large units; on a more extensive scale than had seemed possible in agriculture or had been attained in manufacture. Great fleets of vessels had been organized, not because capital ran into commercial channels in large quantities, but because of dangers encountered in individual trading at a distance. There is more than a superficial similarity between the wheat fleets of republican Rome sailing from Alexandria and the Spanish vessels laden with silver crossing from Panama. Pirates preyed on both. As recently as the fifteenth century new methods of accumulating and using wealth had come into existence, foreshadowing the amazing and profitable credit operations of today. Banking, starting in Italy, had spread everywhere, although only three American banks flourished at the time Washington was inaugurated President. With the opening of new lands by Columbus and Da Gama huge commercial companies had been chartered, seeking profitable dominion among non-Christian peoples. The Dutch East India Company, the British company which controlled India to 1857, and the larger colonizing joint stock companies of America were forerunners of the large exporting cartels and trusts of today.

Contrast separates us from our ancestors of the early eighteenth century. They lived simple, quiet but very industrious lives. They never heard the throb of engine or the whir of anything larger than spinning wheels. Most articles were made at home, frequently in the winter, by the dim light of fire or candle. Foods, clothing and furniture represented little that was not produced in the immediate neighborhood. Travel, as now in backwoods districts, was the good fortune of few. It would be tedious to list what they did not have, for the change has been great indeed.

II

INDUSTRIAL AND POLITICAL REVOLUTIONS

The last half of the eighteenth century, interestingly enough, witnessed not only the first climax of the English Industrial Revolution but a great outbreak of political revolutions as well. Probably there is some indirect connection between these two, for both represented that age of reaction against arbitrary rule in government and of business; and both grew mighty with the eighteenth-century concepts of a new individualism. In going its way, each was unconsciously dependent upon the other. *Neither nationalism nor democracy would have thrived in a provincial world. What the Industrial Revolution did to provincialism was the breaking down of isolation barriers,* partly through the demand for wider markets of mass-production products made possible by machine power. New and quicker means of transportation may directly have had even greater influence upon the establishing of new contacts, creating cosmopolitan areas, first, within nations, and later between them. The relationship between industrialism and nationalism was not one-sided, however. The struggle for markets was a contest of nations. The encouragement of manufacturing continued to be a chief object of national policy, except in Great Britain, where it was unnecessary. *Industrial evolution prospered because nations were growing and expanding.*

MECHANICAL-POWER CHANGES BROUGHT ABOUT BY THE INDUSTRIAL REVOLUTION

Introduction   Back of the English Industrial Revolution of two hundred years ago was a long period of preparation and mechanical advance. Hero's five simple machines [1] did not lead to me-

---

[1] The wheel and axle, the lever, the pulley, the wedge, and the endless screw.

chanical progress in the ancient world.   But about the time
that the printing press, with moveable type, started a new
era of intercommunication, cannon and gunpowder made royal
armies possible and created a wide demand for metals and
machine-producing companies   The following age stimulated
invention, as is shown by the long list attributed to Leonardo
da Vinci and his contemporaries.[2]   Before this, in Italy, silk-
winding machines were used together in large numbers, in
what without distortion might be called a factory; and a
machine was perfected with several thousand parts, which
was used in the making of stockings.   Possibly these were
isolated instances of the kind of mechanical changes which
were to be developed very much later in Western Europe.

With the Renaissance began a series of changes which, in
several respects, paved the way for industrial revolution.   In
the Middle Ages there were no large general markets.   Even
if there had been factories using machinery and utilizing
water power, the products turned out would have been too
numerous for sale in the markets then available.   With the
opening up of the New World and the development of better
means of communication, *new large-scale markets*, both
domestic and foreign, came into existence.

Almost more important to an economic revolution worthy
of the name was the discovery or creation of new funds of
capital.   Mining of the precious metals had developed before
America was discovered.   With the addition of large supplies
of silver and some gold from America, the commercial world
was now supplied with abundant media of exchange and with
surplus capital either for lending or for the promotion of industrial enterprise.   A class of *bankers* arose who began to
store funds for those who could not use them themselves,
capital that could be reloaned for new kinds of business.
There was a beginning of near-factories from the days of
Elizabeth, especially on the Continent.   We sometimes think
of the factory system as following the mechanical and industrial advance in England in the middle of the eighteenth century, but a good-sized factory was in operation in Sweden in

[2] A. P. Usher, *A History of Mechanical Invention*, pp. 183–185.

1700, and before that day similar factories, devoted to single or combined processes of manufacturing, were in use in Holland, France, and other countries. In this period also began the new types of *business organization* mentioned at the end of Chapter I.

When Kay improved the shuttle in cotton weaving (1738), none dreamed of the series of inventions in the textile industry to follow. This device abolished hand throwing for the shuttle, substituting a mechanical plan of casting it from side to side. Then came a demand for more yarn to be woven. The need, popularly characterized as the mother of invention, waited a quarter century before an overturned spinning wheel stimulated the thought of a number of wheels on a shaft. Improvements in this spinning jenny made it usable with power, gave a finer and a tougher thread. The improved spinning called for better methods in weaving, and demanded more satisfactory power than either hand, animals, wind, or water had offered. This the steam engine furnished. Soon a power loom, clumsy and slow, was invented by a clergyman. A few years later Whitney's cotton gin greatly increased the supply of cotton itself. So in the span of a half century came these changes in the manufacture of cotton cloth, a real forerunner of the Machine Age.

The Machine Age in its nineteenth century form was one of steel and steam. In the twentieth century, it was rather one of electricity and technology. The development of these mechanical eras was promoted by the eighteenth-century improvements in mining, which gave new and vaster supplies of coal and iron, and by improvements in energy-producing machines. Rather high authorities contend that even if the steam engine had not been made efficient, before 1850 improvements in the utilization of water power would have furnished a sufficient supply of energy usable in factories to have greatly stimulated industrial advance. Because new supplies of coal were available and the steam engine was constantly being improved, less use was made of water power than otherwise would have been. Watt's improvements of a pump, which finally became recognized as a steam engine, covered a period of years, culminating soon after Adam Smith announced his new idea that the wealth of nations depended upon the freedom of enterprise within them and between them. This steam engine was not very effective until after Oliver Evans added a better condenser, and even then it was used for years chiefly in pumping water from mines and as a stationary source of power.

Before the nineteenth century, Fitch sought to apply the steam engine to transportation by water. The fact that we associate Fulton's name with the first successful steamboat (1807) shows how slow was the progress in utilizing these new forms of power. By 1819 the northward voyage of the Mississippi, heretofore closed to upstream traffic, had been accomplished. With the aid of sails, a steamboat had crossed the Atlantic in 1819, and in 1829 Stephenson's "Rocket," an improved locomotive, had made a real success of transportation by land. It is a far cry from these humble beginnings to the thousand-foot steamship, the fifty thousand-ton ocean freighter, the mogul engine, the sixteen-cylinder automobile, and an airplane that can cross America between dawn and dusk or the Atlantic in less than two days.

Formerly historians wrote of the Industrial Revolution as something that had taken place in the eighteenth century in England. Later the term was applied to economic transformations in America, Germany, and other countries. Recently we have come to realize that *the Industrial Revolution is a continuous process, much older than 1760, still in operation,* more effective today than in the past, and possibly holding more in its grasp for the future than we can visualize or imagine. The dominant note of the scientists and engineers who coöperated in writing *Toward Civilization* is the optimistic attitude toward future development. What we have now is still little; the possibilities in days to come are very great.

In the transformation of pre-industrial life into that of to-day invention has taken first place. Some of these improvements have dealt primarily with machinery; some especially with power, which has been used with machines of all kinds and in the field of transportation. In all countries invention

Inventions

has been encouraged by the granting of patent monopolies. Yankee ingenuity may have stood at the head, but the whole world has passed through a furore of inventiveness. A study of the records of any national office shows how cumulative is the movement toward mechanization of the modern world. In 1840 only about a thousand applications were made at Washington. By 1900 the number of patents for that year had risen to 26,499, although almost as many requests were refused. Today 50,000 patents are granted annually in the United States alone.

Invention is not simply cumulative; it is simultaneous. One good turn leads to another as well as deserves that other. In the history of discovery or invention there are few isolated improvements. Each depends on the preceding, and each seems connected with a corresponding discovery by some one else. The next step in invention may not be predictable; but it should be. In *Social Change* [3] William Fielding Ogburn lists 148 almost simultaneous discoveries or inventions. Some of these were really independent of each other, although each set was dependent on some precedent discovery or need. Most of these gains were in the field of science, but the continuity and cumulation of inventions appears in all areas of human endeavor. Two only need be mentioned here. In 1859 Charles Darwin was not the only investigator who wrote on natural selection and variation. Alfred Wallace, working independently but with much less exhaustive research, had reached similar conclusions, the same year. More spectacular was the application for a telephone patent made the same day, March 7, 1876, by Alexander Graham Bell and Elisha Gray. Although Bell's device was more complete than Gray's, the careless methods of the Patent Office left the point of priority in doubt. Not till many years later did Bell win his case in court.

At the beginning industrial advance was slowed down because nations refused to share with each other any improvement made by their people. For example, Great Britain prohibited the exportation of her new machinery, finally plac-

[3] pp. 90–102.

ing a twenty-five-hundred-dollar fine upon any one who was guilty of taking a machine out of the country. Some smuggling, of course, did occur. Later, and particularly in recent years, although the advance in invention has been very great indeed, improvements are frequently not utilized because they render old plants obsolete. Sometimes inventions which would increase the output, reduce cost, or save much to the consumer, or add markedly to his standard of living, are placed upon the shelf or otherwise bought up and suppressed. The reason may be the expense of installing the invention. Its use might interfere with the sale of stocks on hand. A few years ago improved radios were not placed upon the market because the manufacturers had a supply adequate for several years. The new radios, of course, were much cheaper and much better than the old had been. Sometimes the non-use of a new invention controlled by a single company or corporation may be accounted for solely by the desire to avoid payment of large royalties when the use of the older machines does not cost the producer so much.

Invention has "made" the Industrial Revolution largely through changes in machines and power. Electric producers and transformers aid in the utilization of the earth's natural resources. Falling water becomes an electric current which is sent hundreds of miles and may be commercially usable around the globe. With a dynamo to create and a motor to propel, the world is literally moving forward rapidly. With thoroughness, if not suddenly, the dynamic changes of the present period are transforming the old order into a new era.

Agriculture may not have shared equally with manufacturing and transportation in these epoch-making improvements, yet the steel plow has now become a multiple affair quite as much as the first improved spinning wheel. Millet's portrayal of "The Gleaners" still finds its counterpart in many portions of the globe, but the large American ranches devoted to agriculture and collectivized farms in Russia harvest their crops with huge mowers, reapers and combination machines which do daily the work of thousands of peasants.

The railroad, the steamboat, the automobile, and the airplane in their respective fields have developed entirely new types of contact, some unintentional. The telegram, submarine, cable and wireless have opened up new worlds and have brought all mankind closer together. The telephone is an instrument for shortening conferences, for time saving, and for business expansion. Compared with the radio it has both advantages and disadvantages. It is individual and personal, but a two-way channel; whereas its widespreading young brother reaches hundreds of thousands and millions with a general and one-way message. Soon television will be almost as common as radio and almost as inexpensive. How will social organization and procedures, group actions or ideas, be altered by this ability to be seen by, and converse with, friends and followers at a distance, by this opportunity for demagogues or educators or high office seekers or holders to reach their constituents or their public?

Science

If the Industrial Revolution had been purely a matter of mechanics, or of mechanics and power, it would not have changed industry and life as it has. It coincided with an epoch of scientific progress unequalled in all previous ages. Foundations had been laid by earlier investigators. Popular belief to the contrary, medieval scientists had kept alive the spirit of the ancients. During the Renaissance the revival of Greek learning stimulated more independent research. Scientific methods supplanted speculative thought. Copernicus took away our belief of the earth as a center by proving that the sun is the center of our (solar) system. With telescopes and more knowledge Galileo and Newton made it possible to penetrate other universes than ours. Nevertheless, Physics is a comparatively new science, developing with the Industrial Revolution rather than based upon old research. Some of the most important modern industries depend solely or chiefly on applied chemistry.

The name *The New Industrial Revolution* is applied by many writers to the new age of applied science and technology.[4] In Germany, and to a lesser extent in America, the

---

[4] On technics and civilization, see the volume with that title by Lewis Mumford.

scientific departments of the universities have made especial contributions. In America, and to a lesser extent in Europe, the new technics are the work of the research laboratories of the great corporations, or organizations like that of Edison. Improvements in lighting and in sound transmission have come largely from the researches of the wizard of Menlo Park or from work done by the American Telephone scientists or those at work for General or Western Electric. Transmission of electricity, possibly the greatest single transformer of modern life, has been speeded up by old contributions of the Southern California Edison engineers or more recently by the Schenectady group of experts. Wonders never cease. Who before the days of Perry and Amundson and Byrd would have dreamed that the "North Pole" could talk to the "South Pole" and the rest of us listen in? Thousands of laboratories house some unknown modern Prometheus [4a] bringing mankind, let us hope without punishment if without reward, some gift of the reluctant gods.[5]

THE WORLD TRANSFORMED BY THE INDUSTRIAL REVOLUTION AND SCIENCE

Only the person with a well-trained historical sense can envision a world without machines. Whether we are dealing with production, with transportation, or with exchange, we find at every turn evidences of the new mechanics, new forms of power, and new scientific achievements. The modern city seems like that of ancient times; but it would be impossible without the skyscraper and rapid systems of transportation. The modern factory, a machine center, would be useless without steam or electricity. Agriculture is yielding slowly to the new forces. The farmers have made more than a beginning of using new plants, possibly imported from a great distance, better means of cultivation, and coöperative forms of marketing. It is difficult to realize that less than two generations

Industry and transportation

[4a] Prometheus brought from heaven fire, denied to man by Zeus. He was punished by being chained to a rock, each day his liver, nightly renewed, being torn out anew by an eagle.

[5] On further contributions of applied science to industry, the Industrial Revolution, and humanity, see chs. IV, XIX.

have passed since the world thought Darius Green ("and his flying machine") ludicrous, laughed at Jules Verne's *Twenty Thousand Leagues Under the Sea,* and was skeptical of Phineas Fogg, who circled the globe in eighty days. Much more power is used in transportation than in production, possibly as much science and real invention. A world without telephones and radios would seem rather circumscribed even if cloth were cheap and transcontinental trips easy.

In all forms of economic activity a chief change would seem to be large-scale coöperation. This achievement depends upon accumulation of the savings of multitudes; and these multitudes must act as a single group and unit. A few transportation systems include most of the mileage of our great American railways. The employer today is not a promoted workman, but more frequently an organizer and a capitalist dealing not with ten journeymen but with a hundred thousand workers. New opportunities have been opened to individual initiative and enterprise; but to the rank and file there has been standardization of work as well as standardization of machine production.

New classes and levels of living

In this new world, as always before, *classes are organized according to economic standards.* This statement does not mean that a man's status is predetermined by his wealth. It does mean that today as formerly those who have hold a different level from those who have not. Regardless of equity, law or justice, the accumulator of wealth leads or dominates those who do routine tasks. In ancient times and before the beginning of the Industrial Revolution much wealth consisted of landed property. Property was held in families and transmitted from father to son. Except in rare instances the landed aristocracy was debarred from engaging in other enterprise. Inevitably these members of a closed corporation had a hereditary monopoly not only of wealth but also of position and power.

In the preservation of all these privileges, religious sanctions were asked and obtained. The church was more than the organization of those most religious minded. It was an institution dedicated to preserving the *mores* and worshiping the deities who made these *mores* possible. It was but a step from this attitude to that of revering what is because it is God-given and God-sanctioned. In ancient Babylonia, as in France before the Great Revolution, the church not only buttressed existing privilege, but itself controlled much of the land and most of the social policies. In many periods, particularly in antiquity and in medieval times, the church was the preserver and the transmitter of the social heritage. It made reverence for God a means of accentuating its own power rather than of rendering service to those having the greatest need, whether religious, economic, or social.

One indirect transformation brought to modern society by the Industrial Revolution has been a reorganization of all classes, which are primarily economic and secondarily social groups. . Since the beginnings of industrial revolution men have been more money-conscious. The making of money has with most of us become a chief purpose in life rather than just an incident of living. That is one reason why in Europe the landed aristocracy has given way before the industrial capitalist. In America we had few great landed proprietors, especially in the West. If free and abundant land and freehold ownership of small properties had been a permanent rather than a transitory phase of American development, democracy with its old slogan of equality might have become the fact it appeared a century ago. Unfortunately, the occupation of the Mississippi basin did not take place until the Machine Age was well on its way; so agriculture lost its chance to establish a permanent landed democracy. The rural population may still be made up to a great extent of small proprietors, but the cities are filled with wage-earners, at low salaries and without social standing. More than one-half of our total population is proletarian and many tenant farmers are little better off than peasants.

One criticism aimed at the modern age stresses the widening gap between those near the top and those at the bottom. Compared with the age of slavery, the gap seems small. The man with billions to his credit and with tens of billions at his command, after all, can use very little that is not enjoyed

to some extent by an overwhelming majority of the population in the more progressive western countries. It may be
true that today the rich are growing richer and the poor are
growing poorer. It certainly is true that unemployment is
too common. Besides the "submerged tenth" myriads lack
food.

In general, however, *the Industrial Revolution both directly
and indirectly has brought life to a higher level.* Directly,
improvement reflects the increase in the return of labor and
the decrease in the hours devoted to toil. In turn this has
meant more leisure. Indirectly, the economic revolution has
made life more worthwhile. Increased wages and leisure have
opened up new channels of interest and entertainment. It
it well enough to say that a dollar in Queen Anne's time
would go as far as five or ten today, but the average man
can buy more goods today than he could two hundred years
ago. Moreover, no dollar of that period could have annihilated distance by a telephone call or have magnified candle light into the rays of an incandescent globe. The weary
traveler and his horse could cover in a day only the space we
leave behind in an hour; and we do it with much more comfort. If time is money, the modern man earns as well as
spends and saves more wisely and effectively than Poor
Richard could have proposed. If one wishes to discover how
far humanity has progressed in the last half century, let him
make a list of a dozen or score of necessities that did not
exist a half century ago. Let him read the first chapter of
Stuart Chase's *Men and Machines,* following the author
through a three-hour series of contacts with the new mechanical world.

The standard of living is too low for more than three-
quarters of the American people, for more than nine-tenths
of Europeans, and for practically all other races. Compared
with the past, however, standards are relatively high and
actually very high. Whatever ill the Industrial Revolution
seems to have brought to those who sweat in the monotony of
factory or shop, it has made up in greater general training,

larger actual income in consumers' goods, and greater opportunities in the non-working hours.

Interestingly enough, the greatest influence of the Machine
Age and of science may be found not in a world of mechanics
and power, but in *the training, ideas, and group actions of
people today.* Universal education is still an ideal, illiteracy
dogs our steps at every turn; and ignorance is a foe of all
advance. Nevertheless, compulsory education is on its way,
and this compulsion has been progressing from primary to
grammar levels, and is reaching on into secondary education.
In our own day it may demand some collegiate studies or a
technical equivalent. The new science has both reduced infant mortality and added to the span of human life. The
years of active work need not begin so early, leaving time
for preparation which may quadruple individual accomplishment. Not upon the individual, however, is the chief effect,
but upon society in general. Social classes still exist and will
be maintained, perhaps to the end of time; but the type of
rule desired by a landed aristocracy in days of limited inter-
communication must yield to a government as large scale as
production, as universal as education, and as efficient as modern industrial science.

Ideas are products. Or do you prefer to call them by-products? They may be chiefly elements of social heritage, products of the past little changed in the transmission to the
present. If life is transformed mechanically, scientifically,
politically, and socially, ideas will not lag forever in the *mores*
of antiquity. A patriarchal system of government and of
society is possible only so long as agriculture dominates
human life. When the farm yields to the factory, new reorganization is necessary because old institutions are inadequate and old ideas no longer prevail. Probably several
decades, possibly several centuries will elapse before a new
concept will be accepted regarding a better system to replace
a patriarchal type of life and organization.

Go back five hundred years and note how the individualism
of the Renaissance replaced the collectivism of all preceding
ages. Even now this individualism has not penetrated every

(margin note) Indirect changes through new ideas

corner of human endeavor. But reaction has already started against it. Society seeks a new type of socialization, but it wants one which does not demand the suppression of individualism.

Certainly the isolation and provincialism of the farm, and of the thought that goes with farm life, are yielding to *a new urban cosmopolitanism which may easily break with many favored traditions.* Since science has transformed our knowledge of the things smallest and of the universe that is no longer solar, and of other universes beyond, we can no longer think in the terms of even the scholars or philosophers of the great Renaissance. If mass education brings to the dullest of our youth ideas unknown a century ago, his outlook cannot be that of his grandfather, even if the conditions of his life might be similar. The daily press keeps us on the *qui vive,* alert to hear yesterday's happenings in Berlin, Rome or Westminster, or on the Chinese front. If dissatisfaction develops or spreads in Russia, Brazil, or India, we can no longer be indifferent to the play of forces which put those people in revolt against the order no longer meeting their needs. Two centuries ago the call of humanity might have remained unheard in the neighboring district over the hill, but modern life, much interwoven, with close contacts may not ignore real needs brought to our attention by telegraph and press. The new world that the Industrial Revolution is bringing is a different and a larger world, possibly a better one. But the revolution in the industrial field was only one of many. The eighteenth century ushered in a new era of political revolutions. Industrial and political reorganization together have made use of two of the greatest ideas or institutions of modern times, individualism and nationalism.

THE MOVEMENT TOWARD NATIONALISM AND INDIVIDUALISM

Nationalism   When history dawned in Egypt, men were living in united groups under a consolidated government. The area over which a pharaoh ruled was large, and the organization of his political system, at least by the time of the Egyptian Empire,[6] was almost as elaborate and as differentiated as was that of a European monarch a half century ago. The science of government seemed almost as complete when explained by the keen mind of Aristotle[7] as in the writings of Bentham[8] four generations back. Nevertheless, the ages from Menes[9] to Wilhelm of Germany presented a series of changes which anticipated though vaguely the actual transformation of the nineteenth century and the problem of political reorganization in the twentieth.

In the middle of the nineteenth century governments may have been formed as they were fifty centuries earlier, but the groups governed were *organized* in a modern way rather than an ancient. The modern state has been a natural development from the feudal state. In medieval times people were governed in countries with an hereditary king as the political figurehead. Political authority rested with a noble who controlled his local estate isolated from its neighbors by impassable roads, and by limited community requirements. Politics and good government were the least of the interests of a noble little concerned with his tenants, but vitally interested in warfare. Then came an economic revolution. Wider markets developed as Crusaders penetrated the East. Da Gama led the way around Africa, and Columbus opened up a new world in the West. Small community economy gave place to a "national" economy. The kings ceased to be suzerains of feudal vassals; they became sovereigns of more or less loyal subjects. When the rank and file of the people supported the king rather than the immediate lord, monarchy triumphed, as it did easily in England, beginning with Henry VII,[10] and as it did after a long struggle in France, following the successes of Joan of Arc.[11] East of the Rhine there was

[6] Fifteenth and fourteenth centuries before Christ.
[7] The Greek philosopher, 384–322 B.C.
[8] An English economist of the early nineteenth century.
[9] The first king of united Egypt, 3400 B.C.
[10] The first of the Tudor kings and the earliest of the English Renaissance monarchs (1485–1509).
[11] As a young girl Joan of Arc (1412–1431) inspired and led to victory the French troops that were being defeated by the English in the Hundred Years' War.

no such transformation: here feudalism, weak monarchies, and personal serfdom survived even to the nineteenth century.

The lever which pried continental Europe loose from post-medieval feudalism was the great French Revolution of 1789. Itself an evidence of nationalism, the revolution reorganized the French nation on the basis of the people rather than on unity through a monarch. The leaven of national unity spread to Italy, to Spain, and to Germany, which rallied *en masse* against attempted control by Napoleon. Nationality as an idea had to precede nationalism as an organization; and only in the mid-nineteenth century did Germany and Italy attain national unity. Gradually other peoples and races farther east sought this same end, although they did not succeed so fully. The twentieth century has echoed and reëchoed with the struggles between former ruling autocracies and racial or national groups demanding, and sometimes acquiring, self-determination.

We have stressed *industrialism* with its corollary of capitalism, but without much stress on capitalism, and we are stressing *nationalism*, with some attention to democracy and individualism. For our purpose we are treating these two as the important elements in the historical background of contemporaneous civilization. Later [12] nationalism is examined more fully and contrasted with internationalism, as well as with the precedent localism which it replaced.

Nationalism is not easy to define, because few authorities agree upon either a definition or an explanation. As we shall use the term, it applies to the organization of "racial" groups, within definite territories, who are conscious of their existence as a society and as a people with fairly common ideas and ideals, separate from any other modern racial or politically organized society. In their political organization, at least before the advent of democracy, most nations were not essentially different from the monarch-ruled states or societies of the post-Renaissance period or, in fact, of fairly ancient times. From the standpoint of *racial unity*, of *common in-*

[12] Ch. XV.

terests, and of *independent existence as a state* within the modern world, the modern nation is quite different from any of its predecessors before the eighteenth century. Even as early as 1776, Adam Smith used as the title of his epoch-making book on the comparatively new science of economics the term, "The Wealth of *Nations.*" At that time it may well be questioned whether any of these people, except those of England, deserved the name "nation," although the French people were gradually becoming conscious of their nationality, which they asserted very emphatically in and after 1789. In America the *organization* of a nation existed presumably under the Constitution of 1787, but the American people did not emerge as a true nation until they had destroyed slavery and formed a true Union after a civil war.

In the modern development of society politically, there has been *a readjustment of the interrelations of individual and group.* Ancient races made almost a religious fetish of the idea of group solidarity. The family, the clan, and later the tribe, was everything; the individual was a social nonentity. The Greeks philosophized individualism, although they did not practice it. Christ taught individualism, stressing the value of the human soul. Individual religion and individual salvation, however, yielded to the need of coöperation, as the early Christians fought persecution and sought church advancement. When the Christian church gained recognition of itself as the official religion of the Roman Empire, it subordinated individual religious problems to collective political progress. Later the Church borrowed from its heathen friends the concept of an empire which was called religious but was built upon the model of the Roman imperial organization, under an imperial bishop. With a universal medieval church, both political and philanthropic, the individual took little part in religious services and did not dare to go counter to rite or dogma served out to him. Throughout the whole medieval period the religious individualism taught by Jesus lay dormant.[13]

The individual and group life

[13] The most widespread protest against the medieval church was the Waldensian movement; the most vigorous protest, the Albigensian crusade.

The Great Renaissance was in a true sense an attempted renaissance of the individual. Almost all historical movements have started as a protest against the preceding régime. The attempt to reorganize medieval collectivism not only created modern monarchies out of feudal states but it also developed, in the philosophy of the humanists, in the religious ideas of Luther, and in the religious organization of Calvin, a true social individualism. A new society appears: not simply a mass, but a group of members, important as individuals. Centuries elapsed, however, before these ideas penetrated beyond the confines of a few New England towns or the churches of some of the more progressive Protestant sects. The Puritans led the way, but, stiff-necked as they had to be, they did not lead very far. The Anabaptists in Holland and Roger Williams in America carried this idea of individual religious freedom to its logical conclusion. What gain to change from a Church Universal, with an imperial pope, to a church national, with a royal dictator. *The seventeenth century brought England constitutional government; and the struggle made thinkers like Milton and Locke advocate the new political individualism.* The French philosophers popularized rights of man in individual dogma; but the American politicians made it personal and practical. In our "Declaration" we mentioned equality and individual rights, and the consequent right of self-government, as reason for overthrowing the rule of Great Britain. When the French Revolutionists borrowed the philosopher's ideas and their phraseology, "liberty, equality, fraternity" became a motto and a goal for half the western world.

Democracy: nationalist and individualist

Eighteenth century democracy developed slowly but logically. In America free land made this possible; in France extensive individual ownership of farm property; in England industrial equality of workers.

In America the frontier states were the first to abolish the old land ownership or property qualifications for voters. In time property, even property in land, furnished a rather meaningless distinction because land was plentiful and almost free. In the West it could be had for the taking if not for the asking; hence the frontier with its economic equality and socially leveling influences gave us manhood suffrage. This idea spread eastward until by 1840 white men voted almost everywhere in America. The Civil War not only freed the slaves and made them citizens, but sought to confer the elective franchise in order to protect both their freedom and their citizenship. The following half century carried this idea of individualist democracy one step farther. Myriads of changes entered into all phases of social life and business; they brought women a new status in the family and in industry. The World War made adult suffrage inevitable, the Nineteenth Amendment doing for women what the Fifteenth had proclaimed for men regardless of "race, color, or previous condition of servitude." However, it did not equalize *civil* rights for women, as those have not yet been gained in full except in a few states.

With greater hesitation the older states of Europe entered into the heritage of the new age. Old bonds were severed reluctantly. Long ago France tried to embody in law her revolutionary motto, and temporarily she made all men voters. Not until the Third Republic did France finally adopt manhood suffrage, about the time that Germany accepted the same standard. With true British conservatism England slowly extended the suffrage to householders and to lodgers; but not until 1918 did she really give the right to voters as men rather than as occupiers of property. In the same year five million women were added to the British polling lists, the franchise being extended still further ten years later.

Individualist democracy brought universal suffrage to women as well as men earlier in northern European countries than elsewhere. The Scandinavian peoples were first, before the World War; but that war marks an epoch for voters as well as for races. In conferring the elective franchise after 1918 Germany, Russia, and many lesser states made no distinction between the sexes. If democracy were chiefly a matter of extended franchise, the World War brought democracy even if it did not make the world safe for what there already was of it.

Important Revolutions in America during the Last Century

Changes brought by the Industrial Revolution and by political reorganization will be more clearly understood in relation to America before and after the World War if we examine sketchily the major transitions in recent American history before 1918. They are interesting because they show the interplay of economic and political forces at work in American experience. Contrary to our older beliefs, revolutionary transitions in America are not distinctively eighteenth-century phenomena. The American Revolution of that period, consisting of the revolutionary break with England and the revolutionary organization of a federal union, was not more important than the revolutionary changes brought about since 1850. Apparently these are political movements, or at least they come to climaxes in political campaigns and in part show real changes in the American political system or Constitution. The underlying forces in all of them, however, are economic. The *conflict* which culminates in each period is between successive types of economic institutions or "cultures." The outcomes are largely responsible for the shift in America *from a modified agricultural civilization toward the industrial civilization* which we have been working out in very recent years.[14]

The Civil War revolution

The changing world today is, therefore, not a thing apart. It is explained by previous revolutionary transitions as well as by that through which we are passing. One uses the word "revolution" advisedly and with hesitation; but accepts it without distortion because it expresses the real nature of these *drastic transitions in American experience*. To hesitate, or quibble, in its use might prove us unworthy to face fact or meet the issue squarely. If we will not do that, we add greatly to the difficulties that today confront us.

The two serious transitions of the nineteenth century went to the foundations of our political and business systems and our social order. The first was the "irrepressible conflict"

[14] See ch. IV, "Agricultural Civilization and the Present World."

between freedom and slavery. The second was the even more 2
fundamental, titanic contest between the old agriculturalism
and the new industrialism. A third, the present, is involved 3
in the reorganization of industrial capitalism. We hope that
from this transit will emerge a Twentieth-Century Renaissance. Such an outcome is a problem and responsibility of
the American people in our day.

The first great revolutionary conflict under the Constitution culminated in a Civil War. Viewed politically there had
been a struggle for supremacy between state sovereignty and
national sovereignty. When this neared a climax, *the contest
was between the slave plantation South,* which supported
state sovereignty as a means of protecting its ancient and
outworn system, and *the free North of farmers and industrialists.* The North was not a unit; it was made up of two
totally dissimilar elements, both free. One was the agricultural West, a land peopled by freehold farmers, "the first
Americans," the first of the world's races to develop a true
rural democracy. The other group of the North concentrated
on the new industry, though indirectly interested in commerce
and banking. Because it included a large and rapidly growing body of free workers, it made alliance with free farmers
against slavery.

The Civil War resulted in the overthrow of slavery and
state sovereignty. It created a new union, agriculturally
free; but facing forward toward a new industrial society.

This country of ours was born in individualism and nour- The agri-
ished in the spread of the frontier, a distinctly individualistic cultural-
environment. So long as there were free lands in the West, revolution
individualistic rural democracy moved forward with giant
strides and gave to all America, and to part of Europe, new
standards of rule by the people. As the frontier was ending
and free lands ceased to exist, cities sprang up, especially
throughout our northeastern area. These cities grew as industrial and commercial centers; they became banking communities and centers of capitalism. A quarter century after
the victory over the slave South, the agricultural West saw
a decline of its influence in American affairs; for industry

and capitalism were more concentrated, better organized, and had greater wealth. *Before the nineteenth century closed, industrial capitalism and agriculturalism came to a showdown.* A prolonged depression, in many ways like that of the recent years, and a great presidential campaign, obliterated party lines and hastened the agricultural debacle. The North-East stood for gold, the protective tariff, and capitalistic domination. The West and South enlisted under the banner of debtors, and the two "lost causes," agriculturalism and silver.

The triumph of industrial capitalism over agriculturalism continued and was not challenged in the succeeding generation; and the sway of the industrial capitalist was not changed. Not in the beginnings of invention and of the factory, but in this decline of agriculturalism and emergence of industrialism do we find *the real industrial revolution.*

The subordination of agriculturalism to industrialism was more than the triumph of one socio-economic system over another. It was the beginning of the end of the world's greatest historic civilization. Agriculturalism had its beginnings when man first learned how to plow, sow fields, and reap harvests. Then began use of buildings, settled abodes, permanent group organization and all the problems calling for definite laws, group religion, and well-knit social organization.

This civilization, several thousand years old, continued as the dominant force in the life of humanity with comparatively little change to the eighteenth century. The plows and spinning wheels of three thousand B. C. were not unlike those used by our forefathers two hundred years ago. Science had been born but it did not affect vitally the work or the lives of those living. But with the great Renaissance a really new science arose; and, when post-Renaissance inventions applied new forms of power, the old order was doomed.[15]

[15] The French Revolution, by which the *ancien régime,* surviving from the medieval ages, was replaced by a modern system of national reorganization, and the American revolution, with its ideas of equality, were only by-products of this ancient civilization. They produced no new civilization which sooner or later was destined, at least among western peoples, to con-

Industrialism grew great, not simply because of machines and new types of power, but also because people believed in individual enterprise and opportunities. This individualism in its turn had arisen in protest against medieval collectivism and during the eighteenth century against political and economic absolutism. In growing great it gradually undermined the foundations upon which it was built, because it could not assume giant proportions until it made use of the collected savings of hundreds, thousands, and hundreds of thousands even in a single corporation; and *this type of collectivism is the opposite of individualism.* Large-scale production therefore gave the death blow to any idea that competition is desirable or that business individualism is the best means of producing the maximum of wealth. Not only, therefore, did individualism tend to destroy itself in business, but science had the same effect. Originally, science was the creator both in improving inventions and in devising new and better and greater sources of power. But, as machines became larger and larger and machines were invented to make new machines, and as power became utilized more and more efficiently and became utilized at greater and greater distances from its source, large-scale industries competed with one another for survival. This competition of the industrial giants, so efficient that they did not need many workers and so productive that they could not sell all their goods, has created our present industrial impasse. Out of the dilemmas of industrial capitalism has grown the third great American revolution, brought into prominence by the World War, through which we are passing.

test the supremacy of agriculturalism, to attempt strangling the older system, and eventually to subordinate it, as has been done in America and western Europe in the twentieth century.

III

THE WORLD WAR AS AN EPITOME OF
CONTEMPORANEOUS CIVILIZATION

The cause of the World War was contemporaneous civilization. Neither is understandable without the other; at least the war would have been different under a different civilization, and the changes in civilization since 1918 are due greatly to that titanic conflict. The largest *direct* cause of the war was the conflict between the great alliances, the Triple Alliance and the Triple Entente. These alliances had been formed nominally for protective reasons, to prevent the important nations from being overwhelmed by powerful and dangerous neighbor enemies. This ostensible negative purpose was largely an excuse for an active, *aggressive nationalism*. Each nation was seeking not only to protect its nationalism regardless of consequences to others, but also was carrying on an offensive policy of foreign relations, military and naval armament, colonial expansion, exploitation of subject peoples or of races in controlled areas, and an imperialism which was partly political but chiefly economic. Without the Industrial Revolution and its vast expansion of large-scale industry, there would not have been the world-wide search for cheap raw materials and the still more extensive attempt to gain and control *world-wide markets* for the sale of finished products. In 1914 if not in later years, to many interested observers, the chief cause of the war appeared to be this terrible international competition for trade and profit.

CAUSES

NATIONALISM AND MILITARISM

Nationalism   Intertwined with other elements of modern civilization as a cause of world war was nationalism. Nationalism started

46

as a post-product of feudalism. As means of communication improved in the late Middle Ages and as the need for people to work together on a larger scale became imperative, the king appealed to the business sense of his subjects as well as to their racial conceit. He was able to rally to his standard most classes in most sections of his country. Royal progress capitalized both racial pride and business cupidity. It offered new trade opportunities and created a national selfishness which appealed to human nature.

Monarchy is not to be confused with nationalism, but without the development of monarchy, growing more absolute during the sixteenth and seventeenth centuries and changing into constitutional government, it probably would not have been possible for nationalism to have developed as it has done since the seventeenth century. Nationalism is not in itself a cause of war. Nationalism, however, fell heir to the feuds between the dynasties that ruled the great states of two or three centuries ago. Nationalism of other races or groups than these important powers was militaristic because they sought freedom from oppression by rulers who were not representatives of their own nation. Nationalism also fell heir to the struggle among the European states for a balance of power. Add to these forces and motives the struggle for national systems of colonies and for national expansion of trade, and the stage is set for nationalism as an important cause of war in the early twentieth century.

Any institution or organization persists unless it meets forces more powerful than itself. It may have outgrown the environment from which it developed, and it may have failed to adapt itself to the new changing conditions, especially in a world revolutionized by machine-power industry. Although nationalism had not been organized widely by the middle of the nineteenth century, already forces were at work toward a larger and better form of political group organization than it represented. Consequently when Germany and Italy achieved national unity in government, they at once encountered problems due to inter-nation competition.

The powers of Europe were united and presented a united

front chiefly in connection with the near-Eastern question and occasionally against Russia's ambitions and plans for Constantinople and in the Balkans. In practically all other respects they had few interests in common and were not very willing to work together. This is true whether we are speaking of statecraft as diplomatic means to gain the nation's selfish political ends or are concerned with foreign policies which were distinctively economic in character.

In Germany nationalism completed political organization of the German people through a policy of "blood and iron," a seventeenth century instrument. The resultant empire produced by Germany had many characteristics of seventeenth-century absolute monarchy; and her nationalism was too much one controlled by government, instead of one organized by a people. Possibly those traits fitted her well to combat the opposition aroused by her or against her in Europe. Possibly, also, they were helpful in gaining colonies in spite of her late entry in a new scramble for colonial empire, which was not unlike that of the sixteenth and seventeenth centuries. Certainly in the field of international commerce autocracy could plan more effectively and carry out more successfully than disorganized democracy. But nothing could repair the delayed start of Germany in the field of international competition. Consequently her search for a "place in the sun" made her seem the aggressor whether she was that or not.

Germany's national development upset the older order (almost an ancient régime) and threatened to replace the balance of power among the nations by her hegemony not simply on the continent of Europe but throughout the world. Her aggressiveness aroused the fear of her neighbors and developed an active defense on their part to protect themselves against her aggressive offense.

This does not mean that Germany caused the war. To assert that as a fact is to glorify the Teutonic empire and magnify her influence. It means simply that the late development of German nationalism and the peculiar forms that nationalism took in that country were more direct causes of the war than nationalism elsewhere. The peculiar combination of autocracy and economic development which characterized Germany probably constituted a more important cause of conflict than any other single situation or condition. To what extent Germany should be blamed for copying and exaggerating the methods and successes of her neighbors will be left probably to the judgments of individuals and of different national groups, no two of which will agree.

The old nationalism, as represented especially by England and France, but to some extent by Italy, was more democratic and consequently more liberal and progressive, if not more human, than this nationalism of Germany. The French and British peoples had fought out some of their national ambitions and plans and were ready to adopt more modern methods in the solution of new national and economic problems. Having gained colonies in past centuries, having recently added possessions in Africa and elsewhere, they stood for the maintenance of the *status quo.* When German speed and enterprise threatened their sources of raw materials and their markets, they were as willing as Germany to use the drastic methods of a bygone day.

Militarism can hardly be considered a distinct cause of war Militarism *or element of modern civilization.* It is rather a phase of the old nationalism reënforced by modernized methods, organizations, and scientific means of destruction. In fact, although force is a characteristic of many modern aggressive nations, in their internal policies as well as in foreign relations, it was the weapon of kings long before their peoples became nations. Ever since there have been modern kings, there have been armies gathered under their banners. The modern army and modern warfare came in with the use of gunpowder, muskets, and cannon, reënforced by royal treasuries out of which "national" rather than feudal troops could be paid. Modern military organization consists not only of standing armies but of large, well-equipped navies and of general staffs, which are really a part of the government. Military conscription was used by Prussia in the Napoleonic wars but was not adopted generally until the latter part of the nineteenth century, first in Germany and then in other countries. It is a necessity of rampant nationalism; and it is fairer than voluntary enlistment for democratic nationalism.

Superiority in naval armament occurred first in England. England, with her insular position and far-flung empire, was determined to have a navy which was very much larger than that of any other country. In the twentieth century Germany insisted upon having as large a navy as she wanted and needed.

After the Agadir Affair in Morocco (1911), a new struggle for land armament occurred on the Continent. Considerable controversy has arisen over the responsibility for this new development.[1] Both Germany and France have tried to shift blame to the other, oddly enough each being willing to yield priority in this race for a larger military force. The increased period of conscription from two to three years in France was laid to the door of Germany because it was claimed that Germany first began to increase her standing army. On the other hand, Germany has maintained that she had made only a partial increase in her army until it was known that France was to adopt a three-year rule. Then she acted. Ex-Chancellor Marx and other Germans assert that in France the war fever was at its height before the war broke out because France wanted war. People who visited Germany after 1911 insist that military preparations were active, and the war spirit was rampant long before the war broke out. Probably Russia, humiliated by Japan and reorganizing her army after 1905, was in a sense quite as militaristic as either Germany or France. Her army was certainly in better condition for mobilization than the Germans believed possible. Technical historians would place upon Russian mobilization of July 30, 1914, the actual blame for beginning hostilities. But Germany was able to mobilize her first line in twenty hours. Britain was able to send a hundred thousand men out of her small army into France within a few days after hostilities began. In point of fact, Great Britain had practically mobilized her navy before the first of August.

---

[1] Munition makers are now being held responsible for stirring up controversies and arousing national rivalry and hatreds.

Were any of these pots and kettles anything but black? Even if armies have been smaller since 1919 than before the war, are large standing forces needful with millions of ex-soldiers ready as reserves? Will militarism, from Russia, the Far East, or the older powers, decide the controversies and dominate the civilization of the near future? Will the science that has made war appalling threaten total destruction to the people who are drawn into another world conflict? Will militarism, with or without alliances, make *nationalism* the chief threat to the peace of the world?

ECONOMIC IMPERIALISM

The Industrial Revolution underlies the conflict of nations as well as the general material progress of nations in modern times. Without the development of machinery and the use of new forms of power and transportation industrial expansion in Great Britain, Germany, and the United States would not have led to keen economic rivalry throughout the world. To protect national industry and international trade, tariffs, subsidies, and international credit institutions were created; but they made economic conflict between nations easy or inevitable.

Beginning with the discovery of the New World and continuing to the opening up of Africa, the progressive nations of Europe "meekly" sought to inherit the earth by creating colonies, by acquiring protectorates, or by dominating spheres of influence. The *colonial expansion* of Portugal, Holland, England, France, and, in modern times, Germany and the United States has gone hand in hand with the extension of *national commerce*. Imperialism, including economic imperialism, has therefore been an important characteristic of modern life, and particularly of national expansion. The relation of mother country to colony has usually been that of a governing power exploiting a subject territory.

By continuing the old policies of seizing territory when opportunity offered and of developing home industries, the European nations were able to secure extensive supplies of raw materials, manufacture them without too much competi-

Struggle for commerce and colonies

tion from the outside, and sell them to their own people and in their colonies without the keenest competition. The success of these ventures induced them to follow the same plans outside of country and empire. They searched for and purchased raw materials in the best and cheapest markets. As time went on, each produced far more than its own people, including those in its colonies, could possibly use. *A new world-wide struggle for more business* was the result. It can hardly be said that this began with the attempt to secure cheaper raw materials; rather it included that; for the rivalry found its keenest expression in the marketing of goods. In *Imperialism and World Politics,* Parker T. Moon stresses the numerous interrelations existing between raw materials and imperialism.[2] He quotes the president of the German imperial bank as saying, "The fight for raw materials plays the most important part in world politics, an even greater rôle than before the [World] War." A few years ago the importance of raw materials was illustrated in the rubber industry, largely controlled by British interests. The desire of Germany to secure increasing supplies of iron ore was partly responsible for the Moroccan crisis, which was settled in favor of France in 1906, the controversy and the settlement being important causes of the World War.

Industrial expansion and its markets

It is impossible to understand the pre-war struggle for markets without noting *industrial changes and development in France, England, Germany, and the United States.* France has always devoted herself largely to the manufacture of fine materials, particularly by hand, quality not quantity being her motto. She did not suffer greatly from the keen machine competition of her neighbors. Great Britain owed her tremendous development and power in the early nineteenth century to her commerce rather than to her fleet. Until 1880 she was far ahead of all rivals in manufacturing, in shipping, and in foreign commerce. With that year the protection-fostered manufactures of Germany and the United States be-

[2] Moon, *Imperialism and World Politics,* pp. 542–558.

gan to loom large.[3] Before the World War the trade of
Germany and the United States was creeping up on that of
Great Britain, the total foreign commerce in Great Britain
amounting to something over six billions; that of Germany to
approximately five, and that of the United States to a little
more than four. The well-entrenched English world-wide
commercial system was therefore yielding to the attacks and
assaults of these two great rivals. They might have surpassed
her before 1914 had she not controlled so many colonies and
so much shipping. If economic rivalry was an active cause
of world conflict, how large a part was taken by Great Britain's threatened loss of world economic primacy!

Out of commercial needs grew government policies and attitudes, culminating in naval as well as economic rivalry.
Great Britain's chief need was the importation of foods and
raw materials; Germany's, the necessity of finding markets
for her goods; America's, general expansion sufficient to take
up the slack for the new marvelous prosperity.

Hampered though Germany was in lack of raw materials,
and no large country in Europe is poorer in them, she organized her factories well, called upon her universities to
develop scientific methods, particularly in chemical industries,
and then gave her exporters the greatest possible state aid.
Banks were organized everywhere throughout South America
and territories likely to be favorable for German trade. The
government granted subsidies, protected big trusts, and followed a policy of aiding, abetting, and protecting merchants
at every angle of the competitive game. America was careless of foreign needs; but, with her limitless resources and
huge-scale production, frequently undersold her rivals. In a
true sense before 1914 America was not a real competitor in
this wonderful new game of economic imperialism.

[3] In 1880 Great Britain produced nearly eight million tons of pig iron,
exceeding both Germany with less than three millions and the United
States with less than four. At the outbreak of the World War, Great
Britain's output had risen to only ten million tons, but Germany produced
nearly fifteen millions, and the United States twice that amount. Much
the same story is found in the production of coal. In the generation following 1880 Great Britain's increase was only seventy-five percent, against
nearly three hundred percent in Germany and tenfold for the United States.

Germany asserted that she wanted a place in the sun; that probably included world trade. As a matter of fact, her commercial sun was dimming those that shone upon French and English men of business. England and France had been first in the field in colonizing Africa, because Bismarck, anxious to dominate the continent of Europe, was neglectful of colonial conquests in Africa and elsewhere. When Germany did seek to gain possessions, she may have used more ruthless methods than her rivals had found necessary. The increase in her merchant marine and the building up of a navy seemed to threaten that of Great Britain. She refused consent to a "naval holiday"—to stop building vessels if England would do the same. In many ways she consolidated British fears of the new, great political and economic Germany. Undoubtedly her economic gains, as well as her ambitions in southwestern Asia, were largely responsible for the formation of the *Entente Cordiale* between England and France in 1904 and the completion of the Triple Entente between Great Britain and Russia in 1907.

Closely related to economic imperialism is international finance. In the half century before 1914 new ties had been created by the lending of huge sums by members of the Entente or the Alliance to other countries. These political aims entered not only into the German *Welt Politic* but into the policies of all the powers, least possible of Great Britain, the greatest of the lenders. British gold, half of the annual savings of the people of the British Isles, was invested abroad. Fortunately most of this was purely and distinctly business investment, chiefly in the British colonies. A quarter of the French foreign loans went to Russia and were quite political in character. In fact they were loaned by the one government to the other for the political advantage of both. Loans to the smaller countries of southeastern Europe rarely were separable from attempts to influence their governments or direct their affairs. Eventually "the official circles of lending countries gradually came to envisage the foreign investments of their citizens, not as private financial transactions, but as one of the instruments through which national destiny was

achieved." [4]   The pre-war system of international finance
tended to strengthen alliances, to foster national controversies,
and to make economic and military conflict inevitable.

RACIAL PROBLEMS AND NATIONAL PSYCHOLOGY

Economic imperialism is closely related to other forms of
imperialism, to national world policies, and to diplomatic
rivalries.   To treat one without taking into account another
would be to try to separate the sap of the tree from the tree
itself.   In all of them we find racial attitudes and national
characteristics or peculiarities reflected.

The very essence of national unity is not consolidated territory or a single independent government but *racial solidar-*
ity.   If that is old and of slow growth, it probably shows
itself in deep-seated racial characteristics such as British determination and French superior-mindedness.   When national
success is achieved by a few striking successes, it is likely to
take the aggressive form found in Germany before the World
War.   Racial character, like that of the individual, is many-
sided and complex.   A race that has proved its success in
leadership gains a self-confidence (and arouses an unpleasant
reaction) such as we find in the over-successful individual.

In the *development of national unity,* strong appeals frequently have been made to prejudice and hate.   Only in recent years have American school textbooks reflected anything
but intense hatred and disgust toward that dull but well-
meaning British monarch, George III.   The acme of national
patriotism seems to have been an appeal to fear or to racial
prejudice, a demand for "strafe," "straflichkeit," or "re-
vanche."   Often national prestige has been founded more upon
attempted humiliation of enemies than upon successes of the
home nation.   Short-sighted seeking of national advantage
arouses resentment that is not simply racial but universal.
Notice the antagonisms the United States has created in Latin
America over many years.   Check the hardly forgotten neglect or alienation of European friends and consumers since
the World War and the disregard of Orientals upon whom in

Racial prob-
lems and
policies

[4] Feis, *Europe, the World's Banker, 1870–1914,* p. xvi.

the future we must depend for business development in the Far East.

Past glories or former defeats furnish their own international problem. If a nation has had wider territories than it now possesses, it looks forward to the millennium which will come with the re-acquisition of these lost possessions. Years ago "Italia Irridenta" represented to the Italians the zenith of national desire. Although this goal has not been reached, the Italians have recently acquired lands in which Italians are out-numbered by those of other races. In the Balkan area the Rumanians, the Bulgarians, and the Serbians really expect some day to regain the lands which were part of some ancient empire of theirs in days of their glory. Only when two bodies can occupy the same space will the joint occupancy of these overlapping territories be a possibility—until then there will be conflict over claims or recessions.

Still another mirage as futile as lost power is that of natural boundaries. The best example of this will-o'-the-wisp is the Rhine boundary in relation to France. To give France this fine stream as her eastern limit would mean to include within her territories millions of Germans, including the inhabitants of the Saar valley, who expressed their preference for the Reich in no unmistakable terms (1935). Such an extension would give her practically the whole of the disputed lands of the original Lorraine sub-division of Charlemagne's empire granted to Lothaire in 843 A. D.

Ambitions, antagonisms, and prejudices have, therefore, been prolific causes of misunderstandings and of war. We of America find difficulty in comprehending the ancient feuds that separate European peoples who would like to elbow each other out of the way.

Psychology of western European peoples

National psychology in relation to other nations is expressed rather well in patriotism. Racial characteristics, set by generations or centuries of experience, may be latent and quiescent in times of peace, but in periods of stress and in war they became active and blatant. It is said that human nature is only skin deep, but careful observers of masses of men in battle doubt whether it is even that thick. Strangely enough, *nations* take pride in qualities similar to those of which humanity as individuals is becoming ashamed.

In the study of the last half century one is impressed by three characteristics of the three most important European powers. These may or may not have been important causes of World War; probably they were, but they are forces that will help to make or change the civilization of the future. One of these emotions has been the *fear complex of the French people*. This developed out of a combination of two elements. The first is the old culture of the French, which made them the leaders of Europe for several centuries. The second is the growth in numbers and armament and other forms of military or naval power possessed or gained by neighboring countries. The fear complex of the French was partly responsible for their attitude toward the expanding commercial and colonial authority of Great Britain in the seventeenth, eighteenth, and nineteenth centuries. After Sedan (1870) it concentrated against the growing power of the German Empire. Many French jingo leaders sought to preach a war of revenge; and the whole national psychology of the French people was built anew around the possibility of a new war with Germany. By this crusade the "lost provinces" (Alsace and Lorraine) were to be regained; in it probably invasion by Germany was the constant nightmare. Since the World War international affairs are explicable chiefly in terms of French fear and demand for security.

This inferiority complex of the French contrasted sharply with the *superiority complex of the British and German nations*. Bethman Hollweg and other German leaders accused Earl Grey and the English people of causing the war because Great Britain refused to take sides definitely. In siding with their traditional enemy, France, against the new Leviathan, Germany, but unfortunately not very openly in July, 1914, the people of the British Isles were simply following their traditional policy of joining the enemies of the fastest-growing and most progressive country of the Continent. Yet the British, secure in naval and commercial supremacy were as unprepared for trouble in war as in industry. In 1902, Lord

Roberts, with tears in his eyes, had appealed to Parliament, urging the enlargement of the army and the adoption of military conscription; but the English habit of following tradition was strong. What was good enough for their fathers was good enough for them. It took the invasion of Belgium to cause action by the ministry and to waken the British nation by sounding the tocsin.

Contrasted with the age-old belief of the French in their culture and their newer fear of having that crushed by Kultur; contrasted with the indifference born of belief in their own superiority which possessed the British, was the new-born national egotism of the German race. Modesty was never a Teutonic failing. The success of Bismarck in creating a new Germany, the unusual development of industry and expansion of commerce, made it easy for group egotism to become the dominant note for new German attitudes and policies. One cannot read much of German philosophy or browse through public utterances of their officials without realizing that the Germans believed thoroughly in themselves, their works, and their Kultur. Because as a nation they were young, they saw only one side of the situation. In the opinion of the Entente leaders they were thought to believe, that, as the chosen people, they should go in and possess the lands of their neighbors, compelling them to accept the worship of the new civilization—German Kultur.

The national psychology of a well-developed nation is different from that of one which is still in the making. Before 1914 Austria, Russia, and the new Balkan countries possessed territorial unity and powerful monarchs; but they had no racial or religious unity and no national consciousness. In spite of the fact that they were not yet true nations, they had all the ambitions and more than the ordinary prejudices of real nations. Because the inhabitants of these countries had not gained social solidarity or achieved the like-mindedness of united peoples, they had less control over their governments and less influence over their policies than did the western nations. Given unbridled passion, unscrupulous leadership, and ideals of possible interracial unity; and the stage was set for strife and local, possibly general, war.

National animosity or hatred is raised to the *"nth"* degree when it becomes racial in the larger sense. Between countries there was no such *intense rivalry as existed before 1914 between Pan-Germanism and Pan-Slavism.* Intensified by a struggle for Balkan control, made bitter by thousands of tiny bickerings, this came to a head in the quarrel between Austria and Serbia. It was brought about in July 1914 not only by long-standing differences but by the machinations of Russian trouble-makers, by Slavic societies in Serbia, by the assassination of the Arch-duke Ferdinand, the heir to the Austrian throne, June 28, 1914, but most of all by those who directed the affairs of the Dual (Austro-Hungarian) Monarchy.

INTERNATIONAL INFLUENCES AFFECTING THE WORLD WAR

Before practically all Europe and most of the world was involved in conflict, permanent peace had been expected. Would not the Hague Conference promote peace and the Hague Tribunal prevent war? To make war less inhuman, international agreements had been made, as in Paris in 1856 and at London in 1910. To draw a distinction between civilized and uncivilized warfare is absurd but such a distinction has the best historical authority. Beyond national boundaries agreements are binding only upon the contracting parties who wish to keep them; otherwise they become scraps of paper.

Foremost among direct and immediate causes of war and looming large as attempted international coöperation were the great alliances formed by the European powers. The first of these was the work of Bismarck. Just as he had secured unity of the north German states in a series of events culminating in 1871, so he sought security by a form of international unity soon after the German Empire had been organized. Most authors agree upon the base motives which actuated that statesman in promoting German unity by forcing war upon Denmark (1863), Austria (1866), and France (1870). Some have questioned whether his motives were of

The Triple Alliance and its influence

a higher order in organizing the *Triple Alliance* by alliances with Austria in 1879 and Italy in 1882. To checkmate this powerful group of nations, France and Russia, in 1894, completed a Dual Alliance. Undoubtedly they were actuated both by fear of Germany and by anxiety to increase their own power and prestige. If this Dual Alliance was not an international marriage of convenience, what was it? Money was to be furnished by France in exchange for the promise of soldiers from Russia.

In forming the *Entente Cordiale* in 1904, one would like to think that England and France were free from the sordid motives present in continental diplomacy. When they buried the hatchet, they took a long step forward; when they settled many problems in the New World they did by direct negotiation what had ordinarily been decided by indirect arbitration. Their main purpose, however, had little to do with Newfoundland or with Madagascar. It was concerned with Germany. By the understanding of 1904, Great Britain and France agreed that England should have a free hand in Egypt, where neither had a rightful claim, and that France should be equally dominant in Morocco, where the French rights were even more shadowy.

Germany was quick to sense the danger and was characteristically tactless in her protest. The Kaiser had already aroused English feeling at Damascus in 1898; he had proclaimed himself the friend of all Mohammedans, of whom England had too many in India. German officers had been reorganizing Turkish armies on the borders of English possessions and German capital had financed the notable *Baghdad Bahn.* One branch of this international railway from "Berlin to Bagdad" sought a southern terminus in Medina, opposite England's Egypt; another looked to an opportunity at Bagdad with commercial advantage on the Persian Gulf, not far from India. An international crisis was brought to a head not by the general competition for foreign lands but by the Kaiser's suggestion of German sympathy and support to Morocco when he visited Tangiers, Morocco, in 1905. The Algeciras Conference (1906) sought to smooth out these

Moroccan difficulties. In the voting, Germany had the support only of Austria and lost in influence if not in negotiations. Meanwhile delegates from Great Britain and Russia paved the way for an opposing triple alliance or organization developed out of the Entente Cordiale.

In 1907 the *Triple Entente* of England, France and Russia became fact. England and Russia no longer quarreled about Constantinople, subordinating their differences to prevent Germany's threatened control in the Near East. Taking advantage of a Persian revolution, they reorganized Persia with a Russian sphere in the north, a British sphere in the south, and a temporary Persian belt in the middle. *The Dual Alliance was merged with the Entente Cordiale.* Henceforward, France, Russia and England, the Triple Entente, stood shoulder to shoulder against the Triple Alliance, Germany, Austria and Italy. Europe was divided into two armed camps, each ostensibly seeking peace, but determined to uphold national power and prestige at almost any cost. No longer backed by the most powerful group of nations in Europe, the mailed fist ceased to be the threat it had been. The Triple Entente and conflicts

It does not seem possible that a gunboat dispatched by Germany to Morocco (Agadir Bay) could possibly have brought Europe to the verge of war. Yet it happened. Germany had hoped that England's "understanding" with France was merely understanding. In 1911 she learned her mistake. Great Britain intimated that war against France was war against her; but no nation was prepared for a general conflict. Nineteen hundred eleven rather than 1914 is the turning point in this great struggle between nations, or rather between the two grand alliances, the open conflict between which precipitated the Great War, afterward the World War.

Beginning in 1911 the armed forces of practically all the continental countries were increased. Industrially, financially, commercially, and in other ways, Germany sought enthusiastically from 1911 to 1914 to prepare herself for a serious struggle. In France the government and the War College with single-mindedness of purpose prepared for war. From that time the French War College devoted itself to two things:

a plan of campaign to combat Germany when she invaded France, and the necessity of offensive warfare.

We end our discussion of causes, therefore, as we began: *the cause of world war was the peculiar character of contemporaneous civilization.* The unevenness with which humanity has developed different forms of material or cultural civilization or group organization, especially in nations, accounts in large part for the conflict which involved the most important countries of the globe. Science the benefactor became science the destroyer, making the war progressively more atrocious in the years before the Armistice. The public or social standards of the twentieth century are in many ways superior to those of previous ages; but both business and government pride themselves on sharp and unscrupulous practices which have long been taboo with individuals in their relations with one another. The intrigues of secret diplomacy would not be tolerated, let alone respected, in the methods of our neighbors as citizens. The distinction which some have attempted to draw between civilized warfare and uncivilized warfare represents an attempt to discard exceptionally objectionable practices from previous ages of barbarism.

The rallying cry of *democracy versus autocracy*, sincere and genuine in the hearts of those who believed themselves crusaders, appears after a decade or two an untrue characterization of America's part in this titanic conflict. Certainly nationalism, whether of the independent or of the alliance type, cannot be guiltless of the major share in making a great war inevitable and of dragging in other nations which needed, or thought that they needed, to protect their own power or plans.

Industrial capitalism took an active part in shaping the public policies of rival nations and in deciding that war would advance the interests alike of industrialist and financier. Especially significant as cause of war, therefore, was the economic rivalry behind the most severe business competition. Economic imperialism worthy of the name is as true a product of the Industrial Revolution as are the machines, methods of applied science, and revolutionary developments in transportation, without which modern economic imperialism would have remained retarded, undeveloped and inactive. At the outbreak of the conflict this struggle for economic supremacy covered the whole horizon, but from the vantage point of a later day we discover that in itself it does not explain a world-wide war between nations.

In a real sense the nations reverted to conditions of three thousand years ago in making Jehovah the god of battles for their own tribe, but they did not accept for themselves except as individuals the command of Jehovah, "Thou shalt not kill." Culture and religion were made instruments of patriotism, denying them their proper place in creating a civilization of international peace, progress and goodwill.

Results

COSTS, WINNINGS, LOSSES

The causes of world war might give an excellent explana-   Costs
tion of important elements of contemporaneous civilization. At once we discover [5] that industrial capitalism apparently was not so important a cause of war as it is an element of present-day civilization. Evidently, from the material we have gathered, age-old social habit, re-formed in the molds of national group organization, played a larger part than did industrial capitalism. In examination of the shift from agricultural civilization with its social heritage to our present order [6] it may be possible to trace some of the *forces at work* which caused a world war and were either *destroyed by it, re-diverted through it, or in a new form accentuated by it.*

The influence of the World War in Europe and America since 1919 shows itself through the costs that have been paid and through the successes and failures of the war itself. The price paid in human life and in money affected the later development of the western world. The costs, human and material, were appalling.[7] More than eight and a half million lives were forfeited directly, besides the other millions lost through serious injury, through illness traceable to the war,

[5] Part II.   [6] Chapter IV.
[7] Bogart, E. L., *Direct and Indirect Costs of the Great World War.*

or among civilians through depleted physique. Children born during the war in many cases did not have proper food or care; and the total toll upon the vigor and vitality of humanity in the loss of lives of young men was vividly explained by David Starr Jordan in his study of the vitality costs of the Napoleonic wars.

The actual direct cost of the war in money has been computed at 186 billions, with indirect costs about as much more. In the opinion of many observers, commercially if not governmentally, the costs of the war were soon repaid and the losses almost completely recouped. One reason for this belief is the great inflation of currency during the war and either the extraordinary depreciation or the stabilization of currencies at a small percentage of pre-war values. Germany wiped out most of her debt by the practical annihilation of the value of the mark. In 1926 France stabilized the franc, at one time worth less than two cents of American money, at approximately one-fifth of its pre-war value. In England and in America, where there was no conscious stabilization at a lower value, or internal inflation except that which came with the war, prices remained for a long time far above the 1914 level.

These monetary changes reduced greatly the amounts represented by the post-war debts of the belligerent countries. Difficult as it was to balance national budgets, it has been impossible to agree upon or to pay up international indebtedness. German reparations, planned originally as a huge sum, have with each successive conference been whittled down until little is left.[8] Heavy national interest charges and payments on war claims or war loans are a considerable, if not the largest, part of every national government budget. It would be impossible to estimate the effect of war debts upon national or international policies and psychology. The problem of their payment or non-payment is interwoven with almost all questions taken up in any international economic conference. It affects all plans for national security, disarma-

---

[8] Compare the German and Allied claims regarding the amount that has been paid.

ment, ententes, or other post-war inter-nation problems of a political character. It has constantly threatened the peace of Europe.

Possibly the influence of the war is explained in part by a consideration of who won it or lost it. Possibly the query of who won it may be quite as academic and almost as pointless as an investigation of who caused it.[9] Spengler [10] maintains that no "state" won the World War. He is quite as positive however that "the labor leader won the war." Probably an examination of governments in central and eastern Europe in the years following 1919 would seem to prove his statement. The spread of autocratic government, however, at least in Russia, Italy and Germany, certainly seems to indicate that leaders of a socialist party or type did not keep their winnings long. The quasi-leadership of France, due to alliances and military power, might indicate what forces won the conflict. If industrial capitalism was responsible, in large part, for the war, except for a temporary splurge of the subsequent period of prosperity, it gained a Pyrrhic victory.

Who won the war?

Possibly it is equally academic and pointless to ask the question: "Who lost the war?" Germany seems to have done so if we consider the colonies of which she was deprived and other territories of the German Empire in central Europe which were taken from her. In the years following 1919 Germany seemed to have lost because of her low military standing, her loss of prestige, her dishonored political status and her ruined business abroad if not at home. If Germany did not lose the war, it was about the only thing she did not lose, as the map and post-war records seem to testify. Certainly Germany's problems have entered into almost all post-war crises, at least in Europe.

[9] In the Treaty of Versailles, made without consulting Germany, the Allies agreed upon Germany's war guilt. With the passing of the years and the publication of archives, not including the most valuable documents in British or French possession, the evidence shows rather clearly that no one country or government must bear the responsibility for the war, for all had some share in bringing it about. As already shown, the causes lie much deeper than any pan-racial program or military policy or national diplomacy or international intrigue. William Bennett Munro is not far wrong when he says that the question *"Who caused the war?"* is as dead as the dodo.

[10] Spengler, *The Hour of Decision*, p. 147.

If the "greatest depression in history" can be chalked up on the debit side against the account of the World War, the losses of every country will loom very large indeed. During the last century and a quarter our most serious depressions have followed rather closely upon wars. Probably there is more than an accidental connection between these severe depressions and the preceding wars. If so, all the western peoples lost the war.

A computation therefore of costs, winnings, and losses seems to sum up as follows. It is difficult to discover directly who won or what was won. It is easy to count up the things destroyed. It is necessary to watch even though we may not learn what changes followed the war and how they altered the civilization of the pre-war period. Possibly by the destruction of old institutions, ideas, or practices which should have been abandoned—or at least were no longer necessary or valuable—or possibly by the starting of new institutions or procedures, we shall find the real gains to humanity growing out of this world crisis.

SURVIVING THE WORLD WAR

The war naturally became itself a major cause of disintegration and reorganization. Trends which were hardly visible before this great conflict loomed fairly large after it was over. Tendencies which promised to develop along certain lines were often diverted into new and sometimes radically different channels. In this summary, there is no desire to examine or explain events or changes, from the historical viewpoint, which occurred either in Europe or America after the war and due to the war. *The place of the World War in modern civilization* will hardly be discoverable, however, unless we get at least a glimpse of, first, the extent to which elements of civilization which caused the war survived or were accentuated by that holocaust; secondly, new influences at work growing out of the war itself; and, thirdly, deep-seated changes in human organization, public policies, or social philosophy, really traceable to the war.

Trade before the war was like yet unlike that after the war.[11] If we omit the foreign business Germany lost and America gained, the differences are slight. Great Britain may have fought to protect her trade. If so, she was out of luck, when we consider her difficulty in increasing her exports and her problem in meeting foreign competition after 1920. Possibly the war is not to be blamed for the rapidly increasing industrialization of countries in south-central Europe, or in a minor degree of India, China, and Japan. Certainly the foreign market for manufactured articles has been poorer since 1919 than before 1914. Many observers have counted changes in foreign trade as the chief up-set caused by the war.

Economic changes

Trade changes were part of new shifts in creditor-debtor relations between nations. Through reparations or new loans Germany became debtor to most other western countries. Through war debts all the Allies owed Uncle Sam. Shifts in trade made America the creditor of half the world. Creditors wished to be paid in gold, but France and America had most of the world's supply. Creditor countries often refused to continue credits abroad, or make new investments away from home, thus hurting business in the debtor countries which needed financial help. Creditors would not allow the debtor countries to pay obligations in goods because, as just noted, each country was trying to sell more than it bought. Added to all this was *the attempt to protect economic nationalism,* an inevitable corollary of political self-determinism. Protective tariffs sought to reduce imports, but succeeded chiefly in arousing antagonism with other nations.

If *nationalism* was important as a cause of world war and as an element of the Treaty of Versailles, one would expect that it might not be less important since 1919. At first a wave of internationalism swept Europe, though not official America. This did not last, or, when it did, it was concerned chiefly with attempts to reconcile differences between countries. In each of the powers every problem that was especially economic or international was examined carefully to see how it affected the internal policies and success of that separate

Political changes

[11] See Hansen, A. H., *Economic Stabilization in an Unbalanced World*, I.

nation. Not only were the governments jealous of commercial
gains of rivals, but proposals for economic conferences or disarmament meetings stirred up feeling within the separate
countries against all foreign peoples and instigated demands
from factions, if not from governments themselves, that no
nation should yield to any other. Inter-nation alliances were
made, as the Little Entente of Czechoslavakia, Jugoslavia,
and Rumania, in consultation with France, and the Franco-
Russian agreement or alliance of 1935. Attempts at disarmament were resisted, or the decisions set at naught, by the
refusal of some party, as Japan, to accept the share allotted
to it. Disarmament among the Allies, as promised in the
Versailles Treaty, became a dead letter.

Within the borders of the powers and some other countries
nationalism took on a new form. Possibly it would be more
accurate to say that nationalism revived, in nationalistic
form, some of the worst traits of absolute monarchy. Government policies, especially after the onset of depression,
sought to adopt new nationalist measures, as money standards, trade protection, army expansion, press and school national propaganda. Many of these were urged and adopted
in spite of the way they might injure neighbor countries. In
fact, some of the crowded nations probably changed old
policies into others more nationalist in the hope of injuring
rival or enemy nations. In order to make nationalism more
rampant and successful, some governments became more
narrow and arbitrary, substituting dictatorships for constitutional government and suppressing every faction, movement
or plan that seemed to interfere with their brand of nationalism at home.[12] In a sense, this was a substitution for nationalism of a new type of absolutism. But possibly fascism as
practiced for selfish *national* reasons in Italy and Germany is
only an exaggerated form of the self-contained systems sought
or tried in western Europe and in America.

Did this new pseudo-nationalism mean that constitutional
government has been suffering an eclipse? At the close of
the war the trite phrase of "making the world safe for

[12] See ch. XII.

democracy" seemed to have had real meaning. Germany and all the German states became republican. Many other new constitutions were adopted. Had the war not brought the issue between Great Britain and Ireland to a head, the Irish Free State might have waited a score or more of years for any legal status at all. Before the war rulers took pride in being absolute; afterward they went through the motions expected of constitutional monarchs. Whatever the war may have done for democracy, what it did to kings is conspicuous. Of all of the ruling houses at the opening of the twentieth century, in 1934 those in northern European countries alone are still ruling in about the same way. Possibly the fact that practically no government which started the war survived it may be the best possible reason for not starting another, unless the rulers are too ignorant or unwilling to learn from experience.

Americans are sometimes surprised to discover that the American system of presidential government, with its checks and balances, is little used across the Atlantic. Parliamentary government had made considerable progress before the World War. Apparently it had gained complete sway almost everywhere in the years immediately following. But most of these countries had little experience in responsible government, had no dual party organization [13] suitable for the management of this scheme, and made as little success of it as Italy did during the ten years after Rome had been added to the Italian kingdom.

During the war the democratic countries managed to show an adaptability and a flexibility in handling their problems that the more autocratically ruled peoples did not have. Their resilience under stress and strain may have had little connection with the type of government they used; it may have been far more a part of their educated intelligence, their coöperative interest in public affairs, their sense of long standing social unity and psychological solidarity as nations. Whatever the basis of the people's resistance and response in face of apparent defeat, their governments certainly showed

[13] P. 359.

70 HISTORICAL TRANSFORMATION

the need of some reorganization and re-adaptation even in the best years which preceded the world's greatest depression (1929). The war may have been fought for democracy and won by democratic peoples, but it was not won by democratic methods. In winning a war, losses must be disregarded. Victory demanded concentrated power and thus gave an experience in centralized organization which has been used since in emergencies or as a regular policy. Is militarism less conspicuous since the war than before? The great alliances have disappeared; many smaller alliances and ententes have been formed. Most conspicuous among all the changes brought about by the war was an apparent increase of internationalism.

In central and eastern Europe the swing of the pendulum from absolute to liberal governments, more or less socialistic, lasted an even shorter time than was to be expected. Depression with its attendant problems, national and international, probably gave a new impetus to dictatorships. However, the rise of Mussolini in Italy and of Rivera in Spain soon after the war indicated either the need of arbitrary rule in those countries, possibly to prevent the spread of bolshevism, or the supposed value of fascism as a means of solving their political problems. In any case, reaction has seemed to be in the ascendant outside of the industrial democratic areas of Europe.[14]

Internationalism

What of internationalism, or its component elements, since the World War? Is internationalism threatened by militarism? Germany and Austria were practically disarmed by the Treaties of Versailles and Saint Germain-en-Laye; though long before 1935 Germany had rearmed, and in 1935 Hitler did not hesitate to declare it as a right. The French army is as large as formerly, and the hegemony of France since the war may be due to her army more than to any other or all other causes. The struggle for rearmament in Germany and the desire of other countries to establish huge armies in time of peace have been causes of national and international disputes. President Hoover's appeal for a very sharp reduc-

[14] See ch. XIII.

tion of armaments and all the disarmament conferences have made no dent in the war programs and very little in the war expenditures of most of the European countries. America may have seemed to escape this general tendency, or so we think until we come to notice the naval if not the military budget of the United States. War is unpopular in talk and in pacts, but no nation intends to be caught unprepared.

Has internationalism succumbed to the revival of nationalism in recent years? Nationalism and insistence on national prestige seem hardly less strident than before 1914. Development of policies according to national prejudices and rivalry for national advantage almost dominates the European scene. Revenge, which was the cry of the conquered after the Franco-German War, is probably more conspicuous in Germany today than it was in France a half century ago. Her lost colonies and lost territories, coupled with her opposition to paying war damages and even just debts, coupled also with national jealousies and national ambitions, threaten new war. The fear of war, which before 1914 rose occasionally on the horizon, now threatens close at hand. The Treaty of Versailles, instead of being a peace without victory, was an eighteenth-century nationalistic document, almost of a dynastic character, which contained within itself the seeds of, not one war, but possibly several future wars.

The coöperation of nations in a large-scale coalition ended the war and overthrew Germany in 1918. This coalition did not survive, being purely of a military character; nor did the pre-war grand alliances continue. With the organization of the League of Nations, the Covenant of which was part of the Treaty of Versailles, and the subsequent formation of a World Court, more than fifty countries were brought together in a permanent organization. The League and World Court naturally have been in no sense an international government. The bond between members has been extraordinarily weak, and concerted action by the powers has been due almost entirely to the work of the Council, representative chiefly of a few great powers. Nevertheless, at no time in history has the spirit of internationalism been stronger than since 1919;

and there has been increasing consciousness that world-mindedness is worthwhile.

Conclusion   It would be interesting if one could delve into the causes and nature and outcomes of the World War enough to segregate those which may have contributed something to the transition to an industrial civilization, negatively perhaps. Was the war in any real sense due to a failure of proper development from the old agricultural to a new industrial civilization? In what fields and in what ways did the lag of government in relation to science and industry, or the lag of international political organization in a world becoming commercially internationalized, lead to conflict or become a major element of the struggle? Was individualism responsible for the failure to keep the peace? Did political policies, either autocratic, nationalistic, or insufficiently collectivist, lead to external or internal demands for better adjustments and a fairer reorganization within these fields? Why were the munition makers the truest pre-war internationalists? What caused the failure of socialists absolutely to support any international program of peace when war costs workers so dear? Why did they support national programs contrary to their interests rather than an international policy favorable to their class? Had the world failed to break the bonds of outworn isolated nationalism for the needs of a common humanity? Has it yet?

IV

CIVILIZATION IN TRANSITION

Agricultural Civilization and the Present World

Surviving the World War has been simple compared with Introduction outgrowing traditional civilization. We speak of the civilization of the past as an agricultural product and refer to the last half century as a true transition from an agricultural to an industrial capitalist régime. Out of the old how much have we kept? To what extent is the new really original, distinctly different from the old? As we have rebuilt our civilization, chiefly by a series of unconscious adjustments, have we abandoned the social habits, the action patterns, of our ancestors, in any of their essentials? Even if we tried, could we do that rather successfully? We are transforming our civilization in spots, but undoubtedly it holds us in the grip of thousands of inherited customs and traditions.

The past, which brings us its heritage and prepares us for the present, handicaps us in making fundamental transitions. The serf of the Middle Ages was bound to the land. We of the twentieth century are equally bound to the land and its civilization, that is, held by the bonds of an agricultural civilization started several millenia ago. So closely is economic organization interwoven with the political system and the social order that land and its cultivation gave rise long ago to usages, to forms of government, to law, to religion, and to an intricate system of social life which have survived almost to our day, which may even persist today.

So far as the old agricultural civilization survives, its survivals frequently fit badly into the present times and are rather absurd. James Harvey Robinson, in the last half of *The Mind in the Making*, decries people's reluctance to abandon

73

ideas that are old, although the need for change may be very great. In his belief the progress of mankind is unnecessarily blocked by these traditional drags upon humanity's upward progress. Because we are slow in adopting change, we need not urge that we move slowly, nor really be afraid that we shall discard the old before the new is created. Is there not real danger, however, that, passing not only from a period of agriculturalism to one of industrialization but also from one of individualism into one of greater socialization,[1] some who cling to individualism or who make individualism an excuse might expect to take advantage of these shifts to do what seems right in their own eyes? If no adequate, *substituted standards* have been devised for the old customary norms, whither are these transitions leading us?

Modern investigators are just beginning to realize the extent to which we are using customs and group procedures developed when agriculture and grazing were young. Even so prominent a phase of present civilization as family life or religious thought goes back to the time when the first farmers revolutionized the method of supplying humanity with food. Later we shall consider institutions, patriarchal or primitive in type, which have become to us among the most sacred symbols of life today. Examined in their historical setting, or analyzed to discover their real character, we find many of these far better suited to undeveloped agricultural societies than to a machine world, with its large cities and exceedingly complicated interrelations.

Heritage and Present Need

What is this agricultural civilization to which we refer as though it were a well integrated unit? How long had it existed? Did it have similar characteristics over the whole of its existence? Shall we identify the frontier civilization of colonial or nineteenth-century America with the ages long past, in medieval England, or in classical Rome, or in dawn Egypt?

Certainly the civilization of the early agriculturist did not

[1] See ch. X.

bear a close resemblance to that of later and much more settled times. However, the estate of the Egyptian noble was not radically different from the "latifundia" of the later Roman empire or the feudal estate, or in some respects of the modern British landed property. Methods of cultivation changed little from Babylonian days to the day of George Washington. The Dakota wheat grower of today would probably rejoice at stalks of wheat with heads equal in size to those described by Herodotus, five inches in length, as the regular product of Mesopotamian fields. Or was Herodotus' Babylonian correspondent a pre-Christian prototype of our twentieth-century promoter? In spite of experimental stations and scientific breeding of plants, the average ear of corn today may not be appreciably larger or better than those which John Smith took from the unwilling Indians in the starving time of Jamestown.

Not agricultural methods or products, not even the organization of the farm and the family on the farm, represent the chief heritage from an agricultural society and civilization. For the bequests that it has made us rather do we look to its social organization, its government and its religion.

Food scarcity was a far more serious problem in distinctively agricultural ages than in the later days of commercial inter-change and in the still later periods of industrial productivity and extensive markets. As late as the nineteenth century, local famines were not unknown, chiefly in primitive regions but also among civilized peoples such as those of Western Europe. The twentieth century also has suffered from that calamity among the dense populations of Asia. Poor methods of cultivation and small crops did not leave a sufficient margin of surplus in any one community to meet the demands of famine or pestilence in others. But, when adjacent territories were isolated, because they were separated by natural barriers or by artificial tolls or by lack of any means of communication, local famines were common even though there was plenty in the next valley.

With the coming of commerce, roads inevitably were built. Rivers were used, and oceans were crossed. After the creation

Agricultural economics of scarcity

of the factory, by a touch of the modern Jove (machine power) raw materials, Minerva-like, became quickly full fashioned. Peoples who could manufacture now had huge surpluses for exchange at prices far above actual costs. Limited supplies of food now meant little to any industrial country, unless war blockades prevented a natural exchange of goods.

Even the addition of commerce on the Seven Seas and the substitution of robots for men did not for years and years modernize an *obsolescent economics of scarcity*. Business was dynamic; but most of the technics, business ideas, business regulations, whether in the relationship of employer to employe, of buyer to seller, or owner of capital or property to borrower or renter, remained static. For a long time very little change took place in the customs or in the rules by which these persons or groups dealt with each other.

Law

Dean Pound of the Harvard Law School says that our great problem of law breaking is due to the fact that we are trying to use a rural system of criminal law in an urbanized world. One special difficulty is due to the lag of law in its attempt to keep up with rapidly changing conditions, of which urbanization is an important part. A man can secure the property of others in numerous ways if he is skilled in high finance, if he has the advice of able lawyers and if he works on a sufficiently large scale. His offense may be "good business," not even mentioned in the criminal law, possibly not in the civil codes as well. Corporations, by the use of legal rights as persons, have gained a fair part of the wealth of America; *corporate property has partially supplanted private property in this country.*[2] Yet our whole system of law is built on the concept of private property. This would seem to give legal advantage to the owner of private property, that is, to the average citizen, in the protection of property rights; but this is not the case.[3]

The student of law today finds it convenient to have some acquaintance with the Latin language. Legal phraseology bristles with phrases from that tongue. If this is true in

[2] Pp. 117–118.
[3] P. 392.

America and true in England, what must be the case in western Europe or in Latin America, where the law is much more closely related to the old Roman law of Justinian and earlier codifiers? These Roman laws, as one could see easily if he were to study the process by which they were first developed, undoubtedly were built upon the best of the very much older legal rules. They were supplemented moreover by old ideas of justice and equity, the two being built together into a system which has made the world's finest code of laws. Not only the form of the laws but the legal ideas have survived, whether they fit our present-day needs or not. And they survived because they did fit rather well into the world not only of continental Europe but of England and America so long as the peoples had not departed greatly from the agricultural civilization, organization, ideas, and procedures of their ancestors.

The English developed for themselves, out of their own needs and conditions, quite a different type of law, which we know as *the common law*. The early American colonists brought these laws to America with them, changed them in part to meet the needs of a less settled life, but counted them almost the most precious part of their visible heritage. So far as that law dealt with simple personal relationships it probably does not meet so illy the requirements of the present. So far as it deals with business relationships and with more complicated problems of modern men in their dealings with one another, its modification, revision, and in some cases complete cancellation seem desirable.[4] But, so long as the law stands for accepted rules, an authoritative expression of ways of doing things, it is rather difficult to make any complete change by anything short of revolution.

It would seem as though the American habit of turning out statutes by the hundred, and possibly by the thousand, at each legislative sitting would give us new and up-to-date laws promptly. On the contrary, most of these statutes seem only to modify some minor item, to change a procedure, limit a

[4] On the revision of the common law, consult Stoodley, Bartlett H., in *North American Review*, 194 (1934), pp. 24–30.

penalty, rather than bring in a new idea. If a layman, not an administrator, afterwards a Supreme Court justice, or a Harvard law school man or a Columbia University professor, were to suggest that much of our law is antiquated, out of date, replete with contradictions, and full of injustices, he might immediately be branded an anarchist or worse. Yet, if we have really modified our civilization and ways of living together, common sense would indicate that the abandonment of out-worn rules and practices should not be delayed indefinitely.

Why, then, does law change so slowly? [5] Possibly because it is the very essence of authoritative tradition; possibly because law is custom re-interpreted by courts, rather than statutory additions to the body of law already in existence. If this idea is correct, we perceive at once the difficulty but also the opportunity of re-adapting old laws to new needs. What is as inflexible as custom? What is less likely to give change than judicial decision based upon precedent? What lacks adaptability more than usage interpreted by conservative judges? Yet what is simpler than, by a few sweeping judicial decisions, to change old interpretation when real need arises?

Religion   Whatever the origins of the laws or political institutions in use by any people, it is safe to predict that both, in the beginning if not now, carried religious sanctions. In the past, and especially in medieval and ancient times, religion occupied a broad field that has since become secular. If law is venerated, especially by those whose vested interests it protects, how much more unchangeable must we expect to find the ideas and the standards in the field of religion. We no longer have any state churches; but many other legal or social institutions have not shifted with the years from the religious sphere to the secular. They have remained in the ever decreasing orbit within which religion is recognized as supreme.

Religion possesses not only the authority of law, but its permanence is assured by the divine sanctions upon which it

[5] Pp. 88–90.

is built. The conclusion is almost inevitable that any body of rights, beliefs, ideas, or practices which was considered religious would necessarily be readjusted to new conditions more slowly than almost any other custom or institution. Impossible therefore might it be, first, to evaluate those characteristics of modern nineteenth-century religion which have come down to us from an agricultural civilization. Secondly, we should find it quite as difficult to examine, explain, and determine the influence of industrial civilization upon our present religion. Thirdly, even harder is the discovery of ways in which we can keep religion pure and undefiled and yet make it meet the needs of a new dynamic society.

In the past, religion has depended on authority. But the day of unreasoned and unreasoning authority is gone. Not only modern youth but the western world is in revolt against the bonds of any system and the claims of any institution that finds its authority only in the things it did for peoples long ago. Religion, so far as it has depended on its appeal to the unknown, finds its hold constantly weakened by the marvelous advance of human knowledge. It may take heart that with widening horizons the contacts with the unknown inevitably increase in number and possibly in significance. Religion as ritual plays a constantly smaller part in a practical world. Religion as paternalism is incompatible with modern individualism and with the freest and best expression of social service. Religion as dogma runs counter to the clearest and most enlightened thought of an age that, if slogan-minded, wants modernist motives. Religion as institutionalism finds itself rather a misfit in an urban and industrial world.

If eternal truth is confused with old ecclesiastical systems or with long sanctioned, literal observance of priestly dictates, the past fights religious advance in the present. Fortunately our religious heritage is one of substance as well as form. Spiritual values, always a chief aim of religion, increase in importance as we learn more about creation and the Creator. The brotherhood of man increasingly ceases to be a phrase, because *society rather than the patriarchal family or the clan assumes responsibility as its "brother's keeper."*

Our agricultural ancestors perfected the patriarchal family; and in a way have bequeathed it to us. Many European peoples still cling to a family organization that is distinctively paternalistic, the father dominating wife and children as in old days. Western and Northern Europe have abandoned the harshest features of the patriarchal régime. In the strict sense the old patriarchal family never was transplanted to America but, until industrialism became dominant in this country, the home was not radically different from that of the traditional family.

Modern conditions, even before the present time, have been unsuitable for the family system bequeathed by antiquity. Democracy and the emancipation of woman are corollaries. The individualism that has pervaded all modern thought, aided and abetted by crowded city conditions, has been a centrifugal force that has affected family solidity. Possibly it is responsible to some extent for breaking up the unity of home life. One by one the characteristics of the outgrown patriarchal family disappear, unhonored if recognized as obsolete but deeply regretted when still of some value or part of our present culture pattern.

In the traditional family the father has been legally and often actually the head. He it is who has inherited the property about which the family has been organized; and his word has been law. Marriage has been arranged by the parents, a synonym for a match-making mother, and the alliance has been a family one between a boy and a girl of somewhat the same social status and economic standing. "Who giveth this woman" is a modern survival of transfer of ownership from father to husband. In this family the wife and mother had no separate status, being a dependent; in it children were seen but not heard. At its best it idealized woman, placing her on a pedestal. Man, being worshipful but passionate, kept his ideal even when he maintained a double moral standard.

The traditional family developed differently under different conditions. In the age of the patriarchs, it was a large and fairly homogeneous group isolated by the width of its pastures from any neighbors. In the agricultural age, the family was rather the individual family, cultivating its own lands, living in a permanent home apart from its neighbors, but not necessarily at a distance from them. Possibly the agricultural community, for example the village of modern France or Russia, may have kept the traditions of the patriarchal family alive, whereas the separate farms on western American prairies made its disintegration easy, even in the agricultural stage of existence. Frontier life helped the breaking down of the traditional family; for "family" did not count very much in the back woods or on rolling prairies. Family alliances were not needed to join acre to acre, or farm to farm, if there were other boundless acres beyond. America made the continuation of a patriarchal system unnecessary. Nevertheless, the patriarchal family has left us multifold ideas and traditions.[6]

We must never overlook the debt we owe to humanity in its earlier years or underestimate the influence of habits humanity has acquired in past ages. But, if survivals from antiquity or from the Victorian period in no way longer meet any need, or any want, how obsolete must they be before we change them or the civilization built upon them—the latter being stupid in so far as it does not make necessary adjustments? In the process of reorganization the change from old to new may depend on the antiquity of the institution under view. The earlier may be most in need of rebuilding; the later will undoubtedly yield more quickly to the pressure of new demands.

RECENT MODIFICATIONS OF SOCIAL HERITAGE

Far more modern than law, religion, the patriarchal family, and scarcity economics are individualism, nationalism,[7] and democracy—publicly social concepts, ideas, associations, or institutions, developed by agricultural societies and yet not fully developed until agriculture was well buttressed by commercial

---

[6] On the modern family, see ch. XVI.
[7] On nationalism, see pp. 36–39, and pp. 440–445.

and industrial expansion. Each of these concepts may therefore be dismissed briefly, although each is well worth careful
study.

Individ-
ualism   Individualism [8] apparently is an expression of social *thought*
and inter-action rather than a primary characteristic of social
organization and action. The teachings of Jesus stressed the
worth of the human soul, and His church was the most important institution of the Middle Ages—and yet individualism
gained very little hold until protest was made against the
medieval church and society in the early Renaissance period.
As we have already noted, individualism made very little, except academic, headway until long after the Reformation was
over and a new type of society came into existence. In fact,
the individualism of the eighteenth century may have been
more a protest against the old order into which it broke than
it was a development of that agricultural society. The individualism of the American Revolution was chiefly political,
but the individualism of Adam Smith's school was economic;
and individualism in the social sphere lagged decades, if not a
century or two, behind the other two.

Individualism, "rugged" or "ragged," according to the viewpoint of the critic, made itself a solid part of our racial
philosophy by its economic successes. The frontiersman practiced it; the pioneer farm-owner used it daily and carried it
into his political and social thought or action. Competing
merchants or manufacturers claimed it as their own, when not
too busy lobbying for public help or organizing publicly
created corporations. It became a part, possibly the essence,
of the old Americanism. To it we owe the vision of a new
concept of the individual, his rights and his social opportunities. Not in theory but in fact a new social order was created
out of which a really socialized society might arise, if it could
subordinate individualism to itself. For generations, almost
to the present day, to question it, or the rural democracy
growing out of it, or the shift of dollars dependent on it, was
to question patriotism or challenge deity. It may have been

[8] On declining individualism in relation to increasing socialization, see
pp. 279–299.

a by-product of agricultural civilization; probably its chief victim has been the agriculturist.

Democracy would naturally have very little meaning in societies of ancient times, in which the individual was nothing, the group everything. Yet, agricultural societies, such as existed in America and France, gave us our first modern democracies. Probably the earliest democracy in both America and in France was in the main economic, due to extensive private ownership of land. In France political democracy was indebted to the help of the merchant class in its attempted rise to power, when it sought rights for itself and therefore, due to eighteenth-century philosophy, for others. Frontier America, making use also of that philosophy of the rights of man and rights of self-government, gave us, naturally, a nineteenth-century rural democracy. Whatever may be true in Europe, especially in England where democracy probably grew out of the needs of free and mobile workers, American democracy until the last quarter of a century was unquestionably a product of an agricultural society, if not a part of our heritage from agricultural civilization.

We are still under the spell of names and slogans devised for another day and civilization. Our great-grandfathers thought in terms of the equality chimera of the eighteenth century. As our ancestors thought in their hearts, so do we think today. Unconsciously or subconsciously we boast of the ideas cherished as patriotic by the eighteenth-century idealists and revolutionists. At least we did until the post World War reaction against democracy made us ashamed to idealize it longer. Strangely enough we have but dimly recognized how awkwardly rural, individualist democracy fits into an urban, industrialized world.

The pendulum of social attitudes swings back and forth but we have changed little our points of view, we have scarcely begun to change the habits or ideas which the nineteenth century bequeathed. Like Procrustes of the fable, we are much inclined to cut or stretch the ideas that come from the new age, making them fit the old setting which we have always prized.

NECESSARY READJUSTMENTS OF HERITAGE AND NEW CULTURE

For a dynamic society there are pressing problems of adjustment of old ideas, institutions, or practices to present needs. Who can diagnose conditions, can explain present trends and recent tendencies to determine the essential readaptations in personal relations, in business activities, in the functioning of governments, or in social affairs? Can any person or group decide even tentatively what is best? If we grant that the proposed ideas seem better than those to be discarded, how shall we secure, first of all, a general understanding of the obsolescence of the old, the need of change, and the superiority of the proposed scheme? Granting again complete success in understanding and a fair degree of willingness to make the change, then how may the change be made? How shall we overcome the cultural inertia of associations and institutions that resist all change? Suppose, for example, we decide, as many have, that the English language is a hodge-podge of sound characters unsuited to the expression in word combinations of what we want. Who shall help to find the best substitute or secure ways of agreeing upon its adoption or substitution? And if that be done, how shall we replace our libraries or change our bookplates or create a new written language?

In the material field, aside at least from changing the goods or machines themselves in that field, the transition is comparatively simple—when the old is worn out, have nothing but the new. But how can that be done with institutions? How can we build a new social psychology? With what success shall we tackle the creation of a new world of thought which will function with fair success and be both stable and flexible under new conditions? If we can do that, can we continue to do it indefinitely? Can we make the new fit conditions which are dynamic and therefore change from day to day, or at least from year to year and decade to decade? If we did, how old would any kaleidoscopic pattern be at any given moment?

So much of the process by which old *stereotypes* [8a] are modi-

[8a] For explanation see p. 383.

fied is unconscious that an analysis of structural change, of culture patterns, or of dominant motives becomes an involved process. Even one versed in the history of civilization, though he be also a trained sociologist, finds himself embarrassed in the attempt to identify elements of social heritage which survived from ancient to relatively modern times and have continued in fact well into the nineteenth century. To untangle from the whole web of the present organization or activities of society the strands which represent that heritage in our present changing world is a task for which the historian seems ill-fitted. With him evaluations have always been based upon knowledge of outcomes as well as of beginnings and developments; and the present leaves any future much in doubt.

When a dynamic society makes readjustments, there is first the adaptation of the essentially new to the almost unchangeable old, the conflict or necessary blending of what Glenn Frank calls inflexible tradition and adaptable intelligence. There is also in general a whole series of necessary adjustments of one part to others within the developing civilization. Much stress has been placed, probably too much, upon the economic character of our changing world, and particularly in connection with the shift from individualism toward socialization. In almost any society, economic change almost necessarily precedes shifts that are either social or political. Therefore what is frequently called material "culture" is likely to develop earlier and more easily than a new type of government, any new social grouping of classes, or any kinds of moral culture. The unevenness with which this development has taken place in America during the last century has presented during the depression a major difficulty in the business world. A less evident but far more necessary adaptation is the problem of social control of production and trade.

With these difficulties in mind, note the reasons why the traditional family still survives in many of its essentials, why our criminal law and standards are those of dead-and-gone days, what many have characterized as "the dead hand of the past." Consider the reason why we punish severely the small offender and let the big appropriator of properties escape, if we do not reward him with high office and social position. We shall probably always connect religion and worship with Sunday and with "Sunday churches" more than with almost anything else. Yet the Sunday service of our great grandfathers, at the only time and place at which the members of the community could get together, has much less meaning as such in an urban society, where there is some leisure daily, and time for worship is possibly more common on week-days than on the Sabbath. In the hurried, complex, trying life of today we have constant need of religious inspiration, help, and contact. So far as churches are needed, their doors should never be closed. One might easily run through a long list of other maladjustments of a really serious and significant character.

We can hardly hope to arrive at a clear-cut separation of ancient culture surviving in our social heritage from the modifications introduced by the Industrial Revolution, the development of democracy, or by new world contacts and conflicts. It might be supposed that our task would be simplified through observation of the dependence of culture upon material development among peoples of the past. Attempts, however, at generalization do not show that certain types of economic organization invariably or usually develop into certain kinds of social organization. We may not be justified in drawing any definite conclusion from the kind of government and society which should result from an economic change. The study of Hobhouse,[9] for example, shows a probable connection between the economic conditions of rather primitive races and the social habits or usages of those tribes; but it does not prove an inevitable connection. Nevertheless a primary "culture" that is really "cumulative" because it continues to grow and expand will probably in time compel readjustments to itself. A derivative culture represented, for example, by music or education should be very highly adaptive to the general civilization and needs of its time.[9a]

[9] *The Material Cultures and Social Institutions of the Simpler Peoples.*
[9a] On relation of primary to derivative culture see Ogburn, *Social Change*, 270–275.

Numerous studies fortunately have been made, one of the best of them being *Recent Social Trends*, in which the lag of certain types of social change is very marked when contrasted with the remarkable transformation found in the world of business. Attention is drawn to the fact that *the advance is most notable not simply in the field of business but in that of government as well, and the lag is most conspicuous in the fields of religion and the family.*[10] A more careful study of the materials within these fields would indicate a failure on the part of some of the collaborators to show fully enough the influence of the World War during the last half of this thirty-year period from 1900 to 1930.[11] In the vast materials presented for the general study, or in supplementary volumes, the non-adjustment of government to business, and of society to both, is notable in hundreds of ways. The lack of real coördination within each of the different areas of civilization or culture would undoubtedly be almost as noticeable if one could get the facts, or had the time to examine them and evaluate various kinds of non-adjustments. In the political field alone, although national and state governments are constantly improving the handling of problems common to both, there has been altogether too little coöperative action between the two;[12] for example, in the field of public health regulation. Outside of national control of almost all railroads and control of other public utilities by other governments, little has been done toward starting control of business or social affairs, toward gaining control, toward coördinating state and national controls, or toward working out unified control where that is essential.

It seems fair to assume that even in a dynamic age social heritage will not be modified greatly. It seems reasonable to expect that most of it will be retained. In the field of business new inventions and the profit growing out of their commercial use predetermine not so much the adaptation of an old pro-

New uses of heritage to be retained

---

[10] *Recent Social Trends*, xiv. On lags consult also pp. 309–315.

[11] Rogers, Lindsay, *Crisis Government*, p. 13.

[12] Note the comment of a well-known student of our Constitution, James M. Beck, criticizing the correlation of state and national administration in the enforcement of the XVIIIth Amendment. *Our Wonderland of Bureaucracy*, p. 250.

cedure to a new as possibly the substitution of something new for the older method. The ox-cart and the automobile which uses an internal combustion engine have almost become a traditional illustration of the antithesis between the outworn and the modern substitute.

Law is particularly interesting from a number of angles, some of which have already been indicated. Unquestionably, it touches more different phases of culture than any other cultural element. This is inherent in its nature, for it is not a thing apart, but a statement of social rule or habit, possibly an embodiment of a traditional action pattern used in business, in public coöperation, and in those relations which we consider social. If this is so, the following pertinent questions arise: (1) does the legal rule represent the actual procedure followed in the commercial transaction or the social obligation? Or (2) does the agreement upon a general rule or the enactment of the necessary law take place long after even the majority of those who need the rule have tried in practice to modify the procedure based upon the old law? Or (3) is the rule likely to be made out of hand before the actual need is understood by the majority? In short, *when the need of a modified law arises, does the change accompany the need, follow it tardily or does it anticipate any general recognition of the need?*

These three possibilities probably should be considered both from the theoretical and the practical points of view. Are the laws which we have up-to-date, representing the best practice, conforming to a real need which is both vital and widespread? Do we discover that laws in general, in the present day and in times past, anticipate the problem which already threatens but has not yet become acute. Theoretically the attempt to prepare a rule without wide observation of specific cases usually would lead to a law that might be highly desirable but would not work well. Possibly some wide-spread enthusiasm or an emotional up-set might lead to a law which is not universally desirable or is unwise. Probably the American people would be fairly evenly divided if they tried to explain the necessity for the adoption of the Prohibition amendment. That it was widely desired in 1919 is probably historic fact; even now it is difficult to determine which influenced the adoption of Prohibition most, war patriotism, desire for economic efficiency, or some other less tangible force.

If lag in law is inescapable, our problem is narrowed sharply. Our inquiry then is likely to be: today how much is law lagging, how great are the needs for revision, how serious are the evils created by laws which are out-of-date and possibly obsolete, considering the dynamic changes which have taken place in the fields for which the rules were made? If law is, as has been suggested, largely custom re-interpreted by a judiciary almost inevitably conservative in its outlook, should not something be done to speed up the process of modernizing the law? Then we are confronted with the danger that we may err by making laws before we know just what is agreed upon as probably desirable. Next year the trend may run off on a new, totally different tangent from that followed heretofore, and we have on our hands a perfectly unused but absolutely unusable law.

What the Romans did when they developed the *jus gentium,* and the English when they supplemented the common law with a system of equity, may easily be done in small part within special fields of law at present. One of the outstanding virtues of a federal system such as Americans have is the opportunity for experimentation on a state-wide scale. The more progressive communities need not therefore be held back by those distinctively static or conservative in thought or action, unless the two types are bound together within the same state. A great hindrance in American progress in the past has been the linking together, especially in the Atlantic seaboard states, of the coast area, a tide-water region, and a *hinterland,* as diverse in their interest and demands as the three similar warring parts of the Greek city-states. At present the division of law into two parts, state and national, threatens the necessary unification and integration of a single body of modernized American jurisprudence.

Almost all American states permit their courts, and sometimes the same court, to decide cases in both law and equity.

Some state constitutions provide that if the letter of the law or some technicality dispenses with justice, the technicality and the letter of the law shall be subordinated to its definite purpose. If the American courts followed more the technique of the French judiciary, which pays little attention to precedent, American judicial decisions would be less dominated by the past. A change in spirit rather than in letter therefore might easily be the best means to minimize the lag of law behind social needs.[13]

Because the law covers many readaptations of social heritage, other subjects are not included in this study.

Science and society

Any careful study of a civilization in transition would take into consideration the major causes of change and make some distinction between the fields of primary development and of derivative adjustment. Frequently attention is given almost solely to the rapid transformation of machine-power industry as though it were a distinct field and a thing apart. Undoubtedly in the last two centuries material civilization has advanced more rapidly than any other. But does this mean that material culture was independent of either political reorganization, or, let us say, scientific progress? Ogburn believes, "Certainly a large part of the non-material culture appears to be by nature a method of adjustment either to material culture or to natural environment or to both." [14] And again, "It would seem that a preponderant number of changes are begun in the material culture, causing changes in the non-material culture." [15] In a way American democracy developed just as early as did the industrial or machine revolution in England. Machine-power development went hand in hand with increased knowledge of how to combine power and machines efficiently. Some one has said that much of the mechanical progress of modern times would have been achieved by Leonardo da Vinci had he possessed the scientific knowledge and a few appliances we have today. We who boast of the wonders of twentieth-century aviation might have little

---

[13] In this connection consult suggestions on social equity (Establishing Proper Public Controls, pp. 397–401).
[14] *Social Change,* The Viking Press, p. 271.
[15] *Ibid.,* 275.

to brag about if Leonardo had had an internal combustion engine.

Progress in science, upon which the modern transformation has largely been dependent, is moreover *an interplay between pure science and applied.* Galileo was more successful than any of his predecessors or contemporaries partly because of the mechanical advantage he had from the use of a primitive telescope. As in his day, pure science may lead the way. But each advance may depend not only upon the progress already made in that particular science but possibly and probably upon successful applications of that science, not necessarily in the world of business, but in a practical way.

An example of the interrelations of pure and applied science was brought to the writer's attention some years ago by Walter S. Adams, Director of Mount Wilson Observatory. A well-known astronomer had suggested the possibility of penetrating the heavens much farther than had ever been done before. This was to be accomplished through a new type of telescope. As is well known, photographs of stars or nebulae tens of millions of light years away are taken on small sensitive plates sometimes only an inch or two square. In order to photograph the faintest objects an exposure of six or eight hours is necessary. In addition to using an accurately timed mechanical device, the observer is obliged to keep the star throughout the exposure on exactly the same part of the plate. The apparatus suggested for this new telescopic work, said Adams, might accomplish the desired result but for an inherent defect in the design of the instrument. Provision was not made for adequately shielding the plate from direct skylight and the result was that a fogging took place after an exposure of about two hours. This set a limit upon the length of exposure time which could be used with this instrument.

Possibly astronomy would seem least able to contribute to industrial advance. Without the researches of the astronomical chemists of the sun and the stars several chemical elements would probably still be unknown. This would seem of no commercial significance until we discover that without some of these elements it would have been impossible ever to have invented the neon tube; and without neon signs at night, Main Street would not be Main Street. The geologist seldom capitalizes his knowledge for his own gain. Often his knowledge of strata is invaluable in the location of oil wells. He may be called in to aid in coal development or in mining ventures. Without the help of the chemical engineer, we should have "gone off the gold standard" long ago. With the perfection of the cyanide process of extracting gold from low-grade ores there was a revolution less in gold mining than in the gold supply, better prices, and prosperous business. Politics depends on physics, as Walter Bagehot showed sixty years ago, but is not technology much more dependent on it? When steel replaced wood, buildings and bridges were different in structure as well as in size, strength and appearance. In the field of art alone think of the advance made when reinforced concrete became common. Contrast with the ugly skeletons they replaced the tall graceful or solid towers and the pleasing and artistic arches and balusters.

SUBSTITUTES FOR OUTGROWN INSTITUTIONS AND IDEAS

General

In considering substitutes for social heritage that has become obsolescent *there is no intention of suggesting a reorganization of the social order.* All that is sought is a consideration of some changes already made, with the hope of glimpsing a few trends and tendencies. Probably any examination of recent institutions, contrasted with those which are older, and any evaluation of those institutions in terms of heritage or of readjustment might fail to indicate a trend. Even if it did, the probable future development of that institution would still be more or less in doubt.

A loaf of bread

The transition from the simple rural agricultural existence of a few years ago to the new epoch might well be symbolized by a study of the commonest of all foods—a loaf of bread. Most modern wheat farms have not yet been mechanized, but some have, especially in the American and Canadian northwest and in Russia. Hand labor, which formerly represented considerably more than two-thirds of the cost, has become a constantly smaller percentage of the price of wheat and of the completed loaf. Even where horse-drawn plows are still used and horse-drawn mowers or reapers are in use, the threshing is no longer by hand or by animal hoofs, but by machinery. At least in our western states, tractor-drawn reapers are exceedingly common, and combined reapers and threshers are fairly common.

Even more the loaf of bread itself symbolizes the change from old to new. A half century ago probably ninety-five per cent of all bread was home-made, although the age of "household industry" was a thing of the past for America. The dough was mixed in the kitchen and kneading was done by hand. This substantial and sometimes heavy loaf represented a fair part of the food of the people. They suffered rather little from its indigestibility because they followed the open life. Today most American bread is made in public bakeries and a great deal by machinery. Like other businesses the baking trusts are organized on a large scale and to some extent have merged. In the best establishments hands do not touch the flour or the loaves, the entire process being done mechanically, including the wrapping of the loaf.

Bread typifies many problems and maladjustments in the substitution of new for old. An affair largely individual or family has become the heart of a social readjustment. The rewards to those sharing in the final loaf are badly balanced. The baker and retailer keep half, the other half being divided almost too equally between the farmer, the miller, the transporter and middleman. At each stage of producing the raw materials, social interest or regulation has been becoming constantly more conspicuous. The A. A. A. restricts acreage and limits the supply of wheat. Railway rates are carefully supervised by the I. C. C. The grain elevator was the first of the new businesses affected with a public interest. A law limiting the hours of bakers was, negatively, an important stimulus to social legislation. Bread making is watched carefully by authorities in charge of health, standards of weight, and even price-fixing. The Baking Trust was disapproved under an administration exceedingly friendly to mergers. One of the earliest of all specific international agreements, something that may be very common in the future, was made in 1933 to preserve the price of wheat. The whole dilemma of western civilization might be explained by a loaf of bread.

The rise of democracy Comparing the newer heritage with the older, we discover in the field of politics *the substitution of constitutional government for arbitrary rule.* But comparing the present with the recent past we note *a real modification of that democracy.* The replacement of arbitrary government by constitutional rule might be traced back to Magna Carta, but probably it would be wiser to find its modern beginnings in the Puritan movement and seventeenth-century England. Frontier America, with Puritan influence dominant even in Virginia, represented more constitutional government than did England; but outside of England and America, revolutions were needed before the autocrat was driven from his throne. One would need to be lenient in judgment if he assumed that the form of democracy represented the fact, especially as popular government probably did not arise even in England until well into the nineteenth century. Democracy's vitality proved that democracy was worthwhile; for the western democratic countries successfully weathered the crisis of the World War twenty years ago. Constitutional rule, at least in form, finally spread to parts of central and eastern Europe. Because of tendencies toward dictatorship in that part of the world, we cannot be sure that constitutional government and democracy had been established in those parts of the world.

The present status of democracy abroad and the recent changes to which it has been subjected are too broad a subject for this brief study. To notice recent shifts in a rural democracy that has become urban, let us limit ourselves chiefly to the United States. Here our democracy developed on or near a frontier in which land was abundant and relatively free. The possibility of something approaching economic equality easily led to social and political equality. In fact we can trace through changes in constitutions and in legislation of western American states the series of steps by which a fair degree of democracy, primarily political perhaps, but also more or less economic and social, became the lot of the American people, at least west of the Appalachian Mountains. This democracy was vital not only in its economic origins but in the relative social homogeneity of the rural groups that used it. According to de Tocqueville,[16] the essence of democracy a century ago was the self-government found in the popular election of local officials and the local administration of laws in accordance with the desires of each community.

Much has been said about *individualism* as primarily an economic characteristic or necessity of a *new industrial society* having its beginning a century and a half ago. Advocates of this theory overlook the fact that the frontier, of necessity, is individualistic. They disregard the further fact that self-sufficing farms and self-supporting communities would naturally tend to develop an individualist philosophy out of their practices of being sufficient to themselves. Individualism is as much a characteristic of the political democracy in America as it is of the industrialism existing before the Civil War. In fact, it probably survived longer, if it did not mean more to the people enjoying it, than did an individualist industry.

The democracy that seems ideal and certainly was adequate for a simple, rather primitive community with few outside contacts could hardly be transplanted to an urban society living in a complex world. In the larger American cities the closest neighbors frequently know nothing of each other, except possibly some unfortunate gossip of each other's affairs. That may be gained through the press more often than from those living near. An individualist theory of government, therefore, which stressed the rights of men, offered argument for separation from Great Britain. It did not provide a suitable philosophy for building an integrated, industrialized, complicated society. The political breakdown of rural democracy was hastened by the rise of the city until nearly seventy per cent of the American people came to live in fairly large communities.

[16] *Democracy in America,* 1837.

Since most American cities are industrial rather than commercial, *the Industrial Revolution can claim some real credit or discredit for having started an urbanized, if not a socialized, democracy.* However, industrialism did more than that, for it limited competition and later destroyed it in multitudes of fields of socialized industry. By socializing industry and by dominating the public, which was supposed to be controlled democratically by rulers, popularly chosen, it forced the public to exercise public control over anti-social business practices; in brief, the people were obliged to take one of the steps toward creating a new social as well as urban democracy. Oddly enough, to a very considerable extent, the entering wedge of this socialized democratic control was the protection of competition for bigger and worse business. Even the National Recovery Administration of 1933 provided codes which were called correctly "codes of fair competition."

When the World War was fought to make the world safe for democracy, undoubtedly ninety-nine out of a hundred thought of the old individualist democracy. The returning soldier, unable to get back his job or, especially during the years 1920–22, to find a job of any kind, naturally wondered what was wrong with the protection of individual rights under this old system of democracy. Many besides soldiers, and especially the agriculturists and the small business men, marvelled that under democracy their business was so unprofitable. They could not understand why the people were so heedless to their cries for a square deal.

To many observers an outworn rural democracy and an undeveloped social democracy which has not yet become self-conscious seem to be on the high road to autocracy. Even the minor controls of the N. R. A. have been characterized as regimentation, fascism, or state socialism. An examination of the European situation as well as the American scene shows that autocracies do not seem to thrive in either frontier or industrial areas, but rather grow out of semi-static agricultural conditions. Moreover, democracy has helped to save itself by education in school, at the ballot, and in the public meeting. Few really democratic peoples have reverted to

anything like the old type of absolute rule. Some who practice fascist or bolshevist absolutism never had any real
democracy from which to revert.

One other illustration may be borrowed from the political   Federalism
field. Let us take the question of federalism. Federalism
is a system of government in which the powers are divided
into two spheres, the one national, the other belonging to the
component parts or states. It is too recent a product of
political evolution to be a distinctively agricultural by-product. Agricultural societies as such were never huge. If by
any mischance they were, they were partially held together
by commerce and not by agriculture. So long as peoples were
predominantly agricultural, rather homogeneous, they did
not need a *complex type of political organization.* Federalism
became necessary and desirable when the nation became commercial as well as agricultural, because it covered an extensive
area but included people enough alike to be united into a single
political society.

A tendency toward centralization was quite prominent in
antiquity. To be sure, the centralization of the early historic
period was involuntary, and nine times out of ten the work
of a military conqueror. Modern combinations of political
societies may have grown out of wars; there have been few
exceptions. But war was the accompaniment rather than the
cause. The state which emerged from the process of union
was not as in ancient times a consolidated, harshly ruled affair of subject, conquered provinces. It was probably a union
of states of fairly equal size and population, entered into more
or less voluntarily. For example, if we overlook Prussia, the
North German Confederation of 1867 was composed of such
units. The American Confederation after 1781 was composed
of theoretically equal states and also theoretically independent states which had combined for defense and remained unified for still other reasons.

When the American colonies separated from the mother
country for a common purpose, they formed a union quite
inadequate for either their economic or political needs, even
in time of peace. The Constitutional Convention of 1787

represented the substantial business men of that day; but political separateness for years showed the dominance of agriculture rather than industry. The federal union of 1789 which replaced the Confederation remained in fact a *union of states* until the Civil War. Long after the war, orators and others referred to this Union mistakenly as "these United States." The Civil War, however, established a *balanced federalism* between state and nation, the balance being maintained with a fair degree of success well into the twentieth century. It was not accidental that this *better union* coincided with a great wave of industrial advance.

We notice, however, a change from a federal union dominated by the states before the Civil War to the one afterward which was a well-balanced union. And we discover that gradually that balance was being more and more disturbed because the nation was becoming relatively more important in the federal system. The tendency toward *greater centralization in the American federal state marked the successive stages of industrialization in the United States.* Since the World War represented a contest for industrial supremacy and gave tremendous impetus to the development of industrialism everywhere but particularly in the United States, in the period after the war industrialism advanced with great strides, and centralization continued in many fields. A question which confronts us now is this: if state boundaries are no longer important and if the present states are no longer what W. Y. Elliott calls "economic realities," how much federalism shall we have with a people unwilling to be governed from Washington, and in a country too big to be governed under a centralized system?

Property, private and corporate

The transit of civilization has occurred less in the political field than in the economic, which is the subject of Part II. One illustration must suffice for our conclusion. Private property has a specially prized place in an individualist, industrialized society. The concept, however, of private property is much older than industrialism, carrying us far back into the dim ages. The ownership of private property in a simple semi-agricultural society called for readjustments when the business of that society had to be done in large units and on a large scale. No one person enjoyed sufficient wealth to manage a business running into hundreds of millions or billions. Even if he did, except possibly in the case of the Fords, the Rockefellers, and the Rothschilds, the owner of the capital seldom possessed the managerial ability and commercial foresight to organize, manage, and carry on a growing business. It was necessary therefore to pool capital resources, to secure outside talent, and to develop a business system, chain, or consolidation of huge proportions and moderate intricacy. The *corporation* combined many of these features and has become the most distinctive form of business organization of the modern world.[17] Since it needed legal standing, it was treated as a legal person and afterward endowed with all of the rights of persons and most of the rights of citizens— certainly a fortuitous combination in the age of strident if not rugged individualism, borrowing from the past many rules intended to benefit the small producer and worker.

These four chapters are a quite inadequate treatment of any essential background for a study of contemporaneous civilization and its problems. All that we have attempted to do is to sketch very briefly some of the antecedents of three or four outstanding present-day organizations, institutions, or systems. The selection has really been made with care in order that we may have some inkling, first, of the great depth to which our present civilization reaches, and, secondly, of the comparatively recent development of those phases of industrialism, capitalism, nationalism, and democracy which occupy most of the stage in our view of present-day civilization. Conclusion

With this background it should be somewhat easier to analyze the *conditions* in which we find many existing institutions, some *problems* which confront the American people today, as well as some of the *trends* and *tendencies* which must not be overlooked in an attempt to evaluate what we have and how it is changing. This chapter has been devoted perhaps to the most fundamental of all the *transitions*, but it is treated chiefly as a type of transition which has been taking

[17] On corporation organization and property see pp. 116–118.

place. It furnishes also both background and setting in which
we can examine *lags* of organizations and systems which have
not been moving forward very rapidly. It brings to attention,
especially, *dilemmas* due possibly to advance in one part of a
system and lag in another, or to general lack of harmony between the system as it is developing and the civilization in
which and with which it is obliged to work. Some of the most
important of those dilemmas are our next object of study.

PART II

THE DILEMMA OF
INDUSTRIAL CAPITALISM

INDUSTRIAL CAPITALISM
IN THE LAST GENERATION

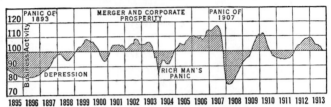

I. BUSINESS ACTIVITY, 1896–1913

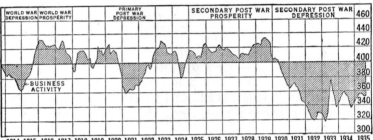

II. BUSINESS ACTIVITY, 1914–1935

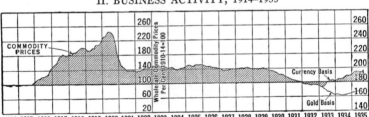

III. COMMODITY PRICES, 1914–1935
(1910–14＝100)

IV. INDUSTRIAL STOCK MARKET ACTIVITY, 1914–1935
Reprinted by permission of the Pacific Company of California.

INTRODUCTION—THE WORLD'S DILEMMA

The present crisis, both an industrial and a financial one, has brought sharply into view the fact that western civilization is facing a real dilemma as well as a passing crisis. The dilemma grows largely out of the fact that we have been moving forward at a very rapid pace. At no time in history, with the possible exception of the period from the beginning of the active use of the printing press through the great Renaissance and Reformation, has humanity ever before made the advance it is making now.[1] We are passing through one of the secondary stages of a transformation from one type of civilization, a rural, agricultural civilization, with its roots probably seven thousand years old, possibly more, into something totally different.

The present dilemma may be more serious than that of late medievalism chiefly because it is not part of a transition primarily *within* a civilization. As we have just seen, we may be experiencing *a real transit from one civilization to another.* Fortunately the dilemma is not so general as the transition. It is rather easily stated, though far from easy to comprehend. It involves both parts of the industrial capitalism which has been dominant in American and world affairs for nearly a half century. There is a dilemma for industrial capitalism as a whole; and as parts of that dilemma there is a

---

[1] Contrast with our day the epoch-making changes of that dynamic age; first the printing press, then the organization within Europe of a number of new national monarchies replacing the old feudal states, then the discovery of America and of the world as a globe. That was a period of very rapid change. According to Thorold Rogers, prices amounted to about five times as much at the end of the XVI century as they were at the beginning. Those changes altered greatly the life of the people and changed many old institutions into something entirely different.

dilemma of industrialism and a dilemma of financialism, as we shall see in chapters V and VI.[2]

Neither industrialism nor financialism can go forward easily or go back at all: this is the heart of their present dilemma. Industrialism has grown so great through improvements of technology in applications of power, and vast sources of capital available, that further increase destroys real possibility of profitable production—and industrialism without profitable production would not be industrialism at all. Machine industry has long faced the situation that it can produce far more than the public can consume. At the same time it is impossible for those with large incomes to spend much of what they receive annually, and there is no good place to invest constantly increasing surpluses. This capital seeking profitable investment causes greater competition. As the total product increases, the margin between cost of production and price at which goods may be sold is decreased. Not a very happy future for present industrialism to face!

Capitalism does not escape the dilemma of its former ally, industrialism. We used to wonder at the idea that a penny invested at compound interest beginning at the time of Christ would amount to several times the total wealth of the world or what that wealth was supposed to be before the crash of 1929. We no longer wonder; we protest. Successive liquidations, especially in times of depression, and finding continuous new sources of wealth through exploitation of coal, oil, and metal deposits apparently postponed the day of reckoning, but they were only a postponement. It looks, however, as though it were close to us now.

Capital has accumulated in huge quantities in the possession of relatively few persons, and there is no longer other income and wealth available in the possessions of all others for the payment of compound interest. Unless we can stop this over-concentration of capital in a few great fortunes, soon there will be danger that capitalist will fall out with financier,

---

[2] Since this book was written, Jerome Davis in *Capitalism and Its Culture* has gathered very numerous illustrations of serious defects and practical abuses in our economic system. These facts help to explain why the dilemma is much worse than it need have been.

and capitalist with capitalist as they compete bitterly with one another for safe investment and productive enterprise. Then the day may arrive when the possessor of capital will be the loser because he has so much. He cannot use it directly himself; he does not know how, and that is not his part of the plan anyway. He will not let others have it, for the abundance of capital thrust upon the producer gives the lender all the risk and almost no interest, the rate being so low. Possibly the only easy way out of the dilemma may be to avoid further excessive accumulations of financial capital by better distribution yearly of the wealth we create year by year. Then we must watch that we do not limit or destroy the amount of capital which is needed to continue the work of our industrial civilization.

Whatever we find it necessary to do, by limiting personal accumulations of capital or by leaving things alone and letting the excesses destroy the value of the capital we have, the future of the financier is none too rosy. Fortunately for us, our chief interest is the present and future of *society*, especially in America.

V

THE DILEMMA OF INDUSTRIALISM

THE AGE OF MACHINES

This new era

How did industrialism reach its present crisis? Causes and conditions demand investigation of recent methods of production. By what course of development did big business attain its present dizzy position? Long as the process must have been, the debacle seems sudden.

We have called ours the Machine Age much as the Victorians referred to theirs as the Age of Steam and Steel. Recent writers put stress upon this as the Power Age or, if they give attention to applied science rather than to machinery, call it the Technological Age.

The new era, especially since the World War, is characterized not only by *an extraordinary development of machinery and power and an almost new technology but also by improved types of organization and larger systems of business coöperation.* These may be chiefly *economic,* as is found in the great mergers, or cartels, or coöperative organizations. They may be *both economic and public,* as the Dawes and Young plans for the rehabilitation of Germany or the new methods for oil conservation in America. They may be *political and social.* The new age is distinguished by closer relations between government and business, and by public regulation for great corporations. It has called for radically new means of public control in domestic and international trade.

Machine expansion

The history of machines takes us back to the beginning of the Industrial Revolution.[1] The success of machines brings

---

[1] We might in fact go back to Hero's five "machines" of very ancient times.

our attention almost immediately to improved water power mechanisms and to Watt's steam engine. Machines operated by power call for *new materials in machine making*. Old hand looms, and other machines operated by hand, had ordinarily been constructed chiefly of wood; but wood did not stand the strain of power. Iron came very much more into use, replaced largely by steel after the inventions of Kelly and Bessemer, about the middle of the nineteenth century, and by alloys of steel later, making much harder tools, or by alloys of other materials, forming much lighter frames, especially for automobiles and airplanes.

Modern machines are made according to standardized patterns. Eli Whitney seems to deserve credit for first developing the idea of *interchangeability of parts*. By manufacturing these parts separately in huge quantities and then assembling them into a complete machine, each worker having a specialized task, modern production has been speeded up greatly. A large part of this business consists in the construction of machines whose primary or sole purpose is the making of other machines. From the business standpoint, a short-sighted policy of making quick profits led to the opposite of the early English system of keeping the inventions secret and at home. Spinning machines and looms have been exported to countries such as India, in which labor is much more abundant and less expensive than in Western Europe and in America. As though this were not enough, international competition increased when machine-making machines also were exported in large numbers.

The culmination of machine development is represented by a machine mechanically perfect and practically free, in the succession of operations, from human aid. As a type of this mechanism one might take a huge rotary press. Huge rolls are fed into one end of this wonderful mechanism, the completed newspaper, magazine, or booklet being turned out and all but delivered to the waiting public at the end of this process. Even more marvelous is the scientist's mechanical men. They "work" the most intricate problems, we should like to say truthfully "even as you and I."

POWER

As the Machine Age is unthinkable without power, some
attention must be given to new forms of power and some to
different sources, especially those becoming prominent in recent years. It is in the field of power utilization that the
modern Aladdins rub their lamps with most startling results.
The steam engine of the stationary type undoubtedly produced most of the power until the close of the nineteenth
century. Its earlier competitor was chiefly some form of
water power, but for large-scale production this competition
was not great. In the last of that century the limitations of
steam led to its replacement to a considerable extent by electricity. Steam can be carried but short distances, and consequently factory buildings depending on steam are crowded
together close to the power house. Inside the buildings floor
space is economized, with as many machines as possible attached by belts to the same power shaft. A half century ago
electricity created by the conversion of steam could be transmitted several miles. Electricity could also be created by
water power or from other sources of energy. The invention
and improvement of the dynamo, greatly improved by Edison,
for creating electricity, and of the motor for utilizing it were
therefore of the highest significance. Before 1929 practically
eighty per cent of all power was electric. Electrically driven
machines can be placed as far apart as desired or in plants
close to the materials each uses. Each machine may have its
own separate switch for starting and stopping, thus economizing costs. A plant with these advantages has more light and
air, as well as better location of machines and factories.
Many new systems of control of machine operation have also
been developed directly or from a distance. A spectacular non-
commercial illustration of this process was the use of a
ray from the star Arcturus to start the machinery of the Century of Progress Exposition at Chicago (1934).

What are *the chief sources of power?* New discoveries or
improvements have utilized coal, oil, natural gas, water
power, and other sources of energy. Sometimes the crude

supply of fuel is burned for direct use of its heat. More and
more the natural resources have been transformed into electricity, which can now be carried great distances to distant
factories, may be distributed to widely scattered small productive units or may be utilized in systems of local or transcontinental transportation.

New forms of power represent not simply a transformation
from one kind of power to another; for they may easily cause
a decentralization of working and living conditions. Why try
to carry on factory work in the fifteenth story of a building
constructed on land worth five thousand dollars a foot front-
age when power is available in the outskirts of a village of
homes and workers, on land that can be purchased for a few
hundred dollars an acre, before the real estate boomers create
artificial values!

When power is measured, we do not refer back to the days
of hand labor but call in man's first successful animal assistant, the horse. A few years ago energy available through
power machines was estimated for the United States at twelve
hundred million horse power and for the industrial nations of
Europe about half as much more although much of this is
non-industrial.

As a source of power, *coal still exceeds all other energy-*   Coal
producing materials. The world supply is vast, but humanity
has been drawing upon these reservoirs at reckless speed and
with inexcusable waste. For many reasons consumption is
not increasing, as little more coal is mined today than a
decade ago. We have been getting constantly more for our
ton, however. In a half century (1840–90) the energy from
coal increased fourfold and the gain did not stop then. The
earth's annual production is in excess of a billion and a half
tons, nearly half of which is the American share. Most of
this is bituminous coal, excellent for its heating qualities, but
containing gases and chemicals of greater value unburned
than burned. Conservationists maintain that if this coal were
distilled rather than burned, an extraordinary saving would be
made through the saving of gas and valuable by-products.
Gilbert and Pogue estimate at a billion dollars annual coal

wastes in the United States.[2] They believe that if the nitrogen, benzol, tar, and other products were separated, an equal amount would be added to our wealth. Of every ton of coal we lose six hundred pounds in extraction, and five hundred and fifty in firing, chiefly in gases going up the stack. Of the balance, George Otis Smith thinks that only seventy-six pounds are actually converted into energy, and that is less than four per cent, so far has the original ton shrunk.

Much recent history has been written in coal. Formerly a chief export of Great Britain, Welsh or English coal has been handicapped by the opening of new continental fields, by the great depth of mines, even in Wales, and by lack of good business organization and methods among the operators. Coal is the heart of Britain's industrial dilemma and responsible for several political crises. Some of us recall the furore created by the Ballinger-Pinchot controversy, in this country. The claim was made that coal supplies on our public lands were being exploited. The dispute was settled by temporarily closing most of these lands to entry. More than once the American anthracite coal monopoly was in the public eye. Now it dominated railroads penetrating the coal fields, now it charged excessive prices and again it became involved in strikes that called for the Big Stick [2a] of presidential intervention.

The American bituminous fields, being much more extensive than our 484 square miles of Pennsylvania anthracite beds, have had far more serious problems. There have been

[2] Gilbert and Pogue, *America's Power Resources,* D. Appleton-Century Co., p. 76, give these figures.

COAL RESERVES OF THE UNITED STATES
CALCULATED TO A PER CAPITA BASIS

	Now underground	Mined to Jan. 1, 1921
	Billion tons	Billion tons
Anthracite coal	190	31
Bituminous coal	15,000	110
Lignite coals	20,000	Virtually untouched

[2a] President Theodore Roosevelt favored the plan: speak softly but use the Big Stick.

too many owners, especially since the World War, even if
somewhat centralized control, too many coal miners, too
many days without employment, too small pay. When the
American conservation movement was at its height, President
Theodore Roosevelt maintained that coal should be treated
as a necessity and a public utility, to be mined under government supervision or management and price-controlled like
any other public utility product. Far-sighted conservationists
and progressives in England look upon some form of government ownership of coal, with drastic reorganization of private
management, as a possible solution of many evils encountered
by Great Britain.

A second source of power is oil. *The problem of oil pro-* Oil
*duction is becoming more serious than that of coal has ever
been.* Owing to our post-medieval practice that he who owns
the surface of the soil owns to the center of the earth within
his land limits, the attempt to utilize oil pools causes unlimited competition and furnishes endless problems. Literally, it is a case of first come, first served. The owner of a
plot of land large enough for an oil derrick might easily drain
millions of wealth from the subterranean property of his
neighbors. In spite of the huge cost of drilling to a depth of
five, eight, or ten thousand feet, wells have been duplicated
inexcusably, oil has been wasted in large quantities, and natural gas of extraordinary value has polluted the atmosphere
for miles around each field.

Oil has entered into international capitalism and into international politics. The fields of Venezuela and of Baku and
Mosul, not to mention those of a little more distant past in
Mexico, have been occasion for an international struggle
among the great powers and of exploitation by huge companies backed by diplomats as well as dollars. At the close
of the World War, Great Britain seemed to have the advantage in this struggle for oil in distant places. With the aid
of the League of Nations, she was able to gain advantage over
Turkey.

In the United States, the oil problem has been particularly
acute. Since "the horse was stolen" by our antiquated laws

regarding the ownership of land and of natural resources, we have tried "to lock the doors" against future losses by concerted agreement of producers coöperating within the states. In Texas, California and some other states restrictive laws or agreements reduced the production greatly. This new type of conservation did not sufficiently limit the production of oil, nor did it stop the waste of natural gas. The problem is a national one rather than a matter for any state. Of what profit is it to keep down production in California, Texas, or Oklahoma, if other American states increase the supply of a commodity already a glut on the market? How can American oil compete with that imported from Venezuela in great tank steamers at a cost of a few cents per barrel?

Before 1933 attempts to conserve oil and natural gas were rather ineffective, although in California production was reduced to half a natural "flow," and in some other states the militia was called out to carry through plans for conservation. President Hoover was heartily in sympathy with the attempt to conserve the oil supply, but Washington did not act until the adoption of the oil provision of the N. I. R. A. law, in 1934 declared unconstitutional. Under a revised law the whole business is for the first time brought under the direction of a single organized body, with Secretary of the Interior Ickes in charge. The petroleum code sought to do more than simply conserve oil, and at the same time natural gas, although that perhaps was the most pressing need of the industry, as indicated above. For a time there was not the same cutthroat competition among drillers and pumpers and others, glutting the market with crude oil or refined gasoline. Some day a revised arrangement will provide for some conservation of supplies, coördination of producing and selling and a full recognition of the public's interest and right in connection with the control of this business.

Probably the public has more vivid recollection of oil scandals than experience with the present oil problem. The fact that a concessionaire is reported to have boasted that he could make a hundred million dollars from oil deposits granted by federal authorities shows the need of honest and watchful administration of public property. The Supreme Court forced a return of these and other oil concessions on public lands. Because of threatened graft, the government could not lease its lands; because of delay, the oil was drained out by private companies operating on the margin of Tea Pot Dome. Because of a lack of public policy, inefficiency in administration, and corruption in high places the public was always the loser.

Water power possesses one quality which oil and coal, un- Water power
luckily, do not possess. It is renewed year by year, and therefore will be inexhaustible to the end of time, if humanity uses a little sense. During the conservation movement under President Theodore Roosevelt, it was estimated that more than five million horse power was then in use. Twenty years later the amount had more than doubled. Now that electricity may be transported great distances, our water falls should have greater value. Some day they may have, but at present other types of fuel are cheaper. Our grandchildren may use from five to ten times as much water power as we have now; but careful students realize that for this generation oil and coal, not water, are the power essentials.

The problem of water power is neither local nor distinctly industrial; it is general, and it is public. Moreover, it is bound up with related problems such as the conservation of forests and headwaters, the development of inland waterways, and probably the canalization of rivers or artificial routes. In 1920, the government at Washington passed the Federal Water Power Act, which permits water power sites on public lands to be rented for a maximum of a half century and requires the payment of an adequate rental.

In the early years of the twentieth century, and particularly after the World War, the expansion of electrical production was one of the noteworthy features of American business. Much of the power was furnished by water. Charges against the group of companies organized into great holding company organizations were numerous. Among them was the seizure and exploitation without proper public reimbursement of valuable water power properties. Because each organization had a monopoly or semi-monopoly within its own district, rates were charged out of all proportion to costs. Within a period of less than five years the charges and profits of huge electrical organizations increased several fold.[3]

During the World War the United States government planned to make nitrates by using the water power of the Tennessee River at Muscle Shoals. After the war, for years Americans were entertained or incensed by the perennial congressional struggle over the Muscle Shoals power dam and fertilizer plant. Around this colossal relic of World War, which was eagerly sought by power interests and the public, centered a gladitorial contest between the "power trust" and those who wished to see Uncle Sam in the rôle of owner and manager. In all probability, new methods of securing nitrates have rendered the nitrate plant obsolete; but the great power dam at Muscle Shoals, with storage and lesser power dams much farther up the Tennessee River, especially the Norris Dam, near Knoxville, gave the people of that area water supplies, electric power, and cheap fertilizer.

In 1933 part of the Roosevelt Recovery Program was a most unusual and interesting experiment in social control. This undertaking, which was only incidentally connected with power, is called the *Tennessee Valley Authority*. It provided for a publicly organized and supervised development project for an area forty thousand square miles in extent. It involved better conservation of water, a more uniform flow at Muscle Shoals, and the creation of publicly created electric power and cheap fertilizer,[4] and other services. On the other side of the continent, irrigation and power were the excuse, flood control the reason, for the huge *Boulder Dam* on the Colorado

[3] The final and in a sense the most objectionable practice of this group of electrical holding companies, designated as the "Power Trust," was the program of propaganda. It was maintained that on the payroll of the organization were distinguished college professors, leaders of national organizations, and even some public officials. Do not understand that these leaders were bribed! They simply received large sums for their articles and for their influence.

[4] This project is proof that the N. R. A., National Recovery Administration, was a reconstruction as well as a recovery program. (See pp. 233–244.)

River—a project consummated after years of propaganda, conference, and state opposition.

For every man, woman, and child in the United States at least ten horse power is available from all sources. Most of this power is represented by automobiles used for pleasure, but a considerable part is available for business. From the standpoint of the industrial civilization of contemporary society, it seems worth while to note, first, the rapid advance in the amount and forms of available power; second, the gain that has come to humanity because *industry had five* (1929) *instead of three and a half* (1914) *horse power which each worker might command* as his servant; third, the reckless use of the sources, most of which cannot be replaced; and fourth, the public problems that have been, are now, or will be interwoven either with misuses of power, or with better organization of industry, or with more effective applications of present-day sources.

Importance of present-day power

From the standpoint of civilization the amount of power or its sources may be far less significant than the social and political by-products. When manufacturing depended primarily upon waterfalls, industry shifted to the neighborhood of streams, especially of natural waterfalls. Around these cataracts there have developed manufacturing centers of fair size. Factory towns of this type were dwarfed when coal replaced water power. The cost of transporting coal gave decided advantage to cities located near good coal deposits. Manchester, the Birminghams and Pittsburgh could manufacture more cheaply than cities depending on a long haul for fuel. It was easier to bring even iron long distances than to pay the high charges of carrying coal by land.

Now that oil and natural gas are being conveyed long distances at little cost, *less attention need be given to concentrated production.* The transformation of fuel into electricity may easily revolutionize the whole organization and character of modern industry. Large machines have advantage over small, large factories over household or community businesses, large-scale production over the old-time shop. Nevertheless, due to electricity smaller manufacturing cities are frequently replacing great industrial centers. In the making of certain products the skilled workman can be more efficient in a single-story plant in a small city than in the nth story of a manufacturing block. In these days of the automobile the worker need not live near the factory. In smaller communities, however, he may have a home of his own on a separate lot, may walk to work and leave the car for members of his family.

The social, educational and cultural advantage of this new type of life may easily be an important characteristic of future civilization in America. Possibly more important will be the opportunities to know one's neighbors, to enjoy new kinds of play, experience, and of family life. More thought and new types of thought may be possible in separation from the crowd. This change is not in any sense a back to the land movement but may carry with it some of the gains which we find in homely, sturdy, rural ways of living. The city may be the hope of democracy; but it is both an area of terrific strains and a cradle for revolts of modern youth. More often than not, at least in European centers, it is a hotbed of socialism or communism.

Development of Large-scale Corporate Business

Commensurate with the increase of power is the *new type of industrial organization on a large scale.* Before the middle of the eighteenth century, there were practically none but household work shops. Before the middle of the nineteenth, there were none, practically, but local shops producing for limited markets. Before the middle of the twentieth century, it is safe to predict that there will be several five-billion-dollar corporations, continent-wide or of international scope.

Much of industrialism's success is due to the organization of corporations. *The corporation is a legal body,* an artificial person, organized for the purpose of combining the capital and resources of many individuals and directed by a group chosen by the holders of stock. Without it many of the gains of modern industrial civilization would have been impossible. Originally all corporations were private and incorporated under separate legislative acts. Corporations are now incorporated under general state laws, subject to the approval and supervision of the authorities of the state which issues the papers. In a sense it is a very extensive and possibly changing partnership, in which the liability of ordinary stockholders and of directors is limited; and which continues regardless of the death of any partner. By the sale of stock and bonds the corporation is enabled to pool the capital of many investors, some of whom prefer security and a definite rate of interest. These buy the bond issues. Others are willing to take the risks and chance the profits of the business undertaking. These buy the stock issues. Today some corporations have hundreds of thousands of stockholders, notably the American Telephone and Telegraph Company with more than 700,000. Some issue much more non-voting stock than participating stock; these corporations may be controlled by a small minority of all stockholders.

As the word implies, the corporation is a body, long ago credited with no soul. But it is not a natural body; it is an artificial creation, a legal product of society. Because it has legal existence, it has privileges, publicly conferred, and under Amendment XIV it possesses all rights of persons, including those of "property." Giant corporations have rights denied to combinations and monopolies, rights which are safeguarded by Supreme Court decisions. Some corporations have been managed, or mismanaged, for the advantage of their directors, who have quite complete control of the company's affairs, in coöperation with the managing officials. Corporation mismanagement has been most conspicuous in the holding company, a corporation organized to hold the stock of a group of affiliated (combined) corporations and thus manage the affairs of the companies thus combined. How shall we modify or reorganize the corporation to keep it from being a Frankenstein [4a]?

The corporation, unfortunately, is not simply an incident of modern business and the present social order. *Already*

The corporation and the dilemma

[4a] Frankenstein was an artificial man-monster, who destroyed the best-loved friends of his creator and finally devoured that creator.

nearly half of American business wealth is corporation-owned rather than privately possessed. According to Berle and Means, private property, as we have understood private ownership, has ceased to be the basic concept of present-day wealth. "Corporate powers over participations and income . . . [represent] the rise of a power which is virtually new in the common law. . . . Private property, as understood in the capitalist system, is rapidly losing its original characteristics. Unless the law stops the wide-open gap which the corporate mechanism has introduced, the entire system has to be revalued." [5] "The translation of perhaps two-thirds of the industrial wealth of the country from individual ownership to ownership by the large, publicly financed corporations vitally changes the lives of property owners, the lives of workers, and the methods of property tenure. The divorce of ownership from control consequent on that process almost necessarily involves a new form of economic organization of society." [6] "Neither the claims of ownership [however] nor those of control can stand against the paramount interests of the community." [7]

Large-scale business

How has America changed from small-scale to large-scale industry? In 1850 the United States boasted 123,000 industrial establishments employing about eight workers apiece and with capital of less than $5,000 each. By 1900 the population of the United States had doubled; the number of establishments had increased fourfold; of workers, five times; of capital, ten times to ten billions; and of products, thirteen times to thirteen billions per year. Large-scale industry is therefore a twentieth-century product. The number of manufacturing establishments has dropped to less than two hundred thousand. Although the population of the United States increased only fifty percent in the first quarter of the twentieth century, capital and price of products increased fivefold.

Naturally, different industries developed at totally different rates. Our largest business, the American Telephone and

[5] *The Modern Corporation and Private Property*, The Macmillan Company, 1932, p. 247.
[6] *Ibid.*, vii–viii.
[7] *Ibid.*, p. 356.

Telegraph Company was non-existent a half century ago. The greatest automobile establishment, and automobiles rank at the top of all manufactured goods, is a product of the last three decades. If we add to the iron and steel manufacturers all other metal goods, including foundry and machine products, except automobiles, we should find that autos are left behind in the race for first place.

Stock slaughtering and meat-packing, our third most productive industry, increased its annual production per establishment from $64,765 in 1850 to more than two million

EARNINGS OF CORPORATIONS IN THE UNITED STATES,[8] 1931
CLASSIFIED BY SIZE

Size (total net assets in thousands of dollars)	Number of reporting corporations	Aggregate net profits after tax	Aggregate compensation of officers	Aggregate net profits after tax plus compensation of officers	Aggregate net profits after tax, relative to total stock equity	Aggregate net profits after tax, plus compensation of officers, relative to total stock equity
		(in millions of dollars)			(in percentage form)	
Under 50	182,447	−415	520	105	−21.7	5.5
50— 100	61,144	−218	312	94	− 9.1	3.9
100— 250	63,428	−353	433	80	− 6.5	1.5
250— 500	31,052	−268	296	28	− 4.6	0.5
500— 1,000	19,335	−271	235	− 36	− 3.9	−0.5
1,000— 5,000	18,345	−591	353	−238	− 3.0	−1.2
5,000—10,000	2,588	−166	99	− 67	− 1.8	−0.7
10,000—50,000	2,117	−104	161	57	− 0.5	0.3
50,000 and over	632	1,507	163	1,670	+ 2.2	2.4

Excluding corporations not reporting balance sheets.

dollars. Cotton factories, in the middle of the nineteenth century, had an average annual product of about $56,000; in 1905, $410,000; in 1923, $1,500,000. In the eleven years following 1914 the output per worker in these factories increased 136 percent. In iron and steel, the output per establishment amounted to more than six million dollars in 1923, and the total product of the United States Steel Corporation in 1920 was valued at a billion and three-quarters.

The wisdom of replacing small business units with large became apparent in the severe depression of 1929–1933. *During the year 1931 the losses of corporations in general were in exact inverse to the size,* as the accompanying table shows.

[8] Table 5, p. 6 Fabricant, *Recent Corporation Profits in the U. S.* (1934), National Bureau of Economic Research, Inc.

Only the very largest corporations made a profit that year. Interestingly enough one of the chief economy gains of merging was the reduction of overhead for the officers of the corporations. This was due chiefly to the decrease in their number, for we have heard much of the excessive salaries paid to those in high position, frequently in six figures, with occasional annual bonuses in seven, as a Senate committee discovered in 1933.[9]

As early as 1922 the Federal Trade Commission reported that "6 companies are shown as controlling about a third of the total developed water power, 8 companies as controlling over three-quarters of the anthracite coal reserves, 30 companies as controlling over a third of the immediate bituminous coal reserves, 2 companies as controlling well over half of the iron-ore reserves, 4 companies controlling nearly half of the copper reserves, and 30 companies controlling over 12 per cent of the petroleum reserves."

The decade after the World War was preëminently a merger-making period.[9a]   Harry W. Laidler reported [10] 7000

---

[9] Senate Committee on Banking and Currency, 1933.

[9a] The merger or the holding company had replaced earlier forms of combination, because most of those had been outlawed or had been declared illegal by the courts. More than a half century ago, captains of industry found it desirable to reduce competition by getting together and agreeing that they would not cut into each other's business. The earlier agreements did not work out very successfully, and were unenforceable in the courts, because at common law monopolies were not permitted. Consequently, these general agreements were replaced by "pools," in which the different managers or operators pooled their earnings and redivided the pool according to agreement. The pools in railroads were largely responsible for the first Interstate Commerce Act and for the earlier anti-trust acts.

When pools were outlawed, the companies which had been combined in a pool placed their securities and business in the hands of trustees: hence these anti-combination laws are usually known as anti-trust laws. Combinations in the form of trusts as well as pools were therefore declared illegal. In the twentieth century, search has been made for new forms of combination which would avoid competition but remain legal. Sometimes a holding company has been organized to take the place of the old trustees, and this has usually been considered lawful. More frequently, the companies have merged, either with the merging companies retaining part of their identity, or through the complete amalgamation of the merging companies, or by the purchase of all securities of the combining companies by a single corporation. The legality of these forms of combination has usually been upheld.

[10] *Current History,* Nov. 1931. All other quotations in the paragraph and most of the details are from Laidler's article. More details are given in his volume on *Concentration in American Industry.*

mergers in manufacturing alone. Two hundred non-financial corporations did 45 percent of the non-financial business of the country. John T. Flynn tabulated [11] 217 mergers in twelve fields controlling 2621 companies with market values of securities Dec. 31, 1929, of $21,655,468,000. Laidler found (1927) 878 grocery chains, "including in their scope 67,000 stores." "Chains now (1931) take care of perhaps one-fifth of the retail business of the nation." In banking "as a result of a decade of this concentration one per cent of the banks of the country control nearly one-half of the total bank resources, while twenty-four New York banks, about one-tenth of one per cent of the total, possess about fifteen per cent of the bank resources of the nation." Three-fourths of the telephones and seven-eighths of the telephone revenue belong to the American Telephone and Telegraph Company and four great financial organizations control more than ninety per cent of the electric power of the United States. Three auto companies produce more than eighty per cent of America's automobiles and two corporations make two-thirds of the people's cigarettes. The large baking companies bake most of America's bread. The list might be prolonged greatly and the menace of monopoly would appear most serious, if interrelated controls were known.

The dependence of the American public upon the large corporations may be indicated by the place of the two hundred largest non-financial corporations doing business in America. In 1930 it was computed that about fifty per cent of all corporate wealth other than banking was controlled by these two hundred largest corporations. This amount was twenty-two per cent of all the wealth of America. Rather more important to the American people as consumers is the fact that in 1929 forty-three per cent of all business was done by these two hundred business giants and that their business exceeded by more than 120 per cent the income of the 800 next largest non-financial corporations.[11a] During the depression the percentage

---

[11] *The New Republic,* July 2, 1930.
[11a] Berle and Means, *The Modern Corporation and Private Property,* ch. III.

of all business done by these huge systems undoubtedly increased because, as shown in the chart on page 119, their business held up much better than that of smaller organizations. The place which these businesses will occupy in the future might be indicated by the fact that from 1920 to 1930 the increase in *their percentage* of all American business was ten per cent—that is from 33 per cent of all business to 43 per cent.

It has been possible to organize business in large units to some extent because of *the holding company*. This is a corporation or other business association which usually does no business itself but holds the stock of a group of affiliated companies and manages their affairs. It gives opportunity for the pooling of capital in very large units, of handling finances easier than the members could, of introducing economies and interrelations which the members could not manage for themselves. These advantages have been utilized most with public utilities; but the holding company is not restricted to any one field. Sometimes the holding company is itself an operating company, as is true with the larger part of the American Telephone and Telegraph Company. From the standpoint of the public the holding company has aroused opposition and criticism because its advantages in financing have led to great inflation of securities, and its control of its member units has limited competition and caused unnecessary increase of prices.

Europe has indulged in large-scale mass production less than America. Writing several years ago, Macrosty, in *The Trust Movement in British Industry*, stated that in iron and steel "the tendency is toward the evolution of comparatively large units in each branch, and then that these units should combine in a loose organization for the regulation of their trade." Charles R. Van Hise declared that in the British textile and chemical industries "combination has extended very far." In tobacco, there is one huge British consolidation. The Germans and the French have a steel cartel somewhat similar in its vast product and market control to the United States Steel Corporation. In Germany, after the

World War, Stimmel and others consolidated industries which were not so concentrated before 1914.

"For a business generation, there has been great and increasing veneration for the principle of Mass Production. To the magic of that phrase has been given much of the credit for the wealth and prosperity of this country. Low unit cost, high wages, good profits were the lusty and charming triplets that drew their sustenance from this fount. American economists and writers joined hands with European observers in concluding that the pass-word to American success was, essentially, Mass Production. Nor does there exist any basis for denying the contribution to American economic well-being which has been made by the system of producing millions of standardized articles at lowest-in-the-world units costs. To those who are secure in their belief that mass production is the absolutely permanent foundation of American supremacy, it would be a shock of no slight magnitude to discover that time is already wearing away that foundation." [12]

An important part of the new world is modern transportation by land, sea, or air.[13] At this time we are concerned chiefly with *large-scale organization of railways,* i.e., the extent of the consolidation movement and the problem of the railroads in recent years. Most of the railroads, before the World War, were owned by eight huge companies. The World War gave new impetus to consolidation movements because all rails were, for more than two years, under management of the authorities at Washington. The return of the railways to their rightful owners was accompanied by a rather revolutionary statute for railway control; *the Transportation Act of 1920.* It permitted mergers. The Ripley commission reported plans for better reorganization and consolidation, and official

Railway consolidation

---

[12] Mazur, Paul, *American Prosperity, Its Causes and Consequences,* The Viking Press, p. 114.

[13] Before the O'Fallon decision (1929) and the depression the investment in American railroads was estimated at more than twenty billions of dollars. When the Supreme Court decided that the Interstate Commerce Commission should base its rates, not upon the original cost, but upon the cost of replacement, the market value of "rails" quickly rose nearly fifty per cent. Even the depression following the panic of 1929 did not bring the market value of railway stocks and bonds much below pre-O'Fallon figures until 1932; then they fell like Ichabod.

action has been taken to expedite the development of huge sectional railway systems. In 1933 a more definite attempt at reorganization, refinancing and rehabilitation was made under the act of that year, with Joseph B. Eastman as co-ordinator. Even this government encouragement and aid, with the removal of unnecessary competition, does not place upon an attractive profit-paying basis railways that were built upon too much credit or were combined with too much high finance.

A very serious and practical problem, that of the railroads, now confronts the American people. These public utilities are still indispensable, in spite of vast sums of public money spent on highways and great development of private bus and freight companies. If, in 1932, the rails earned only a little more than one per cent on their investment, how shall they have the eight per cent on the valuation hinted in Supreme Court decisions? The consumer can pay only so much; and shippers are not like householders who cannot dispense with gas or electricity in their daily routine. If transportation rates are raised too high, business is ruined, not helped. If the rails add to cost of production only what the consumer can afford, then only in prosperity is there profit enough to pay bond-holders and stock owners of these merged railways.

The rails are in a quandry simply because they cannot charge more than the traffic will bear. Even the economies of eliminated competition and profits of combination are not enough. Will improvements in technology solve the problem? It is beside the point to show why the trouble lies in past speculation and exploitation of the railroads. Yet we may not disregard altogether their despoliation, even that of years ago.[14] Possibly the rails, like the canals, have passed their peak! Shall each generation pay full prices on obsolescent machinery and investments of the preceding; or must liquida-

[14] Note just a half dozen flagrant examples. What did the transcontinental roads cost to build, if we take actual costs and not the unearned surpluses of building companies or the profits of the Credit Mobilier? Does the present generation, as well as that of Civil War Reconstruction, have to pay for the pirate operations of the Fisks, Drews, and Goulds? It took Erie a quarter century to recover from the depredations of Wall Street operators, when the heyday of railroads was still in the future.

tion and revaluation readjust at least part of the difficulty? Probably we must decide our public problems by the needs and abilities of our public today. We must not sacrifice the railroads, still important if not so essential as fifty years ago. To charge humanity today for the mistakes of yesterday is both unfair and unjust. Competition consequently is not the chief problem or combination the answer.[15]

To modern, scientifically organized big business we owe the gearing together of many formerly unrelated parts of production, or of production, transportation and sale into a complex and efficient machine. To it also we owe the reduction of wastes, the use of by-products and some real efficiency in creating goods at low costs, supplied to an ever widening public. Recent careful studies seem to indicate that the very large businesses are usually not so efficiently managed as those of medium size. Apparently there is a limit to the profitable combination of separate producing units into a single system. Efficient production involves, naturally, not only a proper calculation of the combinations of materials, power, labor, and other factors of production, but a careful computation of the probable market and the elimination of unnecessary wastes. It has been maintained that the protective tariff has caused heavy losses by permitting us to use old, antiquated machinery and not forcing us to produce with maximum efficiency. Waste due to lack of training of employers and of workers, particularly on American farms, reaches an appalling figure. Unemployment, untrained workers, unnecessary sickness and idleness are productive of extensive waste. From the standpoint of human energy the lack of appeal and incentive probably gives us labor inefficiency of the highest type. The ordinary worker like the ordinary student could probably do

Advantages of large-scale business

[15] A half century ago, when the railways had problems somewhat similar to those of the present, at a time when public regulation was new, many of them went into politics. Those were the days when political machines tried to control state railway commissions and to keep at Washington one senator from each political party. The story is apocryphal but unfortunately rather true to fact. In the gay nineties, a group of senators sat around discussing the death of a distinguished colleague. Following tradition, they spoke well of the dead. One remarked: "Well, boys, he was dependable. We can say of him, he was always true to his trust." Then spoke the cynic: "Shall we mention the name of the trust?"

double what he does. One need not go to the extreme of the Taylor or Brashear efficiency systems. Human nature will not stand being trained too fine or worked too effectively.

One great debt we owe to modern corporate industry is the utilization of by-products. The Standard Oil Company gained part of its unusual financial expansion by utilizing materials or opportunities that rivals threw away. Someone says that any invention worth having is sooner or later secured or copied by this successful semi-monopoly. In popular phraseology, Standard Oil has been outdone, however, by the pork packers, who make use of "everything except the squeal."

After all, *one excellent standard by which we can determine efficient organization of production is to decide whether or not the economic machine creates a product adequate to maintain all those who contribute in the process of production.* If it does not make sufficient appeal to the capitalist to get capital goods or materials for use, if it does not offer sufficient opportunity for an enterpriser to attract managerial ability, if it does not pay a living wage, it cannot reasonably be considered efficient. If it measures values by the yardstick of dollars rather than of utility or of culture, its efficiency is one of technology not of civilization.

The new order, and the new industrial capitalism, has sharp limitations but its influence seems boundless and its ramifications endless. In many cases non-economic by-products of Industrial Revolution are as important as the increase in power or the development of large-scale business. In this period of reorganization the ancient saying represents truth in many fields: "The old order changeth, giving place to the new."

ELEMENTS IN THE INDUSTRIAL DILEMMA

Production and profit

The ancient world achieved much of its success on the basis of slavery. The present world owes even more to the robot. The Roman Empire fell when slavery declined partly because conquest ceased, and because emancipation was accelerated by Christianity. If the modern world declines, it may not be from a lack of robots; it may be, however, from the overabundance of mechanical men. It might well suffer as well as benefit from very great multiplication of power and energy resources that will be utilized.   At twenty words a minute it would have taken ten million copyists seven days to get out a Sunday edition of the New York Times.   It is done by a thousand men working two days each.

Before 1929 we had abundant information regarding the increase in production per worker.   From 1914 to 1925 the actual increase in output in dozens of industries was more than doubled.   The average was more than three per cent a year. Economies introduced since 1929 have replaced expensive man labor by improved machines or new uses of power.   Much as Adam Smith used the shoe industry as a type illustration, attention has been drawn to the fact that our present factories could produce for the American people nine hundred million shoes per year, without overtime work.   This, if true, and it has been questioned, is a larger supply than could be sold under normal conditions.

Instead of working full time industry does not produce what it might.   And the reason is profit!   A small surplus supply of any commodity, as is easily observable in the case of abundant harvests, reduces prices out of all proportion to the amount of this marginal surplus.   We could produce more, and more products that we use daily!   But if we did increase durability the demand for replacement would be reduced indefinitely.   The factories devoted to production of those commodities would not need replacement except at intervals.   The capital used for buildings, machines and other equipment could then be diverted into other channels.   Yet billions of capital are seeking investment at any price, provided the capital is assured security and probable return of the principal.   Attempts to invest most of this capital in profitable enterprise floods the market not necessarily with commodities but with new factories.   These factories increase the present adequate equipment.   They introduce new competition, create new surplus and reduce prices still further.   So the vicious circle continues indefinitely.

If general welfare, with an improved standard of living, is the *desideratum* of our present civilization, *it may be necessary not to scrap as obsolete* the machines and factories which we need, but to modify *those features of an industrial system which fail.* It is small wonder that Veblen, Flanders, and in more recent years the technocrats, have visioned an economic dictatorship which will give us unlimited production, for the sake of production and society, rather than limitation of supply, for the sake of profits and business. Years ago Veblen wrote that production could easily be several times what it was. Both he and Ralph Flanders have drawn attention to the advantages of a technological dictatorship, by which production would be planned and controlled for maximum production. Soddy is among the ablest of the advocates who would use more efficiently energy units prodigally provided by nature. Among the difficulties encountered by technocracy is the fact that only a small proportion of all workers are engaged in production or work of a type which could be radically reorganized by new technology for new and better uses of machinery.

The problem is one of extraordinary complexity, especially since most economic organization and most business activities lie outside of the field that might be filled by robots. As Wesley C. Mitchell has shown, this is a matter for the social engineer. When we consider for a moment the great difficulties encountered in the adaptation of government to economic organization, because the latter is probably primary,[16] and the reëstablishment of multiple relationships of a social nature, it at once becomes clear that a dictatorship of production units fails to envision the whole problem. It would fail to solve our real difficulty in the same degree. Mitchell suggests, in an article some time ago: "If engineers will join with the other professions who are working on the [exceedingly complex social] problem, [of which they consider only a small part,] we shall get on faster. For the present workers need a clearer vision of what is possible in production, and a more constructive attitude of mind. Those needs engineers can supply." [17]

---

[16] Pp. 360–361.
[17] *Mechanical Engineering*, Feb. 1931.

The dilemma of industrialism is in a real sense more a mat-
ter of consumption than of production. Over-production is a
relative term, and it might be fairer to speak of under-consumption. Production, in time of prosperity, may have been
only about seventy-five per cent of capacity to produce; but
if it outran the capacity to consume, it was even then too high.
This phase of the dilemma of industrialism might be stated as
a lack of balance between production and consumption. It
might be due to a general lag of consumption in relation to
production, or it might be rather a lack of consuming power
in a variety of fields. During the recent depression, for example, the demand for *consumption goods* dropped comparatively little from the previous normal level; but the demand
for new house construction, locomotives, factory equipment,
and steel goods in general was very low indeed. Evidently in
troughs of business activity, the real need is a speeding up of
demand for products of these lagging industries. Is the problem in prosperity one of speeding up the general demand to
balance production; and, if so, why can we not do it?

So far as under-consumption is a real contributing cause
to the dilemma of industrialism, it will be avoided, without
question, if the consumers have anything to say about it. The
fact that in 1929 goods worth between six and seven billions
were being bought on installment showed the willingness of
many purchasers to exceed their income in securing autos,
pianos, rugs, radios, refrigerators and other desired commodities. The further fact that a fair part of the personal debt
incurred before 1929 probably was also for houses and other
usable articles, not for investment, shows a willingness to spend
beyond the current income. These expenditures were unwise
because they were beyond the actual income of the purchaser,
including not only income of that day, but, as it turned out,
future income as well.

Evidently then if under-consumption is partly responsible
for the dilemma of industrialism, *the remedy does not lie
simply in more purchases of goods that are produced. Nor
should solution be attempted by reducing production to the
level of actual consumption.* That would usually mean one of

two things (1) slowing down production without lowering prices, or (2) reducing output to make the supply less than the demand and thereby raise prices. The second of these methods would inevitably reduce consumption still further, because if the *total price* paid was the same as formerly, the number of articles purchased would be smaller. That would mean a still further reduction of the existing under-consumption.

A balance of consumption with production in an age of constantly improved technology apparently is no easy task. Without it, however, the dilemma of industrialism gets worse and worse. It would seem as though, with so many human wants far from being satisfied, in fact with so many human beings, even in America, in dire need, the solution should be a simple one, unless shoes, clothing, razor blades, and airplanes are much more durable than they are now. If the sole problem were to dispose of what is produced, there would be no difficulty. If social credit could give us our hearts' desires, there would be no surplus stocks on shop shelves. But when the would-be purchaser must pay a cost plus forty per cent, or one that is 200 per cent above cost, the purchase may not be made for obvious reasons.

Producers cannot afford to manufacture and sell at cost, even if they could sell all their goods. If consumers pay forty per cent more than all costs, including that of raw materials and of final sale, and the forty per cent is taken out of the money or funds available for later purchases, some of the goods manufactured for sale at forty per cent profit cannot be sold, unless the purchaser draws on his future income through installment or other credit. But when that future comes, then his income may be lower than it should be and he cannot buy what he should have purchased, and otherwise could have bought.

Evidently *the dilemma of industrialism, so far as it is represented by under-consumption, is a matter of limited purchasing power in the possession of those who would buy if they could.* From figures given below [18] we can see that the slight

[18] Pp. 131–132.

increase of wages from 1922 to 1929 did not begin to keep pace with the rapid increases of production in those years.[19] That the increased production brought only slight reductions in the prices of those goods is apparent when we compare the increase of three per cent per year in purchasing power with 1.4 percent a year in wages. From this discrepancy between production and consumption, *it looks as though the dilemma of industrialism was chiefly a financial one*—too little income for the average consumer and too much profit for the enterpriser and investor. If that was true in prosperity, what is the fact in depression when the amount actually paid in wages was approximately a half less than in 1925 and dividends nearly a half more? A system which depends, like ours, on *a continued circulation of wealth* [20] needs better *planning of production in relation to consumption* [21] and continued watchfulness to discover ways and means for the increase of consumption.[22]

Possibly the dilemma of industrialism has little to do with the unjust rewards to those who manage it or serve it. *Those who "make money,"* or directly help to make money (wealth), *have been paid generously. Those who furnish most of the ideas,* scientists or engineers, and *those who do most of the work,* the laborers, *have a small share.* Workers outside of the industrial sphere do not count anyway. Since we live under industrial capitalism, those who choose careers in agriculture, art, education, or literature do it at their own loss. Suppose one does become the world's finest musician—"what of it"? To be sure the non-producing folk form more than two-thirds of the population that buy. Whose loss is it if we have a submerged two-thirds consuming class?

For the laborers who do not neglect the main chance, a share in industrial capitalism, what of them? Take only the years of plenty, 1922–1929. "Among employees of manufacturing establishments real wages per capita advanced by 1.4 per cent a year . . . while common stockholders gained at the

Just and unjust payment and out-worn principles

[19] Pp. 118–120.
[20] Pp. 165–167.
[21] Pp. 248–251, 255–256.
[22] On Consumption, see pp. 225–233.

rate of 16.4 per cent a year . . . capital values of invested funds . . . at a rate of 18.8 per cent a year for holders of common stocks." [23] "The aggregate command over goods exercised by manufacturing labor increased at a rate of 3.1 per cent a year between 1922 and 1929; that of 'ownership and management' increased by 7.3 per cent a year." [24]

The great depression would not have been nearly so great but for the unprecedented unemployment in three fields.[25] The first of these was that of the capital industries including steel and other metals, and incidentally the auto manufacturers, railway, factory and store equipment and lumbering. The second was that of the building trades, including not only those who constructed houses, factories and business blocks but those engaged in public works, almost all of which were dicontinued at once. The third was that of the overload occupations, in which the employers were unable to pay regular wages for regular work, or thought they could not. Each man was asked to do not only his own work but also to carry half of that of a man discharged, with repeated cuts in his own wage.

Depression and unemployment have drawn attention sharply to the antiquity of the organization which we have and the archaic laws under which we try to make it work. The excessive maladjustment in bad times shows that when good times return there will still be problems of unemployment and of ill adjustment, because present-day economic organization may be unscientific and even anti-social. Great Britain's plans for permanent unemployment relief would meet with derision in America as a public measure for several reasons. We may have abandoned rugged individualism in business and in much of our political procedure; but we still think in terms of individual rights for making dollars. We scoff at the possibility that, with our almost inexhaustible resources, we cannot continue indefinitely to appropriate, to exploit and to dominate resources and even the supply of labor.

[23] Mills, P. C., *Economic Tendencies in the United States,* National Bureau of Economic Research, Inc., pp. 555–56.
[24] *Ibid.,* p. 550.
[25] Consult table from Ayres, p. 212.

If our industrial capitalist system seems to be based upon rather outworn ideas of individualism, we must remember that business was the first of all the elements of modern society to abandon and therefore to destroy individualism.[26] It may still claim freedom of initiative, freedom of contract, exemption from interference by the public; but it has ceased to exist profitably unless it works harmoniously with a complex society in which alone it finds purchasers and its general market. It has destroyed individualism by a collectivist corporation, developed into combination and consolidation. It has destroyed individualism so far as it may have deprived the workers of freedom of choice and of opportunity of selling their labor to the highest bidder. It has destroyed individualism by exploiting and therefore by dominating the producer of raw materials, and frequently by replacing that producer itself. It has destroyed individualism, and may have undermined itself, if it has limited the necessary purchasing power of the consumer. It has helped to destroy individualism in law and in government, if it has claimed any rights of ancient laws devised for totally different conditions and much more primitive societies.

Industrialism faces a dilemma because it is built on an incorrect principle. We hear much of the contrast between profit and use. It is true. Industrialism has tried for success on the basis of capital, when it should have sought it by working for the public. Industrialism is a system of production. It has made itself great by pooling the public's savings, by constantly improving machines and using better forms of power. *Production has lost sight of its real object—to supply consumers.* May it not be true that it is almost literally losing its life because it has sought to save it, profitably? Better inventions, more labor-saving devices will come year by year. They offer difficulty only because the larger product is not shared, and possibly under the present set up, cannot be shared, with the consuming public. Wages and standards of living have risen: yes. But they have lagged far behind possible output of goods and actual accumulation of profits. Industrialism must change

Why industrialism faces a dilemma

26 See more fully pp. 117–126, 279–282.

its whole policy.[27]   When times are good, the captain of industry expands his business, chiefly by borrowing large sums at moderate rates of interest.   When times are bad, he cannot help us out of the slump because his own book losses are large. In four years of depression all business lost thirty billions.

Does the dilemma of industrialism call for a moratorium on applied science?   Pessimists suggest such a reversion to ancient method and ideas.   Possibly they would, or must, include pure science ahead of applied.   Some people propose as a way out the abandonment of all machines and recent technological advances and improvements.   We could then revert to a semi-medieval plan of an agricultural society, each family living on a small amount of land.   However, the clock of time does not turn backward.   Certainly in time of war, science the creator has become science the destroyer.   Humanity hopes the race to attain civilization will be won by an intelligent people before war, an accompaniment of early civilization, destroys the world's human population, before our civilization can be annihilated.   Science really becomes the destroyer, *if* it creates an impossible situation; if it forces us forward, when beyond us lies the precipice; if industrialism is continually developing into a more and more impossible system; if capitalism and any anti-social interests maintain their privileges at all costs.   Then there is no room left for science except to pass out of the picture, or to complete the work of destruction.   If that is all we can see, something must be wrong with our eyesight.

The World War was fought to make the world safe for democracy; so we said, so we thought.   The outcome made us skeptical of our major premise, and of the real cause, which was contemporaneous civilization.   The World War would not have been fought had humanity still been at an agricultural level.   The World War would not have been fought as it was fought, had it not been an intricate part of a changing civilization built upon ideas hundreds or thousands of years old. The World War might not have been fought, had not industrial capitalism gained advantage from its beginning, from its con-

[27] See IX.

tinuing, from its ending.[28] It has been said that the common soldier "won" the World War, but as a consequence lost his living. *The World War left us with more nationalism, more large-scale competition, more greed, more profit taking, more dilemmas.* It accelerated the movement of which it was a part; and depression was an inevitable consequence of it. Like a blind modern Samson it may help to pull down upon its devotees the whole superstructure of an industrial, capitalistic society.

The standards by which we judge conditions are wrong, like the basic principles. Too often our yardstick is the stock market report. "What did the stock market do today?" is a popular if not a business query. Most of us, including most business men, never see the Babson Chart or Standard Statistics or the Dun-Bradstreet reports. Ignorance of falling prices the world over before 1929, ignorance of business conditions then in Germany and in Great Britain, ignorance of dulling business in U. S. A. made a good excuse for the blunders of the summer and fall of 1929.

Our standards are poor or our standards may be wrong, because many of our business principles may be wrong. They may be wrong because our business psychology is awry. It stands to reason that we shall never get rich as a nation by robbing Peter to pay Paul. If we read *They Told Barron,* we find that many business leaders were interested in gambling more than in keeping business good business. Business undoubtedly exists solely to serve society, for how else can goods be used? Industrialism probably cannot get out of its dilemma until it faces that fact.

The dilemma of industrialism is not simple but complex. Exploitation of public resources counts against industrialism less than the over-multiplication of machines and power units. Domination of workers can be forgiven if work and reasonable income are not denied. Depression can be overcome if pros-

[28] "Our war profiteering sales on credit did not cause the war, but they got us into it, and they made of it a much bigger and a far worse mess than European war need have been. The world today is not suffering from European war losses but from American war financing." Dennis, Lawrence, *Is Capitalism Doomed?* Harper and Brothers, p. 303.

perity creates social surplus and gives momentum for the climb to normalcy. Anti-social corporation mismanagement may lead to prohibition only of exploitation by unscrupulous business managers. Over-production is an evil only to producers. Give society purchasing power and it disappears, as an evil. There now exist three P's—profit-taking, politics, and the public, and the greatest of these is the public. We have tried profiteering and do not like the morning-after taste of depression. If we prefer politicians, we might try rather complete government management, à la socialism. The public we do not know; we have been too busy making money and running other people's affairs. How about a new deal for our own?

VI

THE DILEMMA OF FINANCIALISM

For nearly a half century we have been living under a system, if that is not a misnomer, called industrial capitalism. As indicated in the preceding chapter, industry and finance are not nearly so identical in character, interests, and in aims as most of us have been inclined to believe. An understanding of financialism therefore stresses totally different elements and problems from those considered under industrialism. The dilemma of financialism, while practically a part of that encountered by industry because industrial capitalism has unity in spite of its dual nature, is based upon principles and grows out of techniques quite distinct from those already considered.

Nevertheless the former alliance of these two modern economic giants, their necessary and continued coöperation in fact, and their close interrelations and inevitable interdependence have given to the two together, rather than either alone, the successes, the business influence and the public power which we attribute to industrial capitalism. Industrialism might not have encountered a dilemma if it had not found overwhelming supplies of capital demanding investment. Being new, its opportunities for profit naturally attracted a larger share of that capital than probably should have been put into ordinary industrial enterprise. If that capital had been individual, or even the pooled shares of partners, again industrialism would not have furnished a product far in excess of the capacity of the public to purchase and consume. The dilemma of industrialism has been due in part to capitalism and to corporate capitalism.

THE PLACE OF FINANCIALISM IN A CAPITALISTIC SOCIETY

Circles are not always vicious. The capital which has been poured so lavishly into industrialism is largely a by-product of extraordinary profits and surpluses in the world of machine-power, technological industry. In a single year before 1929 there was saved in America an amount equal to at least twice the estimated wealth of the whole United States in 1850. Talk about increment at a geometrical ratio; we seem almost to have it here. According to Robert R. Doane,[1] the amount of annual savings available to the American capital market for the years 1928 and 1929 was slightly in excess of twenty-one billions annually, and the average from the close of the World War through the panic of 1929 was more than 17½ billions. This of course is not net, because it does not provide for depreciation, losses, and other items that should be deducted. These huge sums saved annually could be used by industry chiefly because of the organization of corporations and opportunities for investment in shares, bonds, or other properties or securities. Its creation and saving depended very greatly upon the coöperation of the government, particularly through laws organizing corporations and permitting, especially after 1927, the organization of banks with special powers in connection with investment, even including "investment" in Wall Street. We earned, we saved, we invested. Everything seemed fine in prosperity; but where did we find ourselves in depression?

Estimated figures for the year 1932 show how compound interest affected the American standard of living, American purchasing power, and therefore American business. Before 1929 we were boasting of a national income totaling nearly ninety billion dollars a year. We estimated our wealth in 1922 at 322 billions, in 1925 at about 360 billions. We did not take into account the fact that in 1929 securities sold on Eastern exchanges, representing corporate and other stocks and bonds that amounted to less than half the wealth of the United States, were priced at an amount exceeding four hundred billions of dollars. Against American actual wealth or fictitious

---

[1] *The Measurement of American Wealth*, p. 112.

paper property, private and public debts had been continually increasing in amount until they totaled an amount estimated at not less than 150 billions, and in some cases guessed to be 218 billions or more. The Dow-Jones "industrials" dropped from 381 [1a] in September, 1929, to 41 in June, 1932. The loss in bonds represented on the Bond Market was less than that. In the case of most corporations Eastern bond losses were not so heavy as those of Western companies.

Where were we, the American people, left by prosperity, extravagance, and optimistic borrowing? Income had plunged from eighty-three billions to thirty-eight billions. But interest was practically unchanged in amount, and taxes which should have been lowered were raised because of needed revenue. Because the American dollar had soared higher and higher, the creditor demanded of the debtor (and not one of us escaped publicly, though we might not suffer privately) nearly one-quarter of the income of the American people for 1932. Taxes took a third. The legislative halls were ringing with demands to lower taxes as a good old American right, but also with requests to raise them in order that some who are hungry should be fed from our "surplus." For the average American family there was left the appalling small annual residue, little more than $650 per family, a net amount barely half of that which the statically-minded economist found the unskilled laborer earned in the years before 1929.

Because *financialism was dependent upon industrialism for capital surpluses, and industrialism was dependent upon financialism in organizing its corporations, promoting the sale of stock and other securities, and in continuing credit,* there has been in the last three-quarters of a century *a close coalition between financialism and industrialism.* The two acted as one against Southern slavery in the middle of the nineteenth century,[2] and against agriculturalism in the late nineteenth.[3] The dependence of industrialism upon financialism grew apace with the development of combinations, especially at the turn of the

Interrelations of industry and finance

[1a] The average price per share of the stock of thirty very important industrial corporations.

[2] Pp. 42–43.

[3] Pp. 43–44.

century. Even before the World War financialism operated
not only as a link between business engaged in production, in
transportation, and in marketing, but also as the directing
member of the business quadrumvirate. Except in the case of
Henry Ford, industrial magnates who proposed business ex-
tensions or arranged reorganizations did so with the approval
and aid of the investment banker.

Before examining more carefully the dilemma of financialism
as shown in the over-development and under-control of banking, the instability of prices and the problem growing out of
debt obligations, let us make some study of the wealth, income,
and savings of the American people.

WEALTH, INCOME AND SAVINGS

Increase of
wealth

"To him that hath shall be given" might very easily be the
text or motto of modern capitalism. Certainly capital has
justified itself by the effective way in which it has increased
the amount of capital goods used to create more wealth and
the volume of consumption goods available for raising the
levels of living by adding comforts to necessities, and former
luxuries to recent comforts. Measured in figures, a single century shows almost unbelievable advance. Even after we make
due allowance for the decrease in the purchasing value of the
dollar, we find a gain marvellous in this country, enormous in
Europe, and great if not easily measurable in the rest of the
world.

In 1850 the wealth of the United States of America was
estimated at only seven billions of dollars. By 1900 this had
increased to $88,000,000,000, fifty-two billions of which was
represented by stationary wealth in the nature of real estate
and improvements. By 1912 American wealth had increased
to $186,000,000,000, a real increase because the value of the
dollar had changed little during those years. Estimates rather
than careful statistics are the only source available since 1922.
In that year the wealth of the United States was estimated
at $320,000,000,000; of the United Kingdom at $120,-
000,000; [4] of France at $60,000,000,000; of Germany at

---

[4] According to Crammond, 88 billions.

$40,000,000,000; and of Italy at $35,000,000,000. In the de-velopment of a North Atlantic civilization of an economic type, which many authorities believe to be the promise and the hope of the future, the preponderance of Uncle Sam is dis-closed by an enormous discrepancy. The figures show our wealth to be greater than that of the other important world powers taken together.

In *an analysis of wealth,* not income, we must consider the different forms in existence and the different sources from year to year and decade to decade. It is not only the taxpayer who, a few years ago, knew that more than half our total wealth consists of land and buildings.[5] After 1922 industry expanded sharply although not so rapidly as the Wall Street bulls would have us believe. Few businesses duplicated the rapid expan-sion of General Motors or of American Can; but, even when the stock-market slump after 1929 was taken into account, most of the active industrial stocks at their lowest still sold for more than they had brought on the market in 1921. The reverse process took place on American farms. The estimated value in 1920 of our productive farm land was almost four times what it had been at the beginning of the century, but by 1925 the fifty-five billion dollar estimate had shrunk to less than thirty-eight billion dollars; and in 1933 what was it worth? Fortunate those who in 1922 owned the stock of the most progressive industrials and unfortunate those who had capital sunk in agricultural lands, frequently mortgaged to the limit.

Who are the people that possess valuable income-yielding property? The Federal Trade Commission made a study of these folk. On the basis of their investigations it was esti-mated that they controlled $242,000,000,000 of our national wealth. Two hundred sixty-eight thousand people, with prop-

---

[5] In 1922 distinctively personal goods at forty billion dollars exceeded the total investment in railroad and factory, thirty-six billions, and manu-factured products for that year, twenty-eight billions. New York was not only the most populous state but also the wealthiest, but of the larger states in an agricultural or industrial area Iowa had the greatest wealth per capita, $4,272.00.

Three hundred fifty-three billions was the estimate of the Federal Trade Commission in 1925.

erty income above $10,000 per year, owned nearly one hundred billion. That is, *six-tenths of one per cent of the population owned forty-two and one-half per cent of all income-producing property and nearly sixty per cent of all the wealth in the United States.* Contrast this with four and three-tenths per cent of income-producing wealth owned by the ordinary laborers, more than twenty-seven million in number. Their share was but $370.00 each, scarcely one-tenth of the per capita wealth of the average New Englander. Had these workers lived in Europe they would have considered themselves fairly prosperous and fortunate. Two reasons exist for this. In the first place per capita wealth is much less in Europe than in America, and second, the income from property goes much farther among people who count their minor purchases in pfennigs or sous rather than in nickels and dimes.[6]

Incomes old and new

A number of studies have been made of national income. Some of these have been very careful and as scientific as the conditions permit. Estimates based upon rather distinct sources are sufficiently alike to justify some fairly definite conclusions. As we should expect, the incomes vary less than inventories of property. A wealthy man who works with hand or brain can add comparatively little to his own income, because that must come chiefly from investments. On the contrary, the professional man, writer, or cartoonist finds his annual income a fairly large part of his total wealth.

Income statistics ought not to be taken as the measure of a man. Between individuals the discrepancies are great and between different types of production there are marked differences. The ordinary wage-earners who in 1924 had only

---

[6] In France a score or two years ago there were only twelve estates of more than 12,000,000 francs; and that was before the franc shrank from pre-war proportions. More than half of the total wealth of that country was in estates of less than 50,000 francs each. In England estates of less than $5,000 constituted only eleven per cent of the total wealth and were the possessions of seven-eighths of the population. Prussia shows a more uneven distribution than that of France, but less than that of Great Britain. Willford King, in one of his early books, "Wealth and Income," compares figures to show that in England the wealthiest two per cent held more of the national wealth than was held by a corresponding two per cent in any other nation. If he could have included a study of the United States as a whole at the present time, America might seem much like England a half century ago.

$10,000,000,000 of income-producing property earned in that year nearly $40,000,000,000, an average of probably $1200 each. The farmers were not the most successful workers, because the cash income for each family that year was only $793.00. In spite of the constantly decreasing appraised value of their land, the farmers received a return of less than two per cent on their investment. Even before the World War agriculture had yielded to manufacturing as our greatest occupation.[7]

It is difficult to estimate the amount of the national income; it is much more difficult to determine actual *savings*.[8] Net savings would seem to be a matter of subtraction. If we could take the total wealth of America one year and deduct it from the total wealth of the following year, we would seem to have not an estimate but proof of the amount actually saved. This is too simple and easy a solution. Wealth involves increase of value in addition to saved income; but we must also take into account depreciation of property or goods which tends to balance the unearned increment found on choice business corners or in the goodwill or in the watered stock of a profitable enterprise.

Savings in relation to income

A better organized society probably would not have the variations in total income such as those we had from 1926 to 1932. Wealth should be somewhat more stable because it should be measured in prices which do not fluctuate as ours did in those years. Apparently savings are no longer a chief essential of an economics of abundance, because we depend

[7] In 1925 the income from agriculture was computed at not more than $5,795,000,000; whereas manufacturing amounted to $9,826,000,000; transportation totaled $3,923,000,000; mercantile business was $7,117,000,000. All other businesses together had the largest income, $14,291,000,000.

[8] In 1900 savings deposits totaled less than two and a half billion dollars and amounted, in 1913, to more than eight and one-half billions; in 1929, they were approaching the thirty billion mark. Second in amount is the actual investment in life insurance policies. Starting with about one and three-quarter billions at the opening of the century, a steady increase gave a total of practically five billions in 1914 and of nearly fifteen billions in 1927. Savings that were utilized in homes show most clearly in the reports of the building and loan associations. For a number of years after 1900, these amounted to little more than five hundred millions, but, especially since 1919, they have increased more sharply than any other form of savings to seven billion dollars.

upon extra production and not upon thrift, first, to meet our expenses, and then to give us a surplus. A brief examination of these three fields, income, wealth and savings, from the 1926 and 1932 points of view might be worth our while.

In 1926 the *income* of the American people was probably between eighty and ninety billions of dollars.[9] In 1932 the National Bureau of Economic Research, in the study made by Simon Kuznets, placed money income produced as a trifle more than thirty-eight billions, later revised to thirty-nine

AGGREGATE SAVINGS OF FAMILIES BY INCOME GROUPS, 1929. EACH FAMILY GROUP REPRESENTS 250,000 FAMILIES—EACH CIRCLE 500 MILLION DOLLARS.
(Committee on Economic Security)

billions. If a society wishes to run its affairs regularly, and if it needs the income of the first period, it can hardly do so on the income of the worst of depression years (1932). Prices fluctuated some, but not nearly so much as the difference between eighty-three billions and thirty-eight billions. This is

[9] In ascertaining income we may be wise to disregard the unusual years before and after the stock panic of 1929. According to the National Bureau of Economic Research the national income for 1926 was slightly less than $90,000,000,000. That represented an increase from 1925 of nearly $10,-000,000,000, and from 1921 of more than $26,000,000,000. However, when we reduce these figures to a 1913 level, because the war changed the value of the dollar as well as the status of Germany, Austria and Russia, we find the increase was only from approximately $32,000,000,000 in 1910 to $53,000,000,000 in 1926. We have no recent statistics available for foreign countries, but for 1910 King estimated the income of Prussia as below six billions, less than twenty per cent that of the United States.

particularly the case with fixed charges such as interest and some salaries. Fifteen million persons out of work and almost as many families dependent upon public aid was the price paid for a non-stabilized or quite inadequate income during depression; and it was too high a price for a well-ordered society to pay.

Wealth may be dismissed more briefly because a change in inventory of wealth did not have the effect upon business or people that changes of income did. This is due to the fact that a considerable part of wealth does not need to circulate, such as houses, clothing, farm implements, and other goods that do not change hands, or need to be replaced, year by year. The chief effect of depression upon wealth was the decided slowing down of this circulation. This congealing or freezing meant a serious problem and in many cases very heavy losses to those whose assets were frozen, but who were forced to pay their debts.

Savings were estimated in 1926 at seventeen billions a year, gross, and possibly four or five billions more. In 1930 excess of costs over income were estimated as being five billions, and in 1932 as nearly ten billions. One expects to have one's personal ledger and the people's ledger show losses as well as gains. These figures, however, presumably represent the actual expenditures in hard times in excess of actual income. They do not give any idea whatever of depleted bank accounts, of homes confiscated by foreclosure, of life savings lost by those who perhaps never would have a chance to save very much again. Please notice that we are considering only financial consequences of a poorly organized or managed economic scheme: no account is taken of wrecked homes, discouraged adults,[10] broken lives and starving children. A friend told the writer his chief regret in 1932 was that during the period of prosperity he did not take a trip to Europe but put

[10] Long before 1929 Judge Robert Scott, then in charge of insanity cases brought before the Los Angeles County courts, told the writer that half the cases of men appearing before him were the results of financial worry. When work and income were provided, an immediate improvement appeared in fifty per cent of those affected.

his money into an investment, which he lost early in the depression. Later, savings that he would have liked to use for a trip around the world he put into another investment. Not only was the equity lost, but creditors came back upon him for additional payments. What an inducement for non-saving!

These losses, inequalities, and injustices could not have been avoided in full; they might have been much lighter under somewhat different banking, investment, and price policies. They probably are due less to the uneven distribution of wealth and the somewhat less uneven distribution of income than they are to our whole capitalistic system regarding debt and the payment of interest, which means compound interest to those persons and institutions who do not spend all of their income. They are most conspicuous and offensive in the severe cyclical changes which seem an inevitable feature of our present economic order.

BANKING POLICIES: THE DILEMMA AND CONTROL

American banking in general

In the indirect use of wealth and income and in the direct provision for the storing and reinvestment of savings, the bank is preëminently the most important institution. A bank aids its depositors and clients in simplifying their dealings as buyers or sellers; it may be even more useful to them in *the creation of credit*. Possibly one special phase of the dilemma in recent years has been the too general substitution of investment credit for business credit. Many bankers have been more interested in selling securities and in lending to speculators on the market than in helping business men finance their purchases of goods.

Banking in Europe is rather different from American banking, largely because it is a semi-state function or activity. Possibly banking had as much to do with the American Revolution as taxes. Certainly some Americans were embittered by the attempt of the English government to regulate certain types of near-banks. Banking in the United States, consequently, has almost always been regarded as a *laissez faire* proposition. To the present time, there has been practically no supervision by any proper authority of the lending operations of most American banks.   Abuses by the states, before 1787, in the issuing of bills of credit or paper money led in the Constitution to a prohibition upon the states forbidding them to issue paper money.

The Constitution gives Congress complete control of the money standard and of monetary problems.   Aside from the First and Second Banks of the United States, however, until the Civil War banking was left entirely with the states.   The right of the national government to charter banks, to control currency, and to supervise banking, was endorsed by the Supreme Court more than a century ago.   Although at the present time most banks are still state banks, the aggregate capital and total resources of the national banks exceeds those of the state banks and trust companies, which in 1921 were two and one-half times as numerous.   Failures after the panic of 1929 were relatively less numerous among national banks than among the state banks.   In spite of the help given in 1932 by the Reconstruction Finance Corporation, the *total number of failures* was very large, more than five thousand before 1933.   This large number of bank failures—more than ten thousand from 1921 to 1934—contrasts strangely with none in England and none in Canada.   A drastic reorganization of banks and banking has been recognized as one of the special pressing needs of the present.

History throws real light on banking problems, trends, and controls.   Before the Civil War there was no national currency except coins, first silver, then gold.   The country was flooded with state bank notes.   Although the Constitution prohibited the states from issuing state paper money, *the state-chartered banks issued literally all kinds of paper money,* good, bad—and usually excessive in amount and of shifting values. *This currency chaos,* fatal to wide-scale business, was remedied by the finance laws of the Civil War, noted just below.   Better a depreciated *national currency,* greenbacks and national bank notes, than state bank currency of no known value and local circulation.   The depreciation did not last, but the inelasticity did.

During the Civil War the government recognized the value

of the banks as a means of marketing securities, and therefore created a system of *national banks* incorporated under national law. Besides ordinary banking privileges, these banks were permitted to issue bank notes against United States bonds held as security. From 1863 to 1913 the notes issued against these bonds represented a fairly large part of the paper currency in use, but the amount varied too little. These national bank notes were freed from the competition of state bank notes, usually issued on very little security. An annual tax of ten per cent was placed upon state bank issues. This currency proved inflexible and therefore inadequate in peak seasons, or during panic, when there was special demand for money, and in depression, when hoarding limited the supply in circulation.

In addition to the *inflexibility of its notes of issue, the national banking system was greatly decentralized.* Except in metropolitan centers each bank served only a local community and had no connection whatever with other banks, except with correspondents either in reserve centers or in New York. A demand therefore arose for a much more highly centralized banking system somewhat similar to the state-controlled central banks of England, France, and Germany. Equal protest was voiced against attempted centralization because the public feared the evil influence of the Money Trust.

The Federal Reserve System   In 1913, with very little coöperation from the bankers themselves, the United States government passed *The Federal Reserve Act.* A Federal Reserve Board of eight members consists of one or two government officials, and college professors or bankers selected by the government. These men direct the general affairs of twelve reserve banks organized in twelve reserve districts, each of which has its own board, chiefly of bankers. Each reserve bank is an organization representing all the national banks and others eligible to become members of that federal reserve bank. This new system pooled the resources of the members to some extent in the reserve bank of their district. But it gave a federal system of coördinated banking highly needed by American business. The old inflexibility of currency gave place to *a new and additional system of bank notes, issued by the Federal Reserve Boards upon commercial paper* submitted to them by the member banks. The World War proved how flexible this scheme was because the amount of note circulation in 1920 was nearly three and one-half billions of dollars, whereas before 1916 all national bank currency had never reached one billion.

An even more effective means of aiding business, whether regular or promotive or semi-speculative or foreign, was *the power of the Federal Reserve Board to determine the rate of discount and re-discount and to take part in open market operations.*[11] In 1927, by the McFadden Act, these powers dealing with investment and semi-speculation were increased considerably. The success of the Federal Reserve System in these fields, however, was much less conspicuous than in *providing business and the public with an extensive currency exceedingly flexible in nature.* In the first place, the Federal Reserve Board did not seem to attract men equal in ability to those who worked with the great financiers in dictating the financial policy of practically all American big business. One of the most serious charges brought against members of the national or regional boards is the actual use of the pooled funds of the public during 1929 to increase speculation rather than to diminish it.[12]

In the use of its power of re-discount and of buying and selling securities on the open market, the Federal Reserve System has a constant influence upon business. The government intended that it should. Consideration of the place and work of banks in an economic order therefore leads to the conclusion that one of the first duties of a national system of banking is *the stabilization not only directly of credit but indirectly of business itself.*

After the World War our currency was both abundant and

The public and control of banking

---

[11] Open-market operations give the Federal Reserve Board opportunity to buy and sell securities, thereby increasing or decreasing funds of banks available for other business. This procedure has very great influence on the amount of credit available in the business world.

[12] On credit and the cycle see Slichter, *Modern Economic Society,* pp. 245–248.

unstable. The fault lies not in the elasticity of the currency issued but in the fact that *most dollars used in business are credit dollars rather than money dollars*. With our numerous and often unsound state banks and our numerous and too speculative national banking organizations, we have been through a period of *credit chaos* similar to the bank note chaos of ninety years ago. The financial problem may not be solved easily, but history shows the trend and the principle of control. Then money was issued,[13] almost irresponsibly, by creatures of the states. It is now provided or regulated solely by national authority. Banking has already been brought chiefly under federal supervision. Nominally the credit chaos can be ended by nationalizing all banks, as we have sought to nationalize all railroads. Actually it can be done only through public-spirited coöperation of all bankers with the government at Washington and through public-spirited support by the people of this coöperative effort. After all, *credit can be controlled only by those who create it.*

Before 1933 there was no separation of speculation from investment, of investment from commercial banking or trust fund operations. In his inaugural President Roosevelt struck hard on no speculation by bankers. "We have witnessed not only the unrestrained use of bank deposits in speculation to the detriment of local credit, but we are also aware that this speculation was encouraged by the government itself. I propose that such speculation be discouraged and prevented." Why not treat bankers, like teachers, as servants of the public? Neither government nor business followed the wise suggestions of experts after the depression a decade ago. They proposed to create surpluses in good times from which we could borrow in poor years. Instead we did the opposite. When joy riding down the long hill of prosperity we stepped on the gas. The ascent of the opposite hillslope found us out of gas, but until 1933 we kept crowding on the brakes of fear and refused to add the oil of constant public coöperation.

[13] See U. S. Constitution, Art. I, Sec. 8, cl. 5, for power of Congress over money and standards.

One of the nicest readjustments of public to business is involved in the discovery through experimentation of a necessary form of bank control by government. We still need our federal system, but banks, except allied banks, in distinctively agricultural states, can no longer exist in isolation. We need coördinated though not centralized banking. "Laissez faire" organization of banks as well as "laissez faire" banking is becoming obsolescent in the present age. Undoubtedly a railway which gives only service as a common carrier is far less of a public utility than a commercial bank which creates, and in a degree controls, credit. *If it has been necessary to have unified, national control of the rails, is decentralized regulation of banks any longer thinkable?* Is there any other business which handles so much of our money, that uses our funds to control "credit dollars" or any dollars? An institution that has exercised, some contend usurped, a sovereign power of the people, would naturally expect to be treated as government, work hand-in-glove with the government, or be subject to the government. *Any argument for control that applies to any other American business would seem to apply with greater force to control of financialism.* Any method of regulation applied to any other economic institution would seem worthy of consideration, in the development of a policy of controlling big banking and large-scale investment. At once we encounter difficulties. With our almost total lack of experience in national regulation of business in general, without a properly trained administrative corps, without any clear concept of what the situation demands or how to go about the regulation of banks or investment corporations, what shall we do first? What shall we try to do later?

The Dilemma Promoted by Money or Credit Policies

More than any one else the banker wants a stabilized dollar. If the dollar fluctuates too much in value, either he is obliged to pay his depositors an excessive sum, or those who borrow from him pay the bank a corresponding excess. In the second case it is possible that the borrower will not be

Kinds of dollars

able to repay the same number of dollars that he borrowed, a larger amount than was loaned to him. Therefore the banker, not able to get the dollars, may be obliged to accept the security, which he may not want. Careless banking was probably responsible for most of the bank failures from 1929 to 1934; but fluctuations in the value of money and difficulty in getting money to repay loans possibly played a very large part. This was especially true because the expansion of banking, and the extension and inflation of credit took place very much more under the state banks in the prosperity period from 1922 to 1929 than under the national banks.[14]

In considering the place of money in augmenting a dilemma of financialism we must take into account the fact that the dollar is not always the same in value and that dollars are always of several different kinds. The first kind is the *hard money dollar* issued by government, usually minted in coins of five or ten, out of gold bullion and circulating at face value, or out of silver or other bullion and circulating at a face value very much above its intrinsic worth. A great deal of this hard money is deposited in vaults at Washington, its place being taken by either gold or silver certificates which are easier to handle, especially if one is dealing with ten thousand dollars at an operation.

In addition to this hard money and its paper representatives, the government also issues a true national currency; these are *government notes* issued on the credit of the United States, usually without much special reserve, like the greenbacks of years ago, some of which are still in existence and three billions of which might have been issued under the inflation amendment of May 12, 1933.[15] Almost as large an

---

(000)
[14] Capital funds of banks in 1922..............$6,575,202
                     National 2,848,465
                     State 3,726,746

In 1929, the total was 9,506,062
                     National 3,593,931
                     State 5,912,000

[15] The Thomas amendment of the Emergency Farm Relief Act provides that in case of emergency, presumably an international one, the President

amount of money as that represented by gold and silver certificates, and very much greater than that of government notes, is the total of federal reserve or national *bank notes* already described.

In addition to government currency and bank currency, we also have *credit dollars*. When a business man pays his bills, he pays by check or bill of exchange, not cash. At least ninety per cent of all American business is done regularly by these means. These credit dollars therefore represent a very much larger amount than government and bank currency do together.

The value of the dollar depends upon the goods or services it will buy. When a building which cost five million to erect in 1927 was sold for a million in 1932, the 1932 dollar purchased too much. If America had done what France did when it stabilized the franc at one-fifth of its pre-war value, we should have the opposite situation in about the same proportion—that the dollar would purchase too little. The value of the dollar depends therefore not chiefly upon what the government says is a dollar, nor upon the number of currency dollars, metallic or paper, issued by the government or by the banks. *The value of the dollar depends* (1) *on the metal content of a dollar,* (2) on *the supply of currency dollars, but even more* (3) *upon the banking supply of credit and the business demand for credit dollars.* Probably that may be the reason why, when the gold content of the dollar was reduced in the spring of 1933, prices did not rise permanently to correspond.[16]

may authorize the Federal Reserve banks to purchase three billions additional obligations of the United States, or failing to do that, have the Treasury issue three billions of United States notes.

[16] "In so far as they [activities conducted under the National Recovery Act] are designed to prevent undercutting in wages and prices and other competitive practices incompatible with a decent minimum standard of living for the worker, they have a humanitarian justification, but they should be viewed in that light. There should be no attempt to impose such regulations on any broader scale with the idea that they are measures of recovery. There should be no illusion with regard to the fact that a general rise in prices through such measures is not a sign of increasing prosperity. It is the rise of prices reflective of increased demand and increased purchasing power which alone can be associated with the process of recovery. The concomitant illusion that a *deliberate* limitation of output, because it

Financialism always faces a crisis and possibly a dilemma in so far as there is a fluctuation in the value of the dollar. If the unit value of the dollar were not determined by a tiny amount of gold or other material but by the cost of purchasing a large number of commondities, in short, a commodity dollar, *if* that could be made practicable and workable, these fluctuations would become negligible *in the purchase of commodities*. But, *in the re-payment of obligations*, especially long-term obligations, the fluctuations would seem appalling either to the debtor if he needed more dollars to pay the amount he borrowed or to the creditor if the amount repaid was smaller in number of dollars though equal in commodities or services that it could command. Evidently we need something more stable than the monetary dollar as our yardstick for measuring values.

Credit and price   To the radical socialist years ago and to many who scorn the name socialist now, the price system, not money, is the root of all evil. The abandonment of the price system involves a drastic supplanting of our present civilization, a method far more drastic than is advocated today by the American socialist. Eventually we may need to substitute something for an ordinary price system. Now the problem seems to be one of prices rather than no prices, of a stabilized standard rather than one that falls in prosperity and rises in depression, when it should do exactly the opposite. Some light may be thrown on our problem of business based on a coin system by the dilemma created 2500 years ago by the *first use of coins*. Substitution of money for barter and semi-barter upset all old business methods and relationships. In Greece there arose a demand for a written law. But when the old laws were recorded, it was found they were "written in blood," so obsolete and harsh were they. A generation passed before the Athenians selected as dictator a poet whose verses had depicted the evils and pilloried the beneficiaries of dynamic economic changes. Solon's first act was to wipe out

raises prices, helps toward recovery is a still more dangerous fallacy." Columbia University Commission, *Economic Reconstruction,* Columbia University Press, p. 17.

debt slavery and cancel debts. For fear the same persons would regain control and reëstablish old injustices, he then, but not till then, changed the constitution, the real beginning of Athenian democracy. In truth Solon left us two legacies: modern democracy, yes, but chiefly the necessity of drastic economic reform before that for political reorganization arises.

The price system is not just a price system. It is a tool of the ruling economic class or group. Rulers use it to increase their power, if they can control the men who manage business. Business men do so, especially if in selling they can charge prices that really amount to "consumer tribute." Slichter has shown that the nature of prices will be different if labor is in control, or if the consumer has the upper hand. Today "the reason why *price* is the supreme guide and organizer of production, the medium in which costs and benefits are computed, is *because it accurately reflects the interests of the class which, under existing economic arrangements, directs and controls production,*—that is, the propertied or capitalist class . . . they [want] the largest net money income; and they employ the methods of production, whether injurious to the community or not, which entail the least money cost." [17]

Prices are therefore an important cause, as well as incident, of the business cycle. Every one makes profit with rising prices. But who will manufacture largely for a market in which the goods will be cheaper in six months? Who will buy, except from month to month, if he can later purchase for less? Thorp and Mitchell have shown that in periods of falling prices the years of poor business exceed those in which business was good. The cyanide process of extracting gold from discarded tailings ended the great depression of the nineties. It really ended a twenty-five year slump in world business due to the constantly increasing value of gold.

The fault of the banks, of our credit system, and even of our money economy lies less with the financiers than with

[17] Slichter, S. H., *Modern Economic Society*, Henry Holt & Co., Inc., p. 62; italics in the original.

ourselves. Our own wild desire to "get rich quick" and our own mad rush to make dollars by borrowing leaves us no alibi. The debtor-creditor situation may be blamed upon the American public rather than upon the banks; but the fault really lies in our whole industrial capitalist system. If not, why is it that the assets of all of us have been less than our liabilities? Of course, we say that was just a temporary situation. The relief was found when prices rose. Prices might not have fallen greatly had they not been reckoned in $23\frac{22}{100}$ grains of gold, a coin which we do not use, and a standard by which we measure not only all prices but all deferred payments. If debts could be paid, as they should be paid, in terms of purchasing power, there would be no debtor-creditor problem such as we have had in recent years. France would not have asked for a deferred payment on the interest part of her debt to us. Inflation may be one way out, much as some of those in high authority in government, and most of those in business and finance, have railed against it. Stabilizing the English pound in 1925 at its pre-war value was a mistake because it did not represent fact. It was chiefly beneficial to the creditor class and to those with fixed wages, because the new pound purchased so much more than the old. The attempted remedying of the mistake by going off the gold standard in 1931 was less of an evil than maintenance of this gold standard from 1925 to 1931.

Probably a managed currency has more evils than a gold standard currency—in normal times of prosperity. But those are no longer with us and they may not return, according to the business and money standards existing before 1929. Certainly the crying need of the present time is a money standard more safe and more sensible than that bequeathed to us by the ancient world.

Many ancient and medieval authorities warned against compound interest, even though they did not fully realize what a curse and an evil it might become. Naturally they could not foresee the huge surpluses of capital which would be created under a complex industrial capitalistic civilization. Before considering the question of compound interest, let us examine a few facts about American debts, which have shown up serious weaknesses in our financial structure or procedure.

The Problem and Burden of Debt

The dilemma of financialism probably can be explained better from a study of debt structure and examination of the significance of large-scale, compound interest than in any other way. Taking the first of these subjects, what is the amount and the character of the debt burden? Under our industrial capitalist system with its sharp shifts from heights of prosperity to depths of depression, what is the importance of the debt burden?

Debt increases and kinds of debt

An examination of debts in type periods during the last quarter-century reveals the following: the total debt probably reached its peak at the end of the new era, 1929. At that time it was variously estimated at from about 150 billions to 230 billions of dollars. There had been a sharp increase during the years of prosperity from 1922 to 1929, about equal in amount, but not so high in percentage, as the increment for the years 1914–19. *The debt increase in the war period* was less than half for war costs. The other half was brought about by over-stimulation of business, made extraordinarily active and far more than correspondingly profitable first by the Great War and then afterward by our share in the World War.

The debt increases of the second period (*1922–29*) were due to the ease with which profits were made, the consequent expansion of business, and the wonderful opportunities for profits. Three types of debt increase perhaps are worth mentioning. The first of these was found in the field of finance itself. The increase of indebtedness of financial corporations or organizations, given by the National Industrial Conference Board as eighteen billions of dollars, is greater than that in any other field. This increase of indebtedness and the unusual profits secured from the sale of those bonds represented chiefly a shift from the pockets of investors to some others.

A second marked increase was in the field of private indebtedness linked with land investment. We have already noted [18] the use of electrical power in decentralizing manufacturing centers, because suburban areas offered cheaper rents and better light and air. The workmen naturally followed their work into these outlying industrial districts. More perhaps than industry, the automobile, providing better means of transportation, gave a new impetus to the promotion of residence districts in suburbs or in communities farther away from the commercial centers. In many metropolitan centers, enough suburban lots were offered to accommodate a population several times as great as that of the present metropolis.[19]

A third field was represented by a great expansion of municipal expenditure. Cities vied with each other in spending huge sums on civic centers and on planned schemes for beautiful parks, boulevards, bridges, and other interesting improvements.

Those in charge of these three fields were not the only people guilty of heavy borrowing and unnecessary expending, and even woeful extravagance. A business man certainly could not be blamed if he refinanced his organization, borrowing practically all the new capital. He might pay the promoter an excessive commission; but, if he could borrow money at six per cent, and make profits several times as large, what could he lose, before the depression? In the reorganization of mergers and refinancing, these methods were used very extensively by corporations, the lender practically paying the whole expense.

If this was the first estate of the borrower, what is the last? Let us consider two points. The first is the obvious fact that he who spends borrowed money is simply making a draft upon the future. Instead of following the plan of paying as we go, we make the improvement or raise the level of

---

[18] Pp. 108, 115–116, 457–470.

[19] In another connection attention is drawn to the inexcusable expansion of real estate subdivision (pp. 429, 431). One authority has also computed that frequently a debt of $10,000 on a valuable home property actually represented an investment of $2000 in the property itself. The rest went for commissions and profits. No wonder the price afterward sagged and the present owner cannot pay the debt. Debts representing huge bonuses or graft naturally cannot be repaid from income of the property exploited.

living by using the money with the expectation of drawing it out of future income. Even if the money was expended wisely and for needed improvements, this was unfortunate in the period from 1922–29, because the current income was large. In periods of prosperity surpluses (savings) rather than increasing indebtedness are the necessities of good financing, public, business, or personal. Probably a hundred million people who did not think about that in 1926 were well aware of it in 1932. Since most business and private borrowing is on fairly short terms, three or five years, these obligations became due during the great depression. In many cases they were not renewed, or were renewed only on very severe terms and an amortized arrangement substituted for a straight loan.

So far as the payments were made for unwise or unneces- Debt
sary improvements, or for consumption goods such as short- problems
lived autos or cheap furniture, the price paid was of course an appallingly high one. During the years after 1929 many borrowers were obliged to continue paying, *annually*, interest and installments of principal almost equal to the 1931 or 1932 cost of the article for which these excessive payments were being made.[19a] Unfortunately, among those who suffered most because the original cost was very heavy and the depreciation a large per cent of the original cost were home-owners, particularly in the suburbs. When these home buyers lost their jobs, or had their pay cut three or four times to probably less than half of the former income, their plight was serious indeed. Even before March 4, 1933, after the railroads, banks and insurance companies had drawn more than a billion for loans out of the public treasury, 125 million dollars was appropriated for these sufferers.

The second difficulty which the borrower encountered in the period after 1929 is this: the decrease in values wiped out all the equity of a large percentage of borrowers in their property or securities, but it likewise left the whole society

---

[19a] Evidence presented before the Senate committee on Banking and Currency, 1933, furnished examples of this type of over-payment by bank employes, not bank officials.

in a state of practical insolvency. In 1929 the public debts of all the governments were more than thirty billions. With the constant need of relief for needy families the face value of these debts was increased, during the depression, to about forty billions. More than thirteen hundred cities, counties and other public corporations defaulted on part interest or on the payment of principal. Whether a person owed anything or not, personally or through any business which was "in the red," if he had any property, he shared in this general obligation.

Before considering the economic and legal principles upon which even interest payments are based, let us ask this question: What are the debts incurred since 1916 worth? These debts are of several kinds. The first of these is Uncle Sam's debt, still represented, strangely enough, by liberty bonds. These are worth more than they brought to Uncle Sam because the market price is higher and the dollars they represent will purchase nearly twice as much, at least in 1934. A second type of debt is represented by American foreign loans. The foreign debts are either government debts to our government or foreign securities purchased by American investors. They interest us as creditors, not as debtors. One is worth about as little as the other.

The financial indebtedness represented by eighteen billions of securities is worth more than foreign debts. A very considerable part of it however has been absolutely wiped off the financial record. A large number of these investment organizations, especially in Chicago and on the West Coast, have gone out of business, at least so far as paying debts is concerned. Probably the experience of these two optimistic areas has been duplicated in small part by the experience of a vast number of other communities. In times of prosperity it is easy to overrate one's assets and to picture a very rosy future. "Caveat emptor" indeed! How much would it cost to buy up on the market all the bonds or certificates of these non-defunct financial companies at the present time? And the defunct companies; what of their securities? For one of the greatest holding companies of all time the receivers decided that the *cost* of discovering its assets would exceed the probable value of those assets.

Foreigners and corporations escape much of their debt burden: the one because they cannot pay, or cannot be forced to pay; the other because their debts are only the market value of their bonds. *The private debtor,* however, *is not so fortunate* in being able to avoid the operation of old law. He either pays or loses his property. If he has other property besides that given as security, under the deficiency judgment laws of the states and the clause of the United States Constitution forbidding non-cancellation of the obligations of contract by the states, he may have the rest of his wealth confiscated to pay the difference between what he borrowed and what his security brings.

In the Recovery Program considerable relief has been granted to some types of debtors on the ground that if a debt cannot be paid it is better to collect part. Some of the states passed laws postponing the collection of matured principal provided interest and taxes were kept up. In the Minnesota case (1933) the Supreme Court of the United States upheld this postponement. In a few other states the deficiency judgment laws were temporarily suspended on *new* loans, that is, on loans made after the law was passed. Several relief measures have been provided in the N. R. A. One of these is concerned with the aid granted in refinancing farm loans. Another substitutes for bankruptcies court agreements with two-thirds of the creditors. These arrangements have usually been made either for corporations or for farmers, not for other debtors.

In the consideration of these problems two things must be kept clearly in mind. Except in peak periods of prosperity, *these debts cannot and will not be paid.* In most cases the only way they *could be paid* would be out of income. Either they will be refinanced at the original amounts plus unpaid interest or they will be cancelled by new refinancing corresponding to the present values of the security. Then the borrower, the lender, or both, will accept the loss. A second point to be considered is that the debt problem is not pri-

marily a debtor affair. Widows and orphans, those who are
old and probably never will earn again, have put most of
their savings either into savings banks, many of which failed
between 1929 and 1935, or into insurance companies, many
of which have been on the ragged edge for several years.
They may have purchased business bonds which have lost
most of their value, or made private loans with the necessity
in many cases of taking over the property, badly run down,
heavily encumbered with taxes, and over-burdened with unpaid interest. A third thing is represented by our law that
a dollar is a dollar, that a dollar borrowed gathers interest,
which if reinvested is compounded.

The Impossibility of Large-Scale, Compound Interest

Why the
past has
escaped

Why isn't compound interest possible as well as necessary?
Why cannot large-scale capitalists use this best possible inducement to saving?

The forty thousand pounds that Queen Elizabeth put into
the India Company, at compound interest represented to
Keynes an amount equal to all British investment abroad
today. The penny of Jesus' time, compounded yearly, would
have absorbed many times all present wealth. The law of
fact should nullify the law of statute, or what is a universe for?

*Why is large-scale compound interest the long-term ele-
ment which makes capitalism impossible?* Possibly a second
question should be included and answered first. How does it
happen that if the laws are the same as they have been in
the past and the principle of compound interest has not
changed, this dilemma did not arise ages ago? *Long-time*
compound interest is identical now with what it has been.
But compound interest for *large-scale surpluses* and investments is a characteristic of the twentieth century, not of
earlier periods. Before our day most great fortunes were not
only personal but they were personally acquired. The old
saying "from shirt sleeves to shirt sleeves in three generations" shows why these short-lived personal fortunes rarely
threatened the savings of ordinary folk. Long-time com-

pound interest never developed as a menace to society because the great fortunes of one century dwindled even though
they seemed to give place to others equally large or larger.
With the creation of the corporation and less dependence
upon the initiative, business ability, and financial skill of
some captain of industry or finance, the continuation of huge
fortunes, for which capable leadership possibly may be purchased, is no longer left so much to chance. The American
method of distributing the estate of a deceased magnate
among many children and others, rather than holding it intact
for an oldest son, might counteract in part this accumulation
of huge sums by a single person. But frequently related
families pool their resources in order not to lose what to them
is an unexampled opportunity for gaining more and more
from those who would then have correspondingly less and less.

Other ways in which past generations escaped the penalties
of compound interest were numerous. One of these has been
confiscation. This was wholesale when vigorous young races
like the German tribes 1500 years ago conquered older
wealthier races of declining vitality; to a lesser degree ordinary war, pestilence, fire or other calamity likewise caused a
real destruction of wealth. The constant depreciation of the
money unit has gone a long way toward postponing the day
of reckoning. Good proof that coins have continually lost
value is shown by the old French adage that a valueless article
was not worth a *sou marquis,* a throw-back to the days when
feudal nobles coined their own money. The English pound
and the French pound, livre or franc, certainly call for anti-
quarian help to discover how a pound of silver or gold ever
degenerated to present depths. New methods of mining, especially through use of machinery and chemistry, coupled with
the retention of the age-old gold and silver standards, have
reduced greatly the purchasing price of current coins. Compared with the dollar of a half century ago, the dollar of
1929 seemed to purchase very little, but the dollars of that
day did not impress people then as wonderful. One recalls
the story of the Secretary of the Treasury who was showing
some friends over a historic battlefield. As they looked across

the Rappahannock, the guide repeated his well-worn story that on that spot George Washington had stood and thrown a dollar which landed on the opposite bank nearly a half mile distant. The guests looked at each other, incredulous, and then the Secretary, with a twinkle in his eye, remarked, "Well, gentlemen, we always heard that a dollar would go a good deal farther in those days."

A third group of reasons why the past did not suffer as we are from large-scale, long-time interest is the fact that those in authority rarely took the bankers into account except as creditors. Certainly the Jew was entitled to no consideration from a Christian noble or monarch. In spite of ancient debt-slavery and rather recent debtor prisons, the laws were less favorable to the creditor than are some more recent constitutional provisions or legislation. Bankruptcies occurred even though the bankrupt did not have modern opportunities of starting again. Bankruptcies by governments are not unknown even in American states, several of which repudiated their obligations in one great depression one hundred years ago and in another following the Civil War. By arbitrarily wiping debts off the slate, it made very little difference what the law of the state or of physics or of finance might have been.

Why the present cannot

Turning to the other side of the picture, we find long-time, large-scale interest is a menace because it is first of all large-scale. In the past, scarcity seldom created or left any surplus. That which survived one period or one type of business usually disappeared in a succeeding period or when applied in other occupation. The margin of income above outgo was not large enough to carry over well. Possibly our own increased wants and easily developed extravagance may do the same thing with the greater product of our scientifically developed machine-power industry. Fortunately perhaps, in the accumulation of capital necessary for the operation of our present economic order the surpluses were not evenly distributed and therefore were saved to a very great extent.

Naturally the very wealthy save the greatest *proportion* of income, but the *totals* of the fairly well-to-do Americans are greater. Even rather conservative students estimate that not less than three-fourths of all income of millionaires [20] is saved. Less careful students make a much higher estimate of their actual savings available as capital. Of those with annual incomes over $250,000 undoubtedly more than half is saved in ordinary times. In fact, those whose income is from ten to two hundred and fifty thousand are believed to save from a fifth to a half of what they get. These classes whose income is more than ten thousand a year therefore probably saved from forty to sixty per cent of all that was saved yearly in the United States—before 1929. Because they did not use it or could not use it in ordinary times, society's surplus capital has become not a constant but an increasing amount. It is beside the point to note that this capital is being used constantly more and more effectively from the standpoint of the goods created and could be used very much more effectively than it is. What is significant is that these accretions to capital, if compounded annually, as they are for those who can save every year, will under our present laws and present economic scheme leave nothing or less than nothing for the rest of society. Of all modern possessions only wealth compounded annually increases in a geometrical ratio. Years ago Soddy showed that *a ball of gold five inches in diameter, compounded annually for a thousand years, would then be a ball of gold equal in size to our earth. If compound interest is not a fact, and cannot be fact, why is it law and why was it the basis of new era financialism?*

Capitalism is a system devised to prevent real circulation of wealth! In a world in which capital was scarce, saving was prerequisite to any advance. Without it capital goods did not exist, the materials as well as the means of production were lacking. In the modern world capital cripples us by its abundance. There cannot be too much? Of course not. But its accumulation in a few hands, and its use *under the system and laws made when capital was scarce* is more than misfortune—it is calamity.

[20] The term millonaire frequently means one with an annual income of a million or more.

Need of
better
circulation
of wealth

Capital is like the oceans of the globe. Wealth circulation is fluid, like the rains, the rivers and the moisture-soaked earth. More than three-fourths of the earth's surface is water. Its average depth is several thousand feet. Life, and the enjoyment of useful work, depends on the rains. They must come from this large water supply at no very great intervals, to all inhabited areas, to make them habitable. Let the available rain fail, or its substitute be less than two feet annually, and dire consequences follow. Let it be more than six or eight feet per year, then crops rot and health suffers. Most of the people of western nations live and work in areas with a rainfall varying from thirty inches to sixty. What happens when a plain is too far from great lakes or oceans, or high mountain ranges cut off moist winds? Let the inhabitants of Gobi and Sahara answer. What happens also when too much of this life-preserving, business-stimulating moisture remains, salted down, in the great ocean reservoirs? Page the 1931 debtor. What happens when the vapor-lifting power of the sun is lost, when the inaccessibility of the general supply brings no moisture-bearing winds, when the recurring prosperous and necessary rains fail to materialize? First distress, then famine, then death; for those who cannot flee the destruction!

Capitalism has promoted the storage of surplus. There are oceans of static wealth, salted down. Industrial capitalism has lost its power to return necessary wealth to those who use it as consumers. It has failed to relift the necessary minimum of circulating wealth fluid to keep humanity active, productive, and prosperous. The level of the capitalistic sea has been rising, flooding and threatening to destroy the chief producing areas which had been established by the old order of civilization. Agriculture finds itself almost submerged by the rising waters of industrial capitalism.

Inland drought follows drought. If rains fall, they are naturally lighter in the valleys than in the hills. But in the mountain canyons check dams of natural scarcity barriers, which in the old days held back flood waters, have been allowed to fall to pieces. They interfered with profits and the collection of interest. Storage reservoirs have ceased to exist, for dams may have been blown up in the name of prosperity. The inhabitants of plain and valley have sought to rebuild check and storage dams; they have been prevented by capitalist-controlled laws or court decisions. If they urge the rebuilding, their attention is drawn to the expense and the uselessness. The rainfall does not warrant such extravagance. What water there is flows back swiftly to the sea. It tarries not for the irrigation of fields between mountains and ocean. Rivers have been deepened, possibly at public expense. Life-preserving capital has been kept in main channels, by closing sluice gates, when low income and inheritance tax rates prevented its natural return to the tillers of the soil or their co-workers in field or factory. The system devised centuries ago for capital accumulation has been kept because it aided business—and what other excuse was necessary? It has been kept even when the rushing waters through open channels prevented circulation of wealth to the producers who needed it most. Even while prosperity boomed, it was kept by capitalist financiers to control the affairs of former allies, the industrialists. It was kept in depression when the drawing power of prosperity's business sun was low and what was a mighty torrent sweeping to the sea had become a tiny streamlet or an underground current. The oceans are fuller than ever before, but it is of little value there.

Conclusion

An analysis of conditions as they are, a listing of evils that glare at us is simple compared with the creation of a substitute for the industrial capitalism we possess. *In a modern, complex society one new slight change in one part demands also many a slight readjustment in almost every part of that particular organization.* A major change anywhere demands further possible reorganization, possibly not so slight, even in less closely related parts of the social system. Economists are more conservative than the rest of us, except those with vested interests. And if economics was ever a "dismal science" or a dismaying science, that time is now. Economists realize better than the rest of us that when we tinker with one part, we destroy the operation or at least the efficiency of another. Unquestionably there are serious evils which must be faced, and, if possible, remedied. One of these is the acute problem of unemployment.[21] A second is the related but exactly opposite one of over-production.[22] A third is the unwise accumulation of wealth and of free capital, needing investment, in the hands of a few.[23] Industrialism, as we have seen, is top-heavy. It rests on the basis of the machine, which seems no longer able to carry the load which it has created. If a way can be found by which machines shall not be limited in their capacity for wise production, standards of living can be raised greatly, as the technologists insist. It rests also, like a pyramid on the gold dollar; [24] and the pyramiding has not been solely in inflating credit but in building a top-heavy capitalist civilization.

"To the victors belong the spoils" was supposed to have passed out of American politics at least a half century ago, with the enactment of the first Civil Service law. It must pass out of industrialism and of capitalism as well. We can take no pride in recent conditions in which returns and income have been largely in inverse proportion to the sacrifices made, the efforts offered, and the unpleasant conditions encountered. An enlightened twentieth century should not need to ask the underpaid workers "Why do they work so hard?",[25] or cut the salary of the underpaid teacher, who is underpaid, let us hope, simply because his product has no direct pecuniary value. Too bad if our leaders have sold themselves to a system with no standard but wealth.

It may be necessary, as the socialists claim, to substitute use for profit or, as the technocrats insist, to do away with money and the price system. As free-born American citizens, most of us hope that evils can be purged from the present social order without overthrowing it, that we may not lose

---

[21] Pp. 132, 211–225.
[22] Pp. 126–134.
[23] Pp. 104–105, 162–167.
[24] Pp. 147–157.
[25] Lynd and Lynd, *Middletown*, ch. VIII.

the individuality of personal achievement, that we may secure special reward for special effort. These traits of our
present system we prize greatly. Possibly the old laws and
usages and court decisions can be turned to the advantage of
society instead of being appropriated so much by big business. In later chapters,[26] we shall examine some methods used
in public regulation of undesirable practices, some of them
existing from time immemorial. We shall attempt to discover
legal ideas or principles which are really at hand for necessary and desirable social reorganization.[27] Existing laws and
court decisions may provide an entering wedge by which society may set apart the excesses and the evils of industrial
capitalism, thereby keeping that which is good, and reorganizing our economic system to make it the servant instead of
the master of society.

The dilemma of western civilization, particularly in America, is one chiefly of production and of finance. The first
reconstruction must be in the field of economics. Inseparable
from that are the problems of the society and government
which have made big business a dominant factor. But a
civilization is more than material or public; it is a matter of
life and of culture as well. To understand the whole need
and problem of reorganization it is necessary to make an
integrated study of the whole social order in its many phases.
Among these is that group of international forces which
may be of first significance in helping us decide, or forcing us
to accept, solutions that may be final even if no better than
the outcome of world war.

[26] See XI–XIV.
[27] See XI and XIII.

VII

INTERNATIONAL FORCES AFFECTING INDUSTRIAL CAPITALISM

The dilemma of industrial capitalism has been treated almost solely from the American point of view; but, although the problem is more acute in America than in Europe, it affects all peoples who are living under western civilization. Business is bigger in the United States than in England or Germany; the problem of financialism, except for banking under a federal form of government, is hardly more acute here than in the British Isles. The former success of both industry and finance was due in part to an expansion of international trade, the exploitation of peoples who furnished raw materials, an unscrupulous struggle for markets and control of investments outside of the country that had a capital surplus. The fate of industrial capitalism and of western civilization may not be decided by unsolved dilemmas or by any action, or failure to act, of western countries. Russian bolshevism and Far Eastern orientalism may not be so modern or so virile as western capitalism; but by sheer force of numbers or by severe competition of endless hordes of workers they may force the decline of our more developed but effete civilization. Nevertheless, if disaster comes, it will be due more to internal dissention and inherent weaknesses in our civilization, disregarded and unremedied.

INTERNATIONAL CAPITALISM AND NATIONAL POLICIES

International capitalism

American capitalism cannot be separated from capitalism in western Europe. The world is too small for Chinese walls around national economic systems. Governments may survive if they follow a policy of partial isolation; business cannot. The day of isolated economic nationalism not only is

170

past, but is a long time past. Will it come again? This is shown first of all by the remarkable increase of foreign commerce. In the century from the fall of Napoleon to the beginning of the World War, the expansion was twenty-five fold. After the World War, development was relatively even more rapid than at any previous period. The change to economic internationalism is shown by the growth of foreign investments. Twenty years ago other countries owed the United States a bare two billions; now the amount, including war debts, is nearly thirty billions on paper. In Great Britain, long the most important of all investing nations, the investments nearly doubled after 1915. In a five-year period, 1924–1929, the foreign loans of creditor countries amounted to more than a billion and a half dollars a year, or nearly eight billions in all.

Economic internationalism is far more than economic imperialism, though it includes that. It represents not only a dependence in a business way of a colony on a mother country and of a *debtor nation upon a creditor;* but business in one country is simply part of business in others. Note the *international spasm* which occurred when Baring Brothers failed as long ago as 1890. Watch the periods of prosperity and depression in the different countries before 1870 and since. In the last half century they practically all go up or down together. Those persons who question the value of internationalism cannot easily overlook the fact that now the business barometer rises and falls over continental areas, if not over the entire civilized world. Again and again since 1929 have we had proof of the links between Europe and America. Withdrawal of English investment from the New York stock market in the fall of 1929 had much to do with starting that fatal crash. In May, 1930, the foreign situation did as much as the domestic to end the slight splurge of that year. The failure of the *Credit Anstald* in Vienna in May, 1931, nearly wrecked the banks of Germany, caused Britain to go off the gold standard and was the beginning of a new financial crisis, distinct from the industrial crisis of 1930.

The interplay of economic forces between nations is not

explained simply by investments or by economic shocks. In spite of *tariffs* there are international price levels, and because of tariffs there are international price problems. The failure of the Austrian bank caused financial upset less than the Hawley-Smoot tariff (1930) destroyed industrial harmony. Not fewer than thirty retaliatory tariffs were levied because of this unwise increase in tariff rates. The suggestion has been made that we should raise some tariff rates still higher because most countries have gone far off the gold standard. Among these people, wages are still paid more or less on the old scale; hence their products cost relatively less than ours. But, raising the tariff would simply decrease still further our business abroad. Figures given in President Hoover's 1932 message to Congress show how ordinary business had dropped off only about a third from the 1925–28 level. Foreign trade on the contrary had dropped to one-third of its former amount.

America still tries to use the old national psychology of a debtor country. This is especially objectionable in connection with the tariff. *Creditor countries must continually seek abroad investment for part of the interest due from abroad; and probably for some of their other surplus wealth.* Two things are incompatable—exporting more than we import on the one hand, and continually reinvesting abroad on the other. Serving both God and Mammon is not more difficult than this dual impossibility. How long before the American people will wake up and begin to realize that creditors must continue to buy or invest abroad—or cease to be creditors!

America self-contained?

If capitalism is international, its problem can never be settled solely by what America does.[1] Yet American leadership is exceedingly important because of her wealth, resources, and potential, if not actual, foreign commerce and investment. Sir Arthur Salter believes the great mistake consists in trying to manage world business with an organization and policies that are distinctively national. Most international economists agreed that in 1933 an increase in the international price

[1] On American solution of American problems, even those of an international character, see Beard, C. A., *The Open Door at Home.*

level was a first requisite of recovery. Probably most of them and most national economists would admit that a permanent raising of the price level is necessary before we reorganize our economic system, industrial and capitalistic. In the opinion of many economists, the coöperation of central banks would go a long way in improving and stabilizing national currencies. Just as capitalists have been disregarding business because they wanted too great profit or did not know how to handle big finance, except as high finance, so the nations have selfishly refused to work together for the improvement of international business. Quoting from Salter, "No international currency control, however, can be satisfactory in a world whose commercial policies are essentially national, and some control in the direction of foreign lending also is probably an essential counterpart of it." [2] Since 1932 some genuine attempts have been made to stabilize currencies on more than a nation-wide scale. Many governments desire such stabilization, but each seems unwilling to agree to any plan of stabilization unless it has an advantage over the others in the plan upon which they agree.

European capital does not suffer as does American capital from an over-surplus or from unnecessary accumulation of gold, except, of course, in France. Nevertheless, all countries of western civilization have reached an impasse, due to poor distribution of wealth and over-accumulation of debts. Creditor countries no longer are lending; they are trying to collect debts, most of which are uncollectable, at least in part. Even interest may be permanently uncollectable in full amount. Walter Lippmann is authority for the statement that British sentiment turned sharply against us when Britain was obliged to ship us nearly a hundred millions of gold in December, 1932. Parleys between Washington and London or Washington and Paris may reduce still further the interest on the war debts. Do not forget that, so far, the *principal of our war debts* has not been reduced for the important countries.

We need not accept the argument that we should cancel the war debts as part of our share of the war costs. We may be

[2] *Recovery, The Second Effort,* D. Appleton-Century Co., p. 94.

willing to reduce interest and principal, or both, in proportion to European reductions in expenditures for war. Foreign debtors are exactly like American debtors. Under present conditions and with present prices, debts simply cannot be paid in full. The problem is not chiefly one of depression. We may possibly work out of depression with the creditors' claims still more or less intact. But we certainly will not get far toward permanent prosperity nor any way toward desirable re-organization until we face two ugly facts. The first of these is that America and the rest of the western world cannot continue to collect high rates of interest on huge accumulations of capital. The second is that although America may lead the way, something it seems absolutely unwilling to do except on its own terms, probably the problem can never be solved by any one country without at least considerable coöperation from the others.

The world managed to get out of the series of depressions from 1870 to 1897 by finding a new method of getting gold out of rather poor ores. The increase in the quantity of gold raised prices and started America and the world on the high road toward at least some kind of prosperity. In all probability the western world will not get out of the present series of price depressions, involving industry, finance and other economic interests, without adopting some monetary units or standards which will either stabilize prices on a higher level or give us continually rising prices. Some type of managed currency might do this, especially with coöperation among nations, provided it is done for the profit of the public and not for the political or business advantage of the managers. What degree of international economic coöperation is essential for an escape from the evils of our present economic order?

International Commercial Competition and Imperialism

Struggle for colonies and markets

An understanding of international economic forces of the present is impossible without some background of inter-nation struggles for colonies, materials, and markets. In the past this has centered around the group of policies we may call economic imperialism. The development of economic imperialism is connected with colonial empires and with European domination of non-Christian races but it is even more concerned with an international struggle for general markets and trade. For several centuries the commercial opportunities of different countries were limited because all colonies were closed to the trade of any except the mother country; and many non-Christian countries were closed absolutely to "foreign devils." The trade which they had with one another they sought to limit because they did not want to import more than necessity demanded.

In the last century there has been a better realization, although still far from perfect, that trade between nations, like exchange between individuals, is of mutual advantage. More than all, even statesmen are coming to recognize the economic truth that you cannot sell unless you buy in exchange either directly or through some other form of expenditure. *The world's trade today is primarily a trade between civilized and independent countries rather than between mother countries and colonies or between great powers and dependent races.* It is not free and unhampered, because it is limited almost everywhere by protective tariffs, bounties and subsidies that protect home industry, national shipping or home-promoted banking.

In the struggle for markets several elements enter in. One of these consists of manufactured goods which have a ready market in foreign countries that have desired articles for sale in return. Formerly English cotton goods found their way into almost all the world's markets. A large part of England's problem today grows out of the failure of English cotton manufacturers to compete with the more abundant and cheaper, though less skilled, labor of new peoples who are using the newest type of spinning machines and looms.

A second element includes the whole procedure of marketing. Those peoples who control their own shipping have a primary advantage over those who must depend upon exportation of their goods in foreign bottoms. The most successful firms engaged in foreign trade act through branches of the home corporation or establish good business contacts with local mercantile houses. Merchants who, like the old American exporters, never studied the needs and wishes of foreign buyers could not easily compete with English or German shippers who understood the local markets, gave each people the type of goods they preferred, and had expert salesmen who knew the language and psychology of the customers as well as the quality of the goods to be sold.

A third element is the credit system under which goods are purchased. Again the old American exporter was rather downright in his attitude. He tried to sell to foreigners as he did to American consumers, on thirty-day credit or upon sight drafts. The new American procedure takes account of seasonal crops, of banking facilities, of the credit processes used in the countries to which the goods are shipped. Occasionally Americans have followed the lead of the Germans; they have organized branch banks for the promotion of credit operations.

A fourth element consists of government aid. This involves general foreign policies, extensive and active consular assistance, bounties or special concessions, and even aggressive, special diplomatic intervention.

Economic imperialism is no new thing. When the city-states of the Euphrates basin conquered their neighbors, commercial empires were created by economic domination of one group by another. Later empires of the ancient world and of the post-Renaissance period were less dominantly commercial; but the motive was always present because political power is desired less as an end in itself than as a means toward economic gain for the ruling classes.

The late nineteenth century saw a second great struggle for *colonial empires* similar to that of the sixteenth and seventeenth centuries. The sphere of conquest was no longer America and the Indies; Africa played the chief part in this new drama of expansion. In this new struggle for colonial empire, as in the case of America before our Revolutionary War, we find the country opened up by missionaries and explorers, and land grants given to chartered commercial companies. Each nation sought to seize the mouths of important

Development
of modern
economic
imperialism

rivers or take possession of commercial harbors, thus controlling the "Hinterland." Again the control was characterized by exploitation of economic resources of the country rather than attempts at true colonization. In many cases the governments looked on with indifference or disdain.

An entirely different type of economic imperial expansion occurred chiefly in Asia among the most populous of the world's peoples, with the most ancient of present-day civilizations. India came into this history rather early when several countries established trading posts at favorable points on the Indian coast. The motives were largely economic and the initial work of the British was done under a trading company, the English East India Company, chartered under Queen Elizabeth. Before Ghandi and foreign observers called attention to British exploitation, the world looked upon the British colonial policy as rather unselfish and British rule in India as a form of benevolent assimilation. We realize now that the white man's burden was accepted in part because of opportunities for graft, profit, and sometimes merciless disregard of Indian rights. If these things are true in British India, what is the fact in other imperial possessions of England in less civilized places, and of other countries in the vast heathen areas they control?

Russia had already expanded to the Pacific before she came into conflict with Britain for territories north and northwest of India. The Triple Entente was completed by the outrageous division of Persia into three spheres of influence, two of them non-Persian. Russia's attempt to gain an ice-free port on the Pacific met with temporary success when she acquired Port Arthur in Manchuria after forcing Japan to relinquish her conquest in that region. But Japan had expansion ideas of her own and trained armies to back her ambition. Sequel: Russia lost control of Manchuria. Japan first annexed Korea for good measure, then, in 1933, set up a Manchu-headed protectorate of Manchukuo in the face of League and world protests.

The struggle for territories or spheres of influence in China makes clear the cynical remark of a Chinese official that the greatest evil or curse China has encountered in our generation is western civilization. Nearly a century ago, with Hongkong as a base, attempt was made to force opium upon the Chinese. Would that the Christian world could blame upon industrial capitalism the succession of land seizures and plunderings in which even America took some part! One wonders what part China will have in the reorganization of western civilization!

These few superficial touches must stand as representing the picture of foreign domination and exploitation of heathen races not well enough organized politically or sufficiently trained in a military way to ward off the invasion of Christian commercial Huns.[3]

Economic imperialism and America Americans always think of themselves as non-imperialistic if not anti-imperialistic. It was with reluctance we abandoned our nineteenth-century policy of "splendid isolation." In the fall of 1898 when the American troops were occupying Spanish soil in Cuba, in Porto Rico and around Manila, many of our people had disinclination to take over foreign soil. Only a few wished to expand into these new fields. Once the Philippines had been acquired, however, the American mind refused to turn the clock backward. In the election of 1900 the imperialists won a striking victory, whether for imperialist reasons or not we do not know. A policy of "thorough" was inaugurated which was supported in Congress and in the courts. The newly acquired possessions were not parts of the United States, they were colonies in fact if not in name.

For nearly a century under the Monroe Doctrine we had kept Europe out of Latin-American politics. We almost prevented the collection of just debts, except by ineffective means which left our southern neighbors the capital and European creditors the experience. A closer acquaintance with Latin-American affairs and finances convinced us that Latin Americans should not be allowed to pay their debts or not as they pleased. This change of heart probably accompanied the investment of rapidly growing sums of American money in Mexico, the West Indies, Central America and to some extent

[3] This term was first used by a German prince in connection with German expansion in China (1898).

in South America. It may have been influenced by the previous failures of our government to protect properly the lives and property of our nationals south of the Rio Grande. One could cheerfully disregard the failure of Latin Americans to pay European shylocks; but when conservative American bankers loaned hard-earned dollars to owners of sugar plantations or silver mines, revolutionary turbulence or recurring bankruptcy jeopardized sound business.

At first we asserted that debts be paid. If an established government did not make business possible, Uncle Sam might establish dependable systems of rule. Within a short year or two we found ourselves as receivers or trustees in Santo Domingo (1907), trying to maintain order and collect customs. This money was to be used for the double purpose of paying officials of that republic and at least the interest on foreign and American obligations. A few years later a somewhat similar policy was followed in the neighboring republic of Haiti (1916). We had already established a protectorate over Cuba when we gave ourselves special economic privileges there in 1901, starting trouble that became serious in 1933. Nicaragua next engaged our attention because we still wanted an alternative route for a ship canal. The American people are not proud of the part played by the American marines as upholders of Nicaraguan officials acceptable to the United States and as protectors of other American "rights." *Caribbean protectorates certainly represent a far departure from nineteenth-century American policies.* If they were not American, they would seem to represent imperialism and also intervention with self-determinism.

The Caribbean Sea may be destined eventually to be an American lake, that is, a body of water completely surrounded by American investments under rulers acceptable to American capitalists. There certainly is an inconsistency between our pretence of keeping our old ideas of separateness when "peaceful penetration" has gone to such lengths in the Caribbean area and in Mexico. American economic interests abroad have led to a policy of "dollar diplomacy" which for a generation was practically continuous except for a slight deviation under Wilson, the Democrat.

In spite of tendencies toward managing other people's business, some Americans insist that they believe thoroughly in America as a separate nation wedded to democracy and sufficient unto itself. This policy, "splendid isolation" or its substitute, not only disregards the imperialist tendencies just cited but does not take into account the new world of business relations of an international character.[4] Since governmental activities affecting business necessarily are economic as well as political, the public should accept foreign policies which will be consistent with the new economic internationalism. Certainly they must not interfere with it sharply.

With the one hand we reach out for more world trade; with the other we build up tariff walls which shut out desirable imports and shut in possible exports. We seek to promote the investment of American capital abroad; yet we have supported with popular clamor almost every policy which antagonizes the people among whom we would invest or to whom we wish to sell. *In the period following the World War there was a sharp reaction against Mr. Wilson's "forward-looking" internationalism.* Time after time we carelessly alienated Europeans with whom we had been having intimate contacts, for fear we might be entangled in European alliances, economic or political. Again and again we antagonized people of Latin America or the Far East on whom we are depending more and more as the years pass for success in our own business. Just after the World War, when America had the lead in the international field and might have been a potential leader in the world of politics, we frequently made enemies of those with whom we were working.

Some of those peoples, now dependent upon us, may when the wheel turns dictate to us the terms on which we may purchase their raw materials or conditions under which they will accept our surplus products. Evidently the present needs a greater understanding of the new unity and interdependence

[4] Pp. 457–470.

of all nations. This knowledge should bring a broader and more tolerant attitude toward all foreign races. A new national psychology would help us modify our international policies, making our actions more consistent with the requirements, not only of capitalists interested in foreign business, but of America among the nations. Or would that be contrary to the traditional concept of the idea of the American interest and contrary to that interest itself in the future?

INTERNATIONAL TRADE AND ECONOMIC INTERNATIONALISM

Economic internationalism finds one of its most interesting problems in the uneven distribution of the world's supply of minerals. Because international politics must work chiefly through national channels, each country capitalizes its own supply of raw materials. Through treaties as well as through bills of exchange its customers bargain for favorable terms on minerals necessary for their industry and work. Fortunate is that country which possesses within its own territory an abundance of those minerals absolutely essential to modern economic life. Unfortunate is that land which does not contain enough iron, coal, copper, or other mineral necessities; almost hat-in-hand it must ask favors from its more fortunate rivals.

The struggle for raw materials

From the standpoint of raw materials few countries are practically independent. Russia and China, possible economic giants of the future, because of their very area may possess most of the mineral requirements for industrial success. Their development problem will be that for a future generation, not for ours. The United States may thank its size for possession of fuels, one of the world's best iron fields, wonderful supplies of copper and most of the other minerals used in ordinary industrial transactions. Great Britain has fine coals, although her mines, deep and poorly managed, provide poor competition for the newer supplies of continental fuels. Her iron, although fairly abundant is not of high grade, her supplies of tin are still unsurpassed; but she is lacking in most other necessary minerals. On the Continent, had Charlemagne's empire descended to a single grandson, or the

English system of primogeniture been in effect, one of the world's best supplies of iron and coal might have been developed under a single government. Union of the Rhine and Meuse basins under one ruler might have given to the lucky owner of Lorraine iron and of Westphalian coal the industrial primacy in the present world. The prize of iron in Lorraine and potash in Alsace has been more than a minor element in two modern wars, as shown by the transfer of Alsace-Lorraine twice in a half century. Without Briey iron, and without the Silesian coal fields transferred to Poland, Germany is no longer a great producer of industrial minerals. Italy does not rank high in minerals but France, in spite of the destruction of the coal mines around Reims, has now become a joint-controller of the destiny of the largest economic organization of the whole world.

Coal and oil as type problems

If we seem to be exaggerating the importance of minerals in economic internationalism, keep in mind that *one-third of present-day commerce between nations is made up of coal, oil or metals*. In these days of high tariff walls this trade is not simple, having both political import and industrial significance. The fact that France and Germany, enemies over a period of at least three centuries, have organized the Continental Steel cartel, even though they may not have married Lorraine iron to Westphalian coal, shows the inter-relation of business needs with political and possibly diplomatic agreements. Britain's plight and the enormous increase in the use of the "dole" grows partly out of her failure to secure adequate foreign markets for Welsh coal. So well balanced and so highly sensitive is modern business that an increase of Russian wheat shipped to America or of Cuban or Hawaiian sugar to Germany or Russia may upset the most important occupation of a fairly large region and influence the whole business system of the country injured by the new competition.

At the close of the World War it appeared as though the struggle for economic supremacy would simmer down to an international struggle for supplies of oil. America viewed with alarm attempts of British capitalists and, in fact, the

British government to secure control of the world's best supplies of this valuable fluid which was becoming constantly more important in international affairs.

Looking back over the intervening years we find that we then overrated the danger of British competition and the importance of owning or dominating fields rather remote from the ordinary channels of trade. Oil is a product of the western hemisphere rather than the eastern. The known supplies are located chiefly in the United States, in Venezuela, in Russia near the Caspian, and in Mesopotamia. Undoubtedly the American supplies are better known and, judging from the flood of black fuel, far better developed than those of any other country. The United States now produces about two-thirds of the world's supply of oil and but for its policy of restriction could easily furnish all that the world needs day by day. The Mexican oil fields were a flash in the pan, filling a larger place in North American politics than in the world's industry. The Venezuela production is now second in amount to that of the United States. Those oil pools are a good future prospect. Russia is developing the Baku supplies chiefly for export because she needs cash. The Mosul area was a bone of contention between Turkey and the British mandate of Mesopotamia; but the League cast its weighty influence in favor of its most prominent member against a Moslem contestant. Standard Oil of New York still outsells its competitors in supplying the China trade. In most of the world it meets with stiff competition from the Dutch Shell, which belies its name because the stock is owned largely by the British government and some British companies.

Resources may be chemical as well as mineral and indirect products of the soil instead of those taken from nature's stores set aside hundreds of millions of years ago. Among the most interesting of these goods is rubber, a product brought to the attention of civilized man through the crude labors of the pre-Columbian Indian of Central America. England's monopoly of rubber supplies apparently has been check-mated by the Liberian successes of Firestone, by the development of other rubber plantations, and the threatened cultivation of

Edison's substitutes. We need not enumerate the cereal products of soil resources.

A half century ago Great Britain was far in the lead in the world's trade. London was accepted without question as the world's financial center and as the clearing house for practically all countries. Before the World War the trade of Great Britain was still easily first, amounting to nearly seven billions of dollars per year. Germany was a fair second with about five billions and the United States was a good third with about four billions. In the year 1928 these positions were only slightly reversed and the total volume of trade had increased only nominally—not very much actually because the dollar and the pound had decreased in purchasing value. Four countries have nearly half of the world's foreign trade.[5]

If we were to make *an analysis of the commerce of world powers before the World War, immediately following that conflict, and at the present time,* we should quickly discover some outstanding characteristics. Great Britain's trade has always consisted far more of imports than of exports. Even if we take the single item of food, more than two-thirds of her supply is raised abroad. England depends upon the outside world for raw materials for both man and machine. We Americans, proud of our rapid growth in population and business, usually overlook the fact that in the last seventy years Germany's foreign trade has made more progress than our own. This seems a sharp blow to strident patriotism until a thoughtful American comes back with the rebuttal that Germany is a small country of limited resources. Therefore, in central Europe interregional trade becomes foreign;

[5] In 1928 Great Britain stood first with approximately ten billions, America second with more than nine billions and Germany a fairly poor third with more than six billions. France had increased her three billions in 1913 to more than four billions; but she has never ranked either industrially or commercially with her more powerful rivals. In 1913 the world's exports were listed as something more than twenty billions, imports at about twenty-one and one-half billions. In 1928 exports had increased to thirty-three billions, imports to thirty-five billions. As all commodities were sent from one country and into another, the difference represents the extra cost of transportation and probably the addition of customs duties.

raw materials must be brought in, being exchanged for manufactured goods.

American trade with Latin America has been over-advertised. Aside from Japan our chief customers do not lie to the south and west but to the east and to the north. Europe does not have so high a percentage of our business as it did a few years ago. It still has almost as much as the rest of the world taken together, but our imports from Japan exceed those from Great Britain. Canada gives us more trade than any European country. Latin America is a better seller than buyer, largely due to our very great consumption of coffee and sugar.

The most important change in American commerce has been neither in quantity nor in location but in the character of the goods exported. In 1880 crude materials and food stuffs included three-fifths of our total exports. By 1928 crude materials had increased six times, food stuffs scarcely any; but the two together amounted to less than thirty per cent of all exports. In 1880, going back again one-half century, finished manufacturers were less than one hundred million per year and partial manufacturers only one-third as much. In 1929, on the contrary, partially manufactured goods totaled $729,000,000, finished manufactures, $2,532,000,000. *Whereas exports of food stuffs had remained nearly stationary in those fifty years, the value of manufactured articles had increased twenty-five times.*

The figures that are given above are enlightening in several ways. They illustrate not only the struggle for the world market but stress also the economic interdependence of nations. Within countries and among individuals the present age is one of specialization. The nation which is a "jack of all trades," or which is content with a national economy similar to the old household industry, has fallen far behind its neighbors who have accumulated huge units of capital, and have built large factories for the manufacture of special commodities. The commercially successful countries are perfecting the relations between agriculture and food supply, industry with its products necessary for daily use, transporta-

Inter-nation dependence and problems

tion which keeps a balance between buyer and seller at a distance, and banking which helps finance the whole process. Whether we watch the intricate channels by which J. Russell Smith [6] brings us our daily breakfast, or the almost equally complicated routes by which we acquire inventions of the mechanical age called to our attention by Stuart Chase,[7] we must realize that we are the debtors of all nations as well as the heir of all ages. This free exchange of goods is much more delicate and desirable than most of us realize. Take for example a semi-perishable commodity like butter. The price varies little from center to center, although less than one per cent of the total sales represents interregional trade. Experts tell us that the price variation almost exactly equals the transportation and tariff costs added to the original price.

The economic bonds created by commercial interexchange know no national political boundaries. Tariff walls may separate the people of our northern border from those in Canada, but even that barrier does not prevent the daily passage of hundreds of automobiles from Vancouver to Bellingham, or the trade in necessary products between Buffalo and Toronto. Had Ontario and New York or British Columbia and Washington been fairly near but rather different in climate and products, the necessary exchange between the two and interdependence upon one another would have been far more marked than it is. Industrial countries and agricultural regions become thus interdependent, and the bonds between them can be severed only with serious loss on both sides. If we doubt the importance of modern trade in creating internationalism, note that more than twenty centuries elapsed between the development of trade codes for different peoples established in ancient Rhodes and the formulation of our first modern international law by Grotius (1625). How far it has developed since his day!

Economic internationalism of the present is a complex of conflicting forces as well as coöperating influences. Many of these are political rather than economic. Some are national;

[6] See foot-note p. 209.
[7] *Men and Machines*, ch. I.

others grow out of international relations. Since the World War there has been a revival of tariffs, especially since 1925. *Every nation has the urge to manufacture,* but even now its markets are growing narrower decade by decade. Each wants to hedge in its food supply by tariff fences. Tariff changes have been constant. The Hawley-Smoot tariff of 1930 started almost a tariff war. It did not cause the industrial depression of that year, but it added to business stagnation and delayed recovery! The World Economic Conference of 1927 had some excellent ideas about tariffs, urging that there should be a general lowering of the barriers.

Evidently an *international conference on tariffs* alone would be helpful, with a board to help restore trade by reducing friction between nations and by making tariff walls lower or more reasonable. This concert of nations needs to understand *the problem that international trade represents today.* How much is that trade needed? To what extent must countries depend on others for goods they cannot produce easily? To what extent do they depend on one another for markets in which to sell surpluses? If a tariff on olives benefits the growers of only two per cent of all olives consumed in America, would it not be wiser to pay those growers bounties? The problem seems to be less a lowering of tariffs than a *readjustment of each nation, and all together,* to fit the needs of the changing world. And it is safe to say that this new world is neither one of "self-sufficing" nations nor of anything like free trade.

One serious difficulty encountered in the new age is the survival of old *national economic psychology.* Countries like the United States that formerly were debtors changed abruptly into creditors. There was no corresponding change of idea that we should import more than we export or that we should continue to lend abroad in bad times as well as good. The old slogans of "protection" and "favorable balance of trade" swing elections. Yet the "protection" may be on articles that need no protection or that cannot be protected. We can export only when we accept something in return. If we will not have *commodity imports,* we must re-invest abroad to cover the excess of exports, but also to include the interest on our present huge foreign investments. To refuse to import, or to encourage monetary or financial conditions that make the United States a poor market to sell in, simply strangles foreign trade at a time when the domestic market cannot absorb all of the supply that is produced. A careful study of international trade under varying conditions shows that commerce continues to expand even when a nation tries to stop imports by substituting *synthetic products* of its own factories for natural articles formerly imported. In inter-nation commerce the future does not call for more and worse uses of an economics of scarcity. This is no time for self-seeking politicians or for vote-getting demagogues. We need statesmen who understand business and public affairs, within the nation and outside.

Elements of economic internationalism

Which shall we have, national pride or international trade? After 1930 the situation was aggravated by the financial depression of 1931, which almost stopped the further extension of credit from creditor to debtor countries. Sir Arthur Salter maintains that the failure to continue borrowing was an important cause of the financial crisis.[8] But the early depression led to further lack of confidence, less buying, a further drop of prices and still greater depression. An almost complete cancellation of reparation debts and some other international obligations might ease the burden. Monetary and financial reforms that would restore better prices would stimulate buying, producing, and thus reduce unemployment and want. In 1934 Raymond L. Buell suggested that a public works program undertaken by one nation would probably succeed only when several countries coöperate. If a half dozen spent billions each, the gains of all might again have restored business at a going level.

The causes of the difficulty are interwoven and became aggravated with falling prices and the depression. The conditions which underlie our problem show at their worst in international relations; their removal or improvement is hampered

[8] Salter, *Recovery: The Second Effort*, p. 59.

by national selfishness not found in the solution of domestic problems.[9]

International commerce has already led the way toward a better understanding of the needs of other peoples; and the opportunities which business must have may lead to national or international unity. As early as 1834 the German Zollverein had created an *economically united Germany* which remained separated politically for a generation; and then became united only as a result of three bloody wars. The economic forces which led to the Constitutional Convention of 1787 were more than an excuse for the formation of a new and better union. Railways cross international boundaries without hesitation and literally bind countries together with links of steel. In the future, international federations may become an economic necessity and economic interdependence may be the basis of a true international government.

The opening of the Suez Canal was an event of tremendous importance not even equalled by the cutting in two of the American continent by the Panama Canal in 1913. From the international point of view these new channels were important in shortening routes, improving trade and in giving concerted interest to increasing trade. Even more important were the new international problems and attitudes connected with this new type of waterway. The internationalization of the Suez Canal was made complete because Egypt fifty years ago was much less a British state than it is now even under its own king. The Panama Canal, presumably internationalized under an agreement with Great Britain, has been turned into an American lake or river without arousing protest from the world's commercial leaders.

[9] The revival of international trade and the restoration of international credit have led to numerous suggestions regarding the Bank for International Settlements. This banking institution, created by the Young Plan in 1928, has already done much more than handle the finances of German reparations. In many ways it has coöperated unofficially with the central banks of several countries. J. M. Keynes, the distinguished English economist, suggests that the central banks work together by holding a considerable part of their legal reserves with the International bank or with each other. Many other plans have been proposed to economize use of the world's supply of gold, which is badly distributed. United States and France, in 1935, had three-fifths of the whole supply.

So far as economy goes, the influence upon channels of trade developed by these new means of transportation and these bodies of water has been negligible. *More than ever before trade follows a few routes,* the largest number of which extend from New York Harbor to the English Channel. Charles Kenneth Leith makes interesting comment on this situation.[10] In their stimulating book, *The Giant of the Western World,* Miller and Hill particularly stress the creation before 1929 of a new type of international business centering in the north Atlantic.[11] They cite numerous reasons why the trade has shifted from the eastern shores of the Atlantic to the western, a dominance predicted by a Frenchman and others at the close of the World War.[12] During that conflict German submarines interfered with British commerce and shipping. What more natural, therefore, than that New York seized the opportunity to become the world's leading port and for *the duration of the war transferred from London to lower New York the clearing house center for all international trade.* The imperial dollar replaced the pound sterling as the standard by which the world's business was computed. The New York banks rather than the Bank of England financed daily transactions and occasionally invested heavily abroad. The Bank of France, temporarily overwhelmed by a quantity of paper whose value no gold reserve could maintain, lost for the time being its capacity to decide important issues by shipments of gold. England has regained the leadership in foreign trade and *now most of the world looks to Lombard Street rather than Wall Street* for credit and solution of trade problems.[13]

[10] Leith, *World Minerals and World Politics,* p. 13.
[11] Miller and Hill, ch. XIII.
[12] "Formerly it was Europe that dominated all races and imposed her civilization upon them, extending her influence to the most extreme limits. As a result, however, of the frequent wars in which she has taken part, the creation of new routes, the formation of new capitals, and the spread of the industrial régime, Europe's hegemony has been seriously checked. From some points of view she has come to appear like a colony of young America, her god-daughter." Herriot, *The United States of Europe,* The Viking Press, pp. 3–4, quoting Dermangeon, *The Decline of Europe* (1920).
[13] When Britain suspended gold payments, in the fall of 1931, she seemed to lose this supremacy again. Of the shift from London to New York, Benjamin M. Anderson remarks: "I have no desire to disparage the achieve-

INTERNATIONAL BUSINESS ORGANIZATION AND CONTROLS

Uncle Sam, Colossus, deserves his title in the field of large-scale production.   Even before the American public lost its antagonism to the idea of trusts and huge corporations, the government at Washington was using dollar diplomacy to promote American business abroad.   The acquisition of the Philippines, the construction of the Panama Canal within territory split off from Colombia, and protectorates in the Caribbean region called for a new type of policies and statecraft toward other countries.   In the Webb-Pomerene and Edge Acts Congress lifted the ban placed upon combinations by the Sherman Anti-trust law.[14]   Producers and bankers were permitted to work together for the sale of American goods even though their actions would have been illegal in the United States.   Sewing machines, and frequently automobiles, sold in China lower than they were priced in Chicago or New Orleans.   Germany was not permitted to go into Venezuela in 1903 to collect her alleged debts, although the policies of the debtor organizations were worse than those prohibited by law in the American states.

The replacement of trusts by mergers and giant corporations was of more domestic concern than international import.   Nevertheless, a company which reckons its capital in ten figures and its annual business in the same, would naturally not be content with a *national market,* which might not absorb its entire product.   Standard Oil of New York may be a separate company, unrelated since the Rule of Reason decision of 1911 to its fellows of somewhat similar name.   Yet it is odd that the others have competed very little with this

International cartels

ments of the United States in finance, or the technical knowledge of markets which our trained merchants and dealers possess, but it is no disparagement of our own economic organization to say that it is inadequately prepared to take up on short notice the problems with which London has been dealing for a hundred years.   We need London, and we are still accustomed to lean on London, even though our need for her be not as great as it was in the pre-war period." *What England and Germany Mean to the United States,* The Chase National Bank, p. 5.

[14] The Sherman Anti-Trust Law of 1890, reinforced by the Clayton Act of 1914, prohibited monopolies and combinations in restraint of interstate trade.

New York branch in supplying kerosene to the Chinese, gasoline to Mexicans, and fuel oils in Latin America. In 1902 the United States Steel Company had no foreign reason for being our first billion-dollar trust; but since the World War there has risen a competitor that does practically as much business, has better supplies of iron and can secure cheaper labor for longer hours.

Those who hope for a new Europe, a united Europe, believe that, as political Germany came as a by-product of an economically united Germany, *a federated Europe may come in the path of economic coöperation.* The international cartel is no new thing, but its chief development has come as a post-war product. These cartels do not merge the individual companies that are combined but enable separate producing organizations to work together. They divide territory or split up proceeds much as was done by the old-fashioned pool, forbidden by American law a half century ago. England has been drawn very little into the continental vortex; but several cartels have been developed by Central Europe; and in some instances other countries of the Continent are involved. In Europe international cartels are necessary because of the uneven distribution of minerals and supplies of trained or skilled labor. In some lands there has been sharp advance in scientific and technical knowledge but the possessors of this technic have not always had the capital or the goods with which to carry on the work at its best.

A few years ago one of the most spectacular of these organizations, not a cartel at all or a merger, was the Swedish Match Trust. This company had a monopoly of the match manufacture of the world, since ninety per cent of all matches struck were manufactured by companies under this trust, which did business under the clever manipulation of Ivar Kreuger, promoter par excellence and swindler exceptional. Less effective in their control of production or marketing are cartels which are paving the way for the economic unity of Europe. Almost as complete a monopoly is the European potash cartel, which controls the potash deposits of Alsace and dominates the potash markets of the world. Strangely enough it is controlled by French and German governments. If the politicians of these two nations can work on such a large scale, what becomes impossible first in the realm of business, next in that of politics!

An important degree of control of world markets is exercised by the Continental Steel cartel, a Franco-German organization. Attempts have been made to bring into even closer relationships than now exist the Lorraine iron fields and the huge deposits of coal in the Ruhr Valley. In spite of the incompleteness of these efforts, this *International Steel cartel* produced in 1925 more than twenty-five billions of the ninety billions tons of steels made in that year. Between them, the United States Steel Corporation and the Continental Steel cartel produced about three-fifths of the total supply of the world. One of the problems of managing a cartel, as was discovered by the American pool of ill repute, is the impossibility of fixing a quota which stays fixed and satisfactory. Germany started with the arrangement that she should provide about four-tenths of the whole supply of steel, France a little more than three-tenths. But the German factories, placed in close proximity to Westphalian coal and working on wages that were low because of the depressed value of the mark, proceeded to turn out considerably more than their share and more than could possibly be allotted to the German companies.

The time may come when huge mergers and international cartels may solve some international problems of the present industrial nations.[15] One student of cartels who has himself been organizer and manager of a number during the last quarter-century believes that price stabilization can be aided more by cartels than through any other agency. "One of the most important economic advantages to be derived from the cartel organization is the possibility of establishing a *relative stability of prices,* either through direct regulation of prices or indirectly through a regulation of output. The significance of such stability for the economic recovery of America can-

Will cartels save Western civilization?

[15] Provided, of course, that the cartels do not increase for the nations collectively the dilemma of industrialism, pp. 126–136.

not be over-emphasized in view of the present situation." [16]

"The history of the cartel movement reveals the highly interesting fact that 'cartels breed cartels.' In other countries the organization of a cartel in a mining industry (coal, iron ore, etc.) often leads to a cartelization of the steel or other *raw material industries,* followed by a similar organization in the *finishing* industry, and often extends into the corresponding *wholesale* or even *retail trades.*" [17] What the cartel might be able to do in connection with international problems would depend in part upon whether each nation worked out separately for itself almost all of its business problems. If it did attempt that, and could do it, naturally national cartels rather than international cartels would be the means by which it would be undertaken.

In this country it would seem as though the cartel is not necessarily the solution when so many mergers have consolidated similar businesses on a horizontal plan and such a large number of trade associations [17a] have organized, bringing together almost all the businesses connected with a particular type of production or exchange. However, if cartels have succeeded in stabilizing both production and prices, if they have been able to do that by the use of modern rather than older methods, and if they have done it for the public benefit instead of for private gain, certainly the cartels should not be overlooked in the attempt to solve our pressing problems. We have no assurance that most of these problems can be solved by each nation for itself. In that case, might it not be wise to have mergers of an international character? Trade associations developed within the United States perhaps will not, or should not, expand into Great Britain, France, and Germany. Yet, the international cartel might make possible a

---

[16] Bruno Burn, *Codes, Cartels, and National Planning,* McGraw-Hill Book Co., p. 169.

[17] *Ibid.,* p. 156.

[17a] The trade association is of fairly recent development. In 1933 there were about two hundred of national scope, besides more than a thousand others. The N. I. R. A. of that year doubled the number of national organizations. Since 1925 trade associations have been legal under the Sherman Anti-Trust Act unless they directly controlled prices or indirectly attempted to influence them.

restoration or a re-creation of inter-nation business in the best way and at the optimum desirable level.

In the next half century western industrial capitalism may need to set its house in order or build about itself a Chinese Wall. Otherwise it might well face impossible competition because of any one of a large number of forces coming from outside of its present orbit. The world is much larger than the area of North Atlantic capitalism. Even though the present world powers are one another's best customers, they may not be permitted permanently to monopolize the world market. They may have to face the competition of the "Yellow Peril" or the "Red Menace." *Western capitalism might then occupy the unenviable position that agriculture now holds.* It might be a "back number," out of date, possibly "out of the running." The Five-Year Plan of Russia has led to other five-year plans. If they succeed, and success is by no means impossible, a communistic state under dictator leadership with millions of helots at its command—a system which free Americans would not tolerate—might easily overpower industrial capitalism if that is poorly integrated, too much concerned with profits and hampered by a free, intelligent and constantly better educated proletariat. What will happen when the Orient gains capital, makes use of western machinery and organization and finds effective leadership such as that of aggressive Japan?

England is already suffering from the competition of India and her millions of potential workers. India grows her own supply of cotton; Britain must bring hers four or five thousand miles from our Gulf ports. The greed of American or European manufacturers who export machinery to any customers may easily be a boomerang which will hurt cruelly the unwise exporter or any person or business dependent upon him or manufacturers who use his machinery. Even more suicidal is the tendency to export machine-making machinery. One may not kill the goose that lays golden eggs; but, if the eggs themselves are sold and raise up for their new owner a crop of geese capable of laying this profitable commodity, who then is the goose? The possession of this type of poultry will cease to possess value.

International investments

In this new world of capital there have been a large number of international problems involving investment rather than trade. The almost limitless resources of the United States furnished so great an opportunity that American capital formerly found better opportunities here than abroad, just as it has always secured higher rates of interest in the American West than in the East. Any people that accumulates from fifteen to twenty billion dollars surplus per year in prosperity sooner or later reaches a point of diminishing returns beyond which the further accumulation of capital reduces the return on the capital it possesses. Just as the growers of wheat and cotton and the producers of oil have found necessary a limitation of output, so the accumulators of capital may encounter a situation in which *reduction of further surplus of capital* may be the most pressing necessity.

The uneven distribution of wealth in Europe has caused large investments abroad by many European governments and nationals. These have increased greatly in the last half century, particularly the investments made by Englishmen and Frenchmen in many parts of the globe. A half century ago English foreign investment was but little more than six billion dollars. In 1900 it was twelve billions and in 1925 twenty-two billions, plus a war debt of eight billions more. This exceeded even the very large post-war investments of America. Among continental countries France stood first, with total investments before the World War of about eight billions, chiefly in Russia and Turkey. Germany's foreign investment, before she became involved in world conflict, was slightly smaller than that of France. We must not make the mistake, therefore, of thinking that Europe as a whole has changed from a creditor continent into a debtor region. Although she borrowed from America during the World War and has borrowed since, as far as business is concerned a balance of the ledger shows the world owes Europe more than her indebtedness to all the countries on other continents.

Rather more interesting to us is *our abrupt change from a debtor condition to that of an international creditor.* In colonial times the American colonies had practically no capital of their own. They were dependent almost entirely upon the opportunities which a new country offered to those who preferred large returns to investment security. Comparatively few of the early trading companies made money. Even the thrifty Dutch maintained that if it had not been for piracy—they did not call it that—on the Spanish Main, the Dutch West India Company could not have continued in business.

When the first United States Bank was organized, it was not an American or a government institution. It was not only organized on the British model but was largely financed by British capital. In 1850 joint American and British control of an inter-oceanic canal was proposed, because British investors were expected to furnish the necessary money for constructing this "Big Ditch." Economically the expansion of American industry after the Civil War was an independent movement; but railways and even more solid investments made an appeal abroad, bringing us more capital than had been invested by Europe formerly. Before the Great War gave us a huge business in munitions, it is estimated that we were indebted for four billions of our capital to foreign investors.[18] The best way that Europeans could pay a considerable part of the debt incurred during the Great War or the later World War consisted in a repurchase by America of securities owned abroad. Within a short time foreign investments in the United States decreased sharply, and American investments abroad even in Europe increased by leaps and bounds. During the war advances were made to foreign governments by America, a sum which has increased through failure to pay interest or reduce principal. These *war debts,* however, are political and governmental. They were supplemented by *commercial debts* incurred by foreigners who needed money which could not be secured from Europe. So rapidly has Uncle Sam become the world's banker that before 1930 this latter sum was estimated at approximately fourteen billion dollars, and it had been increasing at the rate of more than a billion dollars a year.

[18] At that time American investors held foreign securities or properties worth about two billions.

Our investments abroad have been made not only in Europe itself but in Canada, Mexico, Cuba, South America and, to a lesser degree, the lands across the Pacific. Even in Europe, however, major enterprises seldom are undertaken without requesting if not accepting American money. The whole question of reorganizing German finances and of refunding the war debt involved in the *problem of reparations* hinged to a considerable extent on the possibility of asking Uncle Sam for loans sufficient to finance these enterprises. The German business crisis of 1931 was averted largely by the prompt action of the Hoover administration in postponing debt payments for a year and by American coöperation in the international conference in London.

International loans tell a small part of the story of international banking and economic dependence. Alphonse XIII could not leave his throne without the stock market receiving a distinct shock. Some of us have not yet ceased blaming the Hatry failure for the stock market collapse of 1929. Even before that occurred Roger Babson had been warning us that the future of business was uncertain, that bonds were better than stocks, that speculation was unsafe. The Hatry failure caused a demand for ready money. This demand was met in part by the sale of British-owned securities in Wall Street. A few months later the sharp stock slump of May, 1930, was attributed again to the desire of New York banks for foreign investments more attractive than the market for call loans in lower New York. Threats of business trouble in Germany in June, 1931, and the relief offered by the Hoover one-year moratorium again gave evidence that *national bourses are directly affected by international business.*

More widespread than any previous depression was that which followed the stock market debacle of 1929.[19] Recovery in 1933 was not simply American; it was general. The world, at least the North-Atlantic part of it, is becoming more and more knit together in most of its affairs, particularly those concerning big business and industrial capitalism.

[19] For the influence of the American depression on business stagnation outside of Germany and Great Britain, consult, *The Course and Phases of the World Economic Depression,* ch. V.

RECOVERY AT HOME AND ABROAD [20]

(Comparison of Dec. 1933 with Feb. 1933[1] with % of improvement)

	U. S. A.	Canada	Great Britain	Germany
Industrial production	20	26*	3[3]	18*
Factory employment	21	19	22[4]	32[4]
Factory payrolls	32			
Building	22[2]			
Agricultural prices	36	40	none?	—[5]
Wholesale prices	18	9	4	5
Exports[6]	80	93	6	−14
Imports	59	50	29	−11

[1] Or Dec. 1932, whichever is lower. Feb. 1933 indicated by *.
[2] Comparison between last six months of 1932 and of 1933.
[3] 1932 compared with 1933.
[4] Reduction in registered unemployment.
[5] Under laws of Sept. 1933 controlled, "just" prices.
[6] World trade for 1933 showed a loss of more than 10% over 1932.
Statistics from World Economic Review, U. S. Dept. of Commerce, 1934.

In the inter-nation economic relations of recent years the clash between *economic nationalism* and *economic internationalism* has been conspicuous. The London Conference of 1933 failed to accomplish much because nations and groups of nations were primarily interested in those economic problems which seemed to embody their real difficulty. Some favored the plans suggested at the Economic Conference at Geneva in 1927, for lower and more uniform tariffs. Others concentrated on an increase of the price level, and were opposed by the gold group that wished to keep prices low. Probably no action would have been taken; but any possible decision was ended by President Roosevelt's refusal to consider any plan for international currency stabilization until America had worked out an arrangement for better prices in the United States.

Statesmen in conference represented economic national preferences. The world's business continued along lines showing sharp and increasing interrelations. The low point of the depression was reached earlier in Germany than elsewhere, since Germany had felt the depression in 1927, when the rest

Conclusion: What should America choose?

[20] For much fuller details on the extent of depression and the relative degree of 1933 recovery in America and abroad, *see* Berle, Dickinson, Sachs, *America's Recovery Program,* pp. 114, 148.

of the world was still prosperous. Recovery in Germany was not so rapid as in Great Britain, Canada and the United States, in which no real gain was observable until the year 1933 or possibly later. In America and in Great Britain February or March, 1933, represented the nadir of the depression period; and the subsequent spring and summer marked the sharpest recovery, although greater in this country and Canada than in Europe. If some of England's business improvement had not preceded the Roosevelt New Deal, we should attribute world recovery in 1933 to American leadership and show that national action must precede international and, also, that it determines what the foreign action shall be. At least the close interrelation of business affairs in many countries appears when we note that since 1870 every great depression in any great power has been accompanied by *world-wide changes from prosperity to depression.*

Does the course of international business in recent years show that each nation should go its own way, or just the opposite? Has international trade lost its former significance? Will the future furnish a smaller foreign market for American surplus products? If so, will the debacle of industrialism and capitalism be hastened or postponed? Secretary Wallace has vividly portrayed the need that "America must choose" between [21] "self-containment, full participation in world trade, or a planned middle course." Which do you think it should be?

[21] H. A. Wallace, *America Must Choose,* World Affairs Pamphlets, No. 3, 1934.

VIII

NEEDS, PURPOSES AND MEANS OF ECONOMIC REORGANIZATION

Transition from any economic order to any other is bound to be accompanied by sacrifices, losses, and disadvantages, for numerous groups and classes. A hundred years ago, English workers of the old type formed mobs and destroyed the machines which were taking away their livelihood. The American public today cannot do that in fact, and by violence. If we are wise we shall probably build on what we have, studying carefully the adjustments of new to old. Before introducing necessary changes we should capitalize the elements of both the existing political system and business organization. It is not simply a lack of organization or an unwillingness to act that has created the plight of large classes and groups in America. Our lack is a limited understanding of our system, a faulty psychology in relation to our problem and our necessary attitudes, and a failure to realize the fact that without some rather drastic reorganization the American situation may become constantly worse, although relieved by occasional and partial improvement.

The Plight of the Farmer

The difficulties and problems of the American farmer have stood in high relief the last fifteen years. Interestingly enough, from the business point of view, the first twenty years of this century were the most successful and profitable he ever enjoyed. This is the more odd because in a way the close of the nineteenth century marked the end of the farmer's special influence in politics and the passing of the American rural family as the typical social unit of our country; and

American agriculture after the World War

the first part of the twentieth saw the loss of most of the foreign market for cereals.

In the year 1900, the value of all farm property was only twenty billions, whereas in 1920 that property was appraised at seventy-eight billions, nearly a four-fold increase. Undoubtedly the actual increase in value had been considerably less than these figures, which reminds us of urban real estate boom prices before 1929. During those years the number of farms had increased slightly, but the farm population had dropped sharply. If one were making a comparison between 1880 and 1930, in that half century the farm population of America decreased from practically fifty per cent of the total to a little more than twenty-one per cent.

The reason for the high appraisement of farm lands is seen when we compare the value of farm crops in 1900, a little more than three billions, with the estimated value in the banner year, 1919, sixteen and a half billions. The war, of course, had been responsible for an increase in agricultural products, accompanied by most unusual prices. Wheat was held to $2.20 a bushel plus freight rates, although in 1930 wheat sold for one dollar, and in 1932 it touched the lowest price in the history of the last four centuries, practically forty cents a bushel, about the labor cost of planting and harvesting by older methods.

From shortly after the close of the World War to the depths of "the greatest depression in history" American agriculture declined steadily. A great deal has been said about the loss of foreign markets as the cause of that decline of agriculture. A study of figures, however, shows quickly and clearly that American grain farmers lost their foreign markets to their Canadian, Argentine, and other competitors in the first twelve years of the twentieth century,[1] not in the twelve years following the World War.[2]

---

[1] Canada increased her wheat production tenfold from 1900 to 1928. Argentine and Australian wheat crops in 1913 stood at more than double the 1900 figures.

[2] Under the stimulus of the World War, agricultural exports totaled 2,859 million dollars in one year. This condition was purely temporary. When it ended, agriculture should have been in much the state it was before the war.

A second explanation of the decline of farm profits from the peak at the close of the World War is the mechanization of American farms. In the ten years from 1918 to 1928, the number of tractors in America increased ten times, until the total number was nearly a million. Farmers of the corn belt made use of new machinery which cut the standing corn, shelled the ears, and prepared the rest of the stalk for the silos, all in one series of operations. The use of giant plows and machine methods on farms such as that of Thomas Campbell in Montana is well known. The labor cost on a thousand acres was reduced to three hundred and fifty dollars. By older methods seventy acres would have cost as much. Beginning about a half century ago, California farms made use of instruments to avoid separate threshing machines. With later improvements these combines greatly simplified the procedure in cutting, binding, and threshing the wheat, reducing the cost to about a third of what it had been before. These examples of new and better machines and power illustrate the reduced costs of American farming, especially in the wheat area, and to a lesser extent in the corn belt. This increased use of machinery naturally created keen competition and a glutted market.

After the World War, if the majority of American farmers had been scientifically trained, or if most farms had used good tractors with up-to-date machines, still larger bumper crops might have caused still greater bumper losses, all in that greatest of all prosperity periods from 1922 to 1929. Farms did not increase in size, however, the average for the United States being only 150 acres; and that size has remained fairly constant for thirty or forty years. Since averages are misleading, we should look at the figures to see that forty per cent of the farms are fifty acres or less and fifty-five per cent of the farms are one hundred acres or less. The average is caused by a comparatively small number of rather large farms. Taking into account the fact that tractors and combines, considering only one combination of power and machinery, can be used only on farms of one hundred acres or more and only for certain types of crops, we can see that reductions in cost would not necessarily lead to unusual profits for the average farmer.

When we examine the reports of the United States Department of Agriculture, we find that the farmer's plight after 1920 was a real one and a very serious one. That department took some ten thousand farms of an average size of three hundred acres, but even with reduced appraisements of farm property the return gave the farmer less than two per cent on his investment. After taxes and interest on loans had been paid, the labor return for the farmer and his family was very much less than a thousand dollars and frequently under eight hundred dollars for the farm household. When we keep in mind the fact that the average rather unskilled American laborer was making in those years about twelve hundred dollars per year, that the farmer was taking all the risks of drought, pestilence, and uncertain markets, this absurdly low return gives us an appalling picture of the American agricultural situation.

If we approach the subject from another angle, we discover, first, that farm lands lost in value, at least appraised value, a very considerable part of their 1920 price at a time when all other American property was increasing fairly rapidly or rather rapidly in value. After 1929 the loss in farm value was so great that estimates are practically meaningless. Secondly, even in the years from 1920 to 1930 a farmer paid for commodities that he bought relatively more than he received for farm products. If the prices in 1920 were treated as base, the prices paid in 1927 were twenty per cent higher than those received, and in 1932 were nearly double. That is, in 1932 the farmer's dollar—and remember how few he had—purchased only half what it did in 1920. During those years, the wages paid to farm workers held up better than prices of farm products. Taxes in 1927 were 160 per cent higher than taxes in 1914, and in 1932 taxes on agricultural land were more than double what they had been in 1914, although prices were only 57 per cent of the 1914 prices, the total value of all farm crops in 1932 being $4,200,000,000.

Much has been said about the farm debt and its burden

upon the American farmer. Certainly much history of recent
years has developed out of attempted foreclosure, in farmer
strikes and boycotts and in legal decisions upholding foreclosure or preventing the taking of farm property for the payment of notes. In the years from 1922 to 1929, when almost all
other debts except Uncle Sam's Liberty Bonds were increasing
in amount, the farmer's debt decreased slightly. This was
not due to prosperity; in fact, in most cases it proved exactly
the opposite. Nearly three-fifths of this debt was secured by
farms in the North-Central region. Surprisingly enough,
practically three-fifths of the American farms are absolutely
free from mortgage.

Certainly it is impossible for any business to continue on
so small a return on its investment and so limited an income
for its workers and enterprisers. From the economic point
of view the situation may have been relieved some by the
extraordinary increase in the number of tenant farms; from
the social viewpoint the loss from that change is ours. Each
census until 1920 showed an increase in the *number* of owners
who managed their own farms, but the *percentage* of tenants
has increased steadily from about one-fourth in 1880 to approximately two-fifths fifty years later. Evidently the freehold farm of the grandfathers is gradually, if slowly, becoming a thing of the past. Certainly agriculture has no rights
which the industrial capitalist seems bound to respect—or
at least before the eighth of November, 1932.

In those tremulous years following the World War, the
farmer may not have gained much public help; but, if he
did not, it was not his own fault. Soon after the war the
War Finance Corporation was resurrected largely for the purpose of increasing the sales of agricultural products abroad.
The Farm Block struggled for years to secure legislation in
Congress favorable to farm interests. Considering the fact
that the farmers worked well together, and the Republicans
did not have a working majority without them, the wonder
grows that they did not secure more legislation, and more
favorable legislation, than they did. A considerable gain was
made in connection with *farm credits;* before depression ar-

rived nearly two billions was being loaned directly or indirectly to farmers from the public treasury. The advantage
to the farmer was less that one-sixth of his debt was now
held by the government, than that loans made at reasonable
rates by Uncle Sam reduced the rate of interest which he paid
to private parties or to banks and insurance companies and
other investment organizations. During those years, members
of Congress, especially McNary and Haugen, struggled val-
iantly to secure relief, especially in connection with the marketing of agricultural goods. If their bills managed to get
through Congress, and some of them did, successive presidents vetoed them with unfailing regularity and constantly
more elaborate veto argument. During the depression, large
sums of money were lost by the government in the purchase
of wheat or cotton at market prices when re-sold on a very
sharply falling market.

Relief since
the Roosevelt
inauguration
March 4, 1933, dawned like a rising sun on the horizon of
the American people, including the distracted farmer. Comparatively little positive relief had been promised by the in-
coming administration. One of its first acts, however, was
the enactment of the Agricultural Adjustment Act,[3] in a field
especially close to the heart of President Roosevelt, who as
governor of New York and later has worked unceasingly for
a squarer deal for the farmer. The primary purpose in the
minds of the proposers of this interesting scheme of public
aid was undoubtedly the raising of farm prices above the
level of necessary costs. Suggestion was made that if possible
prices should be brought back to the 1911–13 point. Wheat,
which had been sluggish at about thirty-three cents rose
eventually to more than one dollar a bushel, although it did
not stay at so high a price as that. Corn, which had sold on
the farm for less than ten cents a bushel, when there was any
sale for it, staggered upward to forty cents. Cotton, which
had been a drug on the market at six cents, managed to
touch fourteen cents before it fell back into a more natural
price level.

These gains came indirectly through the revival of business

[3] On the Agricultural Adjustment Act, see also pp. 237–238.

and the restoration of public confidence. They were even
more traceable to the new government proposals. In part
these were due to reduction in acreage, a procedure which
proved not essential in 1934 by the prolonged drought of
that year. The wheat farmers were paid something in lieu
of a rental on land removed from cultivation, if acreage were
reduced, and were entitled to the benefits of a processing tax
handled through the millers and other middlemen and paid
later by consumers. The American problem with wheat was
simplified by the agreement reached in August, 1933, that
Argentine, Australia, and Canada would also reduce substan-
tially their exports of wheat. On the contrary, the plowing
under of growing cotton plants at the request of the Agricultural Administration and the failure to plant as many acres as
usual did not benefit by a similar international protective
agreement. Since the United States has produced more than
three-fifths of the world's cotton, more than half of which
it exported before 1933, foreign countries such as Argentine
can easily take advantage of our reduction to supply more
of the world demand. R. L. Buell maintains that for every
acre taken out of cultivation in the Gulf states, Argentine
planted a substitute acre.

The relief of American agriculture has been aided also by
the new measures of refinancing,[4] which need not be detailed
here. Undoubtedly, the American farmer would manage to
survive, if not to succeed, provided some means is assured of giving him a real margin of sales above actual costs.
Collectively, the farming world would benefit greatly by co-
operation or combination. Some observers accused the farmers
of causing the great depression because they refused or failed
to reduce crops at a time when all other producers were cutting output and merchants were reducing sharply their stocks
of goods. Unlimited competition certainly is no better for
the farmer than it was for American industry a quarter or a
half century ago. This is especially true when we have
many tiny farms cultivating much marginal land and using

* Pp. 242–243.

antiquated methods, including the failure to provide up-to-date and labor-saving machines and power.

A second phase of the farm problem is connected with the international market. Two schools are arguing very vigorously in favor of "America Self-Contained" or American co-operation in every possible way with other countries. As Secretary Wallace has so vividly pointed out, "America must choose," and upon the choice will depend to some degree the prosperity of American agriculture in the future. If governments assume as part of their twentieth-century function, at least in the second third of the century, an obligation to prevent free and unlimited competition injurious to business, certainly the farmer is entitled to the benefit of any help that can or should be given. Whether this occupation of using the soil as well as other business shall be left to depend upon the rather unrestricted operation of supply and demand probably cannot be worked out immediately. Relief which is of a semi-dole nature, or relief which depends as much as the Agricultural Adjustment Act did upon creating artificial scarcity, would hardly seem likely to solve the problem of the American farmer in our day. The fact that bigger and better managed farms would give more food than we can eat or than the farmer can sell at home or abroad indicates a needed readjustment of our whole farm set-up. Certainly, this is no problem primarily of a business nature. It must be political because our traditional democracy was a product of the farm and the agricultural problem as a whole is a public one. It is unquestionably social also, for the reason that the freehold farmer made up the great bulk of the middle class [5] of the mid-nineteenth century. The plight of the farmer involves almost every part of our present civilization and throws light on the price paid in this period of transition by the most important class in the old order.

Agriculture as the Cinderella of the Machine Age

Why is agriculture the Cinderella of the Machine Age? Our farmer ancestors produced their civilization and bequeathed it to us, but the modern farmer finds himself hampered rather than benefited by what his ancestors have done

[5] Pp. 372–381.

for us. He finds himself caught in the toils of an economic machine of which he seems an unimportant part. Nevertheless he has not made capital of the fact that only a very few days may stand between the ordinary well-being of our cities and starvation, should the flow of food cease.

This poor relation of the modern capitalist is himself capitalist, enterpriser, worker, and often marketer. The farmer is a *capitalist*, but he has little capital. If he wishes to improve his buildings or equipment, he usually must borrow. The days of the fifteen per cent mortgage no longer harass the Kansas farmer, thanks to the Farm Loan Board and the Federal Land Banks. Sometimes he has been able to borrow —not at the call money rates of Wall Street—but for as little as his city cousin pays his banker. Often he is a renter, without capital even for necessary farm equipment. He is an *enterpriser*, but there are so many of him that, like the corner groceryman of a generation ago, he succeeds well only when he supplies a local market. If he comes, as he usually does, in competition with others at a great distance, possibly in a foreign country, he is in danger of getting only a fraction of the cost of production. As an enterpriser he manages business with risks almost unequalled in other occupations. Unfavorable weather, unknown markets, and many other factors enter into his problem. He is *laborer*, but to judge by his net returns, a poor one unworthy of his hire!

The interregional breakfast [6] of the average man may be the farmer's tragedy. This is not because the ordinary American depends upon hated foreigners for his food, but because the

[6] "The man of today starts his breakfast with an orange from California or Florida, or a banana from Central America, or an apple from Oregon, Virginia, or New York. He takes a shredded wheat biscuit made in Niagara Falls from Dakota wheat. He sugars it with the extract of Cuban cane. He puts Wisconsin butter on bread baked of Minneapolis wheat flour, mixed with Illinois corn flour. He has a potato. In June it comes from Virginia, in July from New Jersey, in November from New York, Maine or Michigan. If he indulges in meat, it is a lamb chop from a frisky little beast born on the high plains near the Rocky Mountains, and fattened in an Illinois feed lot before going up to Chicago to be inspected, slaughtered and refrigerated. He warms and wakes himself up with a cup of coffee from Brazil (called Mocha perhaps) or tea from Ceylon or Japan, or cocoa from Equador or the coast of Guinea." Smith, *The World's Food Resources*, p. 7.

farmer has never made himself a successful part of our great system of exchange. Coöperative organizations, such as the Southern California Citrus Association, have helped their members greatly. With the aid of the government they have limited charges in transportation; by working as a unit, they have helped to maintain prices in eastern markets; by knowing facts of foreign competition, they have gained political support against importers. These associations are the exception, both in number and in type of farming they include. Again consider the wheat farmer. Formerly the farmer did not plow his land and harvest his crop at a labor cost of less than forty cents a bushel. An acre of wheat nets him, for the United States in general, about eighteen bushels. Its total cost of production to the consumer is more likely to exceed a dollar per bushel than be below that figure. Being at a distance from the centers of population, his goods must be transported hundreds or thousands of miles. The railroad and the elevator man take their toll, their charges being controlled by public agents. The miller adds his mite; and, if we believe a careful investigation, it is one-third as great in a few hours as the farmer's profit of many months. The real magician, however, is the baker. To his flour he adds other ingredients and a little heat, and behold, his addition to the price is almost as great as that of all those who have gone before him! The loaf of bread, which may cost the consumer ten cents, has given to some member of the baking trust the greater share of this insignificant dime. The farmer is lucky if he gets two cents from the total.[7]

Figuratively speaking, agriculture is the Cinderella for its three younger sisters: industry, commerce, and banking. The public has now forced the last to give the American farmer the necessary capital, at a reasonable rate of interest. Apparently the public again makes railroad rates low enough, so that grain and other foods can be marketed. As a small-scale operator, the farmer seems unable to compete with groups whose capital amounts to billions and the value of whose products threatens to reach eight figures annually.

[7] *Competition and Profits in Bread and Flour.*

In the management of the economic order and hence other affairs of the Machine Age, the farmer has lost the control which in a sense he enjoyed in the last half century. Turn about would seem fair play, and agriculture cannot expect to dominate our lives as it did that of our ancestors. Age-old agricultural civilization already has too many undesirable and vicious holds upon our thoughts, our attitudes, and our social responses. But if we make the present-day farmer— very often a tenant farmer—the scapegoat for the maladjustments of agriculture in the Machine Age, he will be tempted to withhold from us the food essentials, without which machines and power are useless. A shortsighted policy, this which we have been following! No paper profits of huge trusts can possibly justify this neglect or ill-treatment of the American farmer. Yet our agriculturists are far better off, relatively, than those abroad, even though (or because) the Machine Age has made more progress in America than in Europe or Asia.

It was the freehold farmer who saved England from feudalism and despotism; it was the frontier farmer who ushered in American democracy. The farmer is the foundation upon which even our present-day civilization rests; but frequently he is inexperienced and unscientific, invariably unrewarded and unsung.

The Plight of the Worker

Never having reached the heights formerly enjoyed by the farmer, the worker could not fall so far. It probably hurts just as keenly to lose a little as to lose much, if that little is all one has; especially if the loss means no income at all, with public charity the only alternative. In the early years of the depression, following the stock panic of 1929, public attention was centered on the crisis in unemployment. The new public conscience of the American people and new attitude of the American government are shown first by the attempt to keep workers employed in spite of the lack of regular business. This was practically the first depression in history in which the first effect of depression was not forced and pro-

Unemployment, especially in depression

longed unemployment.[8]   The actual total of those out of employment, or being employed very little compared with ordinary times, probably will never be known.   Estimates in
the United States run close to fifteen millions, out of a total
of less than fifty million workers employed and employable.
In 1932 the payroll of the United States Steel Corporation
dropped to half what it was at the end of 1931.   In 1932,
steel, formerly thought the "barometer of trade," paid out in
wages only 166 millions compared with 730 millions in 1929.
In 1933, with a revival of employment, three-fifths of the
workers in the heavy industries and in the building industries
were still out of work, although the number of those producing consumer's goods, or in retail trade, had come back somewhat nearer normal.   The extent of unemployment in different
types of occupations is clearly presented by Leonard P. Ayres.[9]

Percentages [employed]

Consumption Goods	1929	1933	*Durable Goods*	1929	1933
Agriculture........	10.47	10.47	Lumbermen.........	.18	.03
Fishermen, etc......	.07	.07	Miners	.57	.33
Mining............	.41	.37	Manufacturing and		
Manufacturing and			Mechanical........	5.06	2.93
Mechanical.....	5.03	4.53	Construction.........	4.03	.69
Total............	15.98	15.44	Total..............	9.84	3.98

Numbers [unemployed]

Producers of Consumption Goods....................	538,000
Producers of Durable Goods........................	5,860,000
Providers of Services..............................	5,868,000
Total...	12,266,000

Abroad, unemployment was both worse and better than in
America.   In Germany the unemployment situation had been
bad before 1929 but became very much worse after that time,
with five million unemployed as early as February, 1931,
thirty per cent of all workers.   In Great Britain it was not
so great, but was estimated in 1931 at two and two-thirds
million.   Later, on January 1, 1933, almost three million of
insured workers in Great Britain were out of work, twenty-

[8] Even with the pressure from Washington and the influence of public
opinion employment dropped so rapidly that Ethelbert Stewart's figures
showed only forty per cent of workers in manufacturing on July 1, 1931,
compared with the number at work two years earlier.
[9] *The Economics of Recovery*, pp. 173–74, 175.

three per cent of the total number. In France employment continued about as usual, including work given to more than two million Italians and others, who were employed in France after the war, but who lost their jobs in 1931, 32, 33. Being a country of small producers and shopkeepers, the French did not suffer the extreme depths of an industrial-capitalist depression.

In the depth of the depression and for an average of at least a year about thirty per cent of all American workers were unemployed.[10] If there were any savings left as late as 1932, they did not last long under this draft. During that year the amount spent for relief could not have been much less than the $800,000,000 of 1933. For all workers, the seventy per cent still employed, payrolls were only two-fifths of what they had been.[11] In ordinary times payrolls may run from fifty per cent to fifty-five per cent of all business expenditures; but they are also practically the whole earned income for workers and wage earners of more than seventy per cent of the families in America.

The plight of the worker is greatest because of *cyclical unemployment*, the major cycles averaging about ten years, with minor cycles in the interim. The plight of the worker is much more than that; for back of the cycles is a great deal of *seasonal unemployment* or *technological unemployment*. All three of these causes count because they indicate the shift from the old type of non-specialized or small-scale business to mechanized industry, to large-scale systems of transportation and sales dominated by industrial capitalism. The plight does not call for relief, either charity or public dole, but for *some form of stabilized income*, possibly through unemployment insurance but probably through a permanent readjustment of work loads and wages. These in turn will not be easily devised so long as industrial capitalism faces dilemmas similar to those of the present.

In the lives and thought of the workers, few evils of the capitalist régime are more serious than the danger of losing

Unemployment: causes and costs

[10] Kuznets, *National Income*, 1929–1932.
[11] *Federal Reserve Report*. Kuznets gives 64.5%; but Kuznets' figures for wages in 1932 were higher than King's or Douglas' before 1929.

a job, or the critical struggle through which a family goes when the chief earner is unemployed. The need for workers may be constant, but if the supply is unusually large no individual feels that his position is secure. For the ordinary worker, at least before 1933, there are no laws, rules, or customs which compel an employer to give advance notice of discharge, to present to the employee reasons for discontinuance of work; no opportunity before an impartial tribunal to explain the success of the discharged worker or the needs of his family.

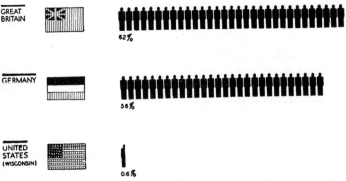

GREAT BRITAIN

62%

GERMANY

56%

UNITED STATES (WISCONSIN)

0.6%

WORKERS OF OTHER COUNTRIES AND THE UNITED STATES PROTECTED BY UN-
EMPLOYMENT INSURANCE
(Each Figure Represents 2 Per Cent of Total)

Objectively, unemployment brings with it a total cessation of income except to those who have unemployment insurance in their union or under the government. This number is large in Europe; only three-fifths of one per cent in the United States, outside of Union help. When unemployment is great, a sharp decrease occurs in the purchase of even the necessaries, such as bread, milk, and other nourishing foods. Subjectively, there is not only the pinch of poverty and the worry over the next meal, but the fear that unemployment may continue indefinitely. When the problem is an individual one, due to the discharge of a worker for personal reasons, the difficulty is still more serious. If a man loses his job without special reason or because his employer objects to him personally, he has great difficulty in securing reëmployment, especially in these days of great corporations.

Unemployment may be due to various reasons. Many of these are personal, but more are economic. Some businesses are inevitably seasonal, but some that were seasonal have become regular through foresight and applied science. In cold climates the building trades are less active in the winter months. Agriculture, although highly seasonal, usually carries a fairly permanent force of workers, although needing extra help in peak seasons. The making of toys or other Christmas gifts, the work of those who satisfy the needs of fashion, and multitudes of others find the demand for their services much greater at certain times of year than at others. A great deal of unemployment is caused in businesses which have continued peak loads over several months, or possibly recurring peaks at irregular intervals. For example, consider the unloading of vessels in harbors. If each wharf company maintains a definite substitute list of extra roustabouts, the percentage of unemployed in that community is likely to run thirty or forty per cent. One of the major causes of disagreement between the San Francisco stevedores and the shipping interests in 1934 was not the pay but the right of the workers to be taken in regular order. The companies agreed on wages but wished to pick their men.

One of our largest extractive industries, that of coal mining, furnishes the best possible example of unemployment due to heavy seasonal demands. The number of working days of the average British or American miner is likely to be considerably less than two hundred per year. For American miners, in only two years out of thirty did unemployment average as low as twenty-four per cent of the regular time, and in nine of the thirty it was higher than thirty-five per cent.

Much has been written and said about technological unemployment. A study of a machine-organized business like the A. O. Smith Corporation shows how a worker or two can now do the tasks formerly assigned to hundreds of men. If technological advance had proceeded as rapidly as scientific invention made possible, this increase of technological unemployment would have been very much greater than it has been.[11a] Special studies within limited fields seem to indicate that the amount of technological unemployment has actually been very greatly overestimated.[12] In the printing trade, in which hand composition has been replaced by machines, and small presses by huge complicated rotary presses, the number of persons displaced has been relatively small. If an investigation were made also of the producers of materials, the persons now employed in distributing the products of these printing establishments, and all others to whom new jobs were granted indirectly, we should probably find more people now employed in preparing materials for paper, in making paper and other printing supplies, in the process of composition and printing, in the distribution of papers or books, and all other by-occupations, than were employed before.

A study of the age and sex of workers perhaps throws some light upon the question of unemployment. If we had figures of a century ago in cities, we probably should find as large a percentage of women and certainly children working then as now. Each census reports a somewhat larger percentage of women workers than the preceding, the increase from 1900 to 1930 being double, with a total in 1930 of ten and a half million. Many of these are married women, some of whose husbands are working, the increase in the number of married women since 1900 being twice as rapid as that of women in general. Studies by Miss Kyrk and others, however, seem to show that the number of these workers is much smaller than we have imagined and that they are not a major cause of unemployment for others.[13]

[11a] See Polokov, *The Power Age.*

[12] On technological unemployment Douglas and Director after a rather elaborate argument sum up as follows: "In the long run therefore the improvement in machinery in a given industry and the greater efficiency of management do not throw workers permanently out of employment nor create permanent technological unemployment. Instead they raise the national income and enable the level of earnings and of individual incomes to rise." *The Problem of Unemployment,* p. 141.

[13] The problem of employment and non-employment for women who have prepared for a profession is more than economic, it is an important personal and social problem in our present world. It enters into the probability of marriage and possibly into the success of marriage.

A pertinent question is this: Is the worker a victim of the Industrial Revolution as such, of individualism as a basis of business organization, of industrial capitalism as the modern phase of our economic and social order, or of what else? Attention has been concentrated on industrial capitalism from the standpoint of production and from the standpoint of financialism. To what extent is industrial capitalism directly or indirectly responsible for unemployment? Certainly workers are as skilled as formerly and are better educated. Probably there is less intemperance and more desire to maintain efficiency, if less industry, than in previous times. On the contrary, labor is less varied and diversified, and, being more specialized or technical, there is less possibility of shift from one job to another.

The Industrial Revolution certainly has been responsible for technological unemployment. It has also been responsible for thousands of new kinds of jobs and for distant contacts which were impossible under the pre-industrial conditions. Individualism coupled with industrial capitalism has placed the worker at a disadvantage in bargaining, and therefore possibly in getting and certainly in keeping the job. So far as individualism has expanded business, and through initiative increased opportunities for investing capital or creating new markets, it has probably helped as many workers as it has injured. From the standpoint of the worker, industrial capitalism has shown most of the faults and few of the merits of a technological age.

Advantage has been taken of freedom of contract and of large-scale organization to exploit all workers, except possibly those that are well organized. Organization of labor has been fought by law through a series of victories for the public and labor for more than a hundred years. It is difficult for many who praise and benefit by large-scale corporate business to realize that labor is as much entitled as capital to collective organization and legal protection. In gaining its ends labor uses methods that are underhanded and warlike, rather similar to some by which business crushed its way to success, but reprehensible in a socialized order.

After what we have suffered from "capital," must we pass through a corresponding period of "labor" dominance? A society organized by and for labor would be as unsocial as industrial capitalism, without the excuse, productivity, and the probable success. If the public does not allow labor to take its affairs in its own hands, it owes labor the square deal of a reorganized capitalistic system in which capital does not keep the spoils gained by methods now denied to labor. Particularly the worker should not suffer the disadvantages of industrial capitalism in depression, and it should not pay the price exacted through the dilemmas of both industrialism and capitalism.

Shall we have unemployment always with us?

A competitive, profit-making system is far less satisfactory from the employment angle than from the production point of view—and it fails in depression if not in prosperity as a going, productive concern. To secure recovery, all kinds of expedients have been used to provide employment, thereby hoping to increase purchasing power. "Busy" work has been offered as a means of relief, and it certainly is better than outright charity, although the work done is of little social or economic value. Public works are planned and speeded up on a large scale. The N. I. R. A.[13a] and other plans have spread employment, helping to get several million more workers on the payrolls; but the payrolls themselves did not increase as rapidly as the added number of workers. In other words, total income per worker was slightly lower in the fall of 1933 than in that of 1932, although a great amount of unemployment had been relieved.

If we get permanently out of the depression and no longer depend on emergency measures, how shall we get more regular employment on a more sensible basis than in the past? When the whole economic order starts to function again, normally as in the past, workers will be needed because there will be demand for the goods they produce or the services they render. But, if we allow ourselves to return to the business system we had before 1929, we shall always have some non-employment and much unfair payment of the majority of the

[13a] National Industrial Recovery Administration, pp. 233–244.

workers. The trouble lies chiefly in the fact that, in order to create profits, our economic system produces far below its capacity. It plans deliberately to keep supply less than demand, thereby increasing the price of each unit of the supply or product. Strange as it seems, the remedy may be found in speeding up our machine industry.

How is more production possible when our chief difficulty is over-production [14] and technological unemployment? The answer is illustrated by striking fact. In depression, men in the bread line found themselves knee-deep in wheat; and the only thing we seemed capable of doing was to sweep away the wheat. We know how to reduce the supply but not to use a surplus, much as that is needed. We have low wages and non-employment because payrolls, like profit, must come out of what we produce. We limit production when it should be increased for general welfare, because that is the only way we know of making profit. And in increasing profit we leave the workman holding the sack. We do more than that—by curtailing output, we reduce levels of living that might be raised and therefore lower standards of living. Our stupid civilization is stupid partly because we allow an outworn economics of scarcity to decide production in an age of plenty.[15] Machines and power and other forms of applied science have changed the face of the earth—or would if our business and other public leaders would let them.

Under our present set up we have unwisely reduced purchasing power much below its natural level, largely by our failure to equalize working loads. Consider only two things: (1) the working hours of machine workers and non-machine workers; (2) the pay or return of those who work with money compared with that of those who work with mind. A man who formerly used hand tools and now has a high-powered machine naturally turns out many times as many articles as formerly. As the *general* demand has increased only a little, his services, or those of his fellow workmen, may be needed

[14] In 1929 it was estimated that production was nearly 80 per cent of capacity. Nourse E. G. *et al, America's Capacity to Produce*, 164–170, 301–304.
[15] See IX, C.

three or four hours a day instead of ten. His wages, because of the great increase and value of his output, probably have gone up. Through luck he might seem in a position to command a much higher wage for much shorter hours, and he does if he can keep a job. In the meantime an associate, who does not use new machines or power, is expected by his employer somehow to increase his output. To do that he carries a heavier load, usually for the same number of hours as formerly, and at the same wage as before. His level of living has been improved by the cheaper goods of his machine-working friend but, relatively and actually, he is less well paid than formerly because he must try to meet his friend's competition—and it can't be done.

The first remedy we must apply to the production system—from the standpoint of workers—is to have all workers—and consumers and society—share *directly* and *fully* in the *gains* of new improvements in production. *All* wages must come out of production or income; only in depression would we think of trying to pay workers, on a large scale, temporarily out of capital. When any industry, or all industry in general, has found new means of increasing output without increased costs, it has kept for its financial supporters, for its managers, and for its employees who were not discharged, most of these advantages. It may seem Utopian to expect these industries to share their gains with the rest of the nation, or nations. They have not always done it, or done it very much, and they are paying the price because the workers outside their industry, or all industry, cannot buy their products. It would be just to pay all workers the same for similar hours and effort. Under competition, in a society less dynamic than ours, that has happened more or less, at least after a generation. Until business arranges equalized pay and loads, it will suffer repeated and constantly recurring losses, for it has not discovered the necessity of sharing its improvements with those who buy its goods.

The farmer and his help have been worked hard, if not so hard as in pioneer days, at a third the compensation that the machine worker has commanded. It is a pity, if the *govern-*

ment must step in and insist that equal pay shall go with equal work.

The unwisdom of our present scheme of things is shown by comparing the pay, reward, or return of those who work with money and those who work with mind. A lawyer's fee depends far more on his client's ability to pay than on the real value of his legal advice. Naturally, when his suggestion about getting ahead of the law nets his client a million dollars, he can charge well for his services. The big banker who persuaded, or forced, his affiliated companies or clients to take over dubious securities could claim a large slice of profits for his honored name. The broker, dealing in speculative stocks in 1928, despised the hard-working secretary. The one whose services were socially most valuable did not make a tithe of the other's commissions. Teaching loads kept increasing because industrial capitalism was unwilling to share with the schools the enormous profits of capitalistic, machine industry. By setting money-snatchers to work productively and lowering the loads of the millions of brain workers, there would be a great spread of employment. And there should be plenty of income for every one if we do not limit production to increase profit.

The solution cannot be worked out in depression. Nor can it be applied after recovery if both recovery or reconstruction proceed along the same old lines. We have not only reduced income and wealth in our search of profit, but we have destroyed purchasing power in order to pile up surplus for the elect. We need more production, not less. In order that increased wage income should not be taken out of industrial-capitalist surplus, a speeding up of productive industry is necessary. We must have a smaller share for those who personally contribute little, and less burden in paying public expenses for those who work for wage or salary. No one employer or industry could expect, working separately, to get these results. Public and business would need to work together, coöperating and coördinating on a huge scale, with much saner and more socialized purposes in mind than industry has been willing to attempt. If the unemployment problem could be solved in this way, industrialism would escape other penalties than non-employment, involved in her present dilemma. More purchasing power, greater demand, higher prices: once we regain these and keep them steadily rising, the economic machine will work more smoothly and efficiently than ever before. Now business is losing for fear others may gain.

Acute as the unemployment evil is, Americans have been slowest among all civilized peoples in accepting public responsibility or in devising general methods to remedy the fault. One reason has been the relatively high wages of American workers, with the possibility of some savings out of the normal wage. A second reason undoubtedly has been the relatively limited supply of American labor, because we have needed workers to develop almost limitless natural resources and to utilize great amounts of available capital. Yet, without further improvements in technology, it is probably possible for American industry, with all factors working at average speed and all workers employed for an eight to ten hour day, to produce twice as many goods as either the domestic or foreign market can absorb under present conditions. Both capital and the public are facing this serious problem of guaranteeing to every willing and capable worker not a living wage, but an opportunity to earn a living.

Capitalism, trained in individualism, harks back to an outworn economy in which the employer hired and discharged whom and when he wished, because both the capital and the business were his. This is no longer true of large corporations. The resources utilized, regardless of ownership, are frequently in essence public resources, although the people's legal title may long since have lapsed. The capital furnished, by the purchase of stock or of bonds, equally represents a pooling of funds of the public. The captain of industry is more trustee than owner. Even if he were exclusively owner, the worker, the employe, is no wage slave but a human being, usually "free, white, and twenty-one."

Europe with her teeming millions and limited capital has been compelled to find a way, and even in individualist England it has taken the form of state insurance. Germany made more initial progress, but the best example of European benefit during unemployment is Great Britain. Soon after the opening of the twentieth century England tried an experimental scheme of insuring about two million people in the seasonal industries. This plan has gradually been extended so that in most occupations the men, women, and children make weekly contributions which are nearly doubled by the state and more than equalled by the employer. Out of these funds, those who are out of work and have made an honest effort to secure employment may get a weekly benefit with a maximum of seventeen shillings, provided they have made a certain number of contributions in previous years, are in businesses that could possibly provide employment, and have not recently been idlers or beneficiaries of public charity. By the joint use of reëmployment bureaus and placement bureaus unemployment in England has been reduced.

A great deal of ignorance has existed regarding the English "dole," which really did not exist until depression grew very bad. Criticisms have been leveled at it by those who have not taken the trouble to understand its purpose or its character. Any system of that type is subject to abuses, but its careful administration is shown by the fact that nearly a half-million claims of unemployed persons were rejected in 1925, a fairly typical year. In 1929, fewer than a million workers were supplied with definite benefits under these stated and previously understood conditions. How much better than the situation existing a century ago, when fifty thousand of the three-hundred thousand workers in London depended winter after winter for food upon the charity soup kitchens! Of this insurance system Douglas and Director state: "None but a person with a strong class bias has accused unemployment insurance as fostering a distaste for work and a preference for benefits among British workers. . . . But there are some grounds for believing that the insurance system strengthens the resistance of the trade unions against wage cuts which might otherwise take place and reduce the volume of unemployment, and that the payment of benefits for partial unemployment tends to increase the practice of it."[16]

From the standpoint of capitalism the English system is tentative and experimental, but it involves two or three principles which probably will enter into the necessary attempt to solve this world-wide problem. If no solution is found for unemployment, capitalism will discover that this problem will take first place in our economic world. If capitalism fails voluntarily and collectively to accept the solution of unemployment as its job, the public will necessarily step in and take control. Even though most of our active wealth and a very considerable part of our industry, transportation and trade, and banking are now dominated by a single group of business men, it is doubtful whether, regardless of their desire, it would be possible for them to work out and put into effect a scheme which would insure work for every man, or when that is impossible an adequate income. *Evidently the responsibility is either theirs or it is a public and a social one.* But it must probably be exercised through business because if it is not done through business, it must be completed directly by government. But if government *must* do that, it must be allowed also to have a "say" in the partial employment furnished by business. Socially no part of society can take what it likes, when it likes, and make the public do the rest and foot the bill. That is too much "heads I win, tails you lose." In all history only modern business has ever imagined a possible escape of the economic order from this obligation. Because the modern world has given workers freedom and has added welfare to the vocabulary of its obligation, it has not freed the wealth-owning and employing class from a responsibility which was accepted by the land-owning aristocrat, feudal lord of the manor, and even the slave owner.

The problem which we must work out is not so much whether capitalism shall be held to this duty but rather how public and employer and employe shall make the thing workable. Free public but compulsory education, analogous to this necessary public guarantee of employment for all who

[16] Douglas and Director, *The Problem of Unemployment*, p. 425.

want work, should coöperate not only in preparing workers but also in explaining conditions and in making clear the problem. This is part of a very much larger problem. As we shall see,[17] semi-starvation or under-nourishment is the lot of most of mankind if not of many in civilized countries. If we turn over to industrial capitalism the task of producing and distributing goods; even more, if it arrogates that task to itself, must it not accept this responsibility, that humanity shall be kept busy, at useful and regular work, and shall have a chance to provide itself with necessary food, on a self-respecting basis?

The plight of the worker has been discussed almost solely from the standpoint of necessary work and income for all employables. It is much more than that; and the public's interest in other phases of the worker's problem may be very important. At least we should keep in mind the right of bargaining, and the rights of labor, with the limitation of its rights, in industrial disputes. In examining these subjects we should not make the mistake of treating them solely from the standpoint of the worker. If it takes two to make a bargain or to start a quarrel, in this day and age the two parties, capital and labor, may not do as they please if their actions, or the acts of either, are anti-social or contrary to the public good. In these problems, as in those considered at length, we must never lose sight of the necessary interdependence of labor, business and the public.

THE PLIGHT OF THE CONSUMER

The plight of the consumer is real. Unquestionably, more than half of all American farmers for the last ten or fifteen years have found their selling dollars quite inadequate to cover even their most essential needs. In ordinary times some workers are always unemployed and millions of others have barely a living wage. In depression several million casual laborers and a large number of real workers, unemployed, suffer even greater disability because their income, frequently for months on end, is actually *nil*. It is not the

The place and the dilemma of the consumer

[17] Pp. 420–424.

agricultural victims of industrial advance, however, or the occasional prosperity sufferers, and far more than occasional depression victims, whose plight needs special attention, although these farmers and workers with low or no incomes add just that much to the plight of the consumer in general. The day of "consumer tribute" should be over.

Like industrialism and financialism the consuming public has a dilemma. Possibly it would be more accurate to say that the dilemma of the consumer is a vital part of the dilemma of industrialism.[18] Industrialism would not worry half so much if it could speed up industry and sell its goods. The consumer's dilemma, the other side of that, would quickly disappear if he could purchase more and cheaper goods, not at the peaks of prosperity, but continually. Mass production augments the dilemma of the industrialist because the production increases so rapidly that it becomes impossible to sell all the goods produced. The dilemma of the consumer grows out of the fact that mass consumption is not one of the successful technics of a technological civilization. The answer would seem simple, namely, that whatever is produced, if produced with an eye to the demand, could and would be taken over by the consumer. If all consumers shared in the benefits of improvements in technology and even the average worker, not alone highly unionized labor in industry, benefited by an increase of wages or income or purchasing power, possibly and probably mass consumption would not have lagged so woefully behind mass production.

The whole problem brings us back to the poor circulation of wealth [19] in a society bristling with maladjustments between the old habits and the new techniques. Poor distribution and unwise legislation are but single items in the catalog of difficulties. Even acute depression following spendthrift speculation is not the real problem. If the industrial-capitalist machine slows down a little, some parts of the machinery threaten to stop altogether; and then the whole machine hesitates and works spasmodically. It would seem as though a decrease of

[18] Pp. 129–131.
[19] Pp. 166–167.

work and wages by one-quarter would give us three-quarters the business activity we had before. Some statistically minded person has figured out, for one small community, that this one-quarter cut for all workers in the village reduced business much more than one-quarter. Those from whom the workers purchased groceries or clothing suffered more than a quarter reduction in business. They in turn purchased not three-quarters as much as formerly but a smaller amount. By the time we reached the dependents or sellers four removes from the original worker we find the business of the community less than half of what it was. An examination of statistics for the years 1930 to 1932 serves to bear out these conclusions, although possibly not to that extent.

The hope of permanent recovery lies in the opposite of this progressive slowing-down process; it consists of a cumulative speeding-up process. Instead of the twenty-five per cent cut, with its fifty or sixty per cent effect on the business of the community, a twenty-five per cent addition to purchasing power would multiply itself according to the series of successive purchases it made possible. Just as "nothing succeeds like success," so nothing stimulates circulation of wealth like more and more circulation of wealth. The process is not simply continuous; it is cumulative. The problem is first to keep the upgrade moderate but unceasing. That can only be done by stabilizing business, limiting its heights and if possible avoiding its depths. To do that means better distribution of the product, that is, allocation of their share of the total production of society to worker, farmer, and others as consumer income. It means more fundamental changes, as limitation of excessive profits and the avoidance of unnecessary and concentrated accumulations of capital.

In the earlier part of the Roosevelt Recovery Program special stress was placed upon an increase of purchasing power as the chief means of reviving business. Later, public employment, either emergency or on public works, was characterized as "priming the pump" so that permanently a flow of life-giving wealth would continue if not remain steady. This well-meant and rather successfully directed effort did

Public protection for the consumer

stimulate buying, especially in the summer of 1933. But an examination of the figures for the summer of 1934 shows a greater increase in prices than of purchasing power of the consumer. In one of President Roosevelt's earlier heart-to-heart talks, he drew attention to a five-cent processing tax that was excuse for a two-dollar increase in the price of a cotton shirt. This secondary purpose of recovery, of restoring if possible and as soon as possible the price level of 1926, seemed therefore to defeat the primary object of giving work and making general consumption more easily possible. The vicious circle still pursues us: purchasing power is only income, and income must come out of production; production may increase simply by having a greater quantity, but we ordinarily measure it not in units of goods, but in the prices those goods command. Certainly the last estate of that recovery scheme did not seem much better than the first, particularly as the percentage of recovery in most lines in America was not much greater than that attained during these same months in Canada, in Great Britain, and even in Germany.[20]

The attempt to aid the consumer by government action brings up the question: Can that be done without depriving the buyer of his age-old right to protect his interest by bargaining? If we substitute public control of business for capitalistic, shall we not limit what little competition is left, including that between seller and buyer? Will the public protection of the consumer be as valuable to him as his own bargaining power has been? Walton H. Hamilton, working with the Consumers' Advisory Board of the N. R. A. declares: "In a shift from the market to a board as the agency of price-making, the problem of the consumer is simple and clear-cut. He cannot afford to barter the safeguards which he possesses under competitive arrangements for less than an equivalent. He is one of two parties to a bargain about the production and sale of goods. He has enjoyed, and should possess, equal authority with the seller in determining the conditions of sale. To accept less than this would be the sacrifice of a right

[20] Pp. 198–199.

which it has been the intent of public policy to invest in the consumer." [21]

In this brief summary it is impossible to consider even in a fragmentary way the difficulties which the consumer has in getting his money's worth. The Pure Food and Drugs Acts passed by the national government and the states have sought to protect the buyer from injurious and poisonous foods and drugs. They may not afford this protection for the reason that penalties are placed upon manufacturers only in case the goods are misbranded; and in administration of the law misbranding must be serious indeed before penalty is assessed. The American Medical Association has brought to public attention large numbers of near-drugs in which the consumer gets very little of the drug or antiseptic desired, at a price many times that which should be charged. The National Bureau of Standards has done wonderful work in protecting Uncle Sam, and other government agencies which make use of the research of the Bureau, from buying goods at a cost out of all proportion to their value. Consumer's Research Inc. has grown powerful during the depression and has simplified for millions choices between different brands or articles. The "best may be the cheapest" but the highest priced is often far from the best. Some other organizations have also added their suggestions. Magazines and books have been written for the express purpose of giving consumers some idea of the merits of competing goods.

Evidently one of the greatest needs is to reverse the old saying, "caveat emptor," [22] and place the responsibility and burden of proof where they belong today, making the term "caveat vendor." [23] In our present complex society the buyer cannot possibly know the respective merits of competing types of radio, or brands of breakfast food, or of silk and woolen goods. Particularly is this the case in these days of miracle cotton. This wonderful product, "made in America," is first of all used for infinite varieties of cotton goods. It

[21] From Walton H. Hamilton's article on "Consumer Interest in Price-fixing" in the *Survey Graphic*, February, 1934, p. 80.
[22] Let the buyer beware.
[23] Let the seller beware.

may be the chief ingredient of linen handkerchiefs. Mercerize it and it produces silk stockings. Camouflage it and it reappears as woolen cloth. Add a few chemicals and it becomes gun cotton, a high explosive. Crush its seed and lo, "olive oil" is the result, or something sold as a substitute for that. Advertisers who sell rayon or cotton as pure silk, who advertise, but of course do not label, applesauce with a little coloring and flavoring as expensive jelly, naturally can delude a public which is ignorant of the contents of the goods purchased.

Consumption
à la mode

In determining the folly of the consumer and removable faults in consumption, the psychology of the consumer must always be taken into account. This is capitalized by the seller in installment buying, by virtue of the small sacrifice needed to acquire an article very much desired until the collector keeps coming, when it is too late to change. High pressure salesmanship goes a long way toward stimulating as well as using this desire side of human nature. Human weakness is played up in the rivalry shown not in neighborhoods only, but between friends or acquaintances at a distance. This is especially valuable in the whole field in which demand is exceedingly flexible, as in high-priced household ornaments, fine clothing, up-to-date autos, not to mention summer cottages, steam yachts and other necessities. Many a person has told the writer at holiday season that he would have abandoned the sending of Christmas cards but for the fear he would lose social prestige by failing to do what his friends did. An especial appeal to cupidity is offered by the numerous sales, most of which on bargain days are misleading because goods are not offered much below regular prices. Under the pressure of mob competition purchasers usually go away with things they would never have bought in soberer moments.

The consumer would like to blame his plight upon the system rather than upon himself. In considering his alibi we should take into account several items in the consumption program. A family with growing daughters or ambitious sons wishes to live in a good neighborhood, and many former luxuries become social necessities because of neighbor's real or supposed standards of living. There is nothing new about "keeping up with the Joneses." Three generations ago William Allen Butler aroused sympathy for "Miss Flora Mc-Flimsey of Madison Square," with "nothing to wear." And Oliver Wendell Holmes, Sr., asked for little "here below," "a brown stone front," for example.

It is an interesting and curious fact that although the percentage of income [24] spent by families on food, and to a lesser degree, clothing, decreases with a real increase of income, the amount spent for housing remains either constant or increases until the income reaches five figures.[25] The more expensive the home, the greater the probability of a very high percentage of deferred payment. The plight of home-buyers who purchased before 1929 and had to make payments during the early thirties was pitiable; Washington was called on for relief for homes worth up to twenty thousand dollars. Counting only personal or household goods of a moveable character, installment buying amounted to more than seven million dollars at the time of the stock panic.

"The consumer's case against the modern market can be summed up thus: (1) It provides no source of reliable information about new discoveries. The average consumer readily confuses violet ray generators with ultra-violet ray generators, and knows nothing accurate about the value of either. As inventions increase in number and complexity, the ignorance of consumers becomes relatively greater. (2) It centers increasing attention upon style as distinct from

[24] Pp. 483–485.
[25] The amount spent for food in the years before 1929 was probably in the neighborhood of twenty billion dollars a year. Figures given by Lynd in *Recent Social Trends* (p. 889) are 17 billions; by Doane in *Measurement of American Wealth* (p. 73), quite a little above 20 billions. Doane's figures for housing are but little lower than for food, although Lynd's are but 8 billion. Clothing in Doane's scale was between 8 and 9 billions, about the same as Lynd's. Transportation, Lynd gives at 8½ billions, Doane at more than 13. Doane's figures for everything including government amount to practically 90 billions, whereas Lynd's figures amount to 73.3 billions (p. 889, *R.S.T.*). As the national income for that year has been usually computed at about 85 billions, out of which Doane admits (p. 123) that more than 19 billions were saved, it probably is better to make use of Lynd's figures than of the other.

serviceability, creating an artificial obsolescence in household fixtures and durable equipment no less than in clothes, producing a profound dissatisfaction with whatever the consumer has already acquired. (3) It floods the market with untested devices of all sorts, with novelties and doodads that use up the consumer's purchasing power without giving him anything substantial in return, and in some cases with downright quackeries. (4) It creates psychological values which are more and more divorced from the physical requirements of comfortable living, and which make these harder to attain. (5) It is driving unadvertised articles out of the market even though many of them may be cheaper than their advertised equivalents and some of them more nearly standardized and uniform in quality. (6) It cultivates impulsive and emotional buying, making the use of reasonable comparison practically impossible for the ignorant and *démodé* for the more sophisticated." [26]

A word about coöperative consumer organizations. They are few and far between in America, possibly because of our individualistic attitudes and partly because nature has given us fair incomes during most periods. Consumer coöperation, however, has made some progress in the United States, although not nearly so much as in England, and far less than in Sweden and Denmark. As already suggested, Scandinavian democracy may easily be traceable to coöperative attempts to protect consumers and give them a real voice in the conduct of affairs, general if not public. Possibly Scandinavian experience in consumer-controlled production and capitalism may point the way toward an economic reorganization that is just what America wants. Beginning in 1931 Sweden tried stabilizing currency in relation to consumer prices, with a marked degree of success.

It may be that the consumer, like the farmer, is a victim of our technological civilization for the excellent reason that the people who do most of the buying have not been getting their share of new wealth and income—that industrial advance has been too busy making gains and has therefore for-

[26] Atkins, W. E. *et al, Economic Behavior,* Houghton, Mifflin Co., II, p. 27.

gotten both the farmer, as producer, and the consumer.[27] The consumer will be benefited without doubt if he is free from high-pressure salesmanship, free from production of diverse and inexcusably costly goods made to attract the eye or appeal to pride, and if his income can be kept steadily increasing. Wastes in buying are probably much more serious than wastes in manufacturing. Possibly even the extraordinary sums paid for the rather unproductive work of middlemen are less of a loss than faulty and unwise buying. Although the large number of middlemen takes up the slack of the unemployed, what would happen if most of these were put into productive industry or into other productive work?

Some obvious and inexcusable burdens are placed upon the ordinary consumer which ought not to be part of his load in a modern sensible civilization. Perhaps the greatest of these is the burden of consumer taxation. Curiously enough, most of the new and "best" taxes are consumer laws—the gasoline tax and the sales tax. The one would not be so bad except that its use does not relieve the general burden upon the taxpayer, being spent too exclusively on roads used by the buyers of gasoline. The other, however, hits hardest those least able to pay, like any other tax on consumption, even though expenditure is income in reverse. A second inexcusable burden is the high cost of debt. Prosperity may come and prosperity may go, but interest payments and foreclosures go on forever. Notice, for example, how constant was the amount paid out in interest in 1932 compared with the years before 1929, a reduction of only three per cent, whereas all other expenditures were practically reduced to half.

Recovery in Relation to Reorganization

The distress of these three groups was reason as well as excuse for the "New Deal," which was the outstanding characteristic of President Roosevelt's first two years. The legislative program included more than a score of acts, usually with a two-year limit, providing relief, temporary remedies, or experimental plans. In this sketch there is no desire to

[27] Pp. 129–136, 248–251.

examine or analyze these measures or consider the administrative procedure by which the plight of these classes or others was relieved. We need ask ourselves only three or four questions. First, what was the general nature of the "New Deal"? Second, what were the purposes of the Roosevelt Recovery Program, including the temporary relief measures? Third, what were the policies suggested? And fourth, what were some failures and successes of the N. R. A. (National Recovery Administration)?

Recovery and reconstruction

The problem made clear by prosperity and depression need not be reëxamined, although an historical introduction from this angle would be very helpful in understanding what President Roosevelt and the "brain trust" tried to do. We have already noticed some characteristics of the "New Era" or period of prosperity from 1922–29. Under the Dilemma of Industrialism and the Dilemma of Financialism we have also considered some of the lessons prosperity should have taught, and have tried to make clear the menace which would be involved in the possible return of the "New Era" type of prosperity. The world's greatest depression has been considered from a number of angles although no study of successive phases in its development has been made, either for its understanding or as the basis of the "New Deal" policies. Probably we should consider the question of whether from the standpoint of 1932 recovery or reconstruction had priority. In 1932 that was important. Was reconstruction possible in a subnormal period? If we gained recovery without reconstruction, how was our situation different from what we had before 1929?

Recovery seemed the first thing, but a recovery without some plans for reorganization of our economic and social system would have placed Roosevelt with Coolidge as the man of the lost opportunity.[28] Only time can render a verdict on the degree of success of the N. R. A. As a skillfully planned and practical attempt to get out of depression and

[28] Reconstruction during prosperity would have avoided many of the ills we had after 1929.

get out on the right side, it must be recognized as a valiant experiment of a high order.

The real problem confronting Washington was not the priority of recovery or reconstruction, not even the constitutionality of the N. R. A., but the extent to which the recovery program should be purely or chiefly for recovery or only incidentally for recovery but largely for reorganization. The answer to that will be apparent from the brief discussion of purposes and policies given later.

Sweeping and comprehensive the recovery program of 1933 seemed to be. Those Rip Van Winkles who thought in terms of unlimited competition waked up to a scene totally dissimilar from that of pre-slumber days. Price-fixing for many industries, with some price-boosts for agriculture, minimum wage-scales, and maximum hour schedules savored of nth degree paternalism. Coercion may have been the last desire of President Roosevelt and General Johnson; but a new world seemed to spring into being when each industry developed trade associations and became a semi-monopoly, with the consent of the governed. Was the government of 1933–35 more of a partner than it was in the do-nothing days before 1929?

More specifically, did the Roosevelt Program avoid the pitfalls of past government mistakes, failures, or limitations? Was corporation business, created and directed under authority of the states, legally and actually made responsible to the American people through the national government? Did the farmer get a square as well as a new deal? Did labor find work as well as safeguards? Were savings and investments really made safe? Were the real dilemmas of either industrialism or financialism reached? So far as these queries call for reorganization, the answer is "no," for the program was chiefly of recovery, if not solely for that purpose.

Fairness limits us to the first of the questions above. It seemed right that the public should be considered in industry for a change. It seemed fair that business which is interstate or on a national scale should look to Uncle Sam for regulation, as the railways have done since the Shreveport

and Wisconsin decisions.[29] National creation of national corporations, with control by the national authorities, seems
inevitable in a country of wide-spread markets and concentrated business. A "New Deal" should not be an opportunity for deserving partisans or for political favoritism
to friendly mergers or banks. With horror some looked upon
the plan as an excuse for a group of threatened politico-economic monopolies to become government-approved trade associations.

Money, credit and banking present a different group of
problems from those found in industry and labor. The United
States has been trying to do what the Macmillan report urged
in England some years ago—raise prices to a level that will
lighten the burden of debt and quicken market transactions. For debtor relief the President quickly let us slide off
the gold standard, and Congress suspended the operation of
the clauses in bonds or mortgages that obligations be paid in
gold. Congress and some state legislatures tried to stop fore-
closures and to aid refinancing of mortgage-burdened homes
and farms. The Recovery Program thus sought chiefly recovery. Although it placed very severe restrictions on exploitation of an investing public, it did not go, and probably
could not go, to the heart of the dilemma of financialism.

The Roose-
velt Recovery
Program as
relief
One of the darkest hours in the history of the American
people was that late winter period of 1932–33 when the banks
seemed to be going to pieces, and, in spite of the upward
trend already observable in business, fear and discouragement
obsessed the American mind. To one reading now Roosevelt's *Looking Forward,* we can see in his campaign speeches
the suggestion of a large number of the measures or
remedies which he believed should be applied to bring the
depressed American public back to health. The inaugural
address radiated cheer and optimism; at once the psychological attitude of the American people changed. Fear gave place
to faith, and discouragement to hope. Even the closing of

[29] Under the N. I. R. A. an individual corporation that competed unfairly,
profiteered, or otherwise injured its field of business or harmed society,
might be licensed by the national authorities. This license might be cancelled when anti-social practices were used.

every bank in America for a few days did not seem to dampen the ardor with which the people seemed ready to rally in support of the President and his program. The purposes of the Roosevelt Recovery Program might be explained by citing the provisions of some of these acts. For example, the Agricultural Adjustment Act of May 12, 1933, provided:

It is hereby declared to be the policy of Congress—
    (1) To establish and maintain such balance between the production and consumption of agricultural commodities, and such marketing conditions therefor, as will reëstablish prices to farmers at a level that will give agricultural commodities a purchasing power with respect to articles that farmers buy, equivalent to the purchasing power of agricultural commodities in the base period. The base period in the case of all agricultural commodities except tobacco shall be the prewar period of August 1909–July 1914.

The National Industrial Recovery Act Declaration of Policy was as follows:

Sec. 1. A national emergency productive of widespread unemployment and disorganization of industry, which burdens interstate and foreign commerce, affects the public welfare, and undermines the standards of living of the American people is hereby declared to exist. It is hereby declared to be the policy of Congress to remove obstructions to the free flow of interstate and foreign commerce which tend to diminish the amount thereof; and to provide for the general welfare by promoting the organization of industry for the purpose of coöperative action among trade groups, to induce and maintain united action of labor and management under adequate governmental sanctions and supervision, to eliminate unfair competitive practices, to promote the fullest possible utilization of the present productive capacity of industries, to avoid undue restriction of production (except as may be temporarily required), to increase the consumption of industrial and agricultural products by increasing purchasing power, to reduce and relieve unemployment, to improve standards of labor, and otherwise to rehabilitate industry and to conserve natural resources.

From the statements of purposes given therefore we can see that the aim of the government at Washington was first to give *relief to the workers, the farmers, and the consumers* whose plight we have just examined. Since part of the farm problem was connected with debts and the attempted fore-closures of mortgages, an important cause of agricultural dis-tress for the farmer in addition to home-owners, emergency measures were passed in order to try to save homes and farms. The A. A. A. (Agricultural Adjustment Administra-tion) was the most important of the farm relief organizations. Its object was purely temporary and its economics was of the least desirable scarcity variety. For a number of agricultural products the acreage was to be reduced or the supply to be arbitrarily limited. For the farmers who coöperated, the A. A. A. by processing taxes both raised the price of the wheat, corn or cotton and rewarded the agriculturalists who helped keep the supply down in amount.

Part of the Recovery Act was the provision for a huge *pub-lic works* program. The express purpose of this measure was employment for those whose jobs had been missing since local public works improvements had been discontinued in 1929 and 1930. Temporary employment was given by the C. C. C. (Civilian Conservation Corps), by the C. W. A. (Civil Works Administration), a temporary but remarkable employment ex-periment that reached four millions of the able-bodied unem-ployed, both skilled and unskilled. The relief was real, though too often the results gave point to the quip about "manicuring the roads." Through the payment from the pub-lic treasury of these emergency workers, through the shorten-ing of hours in many businesses, and through the actual if not rapid improvement in business, the number permanently un-employed was reduced from the neighborhood of fifteen mil-lions to not more than six or eight millions. The relief granted apparently was very much greater than the new pur-chasing power created, possibly and probably because the purchasing power was applied in business which had not been hit hardest by the depression.

If much space is devoted here to the *consumer,* he will have a far greater amount of attention than that he was actually able to get under the N. R. A. This was in no way the fault of the planners of recovery policies or of the able people in charge of the consumer groups. The fault lies first in the fact that the consumer was not properly or adequately represented in the boards that did the work. It lies very much more in the fact that the American consumer is not organized, does not know his problem or his needs well enough. The problem is due even more to the fact that we cannot start with the consumer even though his wants are the basis of all sales, and the sales are of goods produced to satisfy his needs. In the summer of 1933 the consumer found that his plight in recovery was just as great as it had been in depression and in prosperity. Apparently society must do something about it.

The N. I. R. A., although only a part of a statute, was by all odds the outstanding feature of the Roosevelt Recovery Program. An important purpose of N. I. R. A. was remedy for the ills of labor. When the law was proposed, Congress, which had already passed through the Senate the Black Act providing for a thirty-hour week in industry, immediately substituted for that the labor provisions of the N. I. R. A. statute. However, we must not lose sight of the fact that the National Industrial Recovery Act was passed almost as much at the suggestion of big business, which wished to get rid of the anti-trust laws, as it was for the benefit of labor.

Industrial and financial programs

The Act provided for the organization of *codes of fair competition* which should be made by associations truly representative of the business for which the code was prepared.[30] After the code had been made, possibly with the coöperation of General Johnson's staff in Washington, the approval of the President was necessary. In the codes and in the President's

---

[30] In the making of the codes, nearly a thousand of which were suggested and several hundred made, the first problem was to get a group actually representing the industry or business. The two hundred national trade associations grew to four hundred. An attempt was made to see that the representatives really indirectly represented at least half of the firms engaged and doing a still larger part of the business in that field, measured in dollars. For a long time those businesses that did not have codes of their own were brought under the President's reëmployment agreement, or the blanket code.

Reëmployment agreement, the thirty-hour week was abandoned for a thirty-five-hour week for laborers and skilled mechanics and a forty-hour week in clerical and commercial positions. The reduction in hours was intended largely for the purpose of spreading employment, although it frequently resulted chiefly in an increase of load per hour. Another provision of the blanket code and of most of the other codes was a minimum wage per hour or week, since modified or abandoned. The basic minimum was thirty cents per hour but attempt was made to limit that to as few industries as possible and to make forty cents per hour, or twelve dollars per week, the minimum. The minimum was higher than this in cities. The whole code structure was swept away by the Supreme Court by a unanimous decision in the Schechter case (1935) because the codes were not made by Congress, and because they dealt with powers of the states.

In order that labor might not be deprived of its long-standing right to bargain for better wages, a right which had been used successfully only by well organized labor, clause 7a of the codes provided for *collective bargaining* by unions that were neither organized by the company nor dominated by the government. The right of collective bargaining gave to very many labor groups a desire to secure by concerted action higher wages than the law prescribed as the low level. Probably no period in our history saw so many strikes as took place just after the application of the N. I. R. A. codes. Probably no period in American history, considering how subnormal business still was at that time, gave labor a squarer deal than it received under this arrangement and subsequent laws.[31]

Under the codes *business was permitted to combine, concentrate, or at least work concertedly* as never before in American experience. To a great many this substitution of

[31] In the opinion of many the high wages and shorter week prescribed by the code became a burden which made continuance in business impossible. For others, looking forward to a possible return of prosperity, this drag of public interference spoiled any desirable drive forward to make business normal. Why regain prosperity if the enterpriser's share was cut so sharply? Why not wait until more favorable opportunity arose?

concentrated action for competition made probable a degree of monopoly which, under other conditions at Washington, might threaten the safety as well as the welfare of the dependent classes or businesses in the United States. Naturally the advantage in code making and administration was with the large, well organized industries rather than with their smaller competitors. The reports of the Darrow Committee, incomplete and possibly distorted, called attention to what the little fellow was not getting out of code administration. Considering the propaganda methods and patriotic appeals for the support of the "blue eagle," business was disappointed at the slowness of improvement. The worker, the consumer, and the farmer expected considerably more than they received.

Financial regulation was almost as much a part of the N. R. A. as was labor protection and business stimulation. The epoch-making series of statutes passed by the special session of Congress that met March 9, 1933, started with an emergency finance law and ended with the Bank Act of 1933. A primary object of financial legislation was the safeguarding of investments. The Securities Act made promoter and sellers responsible for misstatements about any of the stocks or bonds they sold. More than twenty years ago the Pujo Committee had shown the character of many investments and the way investment bankers use other people's money.[32] Reports [33] of the Industrial Commission years before, of the I. C. C. (The Interstate Commerce Commission), of the Federal Trade Commission [34] and of Senate committees, particularly that of 1933, showed ways in which the public had been persuaded to purchase securities at a price far above their value. As much of this exploitation had been supplemented by further shearing of the lambs on Wall Street, the Stock Market Act sought to end the worst of the anti-social practices of the stock exchange. These laws limited for a time new forms of credit and active trading on 'change. As American busi-

[32] See Brandeis, *Other People's Money.*
[33] Extracts from some of these reports are given in Flügel and Faulkner, *Readings in the Economic and Social History of the United States*, ch. XIV.
[34] Thompson, *Confessions of the Power Trust*, gathers evidence on ways the electric power companies operated against the public interest.

ness follows the stock market even more than stocks reflect business, this legislation retarded rather than promoted recovery. It proved further that the New Deal sought reorganization rather than courted recovery at any cost.

A real attempt was made to raise prices and thus both promote recovery and stabilize business on new levels. One law repealed the gold clause in all contracts.[35] A series of laws or administrative measures took us off the gold standard, raised the government price of gold from $20.68 an ounce to $35.00, provided for more currency, and arranged for a maximum of twenty-five per cent of silver in the government's cash reserves. Temporarily bank deposits were guaranteed.

Under the new safeguards savings should be safer, if human folly in investment does not reach too high a level; and both debtors and creditors will gain if interest can be paid and foreclosure avoided. A cheaper dollar and easier credit should postpone the submergence of the social order by the rising sea of surplus capital. Unless too many of us, and politicians, and juries, representing the old American psychology, interfere, producer and consumer may reduce financial influence in our economic system. Probably any more drastic reorganization might have defeated the purposes and blocked the success of the Recovery Program.

For the relief of distressed business, in 1932 the Reconstruction Finance Corporation had been organized, being in a way a revival of the post-war organization. Before the Roosevelt inauguration this body had loaned almost two billions of dollars, chiefly to banks and railroads. Under the Roosevelt administration the amount was increased until Uncle Sam looked almost like a trustee of some corporations. Supplementing the loans of R. F. C. were those authorized under relief for farmers and other debtors. The Home Loan Board, organized under President Hoover, was supplemented by the act of June 13, 1933. The Farm Credit Act provided aid in the refinancing of farm mortgages, not by the government but with some public guarantees. Debt-ridden corpora-

---

[35] That is, if a contract provided for payment in gold dollars, currency must be accepted as substitute.

tions and farmers obtained relief if creditors representing two-thirds of a debtor's obligations were able to agree on what should be paid.

Not only did Congress and the Administration aid the farmer distressed with debt, but the state legislatures also passed numerous relief measures postponing foreclosure and other drastic collection of matured debt. As an emergency measure the Minnesota mortgage law was upheld by the United States Supreme Court by a vote of six to three. Most provisions of the National Recovery Acts failed to come before the United States Supreme Court, and the question therefore of their constitutionality probably will never be determined because of the time limit of the spring of 1935.

Did the Roosevelt Program succeed? Did the needed integration of public, government, and business take place? Possibly its success or non-success depended on our ability to administer the projects we planned. Even the most braggart Americans must admit that government administration is nothing to boast about. The heritage of individualism survives in the American demand that the people be let alone, even though they be condemned in the process. Consequently administration is admittedly the weakest part of our public system. By an excess of legislation and boosting we camouflage our failures in law enforcement and law observance. What do we need to help us temporarily—without experience as we are in the best organization and procedure in administration of public affairs? It took the Interstate Commerce Commission twenty years to gain the power or learn the technique of regulating the railroads. And the plight of the rails now looks as though the job has not been done well yet! Until we can get coöperation of all the related bureaus or departments that must tackle the same problem, or almost as necessary coördination between the courts and administrative departments,[36] we cannot expect to have the much more difficult coördination between government and business.

What success the N. R. A.?

[36] The Los Angeles Gas and Electric case (1933) represented a new willingness of the courts to accept the findings of a state utility commission, a real departure from the judicial refusals of the post-war period.

The Roosevelt Recovery Program was a direct challenge to the depression and to American competitive business. What shall accompany it, or follow it, to make industrial capitalism safe for the western world? In the attempt to get a balanced budget, unemployment, for example of scientific experts in government employ, was increased, and teachers and others publicly employed throughout the country had money wages reduced and real wages cut very sharply. The construction of a semi-artificial system of public works, supported by huge borrowings, cannot be more than a temporary substitute for the real article. Both industry and government have set bad examples of economizing by doubling-up loads instead of spreading employment. The President and General Johnson tried, unconstitutionally as it appeared, to get codes for co-operative industry and labor, not to reallocate production more wisely; but the chief industrial purpose was anti-competitive rather than to protect consumption under planned production. The solution for labor, if there is one, will come through social engineering, rather than just shorter hours in the present set-up.[37]

It took a long time to divert the world's merchant marines from piracy to helpful international exchange, as the primary business of trade. It should not take so long to re-convert the successors of nineteenth-century chiefs who preyed on credit, industry, and the public. Moving the financial capital from lower New York to Washington cannot help unless Washington can run our financial affairs better than Wall Street has done. What we need is an integration of government and finance, not a substitution of one for the other. As yet we have barely made a dent either in control of financialism, in making new plans for taxing unwise surpluses until they become innocuous, or in discarding impossible, unworkable principles of industrial capitalism. Evidently we need some new theory, as well as new practices, in our western, Christian, capitalist civilization.

[37] See IX.

IX

A NEW PUBLIC ECONOMICS OF PLENTY

The plight of farmer, worker and consumer, and the dilemma of industrialism and of financialism which is largely responsible for their specific problems, would not have developed to the present impasse but for the principles on which our present economic order is built. We find ourselves in the position of the manufacturer who has tried to construct a permanent building with enduring machinery; who then finds both his machinery and his building rendered obsolete by changes he could not foresee. Civilization cannot be scrapped like out-of-date factories, so what are we to do about it? When the theory on which we have been working shows itself to be contrary to fact, there is only one thing to be done— try another. The temptation will be to experiment with the opposite; that's humanity's favorite way. From paternalism we swing to free enterprise, from monopoly to competition. Now what?

OUR ECONOMIC HERITAGE

The World War proved that much of our old economic theory was wrong or did not correspond with fact. At that time prices did not follow the curves laid down for them when we applied the economic principles we had thought universal and permanent. The post-war period and the depression emphasized more fully the need of understanding those tenets which more truly and accurately represent what we are doing. Even more we have come to realize the desirability of getting at those underlying principles which will rid us of some evils we now suffer, if we can know those principles and use them. These will then replace outworn ideas with some that are more modern, and will show how to benefit the pub-

Principles of the old industrialized society

lic rather than business, which is after all a means rather than an end. Without any expectation of solving any problems or of dissolving any dilemma but of trying to see the situation as a whole somewhat more clearly, let us consider very briefly

1　some principles of the old industrialized society
2　social economics *vs.* an economics for business
3　the need of economic planning
4　how far we have gone toward a public economics
5　how far we have gone toward an economics of plenty
6　social engineering.

Individualism as a theory and *laissez faire* as a policy will be examined later at some length [1] and need not be considered fully here. Truly both the theory and the practice are used very much less than formerly. Undoubtedly we do not yet realize how much we have abandoned them, though the depression has helped to wake us up.

Free contract is a desirable if not an essential feature of any successful economic society. The difficulty is to have it free when the parties are so unequal as in our day. To be just and fair a contract should give what it declares, "value received." The farmer, the worker, and the consumer are wondering why they did not get it.

Private enterprise and initiative stimulate interest, give the capable a chance and change static business or social organization into dynamic. The land of the free has it, for those who can invent, and keep the invention, for those who play the game, perhaps for those whose field is not already semi-monopolized. The small business man has his troubles, with local organizations that give no outsider a chance, under codes or substitutes that protect chiefly the average producer or seller.

Free competition was sharply in contrast with paternalism and monopoly of court favorites of the pre-"laissez faire" period. Free competition, somewhat like contract, assumed if it did not assure the power of equal bargaining. This

[1] See X.

was most easily secured for producer against producer, seller and buyer. It was less easy to protect seller against seller and buyer against buyer. It has been hardest of all, in days not far gone, to safeguard buyer against producer and seller. In a close hundred yard dash the judges try to pick out those in first, second and third places, for all cannot watch first only. New electric checks show a fair percentage of error. The judges of our economic competition have had their eyes too much on the modern winners, the producers. When producers only are in the race, they try to weed out those who jump the gun, "box" the fleetest or foul their competitors. They pay very little attention to crude tactics in the other races. We have often failed to appoint judges of fair competition to protect consumers; and sometimes groups of workers have not even had rules for their protection.

Combination was a coöperative substitute for competition under "laissez faire." Being undertaken as a means of securing profits which were threatened by too much competition, it had difficulty in evading the law of an individualist society. Gentlemen's agreements were replaced by pools, pools by trustee organization, trusts by holding companies, and holding companies by mergers. Mergers were held legal but gave way to code boards. So coöperation, of a sort, has emerged because business needed to limit competition.

Private property has yielded to corporate property or publicly regulated property, much as competition has shifted to combinations and for the same reason—profit.[2] Grover Cleveland referred to public office as a public trust. Private property, right of combination, freedom of contract carry the same obligation—those who hold, have, or make have corresponding public responsibilities. Their responsibility to society is negative, that of our elected or appointed officials positive. Even those having economically important trusts need not give account of their stewardship, or be held directly responsible to the public, as an official must, in theory. The whole theory of "laissez faire" is opposed to such a concept, for business was to be "let alone" because it was

[2] On corporate property, see pp. 117–118.

none of society's affair. "Laissez faire" seems to be passing therefore because business needed public help to keep going; because it forgot that business was only part of a social order. Ours is a problem of how our economic system shall be reorganized to survive, and in surviving serve humanity and itself better.

In two or three places[3] we have indicated the problems and maladjustments which have grown out of lags in our social system. Probably popular opinion is right in stressing "cultural lag" as the greatest and most objectionable of these. Frequently a major problem which is primarily economic is due to the *partial abandonment in some fields of these principles of the old economics,* with *their retention in full force in other fields of business organization or relations.*

We speak of competition as more or less a spent force, but as already indicated,[4] the competition which has been eliminated is largely between large producer and large producer or between large railway systems. The competition between consumer and consumer, between worker and worker, between farmer and farmer existed in 1932 almost as completely as it did in 1882, about the beginning of the industrial consolidation, that is, the beginning of a movement in *production* which greatly reduced competition.

Particular attention might and should be given to the *lag of distribution in relation to production.* As stated later,[5] this should not be over-stressed because distribution without regard to production is rather meaningless. However, in our world of potential plenty, with so-called over-production common, due to a very great increase in technological production, the question of poor distribution looms as one of the greatest problems for our generation. If we keep in mind the fact that competition has disappeared in production very much more than it has been reduced in distribution and consumption, we see at once why distribution is a puzzle to us, but at the same time see a way out.

[3] Pp. 76–78, 85–90.
[4] Esp. p. 133.
[5] Pp. 263–265, 309–311.

The capitalist and the industrialist have the direct advantages of the new power and technology as well as the indirect advantages of combination. The combination works to the disadvantage of the farmer and the worker and the consumer, who compete against each other as well as against the industrialist. Until that competition is limited, or each of these groups, or all together, can compete on equal terms with those directly in charge of production, the industrial capitalists alone will enjoy most of the fruits of the new industrial revolution. Farmer, worker, and consumer will still be contenting themselves with little more than they would have had under an economics of scarcity. And the reason is plain: in a sense they are still using economic principles, or technics, of the age of scarcity.

One reason that the *unorganized farmers* and the *semi-organized producers of other raw materials* for production do not have the share to which they are entitled in the process of distribution is the necessity of bargaining with the *organized producers* in disposing of their materials. Not only do they compete with one another; but, what is even more important, the old idea of freedom of contract restrains them from bargaining as equals with well organized producing or selling groups—it therefore gives advantage to these groups with which they bargain. In short, the survival of those two principles, rather *unlimited competition* and *free contract*, accounts to a very large degree for the handicap which prevents the farmer and the miner and the separate oil producer from getting his money's worth for the materials that he turns over to the "industrialist" who prepares the materials for the general market.

Even more striking has been the unfairness observed in the dealings of any large corporate group with workers. One would think that, especially in a democratic system, with presumably popular government, the workers, who form an overwhelming majority of the voters, would make rules especially favorable to themselves. As we shall see later,[6] the proletariat has almost no representatives in Congress and probably com-

[6] P. 346.

paratively few in the state legislatures. Wealth, and the power that goes with wealth, shows plainly in the survival of the old economic principles in the law and in judicial decisions.

If capital in relation to labor had only a legal advantage, the handicap of labor would be removed sooner rather than later. Remove legal handicaps and unfair competition to which the workers are exposed, and labor would still be at a disadvantage. Apparently the American public, including perhaps some of the fairly unskilled laborers, is sold to the idea that although combination, and organization and concentration, is quite the proper thing for manufacturing, for railroads, and for banking, something is all wrong about too extensive combination or organization of workers, or group bargaining of workers with employers—collective bargaining. It would be a miracle if unorganized labor, dealing with greatly organized capital and industrial groups, powerful in part because wealthy, had its fair share in the distribution of the product. The remedy? Why not try the removal of some of the handicaps and disabilities of the worker and if possible of the groups furnishing materials? That might help in part; but it would not create, for labor, conditions of an economics of plenty.

The consumer stands in practically the same relation to the industrialist-capitalist groups as do the producers of raw materials, including the farmer, and the relatively unorganized workers. That is, the consumer is handicapped by the principles of the old economics, especially these two of unlimited competition and contract. It may seem rather absurd to dignify by the name of contract the ordinary purchase and sale of goods, but that is in a sense what takes place in an *agreement* between buyer and seller. And in almost all purchases that take place today the buyer does not really have much bargaining power. He usually pays the price which is charged—he either takes the article or leaves it. In other words, although the buyers might in a sense compete against each other, if the supply were scarce, where that is abundant—and usually under technological production it is over-abundant—they usually have no real competition with the seller.

Occasionally *producers of raw materials* get together and agree not to take less than a certain sum for their goods. Even before 1933 only one fairly *unskilled worker* out of ten was connected with a labor union. But the *consumers* have had faith in the government to protect them from faulty goods and have depended upon the advertisers to know when they were getting their money's worth. For a twentieth-century society this child-like faith has had its own reward, and too often instead of "value received" the buyer gets the worst of the bargain.

Consumer disadvantage might be overlooked in this shift from an old type of business to a new, but for the fact that frequently it is so *costly to business*,[7] and always it is a loss to society. The fact that production has the advantage of combination and of other new methods and procedures is not to be counted against it. It would seem stupid, if one could invest money more wisely and manufacture more cheaply and in greater quantity to cling to any old, outworn method. If we could, we should like to duplicate in consumption the methods of the new industrial capitalism in production. That of course is not possible. Proper consumption is not a matter of power or technology.

If it is necessary to give the consumer a fairer deal for the benefit of business and the public, it may be done directly in the process of buying or indirectly through the public. Preferably the decreases of cost and greater production should come automatically to consumers rather than by artificial combination of buyers or through very much government interference.[8]

SOCIAL ECONOMICS VERSUS AN ECONOMICS FOR BUSINESS

One does not need to generalize on the limitations of the old business theories and practices nor to show very much how the ideas accepted as old principles have proved to be

New principles for old

---

[7] Pp. 126–128, 155–157. See also pp. 253 *et. seq.*
[8] On this consult W. H. Hamilton, p. 229.

false in theory and a failure in practice. The brief sketch just given illustrates the shift from old ideas toward new, with the lag in essential fields of business, a lag that should be reduced if not removed. That some of these principles are false or unusable has been shown by the length and depth of the depression, the inability of production in ordinary times to continue producing semi-normally, the inescapable fact that financialism could not re-invest unspendable surpluses at compound interest. "If, as many maintain, the extraordinary extent of the world depression is in part explicable by the accelerated tempo of technical advance, the situation is even more ironical in that the very capacity to produce has retarded the activity of production." [9] Business men engaged in production and the investor are in a sense therefore the worst losers from this failure to recognize faulty economic practices used in the past. In the first three depression years, the losses of American business men were computed at twenty-three billion dollars.

Whether these faulty applications of old economic theory are a necessary outgrowth of an individualist economics, or whether individualism is a necessary accompaniment of these principles, which do not work in the modern world, or whether the connection is a semi-accidental one between the old types of business and individualism, the fact remains that the passing of individualism [10] is marking the end of this old economics. The replacement of agriculturalism by industrialism [11] probably counts even in changing our economic ideas. Points of diminishing returns [12] are totally different, and much

[9] Columbia University syllabus on *Introduction to Contemporary Problems in the United States*, Vol. II (1934 edition), p. 413. MacIver, *Economic Reconstruction*, p. 13.

[10] Pp. 279–283.   [11] Pp. 92–100.

[12] In growing wheat or weaving cloth the amount of capital and labor can at first be increased, giving a constantly larger return for each unit of capital and/or labor that is used. Finally the addition of any more capital and/or labor may give a *larger total* return but not so large an additional return for the use of that last unit of labor or capital. This point in each occupation is called *the point of diminishing returns* because the added units used in production give a diminished return compared with the earlier units that were used. On an *acre of wheat* this point of diminishing returns may come with five dollars of capital and five dollars of labor; with a *textile factory*, it might not be reached until the materials amounted to $300,000 and the labor $200,000 annually.

higher, under machine-power production from what they were in the business of an agricultural society. As we have noticed, free enterprise no longer exists in fields of business controlled by mergers or dominated by mergers under codes, private property is fast yielding to corporate property, and the organization of labor as well as of capital makes the old private contract seem rather absurd. "Laissez faire," therefore, like mercantilism, is likely to be chiefly valuable as history.

Possibly the new economics must find its salvation if not its justification in profits. Business economics has sought huge surpluses of capital. Woe betide the modern world if capital again becomes insufficient, as it was in past ages. If that happens, we shall again be in a period of scarcity, without adequate factories, proper machinery, and necessary free capital. Unquestionably, however, the only way in which profits have been possible from the producer's point of view is, first, to limit the amount of capital invested, and, second, to limit the productive use of that capital in making goods. *If that is done, however, we are again back in a period of scarcity; only this time it is artificial scarcity, created by limitation of output, and not a natural scarcity due to inadequate capital and poor means of creating goods.*

If one could consider the use of goods without profits, one might consider what that would accomplish. Certainly a business scheme of that kind would seem to call for an nth degree of planning. There would need to be a decided improvement and re-allocation in the division of wealth and income. *If much profit-making tends to destroy profit and even sales by reducing the purchasing power of most people,* business would benefit by greater diffusion of income and correspondingly higher purchasing power. Necessary as a margin of receipts above costs is to all business, profit would seem to be a by-product rather than an end of good business. Evidently *business and public need a better standard than high profits* (1) *for investment in new enterprise,* (2) *for determination of the quantity of goods to be produced,* (3) *for the fixing of maximum prices.* At this writing (June, 1935), even

for recovery, prices and in lesser degree wages have advanced rather rapidly toward normal levels, and in thus advancing have retarded business improvement and the spread of employment. By advancing artificially they seem to have retarded recovery and made use of a defective and undesirable economics of scarcity.

Possibly by producing chiefly for the present and not with an eye on the future, speeding up production as much as possible, and getting larger net returns from increased sales at relatively low prices, the level of living might be raised measurably, possibly immeasurably, for all concerned.

Possibilities of a reorganized capitalism

Our interest is not in a totally different social order. Rather is it centered in a new type of capitalistic society with business motives, if not business methods, analogous to those of the present *but* organized on a public economics of plenty rather than on a private economics of scarcity. Far be it from the present writer to point out either the main principles or even the chief ideas of this new type, which it seems must inevitably replace the old. A few suggestions however may be offered. First of all are the negative lessons, the limitations of the present system. To understand them in some small measure has been the object of Part II of this study. To comprehend them more fully, we might go even farther than has already been done to ascertain the failures of the old scarcity economics. We might do this if we could discover the extent to which they are due, first, to wrong economic theory, secondly, primarily to anti-social practices, and thirdly, just to profit-taking.[13]

From a positive point of view certain principles or ideas must be examined. The first of these is individualism. In a sense individualist philosophy permeates the whole system; or at least it did. In Chapter X several suggestions will be given on substitutes actually developed or in process.

A second suggestion undoubtedly would concern itself with less stress upon production and a great deal more upon distribution. Too much has been written during the last genera-

[13] Possibly the most interesting recent study of economic reorganization is that of the MacIver Committee on that subject, *Economic Reconstruction*.

tion about failures of distribution, as though a better scheme of distribution will solve the problem. It will not. Economic distribution is, after all, nothing but a phase of production. If it is not linked closely and inseparably with production, the distribution will lead us nowhere. A better scheme of distribution in 1932 would never have solved any major problem due to the fact that there was so little to distribute. In fact, if the National Bureau of Economic Research has not been misinformed, wages held up better than business income. Better distribution before 1929 would not have been amiss. At least it would have added to our business methods more social consideration for the largest class with purchasing power. By adding to the workers' capacity for consumption, who knows how much less severe the depression might have been!

In the third place, consideration might be given, therefore, to a better balance between production, distribution, and consumption.[14] Herein perhaps lies a fatal weakness of the old scheme. It concentrated on increasing power production, wisely, but neglected the workers and the consumers almost to the point of exploiting them. Its managers seemed not to realize that production, including distribution, and consumption are supplementary, if not identical, in their interests.[15] Each should gain from the advance of the other, because one loses as the others are either retarded or keep more than their share of the thing they do together.

The old business system was like one of the old less expensive type of automobiles; the engine was so powerful that the differential could not stand the strain and the car itself was soon shaken to pieces. Every car owner wants power, especially on grades, but he also wants mileage, per gallon and per car, style, comfort and durability. Much has been written about lack of purchasing power (possibly the mileage per gallon of society). We must not try to get it by itself. If the old economic order failed because it tried to produce

---

[14] See pp. 129–131. See also pp. 248–251.
[15] On an economics controlled in the interest of different classes, see S. H. Slichter, *Modern Economic Society*, ch. IV.

for a maximum profit, in the new economic order we must fight shy of attempting to solve the world's economic problem by *direct* creation of purchasing power. Possibly the relief of the years beginning in 1933 might prime the pump of a satisfactorily flowing well of production. But who wants to prime a pump which is flowing? Rather are we concerned with keeping it operating and in giving the supply to those who not only need it but can use it wisely, and for the public good as well as their own.

A fourth idea which probably must be considered is that any reversion to business for business' sake is likely to be just as fatal as the scheme we had before the great depression. As already shown, business is a small part of the economic and social program; it is a means, not an end in itself. It cannot stabilize itself, and values and prices, by watching only business and overlooking the public it is serving, as it has often done in the past. Why stage Hamlet at all if Hamlet himself (society) is to be left out?

Enough has been said, little as it has been, to indicate that this new economics is a matter for captains of industry who recognize their social responsibility and who are controlled as public agents, for financiers who place necessary service ahead of profit, and who accept obligations as well as responsibility to a public which they serve.

Possibly this social reorganization in .which business and government become more closely united, in which society is not a thing apart but a unit of which government and business are integral parts, would seem to create a new socialism. That term, however, usually is concerned with a state organized primarily through its government, a state in which force perhaps must be used vigorously as in a fascist state or in the state visualized by Spengler.

THE NEED OF ECONOMIC PLANNING

Planning,
old and new

The shift from individualism toward a socialized society theoretically is marked by a demand for economic planning. The evils of unrestricted competition and undirected *production* might be avoided in part by a more careful organization of production and business procedure. The American business scene before 1929 was not nearly so planless as it seemed. An examination of concentration in American business [16] shows that, in the majority of fields, some one organization or set of corporations or combinations controlled much of the market. It frequently decided some prices, possibly some production and the allocation of products within the areas over which they were sold.

Even under our old apparently planless scheme business direction by semi-monopolies was not the ultimate one. The "Money Trust" was back of most *organization of new industrial plants or railroads,* and decided *possible expansions* of business through *the granting or withholding of credit.* This direction, supervision, control, or whatever it might be called, was in consequence far better organized and far more centralized than any supervision of a business by itself or by some of its managers. The very high concentration of money power in the hands of a few great banking houses and their friends gave a unity to new investments and a direction of business affairs which probably will not be attained by the majority of the proposed economic plans.

The first question we perhaps should ask ourselves is whether planned economics is possible under American business practices and under American law. Beard and a number of others believe their plans could be put into effect without change in the written Constitution. So flexible is our unwritten constitution that this seems probable. Modification of American law, however, is a slightly different story. Certainly a number of new Congressional statutes would be necessary, and undoubtedly a very great change in American administration would be needed. Assuming therefore the legal and constitutional possibilities of planning, could it be done under American business as organized at present? The codes of the N. I. R. A. are part of our answer. If they were not a type of planning, what were they? These acts were temporary and their constitutionality was not accepted by the United States Supreme Court.

[16] Pp. 118–126.

Elements to be considered in planning

The demand for planning probably grew out of the dilemma of industrialism and the failure to market most of the goods that could be produced rather than out of other public needs. Is the purpose of a planned economy, however, primarily an attempt to plan production? Yes and no. No, because past planning has included national policies, many phases of municipal interests, public works and taxation, in addition to social by-products of economic planning. Yes, because in all probability the whole business world hinges upon the action of industry rather than even upon American finance or upon the actions of labor or the attitudes of the consumer. In industry we have the direct and most conspicuous advantages of our scientific use of machines and power. Mass production more than any other one thing has changed the face of the world and standards of living. If we are to gain the real advantage of a machine-power, technological age, certainly the greatest need is of more and better production. But of what use is that when we are already producing in a number of fields [17] approximately twice as much as we use in times of prosperity and could easily have made several times as much as could be sold in depression.

The planning of production seems rather pointless if all that we do is to *limit supplies to actual demands*. This is nothing but a wholesale application of an economics of scarcity, and an economics of scarcity represents most of the stupidities of our present scheme with few of the benefits we ought to gain. From the standpoint of production, therefore, the first requirement of a planned economy would seem to be production on the basis of an economics of plenty, as Stuart Chase hinted years ago and has since explained more fully. Swope, LaFollette, and others would probably leave more to the self-governing industries than to any outside authority. Some plan of economic board or parliament, such as Germany had, on paper at least, and J. M. Clark suggested soon after the war, a plan which Beard, Soule, and others approve, prob-

[17] In 1929 American industry in general was producing nearly 80% of capacity (Nourse *et al., America's Capacity to Produce,* pp. 164–170; p. 303). In 1932 production was of course much lower.

ably would be desirable and probably would be necessary. Experience with the N. I. R. A. organization and work seems to indicate that this organization should be not only properly representative of the industries concerned but should represent labor and the public, both from the public point of view and especially in relation to consumers. Let us hope the consumer would not be left quite so much in the cold as he has been under the N. R. A., through no fault of those in charge of the program of consumption, but as an inevitable feature of our past mismanagement of affairs concerning both business and the public.

If our failure to protect the *consumer,* and that is one of the conspicuous features of the Roosevelt Recovery Program, is especially prominent, that should certainly be one of the characteristics of any scheme of economic planning. The report of W. F. Ogburn, when he resigned from the Consumers Board in August, 1933, and later reports of these consumers' organizations ought to be read to see what special difficulties they encountered. Apparently a properly planned scheme from the standpoint of the consumer must take into account the whole scheme and not primarily the consumer.

A planned economy would represent little planning if it ignored *labor.* Several features of the *N. I. R. A. codes* represented ideas similar to those of the plans. One of these was a minimum wage and a maximum hour day or week. Of what value a minimum wage, if there is no work? Emergency employment has been necessary, especially through the *C. W. A.* and *F. E. R. A.*[18] It has been proposed in England that a scheme of permanent unemployment insurance will be necessary in that country because of international competition and the reduced market abroad for British-made goods. Will that become a public necessity for the United States? If so, any plan must provide for it. The protection of the rights of labor under the N. I. R. A. was supposed to be looked after by the clause in favor of collective bargaining, since collective action of employers has been fact for many years. However, any plan which organizes the employers and employes into two

[18] C. W. A. = Civil Works Administration. F. E. R. A. = Federal Emergency Relief Administration.

large camps is likely to succeed about as well as did the Triple Alliance and the Triple Entente before 1914.[19] The chief Recovery statute arranged a vast scheme of public works. In the opinion of several internationalists this probably would be effective only when made part of an international program. Is it solely or chiefly for either recovery or for labor that the public works feature of economic planning should be on a super-national scale? Or must any successful planning or reorganization be international?

For consumers and for laborers and for farmers and for producers of raw materials other than those that are agricultural, a planning of *distribution* apparently is of the highest importance. This point has been considered and will be treated under a "public economics of plenty." Any plan which considers production, even with ample consideration of labor and the consumer, but with a neglect of finance, is likely to fall very far short of any twentieth-century standards in the requirements for planning. We have already noted in several connections the interlocking of direct production in manufacturing, indirect production in transportation of goods, the selling of the goods and the financing of all three, showing the high interrelations of all four. In addition to the coöperation of the financiers with industrialists and railroad managers, of real significance are the plans for stabilized prices and the provisions for credit, including bank or credit regulation, and the whole scheme of currency, whether it be cash, or business currency, or a managed currency or a system of managed credit.

How Far We Have Gone or Can Go Toward a New Public Economics of Plenty

A new public economics

A new economics which is public would not necessarily be identical with a new economics of plenty. The public would probably put stress upon public interest and would follow that up probably with the protection of public rights. *If it is true that a much closer and better interrelation of production, distribution, and consumption should be worked out, and could*

[19] Pp. 59–62.

be worked out, it can easily be seen that most large business might be affected with a public interest. A corporation that is producing is not making goods because it loves to work but rather, through the concerted efforts of all under its direction, including the worker and the furnisher of capital, primarily for the consuming public. The public has not only an interest because of the importance of consumption and the universality of the consumer, but a further interest nowadays because many businesses involve work or methods which may be contrary to the public good. If, for example, the commodity produced and sold is a necessity, if most of the supply is furnished by a single organization or group of companies, the public should have good service or goods at reasonable prices. If the public's interest in the business is a *major part* of the *process* of making, transporting, or selling the goods, then it seems fair to state that such a business, as well as a public utility or a monopoly, is "affected with a public interest." Certainly a society, most of whose business is in any way of this type, would refuse to have it done according to irresponsible, individualistic methods. "Rugged individualism" has therefore become "ragged" if the public is disregarded. Under the caption "Establishing Proper Public Controls" we shall consider this topic from several angles.[20]

Public interest, with its corollary, public right, does not mean public management. Business management in general is a highly specialized technical affair. There would be inexcusable loss if we supplanted present methods of training and selecting those in charge, and let Washington do it. The Interstate Commerce Commission has made a fair success of deciding when rates are exorbitant or fixing the maximum limit of the rates which shall be satisfactory under certain circumstances. The making of actual railroad rates, however, is a remarkably difficult and intricate proposition. A specialist in charge of ten thousand rates would find that if a hundred of those were changed by him or for him, probably several hundred and possibly several thousand other readjustments would be necessary. Any inexperienced government official

[20] Pp. 397–401.

who tried to interfere with existing rates and substitute others would make a tremendous mess of the job.

So long as we have a price system, and so long as businesses can be kept running only if there is a margin of income above expenditure, the most skilled, careful and competent management is absolutely necessary. For the year 1931 the Standard Oil Company of New Jersey, the largest of the American oil companies, doing a business of more than a billion dollars, showed a net profit of less than ten million. The figures for 1933 gave only a slightly larger margin. What public official would be likely to organize and manage a business of that magnitude and avoid a deficit? Possibly he would make a good showing by leaving out many items of expenditure, interest on capital, loss through depreciation and taxes, from which a public enterprise might be exempt, showing a balance on the credit side of the ledger.

The public's share in a new economics may not be due to contributions of ideas and principles by the public's representatives. Elected officials or their appointed supporters, with the possible exception of an occasional President or scientific expert, will leave that task to the "professors," although good public administrators have made a real art of it. The public's share, however, will be great in determining the rules under which the game shall be played and in modifying those rules. This may happen as new needs arise. As the public's interests become increasingly evident, constant improvement should mark the ways in which the thing is done for greater benefit to the people. The public's share will also be observable in the negative, and possibly the positive, administration of the activity. Positively, this will be the prevention as well as the prohibition of unfair practices, unscrupulous personal actions, and anti-social services, where social services should have been rendered but were not. It may be positive also in absolute prescription of things which must be undertaken and accomplished. It is more likely to be negative, however, especially in leaving to others the work to be done.

The gathering of capital, the organization of management,

the creation of goods, selling of commodities—all these, public affairs in a way, need not be done by those directly chosen by the public or directly responsible to it. The leaders are and must be held responsible. The followers may be, in the phrase of a generation ago, "soldiers of the common good"— workers in the great army of public service. But even in public utility organizations and possibly even in public businesses they serve the public without necessarily working for it directly.

In carrying out the public's part in a new economics one of the first requirements might be a reorganized scheme of production in relation to distribution or, if the reader prefers, a reorganized distribution in relation to production. In determining production, why not follow the war-time scheme of dividing different industries into those most essential, those desirable, and those unnecessary? Goods especially important in war are of little value in peace; but the principle remains the same. Socially, certain goods are infinitely more desirable than others, whereas much of what we now produce is socially wasteful. Unless war is more important or desirable than peace, why not attempt in time of peace what proved feasible, even if it could not be well administered, in time of war? Without a wise allocation of resources, capital and labor to production, and other business, it will be impossible to gain a public economics or to develop an economics of plenty.

Reorganization of production and distribution

How shall better distribution be made? How shall each element of production have its share of the goods or services it helps to create? It may not be so easy for the public as it has been for the capitalist boss, whoever or whatever that may be, to apportion out the share for each. If it is possible, however, this allocation to the producer of raw materials, to the laborer, to the business manager, and to the furnisher of free capital, should be done in the *process* rather than later. The socialist would probably handle the matter by the decision of a legislative or economic parliament, supplemented by the decrees of a public official. Unless the members of law-deciding and administrative public groups are more capable and less subject to influence than many present business leaders or politicians, we could be sure that the job would not be well and justly done. Possibly we shall never escape the poverty of both public and business leadership which has distinguished so much of our past. Possibly it cannot be done at all well, except through a profit-granting scheme; but it must be done better, with fairer distribution to the worker and with better protection of the consumer, if we are to make our new economics better than the old.

Distribution can be redirected and controlled by more just and more modern laws and by a more effective system of regulation. We can insist upon public and uniform systems of accounting, not only in the affairs of public utilities, but of any business affected with a public interest. Certainly the public should see that natural resources, which are not misnamed if they are called public resources, are not exploited and made the objects of extraordinary private gain. It seems fair that they should not be taken from an unsuspecting public, so that in return we are pleased to pay an exorbitant price for what really belongs to us. Certainly legal but sharp practices will cease, if the method ceases to be profitable to the sharper. Sharp but illegal practices can be forbidden, as they have been in part by the laws, by administrative bodies and by the courts. Each of these limitations or restrictions, prohibitions, or other methods of control would help to make fair distribution within the process itself and not as an after product. As we create and as we use, we could then decide the share which should go to each taking part in production. We could thus also reduce the amount paid unnecessarily by the purchaser of these goods or services.

Taxation provides a simpler means of avoiding marked and unjust inequalities in the distribution of wealth. *Distribution in the process could then be supplemented by redistribution afterward.* Taxation might be a remedy where the process cannot be made just and fair. Most taxes would touch only the current production; but some would eventually get rid of the heavy excess of wealth now overburdening a few members of society. If no one were allowed to inherit more than one million dollars, and if the inheritance rates on bequests above fifty or one hundred thousand were made progressively larger, there would be no really swollen fortunes transmitted from generation to generation. The accumulation of vast sums in the hands of those who contributed nothing to its accumulation also would be reduced. A very heavy tax might be placed upon the income from unearned sources, such as the unearned increment of land or natural resources, or the unearned income from large-scale investment. The non-payment of income taxes, like parking near a fire plug, has been a means of punishing far more serious social evils, as in the case of Al Capone. The collection of an income tax can easily be made to include the evils themselves. If an excess profits tax must be paid, there will be little temptation to make large profits by reducing output. This tax might reduce to a minimum the temptation for people to become one-thousand-percent Americans by gouging the consumer for several prices. Exorbitant or unwarranted profits could be reached and therefore discouraged, not in the process itself, but before the profiteer becomes the beneficiary of his shy-locking. *The dilemma of capitalism probably would be solved in large part* if public control prevented the accumulation of unearned profits among producers, and the policy of profit-taking among financiers and others.

Of course the American people and government would be obliged really to use public *administration*. Willingness to have our affairs administered would not be enough, for administrators must be trained; and experience of a nation in good administration cannot be acquired in a decade, possibly not in a generation. Reorganization would call for wise leadership, real understanding of needs, trends and problems, popular patience with inevitable mistakes during experimentation, and public coöperation of a high degree.

An economics of plenty should, and probably can, shift from a reduction of output to a *stimulation of production*. This would involve, at the least, greater care in the increase of plants in any field, utilization of the best possible machinery, and stimulation of markets to insure a demand equal to the actual, and potential, supply. Conservation of raw materials

An
economics
of plenty

might seem more important for the future than for the present. But failure either to make the most of any supply of materials, or an inadequate compensation for those furnishing the materials, would jeopardize the success of any new and better plan of production. Miners and lumbermen as well as farmers have been sufferers under our present scheme of playing the middle against both ends. A better use of the products of extractive industries and better returns for those engaged in these occupations will help. Wholesale exploitation of timber lands, mining and oil resources, so far as that has already taken place, cannot be remedied, except in part. Something can be done to keep for the public the vast deposits of coal and other minerals on the public domain. Much can be added to the past work of reforestation and other means of preventing further soil erosion. Marginal lands can be left out of a concerted efficiency farm program. *At every turn an economics of plenty calls for a public economics of the highest type.* But an economics of plenty, easily obtainable in production, may not be possible in other economic fields. Only production can make effective use of applied science, improved technology, and machine-power. The gains of the last two or three centuries apply little to distribution (which is not transportation or exchange but division of product) or to consumption. Fortunately, distribution is only another part of production and consumption is directly dependent on production. Otherwise a new economics in production alone could not create an age of plenty. Nor will it do so unless the new gains of production are carried over rather fully into the fields of distribution and consumption. Hence the need of a new *public* economics.

The conservation of *resources* is especially necessary and important in connection with power. In no field have the interests of society been neglected, at least before the twentieth century, as in this one. We should repeal antiquated laws dealing with title to deep-lying oils or coals or to valuable water-power sites. The Creator did not provide those for profiteers, who in turn by their seizure created a scarcity for the public—assuming of course that the public would and could have used them better than an enterprising exploiter did. In power production and utilization lies possibly the greatest opportunity to create an age of plenty.

Not at the mine or at the factory, however, but in the *market* probably lies the crux of the shift from an economics of scarcity to one of plenty. Some engineers and the ultra-reformers would try to sidestep this problem by substituting some other standard than price, because the maintenance of price has usually been dependent on scarcity, natural or artificial. Probably for commodities with a more or less fixed demand a real increase of supply would destroy prices high enough to justify production. But with millions half-starved even in the United States of America, and with many more millions under-nourished, is the demand inelastic for even those foods of which we never want more than a moderate amount? Before Ford, almost any thoughtful person would have denied the possibility of putting a garage on every lot and a car in every garage. A generation ago John Graham Brooks cited the case of a Cape Cod fisherman. "Yes, that's the trouble. My father wanted fifteen things. He didn't get 'em all. He got about ten and worried considerable because he didn't get the other five. Now I want forty things, and I get thirty; but I worry more about the ten I can't get than the old man used to about the five he couldn't get." Unsatisfied wants would make any potential demand elasticity itself. The problem is to make it effective by a juster sharing of the product created, thus increasing purchasing power, and keeping wealth at an optimum circulation.

An economics of plenty should free the worker and the consumer from some part of the plight in which each finds himself. A specific suggestion of the writer's he believes would go a long way toward stabilizing employment and purchasing power. This is the equalization of loads and rewards for all workers.[21] As H. W. Van Loon asks: "Is there really much chance of a reasonable world as long as we insist on buying our material possessions at ten grand and our intellectual ideals at ten cents?" A smoothing of the business cycle might

[21] Pp. 131–132.

make possible a progressive, upward continuance of a better and more general circulation of wealth. Albert L. Deane has some very interesting suggestions on supplemental compensation to make consumption balance production, and by sustaining consumption to gain a lasting Recovery.[22] If possible we must avoid artificial means, even public controls or government planning. If we are to get the best results, the capacities as well as the wants of consumers must be capitalized, of workers as well as consumers. Education and other opportunities for training or understanding should help. Human interests and drives are so often neglected at present. As parts of a great economic and social machine most of us are less efficient than an old steam engine, rated as less than ten per cent effective.

An economics of plenty probably should concern itself chiefly with ways and means of creating a better material culture and using it more successfully. This is the beginning but only a beginning. The joy of achieving should have a part in the work of each contributor just as anticipation is often more vivid and more satisfying than realization. Our possessions too often possess us. Then why roll up more treasures on earth! If the civilization is to be ours, why not put more into it as well as get more out, as giving frequently brings us more than receiving. In brief, how much better, and better off, shall *we* be if we achieve an age of plenty than we were in one of scarcity?

SOCIAL ENGINEERING

The problem of the social engineer

Making better use of what we have, regenerated, regimented or reconstructed, is the job of the social engineer. The name is accepted because the task calls for an engineer and the purpose is not more science, larger buildings, or faster automobiles, but human betterment. Better and newer ethical standards are quite as necessary as cheaper radios; more comfortable houses should mean greater happiness, more real companionship and leisure for culture. Obsessed as Americans are by a mania for speed and reverence for size,

[22] *Survey Graphic,* October, 1933, p. 623.

the social engineer needs the faculty of getting an overview of all parts of the American scene, the capacity to see life clearly and see it whole, the ability to suggest wise adjustments and help us integrate changing elements of our civilization. Just now, after rapid material advances from our old bases, we are like a victorious army, ready to consolidate our gains. He ought to help.

A well balanced society is as important to a nation as a well balanced personality and character are to an individual. The proper adjustment of one part to another is difficult in proportion to the attempt to combine old with new or profit-seeking with welfare service. Even production planning is better than either unorganized competition or predatory combination. Give us a better balanced and more unified society, with less thought of gain, and more of progress; *capital industrialism then can become a real part of civilization instead of civilization being a by-product of industrial capitalism.*

The nation must first of all be well organized. America is almost as short on organization as it is long on organizations. Our fear of control and of authority, due to our frontier conditions and to English tyranny in the eighteenth century, causes us to dread enough organization to make our social "order" efficient. Undoubtedly our legislators make too many new and impossible rules. But that is proof of poor organization rather than of good government. One reason we have followed the plan of leaving things alone and letting them develop as they would has been our unwillingness to tackle reorganization because one change leads to many unforeseen realignments. *Adaptations in social relationships are necessary,* but we cannot tell easily whether they are good or not as we can in business. Economic adjustments have been worked out through money successes or failures in a system built upon competition and profits. Those that succeeded went far financially; those that could not, dropped out. In this manner evolved our economic order. Or do you prefer to call it our economic chaos?

Social engineering covers general organization and reorganization and at least the more important as well as some of the less important relations and forms of interdependence in our complex world. The technical engineer could produce for use more and finer goods than the enterpriser who refuses for fear of spoiling profit. But an engineer is primarily concerned in efficiency rather than social development or public welfare. *The purposes of technology and of human engineering, too, are sharply at variance.* If *readjustments* are more necessary in distributing income than in greater production of goods, they are more necessary to increase purchasing power than to improve markets. Unquestionably, the first important task before us is economic reorganization. But a real part of that, not to be separated from it, is some modernization and re-statement of our laws, some reorganization of our government. Who will provide, in place of an economics of competition, the principles of a Public Economics? A political system which gives us too many grafters will not manage wisely or well any organization we may devise for promoting public welfare. But we have, or can secure, capable and honest leaders in public life and in American business. Possibly we cannot rebuild our social order on safer and saner lines, according to wiser principles. But *at least we can negatively avoid the disastrous dilemmas which threaten to destroy what civilization we have.*

The individual and the new society

One first thing we must do is to make our members self-supporting and self-respecting. That is not possible in an industrial system where willing workers find no work. It is not possible in a political system in which the voter is a rubber stamp, with half of the citizens not bothering to get out the ink pad. Almost as important as finding jobs and giving a share both in business and government is a much juster division of goods and a fairer share of services. Our rewards have often been in inverse proportion to effort and social value. He who has worked with wealth or has wealth with which to work gets a huge return. He who makes life worthwhile or prepares for the appreciation of worthwhile things gets very little. Least of all is given to those who do the most disagreeable tasks, under the most unpleasant conditions, possibly for the longest hours. After all that has been written on purchasing power, under-consumption and unemployment, it seems unnecessary to stress necessities. We certainly have had enough of a poorly managed world which can continue to be a going concern only while the worker makes a profit for someone else.

We have been speaking of workers; we must not neglect those not old enough or well enough, or too old, to work. How many people have cried out during depression: "Would that I had not attempted to save," especially if they borrowed to make that saving seem worthwhile. The savings now are lost. The borrowings have been a constant burden and may be a mortgage upon the future as well as a menace to the security of those who have done their share of life's work. They are frequently facing a time without income and without hope. It is not necessarily true that their loss has been some one else's gain, because the little home may have passed into the hands of some one who cannot use it and does not want it; and the savings have simply been dissipated into the current of expenditure which will never return to benefit the savers or their posterity.

While society is doing something for its members, we might well ask what is the individual doing for himself? Social insurance or public coördination for business may easily degenerate into a "dole." If society is responsible for production, education, work, income, health and leisure, how much better off is the "beneficiary," who need not exert himself, or at least not very much, for these advantages. Some one will be out of luck if society is like the rich self-made man who wishes to save his children the sacrifices and hardships of his youth. We shall not be indebted very much to the social engineer who makes life too easy, removes opportunities as well as temptations, replaces social assistance for self-help. The decline of individualism, a philosophy, will involve too high a price if the individual under the new order has less training, less self-direction, less self-control, less individuality. The place of the individual in society, and the part he has in its work and progress, will depend upon the responsibility he assumes as much as upon our reorganized society.

It is possible that the solution of our difficulty may depend in large part upon our *finding better proportions of the materials of civilization out of which we can rebuild our economic and social system.* If the footrule by which we have measured values and decided worthwhile actions is too simple and too material, we may need one that is composite. Such a standard probably would not be furnished by the engineer, the captain of industry or the money king, whose real contributions have been made too much with an eye on the year's ledger balance. Their mistake is largely the poor proportions of the "culture" elements which they mixed in producing our "business civilization." Hence the need of the human engineer for the present and future.

Shall the social engineer be specialist or general director? There is need of both. The technique of any phase of social engineering may seem less intricate than that of material engineering. The definiteness of the task set for the technical engineer is missing. But the mastery of social engineering, or any part of it, while apparently simpler, because more vague, is correspondingly more difficult. The social engineer deals not with clear cut mathematical formulae and solvable equations but with human materials and problems in which the unknown quantities exceed the possible equations that can be stated. Instead of definite answers, the human engineer is continually confronted with conditions. *If* human nature permits, if group organization may be unified sufficiently, if social controls can be developed and made to work, then certain problems may be solved in certain desirable ways. The generalizations which the social engineer must find and try to administer will be discovered only with the most careful research and with infinite patience.

Unless those who make the almost numberless *specific studies* of social conditions and human problems are capable, trained and working in a limited field, the data with which *the general engineer* works will be faulty and his conclusions erroneous and valueless. If, on the contrary, *the detailed research worker* lacks a fair understanding of past or present, his studies may well be beside the point, of static affairs—or worse, of dynamic affairs treated as static—of human changes with humanity left out. On a great host of scientific assistants the specialist must depend for his materials; on his own skill, outlook, insight and understanding will depend the accuracy of his findings and the value of his suggestions. His contribution to the working out of a cultural reorganization may be within a tiny field of work but may furnish the key to the solution of related problems over a wide area of human endeavor.

Failures in our present set-up point the need in future engineering. Had most business leaders had the inventiveness, adaptability and capacity for advance shown by many technical experts, we should be farther on our way to a more successful and satisfactory civilization. *The social engineer as specialist* must be allowed to provide the proper material and suggest its proper use and its place in the whole scheme. But the scheme as a whole, or parts of it that are general, not detailed, are the responsibility of *the directing social engineer* or a coördinated group of engineers, working out plans and making them effective in rather large fields of social action. Their success may well depend less upon their ability than upon their comprehension of human needs, upon a knowledge of trends in civilization, upon an understanding of the proportions in which cultural elements should be combined and may be combined. Moreover, the social engineer may find that with all these he fails, though he might have succeeded had he added to them imagination of probable future changes in our dynamic world and a vision of its possibilities.

X

OLD AND NEW IN TRANSITION

Introduction The problems and dilemmas of industrialism and capitalism probably developed to the critical stage actually attained in America because society had only recently devoted itself to industrial capitalism. They probably would not have developed to the point beyond which it seems impossible to go in either the industrial or financial field were not an individualistic society becoming well socialized. In all probability part of the dilemma encountered by both industrialism and capitalism is due to the fact that in the World War period both had become more highly organized, centralized, and collectivized than had our government,[1] and the American people, or any of our non-economic institutions.

In an early chapter [2] we left the third great revolution in recent American history until later chapters. This is symbolized by *a conflict between industrialism and capitalism,* but it has been almost as much a contest between either or both and the American public. The World War speeded up business concentration, the centralization of business in huge units continuing on actively through the "New Era" that followed.[3] Financialism grew great possibly more in promoting mergers and in controlling a new, more flexible credit system than was possible with the slower and smaller business changes of the pre-war period. If the World War had threatened to promote democracy, it probably could have done so [4] only at the expense of industrial capitalism. As the victory was not with democracy, the prosperity of the "New Era" period therefore

---

[1] *Cf.* Integral and economic nationalism, Hayes, C. J. H., *The Historical Evolution of Modern Nationalism,* chs. VI and VII.
[2] See end of ch. II.
[3] Pp. 120–122.
[4] Pp. 318–319.

seemed to industrial capitalism to be a paradise regained. In depression after 1929 temporarily at least the business world seemed to face a paradise lost.

After the depression came, industrial capitalism was much concerned with a real solution of the dilemma and made decided effort toward that solution. If the leaders in both the industrial and the financial field were ready and willing to make all necessary changes and sacrifice, the way out *might* be found without very great difficulty. Big business leaders, with all their extraordinary keenness when profit lures, may not have shown great understanding in grasping fundamentals and in attacking vital problems. Moreover, in the past whether the proposed change was the Federal Reserve, which succeeded, or industrial reconstruction, which failed, the business powers fought even minor reforms that seemed to threaten their right to do exactly as they pleased. Seldom did they voluntarily make changes which would seem to meet public pressing needs, although at the beginning they cooperated rather well with the Roosevelt administration in the N. R. A.

In the evolution of industrial capitalism, in the late development of a conflict of interests between the two parts, industrialism and financialism, and in the demand of *each* that it should keep what it had, or change it only at its own request, we find expression of a system of *business individualism* undirected by public agencies and little hampered by public control. Ideas, such as individualism and older techniques used rather successfully to the end of the nineteenth century fitted continually less and less satisfactorily into a world being transformed by technological advance. New contacts were being created, new links formed, new unions cemented, partly as a result of the Industrial Revolution out of which both modern industrialism and capitalism emerged. *As social relations became more complex, the need of social solidarity increased* in all nations, and possibly throughout the western civilized world. In this development no force played a larger part than did big business. Applications of science constantly reduced distances between states and between nations, creating yearly new bonds between them. The small factory gave way to the large plant, finally merging into huge semi-monopolistic corporations which knew little competition and exercised rather autocratic authority. So far as the old individualism has been destroyed, or so much as it has yielded to more socialized actions or more concentrated social organization, curiously enough the change is largely the work of the huge business mergers and of concentrated financial control.

If industrialism and financialism have paved the way for socialization by using it in place of a discarded individualism, why then is there so serious and public a problem of making a shift from an individualist society to a rather highly socialized one? First of all, *the need of socialization, great as it is, is not so well understood in the fields of education and social relations* as in any kind of business, though probably the need of socialization is greater. Any intelligent, cautious attempt to secure this socialization encounters *opposition from the forces of cultural inertia,* more obstinate in social than in business fields. In short, in political and social relations and institutions the necessity for change is not so obvious, and the gain from it is not an easily perceived one like profit, but a general and vague one of a better government or a better society.[5]

In the second place, we must take into account the fact that *gradually reorganization will follow* as a natural consequence the slow but inevitable shift away from an individualist system toward one represented by general though gradual socialization. Later we hope to consider some of the trends which have already been indicated,[6] trends through which we can trace this shift.

In the third place, reorganization may be studied in connection with *the process of social coördination or group organization which is replacing the old bourgeoisie civilization* of individualist America. If we can, we must ascertain the place which the middle class has played in the democratically-

[5] Pp. 81–90.
[6] Pp. 309–319.

minded society of the nineteenth century. We must also consider the question whether a middle class is essential in a socialized society of the twentieth century.[7]

It will not be amiss, fourthly, to examine *the part played in this social organization by the public through government.* The satisfaction of public needs calls for new and better coördination of the agencies which make and administer the laws, whether in state or nation, and the creation of better controls by those public agents of or over business or social groups whose combined interaction represents society at work.[8]

THE RISE AND FALL OF INDIVIDUALISM

We have already noticed [9] the beginnings of modern individualism and have considered the Renaissance and late eighteenth-century periods as reactions against the society or the policies of an earlier day. To be the opposite of an old, unsatisfactory, and outworn scheme is a rather poor excuse for any new institution or system. Individualism therefore needed to justify itself as worthwhile in other ways than freeing people from a pre-existing collectivized society or oppressive and arbitrary political and economic absolutism.

The value of individualism in the old American system

In examining the origin and development of American individualism most writers stress either business individualism or the frontier. In a way the frontier was just as much an economic force as was free and unhampered business enterprise. But the frontier had nothing to do with industry and everything with political democracy of the nineteenth century. If individualism in the industrial arena claimed to be earlier than that in the political field or more important in the creation of nineteenth-century America, its claim might be disputed at once. Certainly individualized industrialism does not have nearly so clear a case as most writers give it.

Is individualism more necessary in a rather primitive society than in one well developed? As a people become well organized and integrated, is individualism of greater or less

[7] See pp. 379–381.
[8] See pp. 319–325, 335–342, 397–403.
[9] Pp. 39–40, 82–83.

consequence? Eighteenth-century America certainly found economic individualism much to its liking. The old British laws of trade, poorly enforced as they were, represented an application of mercantilism most distasteful to the colonists in theory and in fact. By separating from Great Britain we seemed to get rid of the mercantilism used by a European country in her colonial policy. In those days business was on a small scale, and the frontier was close to the Atlantic coast. The overthrow of English control and the demand for personal rights seemed to leave American business men almost unlimited private initiative, freed private property from oppressive foreign taxes or regulations, and left us little competition except that which we ourselves provided. Once rid of English rule, our new *state legislatures* had opportunity to replace some old laws with new. Not many laws were passed because, if legislation was scarce, the rights of man flourished, especially when they were safeguarded by constitutional bills of rights.

The *national government* had a clean slate upon which to write any laws it chose to make, since there had never been any earlier national government in America. Even the slogan "a government of laws and not of men" did not produce much legislation for that generation which thought the less government the better. Did this old individualism actually give more "liberty under law," or did it just give more liberty? Apparently it represented a decided advance over any previous political scheme.

Worthwhile was legislation a century ago, freeing the individual from the limitations that poorer and lesser members of society had carried from time immemorial.[10] Without it probably religious toleration would not have been changed into religious freedom. Without it education might not have been free,[11] might have failed to become universal, might have lost sight of the importance of the individual in the process of training. Were there, however, actually greater opportunities under individualism in the eighteenth century, in the late nine-

[10] Pp. 286–291, 387–397.
[11] See ch. XVII.

teenth, and in the early twentieth than had existed previously or might have existed with more public regulation? Moreover, to what extent did personal individualism, individualism as a social theory, and a philosophy of individualism follow in the wake of economic and political individualism? What do you think?

One of the first safeguards of the individual created in the state constitutions as early as June, 1776, was the insertion in those constitutions of *bills of rights* for citizens. A similar bill of rights was added to the United States Constitution in 1791. The form in which these rights were expressed changed in the nineteenth century from a statement that citizens should have those rights to a statement that the citizens did have them, certainly an increase of safeguard. *These rights, however, were* solely *rights that the individual citizen had against government.* Americans who formerly had protested against interference by those who were enforcing British law were equally anxious to avoid annoying enforcement of American laws as well. Nothing was said about non-political rights such as those connected with health or with the work of the individual. As science provided new understanding of health needs and of health problems, the protection of individual and public health became more and more a matter of public interest. More important even than health was life and freedom from injury, now increasingly threatened by the use of power-machines in factories and on streets and railroads.

In a real sense the protection of the lives and health of workers formed a transition from the protection of individual rights of the constitutional type against government to the protection of the economic rights of workers and the social rights of citizens in general. Seldom did these safeguards get into either state or national constitution except as parts of the unwritten constitutions embodied in important laws and judicial decisions. In a true way *these modern rights of workers against industry* were analogous to the earlier rights of citizens against government. Just as an individualist theory of politics had protected those earlier civic rights against arbitrary administration of law, so now these newer social

Individualism in the American system after 1776; (1) political or economic rights [12] were somewhat similarly protected against arbitrary administration of business.

This new "individualism" grows out of the old, yet it is almost its opposite. Furthermore, when public health is named as a chief basis of action by government and safeguarded through an unwritten if not a written constitution, a still larger and more important element develops—the right of society to protect itself, regardless of the limitations which that protective action may place upon the individual in his relations with other individuals or with society. In the field of individual rights, therefore, more or less for the purpose of protecting the rights of *citizens in society* we have a shift from a philosophy of individualism to one of public welfare and socialization.

(2) economic   The protection of workers in the safeguarding of life and limb was a forerunner by a narrow time margin of many other safeguards of workers as individuals or as groups. Rugged individualism claimed as the very heart of its program an absolutely untrammelled *freedom of contract* and unlimited competition. From past times we inherit the idea that contract is free only if made between equals. In olden days the disparity between buyer and seller or between employer and employe was slight. With the development of bigger and bigger business it became constantly more a legal fiction. Consumers found increasing difficulty in making bargains with producers. Even before the World War employes were handicapped in securing work except near their homes, and possibly only with branches of a single great trust. As late as 1923 the United States Supreme Court refused to uphold minimum wage laws for women, on the ground that the law interfered with freedom of contract of the employer. But in general the courts recognized that perfect freedom of contract presupposed equality of the parties, which might not exist in a highly organized and integrated industrial society.

The protection of individual rights through *business competition* has been a main purpose of some of the most liberal and forward-looking government agencies, as for example the

[12] Pp. 288–291.

Federal Trade Commission. The guarantee of competition means rather little however when before 1925 the Federal Trade Commission itself reported [13] that in a large number of fields a very small number of corporations had almost whole control. If these corporations were interrelated directly or through financial supervision, this control became semi-monopolistic. Of possibly more value to business but an almost greater means of destroying the individualism upon which it was based was the right recognized by the Fourteenth Amendment, and accepted by the courts, that corporations are entitled to all the legal rights of persons under American law. In the period following the Civil War this did not seem of prime significance because the corporations were still young, fairly small, and struggling. In the period following the World War, however, corporations, formed into mergers and practically monopolies, were allowed by court decision to do things prohibited to combinations.[14]

How can individualism be the basis of big business when business is destroying individualism in these ways and others? Business may dictate contracts to individuals when there is no equality between parties and therefore no free contract. It may claim rights of competition when in the fields of most big business little is left, except possibly between the giants in those fields or between the industrialist and the financier. Certainly legal protection of competition was never intended for that type of titanic conflict. It may claim protection of the law in its financial operations and yet it may gain freedom from many debt obligations when the market price of securities is lowered. The individuals for whom a special corporation may be organized may pay light taxes instead of the heavy income taxes required of individuals. The last that we shall mention, but not the last that might be included, is the claiming of individual rights to private property by corporations whose property is not private. We can easily see therefore how the individual business man for whom this system of individualism was created is finding that the corporation as

[13] P. 120.
[14] Pp. 322–323.

a person is nullifying some of his individual rights, and possibly depriving him legally of his property. In other words, economically if not politically the individual is hoist on his own petard.

This brief summary indicates trends from an individualist order toward a more highly socialized order both in the so-called political field of citizen rights and in the economic field. It is possible to discern ways in which *the old individualism is responsible for the decline of individualism* as a theory, a policy, or a system. Is the opposite of that true? In other words, for the increase of socialization is individualism usually responsible? Probably not; but if not, what is? Is socialization due to a growing complexity of relations between individual and individual, group and group, nation and nation, and the development of a highly organized, integrated social order?

Before leaving this topic, we might inquire whether on the basis of an individualist philosophy a modern society can be built or rebuilt. If so, will this be done by purely voluntary coöperation? Or can we, without abandoning individualism, have coöperation that is more or less compulsory? Whatever therefore the nature of the coöperation that is necessary, can it be secured under the principles of an individualist philosophy? What do you think? Possibly we can decide better after an examination of some shifts that have actually taken place in America.

A pertinent question might bring up the place of nationalism [15] and of fascism [16] in this process of growing socialization. In the nineteenth century and in eastern Europe in the early twentieth, nationalism stood for more rights of races to self-determination. A group that had many interests and ideas in common, including race, sought to gain a group organization and a single national government for itself, separate from the old oppressive government under which it had lived, and distinct from its neighbors. These new "upstart" nations and the older nations have grown constantly more self-conscious

15 See pp. 440–445.
16 See pp. 361–365.

and self-sufficient. They have intentionally promoted uniform laws throughout their territory, reorganized customs to get rid of many local differences and provincialisms, and standardized school instruction, patriotic thought, and business methods. This artificial "socialization," especially of those peoples whose nationalism has been rampant, has caused competition among nations to get more, and more concentrated, nationalism. Most of all, and worst of all, dictators or others have used nationalism as an opportunity to indoctrinate the people under their sway with the ideas and plans of some small faction. They have created a pseudo-socialization which has uniformity and unreasoned standardization in place of true social solidarity, developed out of voluntary coöperation of freely acting individuals.

If America is to avoid the disintegration of the old individualism on the one hand and, on the other, the extreme of lock-step nationalization, in school, in business and in society, science and education should not fall as short as they have done of reaching their highest goal. In the future they can certainly be utilized very much better, not in the development of a material "culture" which will create more dollars, but for a better civilization which shall be material chiefly as a means of gaining culture. In creating public opinion and changing their idea of nationality the people should watch slogans and evade pressure politics which present substitute class demands and pretend that they represent the public will.

For the individual and for society the *understanding of what is involved in new standards* will be a considerable part of this task of socialization and reorganization. Those standards are necessary which will help the individual develop himself wisely and well, and help society find and do what is fair, just, and best, since those will be ethical. Possibly many older standards, because they are not up-to-date, are not ethical. Is that probable?

Growing Socialization in America

To make clearer the trend from an individualist philosophy of society toward a more highly socialized one, possibly attention might be drawn to some outstanding changes in suc-

Periods of increasing socialization in American history

cessive periods of twentieth-century America. Undoubtedly there will be some repetition of material already given, just as there has been in these accounts just presented. At the turn of the century these trends were already observable. Trusts had been organized in the early eighties, but the great period of big business reorganization started with the depression of 1893 and gained rapid headway after the Spanish-American War. Competition was lessened among the smaller units even if increased between the great combinations. The trend of business caused the President of the early years of this century, Theodore Roosevelt, to urge better railroad control, protection of natural resources from graft and exploitation—in brief, conservation—and at least in gesture, the better regulation of this big business. Those years, moreover, saw the states passing and the Supreme Court approving numerous types of social legislation, particularly workman's compensation and child labor laws, and shorter hours for women. These changes represent a real shift from the old order toward a new.

The second period might be represented by the World War. Individualism in Great Britain and America never could go back to its pre-war freedom. In the raising of armies, voluntary enlistment yielded very quickly to a juster and fairer selective draft. The right of society to the military services of its young men was not exercised in the Revolutionary War, as represented by the poor showing of enlistments, nor greatly in the Civil War, in which only the younger generation was fully represented on both sides. In 1917 there was little demand for and no recognition of the fact that property has war obligations as well as adult citizens, if they were not too old. Yet, even here property was called upon to make real contributions, as in the high rate for income taxes, or real sacrifices as in the purchase of liberty loans or the withdrawal from production of marginal plants or plants in non-essential industries. The organization of the railroads into a single nationally controlled system typifies the public demand that socio-economic agencies can be requisitioned or commandeered for public use and that a unified organization and control when publicly necessary is the public's right. These few illustrations must suffice.

In the third period, that of prosperity, especially from 1922–29, it would seem as though individualism again was re-asserting itself. Certainly there was little government interference even when business used distinctively unsocial methods at home and abroad. The power of the Department of State was used to promote foreign business, especially in Latin America; at times it gave permission for Americans to expend good money on doubtful investments abroad. Socialization seems less noticeable during this new era; but socialization may have been hastened more by business consolidation during those years than in any other period. Moreover, the reaction against profit-taking during this period, although not observable until depression, may make that time of prosperity one of the epoch-making periods of progressive advance.

The fourth period which represents increased socialization was "the greatest depression in history." If any experience of the last two generations has shown up so sharply the evils of individualism especially through the dilemmas of industrialism and financialism, the writer does not know those facts.[17] Probably most of the criticisms hurled at the existing order dealt chiefly with industrialism and were awakened by the armies of unemployed and the interminable bread lines. The debt problem may have caused almost as much feeling against the investment financiers, but it did not give an equal understanding of the problem or show up so well the weaknesses of the existing system. The world-wide extent of depression brought into relief the problem of attempting to create a social order, not local or even national, but at least as wide as western civilization, which was built upon so slender and temporary a foundation as that furnished by present-day capitalism.

The fifth period, that of recovery and reorganization, has

---

[17] Compare, however, the revelations of the anti-social business practices found in the reports of the Pujo Committee, the I. C. C., the Federal Trade Commission, and successive Senate committees.

hardly begun at this writing. Recovery and reorganization
have numerous ideas in common. Recovery puts more emphasis upon practical relief, reorganization upon remedying
the difficulty which lies back of the distress. Both give special
attention to public responsibility in connection with either the
relief or the remedy. Both seek some readjustment by which
the plight of the farmer and the plight of the worker shall be
lessened. At the beginning of the Roosevelt Recovery Administration first attention was given to increase of purchasing power. In actual administration of the Recovery Program
this was postponed if not neglected, because it could not
be attacked and secured directly. So contrary to the plans
and methods of the old individualist non-interference was the
Recovery Program, at least in America, that many conservatives raised the cry of regimentation, fascism, and socialism.
How much the codes have represented economic planning and
how much of it they should have embodied is a moot question.
More necessary is the query: To what extent should recovery
have been a primary object and the chief goal of reconstruction? If recovery necessarily preceded reconstruction, although valueless without a move in the direction of greater
socialization, how much did the recovery period work out
principles of social engineering?

Social
legislation

The shift away from individualism might be represented
in a large number of fields and by numerous series of studies. In this brief account we shall limit ourselves to two:
social legislation and public education.

In the eighteenth century, as in most of those earlier, the
common man possessed comparatively few rights against government officials or against groups of his fellows who sought
to exploit him. As we have seen,[18] the individual was protected against government in England and in America, beginning with the Revolution of 1688 and continuing on with
the American Revolution and later constitutions, from *arbitrary interference by government officials*. As we shall notice,[19] the means of safeguarding the individual through new

[18] Pp. 279–280.
[19] Pp. 382–397.

laws or by court action improved constantly as more and more members of society were permitted to share in the election of public officials or in the management of public affairs. From the eighteenth century to the twentieth the nominal control of American affairs was shifted from the landowners, first to property owners and then beginning about 1820 to white male citizens. In 1870 the elective franchise was extended to all male adults, giving manhood suffrage, and exactly fifty years later to all women as well, offering universal adult suffrage. In the meantime, the share which these voters had in government was constantly increasing. At first the voters elected only direct representatives in the legislature and occasionally some others. A hundred years ago many local officials and a large number of state administrators were elected instead of appointed; and some judges also were popularly elected. This *popular participation of voters through electing most of the important officials* proved to be inadequate. In the early twentieth century new means of voter control were devised, as is shown in the right to hold direct primary elections, in the permission to introduce and check laws and constitutions, the initiative and referendum, and occasionally to recall elected officials, including judges.

The process of socialization which we are now considering culminated in two periods, nearly a century apart, in each of which extension of popular government was followed by social legislation. The first of these periods is the second quarter of the nineteenth century, the beginnings of white manhood suffrage, and the other, the first quarter of the twentieth, the time of more "rule of the people." If the writer may be permitted to quote from a summary which he wrote a generation ago, the equalization of rights, at least for white men, first became rather noticeable a century ago. "It was inevitable that sooner or later class privileges should disappear. We have noticed already that religious qualifications for the franchise had been the first to go, and that property was not required of voters to any extent. Laws of inheritance no longer gave the eldest son a special share. Imprisonment for debt had been discontinued gradually after 1776, and was used very little in 1840. The newer states were beginning to make homesteads exempt from seizure by creditors. Through constitutional provision or statute some states were following the example of the national government which in 1840 made ten hours a day's labor for its employees, but most changes of this character came later, after the Civil War. In some cases the [state] constitutions expressly stated that married women might hold property in their own names, and gave them certain other specific rights before the law and in inheritance. The movement in favor of *equalization* [*of rights*] *among white men* was almost universal, though less pronounced in the older and more conservative sections." [20]

In the twentieth century a new type of social legislation was evolved. It represents a further degree of socialization, and particularly a *growing acceptance of social obligation*. In the nineteenth century, as soon as men gained the right to vote, they were content to remove disabilities under which they and their fellows had labored for centuries, or possibly from time immemorial. In the twentieth century, on the contrary, the legislation is more distinctively *humanitarian* for classes that have not yet gained an adequate share in government or that probably never would gain such a share, and it was passed with the expressed intention of *social betterment*.

Protective legislation for children in England would carry us back into the eighteenth century. But many years elapsed before there was any protective legislation for any but poorhouse apprentices. Until just about a century ago the children who came from homes really were not safeguarded by any laws, passed to shorten their hours of labor or to improve their conditions of work. Almost immediately English child labor legislation was supplemented by protective laws for women workers. Why the United States, the most democratic and progressive of all countries, did nothing in the nineteenth century is an interesting question. Were individualism and a general policy of *laissez faire* chiefly responsible, or did our lawmakers feel that special labor legislation was unnecessary

[20] R. L. Ashley, *American History*, 1907, p. 329.

because of the higher American standard of living? In any case, the twentieth century opened with almost no public action in favor of workers who needed protection from exploitation.

Child labor received first attention. Through the work of Owen R. Lovejoy and others the public was aroused to the extent and evils of child labor. By 1905 child labor laws were enacted in increasing number and with increasing interest. In one year, 1913, child labor laws were passed in thirty-one states. Many of these, of course, were simply improvements of earlier laws. Originally states were content to prohibit child labor below the age of twelve and for ten hours a day. Gradually fourteen came to be the accepted age limit, except in a very few states; and ordinarily the eight-hour day was demanded, with night work forbidden. Twice Congress sought to prohibit the transportation from state to state of child-made goods. But both measures encountered constitutional difficulties and were declared null and void by the United States Supreme Court. In 1924 a child labor amendment was proposed to the United States Constitution. Before 1933 this had been approved by only six states; but, with the new interest aroused under the N. R. A., the number of ratifying states increased rapidly in subsequent years.

Agitation for the prohibition of child work over a generation accomplished much less than the laws prescribed because in most states there was no adequate inspection. Very few states had birth certificates to prove the age of children, and the sentiment of factory owners and of parents, as well as occasionally of children, was against any interference with personal liberty. When the employment provisions of the N. I. R. A. codes prescribed a minimum wage per hour for workers including children, child labor suddenly disappeared. Our social obligation to children apparently has not been so strong a motive with the American public as the call of dollars.

Protection of women workers had a shorter but much less successful history. In the nineteenth century some laws were passed; but usually they were not approved by the courts. In 1905 an Oregon law forbidding work by women for more than ten hours in any one day was upheld by the Supreme Court of the United States, in the first of a series of *epoch-making protective health decisions*. At the present time only a few states prescribe an eight-hour day as a maximum, although a larger number limit the work of women to nine or ten hours; but almost as many states have no restrictive legislation whatsoever. A much less extensive movement tried to prescribe *a minimum wage for women workers*. This flurry was chiefly a 1913 movement and affected at that time thirteen states. Later Congress made a similar law for the District of Columbia. This was declared unconstitutional by the Supreme Court in 1923, and the following year a similar law from the state of Arizona was overruled. Curiously enough, although the states had done so little to protect women in their bargaining power and other ways, except for hours, the N. I. R. A. prescribed a minimum wage not only for women but for men. This was one of the temporary provisions of the Recovery Program of 1933.

In Europe social legislation has concerned itself infinitely less with protective laws such as these than it has with protection of workers against accident,[21] disease,[22] unemployment,[23] and old age.[24] A half century ago Germany enacted laws in each of these fields. In 1906 Great Britain followed suit by protecting workers against accident in what is known as workmen's compensation laws. Practically all American states now have some compensation legislation with administrative boards to examine cases and apply the law. And there American social legislation stopped, at least until 1933. Comparatively few states have any regulations in regard to compulsory unemployment insurance. Practically none has made provisions for public sickness insurance of workers. And only a few public systems before 1935 provided for old age, except for paupers. As we note elsewhere, if business cannot or will

[21] I. M. Rubinow, *The Quest for Security*, Book II.
[22] *Ibid.*, Book III.
[23] *Ibid.*, Book V.
[24] *Ibid.*, Book IV.

not provide workers with a job by which they can support themselves and a family, the obligation must be assumed by the public.

These new rights were applied to special classes that could not protect themselves. Literally women and children were first. As we have seen, health was not only the reason but a real legal basis for the enactment of these laws and the acceptance of their constitutionality. Working men had been included, or at least until 1933, only when they were exposed to risk of life and limb, and not when they suffered from diseases other than occupational or could not find work. Society therefore has recognized its obligation to groups needing protection of life or of health. In *People at Work* Frances Perkins makes us see in successive periods a continually growing public interest in the worker and his public protection. She shows progressively the development of public sentiment in successive periods, demanding protection against occupational risks and diseases and a constantly increasing interest in shorter hours and less unemployment.[25] A new idea is entering in: the public protection of the rights of those who could not defend themselves under an individualist system.

Possibly the field of public education offers one of the very best examples of the substitution of social action for that of the individual, with a growing recognition of social responsibility. Until about a hundred years ago there was little attention to education of youth at public expense. Except in some towns in the North and in the West, parents of children paid special rates for school instruction. About 1820 new laws were made favoring the public schools, but it was not until 1837 that Horace Mann, as Commissioner of Education for the Commonwealth of Massachusetts, worked out plans and began to develop a *system*, with schools for teacher training, which really deserves to be considered the beginning of public education in America.

With this tradition behind him,[26] Horace Mann had the

Education

---

[25] Sec. 1.

[26] Possibly we should look back two centuries further to the laws of the Massachusetts general court of 1642 and 1647, in which the separate towns were authorized to maintain grammar schools.

advantage over any educational official or leader in most of the other states. The *period* was especially favorable for the development and spread of a public-school system really organized at public expense, because throughout the United States and western Europe in the generation from 1830 to 1850 there was a growing recognition of the *rights of the common man*.[27] This showed itself partly in the extension of the elective franchise to all white men in this country; but it is clearly apparent in the wave of social legislation which is one of the marked characteristics of American history of a hundred years ago.

It is not easy to determine what connection there might be between the extension of the franchise to the common landless worker and this new interest in giving him the rudiments of a public-school education. Possibly the old but none too valuable slogan that the purpose of public-school education is training for citizenship may have been an important reason for education at public expense. Possibly the interest in public schools was simply part of the growing recognition that society owed its less favored members, including children and, later, women, protection by law from the ignorance and oppression to which they had been subject in preceding centuries. In other words, this may have been simply part of a social legislation program, even though that society did not recognize nearly so fully as ours now its responsibility for proper training of youth and better pre-vision for protection of those who formerly could not protect themselves under the law.

The last half century has seen the rise of public education above the grammar school level and a great change in the character of the public school. As late as 1875 the children who remained in school more than the equivalent of three present school years formed a very small proportion of the population. In 1890 the public high schools of America numbered but 2500, and the total number of students was 200,000 —this number being only two-thirds of all of the secondary school students in the United States. Contrast with these figures those of 1915. Only one out of every seven of those

[27] Macmaster, J. B., *History of the People of the United States*, ch. LXIX.

who entered the first grade graduated from the grammar school and entered high school, and of this number two-thirds failed to graduate. But, in 1915, we find the number of public high schools had increased to 12,000, the number of students to a million and a half, and the percentage of students in public high schools compared with private to more than nine out of ten. By 1935 there were a quarter as many students in the public high schools as in the elementary, and of about a million students in American universities and colleges, at least 200,000 were being educated in public institutions for which practically no tuition was charged.

These rather detailed accounts have been given to show the actual extent to which the public has taken over private education, not simply in elementary but in secondary and still higher institutions of learning. We have not included state teacher-training institutions, in which more than a hundren thousand students are receiving training at the present time at the expense of the public. In themselves these data illustrate an extraordinary increase of public interest and a constantly growing sense of public responsibility. In the more progressive institutions the training represents more individual preparation for life and individual capitalization of abilities than did any of the old training of the individualist period of American experience.

In the larger institutions and in the more crowded cities, and particularly since the beginning of depression, more mass instruction is given. Probably the public school overstresses conformity to type and standardization of methods and of standards for measuring or determining progress. In some systems there may be a great deal of regimentation, with possibly an attempt to substitute patriotic or local propaganda for others that appeal to the public or the school authorities as being anti-social. Indoctrination is not unknown, but the opposite is more common. In fact, of the modern public school as a place for learning some have declared that most of the students learn enough to be opinionated but not enough to be informed.

Misguided are many of the attempts to determine school

courses and procedures by legislation, or by the arbitrary ruling of administrative authority, some of which are political or without clear knowledge of educational needs. Occasionally a mistaken patriotism dictates formulae that must be followed by teachers, or oaths that must be taken by them to insure the teaching of Americanism as the existing government sees it. Nevertheless the whole process represents a distinct shift to socialization and a much clearer recognition than formerly that the American people and the public's representatives in the classroom are responsible for more and better training of the youth of America. If this were done chiefly as training for citizenship, if the chief stresses were on the social heritage, or if the dominant aim were to make permanent the social pattern of any time or social creed, this procedure, often barely escaping indoctrination, would be far less important than it is likely to become, in the process of further socialization and civilization.

SOCIALIZED REORGANIZATION

Individualism's contributions to the reorganization

The transition from an individualist order toward one that is socialized is probably linked in hundreds of ways with the transition [28] from an agricultural society to an industrialized one. Probably the separation of the threads which represent an industrialized reorganization in the transition from agricultural society contrasted with those which represent a greater socialization will not be easy and in most cases probably impossible.

The answer to the question [29] whether a socialized society can be constructed upon principles of individualism might now be considered from several points of view. One of these, and the only one that need be considered here, is the place of the citizen in a modern society. A second is the question of whether democracy,[30] originally a rural, individualist type, in adapting itself to urban, industrialized conditions is not changing primarily from an individualist basis to a socialized one.

[28] See ch. IV.
[29] Pp. 280–282.
[30] See pp. 83, 94–97, and chs. XII and XIII.

A third group of considerations that might be taken into account is the problem not so much of a planned economic order as one directed and controlled for the public instead of primarily by and for business.[31]

In a modern society surely a citizen is not primarily an individual. He is a *member* of the whole society. Even in the smaller groups with which he is connected he is of greater importance as a member of a group than he is as a person. It may really be questioned whether aside from his place in these groups he has any individual *rights*.[32] Is not that term meaningless except in association with others? As a Robinson Crusoe he would need no laws because he had no relationships and could claim no liberties or rights, and have no duties, in relation to others. In short, it might be said that the extent to which a citizen has proper status in a nation and proper relations with others and proper rules under which he acts depends upon *the right kind of group or social organization* more than upon any group *action* intended primarily for individuals.

The character of the individual's place, and the nature of his work, in this group organization naturally depend upon the stage of development of the society, upon whether there is adaptation of the social organization to changing needs, and upon the nation's success in securing wise blending of experience with reason in an attempted social reorganization. The proper status of the member or citizen in any society and proper relations with others undoubtedly are far less a matter of legislation than of *new, practical, socially recognized and approved adjustments.* The extent to which those will be achieved by *personal, voluntary coöperation* of the persons or groups which have relations with one another depends probably upon the experience, wisdom, and intelligence of the people who attempt to work the thing out.

If the social organization under which this citizen lives is like our own, in transition from an old order to a new, it will be necessary to take into account (1) the success already

---

[31] Pp. 260–265, 397–401.
[32] Pp. 387–397.

attained in giving the individual his right place and work in society; and (2) how much either the members or the whole group visualize the requirements and the possibilities of the new state of affairs; and (3) the willingness and the capacity of the individual to find, accept, and make the most of his new place in the new social order. With most of us all these things will probably have to be done for us rather than by us, although without some opportunity for us to share in the doing and without some actual coöperation by us in making our social order more what it should be, we shall never gain experience in self-development or gain power in helping ourselves or others. Then both we and society would lose by our ignorance and our inexperience. Can a society rise higher than the individuals of whom it is the collective whole? What do you think?

It might be worthwhile to inquire whether a society might attain a satisfactory social reorganization, not by changing the bases upon which the new is built, but just by remedial legislation, by concerted neglect of old and poor laws, by disregarding through almost unanimous consent the evils of unjust past political, social or economic institutions and systems. Certainly an individualist society seems to defeat its own purpose if it seeks to leave uncoördinated a large amount of personal initiative, self-direction, and self-development; for, as a consequence, it loses cohesion and unity.

Substitutes for individualism

The corporation, a collective body, an anomaly under a régime of individualism, should be under the obligation to render not only an account, but just service, to the shareholders. This should mean responsible "management" and good management of the business. Directors cannot be permitted to misdirect the affairs of a corporation for their personal advantage or for the gain of other businesses in which they are interested. The corporation possesses the rights of persons and is buttressed by legal safeguards for the protection of private property. As a social beneficiary it enjoys these and other legal advantages, and it should be correspondingly a social benefactor. It can be that if it wishes because of its extensive ownership of property and its wide-spread business, protected by legal and constitutional guarantees and judicial mandates.

The need of socialization and desirable acceptance of social responsibility is most observable in the case of financial corporations. There has been a remarkable improvement in the sense of obligation shown by those who handle the people's money or business affairs. Compare the gain of the "gay nineties" over the "reckless seventies," of the welfare-minded pre-war era over the "gay nineties," and even of the "spendthrift twenties" over the nineteenth century. It took a depression, however, to reveal the shortcomings of money trustees, the actual legal and socially moral delinquencies in missale of funds, misrepresentation of investments and disregard of the rights of depositors and investors. There has already been a gain in the separation of investment banking from commercial banking. Almost observable is a trend toward responsibility of bankers. Temporarily the government has accepted direct responsibility for the safety of bank deposits; but in the long run it might be wise to devise a plan which will help the bankers become responsible for those and other banking functions, because the banks should carry their own responsibilities.

The new Industrial Revolution is tending to counteract the worst characteristics of the old. Electricity, by decentralizing industry, frees labor from much concentrated coercion and threatens the ruin of the slum. In many other ways electricity, through the telephone and radio and numerous labor-saving devices or comfort-bringing gadgets, makes semi-isolated homes outside of tenement areas possible and desirable. The automobile has a major part not only in bringing workers to the work instead of forcing workers to stay near the job, but in carrying workers away from even semi-isolated homes into rural surroundings. If the old individualist society found its chief strength in provincialism, the auto has done its full share in making the old life out-of-date. Eventually, if not now, these changes may counteract over-urbanization, mechanization, standardization, the evils of over-specialization of labor, and mass production. There has been a marked revulsion against mechanized and industrialized mass education. The whole trend is toward more stress upon distribution, less attention to production. It is difficult to estimate the significance of the socialization that is bound to come through *protection of the consumer* rather than aid or promotion of the producer.

In developing a socialized society we naturally wish to keep any characteristic of the old order which fits reasonably well into the new. Numerous examples of economic survivals from the "laissez faire" era are observable in spite of the public controls we have begun to develop.[33] Because of the lag of culture, which is derivative, these survivals are inevitably more numerous in our personal relations, in our religious attitudes, and in our every-day usages. If the group organization of the future possesses an integration that includes flexibility, is there any reason why the individual should not be freer to make more of himself and achieve real success more completely than he did under the rugged individualism of the past?

Social coöperation ought to be able to do at least as much for its members, possibly the regular members and certainly the leaders, as football "interference" gives to him that carries the ball. Naturally more members of the family than just the head wish for advantage from their joint coöperation. If only the principal of the school, from the standpoint of the faculty, or the teachers of the institution, from the standpoint of the students, or the student body officers, from the standpoint of the institution, enjoy these individual opportunities and advantages, the individual *in* the society will benefit only indirectly from new and better coöperation. Group organization ought to represent better recognition of each person's individuality, ought to promote rather than stifle that individuality. Even though it is not conscious of such a purpose, when it gives him the place for which he is fitted, training him carefully and successfully for that sphere, and enables him to find the work which he can do, valuable to himself and helpful for the best development of society, it is

[33] See IX and XI.

foredoomed to success. A socialized society may thus gain a greater mobility than any individualist order could possibly attain.

Capitalization of abilities means the offering of new opportunities for self-expression and self-direction within the limits of the activity which the society sets for itself rather than for its members. There is no reason why, in a system of growing socialization, the new individualism should not be better than the old, because the society cannot achieve its purpose of making humanity safe for humanity, and attain its best stature, unless it does make the most of individual members. So far as the individual is concerned, the point is chiefly that any member benefits from good group organization and the right kind of coöperation between himself and society far more than he can by any independent, uncorrelated attempt to serve himself. This is just another illustration of gaining one's life by disregarding any attempt to save it.

INTERACTION OF FORCES IN READJUSTMENT

As the world outgrows its older institutions or finds it necessary to abandon old ideas, customs, or practices, probably less attention is given to understanding the forces at work than to finding practical solutions. We want results even more than we want comprehension. Sometimes we get the one because our leaders or scholars have the other. If we follow the practice of the past, in nine cases out of ten the new will be a reaction against the old rather than an intelligent adaptation of old to new. With this in mind, looking back at the Reformation, we find it is a protest against authority and collectivism. The leaders wished individualism and exercised authority against disagreeing individuals. In the end, throughout northern Europe, *new authority,* represented usually by Scripture, replaced the old, embodied in the mandates of Mother Church. In the case of the American Revolution, freedom was far more a matter of throwing off the yoke of British semi-arbitrary government than of giving liberty to the common American people, and particularly the

Replacing old with new

Negro slaves. The World War seemed to be fought by democracy against autocracy, but several of the countries on the winning side have found difficulty in avoiding dictatorships, and some of them have not done even that. As an example of reaction from extreme to extreme, what is better than imperialist Russia turned bolshevist?

Probably it would be impossible to find, outside of certain fields of science and some methods of procedure based on invention, a complete replacement of the old heritage by something new and really different. Certainly the present-day family is more like the patriarchal family than many advanced new women would like it to be. Our boasted new education is probably far more a reaction against the formalism and scholasticism of the old classical training than it is psychologically adapted to human nature and sociologically suited to modern requirements. Methods of relief used in the recent depression before 1933 were hardly more than an imitation of poor relief a century ago. One wonders whether relief procedure after the first of March, 1933, might not have real kinship to the old Roman "bread and games." From the point of view of a *remedy*, it seems planless; it does not cut deep into causes. Europe, with millions on the margin of getting a living wage or less, over-supplied with labor, has undoubtedly followed a very sane procedure. It has attempted to anticipate needs and through *social* insurance solve problems which are bound to arise. But that may not be the best American solution.

Private business and corporation finance have capitalized the Industrial Revolution; public finance has lagged woefully. We cannot "point with pride" to the budgets of American governments. The bulk of governmental income comes from taxes upon wealth and not upon income. Certainly no business man would attempt to pay most of his running expenses out of his capital. Society still seems to be playing that game. Moreover, the commonest local tax is called, or miscalled, a tax on general property. It is a heritage from an agricultural society in which most of the property was land, improvements or farm implements, easily discoverable. Most American property is no longer of that type. Inevitably, the general property tax has become a tax upon land and improvements. Even in the fairly normal year of 1926, for the whole United States the tax upon real estate and improvements was at least five times as heavy, from the income point of view, as were all other taxes.

In state and national finance some modernization has taken place, and that modernization has relieved somewhat the burden of taxation upon property. Certainly it is a far cry from the *taille* or road tax of France before the Revolution, worked out by property owners or their assistants, to the gasoline tax which has worked a miracle on the surface of American highways. To some extent income taxes of individuals and of corporations have replaced more antiquated taxes on consumption. How little that type of tax has been modernized is observable in the very great differences in rates between individuals paying as individuals and individuals organized into a body and paying a corporation tax. How little we have escaped consumption taxes is shown by our dependence on tariffs and by the popularity of sales taxes.

The problem of adjustment might involve a study from three angles. First of all, there is the universal and all time difficulty of changing from old to new. *Social heritage must be the basis of all civilization,* but, in all but static societies, a heritage that represents only the past fails in all the nice adaptations needed for the present. Inflexible tradition is the antithesis of reasonable adaptation. If accepted at its full worth, it lacks the main characteristic of any growing organization, flexibility. If accepted, as is almost invariably the case, without thought or study, it may be an unintelligent survival, possibly unsatisfactory and possibly the exact opposite of the thing needed. Conditioned reflexes for society may represent a means of adapting old habit to new needs.

The problem of adjustment includes not only that of new civilization to older but of part within the changing civilization to other part. This is most commonly considered under the caption of advance or lag. In a civilization like that of recent decades and centuries, which is first of all material, the

The problem of adjustment

advance would be expected to occur in direct conquest of nature. How much has that given us *mastery of ourselves as well as our environment, increased our understanding of either human nature or the possibilities of social development?* C. Judson Herrick in his *Introduction to Neurology* [34] contrasts the inflexible neural mechanization of the articulates with the far more adaptable or intelligent nervous organization of the vertebrates. The last chapters of that volume and his whole book on *Brains of Rats and Men* bring into high relief the inestimable *value of an integrated cerebro-spinal nervous system and of a good cortex in keeping, modifying and improving experience.* Some of the best chapters he ever wrote [35] are a masterly exposition on the means of correlation and coördination in making the most of cerebral mechanisms. Not as individuals but collectively do we have the brain to modify old responses and to solve the constantly more intricate readaptations demanded of us. *Collectively do we have the gray matter necessary to coördinate the various elements in a new civilization?*

The real question is not at all what we have had, what we have added unto it but not made part of it, but what we are doing with it, or about it, or about ourselves in connection with it. The old story of the frontiersman and the bear might illustrate the point. The frontiersman had the bear by the tail and was "chasing" him around the tree. A friend, watching the whirling procedure, called out, "Jim, ha' ye got the b'ar?" In jerky tones came the reply: "Sandy, I dunno whether I got the b'ar or the b'ar got I." Certainly our civilization, little as it has been readjusted and readapted to present needs, has in many or most respects been beyond our grasp.

We have depended greatly upon science to adapt our environment constantly better to our needs. Even science can help us little in re-training human nature in the better use of our civilization. Many contend that we must have a moratorium in science in order to give us a chance to catch up.

[34] Pp. 26–36, esp. 34.
[35] *Neurological Foundations of Animal Behavior*, chs. XVII–XX.

Many now are contending that a moratorium in production is equally necessary to give distribution and consumption a chance to develop equally with production. Although the editors of *Recent Social Trends* think there has been little lag of government in connection with business, a study of controls indicates the opposite. Whether this is due to the point we must consider soon,[36] that the public has changed and that *there may not now be a really self-conscious, integrated public to handle problems which are public* and presumably should be handled by a public, the writer certainly is unwilling to state.

Intelligent planning for the future must take into account experiences of the human race, or disregard the lessons of history. The French people, shifting from absolutism to a form of republic, used methods unlike those of the American people, breaking away from a mother country and establishing another republic. Time after time the French worked out the most beautiful types of written constitutions, no one of which lasted, partly because the French had had no experience with written constitutions. But even if the French had had social habits working out in the political field, their constitutions would have been unsuccessful because they paid little attention to practice and much to theory. On the other hand, the Americans built upon what they had had and knew to be workable. One can examine the American Constitution almost in vain to discover any really original characteristics. Though it provided for federalism, under it was organized a national government on a model already proved good in the states. It is replete with devices tried and proved excellent.

It might seem immaterial to inquire how much of the lag or failure of adjustment is our own fault, how much of it is due to a failure of social organization to keep pace with industrial, how much of it is caused by events moving faster than we can either understand them or make arrangements about them. We must then ask ourselves three further questions. First, if we have time, can we make the adaptations and reduce the maladjustments in the transition of civilization?

[36] Pp. 379–381, 385, 398–403.

Second, if we study wisely and well, will our understanding and our endeavor make the integration of a new civilization adaptable to real needs a possibility? Or, third, have we created a Leviathan which we cannot control? Have we had the misfortune to make a Frankenstein which will devour us —at least if we cannot become big enough, wise enough, and strong enough to be master of our own fate and of it?

PART III

PUBLIC REORGANIZATION IN A NEW AGE

INTRODUCTION

Industrial capitalism did not rise, nor can it fall, by itself. Its relations with the public through government alone have been a fairly conspicuous part of the preceding chapters. Its relations with the public, because it has decided standards of living, is one of its chief glories or failures. Before its advent the family had gone its uneventful, if not peaceful, way for centuries. Into the family circle it entered like the serpent in Eden, bringing new knowledge and making the family earn its own way in an unsheltered world by the agony of new experience. To consider changes in government and society solely from the business angle would repeat the mistakes of the pre-1929 business world, overrating both the importance and the influence of economic "culture." Advance in science contributed as much to our understanding of ourselves and of our non-material environment as it added to invention and material progress. Education has freed us from business ideals and standards, little as it may have been an active force in making civilization dynamic. The changing world would present a sorry spectacle if it were chiefly a matter of business successes or of public problems regarding regulation of industry, trade or finance.

To the school that a few decades ago accepted government as the chief end of man, government and politics were ends in themselves. They were the only ends worth seeking and the sole achievements for which groups were formed. In a half century thought shifted from political channels into economic. Freeman's dictum that history is past politics yielded to the phrase, the Machine Age, a period during which the non-economic did not count. In the future we shall probably find less stress upon either government or business. Rather shall we consider human nature as a compelling force organized and modified for social purposes, influenced by political and economic motives, but dominated rather by group needs and desires that are especially and predominantly social.

Already a reorganization of government and society is well under way. Not having reached a peak it may not yet have been confronted by any serious checks or problems such as those facing industry and finance. Nevertheless a perplexing situation is observable in almost all areas of non-material civilization. Democracy, like the old gray mare, "ain't what she used to be." What will she be like tomorrow? Is self-government doomed to disappear from the face of the earth? The family is dissatisfied with past organization, fearful of proposed changes. Each decade, possibly each year, education pushes forward with new plans, especially for a better understanding of society's needs and problems, and better training of youth for grappling with its problems.

A knowledge of background helps in this understanding, provided it does not usurp, as it has in past studies, the center of the stage. Amazingly enough the economic motive looms large in this drama of the past as in that of the present. We shall discover many disruptive forces, and many apparently unrelated trends, possibly away from old norms but without any co-related sense of direction. Consequently and naturally there may be less unity and integration within these numerous dissimilar institutions and "cultures" than may be found in the narrower field of industrial capitalism.

XI

INTERRELATIONS OF POLITICAL AND ECONOMIC ORGANIZATION

ADVANCE OR LAG IN PRESENT-DAY ORGANIZATION

A dynamic society presents an unevenness in its development not characteristic of an old, settled, stabilized order. China has had thirty centuries to unify the business life and rule of her race. Scarcely two generations have elapsed since the Civil War ushered in the complete economic reorganization of America, and scarcely one since big business and expansion started a new epoch in American life. Unless we artificially restrict the new industry, purposely retard those businesses which are active, aggressive and of rapid growth, the lag increases. Elements of civilization today are extremely uneven; even *within a single limited field we find that some part lags* because it fails to keep pace with the unusual progress of some other. Distribution has not made the advance found in production. Organization of business has found difficulty in trailing closely mechanical and technical advance. Laboratory achievements have far outstripped gains in the abilities and skill of artisans. Until the adoption of the Federal Reserve System, credit operations in America were handicapped by antiquated banking procedure. And how much has improved human nature failed to keep step with science and technology!

So much stress is put upon "cultural lag" that most of us overlook these lags and others in the economic field. Probably the dilemma of industrial capitalism, the major dilemmas of industrialism and of capitalism, and many other minor dilemmas or inconsistencies are due to fairly definite lags within some field of business. Attention has already been

Comparisons in the economic field

drawn [1] to the fact that production proper has improved and advanced very much more than distribution. Inventions, whether the improvements were in manufacturing machines or in uses of power, have increased supplies, but no patent office has ever granted permits for corresponding inventions in giving workers and others the share necessary for an economic system to succeed. As noted both in connection with distribution and consumption, the reason they lag behind production proper is not even in the field of technological progress in production. It lies far more in the abandonment by production of principles of economics which were usable a century ago, but which have been abandoned almost solely in the fields of manufacturing and transportation. The worker and the consumer are handicapped by unlimited competition and by freedom of contract of the old type, in their dealings with the producer. Therefore *some social heritage,* which production has automatically sloughed off, *has caused a lag in these other interrelated fields.*

It might be pertinent to inquire whether social heritage particularly in the field of law is partly or chiefly responsible for the lag of political institutions in relation to business, and a similar lag of social institutions in comparison with either the economic order or government. In Part III we shall discover that in spite of the changes in political institutions in the last two centuries there has naturally been no transformation in the nature and organization of government corresponding with that which has occurred in production due to the use of the steam engine, dynamo, and mass-production machines. One great advantage of a profit system is the *automatic substitution of new and good technics for older and less efficient methods.* In government no such automatic replacement occurs. If lag is to be avoided, it would therefore be necessary after thoughtful study, by careful and complete readaptations, to get a political system which would be modern, up-to-date, and socially valuable. Mankind's experience with political invention has not endeared that type of experimentation to him, because paper constitutions and governments rarely are half

---

[1] Ch. V, and especially ch. IX.

as good in fact as they are on paper. Sometimes they are not
so satisfactory as those they replaced, unless the old were outworn or very bad.

Still more marked is the unevenness, advance or lag, found
in a comparison or contrast of economic development with
politics or social life. The output of the worker in many
American industries has doubled since the World War. But,
if the output of the American politician has done the same, it
represents either verbosity or hasty legislation. The pace of
the city youth seems swift but his adjustment to modern conditions is much slower than progress made towards concentration in industry. In the realm of ideas and institutions
we find the lag most pronounced. Especially is this true if we
have built upon some deep-seated ethical principle or religious
concept. In the most thorough-going study of trends and
lags, *Recent Social Trends,* the general editor [2] draws attention
to the fact that of our "great social organizations, two, the
economic and the governmental, are growing at a rapid rate,
while two other historic organizations, the church and the
family, have declined in social significance, although not in
human values."

In social affairs and in cultural ideas and institutions the
social heritage holds us in bondage, with bonds that cannot be
broken even as easily as in the field of government. As we
have already noted, this is particularly true in religion, hardly
less true in ethics, and likely to determine the nature of social
classification in advance. The social classes may seem to
change from generation to generation and from century to century, because the new conditions are different from the old;
but the new classes, like the old, usually represent those at
different economic levels. People can change their governments when they tire of them, but most of the evils of the old
system reappear in the new regardless of any change of form.
In city government we tried to get rid of defects by changing
from the old mayor-council type to the commission form, and
by replacing the commission with a city manager. These
changes did not remedy the most serious problems of munici-

[2] P. xiv.

Lags in
political and
social fields

pal government. Let people attempt to set up new social criteria, social standards, or cultural ideas—to an even greater degree the new is essentially the same as the old, regardless of the change in outward appearances. The failure of the Eighteenth Amendment illustrates the idea.

Means of determining or relieving lags

If it were possible to determine the cultural and other lags which we find in our dynamic society, we might then have knowledge that would help us eliminate some of the dilemmas. At least the adjustments which it would be necessary to make would be observed much more clearly. Probably *comparison of past with present* will be indispensable to understand (1) transitions, (2) specific lags due to advances in some one field without similar corresponding advances in an affiliated field, (3) hindrances that keep one institution laggard when another closely associated with it has gone forward.

It may be advisable, and it might be necessary, to take each element of present-day civilization and determine the extent of the lag, if any, that it represents. For this purpose the writer usually charts these institutions or ideas as pre-twentieth century, pre-World War, pre-depression, or post-depression. *Each period has its own type of lag.* Pre-twentieth century elements have not emerged from agriculturalism, or individualism, or both. Pre-depression traits are usually those that continued to develop from nineteenth-century antecedents and survived the World War. Their economic side probably has been emphasized without regard to social or political consequences. If an institution is post-depression, it would show recent change—any lag would necessarily be in the rest of the system of which it is a closely knit part.

If we have our transitions rather clearly in mind and can identify our institutions or ideas with some recent or more remote specific period of American development, we are in position to make a clearer analysis of the lag: (1) why it exists, (2) how much it includes, (3) whether any public or other concerted social action can help in its modification or removal. When it is more a *relative* than an *actual* lag—that is, due to the advance of the institutions with which it is associated, but whose advance it did not share at all fully—the chances are that good fortune rather than conscious effort and invention will open the door to similar improvement in the system, or part system, we are studying. Simply by taking thought we may not be able to add modernizing cubits to its stature.

On the contrary, if, like production, it gained not only by invention and by new organization but also by changing old laws or principles or by using old laws, possibly unconsciously, to the disadvantage of closely related systems or institutions, a way out is not so difficult. We can then publicly insist that (1) the allied systems be permitted to use or misuse those laws or principles also, (2) the public should limit, not the improvements of the advancing institution but the gains it has made at the expense of its fellows and of society or/and (3) *the public should arbitrarily, until it can be done better and more naturally, close part of the gap due to the lag,* possibly by forcing the advancing system to share its gains with the laggard. *In doing this society must be careful not to drag progressing systems back to the level of those unwilling or unable to advance.*

Because of the unwisdom of cutting loose from moorings which have proved necessary or wise in past generations, we make haste slowly in reorganizing the home or in abandoning forms of church worship or religious convention. Unquestionably the sweep of dynamic modern life carries at least the younger generation forward forcibly at its center, although youth is often very conservative in its *ideas.* Many a time-honored ideal, custom, or institution moves slowly at the edge or stagnates in backwater from which it cannot follow the central current of progress; and it may remain behind until a great flood sweeps it onward.

At no time in history has humanity faced so serious a problem of adjustment or of maintaining proper balance between that which is new and that which is old. The problem, fortunately, may be solved in part by natural realignments, as suggested above in the case of lags. *In the history of the human race economic organization seems to be primary, while*

Needs in politico-economic relations

political and social organization appears to be derivative.[3]   If this is fact, it gives promise of a possible reorganization of government and of society along the lines of the economic transformation that is taking place. Fortunately the form of government which a people develop and the type of social classes which they finally attain seem really dependent upon the character of the business to which they devote themselves. Business in turn is necessarily dependent upon geography, including climate, upon the racial characteristics or temperament of the people, and upon the stage of civilization which the people have reached.

Before the Industrial Revolution, moreover, early modern political reorganization was, from certain angles, more complete than were any industrial or commercial changes. Great as have been the advances made in big business in recent decades, the way had been paved for a new order by at least two stages of revolutionary political evolution. The first of these had been concentration of political power under stabilized or rather successful rulers. To be sure, this political absolutism was a renaissance of an ancient prototype. The second has been the creation of nations organized by their members. The conditions which gave rise to modern democracy and constitutional government probably have disappeared in America if not in western Europe; but a political order which has transformed itself twice in the last five centuries certainly gives promise of capacity for future necessary readjustments. It was not business, rather it was government, that pointed the way towards large-scale units of association. Certainly those characteristics of the modern order that indicate initiative and freedom of action are theoretically as prominent in democracy as in industry. Only in theory, however, are they true in either field.

One serious problem which confronts us today is reconciliation of economic organization and democratic government, and a beginning of reconstruction within these two fields. The

[3] Hobhouse seemed to find a fairly close coördination between the *type* of economic order and of social organization, but his critics do not always agree.

national life of America, and to a lesser extent that of the European peoples, is dominated not by free land or economic equality, but by business logically developed out of the inventions and transformations of the Industrial Revolution. Its successful reorganization in the United States depends greatly on the unity, intelligence and common consciousness of the American people. Free universal education may increase somewhat our adaptability to changing conditions. Yet society is like a glacier which moves slowly. Although it adapts itself to the unevenness of land surfaces, it remains unchanged so long as the climate does not vary greatly—and as yet there has been no marked increase in the temperature of human civilization.

GOVERNMENT AND BUSINESS IN THE PAST

In no fields has the gap between economic advance and political inertia been shown more clearly than (1) in that of inter-nation affairs, and (2) in modern political controls, at least in America.

Since the dawn of history, and probably long before that time, society has been organized largely for economic reasons. It is probable that the first group was a hunting band and that the next may easily have been a pastoral body organized to look after its flocks. Each of these primitive and prehistoric societies depended primarily upon itself for its supply of food and other necessities. Primitive workshops at St. Acheul in the Paleolithic period and at Grande Pressigny in the Neolithic prove that ages ago goods were made for more than a local market. But in general prehistoric man was not organized primarily to search for raw materials or to sell his pottery or tools or fabrics.

The political race for markets

Economic motives must have been present in the organization of the world's first kingdom. We do not know and probably never shall know to what extent the formation of the Egyptian kingdom, especially of upper Egypt, was due to the need of a uniform control of the water supply from the Nile River. Foreign economic interests played a smaller part in the history of Egypt than in that of Babylonia, the latter having been situated on the main highway from the Persian Gulf as a waterway towards the East and the Mediterranean Sea, the great lake of the West. Babylonia, in turn, was less distinctively commercial than Phoenicia or Greece. The Phoenicians, with colonies commercially but not politically dependent upon the mother city, were next to Crete in time and the first important commercial people of whom we have positive records almost from the beginning of their history. A little later the Greeks were building their political organization with an eye upon commercial venture and success. It does not seem a distortion of legend to think that Jason led the first group of merchant adventurers into the Black Sea region to secure valuable cargoes of Russian wool or wheat and prized Danubian products. In all probability the ten-year Trojan war was the earliest known racial contest for the control of the Dardanelles, a problem which caused much disharmony in the attempted Concert of Europe in the last half of the nineteenth century.

The historic period naturally has a thousand examples of the interdependence of political and economic organization. Probably the patriarchal family and the feudal period in Europe illustrate better than most other political and social systems the dependence of all other types of organization upon the economic. Time does not permit a study of these systems;[4] nor have we time to consider the effect of economic

---

[4] In the grazing stage of human experience the multiple family of the patriarch was ideal. Suitable hillsides or meadows were not sufficiently abundant for individual families. A group of father, mother, and small children could not well care for its flocks, and it was absolutely incompetent to protect itself and its prized herds. A large tribe could not maintain its unity and integrity in small valleys or on limited grazing grounds. What resulted? A family larger than the natural one but smaller than the tribe; large enough to protect itself, small enough to find successive pastures for each season. Necessary unity came in relationship of the members to the patriarch; necessary authority in the dominance of this old man. The problem of ownership and continuity was solved through blood relationship and bequests from generation to generation.

The feudal system, characteristic not only of Europe and the Middle Ages but of Egypt in its middle period and of Japan in fairly recent times, likewise illustrates the primacy of economic organization. The European feudal system was based upon land. Land was owned in the name of Deity but held by vassals representing over-lords. Self-sufficing villages were cut off from one-another by lack of means of inter-communication. Each community was thrown back upon its own resources

and political forces and events of the Great Renaissance and Reformation in the discovery and colonization of America. In the history of modern government few changes exercised the influence of the Glorious Revolution in 1688. To all appearances it was solely and exclusively political. A king had ruled his subjects arbitrarily and unjustly. He was driven from the throne, and his successors of necessity ruled as constitutional monarchs. Sixteen hundred eighty-eight is truly the beginning of constitutional government in the modern world. Among early accomplishments of this new and enlightened political order were laws prohibiting the export of manufactured goods from Irish ports or American towns. Following this series of prohibitions could be listed a long line of restrictive measures not directly political but in every case economic. These laws of trade seem to prove conclusively that the king was driven from his throne by economic classes that desired his power to make laws favorable to their businesses. The landed aristocracy was chief of these new governing groups, and it was almost dominant in English affairs to the great reform of 1832.[5] The commercial classes of England should not be understood simply as the exporters, importers or manufacturers. By the grace of God and act of Parliament, the English "corn laws"[6] survived until 1846, a century and a half. They were driven from the English statute books not by political reformers but by the rising

for its supplies of foods and other economic necessities. Politically, it was a unit for protection against enemies, and was therefore dominated by its military head, who controlled its revenues and decided all important matters, even life and death. Its social system was a by-product of landholding in fiefs. The fiefholder was noble. Some of the villagers might be freemen and the predecessors of business and professional classes. Below a hierarchy of privileged or free persons, whose status was after all a product of the soil, were the peasants, sometimes villeins but frequently serfs, little better than slaves. Progress from this state of feudalism occurred politically and socially when *the will of the lord* gave place to *the custom of the manor,* but the shackles of feudal bondage were not struck from medieval society until roads were opened and commerce flowed from end to end of the kingdom.

[5] In the great Reform Act of 1832 the House of Commons was purged of many "rotten boroughs," most of them controlled by nobles. At the same time the number of voters for members of Parliament was increased greatly.

[6] A high protective tariff on wheat.

class of manufacturers who wanted cheaper bread for workers, whose pittance might then be reduced.

Whether one considers the colonial period of American history, the Revolutionary era, the Civil War, or the twentieth century, economic motives always influence and possibly decide political action. Our present Constitution was the work of fairly wealthy men interested in commerce. Their interests were economic but they were fairly disinterested and exceedingly public-spirited, men whose first desire was law and order.[7]

Business and government in recent years

The relations of business and government in the twentieth century are manifold. We have already noted ways and means by which big business has secured the help or coöperation of government in expansion. We have also considered rather briefly the attempted partnership of government and business to secure recovery. So far as the N. R. A. stressed relief rather than recovery, the process of business recovery was not accelerated.

Another side of this legislative link between government and business appeared in the proposed or actual regulation of business by the public. Of sixty-two thousand laws passed in five years by state legislatures, fifty-five thousand dealt with business in some form. Obviously few of these were regulatory, but a large number, possibly a majority, prescribed some rule, or proposed some method modifying business procedure. A favorite practice of many political rings or cliques formerly was the introduction of bills suggesting restrictions on business, possibly a single firm or type of corporation. Ostensibly this was public welfare legislation; actually it was never intended to become law. The threat of its enactment did what was intended, for it brought to politicians special favors or money rewards as inducement for its withdrawal. If the proposed bill was intended to regulate business, even the economic lobbies sometimes did not stop legislatures from passing restrictive legislation. Then the business subject to regulation, like the late nineteenth-century

[7] Beard, *An Economic Interpretation of the Constitution of the United States.*

railways, turned around and secured the appointment, or election, of their own supporters to the administrative commission that enforced the law, in order that it might be left unenforced!

The increase of economic interests of the government can be measured in legislation and in administrative expansion. Is it not possible that the dilemma of industrialism is due in part to past over-stimulation of manufacturing by high tariffs, intended originally to protect infant industries, but retained long after the stage of industrial infancy had passed? "Dollar diplomacy"[8] over most of a quarter-century emulated or surpassed German state-aided projects[9] for foreign investments, business opportunities and surplus markets. Consuls have always been eager to bring to the attention of American merchants favorable opportunities to buy and particularly to sell in the market under their observation. In the decade following the World War our national Department of Commerce developed a marvelous system of bureaus and commissions. Not all duties of these were promotive, for some were restrictive. Some were concerned chiefly with aiding and simplifying business by reducing to a minimum hundreds of diverse standards and types. Compare the galaxy of automobile tires carried by the general dealer in 1920 with the few standardized sizes necessary in 1930. A fair idea of bureaucratic growth at Washington will be apparent if one will examine almost any page of Wooddy's *Growth of the Federal Government, 1915–1932.*

PUBLIC CONTROL OF BUSINESS IN AMERICA

Modern interrelations of business and the public are represented in, if not by, every stage of production and sale, beginning with the creation of raw materials, their manufacture, transportation and their purchase by the final consumer. In an individualist society little heed is given directly to the interests, the rights, or the protection of the public, its members or its working or buying groups. In one more highly social-

[8] Pp. 179–180.
[9] Pp. 53, 54.

ized the stress upon obligations, especially economic obligations, has led to government protection of those who cannot,
under present business conditions, protect themselves. This
protection may be minor, as investigation and publication of
facts, rather superficial, as supervision, or more complete,
as regulation or control.

From the standpoint of business, everything and everybody
is greatly over-controlled. From the standpoint of society,
this control is of things that do not count; it is just moder-
ately successful, like parental supervision of modern youth!
America probably needs improvement and extension of control, even if it be nothing but planning. Shall we get it? If
industrialism and capitalism will not coöperate, the problem
then becomes complicated, especially if they stand on their
legal rights. There is and always will be *a difference between
private right and public interest*. Undoubtedly, in a complex
society such as ours, if we concern ourselves with social needs
or welfare rather than economic gain, multitudes of readjustments must be made. Some will be with the businesses most
affected, others within related businesses. Still others will
follow in social relationships directly concerned with industrial capitalism, or in social or political relationships rather
remote. Ours is a partly integrated as well as complicated
social system; but its complexity makes better integration a
public need.

Because our nineteenth-century ideals in both business
and government were individualistic in theory, the government kept hands off business affairs except for the occasional
laws aiding manufacturers, the semi-occasional bonuses given
to railroads—for example the Pacific railways—and the rather
general opportunities for exploitation of the public domain in
our wasteful and extravagant public land policy.

After the Civil War we became conscious of the need for
regulation of some of these businesses upon which the public
had conferred certain legal advantages and opportunities.
About the first of these for which regulation was devised was
the railroads. Soon after, other public utilities, most of them
local in character, either were regulated in small part or were,

as in the case of water works, taken over and publicly owned and managed. With the Civil War some real supervision of banking took place as we have seen,[10] and there was an end of wild-cat note issues by irresponsible state banks.

Oddly, the publicly-organized corporation had practically no regulation as such. In fact, it was freed from most of the regulation which was attempted by the states, because many states competed for the opportunity to incorporate these companies and to secure as much of their business as possible.[11] The super-corporations, or combinations of manufacturing or commercial units were pursued rather relentlessly by the law-*makers* in anti-trust laws, from the late 1880's onward. Before considering the subject of later public control, we might note the degree of regulation needed in different types of business.

When a business is not commercial but industrial, it has special opportunities for directing economic affairs and taking advantage of those with whom it deals. This is due in part to the elimination years ago of most small producers and to the high concentration within manufacturing industries. If the business man is engaged in producing a public necessity, as electricity, or furnishes a necessary service, as telephone operation or railway transportation, he becomes a public beneficiary and is almost a public servant. He probably enjoys a monopoly or semi-monopoly, and has other public privileges granted to him in his corporation's franchise. These public utilities, whether privately owned and managed or not, under the law are quasi-public organizations. From every angle the public is deeply concerned in them, in the character of their management, in the amount of their charges and in the quality of their service. But if the public attempts supervision or regulation, we find that business, like old Proteus, easily changes its form to elude seizure.[12]

Anyone who controlled any of these more important business organizations would naturally affect the public greatly.

Regulation of different types of business

[10] Pp. 147–148.
[11] Pp. 117–118.
[12] On successive forms of combination and their reorganization to avoid illegality. See p. 120, *n.* 9^a.

Any group that controlled many industries and public utilities would seem to be usurping a function of government. The investment promoter or the credit banker who occupies such a position should be fully responsible for the public consequences of his acts. If he is in addition the arbiter of the fate of the credit dollar, controlling the destinies of price and of money value,[13] he has usurped a most important function of the people's representatives under the Constitution.[14]

The I. C. C. and the Federal Trade Commission In nearly a half-century of trust busting and railway control what did we discover? Obsessed with the evils to be overcome, legislators proceeded with a fine disregard for the economic principles which must be observed. The Granger law-makers were not supposed to be well versed in economic theory, but Congressmen who passed the first Interstate Commerce Act should have heeded the clearly stated dictum of Arthur T. Hadley, that it is impossible to prevent both combination and discrimination. Not until 1920, after experience with a unified, if not well-managed, national system of railroads, do we find Congress willing to agree that both cannot be done. *Since 1920, railway mergers have been encouraged,* to some extent compelled. In the meantime, at least until 1906, the limitations of the law of 1887 prevented railroad control from being anything but a farce. The right of the Interstate Commerce Commission (1906) to *declare maximum rates, and to gather all the evidence,* put teeth into the old law.

Following close upon the original Interstate Commerce Act was a series of national and state anti-trust laws. *The Sherman Anti-Trust Act, 1890, forbade monopolies, combinations, and conspiracies in restraint of interstate trade.* It did not attempt the impossible and try to define these terms. It left that difficult task to the public or to the courts. The courts could not well evolve a complete and satisfactory theory of public policy for control of trusts from the ideas embodied in these successive laws, including the Clayton Act of 1914. In the attempt to apply the law without fear, if not without

[13] See pp. 150–157.
[14] Constitution, Art. I, Sec. 8, Cl. 5.

favor, *single corporations had great advantage over combinations.* In fact, the giant corporations were eventually allowed to do almost anything which was not actually and strictly forbidden by the Constitution and literally prohibited by statute. The creation of the Federal Trade Commission was or should have been a long step in advance. It had the right to investigate methods which were proper or improper and to study, in operation, practices that were illegal or anti-social because they *destroyed competition.* Unfortunately there was a division of authority between the Commission and the national Department of Justice. Between them there was a lack of sympathy and an unwillingness to work together harmoniously. The Attorney General seldom made use of the extensive reports of the Commission. The Commission, in turn, frequently ignored the materials and the arguments brought before it. The Commission repeated the experience of the first I. C. C. As a means of controlling business evils, it was an administrative ornament; it is still in the *publicity stage from which the I. C. C. emerged in 1906.* Its great work was different. It informed the people and at times almost aroused the public.

This exceedingly sketchy treatment and summary show how public control has been quite inadequate to cope with the situation. Coöperation between the three departments of the national government, and between the nation and the states may have been intentionally imperfect. *A federal system of government seems devised to prevent control of industrial Leviathans.* The success of industrial capitalism in the "New Era" as well as good salesmanship made the public indifferent to any of its anti-social public policies. The American people favored big business most of the time; and this popular psychology was reflected in the decisions of our highest courts, whose interpretations frequently become judge-made law.

Evidently the American government, possibly because of the division of authority between the national government and the states, possibly because of the individualist philosophy which has made us anxious to keep hands off almost all public affairs, has resulted in a disastrous neglect of

Public control or public quandary

public duty and responsibility, without which a democratic system of government could not survive. It is a strange commentary on the political psychology of the American nation that price-fixing under the N. R. A., really used in only a very few codes, should have caused serious protest, when for years many a large business had practically been setting prices in its field. It might do this by actually refusing to sell its products below a certain figure, although in the years before the World War the courts tried to prevent this type of monopoly price. It was more likely to set a fairly high figure which smaller concerns were unwilling to contest, or it may be they were glad to follow.

Possibly the clue to a necessary and reasonable policy of public control of business by our government has been foreshadowed by the transportation laws. Because Congress has the power to "regulate commerce . . . among the several states," as early as 1914, in a pathbreaking opinion by Justice Hughes,[15] the states were not allowed, in regulating maximum rates, to interfere with national regulation on interstate railroads. This gave rise to a rather awkward and complicated situation. The Interstate Commerce Commission determined maximum rates between states, and forty-eight state commissions decided corresponding and non-conflicting rates. After the World War the Interstate Commerce Commission was permitted to determine maximum rates and other necessary regulations on *all parts of all interstate railroads.* That is, legally the control of the railways was "nationalized."

For at least a generation and a half the incorporation of business has been an interstate affair, because some states, as New Jersey or Delaware, have issued charters or incorporation papers, frequently of a blanket nature, for corporations doing most or all of their business in other states. For at least most of the years in the twentieth century *business has pushed constantly farther and farther beyond state boundaries.* Most goods found on the shelves of the ordinary "crossroads store" were produced in other states than the one in which they are being sold. Many firms, including practically

[15] The Shreveport Case.

all large businesses and corporations, holding companies or chain systems, disregard state boundaries altogether. If the Supreme Court should apply to twentieth-century conditions a definition of commerce as broad and generous as that which Chief Justice Marshall used in deciding the first Supreme Court case under the commerce clause,[16] there would be little legal problem of adequate public control of modern business. A large part of our business, particularly large-scale business, would be free from much petty, conflicting and annoying state legislation, none too successful from any point of view. Congress would then have charge of *all interstate business;* and the result might be quite as helpful to business as it might be valuable to government and the public.

Industrial Capitalism and Political Democracy
The Problem of Their Reconciliation

If industrial capitalism were in process of dissolution, all over but the funeral, and if political democracy has been steadily on the decline, dead but not buried, a study of better interrelations of the two and much higher coördination between them would have none but historic value. It is quite certain, however, that neither has run its race, although its vitality may be low, temporarily. Possibly the two, reconstructed together, may find a new birth and a new restoration. Working as we must with what we have, a better coördination of the two may be one of the best bases of the society of tomorrow. *The problem*

What elements have present-day economic and political organization in common? Do they make use of *common principles;* if so, which? Have they common methods or usages? Are they *interdependent* to such an extent that they work together in a harmonious and unified way? This is our first question or series. Second, what characteristics of political democracy are *survivals* from past years and incompatible with industrial capitalism as we find it today? Third, what characteristics in industry and capitalism, or industrial civili-

[16] Gibbons *v.* Ogden, 1824.

zation, are *incompatible* with both political democracy and that organization of society which we identify as democratic? Fourth, are there any characteristics of industrial capitalism which represent not growth but regression? To get results, does big business depend upon might rather than right? In short, does big business follow ways, and by-ways, which have no place in modern life, which are carrying it and us backward instead of forward? Fifth, how may industrial capitalism and political democracy proceed in order to secure compatibility with each other? How may they be fitted into a unified group organization which will capitalize human and natural resources, retain most that is worth keeping in our social heritage, and make proper use of all that modern science and business can offer?

Elements common to capitalism and democracy

Machine industry and individualist democracy still represent the period in which they really began to take their present form. In the eighteenth century, as we have seen, the minds of thinking men were engrossed with the specific problem of limiting the autocratic powers exercised by the despotic governments of continental Europe and the semi-despotic government of England. The year 1776 was a great year in the history of free movements. That is the date found upon the rare first edition of Adam Smith's *The Wealth of Nations*. The ideas of this book represented a profound criticism of the old ideas of mercantilism. Smith demanded free enterprise in business. The Industrial Revolution is not identified closely with this date, but about 1776 Watt perfected the first steam engine, which he had reconstructed several years before. Seventeen hundred seventy-six is a central point in that era of rapid invention which was to give the world its first specialized machine industry. On the fourth of July in that year thirteen former British colonies demanded freedom from Great Britain because they believed thoroughly in individualism in politics.

In the beginning and from the beginning modern machine industry and modern political democracy were sharply individualistic, as we have noticed.[17] They represented the prin-

[17] See ch. X.

ciple that the individual is a free person with economic and political rights that should not be hampered by the group. They embodied the idea that in practice the individual should have perfect freedom and initiative in managing his own business and in running his own government, that he should be free from government interference in his personal and business affairs.[18]

Besides individualism, industrial capitalism and political democracy have in common organization in large units. The thirteen colonies were united into a federal state which has grown from an Atlantic seaboard confederation to a continent-wide nation. Not alone in America but in Italy, Germany, Russia and in many other countries there has continued a movement toward territorial unification and national consolidation. In a real sense industry has proceeded along similar lines. Starting on a small scale it gradually and inevitably became organized in larger and larger units, expanding from local to sectional, sectional to national, and sometimes from national to international. The combination might be either horizontal or vertical; [19] occasionally it was both. Because no single individual or ordinary partnership could command the capital necessary for such huge enterprise, legal bodies were created, corporations, acting as artificial persons. Because society encouraged corporations and cartels, it enabled the concentration of capital into billion-dollar companies which went far afield for raw materials and still farther afield in the sale of products.

A third characteristic both have in common has been twentieth-century collectivism. Industry and capital abandoned individualism when competition and private property interfered with profitable corporate business. Individualism has been abandoned in part by democracy, because democracy as group organization in a modern complex world could not be built upon a basis of individual freedom. Both *industrial cap-*

[18] Pp. 277–282.
[19] Combination is horizontal if only plants of the same type are combined. When the combination consolidates successive steps in that type of business, as smelters, plants producing steel plate and finished steel products, it is vertical.

italism and political democracy therefore became somewhat collectivized as a necessity of a modern twentieth-century order, political and economic, if not social. The limitations of an economic and of a political system organized on a basis of every man for himself made a reaction to the opposite extreme probable, whether the change was wise or not. The motives of collectivism in the two fields were totally dissimilar, aside from the fundamental one of self-preservation or continued existence. In business the new purposes were rather materialistic, the desire for more wealth without much attention to the social value of that wealth. In government there was at least some altruistic idea of gaining social solidarity for the general welfare. Or did government and the political parties in control of it accept public service obligations as the best means of winning popular support?

Democracy's
failures in
necessary
adjustment

Few institutions show greater change than present-day democracy. The new elements and the old do not always harmonize; both new and old are frequently incompatible with one another, with industrialism, and with modern needs. Even now in the popular mind the idea of democracy has not shifted far from the eighteenth-century foundations of individualism and equality. So long as rural conditions prevailed in this country, there was real harmony between this theory of democracy and the fact as found in nineteenth-century America. The Civil War destroyed slavery and made all persons born or naturalized in the United States citizens. Yet strangely enough the Fourteenth Amendment, which went a long way toward making the United States a *democratic nation,* also granted a special status to *persons* as well as citizens,[20] and thereby aided economic changes under which equality has disappeared—and individualism is following in its wake. Twentieth-century democracy has sought to continue the old ideas by giving the masses the right to rule. New devices have been created to gain these ends, among them the initiative, the referendum and the direct primary. A further evidence of the socialization of democracy is the protective legislation for children, women, and workingmen.[21] Many

[20] P. 117.   [21] Pp. 284–291.

critics believe that we should have become really democratic had we limited more the elective franchise instead of increasing the powers of all voters.

Democracy is *universal voluntary coöperation*. Modern political democracy was developed in small territorial units and usually in primitive agricultural communities. Actually coöperation in modern America has called for large-scale organization. Our political parties, big and unwieldy as they must be if nation-wide, are organized theoretically from the bottom up but actually from the top down. How can we have voluntary and successful political coöperation if we rule through political parties which are usually boss-ridden? What is there democratic about a concentrated semi-monopolistic authority which is frequently corrupt? In any system of "invisible government" [22] the people do not rule, and representative government becomes highly unrepresentative. An unfair alliance between business and government may degenerate into control of national affairs by predatory trusts and into unspeakable coalitions between ward politicians and racketeers. The blame for this vile situation is placed upon the voters who do not vote. Even in our most important elections not more than half the registered voters bother with the polls, and probably not more than a third of the eligible women voters enjoy this new privilege, which was to have meant so much. But the fault lies much deeper—partly in an attempt to continue rural, frontier, democratic methods in a highly complex, urban, industrialized society.

A corollary of equality would seem to be justice.[23] If democracy succeeds in any respect, it ought at least to give every citizen a square deal from every angle. Instead of being a matter of courts, justice is primarily a balance between the opportunities all should enjoy and the rights which none should infringe. Justice is, therefore, woven into the very fabric of a democracy, political, economic, and social, which is constructed upon right principles. Specifically civil justice is impossible if some enjoy where others are denied. Inequality of wealth is inevitable. It is unjust only when its accumulation deprives others of necessities or when its influence gains for itself by withholding from others. One does not expect a millennium or a Utopia, but at least a modern democratic society must avoid a social hell for any class. Undoubtedly it is necessary to reorganize absolutely a system of jurisprudence in which crime is as poorly defined as it is in this country. One does not need to read the severe strictures of Dean Roscoe Pound or reports of the Wickersham commission [24] to realize that something is radically wrong with our criminal laws and their administration.

The problem of reconciling industrial capitalism and political democracy is many-sided. While big business was growing larger and more efficient, individualist democracy even before the World War found itself incompetent to solve many new and difficult problems. Many observers contrast government that is democratic, and government that is efficient, believing that it cannot be both. Apparently, democracy faces a double task. The first of these is to put its own house in order. If it cannot manage its own affairs, it must find some new plan by which it may reorganize and learn how to rule democratically in the twentieth century and how to direct American affairs for the public good. Second, if economic organization is primary, the democratic Mahomet must go to the mountain because the industrial mountain will not voluntarily move from its foundations to accommodate democracy. But both should be reorganized in order to get rid of incompatible characteristics.

Incompatible character-istics of industrial capitalism

Whatever reorganization industrial capitalism undertakes probably will be due to capitalistic defects and evils now existent.[25] In the future some of these will not be tolerated by society because they are poor business or because they are anti-social or because they interfere with some traits of democracy which the new age should retain or secure. Earned exemptions are their own justification; but in the twentieth

[24] This commission was appointed by President Hoover in 1929 to study law enforcement and observance. It published many volumes of reports.
[25] See chs. V and VI.

century inherited advantages, in the form of wealth, influence, social prestige and other forms of power, must justify themselves and prove that they should be retained.

One characteristic of the modern day is the concentration of wealth in a few hands.[26] Twentieth-century democracy does not place upon equality the same stress that was formerly given to that standard. Nevertheless, we must conclude that our present-day distribution of income does not meet just American standards and that our distribution of wealth cannot be justified unless that distribution is best for the public good.[27] Particularly is it objectionable if it makes impossible general purchasing power that is inadequate to keep business as well as society moving forward. Huge incomes have been possible partly because of interrelations of big business in separate and distinct fields. Against a combination of industry, transportation and banking the American public has as yet discovered no adequate means of action.

Many evils found in our present plan are the natural offspring of a legal system devised for totally different conditions. Interestingly enough these laws are not, as some fortunate people would have us believe, of ancient origin, although they may have been in use in some form millennia ago. Rarely do they antedate the break-up of feudalism and the establishment of modern business. Were not a law necessary for the bequest and inheritance of family property, the accumulation of possessions would cease with the efforts of the capable and energetic founder of the fortune; but, under a law that is socially necessary for the small property owner, large and increasing fortunes may be bequeathed practically intact from generation to generation. The law which encourages private enterprise and safeguards savings would be abandoned by modern society with great reluctance. Eagerly society is seeking some new arrangement by which the public will be better protected against *a concentration of wealth that threatens the future of American Business.*

The Big Four of the modern economic world [28] are actually

---

[26] On wealth and income, see pp. 140–145.
[27] *Cf.* esp. pp. 248–251, 253, 255, 263–265.
[28] Concentrated wealth in industry, transportation, trade, and finance.

wielding in business an autocratic power besides which the political absolutism of Louis XIV seems the work of an amateur. Powerful economic interests have always tried to influence government for their own gain. That our present owners of wealth should overlook the unexampled opportunities that lie before them is not to be expected; to a close observer it is contrary to fact and unreasonable in theory. Any further development of economic organization of the "New Era" type, accompanied by political control would threaten too seriously not only future business but the security and the welfare of the American people. It would involve too great a departure from the underlying principles of any kind of good government, democratic or other.

In addition to old privileges intended for one class and used by another, yesterday and our own day have seen a campaign of acquisition and exploitation of natural resources. It will be kind to forget the inexcusably careless way in which the people's representatives squandered the people's public property. Resources taking millions of years to accumulate are exploited by individuals and corporations as though more could be had for the asking. Semi-monopolies which may control natural resources frequently enjoy additional profits because they are in a better position to dominate a supply of labor, intimidate the other producers of raw materials, or exploit consumers.

Formerly the economist thought that the consuming public could not be dominated by any business, even monopolistic. There seemed to be a price beyond which the buyer would not go! Apparently these economic principles were not based upon fact. During the World War, possibly because the people became accustomed to giving until it hurt, they were able to pay prices two and then three times as high as those paid before the war. Hundreds of thousands of customers, if not millions, purchased at a good round sum modern razors which later in improved form were given away with a tube of shaving cream. Apparently there has been little relation between actual cost of production and prices paid by consumers.

More objectionable than direct economic domination of buyers is popular capitalistic control of the press and other social agencies. If a study could be made of news items actually printed, contrasted with news items that deserve most attention, we should probably find marked discrepancies. Studies have been made to discover differences. Not only does the yellow or the jingo press fall far short of proper standards, but frequently it also shows a gross disregard of public interests. Occasionally there is intentional misrepresentation or suppression of materials for the advantage of certain organizations or interests. No large newspaper takes a chance on having its editorial page ruin its advertising budget. The city editor and the man in charge of telegraphic items display equal zeal in the avoidance of items or points of view which will antagonize large advertisers. In general, newspaper publishing is not a very lucrative occupation. Let news be printed without fear or favor, and profits shrink amazingly. One wonders if the press sometimes is yellow in order that the ledger shall not be red. Big business should have equal opportunity with Chambers of Commerce in spreading propaganda in case it does not become anti-social advertising; but the public has a right to all the news that should be printed as well as "all the news that's fit to print."

In all times business has sought to secure advantage for itself by controlling the making of laws and over-seeing their enforcement. Perhaps we should not probe too closely into the forces behind the transfer of political power from the English king to Parliament in the late seventeenth century. Certainly young patriots would be unwise to know much about the way our government helped its business friends in the late nineteenth century, or in the early twentieth. But what shall we do about it? Do we want a repetition of government by the "best minds"? [29]

Would it be possible to reorganize government, in a democratic way or in any other form of rule, making it reasonably efficient and business-like? From such an herculean task even big business might well shrink. Evidently we are far

Is reconciliation possible?

[29] This expression was applied to the President's Cabinet in 1921.

from a solution of the reorganization of democracy to make it modern, to have it fit twentieth-century conditions, to make it a part of our present dynamic industrial civilization. Evidently we are still farther from an attempted reorganization of big business, to purge it of its grossest evils, to make it public-spirited and self-sacrificing for its own good as well as for the public good, to secure coöperation, voluntary or otherwise, between big business and the political democracy we hope to develop.

In the reconciliation of industrial capitalism and political democracy we must probably not attempt to harmonize the two as they are. They worked together rather coöperatively during the "New Era" period following the World War. The failure of their coalition was not their failure to work together but the effect on civilization resulting from business control of government. Government's aid to business at that time helped to perpetuate rather than eliminate old evils in our economic order and unquestionably increased the dilemma of western civilization. Any return to that alliance would involve too high a price for society and would mean too great a loss in American civilization.

If our social order is to have unity, evidently the two must be harmonized. Any forward-looking reconciliation of the two must take into account a real combination of what, in each field, is most modern, if not undesirable, and what is best for society rather than for business or government by itself, or for the two together. Most of the defects, evils or limitations of each, because they may be out-of-date, impossible to use today, or really anti-social, must be left out of the combination if a more modern social order is to emerge from the reconciliation of industrial capitalism and political democracy. That is one reason why some of the characteristics of each, and their interrelations, have been mentioned in this chapter or in others.[30] We must know first how much any part of either lags behind the rest of that system, behind the

[30] Industrial capitalism, esp. ch. V, VI; political democracy, esp. chs. XII, XIII. International relations requiring coördinated government and business, pp. 457–471.

advance of the other, or behind the general trends of the times.[31] We must know further which features of each that may seem up-to-date owe their success and their modernness to obsolete or unsocial theories or supports. We must know what features of each cannot be reconciled with the needs and the probable changes of a dynamic American civilization.

No single *standard* can be used to measure those characteristics which are compatible with both systems and a desirable social order; but a few must not be overlooked. First, security must take precedence of profit, and stabilization of prosperity. The public and its needs must never yield to private advantage—we have paid too much for neglect of common requirements and social weal. Second, traits of agriculturalism, possibly surviving in democracy, but of course impossible in capital industry, must yield to more modern features found with industrialization; and individualist elements in either the democratic or the capitalist field must probably give way to socialized organization in the other system. Third, the rules of the game, usually embodied in constitutions or statutes, must not be contrary to physical laws or social needs, though nature must yield to nurture, and must not block necessary social reorganization. Fourth, any type of organization or procedure that increases, or even tolerates, the dilemma of western civilization or any essential part of it, must be discarded or greatly modified. Finally, the reconciliation of future democracy with industrial capitalism may involve the creation of new machinery for both government and business. Whatever the form of the entente between the two, it should be friendly, non-militaristic and lasting. That may not be easy for big business; will it be possible for democracy?

POSSIBLE INTEGRATION OF POLITICAL AND ECONOMIC ORGANIZATION

If political democracy and industrial capitalism can be reconciled or harmonized, we shall have gone a long way toward getting an integration of political and economic or- Integration

[31] *Cf.* standards suggested on pp. 312–313.

ganization. In all times past, as we have seen, there has been some kind of correlation between business and government, if only the domination of the one more or less by the other. Possibly it is a misnomer to speak of domination of either political or economic organization by the other as a correlation of the two. For this changing world past correlations also are probably unsatisfactory; because the more perfect the correlation may have been, let us say, of an agrarian organization to an aristocratic or later to a democratic government, the more necessary is some *new* union of the two when the agrarian society shifts into one urbanized and industrialized.

For proof of desirable or possible integration of economic and political organization, we may find it necessary to give chief attention to principles and theory rather than to past experiences. Possibly the present is the poorest possible time for attempting to secure or achieve this unity and therefore create a social solidarity, because the government is changing and pulling in one direction whereas business seems to be pulling in one almost exactly the opposite. If in times past they could not see eye-to-eye, how much better can they in a dynamic world that is unsettling both? The shift from individualism to socialization may increase the difficulty of coordinating the two, but makes clear the cost we pay if the two work at cross purposes. Where government and the economic order are not unified, the public cannot avoid the losses which come because the two are at odds. Government has charge of law, order, and other distinctively public problems; business is concerned with producing goods and maintaining markets; but the public is responsible for both and for their success in working together.

Post-war attempts

That this generation cannot escape an attempt to correlate and coördinate business and government seems obvious from an examination of history since the World War. "Laissez faire" England and America found that in winning the war old types of government yielded to more simplified means of securing action. Military necessity furnished excuse, if it was not the reason, for *the division of businesses into those essential and non-essential,* at least while the war lasted. In the non-essential industries plants were sometimes confiscated or abandoned. In the more essential businesses again military necessity dictated the use of plants, the quantity and the character of products and the interrelations that must exist between agricultural produce, transportation, and banking. These measures were not necessarily limited just to producers, because whereas wheat-growing was stimulated, patriotic appeals were also made to non-producers to observe wheatless as well as meatless days. Free and ready competition between railways yielded first to better coördination under private management; and finally the public took over the railroads. Although the public supervision may not have improved the efficiency of railroad administration, it paved the way for better coördination of the rails.

Society's public needs which are satisfied through either government or business might be coördinated more in time of war than might seem necessary later in time of peace; but the experience of Italy, Germany, and Russia, as well as to a lesser degree that of Great Britain and the United States, disproves this point. Whatever may be the final uses and value of fascism in the post-war period, *fascism has created a system in which government and business are not simply coördinated but in some cases treated as identical.* This is not necessarily a free and voluntary union. The fact that *fascist governments always use force* and depend upon the military arm rather than upon any brain trust indicates a forcible connection between business and government rather than a natural and a desirable alliance of the two. Any ideal system in which the two are properly developed, joined, coördinated, and integrated should be perfected, it would seem, through less arbitrary and more natural, scientific and human means.

Italy and Germany, moreover, err in coördinating a small part of government with a small part of business. There might seem to be a high integration of political and economic organizations in the two countries. From one angle fascism might appear to be an efficient political system and from another a well-directed and well-planned economic order.

When we come to examine the whole scheme,[32] however, we find that this is not the case.   So much power is concentrated in the dictator or in the group immediately associated with him, so much authority is granted to the administrators who carry out the will of these leaders, that the government is unquestionably a partial one, one-sided, in no way conforming to the proper standards of the political organization of a real state, well-organized.

In the same way, but to a larger degree, do we find that the economic part of each of these countries is still less completely used, one could hardly say represented, in *the corporative state* or whatever may seem to be the coördination of the two.   It is estimated that in Italy not a large per cent of the businesses need get together in order to form syndicates, corporations, and confederations.   In other words, if not all businesses are corporated, and only a few of the corporated businesses are recognized by the government as the official economic part of this corporative state, the incompleteness of business organization from the public point of view, and of business coördination with government, is self-evident. If this were not enough, the frequent omission of labor from the organizations that work with government in the corporative state would prove how one-sided is the economic part of the fascist system.   How absolutely unsatisfactory is a system which pretends to include all business and yet leaves much of it out of the fold!

Russia is a better example of a planned society but an even worse proof of the use of force and arbitrary means to gain ends.   Again, as in Italy and in Germany, we seem to have a complete combination of government and business, although it is now *a dictatorship of the proletariat* instead of one by the capitalist group.   Again a policy of exclusion limits the union of political and economic organization to only a part, because all peasants with any property are excluded or banished or put to death, and the early revolution destroyed or undermined the industrial and financial bourgeois classes. The use of arbitrary methods of combining business and gov-

[32] *Cf.* pp. 362–365.

ernment, of arbitrary techniques in upholding the system presumably coördinated, is its own proof of how poorly the job has been done. As Glenn Frank declares,[33] "Force is no substitute for democracy. . . . First, force is no final protection to institutions. . . . Second, force cannot stop the march of ideas. . . . Third, force cannot compel the agreement of the unconvinced. . . . Fourth, force does not, in the long run, destroy the morale of the opposition."

America has always boasted of individualism and therefore would not be expected to show any high coördination of business and government. Instead we usually find as a by-product of individualism and as an inevitable consequence of rapid industrial advance, a domination of government by business, of agriculture by industrial capitalism, and of industrialism by financialism, as already shown. In addition to these undesirable relationships between business and government, we have noticed numerous fields in which the public as represented in government has no part. Through the leaders of big business or banking only has the public been able to make its influence felt in interstate business [34] or unemployment more than state-wide. In short, in these fields, the government itself has no power, and the unorganized public, that is, the consuming class, except through its actual purchases, has almost nothing to say about what shall be done.

Necessary coördination

An integration of business and government would not be a complete merging of the two. Each has its own work and functions, distinct if closely interrelated. Public utilities may be either organized and managed by the public or by private parties. We have numerous examples of each in America and in Europe. Even in public utilities there are definite limits of public regulation or control. Even the I. C. C. with its knowledge and experience should determine simply the minimum and maximum limits of the rates to be charged. Rate-making is an expert, technical, complicated job and not to be decided arbitrarily by those not on the job itself, provided the

[33] Frank, Glenn, *America's Hour of Decision*, Whittlesey House, pp. 40–41.

[34] For a fuller treatment of this problem of interstate business, consult pp. 325, 351, 356, 400–401.

private employe never loses sight of that public interest which makes his railway a public utility. If government must help finance utilities and other business, how long before Uncle Sam will own if not manage these publicly-aided corporations?

The interdependence of government and much business other than that of public utilities is not constant. They are interdependent to the extent that government is dependent on the public for its officials and support, or that business is dependent on the people for the purchase of its goods. The government should not attempt to conduct the business and probably not to organize it—that is the mistake the socialists have made. It should see that it has a chance to organize itself well, not too well—as our present incorporation methods under competing state systems permit. Necessary profit-making should be encouraged, just as excessive profits or accumulated profits that bring business to a dead end should be discouraged or forbidden. Business should have, to work with it, a government as modern and efficient as itself. Government should have the constant coöperation of business as publicly organized and as public-spirited as true democracy.

The universal tendency toward reaction when change comes is illustrated in part by the shift from the American system in 1929 to one that was at least a *partial partnership between business and government after 1932*. The reaction was not nearly so sharp as might seem apparent to casual observers or to business men themselves in the period of recovery beginning with March 1933.

The New Deal was concerned primarily with recovery; only incidentally did it attempt any real coördination, and certainly no complete integration, of political and economic organization. President Roosevelt and the brain trusters were too wise to attempt so complete a reorganization of the old "laissez faire" order. That they were content with half-way measures is shown by the use of an economics of scarcity in the oil plans and in the agricultural adjustment program. Their unwillingness to undertake any real public control of banking and many other types of business shows their conservatism. What little control they did attempt or propose did not seem to be popular. The day had not yet dawned for a reorganization for which the American people were as yet unprepared, and in consequence psychologically and socially unwilling to attempt.

If we are to secure a real integration of political and economic organization, we need a much clearer idea than we ordinarily have of what is public, and the extent to which now or in the past things public have or have not been handled through government. A further proposition must be considered: can interests which have not been handled by the government or through government be distinctively public in character? For example, under what circumstances might economic organization for which no public rules had been made, or administration devised, be public in character? The problem today

In times past the problem was not whether a certain action or function was public and *not* undertaken by the government, but the opposite. That is, the autocratic state of three centuries ago seemed to take for granted the right of arbitrary interference with most of the business and the social life of the peoples who were ruled as subjects. The whole field of personal or group rights or liberties, far from opposing and threatening public security and advance of that day, never was recognized by the benevolent despots as outside the proper scope of government. For example, secret and unfair trials were the rule rather than the exception, at least in Continental Europe until the close of the eighteenth century. The problem today may be almost the opposite.

"Towering above all of these problems is the larger question as to how the division of power and responsibility under our complicated economic and political order shall be brought about. Of particular importance will be the type of rapprochement and rapport on the border line between industry and government. Shall business men becomes rulers, or rulers business men, or shall labor or science rule the older rulers? To some extent this is a problem of social policy; or from another point of view it may be regarded as a problem in the construction of quasi-governmental agencies on the border between old time governmental institutions and economic enterprises. What forms of government-owned corporations may emerge between the lines of the 'purely' political and the 'purely' economic? How shall business bureaucracy be held to greater public responsibility? To what extent may forms of government develop within large industrial or professional groups themselves, what type will these new constructions take and how will they be related to the more formal structure and powers of the more formal government? What shape will administration take under these new conditions of public and semi-public and demi-public sets of powers and organizations? What will be the relation of old time legalism and constitutionalism to these emerging relationships?" [35]

In our attempt to comprehend and work out this whole problem, education should play a very great part. One of the purposes of these studies of ours has been if possible to understand at least a little better than we have done the world today, the trends and shifts from old systems to new, and the emerging order. Education in general is looking more and more not to the attempt to create a new social order but at least through social studies to find out what has been done, what exists now, and what probably may be coming into existence.

[35] C. E. Merriam, quoted from *Recent Social Trends in the United States.* Report of the President's Research Committee on Social Trends, p. 1506.

XII

POLITICAL DEMOCRACY AND SUBSTITUTES

Backgrounds of Democracy

Democracy has always been affiliated with government. In our minds it is associated with eighteenth-century beginnings rather than examined from twentieth-century viewpoints. Whatever democracy may achieve in the fields of industry and social relations, we shall probably always think of it rather literally as popular rule, a political achievement. Whether democracy should be treated as a matter of politics and as distinctively an individualist type of group organization may possibly be determined by consideration of the standards by which democracy is judged or measured.

The rise of democracy

We need not go back to Grecian origins either of the word or of the institution. In the infancy of modern democracy we find that revolutionary America and revolutionary France deified equality. The reason is simple. Most outstanding movements or changes represent abrupt reactions against pre-existing conditions or systems. Eighteenth-century society had been saturated with privilege and inequality. What was more natural, therefore, than the assertion of the Declaration of Independence that "all men are created equal"? To this main hypothesis or theorem we find attached the corollary that equality carries with it certain inalienable rights which every American citizen possesses not by gift of law but inherently. These two, equality and rights of man, claiming legal basis for themselves, were the fulcrum and the lever by which the American patriots and the French third estate pried themselves loose from colonial dependency or the Old Régime.

The nineteenth century found less dissatisfaction than unsatisfaction in the standard of equal rights for all citizens. Of what value rights if they remained negative, without the drive or the opportunity to safeguard civic essentials and to make citizens active members of their community, state and nation. *The extent of popular participation in government became the measure of democratic development.* Property qualifications for voters yielded to a tax-paying requirement; this in turn gave place to universal adult male suffrage. This new democracy began to enlarge the list of those officials who should owe their positions and recognize their responsibility to the whole body of men as their constituency. The color line prominent in the first half of the nineteenth century was presumably wiped away by the bloodshed of the Civil War; manhood suffrage emerged triumphant from the greatest civil conflict of modern times.

The twentieth century found the old democracy inadequate. In law all men participated in the selection of public officials. In fact, only those who had access to the backrooms of the saloons or otherwise stood in with the politicians were admitted to a share in selecting the representatives of the public. Only they and their friends had any part in the nomination— rather the ratification of the appointment—of those who every second or fourth year sacrificed themselves in order that the country might be saved. In the attempt to give the voter a real voice at the polls, the process of election was duplicated in nomination. Real rule of the people not having been attained, other checks upon law-makers and administrators were created. The initiative and referendum gave direct participation in law-making to inexperienced masses; and the recall was a warning to officials who strayed too far from the straight and narrow pathway. To the ladies the responsibilities of these numerous duties seemed too onerous for mere man; and so—usually after pressure—the ballot was shared with the weaker sex.

Not content with these new forms of participation-democracy, there arose, as there did a century ago,[1] a new demand for social legislation. Since the masses were doing much for government according to law, it seemed fair that government should do more for the masses, by more and better laws.

[1] Pp. 286–291.

Accident insurance, sickness insurance, old-age pensions, un-employment insurance, and often many others made up the list of benefits which a democratic society owed to its needy classes. It usually obtained them in Europe, although it did not gain them in America.

The World War brought democracy through constitutional government to hundreds of millions of political serfs. The new political freedom may not be more real in Europe than in America; but the condition of those millions certainly has improved. To make democracy safe for the world was at one time a watch-word corresponding to the rallying cry of Wilson's message in 1917. But of all reactions since the war none has been more serious or more thorough-going than the disdain and contempt in which democracy frequently has been held.

Three characteristics of the old democracy represent its progress to the present time. The first of these is the extension of the franchise, the second is representative government, and the third is responsible government.

Standards for measuring democracy

In the seventeenth century the American colonies, democratically, were far in advance of the Old World. The transfer from England to America represented a shift from aristocratic rule to a semi-democratic form of government. This was due chiefly to the ease with which land could be procured. In the American colonies all landowners, especially those of orthodox faith, had a share in local or colonial government or both. The Declaration of Independence, with all its stress upon equality and the rights of man, did not directly affect the elective franchise. Years elapsed before the standard for voters was changed; then it was the western frontier and not the platitudes of the Declaration which brought the change. Here it was the abundance of land that determined the issue. Haltingly Europe modified suffrage requirements, not granting manhood suffrage everywhere until after the middle of the nineteenth century. The Machine Age was moving rapidly and soon all northern and eastern Europe was taking part in a world-wide movement giving women as well as men a share in the right to elect officials. With the exception of some of the more conservative Latin countries, the civilized world stands committed today to *universal adult suffrage.*

Strangely enough *representative government* has a longer pedigree and a far more ancient origin than the *liberal franchise.* The Anglo-Saxon communities had it. The townships elected representatives to the hundred court and the hundred court to the county or shire mote. In the late Middle Ages towns as well as country sent representatives to the mother of all parliaments, that of England. Before the Pilgrim Fathers landed at Plymouth Rock, Virginia had established a representative assembly on the English plan of two members from each local community. All other colonies followed suit. The English idea of representation was modified. Eventually the colonies and states were divided into districts of something like equal population.[2] From each of these individual territorial districts a single representative, a resident of the district itself, was chosen to speak for a constituency.

The single district plan, even though the districts are not gerrymandered, gives to the leading party a membership in the legislature out of all proportion to its members. Its unfairness to minority parties has led to the formulation of several plans of minority or proportional representation. These have been in use in several countries in Europe and in some of the British Dominions. They are fair but not easily workable. How unrepresentative our plan makes our law-making bodies is shown by A. N. Holcombe.[3] In the 73d Congress 73 senators and 368 congressmen, about 70% of all, belonged to the intermediate classes (the chief element of a "middle class"); but those classes included only 10% of the population. The workers, 52% of all Americans had no representatives in the Senate, and only 7 in the House of Representatives. Fifteen senators and 75 congressmen were listed as capitalists, 17% of all members of Congress for a class with less than 1.7% of the American people.

A new form of representative government is based not upon

[2] Los Angeles county for state senatorial representation is the world's greatest-known exception. Here nearly half the population of the state has one senator out of forty.

[3] *Government in a Planned Democracy,* p. 47.

territory but upon occupation. Notice how this arrangement would change the composition of the houses of Congress and of the state legislatures. Plans for this procedure were suggested in America and in Europe many years ago; but Russia was the first country to make use of it on a large scale. Since most of us believe that the Russian plan was devised for the express purpose of giving the industrial hand-worker a proportionally greater share in the government than he deserved, we probably have not accepted the Russian experiment at its true worth. It must be evident, however, that where the population of the state or of the country is almost entirely concentrated in large cities, the old territorial plan devised for rural districts with diverse interests and distinct needs naturally breaks down.

The name responsible government is given to the ministerial or cabinet system. In America elected public officials are chosen for definite terms. Only by impeachment, recall or some other legal cause of removal may an unsuccessful executive or administrator be removed. This plan is characteristic chiefly of the United States. Latin America seems to have the same system, but a fondness for revolution makes all official tenure insecure. Most states that have become democratic usually have representative legislatures with responsible administrations. The executive branch of the government, instead of being separate as in the United States, is closely united with the national parliament. Whatever party or group of parties can control the popular branch of the national legislature places its leaders in important administrative offices. Kings there may be, but they reign; they do not govern.

Before considering the nature and problems of twentieth-century democracy let us examine the general nature of the political systems of self-rule which have been worked out in America and in western Europe.

PUBLIC ORGANIZATION IN AMERICA

Most Americans know their government so well that any detailed description would be unnecessary in a brief survey of

western civilization. Of real significance, however, in that
civilization is the American plan of a self-governing republic
under a federal system. The people are represented directly
by elected officials only in the law-making branches of national, state and local governments, in the persons of the
chief executives of nation and state, with additional administrative and judicial officials in each of the state, county, and
city governments. There is nothing in America similar to the
cabinet or ministerial form of responsible government.

Checks and
balances

Possibly to a European our dependence upon checks and
balances is the most outstanding characteristic of our political
plan. This division of power is found throughout the entire
system. First of all, the work of governing is divided between
the national government and the states. Within the national
government the tasks of governing are separated into the
three distinct and theoretically independent branches—the
legislative, which makes the laws, the executive, which enforces them, aided by the administrative, which applies them,
and the judicial, which interprets the law involved in cases
brought before it.[4]

Within these branches there are sometimes numerous checks
or balances. The best known of these is the separation of
practically all legislative bodies except those in local governments into two houses, an upper, always called a Senate, and
a lower, usually known as a House of Representatives or an
Assembly. Throughout the states the method of representation in the two houses is identical. Although the Senates are
invariably smaller, the members of both with rare exceptions
are chosen from districts of equal population by the voters
within those districts. In some of the eastern states, in Cali-

---

[4] In reality the checks and balances are not so real as they appear in the
paper constitution. In two respects balances have been or are being destroyed. By the use of the "American doctrine of judicial supremacy,"
that is, the right of the courts to decide finally what our legal system is,
the courts have in the past often tried to decide definitely our *public*
policies. With the increase of public problems rule-making has not seemed
so important, and administration has seemed most necessary. The increase
of power of the American President is noticeable although we do not have
the administrative development and concentrated authority found necessary
in countries of western Europe.

fornia, and for the United States Senate the areas represented in the senates are unequal in size and population.

A second characteristic of American government is the dependence upon written constitutions. These have now become fairly common throughout the civilized world. The written Constitution of the United States is more than the fundamental law of our national government. Most of the provisions of this short and remarkable document, prepared by a group of about fifty men during the summer of 1787, deal with the organization and powers of the three branches of government. The national Constitution, however, implies, and in a degree provides for, a federal system in which the powers of government are divided between the national government and the states. In a few sentences at the beginning of the Fourteenth Amendment the nature of this federal scheme is made somewhat clearer, although still implied rather than expressed. This Constitution of the United States, although exceedingly brief and general, has really been amended only twelve times. The first group of amendments constituted a Bill of Rights and was adopted almost at once as a supplement, and in the popular opinion to remedy a defect in the original.

It is evident that the whole American constitution could not easily be contained in a Constitution, adopted long before the decline of an agricultural civilization, for more or less separated states, isolated by lack of means of communication and covering only the Atlantic slope of our present area. If it remained, as it has, a vital, living constitution, something outside of the original written Constitution must have added life and vitality to this skeleton framework. First of all, there was the need of adaptation and adjustment of the old to the new. Second, as new needs arose a whole group of supplementary arrangements, either in organization or powers or procedure, was inevitable. Usage, growing out of practices tried experimentally and found satisfactory, is a large part of this *unwritten constitution*. Congressional statutes of a constitutional nature are another important part of it. A third outstanding feature of this unwritten constitution is a long series of judicial decisions explaining the original Constitution, re-interpreted to meet the needs of the times as case after case has come before the highest judicial tribunal, the Supreme Court of the United States.

Each of the states has a corresponding written constitution. But in the states the unwritten constitutions are relatively unimportant because the state constitutions are newer, are longer, and usually are amended with great frequency and at great length.

The federal system   Under these constitutions the American people govern themselves in a dual arrangement which we call a federal system. The United States Constitution, chiefly in Section 8, of Article I, enumerates the powers which the Congress of the United States shall exercise. This list would cover about a page of this book. In spite of its brevity, or because, being brief, the statements are general, almost the whole pyramid of national power has been erected on the slender base of these eighteen provisions. The few words, "The Congress shall have power . . . to regulate commerce with foreign nations and among the several states," give the national government the authority and the mandate of the American people to work out most of the policies and solve most of the problems of our dynamic civilization so far as that can be done by making and administering laws. In addition to this *constitutional grant of powers given to Congress and the other branches of the national government,* in the Tenth Amendment *all other powers of government are reserved to the states or left to the people.* This sphere is indefinite and of extraordinary extent, including practically all fields directly touching the lives, relationships, and work of American citizens.

During the whole of our history there has been a shift of center of political gravity from the state governments to the national government. The periods of revolution accentuated each of these shifts. The Civil War practically established a *balance between the national sphere and that of the states in place of the preponderance of the states* before the war of secession. The beginning of the transition from agriculturalism to industrialism brought with it the need of more and better supervision of business affairs by authorities at Washington. The World War taught us, tardily it may be true, but rather thoroughly when the change came, that "commerce" [5] could not be separated from other forms of industry and finance, as it already had included transportation. In American federalism one important trend, already noticed,[6] is that toward centralization. Another important need is some special government for metropolitan areas within states and in regions composed of many states.

The *American system* in contrast with that in use in western Europe *is frequently called the presidential.* This name is given not because our chief executive is called a president but because the term designates any government in which the chief executive is chosen independently of the legislature and is neither responsible to that legislature nor removable by it. The American President is selected for a period of four years in what is unquestionably the best known, the most interesting, and possibly the most approved part of our democratic system of government. Not necessarily because he is independent of Congress, but because he has great power under the Constitution and of necessity in a system like ours, the American presidency is probably the outstanding public office in the world today. Possibly one should except dictators who have arrogated to themselves practically the whole of the government of their countries. But they may be excepted not because "uneasy lies the head that wears a crown" but because uncertain is the tenure of him who claims all power or rule; and therefore his rule does not necessarily represent a system.

The presidency shows its overwhelming importance through the fact that the President is officially the representative of the American people. He, and he alone, is the choice of the whole nation; he, and he alone, stands for America in its dealings with other countries. The President is the head of the largest

The departments of government

---

[5] In the Constitutional Convention (1787) the proposal to have Congress regulate *interstate business* was turned down in favor of *interstate commerce* because (1) "commerce" is a more definite term, and (2) there was at that time no interstate business other than commerce.

[6] Pp. 97–98.

business and administrative group in the world. He may appoint comparatively few of the personnel of the national government, but his policy is the policy of all those whose work includes authority and discretion. In time of peace he therefore administers as well as enforces all national laws, and in time of war as commander-in-chief of army and navy he exercises more authority possibly than any other living person. He controls foreign relations in his capacity to make treaties and in his ability to control conferences, so far as that is the prerogative of any nation or head. He is the spokesman for the United States and of the dominant political party, regardless of the obvious fact that frequently he is one of the minor lights among his political associates. If he is, as several of our Presidents have been, a great psychologist, he becomes a real leader of men in a position ideally fitted for leadership. The trend toward increased authority of the President is one of the most pronounced political tendencies in modern America.

The American Congress consists of a rather mature group of senators, ninety-six in number, two from each state, who devote a real part of their time to discussion of public questions. The Senate has special powers, particularly in relation to foreign affairs, for no treaty may be made without the consent of two-thirds of their number. The senators really control the appointment to most important political positions because Presidential nominees must be confirmed by them before taking office. Their long term, six years, coupled with the fact that the Senate is a continuous body, gives them special influence and prestige.

The House of Representatives is a much larger body, 435 in number, its members chosen for two-year periods from territorial districts within the states. It is so large and unwieldy, although much smaller than the lower houses of most European parliaments, that most of its work is done in committees. It does not have the unity, or the solidarity, or the *esprit de corps* possessed by the American Senate.

The national courts are made up of jurists chosen by the President and confirmed by the Senate and serving for a period of good behavior or life. The highest of these courts, consisting of nine men—at present averaging more than seventy years of age—has the final voice not only on the meaning but on the legality of any rule or act involved in a suit or case brought before them. Unique in the experience of modern peoples is this right of nine jurists to determine through the "American doctrine of judicial supremacy" the nature of the political order under which the people of a great nation live. Almost equally unique is the very high esteem in which this great and impartial tribunal, our Supreme Court, is held not only in this country but abroad. No European government has a judiciary of corresponding authority or prestige.

Within the states the central governments seem like copies of the national because the former are lineal descendants of the revolutionary state governments and the latter was made in imitation of those. State governors are always elected by the voters in an election following a campaign. In the states which are overwhelmingly controlled by one political party, the campaign precedes the primary election. The governors are pale imitations of the President within their own territories. The importance of the office may be judged by the extent to which state governors are chosen President. But in general the state governor is not an official of great power. The state legislatures are always divided into two houses, but are never so large as the American Congress. The terms of office are frequently two years, but the upper house ordinarily has a longer term than the lower. Theoretically the legislatures may make laws on the whole field of civil and criminal law except the tiny but important part left to the national lawmakers. The volume of legislative grist is appallingly large. If fault were found, it would be with the quality and not with the lack of quantity in state legislation. *Too often Americans overlook the importance of the work in law-making done by our state legislatures and the importance in law administration of our local governments.* Almost all cases brought before American courts are tried before state judicial tribunals.

THE PEOPLE AND THEIR GOVERNMENT IN AMERICA

An attempt
to use
democracy
in practice

In the organization and work of this American political system what part do the people actually play? How well does the system as a whole represent them? How successfully does it provide for their interests?[7] How adequately does it keep abreast of the needs of a changing world? How satisfactorily is it carrying out the readjustments necessary to avoid the evils and to gain the advantages of a dynamic civilization?

It would be unreasonable to expect that any political system devised for the government of 125 million people would provide in a real degree for self-government. We are asking the impossible if we expect that number of folk to hold in common the same ideas, desiring the same policies to be put into effect in the same way. In a static civilization with a people who think and act as they are told, who have thought and acted in that way for centuries, such uniformity and unanimity might be possible, at least on the surface. For a rather aggressive, independent group of people like the Americans, it is practically impossible to find any set of standards or policies, except those hallowed by tradition, upon which an overwhelming majority would agree.

How then do we manage to get self-government at all? Largely through the *organization* in *political parties,* to which the business of selecting candidates and electing officials is assigned. The question therefore is less, "How representative of us are the public officials chosen directly by election or indirectly by appointment?" than, "How well do these political parties through which we do our choosing represent us and carry out our wishes?" Until recently the platforms and methods and techniques of the political parties have differed so little from each other that they were truly characterized by a great student of party organization and action as "empty bottles." If it were not for the irony of this negative characterization that the party differences are in the labels, this would seem to indicate no very great diversity in the views,

[7] On some of these points consult ch. XIII.

thoughts, and desires of the American people enrolled under the banners of our two great political parties. Unfortunately, instead of proving either a capacity for self-government or the fact that the people rule, these similarities would indicate on the part of the public a lack of interest and unwillingness to face reality, a lack of determination to make government a real part of a changing social order.

The real interests of the American people would seem therefore not to have been well represented by either political party organization and action or by the work of most of the governments that have been sitting in state during the last generation. One reason for this may be the well known trait of group psychology, that we will follow those who do not offend more readily and more unanimously than we do those who suggest new ideas and upset some of our cherished prejudices. There is more than a grain of truth in the statement that we vote against those who offer a single suggestion we do not like rather than for those who have a great many that we do.

If our public officials have failed to provide for our interests, it may be not because they neglected to consider public office as a public trust, but because we do not know our own interests thoroughly and therefore we support a negative policy rather than one which would carry us forward. This seems contradicted by the facts of outstanding leadership offered by at least three of our recent Presidents. Some political trends of the time were opposed very vigorously by Theodore Roosevelt as President, and his vigorous leadership was accepted gladly by most Americans. Woodrow Wilson's reform legislation during his first year, his policy of postponing war in the second and third, and his international outlook during the later war period had tremendous influence upon Americans in working out new policies, although in the end he went too fast for the majority of the American people. We are too close yet to evaluate the work of Franklin D. Roosevelt, but there is no question of the change of psychology brought about by his "New Deal" in 1933 and of the patriotic support of the Blue Eagle for a season or two.

In foreign relations the American public has found itself
hampered by the division of governmental power between
national and state authorities. It has found itself handicapped also by an attempt to use open diplomacy, which has
resulted in pressure politics through propaganda, press, and
messages to Washington, when the task was the delicate and
expert reconciliation of American demands with foreign
counter-interests. In the handling of foreign relations a democratic people that use a federal system are simply a little
out of luck. The extent to which these disadvantages will
become more serious in a world becoming constantly more
internationalized remains to be seen. Evidently the foreign
problem calls for popular understanding and patience, as
well as a diplomatic training and skill we have never yet
achieved.

Our federal system was wonderful in the past because it
gave opportunities for experimentation and adjustment to
the new needs first felt in special sections. In this recent
crisis and in the future it may act as a brake upon necessary
and wise political adaptations to the economic demands of
present-day America. A good illustration of this lag due to
federalism is shown in the field of economic regulation. Apparently there is need of unified direction, in the public interest, of our larger business interests in several economic
areas, including banking and production as well as transportation. Will the unwritten constitution be expanded by including all of those and labor and a few others under the all
inclusive word "commerce" of article I, section 8, clause 3 of
the United States Constitution? If so, the national government would have the legal and constitutional right to control
large-scale business of any kind.

In general, can we imagine a political organization which
has adapted itself to new needs as well as our federal system
or our unwritten constitution has done? Trace the evolution of American democracy, one of America's outstanding
contributions to the world's political progress, and we find
that it is preëminently the work of states permitted to experiment, the benefits of experience spreading if they were found

good, or popular. The "Fathers" could not possibly have foreseen all changes on land and sea and in air that have taken place since their time. If they could have done so, they could not possibly have reorganized their thought and their plans to handle those changes and problems in the rather wise way in which we have been allowed to do it. With all the present limitations of eighteenth-century political techniques, of checks when we need coördinated efficiency, of party bosses when we need popular leaders, of mass inertia when we need group advance, American democracy and our political system hold the promise of possible, positive reorganization for the future.

Constitutional Government in Western Europe

Constitutional government started earlier in England possibly than in America. But on the continent of Europe its rise has been slow and halting. It would be fruitless to trace the series of changes in different countries by which the popular governments of a few years ago came into existence. For our purpose it is sufficient to characterize them as some form of unified government contrasted with our system of checks and balances. *This system of parliamentary, cabinet, ministerial, or responsible government,* because those terms are similar though not synonymous, may be studied through the type form found in Great Britain, in which it originated.

Unlike our own Constitution, that of Great Britain is unwritten, an historical document carrying us all the way back to Magna Carta (1215), although really originating in the seventeenth century. England still has a hereditary monarch, who reigns but does not rule. The real head of the government is a prime minister, the head of a cabinet whose members he chooses with the coöperation of the leaders of the party or coalition which controls the majority in the lower house of the British Parliament, the House of Commons. Unlike our own President, the British prime minister does not hold office for a definite term, but only so long as he and his cabinet colleagues do actually control a majority in the House of Commons.

The British system

Under the parliamentary form the executive and legislative branches are closely combined, correlated and inter-dependent. The House of Commons practically selects the Cabinet. The Cabinet in its turn decides public policies, in line with the general desires of the Commons, framing all important measures, including the budget, and carrying those bills through Parliament practically without change, except the minor modifications suggested by the Commons and approved by the ministry.

In this system there is therefore more *unity* than in ours, more *responsibility,* and presumably more *efficiency.* There is more unity because there is a single Government instead of, what sometimes happens in America, one Executive, one Senate, one House, and one Supreme Court, each going its own way. There is no house divided against itself in the British political order. There is responsibility because the Cabinet is responsible to the House of Commons for its program and for its continuance in office, because the House of Commons must do what the ministry wishes until it finds a ministry more in line with its own desires. And the members of the House of Commons are responsible to their constituents because their term of office is indefinite, with a maximum of five years. If they get out of touch with the wishes of the British voters, a new election may be held, although one may not be called by the voters themselves. Theoretically there is more efficiency because there are fewer checks.

Is not this system more democratic than our own? Certainly it is more responsive in a way to the popular will. We send our representatives to Washington, and at stated intervals, after a hullaballoo more prolonged though not so rough as the English campaign, we keep them or we turn them out, too frequently according to their skill as politicians or according to our prejudices. Probably tradition counts for as much in the British method of choosing its public representatives as does demagogue psychology—I use that phrase for lack of a better term—in America. Since the English government is very largely in the hands of a well educated, highly trained, and very efficient civil service, it would look as though their system, like ours, is chiefly responsive only on the surface to popular wishes and demands. To find how democratic and how adaptable and up-to-date either plan is, we should need to go much deeper into the subject than is possible in this sketch.

The cabinet system of responsible government has been adopted and used rather successfully by Belgium and France, rather temporarily and unsuccessfully by Italy, and more temporarily and with a procedure not according to the English Hoyle in Germany and in some other countries south and east of Germany. One of the essentials of the British plan is *the need of a two-party system,* one of which, being in the majority, represents the Government, the other being out, serves as an opposition. By one of the curious twists of fate America is the only country in the whole area under western civilization which has and has had throughout most of its political history only two major parties. Even England, at least since the rise of the Irish Question (1886), has had to depend upon alliances in lieu of parties. France tries to organize *blocs* or combinations of factions, but her factions are parliamentary groups instead of being national parties. These coalitions in blocs have been almost entirely of the groups in *power.* Because it has been necessary often to rearrange these coalitions of factions, the foreign public has often had an untrue impression of an apparent lack of stability in the French parliamentary system. Since the overthrow of the Third Napoleonic Empire, cabinets may come and cabinets may go, but the French system works on as usual.

Cabinet government on the Continent

Before the advent of the Nazis, Germany had a larger number of parties than any other country could muster. This was inevitable in a country which before 1867 had no political unity. Before the Hohenzollerns were driven from the German throne (1918), there was no responsible government in Germany, because the Chancellor and his colleagues in the imperial ministry were the tools of the Kaiser, or whoever was the power behind the throne in the German system.

In the years following the Armistice, the Germans adopted the Weimar Constitution (1919), which kept in name a federal system as under the Empire, but which practically created a unitary state in Germany. This constitution was in many ways a socialistic document providing for wide powers of legislation in the social field for *the regular parliament*, and creating in addition *an economic parliament* with supplementary occupational parliaments in agriculture, industry, and other economic fields. Without experience in self-government—and under Bismarck and his successors how could that be acquired?—the post-war German cabinets kept themselves in power provided they had a majority in the Reichstag of the members, excluding the ultra-conservatives and the communists, who sometimes were kind enough not to vote and upset the government. Small wonder is it therefore that Germany reverted rather easily (1933) to a type of government similar to that which the German states had had over several centuries before 1918!

European conditions favorable to constitutional government

If constitutional government could have been created by reaction and fiat, the constitutional systems that followed the World War would have established self-rule in fact as well as in name. It would probably be unfair to expect that these peoples of central, south, and eastern Europe could have changed over-night from absolute government to self-rule. Outside of Czecho-Slovakia it is doubtful whether a serious attempt was made to let the people govern themselves. If so, it obviously did not succeed. There is a true reversion to type, or, if one prefers, a continuity of type, in the arbitrary rule found in most of those countries at the present time. If space permitted, one would like to examine the series of events by which each of these dictatorships was established. One would like also to consider the character of the government created and the nature of the rule established. A few suggestions possibly are in order.

Several years ago, M. Francis Delaisi drew attention to the fact that *constitutional government in Europe coincided almost exactly with those areas which had taken over newer types of economic organization and civilization.* In other words, those parts of Europe devoted to industry were almost identical with the regions in which constitutional government was prevalent. "The zone of industrial Europe was confined to an area which ran from Stockholm through Danzig down to Budapest, then west through the northern part of Italy to Barcelona; from there to Bilbao, straight north to Belfast, across the southern part of Scotland to Bergen, and from there to Stockholm." [8] Outside this area, for a few years following the reactions of the World War controversy, some nominal government by cabinets was in force. Within it arbitrary government has been reëstablished only in the German Reich, and that only since 1933.

We ask ourselves this question. *What is the connection,* if any, *between the existence of constitutional government and the prevalance of industrial capitalism* as the dominant characteristic of the social order? Is the connection almost accidental between industry and self-rule? Has capitalism in Europe been responsible for government by the people? Or do we have a connection between the two in this way: Are the increased wealth and leisure responsible for more literacy and greater interest in, or better understanding of, public affairs really the cause of more popular government in these countries? Has the destruction of old customs, ideas, thoughts, and institutions, for which industrial capitalism is responsible, made the continuance of more absolute government difficult or impossible? Does the rule of the people depend upon the greater intelligence, the more general education, the more progressive outlook of these folk who created, not first an industrial order and then afterward brought their political scheme in line with it, but who, as we saw in America, developed the two together? [9]

Germany, one of the most highly industrialized nations of Europe, has reverted temporarily or for a fairly long period

Tendencies toward dictatorship

---

[8] Quoted from *Les Deux Europes* by Lindsay Rogers, in *Crisis Government*, p. 39.

[9] If there is a connection between these two, is it more general than we have just indicated? Is it in part or chiefly due to the fact that the creation of new contacts and the development of a more complex, interrelated social order, led inevitably to a more delicate, better differentiated, more flexible, and adaptable political order as well? Or is there no *causal* relationship between the industrial societies and those constitutionally governed?

to a system of absolutism. Now it is under a dictator, but possibly later it may be under a royal house. One naturally should remember that although the Germans are at the fore-front in almost all phases of industrial development and probably out in front in scientific advance, their whole psychology and their national idea favors a political state highly organized and ruled by force. In all of their history political habit has been developed only to follow and to obey.[10] If the experience and the preferences of a people of high intelligence and remarkable industrial success have given them very little interest in, or training for, popular rule, their reversion to dictatorship and absolutism would have little meaning for other peoples. One hesitates to be dogmatic because we realize that the French people narrowly escaped the necessity of dictatorship in 1926, when Poincaré organized his cabinet of premiers and stabilized the franc and the French government. One recognizes also the narrow margin by which Ramsay MacDonald, in 1931, failed to establish a semi-dictatorial government in Great Britain. Nevertheless, from the standpoint of other countries that use western civilization, Germany's lag in the political field, comparing with the systems of the rest of the western world as standard, does not seem to indicate a trend toward dictatorship as a substitute for responsible government in Europe.

Italy never had enough responsible government to worry either her or the rest of the world, and her successes in using the system were not overwhelming, at least according to British or American standards. The attempt to avoid communism may have been the excuse for the fascist state established by Mussolini, but the real reason, as possibly again in Germany, was the recency of national unity and the need of a strong hand in developing national policies and solving national problems. The ruling house in Italy won the admiration of the world by its forward-looking attitudes, by its courage and its loyalty; but no one would accuse its rulers of

---

[10] Note, however, that the German economists and philosophers were among the first to stress democracy as a desirable form of government. Consult F. W. Coker, *Recent Political Thought*, p. 86 *et seq.*

possessing either the political intelligence or the governing sagacity which were demanded in Italy after the World War for the proper management of public affairs.

Fascism is interesting in itself as a substitute for democracy and even more as a reaction against the limitations of parliamentary government. Just as parliamentary government and the American system in practice require a two-party system, so *fascism is a one-party plan*. In all of the fascist governments thus far established, that party has been the capitalist group, whose influence in American government we have considered in preceding chapters although we have not traced a somewhat similar but less dominant influence in Great Britain. To some, fascism is capitalist democracy run riot. Even the great influence that capitalism has had in democratic government seemed inadequate either to maintain business or to preserve the commercial power of the country abroad. Especially in Europe, where national rivalry has run high, fascism has been both a means of saving the country from any possible inroads of bolshevism and a patriotic opportunity to gain selfish advantage for the nation against its enemies. The Versailles Treaty, the prolonged depression, and the desire of the Germans to regain business and prestige of pre-World War days helped Hitler to overthrow what little was left of parliamentary government in Germany and establish a fascist system instead.

Fascism abandons any real attempt to use representative government, either responsible or partially responsible. If plebicites are held under a fascist government, they are supervised by the powers that be to insure victory. That more than five millions voted against Hitler's assuming autocratic power in 1934 caused wonder both in Germany and outside. Fascism, depending upon narrow patriotism, stirs up antagonism between nations and would cause internal strife but for the use of the iron hand in putting down disaffection. Being a one-party system, it naturally tends to develop a dictatorship, and one which has little interest in or sympathy for the survivors of any other party or faction. In order to secure an apparently united backing, free discussion, of course, is

suppressed—free speech and a free press being forbidden.
Leaders of non-fascist groups are either imprisoned, exiled,
or put to death. This type of oppression has been noticeable
in fascist countries as well as in bolshevik Russia. From the
American point of view one of the strongest indictments
against fascism and bolshevism is this arbitrary interference
with human liberty, which was an important object of
eighteenth-century American government.

The foundations of fascism are probably both economic and
political, as are those of bolshevism. In the fascist state a
group which is really an economic group seizes political power.
In the organization of the government *theoretically* there is
a high coördination between the economic system and the
political. As we have seen,[11] what actually occurs, as in the
corporative Italian state, is that the corporations are not fully
formed and that certain economic groups dominate political
affairs under the pretense that they represent these economic
associations.[12] Fascism seems to represent the fatal attempt
to *identify* economic power and political power, which R. M.
MacIver, *The Modern State*,[13] shows is impossible.

Many fear that both parliamentary and presidential government may succumb to fascism. Raymond Gram Swing
suggests the following reasons why Great Britain need not
expect a fascist invasion.[14] "Looking at fascism in other European countries [than Great Britain] I find that in the main
they have not succeeded without three pre-conditions. There
has been a widespread pauperization of the middle class, usually by inflation; there is a threat of a left wing seizure of
power which is convincing enough to frighten people with property; and there is advance paralysis in the ordinary machinery
of government." In regard to the last point he suggests that
the fairly large number of factions in England might possibly
develop paralysis in the ordinary machinery of government,
especially if the largest political party of all, the Conservatives, should split up into distinct and separate wings. If his

[11] P. 338.
[12] P. 337.
[13] Ch. IX, i.
[14] *Are Democracies going Fascist?* Foreign Policy Ass'n., p. 297.

standards were applied to America, one need not be told how little fascism is a threat this side of the Atlantic.

Russia overturned the old order far more in appearance than in fact. The vitality of Russian life as a people has resided in the communal organization with more or less communal self-direction, which has existed for a long time, and in germ for centuries. Even under the absolutist tsars this spark of self-rule was kept alive in the management of common interests if not of public affairs within the mir, and to some extent in larger districts. What was therefore more natural than that when a system of despotism, tempered by assassination, disintegrated through its own weight, it should have been replaced by a *dictatorship of the proletariat?* This might have called itself communistic but it never succeeded in applying the principles of communism at all literally and successfully.[15] W. H. Chamberlin, after many years residence in Russia and careful study of the Soviet system, declares [16] that Americans are uninformed if they consider Russia either a "challenge" or a "menace" to the United States. Since the Russian soviet system did not replace a government that was either democratic or semi-democratic, it is not considered in this study, although it is the best possible example of a dictatorship, which is the exact *opposite* of democracy.

NATURE AND PROBLEMS OF TWENTIETH-CENTURY DEMOCRACY

The twentieth century has given America a new democracy. In a real sense this is a social or socialized form of popular rule. It does not yet represent any high degree of perfected group organization. It does not consist of several new forms of popular coöperation in government. It does not represent any high degree of correlation between political and economic power. It does stand for many new types of group responsibility towards its members who cannot protect themselves; for these classes it has stressed public or social welfare.

Among new means by which the people are brought in form if not in fact closer to their leaders has been the direct pri-

Standards of twentieth century democracy

[15] On Russia's government see Munro, W. B., *Governments of Europe*, pp. 767–777.
[16] *Russia's Iron Age*, p. 16.

mary, which has sought to replace the old convention system. By this primary the political party has been made more an organization of party members. An examination of the campaign expenses of senatorial or gubernatorial candidates shows plainly that the direct primary can be no part of the budget of an ordinary citizen. The direct primary may help the voter to select his own preferred candidate; but, unless conditions change, more and more those candidates must be selected from fairly well-to-do persons, or represent organizations with money.

A second form of popular participation is the referendum, often associated with the initiative. The referendum has been used to check the work of state constitutional conventions since 1780, and its other uses are now numerous. The initiative and referendum together may be used to secure laws that legislatures have refused to enact or to defeat undesired laws which legislatures have tried to force upon a reluctant if not an unsuspecting public. The recall of public officials is still another means by which a government that is called democratic becomes more decisively a government of the people.

As the shift has been made from individual democracy to social, a third change has shown itself in social legislation. One would like to think that there had developed a new consciousness which showed a new type of responsibility of the public toward its worthy but weak members or classes. In the older democratic countries the years' since the World War have brought little extension of social insurance. To the newer states of eastern Europe there have come not only written constitutions and representative government, but many forms of welfare experimentation.

These standards for measuring democracy are historical and practical. In no real sense do they determine the nature of democracy or give us real clue to either practical or general problems which democracy is facing today or is likely to encounter in the near future.

Problems of
democracy

When the Greeks under Athenian leadership drove back the Persians from Europe Herodotus explained the victory against overwhelming odds as a triumph of democracy over

autocracy. "It is manifest that not in one but in every respect
the right of free speech is a good thing, if indeed the Athenians, so long as they were under their tyrants, were no better
in war [and in culture] than any of their neighbors, whereas,
so soon as they had got rid of their tyrants they became a
long way the best. This makes it plain that, when subjects,
they were slack because they were only working for a master,
but, when liberated, each became eager to achieve success for
himself." In the modern world no less than the ancient, freedom, a share in self-government, and the opportunity to discuss and direct public affairs is good for the citizen as well
as the state. Mass rule especially of the late nineteenth-
century American type has proved that it is, however, a headless, ignorant, blundering type of self-rule, one which needs
defense but finds only apology.

However unwisely we may praise and laud democracy, especially the American product, a square facing of facts brings
us back to Grover Cleveland's comment, "It is a condition
which confronts us—not a theory." "Invisible government"
is far more characteristic of American public life than we realize. When Elihu Root first used that phrase, he shocked the
American people, for that was the time when, in the popular
mind, democracy had reached its zenith. "They call the system—I don't coin the phrase, I adopt it because it carries its
own meaning—the system we call 'invisible government' . . .
Then Mr. Platt ruled the state; for nigh upon twenty years
he ruled it. It was not the governor; it was not the legislature; it was not any elected officers; it was Mr. Platt. And
the Capitol was not here; it was at 49 Broadway; Mr. Platt
and his lieutenants. . . . The party leader is elected by no
one, accountable to no one, bound by no oath of office, removable by no one. . . . But it is all wrong. It is all wrong
that a government not authorized by the people should be
continued superior to the government that is authorized by
the people." [17]

The discrepancy between boss rule and idealized democratic

[17] *Revised Record, New York State Constitutional Convention,* 1915, IV,
pp. 3501–3502.

government has been a sharp one in most periods of American history. No doubt if we could consult the out-voted minority in a New England colonial town meeting, we should learn some interesting truths about wire-pulling, chicanery, and sharp practice. The ward lieutenant, the captain under whom he works, the political boss whom both obey have more to say about what rules shall be enforced in our cities than many a public official whom we vote into office on election day. The petty law-breaker avoids punishment by standing in with the "organization." The speak-easy and the brothel usually have a fixed payment per month as the price of immunity. With the decline of supervised prostitution the whole system which bridged the narrow gap from the under-world to police headquarters became reorganized. First it was local, then more general, and finally of almost national scope. The extraordinary profits of rum-running and boot-legging under the XVIIIth Amendment gave impetus to this new form of political domination. A system which counted its profits by billions could easily spare hundreds of millions for its friends, the boys that help. Corruption of police force and public official is subterranean; but the underground conflicts between sets of gangsters occasionally rise to the surface and show themselves in assassinations, in street duels, and in machine-gun fights. The sharp increase in the homicide rate in cities now notorious for lawlessness has been almost entirely in gangland.

Far more reprehensible than under-world influence on mal-administration of American affairs is the domination of public representatives and probably of bosses and machines by those who want special favors and are willing to pay for them. Suppose that such an anti-social body is a traction company which desires a franchise on a main street in a great metropolis. Years ago this valuable concession might have been secured by downright bribery. These cruder methods gave way to "influence" over aldermen or their superiors. Eventually control was gained of the political machine which managed the affairs of that community or state.

In national politics we take into account capitalism in general, as well as special lobbyists.[18] Big business and organizations wanting concessions on public land in Mexico or business advantage in Europe are not negligible quantities. Some pressure groups are generally believed to far outweigh the thirty-odd million voters whose interest in government or regard for public opinion [19] sends them to the polls quadrennially if not oftener.

If we look only at problems, we see more failures than successes; but, in spite of the limitations of individualist democracy, most of us believe that we are making progress. Gropingly and much disheartened humanity is finding its upward march toward better government a slow and painful process. Disregard and discard of the old democracy was inevitable because economic revolution, which is making all things different if not new, stresses advance and achievement much more than equality and individual protection. The old democracy tended to bind us by keeping the best at the level of the least capable. Necessary as it may have been for the duller half of humanity, and particularly for the submerged tenth, it did not have the standards of an aggressive and successful society. It kept social talents wrapped in napkins. It did not sow its seed for an abundant harvest or devote its wealth to productive enterprise. With all its failures, however, the old democracy transformed the whole spirit of nations, binding each people together into a self-conscious unit. According to no less an authority than James Bryce, democracy has, "taken all in all, given better practical results than either the Rule of One Man or the Rule of a Class, for it has at least extinguished many of the evils by which they were defaced." [20]

In the recent socialization of democracy the contribution of pre-war America and Europe point the way but do not give the necessary reorganization of popular government. As we

The nature of democracy

---

[18] On lobbyists in Washington consult Frank Kent, *The Great Game of Politics*.

[19] On public opinion and propaganda, see pp. 381–387.

[20] Bryce, *Modern Democracies*, II p. 562. On short-comings of democracy, read Edward McChesney Sait's lecture on "Crumbling Foundations," in his *Democracy*, ch. III.

have seen in the comparison of political democracy with industrial capitalism, the democracy of today and tomorrow must possess the vitality of a successful society and the growth possibilities of expanding industrialism. *Democracy must, therefore, be vitalized as well as socialized.* If democracy fails to reorganize itself and fit the needs of both capitalism and humanity in the twentieth century, it will be relegated to the scrap heap along with the stage coach and the hand loom.

To many folk *democracy is an idea and an ideal* rather than an historical product. It stands for humanity working together at its best. In the "Nemesis of Mediocrity," Ralph Adams Cram gives this explanation of democracy: "True democracy means three things: Abolition of Privilege; Equal Opportunity for All; Utilization of Ability. Unless democracy achieves these things it is not democracy, and no matter how 'progressive' its methods, how apparently democratic its machinery, it may perfectly well be an oligarchy, a kakistocracy or a tyranny. The three imperative desiderata named above may be achieved under a monarchy, they may be lost in a republic, the mechanism does not matter." [21]

Practically *democracy represents voluntary coöperation* shown in national like-mindedness which is unified but not solidified. To some democracy is a spiritual entity. To them it may be a challenge that every political group should measure up to the best that it is and thinks and may achieve. Still others visualize democracy as the greatest and best accomplishment of human organization in state and nation, and possibly world state. To them *democracy is perfected group organization.* It is perfected not only because it is organized from within but also because it is well adapted if not perfectly adapted for the needs for which that group was created. It is perfected organization when each member finds his place with a chance to do the thing he can do best but with opportunity for growth and development—a society in which the interference between individual and group is at a minimum

[21] Quoted in Sait, *Democracy*, D. Appleton-Century Co., pp. 4–5.

and opportunities a maximum.   Even if this be an ideal, it may not be impossible.

Democracy represents opportunity for advance.   It means protection for all by promotion of the best interests of the whole, the best use of every form of ability.   Many of these standards might be thought aristocratic or autocratic, according to the norms of nineteenth-century frontier democracy.   They represent the needs of the new democracy in the highly complex industrial civilization of the twentieth century.

XIII

SOME ESSENTIALS OF MODERN DEMOCRACY

Democracy is more than a matter of officials and political parties. Without considering possibilities that can be found in economic or social democracy, we need to examine (1) the question of what type of society can become, or remain, self-governing, (2) the ways and means by which that public expresses and controls public opinion and propaganda, (3) the relations which must exist between government and citizens if any nation really deserves to be called democratic, and (4) means of controlling non-political affairs that must be publicly controlled.

Not all societies are prepared or fitted to become democratic. We have no assurance that a nation like France or the United States in the nineteenth century, democratic in many senses, continues in the twentieth to possess qualities necessary for the continuance of self-government. If democracies of the last century succeeded because they were developed upon the foundation of a unified, self-conscious, responsible middle class, we must ask ourselves three questions. What was that middle class which established the old democracy? Is the new democracy equally dependent on a middle class? Does the nineteenth-century bourgeoisie still exist; if it does not, for the successful creation or continuance of a democratic society, what have we in its place?

DEMOCRACY, A MIDDLE CLASS AND THE PUBLIC

Rise of
bourgeoisie
civilization

What was this middle class of the last century; why did it make the old democracy possible; what was that bourgeoisie civilization? A nineteenth-century development, it had deep roots. Possibly the Crusades, with the rise of towns, was the first important change in feudal life which brought in the

372

burgess element as a factor, first in commerce, then in industry. The Commercial Revolution of the Renaissance period probably gave to the bourgeoisie class an influence never gained by the merchants and bankers of earlier days. Perhaps the House of Fugger did not make and un-make kings; yet, without its help, given with a lively sense of business favors to come, Charles of Spain might not have been chosen Holy Roman Emperor in 1519. The opening up of a New World offered commercial opportunities. It brought into prominence a class which would seem to have reached its peak in the great commercial cities of the Middle Ages, as Venice and Lübeck, now eclipsed by the rising monarchies. Then began the reign of the money power which has become so influential in recent years. The religious sanction previously reserved for hard-working monks now was enjoyed, under Calvin's teaching, by industrious and thrifty artisans or merchants. Labor was holy as well as dignified, wealth the portion and the reward of the elect.

Between the rise of constitutional government and the rise of the bourgeoisie there exists probably a very close connection. This is not easily traceable in events in England, except so far as the wealthy merchants married into the families of the landed aristocracy, which took over the reins of power from the Stuart kings. It is more observable in the American and French Revolutions. The Hancocks, Washingtons and others wished to run their own and their neighbors' affairs rather than have the lords of England dictate American policies. Beard's study of the members of the American Constitutional Convention shows a dominant bourgeois influence. The Constitution itself and many of the laws originally framed under it were for the distinct advantage of the business class. The French Revolution was even more a protest of the Third Estate, really a bourgeois group, seeking to gain political power corresponding to its moneyed status, hoping that social place and prestige would follow suit. In many cases those business men shared with other and still more unprivileged classes some slight share in government and the benefit of such meagre welfare legislation as those days provided. In general, however, as they gained power, they used it naturally for the benefit of their own class.

The repeal of the English corn laws, leading eventually to free trade, is a good example of legislation passed to benefit manufacturers by reducing costs of living and of labor; but these laws, by reducing the cost of living, benefited the people in general indirectly as much as they helped the manufacturers directly. American tariff legislation has been more advantageous to the manufacturers than to either the workers, whose wages were high because resources were abundant and laborers few, or to the consumers, who paid higher prices though they were incidentally benefited by the prosperity which seemed to ensue. Any study of recent years shows the evidences of conflict between the business classes and the rest of society, with the advantage of control in the hands of the wealthy who wanted government help. But the captains of industry were aided and abetted by the members of the propertied class in general, who were exceedingly numerous in America; because the middle classes saw a community of interest with these business leaders.

The bourgeoisie: its nature and its ideas

How much did urbanization and industrialization, twin products of the Industrial Revolution, increase the numbers of the bourgeoisie? Or did it augment chiefly the wealth and power of a small class? Arthur N. Holcombe[1] has made quite a careful study of the middle class in America. He has applied the standards used in Europe by Bukharin and to some extent by Geiger. In his tabulation of Americans "according to the method of Bukharin"[2] a little more than half of the total American population is proletarian; but only a quarter of the rural population is in that category. This leaves practically three-fifths of the non-agricultural population classified as proletariat. Of the rural population of fourteen million income earners on farms this might show from eight to ten and a half millions as belonging to the middle classes or higher. That is, from sixty to seventy-five per cent of the farmers might be designated as a middle class.

[1] *The American Party Politics,* ch. IV.
[2] *Ibid.,* p. 96.

On the contrary, in the cities fifty-eight per cent proletarian and two per cent capitalist would leave a maximum of forty per cent of the income earning population as belonging now to a middle class. Of these probably not more than three-fifths to three-fourths would, by any reasonable application of the term, be a real bourgeoisie. In the transition from an agricultural society to an industrialized one, we therefore lost *our old farming middle class as our American type.* For the seventy-five million or so city dwellers less than two million belong to the high or wealthy bourgeoisie and possibly not more than twenty millions are of a lower bourgeoisie type.

With these figures in mind where do we find the line of cleavage between the wealthier members of society and the dwellers of Main Street and of Middletown? If most of them belong to the middle class, must we make a distinction similar to that found in France before the French Revolution, the distinction between the greater nobility and the lesser nobility? How much was the bourgeoisie represented by the big bankers, the great merchants, and the rich manufacturers—how much by the small merchant and the professional classes of the city, or by the great rural middle class representative, the farmer? In short, had the bourgeoisie become more, or less, typical of the American nation and the British people, being identified more, or less, closely with the social mass?

Probably if one wished to make a study of bourgeois civilization at its height, or depth, at its best, or worst, one would wish to characterize Victorian England, or America during the smug eighties, or the France of self-satisfied Frenchmen a generation or two ago. It is not necessary to hold up to ridicule those out-fashioned characteristics of colorless family life, smallness of vision, pious conventionality, respect for tradition, dull disregard of merit or value in the fine arts and in the art of life.

The typical bourgeois took himself and his place in society seriously. His outlook on life was sober-minded and serious-minded, as befitted a substantial member of the church, society and the world of business. He conformed to norms which he and his associates had created. There were few peaks in his virtues because that would have implied variation, which his lack of imagination rendered difficult. His vices were less those of preceding ages than of his own day. He drank too much but that was the prerogative of a gentleman; and he was the pale imitation of the real article of the preceding age of nobles. He aped some of the forms of the gentry, addressing letters to his friends as esquire and thinking of himself by that title. The code of a gentleman entered into most of his relations with his associates, business excepted, and he showed consideration for others, except employes and competitors, for he felt differently about relationships in that arena—that was business.

His sports lacked the coarseness of an earlier day and the hoydenish hilarity of our own. Fourth of July celebrations and orations of that period portrayed his type of thought as well as the patriotism he and his friends displayed. The dignified quadrille and the stately waltz had not given way to the fox trot and the bunny hug, or measured music to jazz. His was a day of drum and trumpet musical endings and sententious death-bed utterances, so unlike the overstudied, inconsequential conclusions of modern novel or movie. He would have been shocked at the familiarity and jocundity of present-day business men's service clubs. A lineal ancestor of Babbitt himself, there was little of Babbitt in his make-up.

The bourgeois's dress was decorous, even more stiff than that of men today. His "lady" was hampered by voluminous folds of dress and encaged in interfering hoops as became the life partner, but not the equal, of a man of weight in his community. His life was artificial, as little human as possible. Fortunate we, especially womankind, freed from such encircling clothes and a circumscribed life, limited by tradition but patterned after the ideas of such a man and such an age! Yet it was the society and age that gave us Darwin and Tennyson and Wagner and Emerson.

Among the obligations under which this mature prig places us are industry, regularity, punctuality, respect for law, duty above everything. He maintained some of the best standards of Puritanism, from which part of Main Street may not have departed widely today. Our age may be mechanized, mass produced, geared to speed and daft about size. Apparently ours is less reaction against theirs than one freed from drudgery by labor-saving devices at home, shop or office, and one partly freed from ingrowing viewpoints by extra leisure. Many things have changed tastes and interests: the auto makes the home point of view the exception, the movies hardly perpetuate bourgeois ideals, the schools may stress back to nature, and prepare for life and leisure rather than for labor!

From the mediocrity of their standards we need no longer pray to be delivered, because they seem to be disappearing or they have disappeared in the vortex of a whirling, changing world. Youthful exuberance, cynical criticism, initiative that disregards both tradition and authority, a tendency to overturn whatever we have—all these have affected the decadence of the bourgeoisie civilization of the late nineteenth century. Yet, with all its dullness and stupid disregard of realities, the solid qualities of those generations placed us under tremendous obligation. Without the coalition of these richer and less well-to-do propertied groups, we might never have had a true middle class. We should have found it very much more difficult to create a political democracy and a mass solidarity which have made at least the American people what it has been. It may be less to the purpose therefore to consider to what extent bourgeoisie characteristics have survived, than to determine whether we need a middle class to carry on, whether we have one, and whether, if the future civilization can be built only upon a middle class foundation, America will meet the test.

Before examining the middle class as such let us consider some groups forming a connecting link between the *haute* and the *petite* bourgeoisie. In the world today we find the old aristocracy based upon landed wealth, ancient title or family struggling for leadership with the *nouveau riche* of industrial capitalism. The decayed gentlewoman may still retain the social primacy which she inherited. More often our Four Hundred is made up of the children or grandchildren of some

Classes in the early twentieth century

successful industrial pioneer. He may not be a social idol, but his ambitious wife and his children, even if they do not marry into European nobility, sometimes rise to high social position. Wealth does not create quality but wealth furnishes leisure and gives opportunity which may bring culture in their train. The leisure class so interestingly brought into the highlight by Thorstein B. Veblen, being entrenched in privileges and in property, seeks to maintain that which is or which it has acquired. It struggles against any innovation which usually represents loss to those who possess. As Veblen suggests, "The fact that the usages, actions and views of the well-to-do leisure class acquire the character of a prescriptive canon of conduct for the rest of society gives added weight and reach to the conservative influence of that class. It makes it incumbent upon all reputable people to follow their lead." [3]

Whatever the future may bring, the middle class remains or becomes important under universal education and democratic government. The fairly prosperous freehold farmer is still our largest single economic group. Collectively this middle class occupies the larger part of the professional world and controls or directs most of the smaller businesses. From the middle classes we usually have drafted our presidents and college professors. As a rule its members are distinguished by uprightness and industry, and now they are well entrenched economically and politically among the conservatives. In society as constituted in the last half century they have been the pillars to uphold the main structure if not the superstructure. In the half century to come it is probable that their lot will not be enviable. Certainly that has been the case with the small-scale merchant who has had to meet large-scale competition. Truly the recent lot of the farmer has not been an enviable one. The middle class has been a name to conjure with; but, if society and industry tend to become more undemocratic, if the proletariat gains its day and its "place in the sun," the bourgeoisie, like the landed aristocracy, may find its chief glory in its past.

[3] Veblen, *The Theory of the Leisure Class*, p. 200.

The complexity of modern industrial society gives opportunities to millions who occupy positions requiring skill but calling for comparatively little discretion.   In a mechanized but scientific civilization these artisans should hold positions of prime importance and be held in special regard.   Without them the whole fabric of present economic society would fall to pieces in short order.   Because their ranks may easily be filled by unskilled workers whose training seems to compensate for a relatively low intelligence, their tenure seems insecure and their position indifferent.   With them, at least in Europe, we are likely to associate the proletariat.   We call this group the lower classes, unintentionally calling attention to the fact that upon them as foundation rests the whole economic structure.   If they possessed any real solidarity even within a single country, or were a small enough group to secede to some sacred mount, they might easily redress the grievances real or imaginary which are theirs, and might hew out huger chunks of income, even if they rose to no higher place in the world.   In the modern industrial world this class illustrates rather well the application of the iron law so well expressed by the Master: "From him that hath not shall be taken even that which he hath."

From these groups or classes is it probable that America can recreate or develop a social solidarity from which a reorganized industrial civilization can be developed?   How will the wealthy and powerful of the present order respond to the changing demands of the times?   Will they, like the nobles of old and the English ruling aristocracy today, accept the responsibility of class, or like their own grandfathers, almost slaves to duty, sacrifice gain for responsibility?   Or will they fight innovation as sacrilege against the Lord's anointed?   Will they, as in their struggle for place and power, consider only themselves?   In that upward race, as a group their political influence was overwhelming, even to exemption from court penalties.   They tried to make themselves solid with the large mass of small property owners, whose interests in part coincided with theirs and on whom they depended for votes.   The legal talent employed to augment capital and

Need or possibility of a real middle class

prestige "by doing illegal things legally," the banking associates of these captains of industry and the vast horde of assistants in related fields of business created a new satellite upper middle class. To these were added also the follower, the admirer, and the imitator—all Americans wish to emulate the success of these economic leaders—and the sycophant. As the industrial giants waxed, the independent free-hold farmers waned. As industry became more and more profitable, agriculture ceased even to pay expenses. Tenant farmers replaced owners. The old agricultural and business groups that made up the nineteenth-century middle class dwindled before the World War, smaller in *proportions*, even if as great in size as formerly.

Increase of wealth, the replacement of hand labor by machine robots, demand for higher standards of living raised the age at which boys and girls went to work and correspondingly swelled the ranks of those obtaining, first, a common school education, and second, both elementary and secondary training. What has the free public school, with its equal opportunities and general standardization in organization of courses and treatment of students done to maintain a middle class? Have mass education and compulsory school attendance tended to counteract the menace of social classification following in the wake of the Industrial Revolution? Have education, patriotism, religion, and other social forces created standards of thought and insisted upon ideas and ideals which make for national unity and social solidarity, even though the currents of the time made for diversity?

We believe individualism is continually being supplanted by socialization. Has this change created a community of ideas, standards, social patterns, or intellectual aims which make the American people a really unified nation? Has the nationalizing process preceded and pre-conditioned the socialization movement, making that the next natural step in American evolution? The connection between a middle class and democracy can be understood only when we examine these social changes as well as the political movements of recent years. If previous history proves anything, *political democracy is a by-product of social and economic conditions rather than itself the determining factor in economic or social change.* If democracy was a product of a middle class life, will the development of a new social democracy, in place of a rather discredited individualist democracy, be possible in the new social order? Will a social democracy help to perpetuate a middle class, either naturally or by the continuance of old rights and privileges, upheld by law or custom?

A further query thrusts itself forward: if the problems of the present, formerly matters concerning chiefly individuals, corporations, or classes, have become more and more public in character, then public relationships must be recognized in law, must enter into the political policies used by government. There must be a real integration of our political and our economic systems.[4] The individual and dependent groups should be protected not chiefly against government, as we once thought, but against any danger that may arise in a huge complex society. This protection is not chiefly negative, to ward off evils, but positive to insure human development, which may be threatened by ignorance, corruption, but especially by what Theodore Roosevelt called "predatory wealth." To safeguard society, public regulation and other forms of public control may become increasingly necessary. Undoubtedly, the need for public control increases as a society becomes complex, the relationships more numerous and intricate, and the parts of the body politic more interdependent upon one another. The nature of public control and the problem of whether control can really be public is in turn not chiefly a matter of what government may attempt or may do, but primarily a problem of *whether socialized action and controls that deserve to be called public* can be developed by any people *who have not developed social solidarity to a point where they deserve to be called "a public."*

Democracy, Public Opinion and Propaganda

The problem of self-government for any society may be first to make itself a public, but it is not secondly chiefly a matter

[4] See XI.

of developing control. The secondary purpose, closely linked with the first, is to secure that *type of organization* and that *degree of development* which will enable the public to understand and express itself and to protect itself, including its members and member groups, from those dangers and conflicts which interfere with its organization and self-expression.

One of the most important means by which it makes itself a self-governing society is the creation of a body of *public opinion* which is an expression of its interest and thought. One of the best ways in which it protects itself is to have just as much, or as little, organization as it needs to do its work, maintaining between the association and the members or member groups a proper balance between what we may call *government* and *liberty*. In this double function of finding and expressing itself on the one hand and of organizing and defending itself on the other, if we leave out external dangers we find two of the serious difficulties are, first, the use of propaganda and other pressure group methods, and, secondly, either too little government or too little liberty. Since this involves us primarily in liberty under the government, the subject will be considered later.[5]

Public opinion in relation to government

If in a democracy the people rule, but go to the ballot boxes only once in two years, how do they rule? An election decides what elective officials there shall be and frequently determines the public policies which shall be followed by the party in power. Back of the election, back of the organization of political parties, back of the candidates and their expressed platforms or policies, lies a mass of ideas, motives, traditions, and other influences constantly and often silently at work. As DeWitt C. Poole declares,[6] "in order to maintain a sound public opinion, three things are essential. The public must have a more or less sustained interest, it must be informed, and its conclusions must be reached mainly by rational processes."

In these days of newspapers, books, recurrent conferences,

[5] Pp. 387–392.
[6] *The Conduct of Foreign Relations under Modern Democratic Conditions*, Yale University Press, p. 129.

movies and radio programs, the past counts [7] but undoubtedly counts less in the formation of public opinion than do organizations, writers, and propagandists in general. Because democratic government is impossible without popular coöperation, those officials who represent the public need to keep their ears rather close to the ground, and to know what the people are thinking and what they want. This need is great for political parties [8] that organize different groups of voters, presumably because they believe in the same principles but possibly because through organization they can gain power and patronage.

It may well be questioned whether this silent or possibly vociferous but underlying force and pressure which we call public opinion may not predetermine the nature of government far more than that may be done by the type of institutions used or the methods of election followed. As Edward McChesney Sait asserts,[9] public opinion "is the propelling force of government." Even in an autocratic society there are limits to the arbitrary rule of a despot. The old saying applied to pre-World War Russia, that its rule was "despotism tempered by assassination" shows that even if the long-suffering public does not revolt, some of the more radical or reckless members may resort to violence. Moreover, all rulers, tyrants or demagogues, find it worthwhile not only to observe but to cultivate public opinion, to discover ways of changing it in their favor, and to make it the response of constantly larger numbers.

Rulers and public opinion

In his volume, *Mobilizing for Chaos*, O. W. Riegel draws attention to the fact that in Europe today more than three

---

[7] The influence of the past is shown rather well by Walter Lippmann in his outstanding volume, *Public Opinion*, p. 81. We follow these set patterns made chiefly unconsciously by our ancestors, and, as Lippmann says, "for the most part we do not first see and then define, we define first and then see. In the great 'blooming, bustling confusion' of the outer world we pick up what our culture has already defined for us, and we tend to perceive that which we have picked out in the form stereotyped for us by our culture." The Macmillan Co. Unquestionably habit patterns, or revered slogans, or cherished practices or ideals play a large part in forming that group of purposes, attitudes, and plans which we sometimes call public opinion.

[8] Pp. 354–355.

[9] *American Parties and Elections*, p. 86.

hundred million people are prevented from forming correct public judgments on public affairs because of the interference with freedom of thought, with full expression of opinion and with public expression in press or by radio of anything except the ideas satisfactory to the rulers. One keen observer, after visiting Germany during Hitler's first year, was asked what marked differences he noted from the earlier régime, and his comment was that all the newspapers were alike. Sometimes a public has the attitude of the tyrant in trying to force the minorities or reluctant classes to accept the general will. Again, it searches out the opinion and the program of a strong leader because its own ideas are vague, unsatisfactory, or unadapted to the crisis it must face. It cannot depend on the demagogue, who is more likely to discover public opinion and chameleon-like adapt himself to it than to make any attempt to create it.

Public sentiment is developed, organized, or coerced more easily, more quickly, and more successfully in dictator-ruled countries or in time of war. If we can study conditions somewhat similar to those of war, we should expect to find the best examples of public sentiment formation. In periods of peace, however, two or three types of conflict affect the public greatly or make a real popular appeal. The first of these occurs when bitter and frequently prolonged controversies and struggles arise between political parties. If all is fair in love and war, the same may be said of politics. When class interests clash, as in sharp or severe conflicts between capital and labor, or in struggles between agrarian groups and industrialists, propaganda thrives, for partisans are both vehement and outspoken.

Public opinion in a democracy

In this study we are particularly interested in noting the dependence of popular government upon public opinion and the relations between public opinion or the forces developing or controlling it and their relationships with democratic government. If absolute rulers hesitate to act counter to public opinion and if present-day dictators seek to control public opinion, we can hardly avoid questioning, first, the relationship between public opinion and any government, and, second, the ways in which democratic government is more influenced by public opinion than is possible in an autocracy.

Possibly we might consider the proposition, is government democratic in proportion to the extent to which it is an expression of public opinion, or is it responsive to the public so far as its wishes can be discovered. If either of those is the case, and particularly if both of them are true, then we might judge democratic government by this triple standard: *the freedom with which public sentiment may be developed, the lack of restraint in its expression, and complete liberty of discussing public interests.* Probably only through perfect freedom of thought and discussion is it possible to train and organize constitutional groups that examine and debate frankly and freely all public questions. Potentially these groups create a balanced government and one that is publicly controlled. One group, the lesser, probably a combination of several minor factions, organizes an opposition which prevents the government from becoming reckless or arbitrary. Without an opposition, a government might soon cease to represent a public and therefore cease to be democratic. Upon an active and live two-party system, such as that used in the parliamentary plan of Great Britain and in the presidential set-up of the United States, depends the preservation of the democratic tradition. Without it there is little possibility for the people to rule in state and national governments.

A subsidized press, especially before the twentieth century, would mean an unfree people. There would be no free channel through which the public might express itself easily. "Boiler plate," distorted news items and perverted editorials would tend to create a public opinion in favor of those who provided the subsidy. The partisan press of the nineteenth century, and to some extent the partisan press of the early twentieth century, may have prevented American democracy from being the real voice of the people.

To what extent is public sentiment reflected correctly in party campaigns and in elections? We think of the nineteenth century preëminently as the great period of democracy. Yet sixty or eighty years ago it was possible to influence elections as we cannot now. The secret ballot came into existence with the modification of the Australian type adopted only ten or twelve years before the end of the nineteenth century. If one reads F. W. Dallinger on the way primaries and caucuses were mismanaged,[10] one wonders not only whether in those days elections represented true expression of public opinion but whether a government which had those origins for its public officials could possibly be called democratic. Formerly it was said that God was on the side of the heaviest battalions. Might it be said that the battalions of voters were on the side of the largest purse? In comparatively few elections in recent years, notably 1928, has the party which spent the largest sums failed to win. Much of this money was spent for speakers and, recently, for the use of the radio. If President Hoover's opening keynote speech in the campaign of 1932 did not change the line-up of Iowa voters as shown by subsequent newspaper polls, it may be questioned whether public sentiment and the opinions of voters have been as greatly influenced by partisan propaganda—by direct voice, radio, or press—as has been imagined.

When it comes, not to elections, but to legislative sessions, in Washington or in the states, how many gubernatorial or presidential administrations can or do act contrary to public opinion? If few governors and Presidents since Grover Cleveland, who was loved for the enemies he made, dare run counter to a strong sentiment against their policies, might it be possible to assert that whether elections represent public opinion accurately or not, actual government almost certainly does? For example, would it be possible to name a half-dozen laws of the most recent session of any state legislature, a half-dozen statutes passed by the latest Congress, which antagonized or misrepresented the public? And if one could find that number of laws or a larger number, would it be possible to decide whether these laws were unrepresentative of public opinion because of boss control, well organized minorities, property interests, or some bodies not so well or-

[10] Dallinger, *Nominations for Elective Office in the United States.*

ganized? It seems probable that special groups might have influence out of proportion to their numbers and importance, but how often will even they succeed without a considerable backing of public sentiment?

Probably if a citizen were asked the distinction between public opinion and *propaganda,* he would refer first to the permanence of the one and the temporariness or recency of the other. He might well paraphrase the old saying about orthodoxy being my "doxy" and heterodoxy being someone else's "doxy." This might apply particularly to political parties,[11] especially among those whose patriotism is chiefly expressed in a paraphrase of an old saying, "my party right or wrong"— a characteristic of party loyalty much more common fifty or a hundred years ago than today. The whole question of political parties is naturally tied up with public opinion, with propaganda, and even more with possible class conflict. As already noted, one of the ablest students of this subject, Arthur N. Holcombe, stresses continually in his recent writings the replacement of sectionalism, and conflict growing out of sectionalism, by *class conflicts.* In the long run, the American political party has represented a combination of groups, thanks to the two-party character of our national party system.

GOVERNMENT IN RELATION TO LIBERTY, JUSTICE AND SECURITY

In the preceding chapter and the preceding part of this chapter, we have indicated many standards by which we shall decide whether a country is democratic or not. Let us examine three further groups of standards. Any society which tries to manage its own affairs without too much pressure from the outside or too much influence or control by hereditary rulers, upstart dictators, or self-appointed rings, finds that it is necessary first of all to get as much government as it needs. We have passed out of the age of individualism into one which probably cannot be described by any definite name or title. In it, however, we are forced regardless of our personal pref-

General

---

[11] On ways in which a political party creates as well as represents public opinion, consult W. B. Graves, *Readings in Public Opinion,* ch. XXV.

erences to admit that unless we want to be ruled by associations which are not primarily political, we must have *a political organization which is well enough organized and has sufficient political authority to manage its own public affairs.*

In the transition from an individualist America to one much more highly socialized, we encounter a problem not only of organizing a government adequate to handle these public problems, but also one of getting a government which will maintain a *maximum desirable liberty* for its members and member groups. The chief popular slogan of 1934, whether representative of public sentiment or not possibly is immaterial, was *security*. In the pet phrases of the two Roosevelts that have occupied the executive chair, "the Square Deal" and "the New Deal," the element of *justice* is stressed. Apparently then, it is essential that democracy secure necessary government (or the right kind and amount of political organization), necessary liberty (a minimum of interference with personal and group rights), adequate security (the minimum essentials of living), and a true brand of democratic justice.[12]

If we had time to examine these four desiderata carefully, we should find that some of the ablest publicists of America have devoted careful thought to a reconciliation of government with liberty.[13] Others, occupying very high public positions, have been almost crusaders for public betterment, which perhaps is a combination of security and wealth. Still others, and one thinks particularly of a recent Chief Justice of the Supreme Court and a justice more recently on the Court, whose lives were devoted to the reconciliation of law with justice.

[12] We have already treated rather fully political organization and social planning or engineering, which naturally would not overlook the right kind of government that a society needs and the right amount of government. In this attempt we have made no study of the proper limits of governmental action, either in general, or in twentieth-century America, or in the troublous but almost constantly changing conditions of the World War, prosperity, depression, and recovery. For any real study of the proper scope, sphere, or limits of government, one would wish to study rather general books on political science.

[13] For example, Burgess, J. W., *The Reconciliation of Government with Liberty.*

Apparently liberty is a term of many meanings. It seems The nature of liberty to be a concept which represents different things in different periods. As used, it frequently embodies the desires of groups or classes which are either above or below average in success and therefore want more than they have or desire things because they do not have them.

Before the twentieth century the term "liberty" ordinarily designated not so much political liberty, which it included, but rather freedom from interference by oppressive government. With modern oppression through the operation of the "coercion of economic forces," and with the rise of big business, which dominates public situations and personal relations sometimes more than government itself, the term has taken on new meaning. Liberty which meant freedom from government interference or freedom under government is therefore supplemented by liberty which is freedom from economic oppression or coercion. It may be opportunity to express opinions or choices or to do as one wishes in a society in which business rather than government is likely to place limitations upon those actions or choices.

In order to understand liberty, apparently it is necessary to get a clearer idea than we usually have of rights and duties, privileges and obligations. Rights and duties grow out of reciprocal relationships.[14] In the multifold relationships which individuals have with one another, and which any individual is likely to have not only with the groups of which he is a member but with other groups or societies, each relationship, if not one-sided, carries with it a bundle of advantages which we are accustomed to call rights. The rights of one person, with the advantages which those rights confer, is only one side of that relationship, since someone else or some group has an obligation almost exactly corresponding with the right of the person we are studying. In other words, rights and duties are not arbitrary. They are simply the two sides of the same relationship. It would be absurd, therefore, to speak of rights without regard to human relationships or

[14] For a simple treatment consult Ashley, R. L., *The New Civics,* ch. I, especially pp. 4–14.

away from the groups within which the relationships exist or become possible.[15]

It would seem to be obvious that rights increase with the number of relationships, since the larger the number of our direct relationships, the more rights we would be likely to possess. If, therefore, a society is rather completely organized so that these relationships are two-sided and systematically arranged and rather well developed, the individual would have more rights than he could possibly possess in a society which was less well developed. In brief, other things being equal, *our liberty increases as society becomes more advanced, better organized and more truly socialized.* The reason many people do not discover this fact is due to two causes: (1) the corresponding increase in our obligations sometimes annoys us more than a greater increase of rights pleases us, and (2) we continually make comparisons with the good old days when we did not have the duties that belong with our neighbors' rights. The freedom from restraint when people lived in isolation, without social contacts or relationships, impresses some of us as an ideal type of liberty.

Liberty under old American democracy

What has all this to do with democracy, and particularly with democracy in the twentieth century? The answer seems rather self-evident. The right kind of group or civic organization which any society should develop or attain would seem to require as a minimum a fair balance between rights and duties among all adult citizens who are fairly intelligent and

[15] It is not necessarily true that liberty is inevitably associated with rights. Certainly the two are not synonymous. J. M. Clark, in *Social Control of Business,* The University of Chicago, makes this distinction rather clear when he says that "property and contract are rights, or bundles of rights, but they turn out on examination to be rather complex relationships between a number of parties, involving an assortment of duties, liabilities, powers, and immunities which require a high degree of discrimination to unravel." (p. 98) "The distinction [between rights and liberties] is all the harder to keep clear because our liberties (or some of them) are protected by rights, so that we 'have a right to' certain of our liberties." (p. 99) After examining rights in relation to duties Clark adds: 'So far as people have no duties toward me or any one else, they are free: liberty begins where duty ends, and *vice versa.* Which means that my rights set the boundaries upon others' liberties." (p. 99) If we have rights only when someone else is likely to have duties, if rights are in many respects indistinguishable from privileges, what is liberty, and when is liberty not liberty? (Commons, J. R., *Legal Foundations of Capitalism,* p. 96) 1924.

responsible. This was not attained in a primitive society under agricultural civilization, in which most of the property, much of the other wealth, and the best of the social positions, with almost all of the corresponding political power, belonged to hereditary groups. The price of their nobility and political power was, of course, the servitude and possibly the oppression of those who did not belong to these upper classes.

Free land gave to frontier and semi-frontier America fairly equal opportunities in the acquiring of landed property and some other forms of wealth. When economic equality helped to break down the barriers of social inequality and resulted eventually in manhood suffrage, potentially it seemed to create a society in which rights and obligations were fairly well balanced. But this state of affairs was too good to last. When industrial capitalism replaced agriculture as the dominant characteristic of American civilization, the surplus wealth of industry created economic inequality which potentially upset the arrangement by which theoretical political equality and nineteenth-century democracy had come into existence.

Apparently under no other socio-political plan than one which is truly democratic is there any probability of securing to the average citizen the minimum of essential rights, or shall we say a minimum embodiment of liberty, which would seem to be fair and just and is desirable.

Liberty guaranteed by the constitutional bills of rights [16] is important today as in past centuries, but other rights and forms of liberty need to be protected as well. It is inevitable that modern government should extend administration more than that in the past. Many are already echoing the cry of Lao Tse, the famous Chinese philosopher, "Inactive administration—happy people; industrious administration—sad people." [17] Each class or group naturally is interested in the liberty that would come from the safeguarding of its rights, not realizing often that its rights may be upheld only by sacrificing some conflicting rights of others. The Supreme Court of the United States brings this out clearly.

[16] P. 279.
[17] *Civil Service Abroad*, p. 162.

"Life, liberty, property, and the equal protection of the laws, grouped together in the Constitution, are so closely related that the deprivation of any one of these separate and independent rights may lessen or extinguish the value of the other three."[17a] It might have added that the protection of any one of the four might also lessen or extinguish the value of one or more of the others.

Evidently liberty is not the simple freedom from governmental interference so many have thought it to be. Constitutional safeguards are necessary and desirable remedies, though law and court action are essential. But they do not cover enough, and they may not touch the most important needs and problems of a twentieth-century society. Regimentation by either business or government is intolerable, but organized and coördinated planning, economic and political, may be unavoidable. A planned economy or polity may increase rights and liberty as much as controlled traffic avoids congestion and keeps the cars moving, though restricting the right of the drivers to move at intervals, for the best interests of all. Years ago E. E. Robinson drew attention to the "need for a national party whose founders conceived its primary function as that of insuring the protection of the citizen in the liberties promised him under the American form of government and of improving and safeguarding the conditions under which the average man and woman must live and work."[18]

DEMOCRACY AND THE SQUARE DEAL

Formerly we thought of democracy chiefly as government *of* the people and *by* the people. Now we are often stressing *for* the people, because our ancestors neglected that side of democracy. In this topic we shall consider only two phases of government's responsibility for right treatment of citizens and groups. As we have seen in the case of conflicting interests, and those conflicts are inescapable because inherent in

[17a] *Smith vs. Texas.*
[18] *Evolution of American Political Parties,* Harcourt, Brace and Company, p. 364.

the nature of group organization, attempts to protect, aid or benefit one person or group may interfere with corresponding protection or security of others associated with them. Security or welfare will be left to the next chapter.

What are the duties of a democratic society to its members in regard to justice and a fair system of taxation? If justice is blind, to insure impartiality, is she also blind to improper pressure and power and influence, inherited or acquired? Does the system of taxation used in America conform to just principles? Are those who pay the public's bills paying their fair share; and, if they pay more, are they getting a square deal in the process?

The term *administration of justice* is usually applied chiefly to the final act of government in the process of law making, law enforcing, and law deciding. But in a broad sense the administration of justice includes the rules that are made and the application of those rules without fear or favor quite as much as it does court decisions. If the law is unfair, an arrest unjust, no judge or jury will find it easy to render a just decision or verdict. *Justice in law and administration*

We have already discussed the question of law, its inevitable lag, and the dangers that arise from its being too specific.[19] Possibly a suggestion or two should be offered regarding the conditions which must be met if law may be considered fair and just. In general, laws should be general, and they should represent permanent rather than temporary needs. Democracy, representing all the people, usually makes too many and too specific laws.

Good law-making should prevent law breaking. If the rules are simple, not too numerous, and reasonably well-known, there is less danger that laws will be broken through ignorance or lack of understanding. That situation has never arisen in modern America. Our problems of law enforcement probably are increasing, but lawlessness may not be on the increase.[20] The newspapers have frequently drawn the public's attention to cases of law breaking and possibly have discouraged crime.

[19] See pp. 76–78, 88–89.
[20] *Cf. Recent Social Trends,* pp. 1123–1137.

The movies probably have done so. However, whole fields of petty misdemeanors, or compounded felonies, racketeering, gang wars, or other crimes not necessarily covered by our laws seem to indicate, at least in some large cities, a reckless disregard either of laws or of the rights of the public. This disregard of proper rules necessary to maintain law and order is not primarily a problem of law enforcement. As President Coolidge stressed repeatedly, the great American need is not more law enforcement but better general law observance.

Nearly two centuries ago Beccaria, an Italian jurist, stressed the value of the certainty rather than the severity of a punishment as the chief deterrent to crime. Later students urged less attention to punishment, more to reform; less to retaliation, more to social justice. Americans are disheartened when they notice the discrepancy between the number of crimes committed and the number of persons arrested, between the number accused and the number convicted. Possibly we are misinformed. Convictions sometimes are secured by the use of the third degree and by other methods which one subcommittee of President Hoover's Wickersham Committee treated under the title, "Enforcing Laws Illegally." Raymond Moley calls attention to the fact that one reason for the small number of convictions is that most accused guilty persons confess.[21] Occasionally investigations like that of Judge Seabury bring to light widespread and long-standing agreements between police and law breakers. Naturally if a $3,000 annual salary is supplemented by graft to make possible a $200,000 increase in bank balance, a great deal of law breaking must have been overlooked, intentionally.

Some police organizations, notably that headed by August Vollmer and those working with the laboratories of some of our larger universities, are trying to make use of new scientific methods of detecting criminals and to some extent of preventing crime. It is too much to ask that our generation will make guardians of the law enforce laws impartially, and become expert crime psychologists. Perhaps it would also be too much if our generation asked the public in general, and

[21] R. Moley, *Our Criminal Courts,* Ch. VII.

churches, business organizations and clubs as well as individual citizens to accept responsibility for reducing the temptation to break laws, to gain an improved attitude toward law observance, and to replace a semi-barbaric system of punishment for offenders with one socially and psychologically safe and sane.

The administration of justice is in our thought less a matter of fair laws or a question of law enforcement for our benefit, than one for the settlement of civil as well as criminal disputes in the courts. *If crime is poorly defined and the penalties for criminal offenses are arbitrary and unjust,* no system of courts can possibly render justice to accused persons regardless of protection of rights by jury trial and other provisions in our constitutions. Most foreign observers, from Alexis de Tocqueville a century ago to the present time, speak in the highest terms both of American courts and of the American bar. Compared with foreign countries, apparently America has a favorable opportunity to dispense justice; but this may not be due to democracy.

Democracy and the administration of justice

A generation ago Judge Taft criticized severely the delays and the difficulties in court procedure which interfered with the administration of justice in America. A generation has passed but most of those delays and difficulties are still part of our system. Many trials are long and slow, although the volume of petty cases which the average judge considers and decides in a day seems appalling to an amateur. Often evidence is manufactured for the benefit of a client. In the trial of notorious cases the wide gulf which separates the skill and ability of high-priced attorneys of private parties sometimes contrasts unfortunately with the bungling and unscientific management of the state's case by the public's ill-paid investigators and attorneys.

Jury trial has always been inseparable from the protection of the people's rights; and it gave legal democracy centuries before modern political democracy came into existence. But jury trial is the first desire if the last resort of the criminal lawyer and the best hope of the guilty person who hopes to escape either severe punishment or a just penalty. In dealing with complicated cases or questions involving high finance, a jury trial is more apt to be a farce than a remedy. If the jury system breaks down when it tackles difficult or important problems of contemporary civilization, must we adopt a less democratic method to protect the public from offenders? Surely the public is as much entitled to a square deal as is the person accused of breaking the law.

A square
deal in
taxes

More briefly we can consider whether the taxpayer has a square deal or not, under our democratic system. No one wishes to pay taxes. Revolts and taxes are closely connected, as noted in the rise of the Dutch Republic, in the French Revolution, and in our own revolution against Great Britain. Today the tax burden is much heavier than it was before the twentieth century. The cost of government has increased by leaps and bounds, and, except the collector, none is so unpopular as the niggardly administrator. Democracies are notoriously extravagant, possibly because those who spend the money do not pay the bills, possibly because those who get the patronage, the business, the spoils, or the relief make spending good politics. Responsibility for economy has never been a trait of American government; formerly the House of Representatives had one committee to raise public funds, fourteen to appropriate them.

In general we should agree that current revenues should come from current income, actual or potential, not from wealth as such. Probably society must admit that *it must come from those who can afford to pay,* not from those whose payments would lower levels of living essentials already low. Whatever the source of public revenues, it must be a present source, not one that formerly had income. In other words, in America a square tax deal means one that is up-to-date, lays an equal burden for taxes, regardless of whether it is expenditure by national or state or local authorities.

A square deal to the taxpayer is not necessarily a low tax. It is rather a just allocation of all taxes to the sources from which they can be paid with least burden, loss and suffering. But a square deal to the public in general includes as low cost of government as conditions permit, our money's worth for the money spent, and surpluses from years of plenty to supply the lack in years of financial famine. A square deal involves a just tax system, really a *system* for nation, state and locality combined; one that is fair as a whole not simply just in spots. The giving of a square deal is an inescapable responsibility of a democratic society. To secure it we shall need the best possible leadership, in school and in business, in government and in society.

Establishing Proper Public Controls

Our ancestors thought of democracy in terms of the individual and believed any government undemocratic which interfered arbitrarily with the individual or with group initiative or action. We in our day think ourselves wiser because we realize that democracy is preëminently a form of group organization. We believe that it rests upon the foundation of the whole society and represents a public, preëminently the largest, finest, and most comprehensive of all group associations. To organize and integrate such a group is inevitably a Herculean task worthy of a free, intelligent, progressive people.

Public authority and necessary social reorganization

In this chapter we have examined some of the conditions without which democracy is impossible or without the continuance of which democracy ceases to exist. Of the numerous other evidences of democracy let us consider just one more, the need of public control of any economic interests which have become public. A reëxamination of conditions of production and finance that we previously studied [22] shows very little interest in, or regard for, the public or the public interest. This is all the more strange because without the support of laws and the advantage of public organization of corporations, without the possibility of nations that separately or together have given a wide-spread market, machine-power industry and high finance could not possibly have developed to the degree which has actually taken place. A serious public problem in a sense is not to interfere with either industrialism or financialism in the managing of their affairs

[22] See chs. V and VI.

which are solely their own. But *it is publicly necessary that this super-economic combination of big businesses, which many students of public affairs think exercises more public power than government itself, coöperate with government and serve the public as it serves its own interests.* If the day of individualism had not passed, we might ask that "laissez faire" be applied against the capitalist, and for the consuming and governing groups, that by leaving them alone, they be allowed to get a standard of living or success in action to which the advance of modern applied science entitles them.

We realize that modern civilization is largely what it is because of improvement in production; but the benefits of the system have largely been lost because production except for consumption is profitless, at least from the social angle. Many suggestions have been offered regarding the actual or possible use of public authority in the reorganization of the social order. One of these deals with the misuse of law for profiteering, when it should be the basis of improved consumption. A 1935 law forbids war profits, in the hope of avoiding agitation for war by munition makers and others. In many cases a slight shift of emphasis in our law, or readaptation in our custom, is all that is necessary to protect the public instead of promoting selfish interests. Possibly if we could utilize Supreme Court decisions involving public welfare as a basis of public action, we could get rid of many of the abuses of a profit-taking capitalism. Better controls can be devised for the corporation, created by the public for better development and management of our economic and possibly social affairs. Society should be allowed to protect itself on the principle that the creator has rights, including controls, regarding the creation, and the created responsibilities and obligations toward the creator.

What constitutes a "public interest"?

Today most business and even some governments are only parts of our whole system. They could not exist apart from the world of affairs. They are truly affected with a public interest. Possibly the best, and the ultimate, solution for public control of modern business may be an extension of the policy already used, toward "business affected with a public

interest." [23]   From time immemorial certain businesses have
been regulated because they seemed to be of this type. According to Chief Justice Taft, business "said to be clothed
with a public interest justifying some public regulation may
be divided into three classes." The first of these consists of
public utilities "carried on under the authority of a public
grant of privileges." The second class includes "certain occupations regarded as exceptional," which had been regulated "from earliest times," and the third involves businesses
which were formerly not treated as public, but for some reason
have come under government regulation.   It has been suggested that public regulation is necessary when the industry
deals with a *common necessity for civilized life,* and that a
second condition exists when there is a *serious restriction of
the consumer's freedom of choice* in buying goods produced
by an industry.[24]

If a definite principle of public interest is the *degree of control* exercised by the business in question over producers of
raw material, or workers, or consumers, regulation of such
businesses should be both necessary and effective.   In our
social order interrelations exist not only between businesses
in the same field (*e.g.,* production) but also in related fields.
Consequently the consumers, the workers, and frequently the
producers of raw materials may be at a disadvantage compared with the person who produces goods or furnishes services.[25]   For most of us there is little opportunity to compare
prices and quality of products.

In spite of the dilemma in which we find ourselves, in spite
of the recognition that the world has changed and we must
change with it, in spite of the need for a drastic reorganization in many of our economic and some of our social institutions, in spite of revival of old laws and reënactment of new
which will protect the public rather than promote profit, the
American people are abandoning and will continue to abandon,

---

[23] On this point consult, however, the article by W. H. Hamilton in
Yale Law Review, 1930.

[24] In *The Public Control of Business,* p. 7, Keezer and May give a list
of businesses "affected with a public interest."

[25] See pp. 129–131, 226–230, 263–265, 309–311.

with great reluctance, any policy which seems to interfere
with individual liberty or initiative, or circumscribe individual
rights. The fact that coercion of economic forces has already
nullified many of the constitutional guarantees of personal
rights seems to be overlooked. We are unwilling, to use John
Maurice Clark's phrase, to make use of legal coercion to stop
economic coercion. The fact that the legal coercion may be
general, social, and public must not be lost to sight even if
when, in business, we think in terms specific, personal, and
private.

*Most large-scale business becomes "clothed with a public
interest" because of its influence in the life of the American
people.* When it deals with a necessity that we must have,
and one which we get usually from a single source, as the
water company that supplies our residence or the telephone
company that connects us with our friends, it represents a
public interest, be it large-scale or small. Then we call it
a *public utility*, and, as we have seen,[26] we regulate it almost
without limit. If it is concerned with necessary fuels, for
which substitutes are not found easily, the existence of public
interest need not be proved, for those businesses are almost
public utilities.

Gas for lighting and for heating has been recognized as a
public necessity, possibly because we must use the streets for
its distribution. As gas has been replaced by electricity,
might it not be true that the "gas" which auto owners must
have for their daily work or pleasure is quite as much a *public
necessity* as illuminating gas. It does not make use of the
public streets, no; but it does make use of the Creator's subterranean lakes of crude oil. Moreover, most of our petroleum, at least the refining of petroleum, is dominated if not
controlled by a group of business men whose first aim is profit
rather than public benefit.

Might not either *monopoly or the wide-spread character of
a business* in these days be almost sufficient to clothe it with
a public interest and to make the protection of public rights
in connection with it a matter of public obligation in a demo-

[26] See ch. V.

cratic society? Price regulation is everywhere a most important feature of "utility" control; but, when a huge corporation or group of corporations actually determines prices, as many of them have done, should those prices not be subject to recheck by government? Equally of public interest are those companies that play "patron" to workers and control "company" towns. Widespread control of price and life is most characteristic of interlocking businesses and holding companies. Especially objectionable are those in public utilities, which are controlled and, if over-pyramided, to be forbidden under the Utilities Act of 1935.

Apparently we need something to supplement our system of common law and statutes and Constitution. We may call this a system of Social Equity. This social equity, like its predecessor in the field of general law, should supplement the law and the Constitution. We have from the past definite principles of right, fairness, and justice. But the old law, because it is old, because it inevitably lags behind present needs, because it may intentionally be diverted for the advantage of some powerful group, is unjust as well as antiquated. The term social equity places great stress upon public protection and general security, needed because times have changed and we cannot quickly alter laws and constitutions. We might take from the decisions of the Supreme Court a few years ago the term public welfare. The much older ideals of public health, safety, and morals often might gain by yielding precedence to it, because these three, coming to us from the ages, may be inadequate in this new age of dynamic changes. *Social equity*

Basically the great need of a democratic people in the solution of this vital public problem of the proper relations of government to business and of a public economics is a new Adam Smith. A century and a half ago he stated economic principles of a new individualism. We should have a restatement of the underlying ideas of a new economic society. "Laissez faire" was a protest against paternalism. Why not modernize Mr. Smith and call him, to accord with the spirit of the age, Adam Smith, Incorporated, in true twentieth-century style. No one individual is equal to the task; how many *The need for leadership* would deny their inability to help restore order from chaos? Five men, at least, are needed to give "legality." For the directorate I should be glad to offer suggestions. Whom would you nominate for the Board of Directors?

If civilization is done over to order, will the end justify the action? No two successive generations see eye to eye. Shall we escape the limitations and twists of our day? Imagine our whole civilization being reconstructed a century or less ago in the best Victorian manner! Their standards of thought and of morality, their monstrosities of furniture and of architecture, their provincialism and their smugness are not ours, but our reorganization might easily be more offensive than theirs would have been. Luckily human life is short, but in these days not short enough to escape the nemesis of our earlier blunders. Evidently we shall need the finest kind of leadership, not only in discovering the significant principles in a public economics of plenty, but also in discovering the significant principles of a new socialized democracy.

The old democracy has yielded to the new partly because it disregarded and feared leadership, whereas the new capitalizes leadership. So anxious were our ancestors to attain equality, they failed to understand or appreciate organization as a first fundamental of any society that was not primitive and simple. With the increasing number of groups necessary to carry on the general work of our people, and the growing complexity of relationships of group to group, of group to the whole society, of member to the whole or to the groups to which he belongs, there is need not only of organization— definite, unitary, and flexible—but of a high degree of co-ordination. In a social unit this means the development of an intricate and integrated set of policies.

The re-formulation of a popular, intelligent, and flexible polity, and the wise and skillful adaptation of these policies in actual administration of affairs is neither within the capacity of the rank and file, nor their task. It is the province of those specially fitted for that work, those geniuses of democracy who know the way, comprehend means of attaining the right goals, and above all are able to carry us with them.

These men have that divine spark we call leadership. Without them and their leadership we grope our way too much. We have the drive, but we do not arrive. If they are of us as well as for us, none need worry about democracy losing its popular character. But if in the dynamic age we forego their guidance, as older generations did, our generation will fail to work out the reorganization, the necessary adjustments, the ability to achieve which will make our present America a successful, self-directing, democratically organized society. Let us not make the mistake of either belittling, neglecting, or refuting leadership.

In conclusion we note again that democracy is not simply a political system; but even as a political system it is an integral part of our economic and social order. As a political system it is democratic only to the extent that it represents the public, if it has a public to represent, and that it accepts its responsibility to that public. This responsibility involves the formation and the management of a good as well as a popular government, a government that is not too much a survival of the past (that would be un-American) and a government that is an integral part of the present social order of America. If this be ideal, or an ideal, we can at least insist that our political parties, and we as American citizens, study and understand the whole set-up and act on a judgment that never forgets responsibility. *How else can we keep or make America truly democratic?*

XIV

WELFARE AS A PUBLIC RESPONSIBILITY

THE QUEST FOR SECURITY

Of what value democracy if only the political forms are ours; of what value a political system "of" and "by" the people unless needed action "for" them is forthcoming; of what value a public if it is obsessed with affairs and successes in the market and not in the lives of the people? The dilemma of industrial capitalism would not have aroused public indignation, or called for public action, had not the plight of worker, farmer and consumer demoralized society, called for new public policies and made some social reorganization inevitable. Unless business is greater than society and that society unmindful of its members, all safeguards of life, health, home, work and vital possessions must be assured, as the primary obligation of the public.

In the mad rush for profit, place, and power, the vast majority sacrifice advancement for security. We love excitement, we crave adventure, we demand entertainment; but of liberty, prosperity, and security, the greatest of these is security. The human heart finds home best. Merchant and citizen insist on safeguards for property and life. Nations stifle ambition lest a grasping diplomacy jeopardize public security. "Safety first" is the slogan that marks the limits of this age of rush and speed. Law and order are the very foundations of the commonwealth.

Personal, Political and Economic Security

Personal security

The quest for security belongs to no epoch, race, sex, or age. It probably is characteristic of passive rather than active societies, of fore-thinking rather than thoughtless peoples,

404

of women rather than men, of childhood and age rather than youth or early manhood.

Psychologically *the desire for security* is a force which constrains us from the cradle to the grave. John B. Watson's studies of very small children bring out strikingly the influence of fear in relation to loud noises and high places. These innate traits, call them instinct or some different but more outlandish name, represent the baby's wish to escape from difficulties and dangers in a world he knows not of. There is little reason back of this urge to withdraw from the problems, difficulties, trials, and tribulations which must be encountered in a complex society of living folk and an environment which is frequently none too kind. Even if we do not succumb to a reversion to infantilism, we may find that it is not in our stars but in our inheritance and inhibitions that we are underlings.

Soul-analysis is too difficult a task to win universal approval; some interpret it from one angle and some stress one thing to the exclusion of others. Most psycho-analysts are agreed upon the quest for security as a major cause of maladjustment with life. In his treatment of the neurotic constitution, Dr. Alfred Adler gives particular attention to this problem. His will to power is little more than an attempt of the person who does not succeed to cover his failure by magnifying himself. After all, this is but an abnormal way to forget that the security which was most desirable has not been acquired. Dr. C. G. Jung stresses our willingness to run away from our problems. This is practically an acceptance of the idea that security shall be purchased even at the sacrifice of responsibility or of an attempt to overcome the difficulty which one faces. Dual personality, whether we follow Dr. Morton Prince or others, is nine times out of ten a reversion to some childish condition in which we believe we attain security, a security that would be denied us if we go forward and upward.

Security is not an abnormal condition nor is it chiefly characteristic of abnormal psychology. The pious person who has intense faith attains it both as a means and an end. Until recent years religion was dominated primarily by fear, a mo-

tive to attain security. Present ills are borne with patience in
order that a future may be secured in which there will be no
tears and trials. But faith is not primarily a religious motive;
it is an underlying confidence in all that we are and in much
that we have. Without it all the uncertainties from Pandora's
Box [1] would keep us from attempting much or achieving anything. Security, therefore, becomes not simply an inactive
motive enabling us to avoid danger, but a positive force driving us to the highest possible goals.

In the simple agricultural life of the past, tradition, if not
lack of opportunity, set narrow limits to the problems which
any individual or any group must face. The modern complex
world bristles with new situations. At every turn we encounter contacts unknown a century ago. Even so simple a
matter as crossing a street may be fraught with danger to
life and limb, and is frequently subject to public regulation
and control. The old classification of pedestrians as the quick
or the dead is typical of a hundred other modern situations
that we meet daily. In school and in factory, in shop or in
office, the strain of a high-geared life causes a wear and tear,
physical as well as nervous, which *makes security especially
necessary* and blessed if rare and difficult of achievement.[1a]

Old political
security

Political history of modern times represents a struggle for
security. Our national Constitution ends with a bill of rights;
our state constitutions begin with those safeguards of personal
liberty. Until democracy pried monarchy loose from its moorings of absolutism, government, unfortunately, meant arbitrary rule. Arbitrary rule in turn was administrative
interference for the advantage gained by someone who had
friends at court or influence in high places. The Greeks gave
us the word tyranny; but in general their tyranny yielded
to some form of popular government, much as absolutism has
been modified by constitutional monarchy, and constitutional

---

[1] After Prometheus stole fire from heaven, Pandora was sent to the
earth with a box containing all kinds of evils, or blessings. The brother
of Prometheus made her his wife. Through curiosity she opened the box,
from which everything escaped save Hope.

[1a] The strains of city life and nervous breakdown are considered by W.
F. Ogburn, *Social Change*, pp. 325–6. Compare urban with rural strains.

rule has found expression in representative government, responsible government and other forms of democracy.

Liberty has seemed the main purpose of government because it is the reverse of tyrannical interference in personal affairs. The opposite of an evil rarely lasts as the basis of group organization. The excesses of the French Revolution made a Napoleon possible. Napoleon proved himself a splendid psychologist and politician when he made use of that fundamental human desire for safety. He was right when he insisted that the French people desired personal freedom, but preferred security to liberty.

We have many theories of government, but all agree that *the most essential function of political rule is protection,* spelled with a small "p." A second purpose which most would accept is *the defining of legal or normal relations between individual and individual.* These relationships are of infinite variety, personal, as that of husband to wife, political, as that of citizen to official, economic, as that of employer to employe or of buyer to seller; social, as that of one member of a community to another. Without naming or analyzing other activities of the state, we can see that these two fundamental functions alone place a premium upon making us individually and collectively secure. The public cannot be responsible for many of the personal gains individuals will be wise in securing; but it cannot evade its responsibility for safeguarding individuals and classes that need its help and protection in this modern world. These types of compulsory security are much more numerous and important than appear at first glance.

International rules are few and unobserved by the strong in time of strife; but international law, and an attempt at international organization, is founded on the idea of national self-preservation. The rights of neutrals in time of war, the rights of persons who were not fighting but were citizens of a belligerent nation, called for the earliest safeguards among nations. Whether we are dealing with life or with property, the desire for protection by due process, by custom if not of law, underlie the agreements nations have made with one another. Examine Germany's motto of a place in the sun or Bethman-Hollweg's insistence that Germany invaded Belgium because her back was against the wall. Contrast with this Belgium's reliance upon international agreement to which both Prussia and Austria were parties, granting security against international interference. She objected and the world protested against turning a treaty into the famous "scrap of paper."

New economic security for workers

The exercise of political advantage is the prerogative of the powerful; the support of public organization, the compulsion of the many. In most of its history humanity has been ruled and has had little share in the ruling. If the sway were just, what more should be expected? After all, government is an underlying, but not an active, part of our daily lives. Without it there would be little order and accomplishment in our daily work. Not government but business or the home decides the routine of the day—the work we undertake, the people we contact, the multitude of experiences we encounter.

In naming economic fundamentals we do not add government to food, clothing, and shelter. Custom controls too many things, but economic necessity not tradition makes these commodities the *sine qua non* of existence. Earning a living and voting are so far from the same level that most of us do not vote, although work is inescapable. There is no time like a depression to emphasize needs and to bring problems into prominence. Any thoughtful far-sighted person might have realized that the prosperity from the World War to the panic of 1929 was a passing phase of human experience. Self-appointed prophets of a new order might proclaim a cessation of business cycles, predicting a cumulative pyramiding of stock-market profits for many years. The tens of thousands who lost make us forget the tens of millions who did not speculate.

The tens of millions who did not speculate included about fifty million workers, for in 1927 the National Bureau of Economic Research found outside of agriculture but 3,677,000 independent employers, professional people or workers independent of an employer. For the others well may Abraham

Epstein have referred to the "specter of insecurity" and urged *"social security through social insurance."* In the study of socialization we have already noted some minor regulations made in America for children, women and workers in hazardous industries. It is a pitiful commentary on the laxity of law administration in the United States that when N. I. R. A. codes made child labor unprofitable it ended most child labor that had been forbidden by state statute for a generation and which Congress had not been allowed by our national Constitution to prohibit. Hours for women are still inexcusably long, only six states having an eight-hour day in 1932, although the N. I. R. A. codes temporarily both shortened and standardized them. Workmen's accident laws apply in most of the states. Aside from these incidental protective helps for labor, we have practically no social insurance in this country. Little or nothing has been done to give some public security against unemployment, sickness, old age or family needs. If more than a score of other civilized countries have established most or all of these types of social insurance, either we must show that they are wrong or assume the burden of proof that democratic America should do at least as much for its needy classes as does semi-democratic Europe. *Nicholas Murray Butler,* in a radio address in 1932, *declared that within ten years all forms of social insurance would be necessary in America.* How rapidly are we coming to understand the reason?

In the rebound from the dangers brought to the fore by the world conflict, we might pardon the disregard of big business for labor or for those who did not add to its profits. Before the war had made us forget everything else, public welfare was the dominant note of most public actions. Welfare is more than security; but it involves at its core the idea of protection of health, a form of security, and the safeguarding of other vital interests of those who cannot safeguard themselves. Four years of depression were better than two decades of prosperity in making clear the public and social responsibility of big business for a better world in which to work. The unemployment crisis of 1930, separated by but nine years from that of 1921, made us employment conscious. *The right to work is just as important as the right to public health.* Formerly considered by our government only an economic condition of no consequence, it may easily become a public obligation, as it has in part of Europe. If the state is responsible for law and order, we might easily accept the doctrine that it is equally responsible that all have the necessities of life. Until recently we have considered poverty the misfortune of the irresponsible. Even when we awake to the fact that it may be the fault of our economic system, we still refuse to accept the obligation as a nation to make poverty impossible in an age of plenty. We treat it by methods that were obsolescent decades ago, as though it were avoidable by its victims. We even refuse by decisions of our highest court to give women workers the benefit of a minimum wage limit. But why maintain, by law or custom, the requirement of a living wage, if no work is provided or none can be procured?

Economic security for those whose need is greatest becomes a general duty. Whether this be charity, the "dole," or employment on public works remains for each group and generation to work out for itself. Apparently the granting of economic security is a public necessity and must be recognized as a public obligation. Some one must now furnish the safeguards formerly provided by the patriarchal family, by a paternalistic clan under a domineering chief, and by the small community, which looked after its own. The Tammany ward boss recognizes his opportunity if not his obligation; as patron he offers help and capitalizes his political power. If the public does not do this in its political capacity, it must do it through the world of business working with our public representatives. If this be socialistic, then we are on our way to that goal; if it be brotherhood of man, we can look forward to a richer and finer Christianity.

Security in Many Fields

It is a simple matter to pass a law or constitutional amendment giving every adult the right to vote. Those who worked for years to secure "votes for women" will disagree violently with so placid an announcement. It is exceedingly difficult, probably impossible, to protect the individual from himself, disregarding his numerous contacts with others. A student of psychology, and all of us consider ourselves good judges of human nature, is amazed not only at how good we are but how much we accomplish. Considering what animal nature and human nature are, social achievements are little short of miraculous. Students of anthropology and archaeology have equal reasons for amazement when they consider the brief interval, scarcely a moment of the time old earth has been in existence, in which humanity has built up its present society and civilization. From the cave man to the skyscraper dweller is but little more than ten thousand years. Instincts and emotions are still here, although much conventionalized and very much restrained; intelligence has developed greatly if we measure by our skillful tests intended to determine that quality. The gain is slight, however, if intelligence be measured by the ability to endure pain, privation, and other hardships, by the ability to find a living in a wilderness or in our highly organized but still competitive society, by the ability as a group to see the needs of our changing world and act accordingly. Modern families are probably more harmonious than those of neolithic days, but present-day groups are bound less by primitive necessity than by choice and desire. The crowd does not call many of us, but the group has an existence just as real as that of the individual. Membership in some society is not a matter of choice, nor does the place which one occupies depend solely upon ability or desire. *One's part in the great game of human existence or of social development depends upon the inevitable relationships within the groups of which we are members,* upon the traditions which we observe, and the goals toward which we are tending.

In this complex but closely-knit system we live and move and have our being. We pass through a period of dependency which is growing longer and longer. Illness or accident overtakes us in the height of our manhood; old age finds us still members but stripped of our ability to participate and contribute in this new world. What substitutes for old safe-

guards are we using?[2] What new types of protection are we
developing because we have more to share and feel bound to
help? In a real sense civilization is modern to the extent that
the public is thoughtful, protective, and humanitarian. The
child is cared for as never before. Those who are ailing are
no longer treated as criminals or put out of the way as burdens. The aged are less fortunate than were those ancestors
who were cared for in life and worshipped when dead; but
they are luckier than the old folk of long ago who were de-

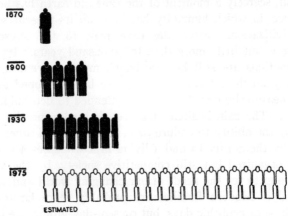

INCREASE IN THE NUMBER OF AGED IN U. S.[2a]

Each Figure Represents One Million Persons 65 Years of Age and Over

spised, neglected, or destroyed when they ceased to be useful.
Consciously or not, society is accepting the obligation for

[2] On the problems and on European attempts to solve them, see I. M.
Rubinow, *The Quest for Security*, Books III, IV.
    One of the most comprehensive measures ever passed by Congress was
the President's Social Security Act (1935) for grants-in-aid to the states
for the benefit of the unemployed, the aged, children, and public health.
Under the administration of a national Social Security Board, from funds
raised through taxes on employer and employe (½% of wages each, 1937,
to 2½% each, 1957) grants are made to the states as part employment
compensation, to be paid through the states. On a 50–50 basis grants of
$15 per month are made to the states for needy, aged persons over 65.
Further grants are provided for children and public health, and are provided through taxes on industry for annuities to retired workers beginning
at 65. This measure should stimulate action by the states toward social
insurance, in order that they may secure this federal aid, although that assistance would not cover all costs.
    [2a] Committee on Economic Security.

those whose need is great in comparison with their ability to provide for themselves.

To most of us, saturated with individualism, the problem of illness or old age seems to be a purely individual matter. We think differently when we examine insurance statistics and discover that at sixty-five only three persons out of a hundred are not dependent on others. If they cannot provide for themselves, who will do it? Their children? But this is the day of filial ingratitude. Urban life does not offer the means as did the old homestead of furnishing a quiet and peaceful place in which to spend one's declining years. It is stretching the point to argue that there are no old folk on the sunny side of eighty. They may look young, but they cannot stand the strain of competition with younger, more active workers—and they look young only in case life does not ask too much.

Throughout our earning days we are confronted with the dilemma: shall we spend or shall we save? The thrift of the old countryman is not necessary in productive and prodigal America. Benjamin Franklin was not the last of the great savers; but ours is an economy of new and greater production rather than one distinctive of thrift. If our income fails to equal our expenditures, the solution is simple: earn more. In time of sickness or depression, or when old age arrives, the unwisdom of this policy is striking—and sickness comes frequently. Seldom does a home with four or five members go through the year without demand after demand for health preservation or relief from sickness. If it isn't the physician, it's the dentist; if it isn't the dentist, it may be the surgeon; if it isn't the surgeon, it may be the undertaker. Few realize how much of a doctor's services are free. Public and privately endowed clinics reduce sharply the cost of diagnosis and treatment, yet the doctor's bills mount and mount and mount. The savings of a year or of five years are gone to pay for doctor, nurse, or hospital. Frequently charges are fitted to the purse of the patient, but carefully planned savings disappear when sickness gains admittance. We do not need to read sensational literature to get facts on the high

Security of savings: need of borrowing

costs of being ill. *The Survey, Harper's Magazine* and other dependable periodicals multiply illustrations of this serious problem. Besides illness comes accident or death; and it costs more to die, ordinarily, than to live.

Sickness is responsible for at least a quarter of the loans made to the small borrower, and these loans total billions annually. In the first place, more than three-quarters of the workers do not have any savings worthy of the name, do not enjoy credit with the banks or ordinary lending organizations. When a bank has to charge a dollar per month for checking accounts below a balance of fifty, one hundred, or five hundred dollars, it cannot afford to carry small loans based upon personal or household collateral. It is much, very much, easier to lend five thousand dollars on good stocks or bonds at six or seven per cent than to finance a much smaller amount for men of no credit and small means. Evans Clark shows that attempts to reduce the legal rate of interest below two per cent a month to the small borrower leads to absolute disregard of the law. Consequently the man in need pays a personal financial company or a pawnbroker a rate much higher than the law should have recognized as necessary.

The question arises: Why should one borrow? The improvident, the greedy, or possibly the farsighted, buy on installment and probably lose when the collector cannot be paid. This is, in a real sense, a form of borrowing and has grown in volume, until in 1929 the amount secured on credit in the United States in this way was estimated at seven billions of dollars. Strangely enough prosperity boosts borrowing, but usually in intervals of idleness for the wage-earner. The amount is stated by Franklin W. Ryan as an average of $250 for actual loans or for deferred payments. It is a little misleading to say that half of what we purchase is on credit when most of us pay our bills after the end of each month; we do not tell how long after.

The problem of the small saver is closely related to that of the small borrower. He has a little money and can save five dollars a week or, occasionally, fifty dollars per month. In what shall he place that? The savings bank presents first aid to the thrifty-minded. Uncle Sam has postal savings banks at most of his post offices. Many schools maintain school savings banks in which tiny savings may be placed from week to week. The savings bank is helpful because investments are likely to be semi-permanent. The penalty on withdrawal is sufficiently high to prevent or discourage the spending of well-earned savings. Savings accounts rarely carry a family very far through illness, depression or disaster.

Savings would be very much more helpful if they could be made more regularly or in larger amounts. They would be both regular and larger if the risks of the investor were not so great. Consider the tens of billions lost by buyers of land or securities during the "New Era" period after the World War. Some investments are undoubtedly safer than others, though with less chance of increase in value. Life insurance or some home builders provide regularity of payments and high incentive to invest. New forms of insurance represent cumulative or endowment savings, as well as provision against death. Ordinary life insurance necessarily carries such high premiums that it usually is out of the reach of the working man. For him and members of his family industrial insurance, or survival insurance, is issued—fifty million policies calling for $800,000,000 yearly in premiums—with an average payment on death of $200. This should be called funeral insurance for there is little or nothing left for the survivors. If the head of the family dies, a widow with small children needs a regular income—or gets public charity! Rubinow calls attention to the fact that in Great Britain, all forms of social insurance in 1928, including some dependency insurance, cost the public only 824 million dollars.[3] Why are we sold to private insurance if public is cheaper, more comprehensive and socially more desirable? One wonders whether commissions, advertising, and insurance company profits explain the reason.

Security of investments

Home ownership is still esteemed highly, even among our urban nomads. This is the more strange because of the heavy

[3] Rubinow, I. M., *The Quest for Security,* 460–475.

losses among the millions who built between 1922 and 1929.[4] If we wish household goods rather than cash on demand, the installment seller provides our needs. There is natural enmity and sharp rivalry between thrift and high-pressure salesmanship. Advertising is a necessity in the modern world; but when we contend that advertising makes "business a civilizer" we are reckoning without the high cost of this particular "tragedy of waste."

The person who has little to invest has small opportunity and little hope to invest wisely. In the first place, the best securities are not offered in small quantities. The investment trust has sought to remedy this evil, but it has substituted a tremendous service charge, and frequently combines wild cat enterprise with good investment. When the public demands of the investment trusts the same degree of care and safety that now guards savings banks, the investment trusts will become the boon of the small investor. A savings bank is in itself simply a lending organization; the investment trust may offer a partnership in highly productive and profitable businesses.

The small investor who declines savings rate, who passes by insurance, whose totals do not justify home building looks about for a good return for his money. "Let the buyer beware" should be put in capitals for the investor. The get-rich-quick operator has found more suckers in this pond of small savers than in all other fields. Without experience the would-be capitalist has bought mine stock, greatly overvalued at one cent a share, oil stock on land to be the subject of future drilling, or some other business represented by beautiful certificates and oily-tongued salesmanship, but with no properties or tangible assets. Those who seek to save a little for old age frequently have been caught in this mill. Savings of two or three hundred a year are put aside in the hope of giving a thousand or more annuity when working days are gone. Long before the time of retirement arrives 99.99 per cent of these investments have become worthless. Of making foolish investments there is no end. As the lamb is led to the

[4] See also later on housing, pp. 429–432.

slaughter, so the margin speculator sees his hard-earned savings put into the coffers of bear or bull. Wall Street is not the slaughter pen it sometimes is pictured, but those who cannot manage high-powered financial machinery should leave it to those who can.[5] Its rules are business-like, and those must stay away whose word is not as good as their bond. Its rules are ruthless, at least to those who do not know how to play the game. Yet Wall Street is an old-fashioned conservative business house compared with the pre-N. R. A. confidence men or many sellers of high-return investments.

In saving as in earning, the time may come when the public must help the individual in gaining security, just as it may be required to offer insurance against unemployment, illness, and old age. The N. R. A.[6] tried to place safeguards on the investments of the public. This was done by the drastic Securities Act, which made promoters and salesmen responsible for the stocks they sell. It is aided by the separation of investment banking from commercial banking. For those who dabble in Wall Street, further safeguards are provided in the Stock Exchange Act. These three acts and greater watchfulness on the part of law-administrators should help the small investor. This is a general problem, a public and probably a social responsibility which we should not shirk. In olden days the patriarchal family looked after its own. In socialist communities the group decides the work and the salary and assumes the obligation. How will capitalistic America find its way out of its present dilemma? Can it work out a plan which does not sacrifice individuality or exclude initiative, yet provides training in the beginning of life, work in the middle, and necessities with some comforts at the end?

The proper use of human resources is an economic and social necessity which must not be primarily negative. From

The proper use of human resources

[5] General business was almost as usual in the years between 1925 and 1929, but thirty leading industrials on the stock market jumped from 100 to 150, from 150 to 200, from 200 to 250, from 250 to 300, from 300 to 350, and almost to 400 before the pyramided prices collapsed to something like the level of values. And when they collapsed, they did not stop at the ground floor; they fell to the third basement.

[6] Pp. 233–244.

the standpoint of business and production, the protection of
life and health, and of personal rights is not the chief consideration, necessary as they may be. Industrial capitalism,
although a human institution rather than an economic mechanism, wishes to use human abilities and desires both in consumption and in production. It must not only refrain from
limiting employment and purchasing power of the people, but
the work provided should be satisfactory and productive.
Adequate preparation must be offered for life work, that it
continue under maximum as well as optimum conditions. If
we are to have *the maximum coöperation of all members of
society,* passively from those who are primarily consumers,
actively from those who contribute labor and time, industrial
capitalism must be, not chiefly a system of creating goods, but
one that makes labor successful and productive by arousing
and keeping workers' interest and by appeals to worthwhile
motives. A century ago the employers, and all of them were
small scale, had the right to hire and fire whom they pleased.
In an integrated society which depends greatly on the development of modern industrialism, the worker should have
not only a chance to work but a fair return for that labor.
Industrial capitalism must provide not only a well organized
system of production but equitable distribution and a wise
adjustment of production to possible consumption. Fair distribution requires that the product of power and machinery
should not go chiefly to those of wealth who control the agents
of production rather than to the public in general. The consumer is entitled to a fair price, within the means which our
capitalist system has given him as his share of produced
goods. The business man is entitled to a special return for
his foresight, skill, and managerial success as well as an extra
margin for the risk taken. The inventor has a special claim
on the gains of scientific discovery, of new forms of power
and of intricate machinery, but the real benefits of these and
more than all else the contributions of natural resources, belong to all.

Possibly in connection with the proper use of human resources capitalism may develop desirable standards of in-

dustrial morality such as L. P. Jacks suggests.[7] "We clearly need an industrial version of morality. I cannot persuade myself that we have it at the present time. . . . Such industrial morality as we have consists of borrowing from the versions aforesaid [political, ecclesiastical, legal]. It exists in unrelated fragments and is not a native growth of the industrial soil. It defines no industrial ideal and is inadequate for industrial guidance. . . . I do not say that industry has no morals; if that were so it would cease to exist; but I do say that what morals it has are hand-to-mouth, hap-hazard, fragmentary, and borrowed from non-industrial sources."

In capitalizing human capacities,[8] we must not blame the capitalist for inherent human faults. Good pay cannot be offered for slovenly service or necessities provided by business for those who will not make an effort. Possibly human nature and work valuable to society are hopelessly at odds. It may be that the human body, in either an economic or a social capacity, is not more efficient than the ordinary steam engine. Those critics may be right who maintain that we work too long and too hard anyway. Most of us hope they are right. The political leader who can prove that the gospel of industry is a spent force will never lack public office. It may be that for real accomplishment at present necessary incentives are lacking. But any proper use of human resources must take into account the fact that compensation in a general way should correspond to the service rendered; it must also consider the need of the contributor especially if he is an adult with dependents. When making out pay checks it is not easy for private competitive business to take into account these different social needs of workers. Possibly we shall agree with that leader who suggested this motto: "From every man according to his ability; to every man according to his needs," if some of us do not know his name. In this age of business civilization security means almost too much the protection

[7] Jacks, *Constructive Citizenship*, Harper and Brothers, pp. 166–167.
[8] In connection with non-economic capitalization of human resources, *see* ch. X, C, 3.

of laborers, as in the days of the Stuart kings it meant the
safeguarding of citizens against arbitrary government.

LEVELS OF LIVING

What Constitutes a Minimum Expenditure for a Decent Standard of Living

General

So far as civilization shall make secure the things we have,
the general level of living should be one of the best standards
for the measurement of its success. The term standard of living is difficult of definition and hard to explain well. It should
be easy to show whether any people have adequate supplies
of food, satisfactory clothing and proper shelter. The conditions under which they live and the comforts they enjoy are
less definite. Their possession of leisure and the means to
spend that time interestingly or profitably are not discovered
readily. Separately none of these things measures a standard
of living; collectively they should do so.

The standard of living of any nation naturally is the standard of the masses rather than the classes. It matters little
how magnificently the very rich may be housed, how much
they may spend on banquets or on luxuries, if the rank and
file of the population do not have a reasonable supply of necessities and are limited in comforts. Standards of living
naturally vary from country to country and from period to
period. They should be superior in lands of unusual resources. Natural advantages do not guarantee any high level
of living; a comparison of China with the United States
proves this point. Far more important than resources is utilization—the possession of modernized, productive technics by
which the soil elements, the mineral deposits, water supplies,
and timbers become actual means of supplying the population
with material goods. Proper organization of business, whether
extractive, manufacturing, or commercial, is a prerequisite for
the change of resources into consumable products. Abundant
and sufficient labor for necessities enters in. Where law and
order are not maintained, where the distribution of the pro-

duced goods is unfair, the level of living suffers. No high standard can be enjoyed without an appreciation of non-material civilization, together with the leisure and the ability to enjoy it. The best standard is developed if good organization waits on resources, and culture on both.

Of living levels food is only one element, but necessarily the most essential. In America we may not be able to determine the family's standard by the quantity and quality of the things it eats, but we can measure its status by the percentage of its income spent for food. In other countries, even some of those in western Europe, food takes a very large part of the family income. Compared with past ages we find, for instance, a change in the diet of the common people from black bread to that made of wheat, possibly of too finely bolted white flour, a decided loss in nutrition. Moreover, on the table of the medieval worker meat was seldom found, poultry never—because fowl were raised for the tables of the nobles—vegetables were scarce and some of those most common with us today were unknown.

Food expenditures

In time of famine and depression we hear constantly of those who are undernourished or on the verge of starvation. Appeals made for public aid, the long bread lines and patronage of free soup kitchens are visible evidences of widespread want. Even in ordinary times—and they may be for most of us eras of prosperity—*the inadequacy of the food supply in great numbers of families is appalling.* Joseph S. Davis and Alonzo E. Taylor believe that the public underestimates greatly the amount of undernourishment of many people, especially children, in the United States. "No country is without its ill-nourished class, which is by no means restricted to the poor, but the extent of the class and the degree of the subnormality vary greatly from country to country." [9] According to J. B. S. Haldane, "About half of the human race at the present time (1928) is suffering from partial starva-

[9] In material by Leo Wolman, *Recent Economic Changes in the United States,* Report of the Committee on Recent Economic Changes of the President's Conference on Unemployment, Herbert Hoover, Chairman; including the reports of a special staff of the National Bureau of Economic Research, McGraw-Hill Book Co., Vol. I, p. 25.

tion, and the first requisite for them is to eat more of the cheapest food they can get." [10]

In the nineteenth century Dr. Engel in Prussia determined the standard of living of a family by the percentage which it spends for food. In the poor families whose budgets Engel examined, he found that more than half the total income went for food. Families higher in the scale devoted a smaller percentage of the family income for food, leaving more for clothes and incidentals. Few Americans spend as much as fifty per cent of their total budget in supplying the table. Before the World War a number of studies showed that for American wage-earners about forty-three per cent of the expenditures covered the food cost. Of the balance nearly eighteen per cent was paid for shelter, thirteen for clothing; and about one-fifth of the total went for sundries.[11] Was the percentage the same before the panic of 1929? Did it remain about the same in 1932? Does that amount keep the family properly fed and nourished? Is our average standard radically higher than that of different countries, and is our present food level different from that of the past?

Again quoting Davis and Taylor: "For many years there has been a significant and practically continuous trend toward smaller food requirements per capita. . . . This decline has occurred largely in energy-producing foods, and chiefly in the quantities needed to maintain body heat and furnish energy for active work." [12] Before the World War the American people daily consumed nearly a half pound of meat per capita. When war came, the public was urged to reduce the consumption, especially by observance of meatless, and wheatless, days. Meat is a protein food with high food value in small bulk, and it was particularly useful for the energy needed by the soldier at the front. At that time our per capita consumption of meat had been fifty per cent greater than that in Great Britain or Germany, much more than

[10] *Ibid.*, I, p. 25.
[11] Engel found that only five per cent of the family income in Prussia was spent for sundries.
[12] *Recent Economic Changes*, Vol. I, p. 27.

double that of France, Belgium or Holland, and more than three times that in Russia. After the war meat consumption again rose in this country, and in time of prosperity the demand was greater for the choice cuts than for cheaper meats. Apparently more poultry and eggs have been consumed. A large consumption of meat has always seemed to indicate a high living level, and the prosperity of the post-war years evidently was reflected in the quantity and cost of meat and allied articles.

According to popular belief bread is just as much the staff of life today as it was when Swift originated that phrase. Startling as it may be, while meat consumption has remained fairly stationary that of wheat has declined somewhat, and corn meal has almost disappeared from the ordinary diet. This is not due chiefly to the high price of bread. It must be due to a substitution of vegetables and fruits or possibly some other articles of food. The sharp fall in the use of corn meal can be accounted for only by an abrupt change in the diet of large numbers of southern families. In spite of a smaller demand for cereals, before the World War more than a quarter of all food consisted of wheat products and more than a third of wheat and other cereals. At that time little more than five per cent of our total food value was represented by vegetables and less than half that small amount by fruits.

A controversy of considerable importance has been waged over sugar; and the World War itself revolutionized sugar production, substituting cane sugar for most of the beet sugar formerly constituting most of the world's supply.[13] This single item of international commerce has created new producing areas and channels of trade for old. The youth of the land, at least the feminine part of it, declares for sugar in no uncertain terms. If a girl has taken a course in practical physi-

---

[13] Before the World War the world's supply of sugar consisted of almost as much beet sugar as cane; in 1928–9 the supply of cane sugar was more than double that of beet sugar, the *increase* being almost wholly in cane sugar.

ology, she cites the tremendously valuable energy-producing characteristics of sugar. The endocrinologists point out its usefulness in any active occupation such as fight or flight, in which the liberation of free sugar from the liver makes for continued successful effort. Whatever the cause, the per capita consumption of sugar in America increased forty-one pounds between 1911 and 1929.

"The large and increased spread between producer's prices and retail prices, which has attracted wide comment, affects producer and consumer in varying degrees from year to year. . . . It is probable that expensive competitive advertising, which has been resorted to both in order to break down inertia of consumers and to expand the market for less staple products of many kinds, and in order to check the decline in consumption of staples, such as bread and meat, is partly reflected in higher food costs. . . . On the whole, the common American diet of today is expensive—probably as compared with simpler diets of earlier years, certainly as compared with a simpler adequate diet today." [14]

Non-food items in individual or family budgets

Less important than food, but even more significant as measuring level of living, is what we wear. To the ordinary American, being well-dressed probably is more important than any other single experience. In keeping up with the Joneses, the family may be more interested in an attractive house, well-furnished, in a desirable neighborhood, and in having an automobile at least as attractive and of as recent model as that permitted by the credit of neighbors. To the individual, personal pride joins with desire for social standing, to be measured in terms of attractive and up-to-date clothing. When the New York manufacturers made the working girl an allowance of two pairs of cotton stockings per year, their assistants did not take into account the fact that most of our girls would not wear stockings that are not sheer or without the gloss of silk. Just as the partially educated person, and I am thinking now particularly of girls, usually writes a good hand regardless of ability to spell, read, or add, so the ambitious youth and adults of America—and most of us like

[14] *Recent Economic Changes*, Vol. I, pp. 49, 50.

to consider ourselves in that class—strive for more attractive if not more expensive clothes.

Probably the reason that *clothing measures American levels rather well* is that, regardless of ambition, taste, or desire, the members of workingmen's families can afford only the most necessary articles. If the thirteen per cent of the total expenditures in pre-war days is correct, and later data seem to show that it is fairly accurate for post-war years as well, how much may be spent on clothing for each of a family of four or five persons? If a girl is working away from home and earning more in proportion than members of a laborer's family possess, how much of her wages can she afford to spend on dresses and other forms of personal adornment? In 1914 one hundred thirty-two dollars was allotted to the family of the ordinary wage-earner. Making allowance for the difference in the later purchasing power of the dollar, that would have given in 1926 a sum of not more than fifty dollars for each member of a family of four or about forty dollars each if the family numbered five. The budget suggestions of the National Industrial Conference Board for 1925 provided nearly sixty dollars each of pre-war value for the clothing of husband and wife.[15] These amounts do not seem excessive. Yet if they are used, what is left for the children? Suppose that some of the young people are girls attending a high school which does not use uniforms. How shall a girl clothe herself in a way that to her seems necessary to maintain her standing and her self-respect?

A number of years ago *The Ladies Home Journal* made an interesting study of what it costs to put a boy or a girl through school. At that time the clothing costs for the girl through high school were estimated at four times the expense necessary for the boy. Although shoes and hats may still be high, the low price of attractive dresses of reasonably good materials should cut that difference sharply. In many cases clothing of the elders must still be made over for the children. Where cash is not available, the home must make a very large percentage of clothing for the elder as well as the younger mem-

[15] *Cost of Living in the United States,* 1914–1926, p. 36.

bers of the family. But the day of home-spun is past; and much homemaking of clothing is an added expense. Only in rare instances are the ways of the Victorian period necessary or economical.

Readers of these pages who frequently pay for a dress, a cloak, or a suit more than the New York manufacturers allotted to the working girl for a year's clothing may be interested in their list of items with allowance for each made in 1926 by those experts. The minimum weekly wage was placed at $12.80; it was suggested that for the girl who works in a factory her allowance for clothing shall be $85.58. If one wonder how she could manage on that amount per year, consider these items. The *annual allowance* for or toward a coat, $14.90; for a wool dress, $6.90; toward a silk dress, $8.32; for one pair oxfords, $4.75; for a winter hat, $2.91; for two union suits, $2.38; for two pairs of silk stockings, $2.08; for two pairs of cotton stockings, fifty-six cents. For the office girl the annual clothing budget was $106.77. The allowance to the working girl for recreation and vacation and sickness under this "fair, American standard" was small.[16]

One must not judge the family of the working man by the vast sums spent by Americans in general for sundries. Yet it may very easily be questioned whether the per capita cost of cigarettes or other forms of tobacco is very much higher for the families of the professional classes than it is for the workman and his son and daughter. Almost the same thing may be said for toilet goods and candy. When we take into account the fact that in 1929 the cigarette manufacturers paid to the national government a tax of three hundred and forty-two million dollars, one can realize how much the American public is spending for this luxury. In 1919, the Secretary of Treasury estimated the expenditures for the different forms of tobacco at more than two billions.

Writers on advertising and on certain businesses tell us that if it were not for the American woman advertising would be cut very sharply indeed, and many of these businesses, even though they produce goods for people in general, would

[16] Materials from *The New Republic*, October 5, 1927, pp. 171–172.

be forced out of business. The estimates of the expenditures
by American women for furs, luxurious clothing, toilet articles, and other feminine dainties have been as high as two
billions annually. Set over against this is the bill for luxurious food of five billion dollars, according to the Treasury
estimate of 1919, and probably men consume more of this
than women. Stuart Chase suggests that we might cut the
Treasury estimate of twenty-two billions for luxuries to a
third and Roger Babson's estimate of fourteen billion dollars
for 1921, a half.[17] Even then we should have one-tenth of
our national income used for these luxuries and semi-luxuries.
These figures have little to do with the workingman and the
ordinary family budget for several reasons. The average
family does not have the money to spend. In most families
the wife and mother is almost invariably not only the most
careful buyer but the most economical purchaser of necessary
goods.

The unskilled laborer worries over necessary limitation of
expenditure because the purse never covers his needs. *The
security that most of us want insured is not necessarily a
living wage, or the right to work, but the standard to which
we either have been accustomed or have hoped to attain, because so many others seem to have it.* Practically no student
of the subject has ever made an estimate of the amount required by a working girl away from home, or by an American
family of five, which is quite so low as the actual income per
year of the working girl before 1933 or the workman's family.
Nevertheless, we should get a totally distorted view of the
American situation if we did not take into account the large
number of comforts which the average American enjoys.

HOUSING

The level of living should include housing as one of its essentials. If a fair per cent of the world's population is below
proper food and clothing standards, their living conditions
are also likely to be low. In England a quarter century ago
one-fifth of the population lived in old, dilapidated, or filthy

Housing
conditions
in America

[17] Chase, *The Tragedy of Waste,* p. 89.

rooms or hovels. In Paris five per cent of the population slept in rooms without windows. In Berlin the slums were worse than those in New York, which had thirteen blocks housing more than one thousand per acre, in tenements, not in modern apartment buildings.

The rural population of America may have more air and light, but many houses are old, poorly heated in winter, unsanitary, needing repair and lacking most real conveniences. According to the United States census of 1920 only "ten per cent of our farms had water piped into the house, and seven per cent had gas or electric lights, and 30.7 per cent had automobiles, and 38.7 per cent had telephones." [18] Geographically there were great differences; 1.1 per cent in Mississippi, 62.9 per cent in Vermont. Modern lighting rated high on the Pacific coast, 19.3; least in west south and central states, 1.9 per cent.

On the social cost of bad housing Mrs. Wood states: "Bad housing conditions which are injurious to health include lack of light (especially sunlight), lack of ventilation, dampness (as in underground dwellings), overcrowding, impure or inadequate water supply, lack of bathing facilities, unsanitary or insufficient toilets, lack of sewer connection, uncleanliness, dilapidation, lack of screens against flies and mosquitoes, inadequate disposal of garbage." [19] Furthermore Mrs. Wood asserts [20] that there is a direct ratio existing between the number of people per room in tenements and infant mortality, especially from gastric and intestinal diseases, respiratory diseases and early infancy. Sometimes diseases that start in the slum, possibly in Europe or Asia, but possibly somewhere west of the Atlantic, spread with virulence throughout the United States. These epidemics are less frequent than formerly thanks to medical science, with little thanks to public understanding of the high cost of bad housing.

Most communities have their shanty towns and some have little else. "Company" houses in mining districts are no-

---

[18] Wood, Edith Elmer, *Recent Trends in American Housing*, p. 30. The Macmillan Co., 1931.
[19] *Ibid.*, p. 4.   [20] *Ibid.*, p. 23.

toriously inadequate. "Generally speaking company towns are unsewered and without a pipe water system for a large majority of the buildings. . . . The typical company house is a single or detached frame house, consisting generally of four rooms. Of the 47,580 buildings for which data were available, 17.3 per cent had modern improvements (bath, water-closet, running water, and gas or electricity), while 39.2 per cent had none, 22.3 per cent had gas or electric light only, and 5.4 per cent had running water only." [21]

In periods of unemployment conditions are even worse. People live in abandoned coke ovens, in hovels without heat or water. A room or a shack that formerly housed a couple now may be all that a family, or even two, can afford. During depression doubling up was an exceedingly common experience. If America has these housing needs,[22] what of the rest of the world? An almost unbelievable gain would have resulted from the labor of the unemployed, if some of it could have been used to repair old homes or build new during the depression years. Apparently we have to have depressions, but do not have to have better homes!

Building and repairing constitute both a seasonal and a cyclical business. Summer is an active period during prosperity. Housing shortage marked the World War and the years immediately following, as it did the late depression era. After the minor depression, 1920–22, there was a furore of building covering one-family dwellings, double apartments and larger dwellings. Suburbs were extended many miles, with some houses offered for sale. Enough dwellings were sold to increase the percentage of home owners in America (outside of farms) in the years 1920 to 1930 from forty to forty-five. This is the more remarkable because the number of families in multiple apartments was considerably larger in 1930 than at the close of the World War.

For homes burdened with mortgage, more than two-fifths of those owned, some relief was granted before 1933. Part of

The problem and attempted relief

[21] *Ibid.*, p. 21.
[22] Except for electrical connections and equipment the number of houses provided with conveniences increases with the size of the city. See Kyrk, *Economic Problems of Family*, p. 5.

the N. R. A. was the creation of the Home Owners Loan Corporation, with capital of two billions, to refinance mortgages on homes to a maximum of $14,000, at five per cent interest. In the first fifteen months, nearly a billion and a half was thus loaned. The National Housing Act provided for loans, chiefly through banks, by which homes could be repaired, modernized and improved by borrowing funds repaid in monthly installments.[23]   Although the building trades have had a greater percentage of workers unemployed than almost any other, building has lagged in recovery. In 1934 it was estimated we already had a house shortage of more than two millions; Doane contended six millions. An N. R. A. code provided a wage-scale for expert workers of at least $1.10 per hour, in the effort to give skilled laborers in that field a suitable wage. If this desirable pay increased costs above desirable levels, the N. R. A. furnished another example of sacrificing recovery for reorganization. The purpose of the whole housing program, however, is a real improvement in living conditions. This may be a part of social reconstruction.

"Let the public keep out" is less well known than "let the buyer beware." It belongs to a worthy period of human development; not the first, for then the member depended constantly on the successes of the group; nor the last, for individual self-help is certainly inadequate today. Already cooperative health measures have reduced the menace of disease in most communities. Already building regulations make fires less frequent and buildings safer against wind, flood or earthquake. Improved tenements are encouraged, although a hundred persons must find a home in older types to one who can be housed in a model and really modern tenement. The real reason why the ninety and nine in the slum area, and about thirty to forty out of a hundred elsewhere, are improperly housed is that landlords will, and possibly should, build only for profits or a good return; and tenants cannot pay rents high enough to assure the right kind of home.

---

[23] This permits home-owners to borrow at a nominal rate of five per cent but actual rate about twice as high for repairs and improvements. The cost must be repaid within twelve months.

Of all houses built in the New Era period the average cost   The economic
was about $7500, and the annual total about three billions.[24]   dilemma of
                                                                    housing
If we accept the dictum that a family should not purchase a
house valued at more than twice its annual income, or rent
one that takes more than one-fifth of its income, how many
American families can afford a home? Forty-six per cent of
them are home-owners, but not of good, modern, up-to-date
houses. Here is a simple problem in arithmetic. In 1926
the American worker, about two-thirds of all earners, made
on the average little more than $1200 per year. On the basis
of our computation, if others in the family earned something, the family could not afford a home worth more than
$3000 [25] or pay more than $25 a month rent. As Mrs.
Wood says, *"The crux of the housing problem is economic.
Under the ordinary laws of supply and demand it is insoluble.
In our modern industrial civilization, the distribution of income is such that a substantial portion of the population cannot pay a commercial rent, much less a commercial purchase
price, for a home fulfilling the minimum health and decency
requirements."* [26] Apparently this is a problem due to a lack
of purchasing power.[27] It seems insoluble unless purchasing
power can be raised, costs reduced, or standards of living modified.

It looks as though housing has its dilemma. If the people
cannot build or buy, and cannot afford to rent, the only kind
of habitation society can afford to let them use, whither the
house-holder? *Europe* tries to find a way out by *subsidizing
builders* or by *building public tenements.* In the decade from
1920 to 1930 Holland rehoused nearly one-fifth of its population. In the years 1919 to 1931 Germany built dwellings for
two and a half millions of her population. Since 1931 Ger-

[24] Figures and estimates vary greatly.
[25] Editors of *Fortune, Housing America,* pp. 33–34. If raw land costs
$3000 an acre, by the time it is improved that cost becomes $11,000 per
salable acre, and by the time that it is fully capitalized and resold becomes
$25,362. If this is divided into seventeen lots 25 x 100 the price of each lot
is $1492. If the lots are 50 x 120, the lot costs more than the average work-
man's family can afford for house and lot.
[26] Wood, Edith Elmer, *Recent Trends in American Housing,* page 1.
(Italics not in original.)
[27] Pp. 129–131.

many has built a large number of six-room separate family dwellings, at an average cost of $800 per family, in place of tenements which formerly cost $2500 for each family that the tenements housed. England did even better. In the fifteen years ending 1934, she constructed 2,175,000 houses with gardens, and in the last year of that period built homes for a million persons. If Europe can undertake publicly to do so much, why has America publicly done nothing?

Germany offered to replace houses in northeastern France destroyed during the war, with standardized houses "made in Germany." The home-loving French peasants did not agree! Years ago Thomas A. Edison promised to make for the multitude mass-produced houses at a cost of about a thousand dollars each. If improvements in automobiles are possible, with constant reduction in price, why cannot more modern homes with all necessary conveniences be produced at a price families can almost afford? And if that cannot be done, does the public have any responsibility to see that America is properly and decently housed?

There is another public angle to this interesting question. The building trades employ in good seasons a million and a quarter workers. The slump in building after 1929 was one of three major causes of unemployment and continued depression. The editors of *Fortune* sum up its importance in the American world of business as follows: "The building industry is the market for the major part of the nation's output of lumber, stone, brick, paper, paint, and glass. It is the second largest purchaser of steel. It creates an almost immediate demand for furniture, carpets, furnaces, household goods, etc. Its total volume in 1926 was over $7,000,000,000 as compared with the gross railroad revenue of $6,449,000,000 and a value for motor vehicles manufactured in 1925 of $3,371,856,-000. And it pays in normal years the largest American wage bill—$3,000,000,000 in 1926. Its failure [and its decline in the depression], therefore, is the concern not of the building industry alone, but of all industry and of all observers of the contemporary scene." [28]

[28] *Housing America*, p. 24.

Here is a public problem, involving millions of families, the success of American business, and the welfare of tens of millions of persons. What are we doing about it?

LIVING LEVELS OF MOST AMERICANS

The American home has changed even if more than a quarter of the houses are old and need modernizing. An inventory of conveniences would set off the present home even more markedly than that of the past. The city apartment has its disadvantages, but low rents compensate some for loss of flowers and land; community heating saves numerous furnace troubles; and the combination of many homes under one roof makes modern cities possible. Popular opinion to the contrary, separate dwellings, most of them with their own yard, are the American rule, not the exception. According to the census of 1930 there were twenty-five million dwellings for thirty million families. Of this number of homes fewer than half were owned by individual families.[29]

Standards in home conveniences

The American's dwelling place may be owned or rented, mortgaged or free; but America is the home of the bathtub. A generation ago the majority of small European hotels had neither public nor private baths. In central Europe whether in Germany or in other countries pride was taken if the inn could boast "Bäder im Hause." Naturally private homes of the older type did not have this convenience and probably do not now. On the contrary, of probably twenty-five million houses for thirty million families there were in 1928 nearly eighteen million bathtubs; undoubtedly that figure includes showers. In the generation just past the Saturday night bath was a preliminary to Sabbath religion. It looks very much as though with us cleanliness has replaced godliness. We must not overlook the several millions without bathroom conveniences, a fair percentage of whom haven't even running water in the house.

An almost identical number of homes were wired for electricity, most of them for light only but many with electric

[29] Census figures on ownership: owned   rented
                                    1930   46.8   44.6

ranges and a still larger number with plugs for electric irons, vacuum cleaners and other household helps. The number of radios which in 1922 was 60,000, in 1928 was 7,500,000, and in 1934 nineteen million. Expenditures for electrical household equipment as refrigerators, washing machines and others jumped from 82 millions in 1919 to 375 millions ten years later. The number of telephones was about half that of bathtubs and of houses wired for electricity. The number of homes equipped with running water was probably somewhat smaller than were those electrically wired, because it is easier

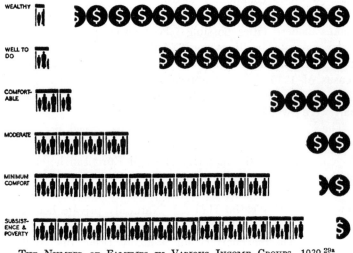

THE NUMBER OF FAMILIES IN VARIOUS INCOME GROUPS, 1929 [29a]
Each Family Group Represents One Million Families, Each Circle $2,000

to carry a wire on a pole than provide a main in the street or road and a connecting pipe that will supply a household with water. Possibly a true comparison of American and European standards may not be made by noting the differences in the daily consumption of water, for waste does not measure high standards. But in northern Europe the daily per capita consumption of water is rarely as high as forty gallons; in the United States it averages more than 100 gallons.

[29a] Committee on Economic Security.

The farm population of the United States is decreasing. Many contend that our leaders, political and business, have been reared on the farms. Certainly the percentage of the population living in cities has been constantly on the increase. In 1925, the Census Bureau estimated that practically seventy-five per cent of our population was urban, although in 1930 only fifty-six per cent lived in cities or villages of more than twenty-five hundred, and only sixty-four per cent in incorporated cities or villages. Evidently there is a sharp movement back to the land, because in 1934 more than a million and three hundred thousand people moved from city to country, only about three hundred thousand less than the number who migrated from country to city.

The modern farm usually is provided with a telephone. The electrical aids frequently include an electrically operated churn, and occasionally, an electric clothes washer or even a dish washer. The farmer himself is even better off than his wife because gasoline furnishes the power not only for the family automobile but for the tractor. Only one-fifth of all families down on the farm resort to horse and buggy. The farm hands do not receive a wage comparable with that of the city worker, but farm labor is not nearly so arduous nor hours so long as were those of the boy on the farm two generations ago. Machinery of all types and kinds is in use as far as the small size of farms or the farmer's limited wealth or borrowing power made its purchase possible or advisable.

The number of American families has had difficulty in keep- ing ahead of the number of passenger automobiles. Many a family has two or more cars, but among workmen at least the more skilled enjoy some kind of automobile. A computation of automobile owners shows that nearly thirty per cent belong to manufacturers, merchants and professional classes, about thirty per cent to foremen, clerks and other skilled workers, and about the same percentage to working men and farmers, leaving only a little more than ten per cent to housewives and others.

The importance of the automobile in present American

civilization can hardly be over-estimated. Standards of living are affected only indirectly by the large number of trucks and busses which have created a totally new group of problems for railroads, as carriers of freight and inter-urban transportation systems. Even more the family automobile has cut into the profits of the street railroads and has made street car tracks unnecessary except on the main city thoroughfares. Directly, the automobile has transformed family life. Even though less than one-tenth of our families have "a second car for the wife," some member of the family can take father to business and call for him. In all probability some one besides the wage-earner is using the family car during the day. The ease with which we may get from place to place promotes leisure even if it may complicate the problems of school principals. Family discord may easily arise from the desire of several members to use the car at the same time. Social problems have increased not only with reckless use of cars in daylight but in extensive night driving by the younger generation.

The beautiful new highways which we owe largely to the automobile may be crowded Sundays; but think of the recreation and variety of experience possible because the family need not sit on the front porch all that day or gossip over connecting fences with neighbors! Less work is done on lawn or in garden because the car is ready, or because it must be made ready. When vacation comes, the car, especially if it has a cabin-trailer, makes possible for the whole family or for a considerable part of it a fairly inexpensive outing to resort at beach or in the mountains, if those are not too distant. Auto camps dot the highways or cluster along the rivers, lakes, or bays. Change of scene and of thought at moderate expense—and even that sometimes cannot be afforded—makes a worthwhile outing, though the job may be less attractive on return.

A decade ago the average American enjoyed a talking machine, frequently miscalled a victrola; even now many families secure their music and other entertainment by replacing records. However, a constantly larger number of homes, now more than one-half of all, possess a radio, which through invention and economic depression has become less and less expensive, smaller, and frequently of the portable type. With a radio in his possession no hermit need enjoy seclusion from his fellows. The problem of allocating the rather limited series of wave lengths has already become a major difficulty due to the competition of broadcasters. Fortunately, national control of transportation and communication had been established before this problem became acute.

To scatter culture broadcast is certainly a modern marvel, even though the opportunity is not fully used. One wonders whether a planned radio arrangement might not be socially much more valuable than one devoted to advertising, one rather highly competitive. Would the English plan of government taxes on machines and government authorized programs give us what we ought to have rather than what we want—and help the Government against its opposition! In a rather inaccessible region at the edge of America's greatest scenic wonder the writer happened to enter the office of the camp one Saturday evening as a raucous voice came over the radio. The desk clerk turned to him with a smile: "You see we are in close touch with civilization." It was the prize fight of the year.

With the changing family and increasing leisure, music was becoming rather a lost art. Because of the mania of Americans for popularized amusement, the movie and the talkie attract their millions to the tens of thousands who attend concerts or symphonies. Not many years need elapse before the American public learns to appreciate the best of popular music and some of the most interesting of that termed classical. Verdi and Strauss never fail to appeal but Wagner, Schubert, and Beethoven will become popular as they are better understood. Our schools are giving more and better music courses, because the radio is bringing opportunities for hearing occasionally some of the best. We have not even reached the gray dawn in the social and public, nay even cultural, possibilities of radio and television.

Shall we have difficulty in getting a reasonable degree of   Conclusion security and in keeping a proper standard of living because some of us, or most of us, think the ways we may be obliged to use in doing that are "un-American"? A half-century ago those who proposed legal innovations were always met by the protest that the suggested plan was "unconstitutional." Before the World War the Chief Justice of the Supreme Court declared that the Constitution must never stand in the way of progress. Since the World War almost as many persons offer objection to rather startlingly new, but possibly necessary changes, as un-American. Our highest interpretative social authority should insist that the system formerly known as American shall encourage the making of changes that seem, after careful consideration, to represent progress. Surely we should go forward, not back, in this land that prides itself on being in the forefront of human advance.

If the world changes, we do not simply wish to change with it. We wish to be a part of the vanguard in any movement that leads us upward and forward. Certainly we should hate to have Americanism identified with haphazard charity, because poverty, if not dire poverty, is the threatened lot of a tenth or more of our people in prosperity and a quarter during depression. If system can be substituted for spasmodic action, coöperation for antagonism, scientific preparation for emergency makeshift, society as well as the victims of social change should have nothing to lose, everything to gain.

One penalty we pay for living in an age of progress in a changing but dynamic civilization is the price that is exacted from the misfits in the new scheme of things, the price paid by the members of society who are less well off under the new order than under the old. The fault may be theirs in part, because they cannot adjust themselves well to the changing economic and social systems; but the loss is ours as well as theirs. If their loss is due to changes which in general represent progress, it would seem fair that society, the real beneficiary of the progress, should accept the obligation to see that they are not submerged by the rising tide of a new civilization. If survival insurance is worth while for the dependants of any earner, *is not assurance of survival minima for all a just requirement of a fair and social-minded society?*

In an age of potential plenty, society enjoys, or can enjoy with a little care, very high standards of welfare. Should it not accept the responsibility to give every one both security and a decent standard of living?   What do you think?

XV

NATIONALISM *vs.* INTERNATIONALISM

One further question on possible public reorganization must be considered. In the political set-up of the future, will the place of the nation be less dominant than it has been? What may be the proper, or necessary, relationship between any nation and all of the others? Little as has been done to organize international government, must international coöperation replace in some degree attempts of each country to regulate its own affairs or decide finally on its economic and social policies as well as those we call political? Will national self-determinism be possible or successful, when the interplay of forces at work among nations may out-balance those of like character within each country? President Wilson could not "keep us out of war." Can the average or unusual President keep us out of international business? Undoubtedly most of these questions cannot be answered now. Probably they will never be answered fully. Nevertheless the future of western civilization will depend upon the nice adjustment of nationalism to internationalism, much as the future of America depends on the proper adaptation of federalism to new American needs and of industrial capitalism to what society requires.

PRESENT-DAY NATIONALISM

The fight of nationalism against provincialism

Historically considered, the way was paved for modern nationalism by the decline of feudalism. The feudal state was weak and decentralized. The feudal king was a mere suzerain over great vassals. The Commercial Revolution, starting with the Crusades and new inventions, did to feudalism what the Industrial Revolution has been doing to modern

440

absolutism. Roads were necessary; isolated communities were no longer self-sufficing. Foreign trade developed, first with the East, then with Africa, then with a new world, eventually covering the whole globe. The medieval kingdoms needed real leaders with new nationwide attitudes and policies. To gain political authority it was necessary to destroy the power of the nobles. To do this a new type of patriotism was awakened and a new type of loyalty created. This was possible only in those countries that had already developed national languages. The royal house emerged sovereign and there was no patriotism but allegiance to the king and to the nation. It is this type of patriotism which to a great extent fought and won or lost the World War. Possibly it lost in Germany and Austria because it was still too close in time and thought to the semi-feudal loyalty that survived in those countries until late in the nineteenth century.

Protest against the feudal decentralization of these nations did not produce nationalism, for that is a product of the last two centuries. The struggle between provincialism and what afterward emerged as nationalism was a slow process. Without a common or "national" language it was difficult or impossible really to unite the people of any country. First came centralization, the sway of one instead of many in each country. The modern monarch may have lost the sacred character which the ancient despot claimed because of descent from a god; but with absolute monarchs claiming rule by divine right, the allegiance of the modern subject has been different only in degree, not in kind, from that of the Roman near-citizen, or the more ancient Egyptian fellah. In time modern thought became less provincial and based on wider and higher standards than were possible before the days of general education for women as well as men, and of worldwide general commerce. A man who reads a newspaper filled with telegraphic items from five continents cannot think as did his ancestors who had to be content with local gossip. The woman who daily eats foods or wears clothing or ornaments produced by at least a dozen different peoples becomes cosmopolitan in her demands if not in her ideas. The Industrial Revolution, attempts at democracy, and technical education have undermined the very foundations of local prejudice and a provincial social heritage. Even in the backward districts of Europe people think in terms of nations rather than of communities, although the community idea fights to the last ditch for its own ideas and ideals. Do we question the vitality of localism? Then let us follow Babbitt to his club or listen to a few civic slogans, or read an occasional Chamber of Commerce broadside. With civic pride aggressive and triumphant, we may be glad that humanity is at least grouped into nations. With human nature what it is, why expect that in a few decades or at the most a century or two people will abandon provincialism for nationalism. One would be optimistic to expect that the people of these *nations* will think of outsiders first and of themselves afterward.

The failure of the pre-war socialists to act as a body regardless of national boundary lines proves that nationalism is vital. The decisions of the Versailles Peace Conference show that leaders have national obligations and still think in terms of national advantage. We need not wait for threats of war to arouse national patriotism, as observed in the speech, in the thought, and in the press of every people in Christendom. The lessons of world war have not made us international minded; they have increased the demand in every country for the protection of the interests of that nation regardless of the losses and the costs to others. National diplomats are no less jealous than formerly of national power. Members of parliaments demand higher rather than lower protective tariffs. In spite of the Kellogg-Briand pact, and of the Washington and London Naval Conferences, and of World Peace Conferences, the race for armament and national prestige in international fields goes on as before.

Sociological and psychological nationalism

Nationalism is a sociological and a psychological fact. If it were only a matter of political organization, there would be less fear for the future. In the last generation the majority of Christian rulers have lost their thrones. We in

America do not realize the extent of the upheaval which has taken place east of the Rhine Valley since the close of the World War. Our fear of bolshevism may prevent our knowing what Russia is doing. Our concentration upon prosperity, depression, or international crises may blind us to the new constitutions and democratic progress in at least half of the Christian world. Lenin, Mussolini, Stalin and Hitler attract more attention than the silent upward trend of humanity—than the release of many peoples from serfdom and from political bondage. If we disregard our obsessions and fears, we may discover that *nationalism is vital* in proportion as it is democratic, progressive, and adapted to modern needs. But much recent nationalism has been anti-democratic and reactionary.

In the very beginning *nationalism was warlike* because it had decentralizing forces to destroy. At present it is warlike because it has prestige to maintain and other enemies to combat. At first it seemed to depend on force, as in the creation of modern Germany. Now it uses force for its ends where national government and policies are dominated by a minority group, as the Nazis, although the public supports that group's nationalist program. At first *it was social* because the manor was too small and the church too big for successful and unified group action. Now it seeks outlets for its ideas and products and wider fields for its type of civilization. Not simply Germany but every nation wants to give its culture the sphere to which it is entitled, in the eyes of its worshippers. In its origin, *nationalism was economic* because the new needs two centuries ago concerned transportation and trade opportunities for the progressive countries. It is economic now because it seeks gain for its nationals as a group, because each nation works within self-erected economic walls. Its economic policies may be no more far-sighted than were those of the mercantilists, seeking gain by keeping outsiders from profit. It may raise tariff barriers so high that real wages are reduced, unemployment increased, and prosperity strangled. Yet, without definite national protective policies, a people might succumb before foreign competition. *Nationalism is political.* In times past it would have been called that and that only. The nation is a public group; the largest and in many ways the finest today; but it may be public-spirited chiefly for its own members. Its diplomacy may be narrow-minded and in-growing. Rather than give up to an international government some power that would benefit all coöperating nations, it is content to permit localism, provincialism, and sectionalism. Its patriotism may be too much "my country right or wrong."

The dangers in nationalism are very real, as shown by the World War and by threats of reprisals and of wars to come. The World War which began in 1914 could not have occurred in the ancient world or in the Europe of Gregory VII or of Innocent III. Medieval people who lived under a Church Universal possessed an organization wider if not nearly so deep as that developed under nationalism. The rise of several live, active, powerful nations, rivals for leadership and power, has led to jealousy, prejudice and intense competition. *Nationalism is psychological.* In that lies the greatest danger and the greatest hope. The danger may arise out of political conservatism and popular superstition. Too many nations are of the Bourbon type; they "learn nothing and forget nothing." Individuals outgrow the past because in youth they are progressive and inevitably slough off many outgrown ideas and attitudes of their elders. A nation lives through its youth only once. Usually it is so busy growing up, seeking man's estate among other nations, that it loses most of its opportunities for new development and advance. When mature, it clings with the doggedness of age to the ideas of its youth, the traditions of its ancestors. Nowhere is the grasp of the dead past so vicious as in the field of national political stagnation and patriotism. Be it reverence for an ancient constitution that no longer really exists or veneration for a dominion that has passed to others, it plays up ignorance and capitalizes false pride. Neurotically refusing to accept reality, its will to power brings the nation decay and its neighbors disaster. Gird the body-politic with the unyielding bands of past glories, add the racial prejudices of age-long struggle and enmity, and we have created a psychological prison from which few nations escape. With these death-dealing forces we must include fear, hate, envy, and all the horde of satellites that prey upon any peoples who have ceased to grow, or who are losing out in the great struggle for worldly gain.

The hope of the future lies in a better understanding of the psychological possibilities of nationalism. The elemental forces of human nature—we call them psychological—which should make men richer and finer and stronger in spirit have not yet been tapped enough for groups to make nations free. If Shakespeare is right in thinking that it is mind which makes the body rich, then knowledge, comprehension, wisdom, impartiality in viewing a nation's own faults, opportunities, and responsibilities; these must be the bases of national progress and success among nations.

Internationalism and Nationalism in the Past

The twentieth century is the battleground for a titanic struggle between nationalism and internationalism. Only recently has there been real need for any combination of groups larger than separate countries. The ancient world created vast masses organized as empires. These were solid, consolidated political societies, with very little differentiation of organization. Even the Roman Republic, a world state before reorganization by the Caesars, was after all only a city-state grown large. Those optimists who expect to reorganize society or government in a decade should consider the length of the period of decentralization which followed the break-up of the Roman Empire. Ten centuries elapsed from the "fall of Rome" to the organization of the first modern monarchies in the late Renaissance.

Reorganization of these Renaissance monarchies into fairly democratic political societies did not take place, except in France and England, until the nineteenth century. The awakening, largely democratic, which has made national groups

Beginnings of internationalism

self-conscious, is yet in its infancy except in America and western Europe. Had not the rule of rather absolute monarchs survived into the twentieth century, the chances are that political groups larger than nations, and different from them, might have been developed in the late nineteenth or early twentieth centuries; Christendom in the Middle Ages showed this possibility. Up to the beginning of the World War there seemed to be more like-mindedness among socialists throughout Europe than among the nationalists living under any one flag. But this was not so. The day of nationalism was by no means past. The World War was largely an expression of nationalism and a demand for more.

Separated as Europe had been for centuries into petty kingdoms, the common problems of all Europeans, particularly those on the Continent, compelled them to coöperate even if only in war. Rivalry between nations over Italy has been named by John Bassett Moore as the beginning of modern internationalism. International rules were formulated as early as the time of Hugo Grotius in the seventeenth century. International law developed around war and dealt chiefly with the limitations put upon belligerents or with the rights of neutrals. Before the nineteenth century the chief international organizations were temporary military coalitions of the eighteenth century to maintain the balance of power.

Super-na-
tionalism in
recent years
At least *three forces coöperated in the late nineteenth-century internationalism.* One of these was a new type of democratic nationalism formed largely from within. A second grew out of the Industrial Revolution, seeking internal development and demanding external markets. A third was the desire to gain by peaceful alliance and benevolent assimilation advantages that in a less enlightened age might have been secured by making war. The great alliances—the one formed by Bismarck and the other organized against his successors—represented this stage of international development. In the attempt to maintain an armed peace on an international scale there was finally precipitated by far the greatest military struggle in history.

The present post-war stage is difficult of definition and even of explanation. The pre-war alliances no longer persist. But every threat of war tends to revive or recreate them.[1] A number of new nations were born, or possibly were created by the winners of the contest; but more than all else, a new spirit has pervaded world politics. There has developed a new understanding of the meaning of nationalism and a real belief in internationalism. A new leaven is at work, even though the direct results of war have frequently been a nationalism more insistent than had existed before. In all probability the League of Nations will be a far more effective agency toward securing international coöperation than was the post-war association of nations a hundred years ago. The World Court may be a court without real authority or power to enforce its decisions; but it seems a true judicial tribunal, not like the Hague Court, a quasi-board of arbitration. More than all else is a different attitude toward internationalism, a new demand for something that leads toward international government. Briand's attempts to obtain security for France may not lead farther than did Bismarck's effort to gain security for the newly united Germany. Yet there is a promise that some kind of coöperation and possibly some new form of organization may be gained by the use of the two great principles of which America has been the world's leading exponent—federalism and democracy.

The League of Nations and International Agreements

In no previous period of history has it been possible to get together so many nations or to secure a political organization of any kind representing a combination of different powers. Before the World War there had been several movements toward something better than separate nations, better than the militant alliances whose clash finally precipitated the World War. When the representatives of the victorious Allies met in Versailles in 1919, it was understood that there should be a general organization to supervise the interests of the Allies and the enforcement of the treaty, if not for the

The League and its work

[1] According to dispatches, Dec. 1934, France and Russia have entered into an alliance against Germany under Hitler.

more general and more altruistic purposes desired by President Wilson. As is well known, the Covenant for the League was made the first part of the Treaty of Peace, and that treaty was rejected by the American Senate largely because the Covenant formed part of it. It was America's desire to continue our policy of avoiding entangling European alliances, especially in the attempted settlement of the numerous difficult disputes between European nations whose interests differed widely.

The League has been accepted at one time by more than sixty nations, including all the major powers except the United States. The organization of the League consists of a Council, an Assembly, and a Secretariat, and it is affiliated with an International Court of Justice. The *Council* consists of permanent members from four great powers and ten other members, three elected annually for a three-year period plus one new member (1934). The Council has met three or four times a year and has been the instrument for considering and deciding rather acute if not major disputes between different members of the League. The *Assembly,* composed of from one to three representatives from each member, one vote per member, meets annually in September at the headquarters of the League, Geneva, in Switzerland. Possibly its debates have resulted in relatively little positive action. Nevertheless, they have presented the arguments on many sides of important problems involving the security or success of world powers and the peace of Europe and the world. Without these preliminary debates it is questionable whether, for example, the Locarno agreements would have been reached easily and successfully, or international pacts have been made [2] which have guaranteed more fully the territorial and financial integrity of nations, or the successful coöperation of the powers.

The *Court of International Justice* is really a court, not like the Hague tribunal, a body from which an arbitration board may be selected. Its fifteen members represent fifteen distinguished jurists from the same number of countries se-

[2] See p. 451.

lected for a period of nine years by the separate majority vote of Council and Assembly. Although the United States has refused to adhere to the World Court because of its affiliation with the League, Americans have always been ably represented on the International bench.

The *International Labor Office* is truly a branch of the League organization. It is a larger body than the Assembly because the membership consists of two to represent each government, as well as one representative for employers and one for employes from each member country. Its organization has been rather successful in promoting some standardization of rules for the workers of the world. All have agreed upon a living wage, most of them make some provision for a weekly day of rest; and in theory they accept the idea of a short working day and the right of labor to seek its own best market.

Associated with the *Secretariat* are a large number of boards and commissions, some of which have been exceedingly active and successful in protecting the interests of refugees, placing checks upon traffic in women, children, or opium, and otherwise promoting the international standards represented by civilization.

Among the activities of the League or its associates have been the solution of a number of national problems, of international disputes, and of international difficulties. An example of the first was the financial rehabilitation of Austria. When that once-powerful state was divided into a number of succession kingdoms, Austria found herself in a serious economic and financial situation. Her urban population formed so large a percentage of the total that food supplies provided by the Austrian rural districts were inadequate. Special international agreements were inevitable, and monetary help was essential. The League proved that there was no carry-over of antagonism against Austria from the war period; and the help was forthcoming.

A good example of disputes settled through the League was that of Silesia. Upper Silesia is inhabited by Germans and Poles. Its business is partly agriculture, partly industry, but largely mining. According to the Versailles Treaty there was to be a plebiscite to determine the status of these people. When it was held, it showed a vote of about seven to five in favor of Germany; but Poland claimed the nearest territories, and on appeal to the League these were assigned to her. The significance of this decision lies chiefly in the importance of the mineral resources granted to Poland.

The Supreme Council, supported by the League, has helped to decide the problem of reparations and of the relations existing between Germany and the other powers. The original plan was to grant to the Allies a very heavy indemnity. This has been whittled down until it amounts to less than $10,000,000,000, little more of which is ever likely to be paid. It might have been better to have accepted the original German proposal of a sum equal to $7,500,000,000 on a cash basis. When France believed that she was not getting her just share of reparations, she occupied the Ruhr Valley for nearly two years. This economic-military occupation did not benefit the French or bring them adequate returns; but it seriously crippled German business.

Under the guidance of Great Britain, a committee from that country, the United States, France, Italy, and Belgium attempted to solve the problem of Germany. Because General Charles G. Dawes was chairman, this group is always known as the Dawes' Commission. Plans for definite amounts of reparation to be paid annually, for the establishment of a central bank in Germany, and for the issuance of mortgage bonds on German investments seemed a solution and yet did not work out well. The Dawes' Report of 1924 was supplemented by that of the Young Commission, again headed by an American, in 1929. The annual payments, provided by the Dawes' Plan but not paid, were to be reduced still further. An attempt was made to stabilize economic conditions within Germany to make the payments possible. Since 1931 no reparations payments have been made.

Another important recent League experience has been the clash with Japan over Manchuria. Japan and China had rival interests in that Chinese province. Japan sought to protect hers by force and established the new kingdom or Japanese protectorate of Manchukuo. A careful investigation was made by the Lytton Commission. When this report condemning Japanese methods was adopted by the League, Japan resigned from the League and carried her campaign into North China proper. The Japanese defiance might seem to forecast disregard of League agreements or suggestions by any of the members, as Italy in regard to Ethiopia in 1935; but it called forth more united support of the League's position than any earlier problem.

Since the World War, *international agreements looking toward economic stability or general peace* have been numerous and important. To many observers European conditions, and in fact those of the world, were unsettled rather than settled by that great conflict and the changes which followed it. The Treaty of Versailles seemed a cause of discord partly because of its severity toward Germany and its attempt to make Germany accept responsibility for a war which civilization caused. France, victorious largely through the support of Great Britain and the United States, belived that even the drastic terms of the Versailles' Treaty did not guarantee her sufficient security against neighbors growing more rapidly than she. The original agreement of France, Great Britain and the United States to guarantee the security of France broke on the rocks of senatorial opposition in the United States. Before the League Assembly the statesmen of central Europe and Aristide Briand, the great foreign minister of France, worked for some peace guarantee which would include French security. Many critics of Gallic plans declare that security is but another name for hegemony, a polite title to cover French alliances and pacts. As substitute for League guarantee of French security, on the 16th of October, 1925, the representatives of Germany, France, Great Britain, and some smaller countries *agreed at Locarno,* in Switzerland, on arbitration treaties between Germany and some of the Allies. In the most important of these the inviolability of the existing frontiers of Germany on the west were guaranteed. Germany and her western neighbors agreed not to resort to war

Some international conferences

except in case of actual breach of these agreements or of difficulties under the League.

Even more important than Locarno, in the eyes of many Americans, was the *Peace Pact* agreed upon in 1928 by Frank B. Kellogg, American Secretary of State, and Briand. This pact has been signed by almost all the important nations of the world; and optimists believe it represents a new stage in the history of world peace. This pact provides:

"The High Contracting Parties solemnly declare in the names of their respective peoples that they condemn recourse to war for the solution of international controversies and renounce it as an instrument of international policy in their relations with one another.

"The High Contracting Parties agree that the settlement or solution of all disputes or conflicts, of whatever nature or of whatever origin they may be, which may arise among them, shall never be sought except by pacific means."

If we expect the problems of the universe to be solved by international conference, it will be necessary to disregard the failures of the conference method in recent years. Undoubtedly international friendships are promoted by these meetings; but goodwill is more often lost by conflicting claims and disputes than gained by concessions or agreements. The economic conferences like that at London in 1933 [3] and the disarmament conferences at Geneva have disclosed an unwillingness on the part of almost all countries to yield any essential point of national honor. And how little it takes to constitute such an essential!

Yet, everything considered, in the light of progress toward international organization and the peaceful settlement of international disputes there can be no question that the period since the World War represents the outstanding international era in the history of humanity.

Conditions of Internationalism—Old and New

The old inter-nationalism

The old internationalism was an affair of military coalitions and semi-military alliances. The new internationalism

[3] See p. 199.

is a matter of world coöperation and possibly of federation. Under the old internationalism secret diplomacy and intrigue occupied first place. The new may not deal solely with open diplomacy but it has hope of fair-mindedness, square-dealing and justice, which were conspicuous by their absence from pre-war diplomacy. In the old days an exchange of discourtesies was marked by a gentle request, backed by a threat of the mailed fist or naval intervention. The new is likely to be influenced more by Wall Street and the market than by these considerations. Prestige and power are likely to come from the Bourse rather than from the parliamentary chamber.

Both the old and the new internationalism grow out of nationalism. In a true sense the word national is, therefore, a political "y" or unknown quantity of the twentieth century. What part will it take in the drama which will be played during the next hundred years? In pre-war Europe nationality had been grafted upon seventeenth-century ideas. The organization of powerful nations had intensified the rivalry of states which were as selfish and self-centered as were the absolute monarchs, the fourteenth French Louis and the Romanoff Catherine. The larger national and general principles of human development and of human welfare were lost to sight in the narrower demand for national supremacy. Nothing was quite so important to Germany as "Deutchland uber Alles;"[4] to France, that she should maintain her dominance and security at all cost; to Britain, that she should rule the wave without let or hindrance. When nations with such ideas and ideals formed two grand alliances, the remedy was at least one degree worse than the disease. Possibly the excesses of the old remedy have cured some part of the disease. Some say that the new remedy is more nationalism. If that statement be correct, and if it means more of the old type nationalism, the good Lord pity the twentieth century! If the remedy is to be found in more nationalism, it must be nationalism of a bigger and finer type. The old unitary

---

[4] Originally this phrase meant the fatherland before any of its member states. Outside of Germany it came to mean Kultur before everything else. This idea has been revived under fascism.

idea of sovereignty should yield something of itself, because a world of national sovereigns means a world of conflict and disorder.

The World War made a continuation of many old systems impossible. In dethroning a score of monarchs it caused a complete internal reorganization of many nations. In spite of an eighteenth-century type of national peace treaties in 1919, a League of Nations was formed and a World Court was organized. The idea of the League came from Europe but the pressure which made it fact was American. Though himself a forward-looking American, President Wilson did not carry with him the support of the great mass of the American people.

Europe's international problem

The first phase of the new internationalism was, therefore, a continuation of distrust not chiefly of European countries for one another but of America toward Europe and Europe toward America. For a time the solution was not clear. America was unwilling, probably unable, to assume the leadership left to her, if not offered. The danger of European entanglements made us fearful of all advance away from nationalism.

Europe could not lead the way to the new day because she was borne down by the burden of tradition, and was obsessed by hate, prejudice and rivalry. Europe could not lead because she had little experience with the two main political ideas which might make a new internationalism possible, democracy and federalism. Although these are predominantly American products, they may be more valuable in developing a new system than in continuing it. Europe's primacy in the field of commerce was threatened by a lack of free capital and control of much international business by American corporations. Even in the twentieth century medievalism has a strangle hold upon Europe in too many fields. Continental geography and continental poverty prevent the easy development of a new type of internationalism. Modern anthropologists may tell us to disregard race, because in reality there are no sharp distinctions among races. Our own satisfaction with things American if not with the American race—a composite of so many different elements—ought to make the European difficulty clearer to us. Though only a few miles may separate the man who lives in France from the man who resides in Germany, a very wide chasm separates the Frenchman from the German. National pride, national antagonism, national psychology, national trade policies are almost insurmountable barriers to a new internationalism.

In a sense *Europe is shortening the way to international coöperation* by the continued meetings of the League Assembly, in the settlement of international disputes either by Hague Court arbitration or by the Council of the League, and more completely and successfully through adjudication by the World Court. In a sense Europe is shortening the way to economic internationalism especially in the development of cartels, active integrated businesses which disregard national boundaries. There is coming into existence an economic United States of Europe. In a sense Europe is shortening the way by agreements such as those at Locarno and proposals as those at the World Economic Conference of 1927.[5] Voluntary coöperation in maintaining peace and in promoting free trade is epochal.

America's influence has especially been used to encourage business and to prevent war. In past ages economic rivalry has had more than its share in causing military conflict. The new internationalism, being founded like the rest of the modern world largely upon an industrial basis, may find it necessary to free itself not only from war but from dangers and threat of war. Humanity, and particularly business leaders, naturally will reason out this problem and if possible avoid conflict, whether it appears necessary or not, if we cannot afford it. This cost is not primarily one of dollars. It is of particular interest to society for it probably involves security and prosperity that is not necessarily commercial: and war might imperil the future of western civilization.

Under the old internationalism many classes besides the munition makers desired and encouraged war. Through it the politicians sought increased authority for themselves and

America and the new internationalism

---

[5] On this consult p. 187.

their government: now they wonder whether a war might not remove them from public office for good. By it business aimed to eliminate rivals. Liberals usually opposed war, and conservatives sometimes welcomed it. But evidently times are changing.

Less negatively in relation to war than positively in relation to industrial civilization is a new internationalism necessary.[6] *A new internationalism is a necessity in view of the future possibility that Europe and America may need to stand together lest they fall together.* Unless the new internationalism at all costs avoids war among the powers of the western world, the gains of western civilization will be lost by what is literally a cut-throat competition among nations. This competition is more disastrous by far than any between nineteenth-century business men or corporations, because while Christian nations are wasting their wealth and power in squabbles with one another, others are getting ready to fight us for world supremacy. The jingoist, the false patriot, the short-sighted business man who stirs up strife between these western countries in the hope of advantage for his nation deserves an extra warm seat in Satan's domain.

The new internationalism may not be made in America; but it probably must be developed under American guidance. It is not enough that we should have developed democracy and federalism and that we possess surplus wealth. Our democracy has stood rather poorly the test of post-war domestic and international problems. Yet democracy should aid in securing future peace and success. In the words of Elihu Root: "The entrance of democracy upon the field of foreign affairs . . . involves a terrible danger as well as a great step in human progress—a step in progress if the democracy is informed; a terrible danger if the democracy is ignorant. An ignorant democracy controlling foreign affairs leads directly to war and the destruction of civilization. An informed democracy insures peace and the progress of civilization." [7]

If we are to rule our own house and lead others, American

[6] See pp. 184–190, 193–195, 198–200, 457–470.
[7] Root, *Men and Policies,* Harvard University Press, p. 495.

democracy may be more successful if it ceases to distrust leadership as tyrannical.   Even better would be the avoidance of rule by groups better organized than our government, more successful, more resourceful, and better equipped with the sinews of politics and of war. America can help world federalization by example rather than by direct action. Politically western Europe has reached only the stage touched by America at the close of the Revolutionary War. It is at a stage to benefit by America's experience in uniting separate states into a "more perfect union." No league of nations can be worthy of the name world state, although it is a form of world organization, and it may be a step toward world government.

While *democratic coöperation and federalism* are slowly taking new form and making converts, business is reaching out into new channels and encountering problems that may not become acute in our generation. It is working up new technology, making new uses of scientific knowledge, and more than all else, acquiring super-national organization. The new internationalism must accept responsibility for the protection not of national industry but of all western industrial civilization. Except so far as the European cartels have performed this path-breaking service, this task will probably be undertaken under American leadership that is primarily economic but inevitably political as well. Then we are confronted with the situation that we have made nationalism "large," as Europe did when it formed the two great alliances before the World War. True internationalism may well be a far larger and less narrow thing than international coöperation of just the western nations—it probably should know no boundaries or limits of race, color or economic systems.

The International Scene

Throughout this treatment of our dynamic civilization we have seen how political and economic forces are interwoven. It is impossible to separate the business interests which have become widespread and really public in character from the political problem of promoting, redirecting, or controlling those affairs in the public interest. Since the World War these problems have become much more complicated than ever before, and a new series of interests or conflicts have arisen. If this is true in domestic or national affairs, is it any less true in those which transcend the boundaries of any one nation?

There is no international government which makes rules, which enforces even international agreements or which administers the political side of these economic affairs. It would seem therefore as though there were no possible problem of nationalism versus internationalism, since the nation-state is everything and everywhere among all western peoples. If separate and distinct individual state systems were declining, that is, if they were becoming relatively less important in the whole international scene, economic and political, then we should expect either more inter-nation coöperation or, potentiality at least, action by groups, alliances or inter-nation leagues to manage (1) affairs which the nations as such have agreed to leave alone, and (2) new business interests which national governments have not been managing or which they find themselves incapable of handling.

In time of war neutral countries have permitted belligerents to control commerce between them and the belligerents, not because it was outside of their legal jurisdiction but because it was outside of the actual field in which they could make their wishes count. In time of peace many countries also have voluntarily surrendered their right to handle as national projects a large number of humanitarian or routine affairs such as the white slave traffic, opium, and an international postal service. These illustrations prove rather conclusively that the powers actually surrendered by the different nations are negligible in either scope or character. The neutrals accept a military necessity. Countries at peace often transfer to international commissions routine problems which do not affect business greatly or in no way can tend to dim national prestige.

In the rivalry for place, power, and trade a large number of forces are at work. National chambers of commerce and large business organizations including banking houses often bring pressure to bear to obtain their share of the world's commerce. A manufacturing concern which can find at home only limited supplies of raw material insists that its government shall make the most favorable treaty terms possible with the nearest country which can furnish those materials cheaply and in abundance. The sale of its goods in the domestic market can be protected only by an international policy, a protective tariff. But its competition with foreign companies outside of the boundaries of this country make it necessary for it to get its materials cheap, not to manufacture at a disadvantage and if possible to under-sell all competitors. If its supplies cost little and its actual cost of production is low, either because of abundant power, cheap labor or improved technology, it may not call upon its government because it can under-sell its rivals almost anywhere in open markets and possibly even compete with those protected by high tariffs. This unusual situation exists in connection with many American manufactures such as those of machinery, automobiles, and by-products of petroleum.

Ordinarily these economic advantages do not exist, particularly in the United States where labor costs are high, in Germany where raw materials are now limited in number, or in China where ancient methods of production are still chiefly in vogue. National governments therefore are called in to protect the business internationalism of the different peoples. In consequence each government tries to secure for its nationals a most-favored nation treaty.[8] When those become common and give no differential advantage to one group of nationals,[9] the government frequently is asked to grant direct advantages. International bankers are brought into the picture to help with the sales and by extending credit promote the extension of this business in countries both civilized and barbarous.

When one great power is dealing with another, no primary

[8] When a treaty contains a "most favored nation" clause, each party automatically grants to the other any later favorable concession permitted by a subsequent treaty to a third party (nation).
[9] Citizens of that nation.

concession is likely to be made by either unless the countries involved are in alliance, in which case sometimes military advantages are swapped for commercial gain or investment opportunity, as was the case with France and Russia before 1914. In dealing with the second-rate powers, however, sometimes one country can have its own way. A large loan perhaps may be floated. The national government, as for example our government at Washington not long after the World War, approved a number of loans made in Latin America handled directly by the bankers and financed by the credulous clients or supporters of these banking institutions. Much of this money was probably absorbed by the Latin governments in political experiments or in fighting revolutions. Even Uncle Sam did not hesitate to foment revolutions if the officials in authority were not willing to make sufficient concessions to the Goliath of the North.

These illustrations show how *statecraft enters into new problems, chiefly business in character, which countries or their nationals have in dealings with one another*. Imagine then the importance of the political side of this problem *if the conditions are not primarily economic but both economic and political* as in deciding the future of the Philippines, possibly a more necessary part of Japanese imperialism than of American foreign interests. Imagine the difficulties that arise when *a situation which cannot possibly be handled by each nation for itself does not receive* in the slightest degree that *coöperation between them* which might make the problem negligible. An example of this type of coöperation was the temporary agreement in regard to wheat made by the chief wheat exporting countries after the London Conference of 1933. Imagine the situation again if these *world states have traditions, plans or ambitions sharply at variance with one another*. France and Germany have coöperated in working out a continental steel cartel in spite of the political bickerings and antagonisms and other conflicts of the two countries. The reason for this is probably the unevenness of distribution of mineral deposits in and near the Rhine valley and the overwhelming economic advantage secured by industrialists who are not separated from each other by national barriers.

In the future there is a possibility that industrialists and financiers everywhere will come to recognize the unity of purpose which should underlie all their actions. Would that these peace agencies could form international alliances as effective and as free from nationalism as the vicious combinations or territorial pools of the munition makers. At least these fiends who prey upon human emotions and weaknesses, when peoples are organized into nation groups, disregard national boundaries in their sales and propaganda even though the disappearance of national boundaries would put them out of business. But what would humanity do if the manufacturers and big bankers benefiting from conditions already considered in Chapters V and VI formed world-wide cliques unhampered by national boundaries or controls?

Many of the problems and dilemmas we have examined are not distinctively American: they are characteristic of all western civilization. A major problem to which we should give attention therefore is this: *if our political organization is distinctively national and is in no true political sense supernational, how can these dilemmas be attacked or be solved by any government which has no authority beyond its own boundaries?* [10]

Must the limits of political organization and of economic controls, if not of economic activities, *be similar, if not identical?* If an economic problem such as unemployment or overproduction affects two adjacent countries, what effect upon the situation will be exercised if each nation acts without regard to the other? If each is considering only its own interests,

Problem of political nationalism with economic internationalism

[10] In regard to Recovery in different countries before July, 1934, M. S. Stewart comments, *Paradoxes of World Recovery*, p. 156, "little progress has been made toward overcoming the fundamental obstacles to a revival of world trade—such as the paralysis of international finance, exchange instability or elimination of trade barriers—without which recovery must be confined to fairly narrow limits. The attempt of a number of the larger countries to resolve the contradictions of their internal economies by competitive currency depreciation has served to accentuate the disequilibria in the states retaining the gold standard. Critics have pointed out that unless this tendency is checked the sharpening of national rivalries must sooner or later pass over into the military sphere. Equally disturbing has been the failure of labor to obtain its share of the fruits of business recovery." Material furnished by Foreign Policy Ass'n.

and those interests differ for racial reasons if not for geographical, or for geographical reasons if not for commercial, will not the use of distinctively nationalist policies not only fail to touch the problem but also bring the two countries into opposition if not into conflict? If between them there is rivalry, for example in securing near-by sources of raw materials or a limited outside market, will not their rivalry engender political antagonism and prevent natural solutions of economic difficulties?

If nations cannot provide themselves with raw materials [11] and must go outside of their own boundaries for a sale of a fair percentage of their products,[12] *economic nationalism must work harmoniously with economic internationalism.* This involves the coöperation of many national governments and possibly of a quasi-world government. Future tariffs may be made not only for the primary purpose of protecting national industry and labor but with a view of promoting to the maximum all the business which any people carry on, whether that is domestic or international. A tariff which limits markets more than it limits foreign competition will be unpatriotic as well as unwise. The North Atlantic countries may find it less necessary to make separate national tariffs against one another than to agree upon a coöperative series of tariffs directed against systems involving a totally different type of politically organized industry or of unlimited labor. In a sense this action might simply magnify nationalism, and might make it cover the whole area of western capitalism; but it might not remedy any serious evils inherited from mercantilism.

Assume *a case where the economic problems cover an area occupied by several countries,* as in central or southern Europe. What happens (1) when each state follows an isolated policy, (2) when some coöperate but the others do nothing or adopt measures inconsistent with those of the coöperating states, (3) if all coöperate but use out-of-date or inadequate methods, and (4) if distinct problems are left to inter-nation political

[11] See pp. 181–183.   [12] See pp. 185–189.

bodies with power of suggestion but no authority within their separate fields.

It requires no knowledge of the present to discover that type 4 is used only for some minor and usually non-economic difficulties. Coöperation is rare enough, but agreement among several countries is likely to be of type 3 because an agreement must usually be made on old accepted bases, which may be valueless today. After 1815 Prussia, with widely scattered principalities, had a situation similar to type 2. She handled it without gloves, in typical Prussian fashion, forming a real customs union. Had she been obliged to wait until all her own principalities and the intervening states had been convinced of the necessity and wisdom of the union, how long might she have waited for voluntary action?

In general, is not a large part of the civilized world in the status described in type 1? How conscious of the problem are most of these western states? How much have they considered modification or internationalization of tariff systems, the adoption of similar, modernized trust controls, the acceptance of inter-nation plans for a wiser exchange of products? How much do patriotism, national pride, desire for nation growth help, or hinder, the creation of an inter-nation organization that will make its first duty the unification of policies and controls in these regions of common problems? If such an organization did make uniform policies, how much would the coöperating countries suffer from either (*a*) a loss of control of their own affairs, or (*b*) the adoption of policies that are too old or too poor for proper control of that nation's public affairs?

Is not one of the greatest dilemmas of the modern western world the failure to have *the areas of political unity*, for the world powers and other nation states, *coincide with the fields in which common or similar economic interests continue* or are developed? In Chapter VII we considered somewhat international rivalry for raw materials and outside investments, together with tariff controversies and other forms of competition. In that treatment comparatively little attention was paid to the major conflict of all, that between *nationalism* as a state organization, directing and controlling the work of the different peoples at home and abroad or directing those public policies which represented for each country as a whole the rules which that nation wishes to follow, and *internationalism,* politically unorganized.

If we concentrated on perfecting political organization, we should undoubtedly make our present state systems finer and stronger than they have been. Should we then find, first, that the great public problems of today within national boundaries would be simplified, and should we probably discover, secondly, that the problems outside of state boundaries would then be less a threat to the peace, prosperity and development of the modern world? Suppose that the western state became *the* chief or sole unit of organization, the state being everything, the citizen nothing, and business interests hardly worth the notice of either citizen or statesman. How much would the rivalry of states, the conflicts between them, the danger of war and threatened destruction be lessened? Would not the *emphasis on the state* as such reduce the probability of that coöperation between nations that seems constantly to be growing greater? Then would not their *chief political objectives* include conflicts with each other for power and prestige and make dilemmas more acute, in the strife for hegemony not only in semi-continental areas but in diplomacy, in culture, and even in quasi-world organization?

America's problem of solving problems more than nation-wide

America must face soon a series of decisions regarding the limits that national economy or national self-sufficiency can accomplish by itself. If we find that our dilemmas are similar to, if not identical with, those of other western world powers, is it probable that any solution of a dilemma by America will be final? The answer may be "yes" but probably is "no." If we find that in attempting to solve an American dilemma the problem may be solved by national action but involves us in affairs outside of the country, will even a tentative solution without possible coöperation of other interested countries be a possibility? For example, if dependence upon the outside world for either raw materials, supplies or foods, as sugar, or other types of dependence, is basic for the continuance of our life or our work, certainly these outside contacts cannot be neglected but must be watched and strengthened. If in addition America depends upon the world for the sale of a surplus without which business cannot continue "as usual," again success not only is closely related to coöperation with other countries but is dependent absolutely upon such coöperation.

Whether the rivalry between nations is a rivalry of *states* represented by short-sighted statecraft or a rivalry of *businesses* influenced chiefly by profit motives, the danger of conflicts must increase in proportion to the number of contacts we have abroad, though they can be made to decrease in proportion to the number of wise national policies worked out in connection with each of these contacts. Rivalry of nations and conflicts between them must not be thought of primarily as economic because they may be racial and they may be distinctively political, so far as any political action or policy may be freed from economic motive. If national interests were freer than most of them are from economic taint, then we should be likely to find ourselves in the "ideal" (?) state which Spengler envisions, if we ever escape from what he considers this most decadent period, in which economic interests take precedence of political.

In Europe statecraft devotes most of its energy not to avoiding conflicts but to gaining national advantage regardless of danger of making enemies or even of stirring up war. America, more fortunately situated, blunders along disregarding international consequences of anything that we do, much as Britain has "muddled through" in war and in peace. We maintain that we are big enough and strong enough, with enough resources, money and people to do as we like; and therefore we watch the first chance rather than even the main chance before us. If war comes, we shall need more friends than these policies have brought us in recent years. We may think that any country such as ours, richer and more powerful than others if almost as populous as any other western state, can make allies if not friends on terms rather favorable to itself. Even then a common sense nationalism would seem to dictate careful study of any international phase of every international situation or problem, economic or political.

Wise statecraft would regard the close interlocking of many domestic problems with foreign and therefore if possible develop domestic policies and foreign which are similar, or at least not antagonistic to each other. As already seen in Part II and in the first of Part III, the problems and dilemmas caused by our dynamic civilization are serious not only in themselves but also because economic changes keep ahead of political regulation. We have already encountered difficulty in working out a nation-wide plan of regulating "bigger and better" business in the best interests of the American people, partly because our public authority is divided into state and national parts. With some authority but not all vested in our national government, how much greater will be *the problem of selecting the right policies for these problems that are more than nation-wide, especially those calling for some or very much international coöperation?* Probably many of these can be worked out by each country for itself, with special attention to its peculiar difficulties and conditions, provided the demanded solutions are not too dissimilar, or the only solution is an inter-nation one.

Americans may feel that because they are in advance of other nations in some kinds of invention and in developing large-scale production we cannot possibly be laggard in protecting public interests or in working out plans for solving pressing needs. When we come to consider, however, what Europe has done in the way of forestalling, not unemployment but its evils, not sickness but its costs, not old age but its penalties, at least in the field of social insurance, we have much to learn from the older countries in which workers encountered these difficulties long before they became acute in America.

We are now encountering problems which have already confronted foreign countries and with which they have experimented. Some of these are problems which they have attempted to solve by disregarding individualism and accepting public responsibility. We shall certainly do well to regārd carefully and highly their difficulties and their solutions, even though we do stress differences between our public organization and methods and those of Europe. Very often their ways are not our ways nor their solutions our solutions. Difficulties that are not simply American but general, which we therefore have in common with other western nations, should be solved by similar methods in different countries, by our methods only in case those are the best for others as well as ourselves. It would seem to behoove Americans therefore not to neglect the experience of mankind, not to treat problems as distinctively American which never can be limited solely to America. If we wish true success, why not apply to these problems the intelligence and the attention which the last generation has given to money making? Of what use to gain the whole world of wealth, and to enjoy the material power which goes with wealth, if we lose the opportunity to find the political and social organization which will keep that wealth from injuring us?

In a sense the problem of coördinating nations and making them work together to solve their common problems is like a very much larger world difficulty. That is, the *relation of each nation to the western world,* chiefly America and western Europe, is very much like that of *the western world as a unit to the whole globe.* As any *nation* is but a *political part* of the *western world,* so the *western world* is but an *economic* or cultural *part of the whole earth.* If each nation finds that it cannot attain its salvation by itself or by its own efforts, then the western world may be obliged to choose between isolation from the rest of the world or proper coöperation with it. America, in working with England, France, and even with Italy and Germany, is dealing with a kindred type of state and society. The western world in its contacts with soviet areas may be dealing with a somewhat similar society, but under a rather distinct type of economic and political order. In our connections with the Oriental peoples, however, the Occidental world is dealing with totally different races, governments, cultures, and economic groups. We must face the issue of how far our internationalism shall be carried;

The western world and other competing systems

whether it will be a narrow one, chiefly limited to western countries, or of world-wide scope.

At present the western states outnumber greatly the soviet societies. Probably Russia and western Europe have far more in common than the conflicts and antagonisms of recent years seem to indicate. Although Russia has aimed to establish a proletarian system in which capitalism is anathema, nevertheless, Russia uses willingly our engineering skills and copies gladly the most advanced technological methods. Whatever conflict there is probably grows out of political and racial rivalry almost as much as it is a contest between economic systems. On the contrary, the conflict between Occidentalism and Orientalism is deep-seated and marked at every point of comparison. The Oriental peoples are more numerous than the Occidental, with low standards and levels of living, with little regard for many of the ideas and principles which western peoples revere or use. If the world became all one huge, undifferentiated market and the Oriental peoples learned in a few years to use western machinery, how long before the American workman and capitalist might be driven out of the game by this cut-throat competition?

If civilization is a race between education and catastrophe, as Wells contended, *how much is the survival of western civilization dependent upon our success in putting our own house in order, how much on avoiding possible conflict with Russian communism or Orientalism, how much on being prepared if that conflict becomes inevitable?* Putting the house of western civilization in order would call for what realignment of nationalism with internationalism, what coöperation of western nations with one another, what sacrifices of national preferences, ambition, and pride on the altar of a common need?

So long as dilemmas outrank solutions and private gain obscures public welfare, are the western nations prepared for emergency, individually or together? How wise then becomes the *national struggle for markets,* national determination to win the petty advantage or the proud goal even if enemies are made of other western peoples? How safe and sane is a *series of policies which occasionally threatens conflict and semi-occasionally indicates war or leads to war?* If western peoples must face possible economic, political and military competition of a soviet system or an Oriental world, they will too late realize the inexcusable folly of wasting their strength and resources in petty squabbles or serious warfare among themselves. Even if they offer a united front to either or both of these competing orders, they will have made nationalism "large" to cover the whole area of "western" civilization. Then a world which is rapidly becoming more and more closely integrated will be divided, as Europe was a quarter-century ago, into armed camps, eventually clashing in a Great War. In a real World War between races and civilization, would western nations survive and western civilizations inevitably triumph? If so, with what loss and at what cost?

It is more necessary to avoid such a titanic struggle than it is to keep from one another's throats the present western powers. If parliamentary government or the American system is breaking down, if the "New Deal" or European fascism cannot properly coördinate government and business, new national policies and even new national organization may be necessary. As Leon C. Marshall has shown rather clearly,[13] western industrial capitalism is rather headless and unorganized and must be reorganized to solve twentieth-century problems. The dilemmas of western civilization are not economic alone or political alone, or national alone. Any attempt to solve them or any part of them by action or reorganization *within the field of that part* will almost certainly fail. Business must be properly coördinated with government or with society in its political capacity. Just as surely nation must be coördinated with nation, because the dilemma is of the whole western civilization and not of any of its parts, territorial or social. If this reorganized and recoördinated western world is then brought as a unit into conflict with other world civilizations, we have made the fatal mistake of leaving out of account again the worlds outside of our

[13] *The Social and Ethical Obligations of Management in the Modern Business Régime,* pp. 177–179.

"world" as we now so frequently leave out of consideration the nations other than our own. *What plans therefore are necessary to make western civilization safe in a world that is much bigger than the sphere of western, capitalist, Christian civilization?*

PART IV

THE TWENTIETH-CENTURY
CULTURAL RENAISSANCE

THE TWENTIETH-CENTURY RENAISSANCE

A Twentieth-Century Renaissance is in the making. We Introduction are too close to understand the transformations that are taking place. The centrifugal forces at work appear especially to be affecting agriculture, the family, and religion. The disintegrating agencies are operating particularly in rural democracy, in personal relationships, and in group standards. In the post-war period a most distressing breakdown is the inability of quasi-sovereign nations to maintain the peace of the world and to solve their common problems. In the recent but we hope transitory period of acute financial distress, the failures of industrial capitalism temporarily loom larger than any other.

As we look back over the civilization of Europe and America preceding the Industrial Revolution, we discover that it was not an integrated product. This is rather surprising because the civilization of the seventeenth century was the resultant of forces that had been at work without great change for several thousand years. The technics and the organization if not the standards of the late neolithic period had persisted in much of their vitality until two hundred years ago. Was a new type of wealth-production represented by the Industrial Revolution adequate to transform business as well as production, government as well as business, society as well as government, culture and civilization as well as society? Whether it was adequate or not must be determined by the result. In great part that knowledge is denied to us because we are still turning pages in the record of this transformation.

If the end is not yet, or even in sight, the most that we can hope to discover from a study of conditions and problems today is, first, the character and the extent of the transforma-

473

tion that has already taken place, and, second, the underlying trends and tendencies from the old order to the new.

Unquestionably there will be a struggle between tradition and the path-breaking ideas which the new science is largely responsible for creating and the new education may be chiefly instrumental in disseminating. Those who are optimistic will expect a larger vision based on a greater understanding of truth. From this should come truer religion and finer ethical standards. Material civilization and the struggle for profits, the attempt to get place and power, the temptation to use knowledge and wealth selfishly would seem to intensify the bitter competition between men due to the survival of animal nature in a human world. Yet, if recent history teaches anything, it brings into relief not only a base struggle for money and prestige among individuals and nations but also a growing interest in welfare and a dawning consciousness of public obligation and responsibility.

The edifice of civilization

A civilization is like an old building representing many periods and different styles of architecture. It may have started as a plain, simple structure without conscious plan or design. The original structure no longer is observable as we gaze upon the present building. Additions have been made as extra stories of the original, or as new wings, cupolas, gables, or façades. At first it may have been a rather simple type of building, consisting of simple traditions and customs for foundation and plain unornamented rooms above. This is doubtful. The original building was made up of many different parts, now so submerged that only a skilled civilization-architect and archaeologist can determine the nature of the foundations or walls and discover the original pillars and doorways. The interior of the rooms may have changed through the cutting out of walls, the filling in of doorways, the opening of new windows. Each period or each epoch has probably redecorated those halls and chambers which are still in use.

A huge cataclysm such as the change from Roman civilization to Teutonic or from medievalism to the modern period probably has torn down much of the exterior and rebuilt it according to the tastes and preferences of that race and day. Possibly the new has simply been superimposed upon the old, with the hope that the outer smear is as truly a new civilization as the reconstructors would like to think it. Occasionally, wreckers and dynamiters like the revolutionaries of the late eighteenth century blow up large parts of the structure with the intention of modernizing and improving it.

In the last hundred years workers with machines, using new types of power, have made marvelous additions and transformations. With efficient tools industrial engineers have built a vast modern edifice with new exits if not entrances. This structure, massive, ugly and utilitarian, stands to business leaders and their host of sycophants as the greatest temple of all time. By skillful landscaping of the immediate environment and the construction of new roads, gates and other approaches, many observers are deceived into thinking this vast structure is about all there is of present-day civilization. Those who "follow the man from Cook's" under the guidance of industrial capitalism see only those products of civilization to which they are exposed in the circuit. They do not press through old weather-beaten doors into older and less scientifically constructed parts of the edifice. Frequently they do not know that an older civilization lies beneath, behind and beyond this huge offshoot of the Industrial Revolution.

The ignorant, the incurious, and the unwary never find their way about this edifice of civilization—a most interesting and wonderful product of human experience. The sentinels of the present order stand guard along these entrance roads, enforcing the mandate "Keep Off the Grass." They never reach the vantage point of the nearby hills from which a clearer and more general glimpse is obtained. Others than the industrial elect may wander out into the adjacent fields and meditate in the shade cast by the world's literary trees. To them this materialistic monstrosity no longer hides the ancient and honorable, though often incongruous, bits of architecture which it sometimes conceals. Those who sit beside pleasant brooks, in which runs the heritage of the race, find that the gentle murmur of the stream soothes nerves made jagged by noise and confusion of a machine civilization. From the outside, they find interest in delving into the real nature of the structure which houses humanity today.

The interior of the house of civilization is as elaborate and confusing as the labyrinths of fable days. Without Ariadne's thread the unskilled investigator rarely returns to a true vision and understanding of the structure as we use it now. Possibly some of the most important galleries, passages, and underground chambers are closed to modern observers. Those who enjoy mystery tales could well search for hidden springs that will push back panels or set aside pictures, giving entrance to secret passages, stair-cases and caverns which would explain the unknown in human experience and development. Even a Sherlock Holmes on the trail of human heritage would scarcely unravel the hidden materials woven into the intricate record of humanity's civilization.

XVI

THE CHANGING FAMILY

If a new possible renaissance is social as well as cultural, Introduction it must take into account the changing family.[1] From early historic times the family has been patriarchal in type and rather permanent in character. In our day its permanence is less conspicuous, for many marriages end in divorce. American families are patronymic, but are they often under the absolute sway of the father? Reaction against the servile position of a dependent wife and mother would seem to have been inevitable when the woman of modern America became economically independent and legally free. One would have expected that she should have escaped her old status promptly when she was recognized as an individual instead of her husband's wife, in the eyes of the law. If these changes have occurred tardily, or have not occurred, is it because tradition holds modern woman to former patterns of conduct, or because she does not claim social independence corresponding with her new possible economic position? Undoubtedly the position of the modern married woman is different, if not so unlike the old status as one might expect. Reaction explains most easily, if not very satisfactorily, the shift from a household of suppressed children to one in which they are irrepressible.

We see at work in the family multitudes of new forces growing out of industrialism, city life, democracy, new standards of living and even new ethical standards. Who would keep static the chief unit of society in all ages? Yet who can measure and counteract dangerous elements of disorganiza-

---

[1] A cultural renaissance would include, at the least, in addition to the subjects treated in Part IV, literature as a mirror of life, art and architecture, music and other esthetics.

tion? Who can capitalize the possibilities of a modernized family in a dynamic society? Who but the family?

The patriarchal family is un-American, the present family is unstable, the future family is yet in doubt. If we could discover the standards or norms according to which family organization must conform, we might have a truer insight into the existing problem. We might be enabled to discover *the type of family that does reflect the underlying needs of this coming age.* Ernest R. Groves, a very successful student of marriage and family, discusses a number of marriage norms underlying American family organization. He treats motives for marriage, justice within the family, self-development in marriage, progress in marriage experience, conditions for growth, and several others.[2]

What standards do we find that apply universally, in both the past and the present? One of these is outstanding, *monogamy.* Comparing with California weather, these monogamic marriages may not be perfect but the others are unusual. Secondly, *permanence* is a characteristic. Even in America divorce affects only one marriage in six and, so many divorcees repeat, not more than one married person in ten. A third has been *companionship of the sexes.* This is derivative from the other two, but they might exist absolutely without it. It may not rise to the level of comradeship; but it cannot exist in over-night marriages. Another characteristic of the normal family is *children.*[3] In civilized society we recognize the right of the child to a family life and only recently have dignified the unfortunate childless couple with the title of family. The old family was an *economic partnership.* The new may well be. There should be a fair conformity to the *family pattern* that society has established or

---

[2] Groves and Ogburn, *American Marriage and Family Relationships,* ch. VII.

[3] In times past the family was large, partly because children were made to work and the larger the family the greater the income. Today standards of living and other factors reduce the number, although research students find larger families in America than in western Europe. If it were not for negroes and immigrants, this might not be true, as the families of college graduates, and especially those in which the mothers have a college education, are usually small.

approved for that age and in that land. The marriage relationship may easily become a major opportunity for *self-development*. The practice of discipline no longer appears in home or school; but the need of self-discipline becomes correspondingly greater. Harmonious family unity depends upon, and aids, an extra measure of self-development.

Intermediate between these accepted family norms and the marriage standards that Ernest R. Groves deems desirable are certain conditions or requirements that seem to underlie family and home life. One of these is a minimum of years and health in which every contestant in the matrimonial race should qualify. Another is enough family unity to justify our use of the terms family and home. If the family is chiefly a physical product, what gain over a group of animals? There must be spiritual unity and interrelations, or human nature and outside distractions will leave the family an historic institution.

The Family as a Reflex of the Stage of Civilization

Literally, the family is the transmitter of the biological heritage; figuratively, it will always be the transmitter of a heritage that is social. In doing that it readapts itself in some degree, usually slight, to the changing character of the age. In brief, it reflects in part the stage of civilization through which it is passing. The eugenists may work out a standard by which the biologically fit alone are permitted to marry. Whether there are other selective or controlling forces actually to improve the biological and the non-biological inheritance, only the future can determine. Even the present seems to show a lessening of the influence of the family in the transmission of social inheritance. The home gives more and more to the school, even in that training which is supposed to be the chief social gain of early youth. The fact that the school does not accept children at an early age compels the home and family to continue this useful process of handing down customs or social inhibitions, and preparing children for life in the group. In a real sense, however, *the culture of each age will be largely that possible in the family circle.* The

The family a transmitter of social heritage

non-material civilization may even be what the family makes it.

In times past, customs were largely a matter of tribe. The tribe as a body, however, contented itself chiefly with the initiation of new members, probably in the period of adolescence, and in the determination of standards and ideals to which youth must conform. Before young men and women were initiated into the sacred rites, the family was entrusted with practically all of the training held dear by the elders. At his mother's knee or over it, the child learned what was right and what was wrong, not in his eyes or even in those of his parents but according to the *mores* of his own people. The mother who failed to follow the dictates of custom and law became an outcast without standing in her own community. Many tribes prohibited marriages with complete strangers, lest irrelevant innovations should destroy the very foundations of that society. A comparison of the customs among different tribes, possibly related in race and not far apart geographically, shows how compelling a force is exercised by taboo or social control. Suffice it to say that originally morals were only the "mores," that is, the accepted customs of any group of people.

Present needs and problems

The place which the family must occupy in human society affects the individual as well as the group. If the present family cannot both attract and hold men and women in a family bond, it must acknowledge its inadequacy under conditions of today. Writers on marriage stress the fact that the family is not absolutely a necessity for the perpetuation of the race. Possibly that may be true from the individual viewpoint, but the younger generation must be members of society. They must therefore not only have a satisfactory biological inheritance but they must also have a reasonably satisfactory social environment, which, for both themselves and others, gives them at least minimum opportunities for individual development and for social membership. By whatever name we may call this arrangement, *it must have many characteristics similar to those of the family found in the past and the present.*

Aside from brain capacity, possibly the most distinctive characteristic of man as man is his *prolonged infancy*. The anthropoid of six months is somewhat like a human child of that age in his physical and to a limited extent his mental development.[4] Gorilla babies and human babies are said to be very much more alike than most of us admit. Beyond the age of six years, however, the anthropoid matures with amazing rapidity, one year carrying him through a period of childhood that with human beings covers another six years. In a third short period, he passes through an adolescent stage which human beings find of extraordinary interest over another six years. If biological necessity therefore predetermines relations of the sexes, it equally predetermines parental care of offspring over a period extending through adolescence.

Modern society must use in marriage and in the family, as in other elements of civilization, those ideals, standards and sanctions which the past has found good and which the present believes valid. Whatever solution is found, it must take into account biological and psychological conditions that youth encounters in the adolescent and post-adolescent period. It must reckon with marriage as a contract of economic character and with the family as an economic group. It must be willing to accept a modification of past social controls, either in the contracting of marriage or in the dissolving of the contract. In this present period of transition, the family today may not be any more successful in meeting these needs than is present industrial capitalism as the best organization of an industrial society. Being a transitory form, the present family is likely to perpetuate many evils of its predecessors, without having developed the proper standards for the most satisfactory organization in the future. Fortunately or unfortunately, *the family of the twentieth century must be the burden bearer and the path breaker*. To it may come the privilege of determining the character which the family shall finally assume.

---

[4] *Cf.* the very interesting experience of Mr. and Mrs. Kellogg with a baby chimpanzee, made a companion of their little son, somewhat older than the ape. Kellogg, W. N. and L. A., *Ape and Child*.

THE FAMILY AS AN ECONOMIC INSTITUTION IN
ANCIENT AND MODERN TIMES

Economic
elements in
the past
and present

In considering the family as a social unit, we frequently overlook its character as an economic partnership. The reasons for the partnership usually are not, and probably should not be, distinctly economic; yet the family has been and will continue to be almost as much economic as social.

Under the patriarchal system, whether in ancient, feudal, or early modern times, marriage was primarily a family alliance; and that was certainly an economic affair. The commonest method of marriage included economic procedure. A girl of marriageable age was considered an asset. The laws and the customs upholding virtue were at heart monetary. The economic nature of the old family is shown in the division of labor between husband and wife, and differences of occupation for the two. The character and form of the family was frequently predetermined by the kind of wife that would be most valuable to the husband. If labor were scarce and women were, as they almost always have been, hard workers, a man who could afford many wives found polygamy economically superior to monogamy. The scarcity of wealth and still more the equality in numbers of the sexes made monogamy general, polygamy the prerogative of the few wealthy leaders.

To what extent has the family continued as an economic institution under a machine civilization? In no period of history has business been exalted so much as it has been during the last two centuries. If the Machine Age has compelled a reorganization of the old family, has it not made the new one more distinctively economic than the old? We should expect this outcome. Certainly the partnership is a truer partnership than formerly, since it is more distinctively a partnership between equals than ever was the case in olden times. It is a partnership between individuals, both of whom are free agents. It is in America, and it is coming to be in Europe, a partnership freely entered into by the principals, not pre-arranged by parents. It may be a partnership in which only one earns, but it is one in which the other shares as never before. In many American states all income earned, and all property acquired, after marriage is shared equally by husband and wife. Women enjoy an economic freedom within marriage which would have been the envy of their grandmothers unto remote times.

Family income has not kept pace with standards of living or with desire for still more gains in living levels. Improvements in education and character have not kept step either with increased income, higher standards of living, or possible pooled resources. Family incomes

In almost every field we have examined we find the sad truth that modern requirements demand incomes that do not exist even in times of prosperity. Budget experts insist on approximately $2000 as the family minimum in ordinary times—and those were known before 1929. Yet three-fifths of American families have never regularly had an income that high. Probably more than one-fifth usually enjoyed only half that yearly income. Only ten per cent of all families have had in good times $5000 a year or more. Of course the families that do not reach four figures at all include many small farmers whose food costs are relatively low,[5] an exceptional proportion of these being colored families in the South. In families with incomes above $3000 more than one adult is usually earning, whereas in the poorer half of the families the head usually brings in from eighty-five per cent to ninety per cent of the money income.[6] In the "New Era" period fairly mature children added appreciably to the family income, frequently raising it from a subsistence level to a comfort level. If one of them contributed the major part of the whole, that person may have decided the location of the home and had a predominant voice in other characteristics of the household.

The woman who has worked for wage or salary becomes discontent in a home that provides her a mere fraction of her former income. If she can earn more than her husband,

[5] In 1929 only 2,636,000 "farm" families out of 5,800,000 had incomes in excess of $1000.
[6] Consult table in Lauck and Sydenstricker, *Conditions of Labor in American Industry*, p. 359.

she is faced with serious alternatives. She can be the traditional woman and the natural woman, a good homemaker and a fine mother. Possibly the sacrifice of a larger income and of a successful career may not mar her happiness or that of her husband or children; but the chances are it does. Another alternative is the continuation in business or profession by a woman who seeks to reconcile home and occupation.[7] If there are no children, modern women are frequently happier outside of the home than within. Often they can earn more than must be paid to a housekeeper or other assistant. Whether the home gains from this income as much as it loses in other ways may be an individual family matter. If the number of women workers increases greatly, society may pay a high price in unemployment, reduced wages, or part-time occupation. When there are children, work outside the home for the mother becomes more difficult, the risk of family disorganization greater, and the difficulties of securing marital happiness more complex.

The family as a consuming unit

If account is taken of the family *as a consuming unit, the home is* even more *important as an economic institution. The collective family budget dwarfs the serious problems presented by municipal and national finance.* · Elimination of waste has always been a wifely occupation, and economy in expenditure shows itself in shopping raids and in Pullman economy. These are inevitable by-products of an experience which has compelled housewives to spend carefully and economically. The problem of budget is frequently the determining factor when a young man and a young woman wish to marry.

Economic pressure probably accounts for the constant *decrease in size of the family.* It explains also, or its absence explains, the varying proportions of income expended for various items.[8] The *norm* for the family in 1790 was about five persons, in 1900, four, in 1930, less than three. The *average*

[7] Miss Hazel Kyrk, *Economic Problems of the Family* (ch. IX), lists the occupational interests of two and a half million married women in 1930. In some studies it was found that a quarter of all married women without children were gainfully employed. Miss Kyrk gives as a major reason for the employment of many married women the increasing spread between the cost of living and the family income.

[8] Consult also ch. XIV, D.

in 1880, however, was five and in 1930 slightly more than four. The typical American family of a half-century ago had one more child than that of today. The average family in America today, according to Paul H. Douglas, is slightly larger than that in western Europe. Two families out of every five have no children or none under 21. One out of five has one child, one of six two, one of ten three, and one of seven more than three.[9] Undoubtedly the chief explanation of small families is the desire to maintain a family standard of living that would be impossible today for larger families.

The expenditures of American families are predetermined very largely by the size of the income and the size of the family. Maurice Leven and his associates[10] give some interesting charts of family expenditure. With a large percentage of even workingmen's families the house costs almost as much as food, although the lower the income the larger the proportional food expenditures.[11] With earners above $3000 housing is frequently the largest single item. With farm families, on the contrary, housing costs are naturally low. Farmers with incomes above $1500 usually have saved more than they have spent for food, especially those who enjoyed at least $3000 per year. Curiously enough, with city families the percentage saved was not so high until the salary or net business return was above $10,000 yearly. These statistics, taken usually from 1929 or earlier budgets, tell a story very different from that discoverable after the great Wall Street panic. The greatest depression of history destroyed old norms, and the normalcy to which we return may be one rather different from that of the "New Era."

WHAT INDUSTRIAL CIVILIZATION IS DOING TO THE FAMILY

The changing world would not be changing very much if the traditional family of an agricultural civilization remained just as it was. If our chief social institution did not adapt itself to the new conditions and needs growing out of the

General causes and nature of changes

[9] Farm families average larger than urban, immigrant than native, colored than white.
[10] *America's Capacity to Consume*, ch. VI.
[11] *Ibid.*, p. 68 *et seq.*

shift to cities and many new business and social opportunities, it would show itself too unadaptable and static for desirable survival. In the process of reorganization there would inevitably be some disorganization of the older system. Among conditions of the Machine Age especially favorable to a disorganized family we may cite:

Political democracy with its former stress upon equality and upon the individual;

the changed city home and outside distractions of urban life;

work away from home for other members of the family than the head;

the changed status of women due to economic and personal independence;

the unrest developed in a highly dynamic period, which has affected almost every channel of business life and of social thought.

An interesting summary of present trends and tendencies underlying and affecting the problem of the present and future family has been given by Howard W. Odum.[12] They cover very much more than the Machine Age itself is doing. A restatement of these with the order slightly changed is as follows:

"Tendencies toward instability of the family due to home conditions brought about by social, economic, industrial, and urban situations.

"A general unrest and tendency towards pessimism in current discussions and a readiness to consider the 'drifting home' or the broken family as normal.

"A tendency of the minority toward anti-social ideas of freedom from childbearing and the *identification*, instead of the *equalization of opportunities*,[13] of the two sexes.

"A retrogressive and paradoxial tendency toward the extension of sex freedom in the direction of indefiniteness of sex relations, thus bringing growth to neither individual nor society."

---

[12] Odum, *Man's Quest for Social Guidance*, Henry Holt and Co., p. 247.
[13] Italics not in original.

Since most people in discussing the disorganized family re- fer to a single phase of it—*divorce*—we should, before considering any of these causes of changing trends, have some idea of the extent of divorce. Compared with the remote past, divorce is increasing at an almost appalling rate. In 1870 there were twenty-nine divorces annually for every 100,-000 Americans; by 1900 the number had risen to seventy-three, and by 1928 to 166. The actual number of divorces increased from 10,962 in 1870 to 201,468 in 1929. The depression decreased the number of divorces (why?), but *the ratio of divorces to marriages* was identical in 1932 and in 1929. American figures should not be taken as typical of other countries, for divorces are still fairly rare in Europe, possibly because their civilization has made less modification of social heritage. Seldom do changes in social organization affect so widely the status of the individual or the group as has this revolutionary breakdown in the permanence of many families. What is back of this disorganization? What does it represent? Is it simply evidence of unrest or does it mean a revolt against the old family organization? Does it reflect a new type of morality; or is it an attempt to replace one type of family with something more satisfactory and successful?

Causes for divorce are found in many of the conditions already explained. They may exist simply in the possibility of alimony, which has represented a husband's obligation to support a wife indefinitely regardless of her age or capacity for self-support. This usage, necessary before recent times, threatens to become a menace, rather than a deterrent, in the new age. It may be a major cause of divorce. Under the patriarchal system, divorce naturally was difficult because a change of partners would upset the whole system of alliances between neighboring families. Religious sects, especially of the Middle Ages and of later times in Roman Catholic countries, strongly disapproved any separation as contrary to the will of God. In colonial America family life was seldom broken except by death, and even a half century ago, a divorced woman made herself little less than a social outcast, regardless of provocation or need.

The old family possessed unusual solidarity. It is not strange that a homogeneous but undifferentiated family group should have developed in prehistoric times when the will of one leader was both an economic and a social necessity. In historic periods characterized by oriental despots and absolute monarchs, this type of family naturally continued. The Industrial Revolution hastened the development of political democracy; it did not create that institution. In the beginning political democracy was built on a foundation of theoretical equality, especially of individual rights. What was more natural, therefore, than that in time the ideas of individualism and of self-direction underlying political democracy should have affected home and family? It would be too absurd for a country to grant woman the right to elect those who control government and have no influence in deciding whom she should marry or how she should continue her membership in home and family! *The new social democracy is different from the old individualist democracy. Is it not possible that it will include the family as part of its own further development? In turn might not its development depend greatly upon what the family becomes and what the democratic family contributes to social democracy in general?*

When most people depended upon agriculture and lived on distinct farms, the home was separate, isolated, and self-sufficing. A great transformation has been brought about by the growth of the city. Possibly the minority of city dwellers now live in detached houses; many occupy flats, apartments, or tenements. How can a family live unto itself and for itself unless it has a home life revolving around its members and no one else? The old homestead on the farm gave this. A suite of four or five rooms is neither a house nor a real home, physically speaking. Hallways must be shared by at least one or more other families, and the building may be the abode of from four to four hundred. *The tenement furnishes fertile soil for family disintegration.* Fortunately divorce does not cause the catastrophe in the city that it would have in the country when it destroyed the old isolated farm family.

More and more is the new home, whether it is found in flat,

apartment or cottage, dependent on outsiders even for necessities such as cooked food. In the eleven years after 1914 the output of the American bakery increased sixty per cent. In 1925 practically a quarter of all food was eaten in restaurants. These figures take little account of the other prepared foods delivered to the house in cartons or escorted to the home in paper sacks. These changes reduce the work of wife and mother, but they do not promote the home life of the urban family. The time necessary for housework has been shortened and lightened by decreasing the size of the family, of the home and of its rooms, but chiefly by a great multitude of labor-saving devices. The mother benefits by this transformation more than do others in the family, but all are affected by it. *The gain in number and character of outside contacts by individual members of the family is secured at the expense of reliance upon one another.* Distractions of city life, however, are far more noticeable in street or in club, at movie and in other places of amusement, than in any apartment. In the opportunities for the development of the individual the challenge of complex city life finds rich reward, but again family unity pays the bill.

In the highly dynamic society in which we are now living the resultant of these economic and social forces is not only shown in material civilization; it appears also in woman's suffrage or in legal equality of the sexes. It arouses an entirely new set of emotional and mental attitudes. It creates a radically different set of beliefs and types of thought. No people has ever been able to change from one kind of life to one totally different without marked unrest. The reasons are obvious; living and civilization depend upon social inheritance, and social heritage perpetuates superstition as well as traditions founded upon fact and wise experience. Customs, institutions or attitudes of past ages may fit illy into a new society, especially one as unlike the agricultural era as is this one of power-mechanics. Inability successfully to add new cloth to old garments or pour new metal into old molds causes first wonder, then uneasiness, then discontent. If conservative, we are at a loss to understand why old institutions have not the value they represented to our ancestors. Otherwise, beliefs that satisfied us in childhood or appeal under patriotic stress seem to us as well as to the younger generation of archaeological value only. In no field except that of religion have these new ideas and attitudes been as disruptive as in the disorganization—not the disintegration—of the home and family. When many disregard convention and tradition, and all are conscious of a breakdown in moral and religious sanctions, why expect a continuance of even the present modification of the old family?

New Problems Affecting Marriage and the Family

The changed status of woman
In one of the most famous decisions of the United States Supreme Court, the Chief Justice decided regarding an individual: he is not a citizen; he is property and he has no legal right which society is bound to respect. What Roger B. Taney said of Dred Scott, a negro, was true of woman under the patriarchal régime. She had no legal status; she was not a citizen; she was property. A contract conveyed her from her father to her husband. In that contract she had no voice and no real share. The man whom she married became under that contract legally her lord and master, himself a free agent. A girl child was valued largely as a material asset to be disposed of to the highest bidder, providing he qualified as a desirable member of the family. This system had important merits; socially, it made for a highly integrated society; economically, it was especially valuable in agricultural communities in keeping farms together rather than having them broken up; morally, it maintained a very high level of feminine virtue. From the standpoint of woman, it prolonged the period of dependence and prevented the development of individuality. It forced her to find her interest in life solely in her home and to express her individuality in negative annoyance and in dominance of house and children.

The Industrial Revolution is undoubtedly in large part responsible for the change from this status of women. Without it there would have been less demand for the modern city, and within that city for factory and shop. Woman's potential or actual economic independence has changed her social standing greatly. A young girl can secure work which severs her dependence upon her home and frequently compels her absence from the paternal roof. Even when she remains with her family, her independent income gives her a rank as a contributing member of an economic group. In the family council her voice is not only heard but heeded; otherwise she withdraws and becomes a self-supporting, self-directing, independent member of society. *Economic opportunity has made possible a position in society for this younger woman which the patriarchal family never anticipated and strongly disapproved.*

Although the new place of woman in society is a by-product of her changed economic condition, nevertheless, modern society has been exceedingly slow to recognize the necessity of accepting that changed status in its customs and in its laws. Women have been indifferent to the need of securing definite recognition of themselves as members of society; rather they have sought distinctive political privileges. A single illustration shows this clearly. Nearly a century ago, when the elective franchise was conferred upon white men in America, the most progressive women leaders demanded the same advantage for themselves. What did they get? The right to vote was withheld, but in many American states they gained recognition that woman is entitled to something as a person. If she has property, then that property is hers, not her father's, while he lives, or her husband's after she marries. Mrs. Pankhurst might not have been a suffragette rioter had the English law made a similar concession.

Gradually women gained legal equality, the right to work, not only in the school room but also before the bar or in the medical laboratory. Some states gave them a nominal half share of the family earnings. As wage-earners and as members of families they secured by law what they were supposed to have had through custom—protection as workers. Hours for labor were finally limited, and the limitation was accepted by the Supreme Court of the United States, not because they were workers, but because they were women. The dangers of social exploitation, due to underpayment of girls and women workers, led in several states to minimum wage laws. The climax of legal gains seemed to come with the Nineteenth Amendment. The suffrage leaders secured approval of adult suffrage for women as well as for men. Oddly enough they overlooked the fact that while they were gaining for women the privilege of voting, their legal membership in society was left insecure. In some states a married woman is not a citizen in a full sense. The joke was on that native woman who years ago worked hard for state-wide suffrage only to find that when she went to the polls she could not vote because her husband was a British subject. This problem reappeared for the married women who gained suffrage in the Nineteenth Amendment but left legal civic status where it was.[14]

The new woman and the new family

From the standpoint of woman the old family was unsatisfactory and unjust. She bore its chief burdens, and she belonged to the sex that paid whether in the home or outside. It is possible that she will never escape either the burdens or the payment; but it is equally certain that she will attempt to do both. Woman's revelation to herself as a person has done more than the Industrial Revolution or the Machine Age to give a new aspect to all her relations. Emancipation seems to have freed her from old social restraints by making her mistress of her own destiny. Before, woman walked in very narrow paths set out for her in remote ages by the society which capitalized her sex for its advantage. Now, as a free agent she seems able to choose, bound though she is by nature, by custom, and by need of social approval. In a new world will woman take advantage of a new freedom? Will the appeal of liberty blind her to the dangers of exercising that too fully and freely? Back to nature has its own place; but civilization is too thin a veneer to be stripped off recklessly. Humanity has paid a high price for the little civilization it has achieved; and much of that civilization has had a very high protective value for women. Women may be emotional, but they have always been noted for their common

[14] Since 1920 there has been some Congressional and state legislation by which the civic status of married women has been improved.

sense in doing the thing which was probably best for them and wisest for their children.

Independence seeks equality. Equality demands an abolition of all discrimination between the sexes. The first thing to go has been the double standard. One would like to think that economic independence, by making women self-supporting, has brought men to the moral level of women. The evidence does not show this. Prostitution has declined. Is it true as some believe that this decline is due to "competition of the amateur"? A strange maladjustment in our thought and laws is noticeable in the attitude of some courts. Tribunals constituted for the administration of justice have unconsciously and unintentionally used their authority to aid these vampires in collecting quasi-blackmail from their prey. This injustice is done because it is necessary, now as it has been in the past, to protect feminine innocence. Under the new order it is not always easy to ascertain which party is victim.

Many who have never heard of Havelock Ellis and have no knowledge of his sincere attempt to understand this critical problem would agree with him that sex relations are the affair of the individuals concerned. Materials gathered by Edward Westermarck indicate that all savage tribes regulate sex relations and prescribe marriage conditions. The extensive researches of Charles W. Margold show that all organized groups exercise social control over sex problems of all their people. Evidently the new woman in the new world will accept two bases for the solution of this important problem: in reaching out toward a more satisfactory civilization, we hope a finer one, she will stress justice and freedom but will accept social control as desirable and protective. Judging from feminine influence in the past the solution of sex problems will be decided by women for women.

From the standpoint of marriage and the family it may be well to remember the old saying that it takes two to make a bargain. Even if only the bride counts at the wedding, man must not be neglected too much as a factor in the family of the future. Men may have changed less than women, in this changing world, for they had less to change, industrially, legally and politically. The family cannot afford to reckon without its host or "head." What would be the use of swinging from a "patriarchal" family to one "matriarchal," if both parties, including the man, are free?

The problem of the new family becomes acute for young people in this new age. Desirable high standards of living postpone the age of marriage. Prolonged school and college training does not reduce it. In the recent depression several million boys and girls have been graduated who have never been able to get permanent jobs. Regardless of whether these young people prefer to marry or not, they cannot do so. Even if these delays or handicaps to marriage did not exist, what would be their attitude toward marriage? The prevalence of birth control may reduce the costs of family life, physical and financial. It may even make possible a "family" life in which both the man and the woman continue their former work, without the care and the joy of children. But does its use increase the desire for marriage or decrease it? If it makes possible temporary alliances or trial marriages, there is certainly a debatable question whether it has helped the changing family. There can hardly be debate that if it has not changed the family somewhat, it certainly will do so.

In school and home scarcely a beginning has been made of the necessary preparation for sane sex life. The transition from an age of silence to one of knowledge bristles with difficulties. At one hand stands the Scyllic danger of shipwreck because modern youth may learn too much. At the other hand lies the whirlpool of inherent drives and passions, unexplained and misunderstood, ready to engulf the ignorant and unskilled mariner in the troubled waters that separate childhood from maturity. If the schools give nothing, they seem negligent. If their instruction is indirect and general, they may fail, as the church does, to establish connection between the lesson taught and the problem faced. If the instruction is direct and pointedly human, it may easily magnify interest in a subject already exaggerated in the thought of many adolescents. Business men are asking, and even demanding, that the schools offer more character instruction. The world, changing from old controls to new, is finding constantly greater demand for the individual to know and face the terrific problems of the new age, individual and social. It is possible that we may measure the success of secondary education in the next generation very largely by its willingness to face and its capacity to work out approaches, treatments and training which will give our youth this necessary help and guidance.

The solution of this difficult problem is social, not educational. For the vast majority there is a constantly lengthening period between the age at which a person becomes sexually mature and that when marriage is possible. New types of education, unusual self-control, and new religious or social sanctions must safeguard necessary standards of morality. A new procedure as well as a new conscience may be required for an ancient problem. A dormant public must arouse to the need of discovering new standards and of working out new culture patterns that fit human nature and represent a gain over the past.

CHANGED ATTITUDES TOWARD THE FAMILY

The Renaissance stressed individualism. Political revolution was started to protect individual rights, but individualism is affecting the family today more than it did Renaissance society or eighteenth-century government. This individualism is not a theoretical one, nor is it concerned primarily with membership in society. Luckily it did not develop among the younger members of America, and to a less extent of Europe, until the individualism of the Renaissance had expended much of its force, until the individualism of the nineteenth century had yielded to economic solidarity and social democracy in the twentieth century. American government may not yet have become highly socialized; but at least our political leaders no longer think primarily in terms of individual freedom. Fortunately, our young people are conscious of their place in modern life. With more and better education, they appreciate the rights of others and the duty all owe to their fellows.

Socialization and the family

The process of socialization, which is a marked characteristic of modern life, gives promise of a better home than that of either past or present. The youth who does not demand some independence in middle adolescence is as unnatural as was scientific child training in the patriarchal family. Temporarily we may have overturned the Pauline injunction to read: parents obey your children in the Lord. But the self-assertion which may be back of the revolt of modern youth against an arbitrary paternalism may be the hopeful sign of a better family and a more unified home. Youthful self-development, together with social maturity of the mother of the family, stands for family growth and advantage. If the best home unity is not a consolidation under some boss, then the modern home is more unified if less solid than the old.

Religion and the family

In the beginning, family and religion may have had no close connection. This is doubtful because sex plays a large part in taboo—although sex is undoubtedly less important than Dr. Sigmund Freud would have us believe—and taboo usually carried with it a religious sanction. However society may have felt at first, long before the dawn of history the family had become an integral part of social organization, and religion was the chiefest phase of social life. In the pre-Christian epoch religion was closely associated with sex and with the family. Ancestor worship was one of the commonest of all primitive religions and practices. The Old Testament and the sacred writings of other races than the Hebrews teem with rites that protect family life and the customs of greatest value to the family.

The Christian era ushered in a new set of standards which almost created a new family. The individual was now a person, was possessed of a human soul, valuable in the sight of God if not of man. Women and slaves made up a large part of the early congregations, and to women came a new sanctity for marriage and the home. In the Sermon on the Mount a very high standard of sexual virtue was urged. When the Christian religion became universal throughout Europe, the permanent monogamous family was assured for at least fifteen centuries.

In theory the Catholic world holds rather literally to severe standards of sex morality after marriage as well as before. Protestantism has been more liberal, and some years ago the Federal Council advocated birth control among married couples. Their plan was not accepted by most Protestant denominations. It is doubtful whether the moral standards of Catholic countries are higher than those of Protestant peoples; but that may be a matter of race rather than of religion.

We live in a changing age which has already affected religion more than it has changed the home. Control of marriage is no longer the prerogative of the church. In some countries a civil wedding is obligatory. A justice of the peace would look ludicrous in threatening damnation to those who do not walk the straight path of the old Catholic Christian virtue. When religion is unnecessary for the making of marriage ties, why have religious scruples about breaking family bonds? Since hell-fire may not punish those who dare unmarry and re-marry, many argue possibly it will not threaten those who do not keep their vows strictly and literally. If religion and the family are to be reunited, the old sanctions may apply but former threats certainly will be futile.

Possible and Probable Family Reorganization

To ultra-conservatives there is no problem of reorganization, simply one of continuing that which the past has held in high esteem. To radicals the problem is not one of reorganization, but largely of discontinuance. The solution probably will lie somewhere between these two extremes. *In all times the influence of social heritage has in the long run outweighed the substitution of sharp social innovation.* Even if for a time society departs widely from past standards, the social structure tends to right itself in ways long acceptable. Sometimes the innovation is more natural, and, for the individual, psychologically more advantageous, even though tradition furnishes set patterns which are easier to follow. In social progress nurture frequently triumphs over nature; or what is civilization for?

Adaptations to modern conditions

Democracy has affected the modern family, and its lessons are valuable to those watching the reorganization of the old family. When western absolutism was replaced by democracy, a boss-ridden family tended to disappear. At present, democracy is facing a crisis; its future is problematic and its success as a permanent form of social organization is questioned.[15] Will the family, becoming democratic, pass through the same stages of uncertainty and disorganization? Success to either home or nation involves the recognition of the fact that democracy is social rather than individual, that it is a form of group organization. The process of creating any institution truly democratic is psychological and sociological rather than personal or political. Personal liberty for the members of a household is possible only when they recognize their dependence upon one another.

In the reorganization of the home, account must be taken of the functions inevitably performed by the family and of the trends and tendencies of modern life affecting those functions. William F. Ogburn gives seven functions as those of the historic family. Two of these, the religious and the educational, have disappeared almost entirely. The protective and the economic functions decline if the parents do not live together or if the children are committed to institutions. The extent to which the other characteristics of the family and the home may continue depends in part upon human nature, in part upon social demands, in part upon shift in the interests and desires of modern society. In the light of changing conditions the accepted norms may be changing also.

When is monogamy not monogamy? If the partners may change like those in an old-fashioned quadrille, the name is meaningless. Many today are worried over the increase of divorce in recent years. The problem is a serious one and must be faced squarely. Is the family, as a social unit, possible without a marked degree of permanence? If the majority follow those flappers who measure their age not by years but by the number of their husbands, no family organization is possible. Instead we have a kaleidoscopic series of

[15] Chs. XII, XIII.

moving pictures of family life—a new type of polygamy with several wives in succession instead of simultaneously. It would be necessary to wait for the resurrection to discover whose wife or husband anyone happened to be, because it would be difficult to determine the fact except at some fleeting moment. Particularly is this true if there are children, and especially children of more than one marriage. To whose family do these unhappy little ones belong? In whose home and under whose guidance will they grow to adulthood?

Paramount as is permanence, we must not make a fetish of it if it can be secured only at the sacrifice of comradeship. It should be a family asset, not a liability. From the standpoint of the man and the woman who marry, family success, probably with some fair degree of permanence, depends upon their fitness to form a permanent partnership, their skill in adapting themselves to each other, their capacity to work out their mutual problems, and their willingness and ability to live together in harmony. Compatibility is an indefinite and elusive trait; but without it no future home is possible.

"Whither mankind" is a pertinent question for the individual as well as for humanity. To one bound to a life of routine there seems a true analogy to the squirrel in the cage, constantly whirling his wheel. A large part of the human race has found its religion in a hope of reward, future because impossible here. It is largely a compensation for the trials and tribulations inseparable from earthly conditions. With the weakening of old controls in many walks of life, the individual and the group must discover and voluntarily use new types of self-control and self-development. Prohibitions are inadequate, for character-achievement is positive not negative. In each one's experience some leadership is inevitable if he is to be free and self-directing. *For home and family life of the future the man and the woman who have gained their full stature by their own self-direction unquestionably will surpass as a good husband and a good wife those led and trained through obedience.* Unless unwilling to accept the discipline offered by the hardships and problems of matrimony, couples of this type should give promise of a successful future home.

Whither the family?

Will "the women of tomorrow hold to standards of equality, companionship, economic partnership and dual responsibility" or will "women's newly won freedom threaten to bring about a disintegration of society, and an increasing aversion to marriage on the part of men"? It takes two to make a bargain. Will men accept the conditions women try to prescribe? Will the pendulum swing from an unjust patriarchal family to one equally unjust but matriarchal? Shall we accept as fact Myrick Booth's list of rights of husband and wife? After enumerating several of the wife, the statement ends: *"Husbands' Rights—None."* The solution of the problem, after all, rests largely with the women. The maternal instinct of woman and her desire to conform will probably overcome her tendency to diverge far from present standards. But if the women leaders of the future are not broader-visioned, and more public-minded, than the average men leaders in the field of present business or politics, we well may fear for the future. To place upon woman the whole responsibility would be as unwise as it is unfair. Too many practical decisions must be made in adolescent years when emotion blinds judgment. Probably the transition period of the mid-twentieth century may be the most difficult. After another generation the worst adjustments may have been made. If we are optimists and have faith in human nature and the future, we shall look for a home and family quite superior to any that past or present has witnessed.

Examined from the standpoint of possible substitutions, rather than that of the family failures, this whole question can be considered more sanely. We need not bother so much then with what is wrong with marriage or what is right with marriage, as to consider, if not marriage as we ordinarily understand the term, then what? Human nature will still remain human nature. Biologists and psychologists always refer to the two great instincts—the desire for food and the sex desire. What is personally beneficial to the individual should be reconciled with what is socially desirable. The problem becomes serious when the modern world must accept a delay in marriage due to an increase in the period of dependence and preparation for life. The difficulty is not simply one of the new woman. It may center even more on the new man, anxious to continue the male dominance of the past, and unwilling to accept standards which spell equality or the standards which women may seek to prescribe.

What might be satisfactory, or at least acceptable, in the case of youthful couples without children, may easily be inexpedient with older couples or in families with them. Plato's care of all children by the state or the plan of Soviet Russia would save us pampered and spoiled darlings. But would it give them lives happy and successful enough to compensate for their impersonal training? In comparing the probable family of the future with the family of the past, in dealing with the norms or standards which are likely to be most satisfactory and successful, the needs of children may well outrank the desires of adults.

From the standpoint of society, what is best? From the standpoint of a changing civilization, what is probable? Humanity gains most when its institutions are most natural, when the members of the group are relatively free and satisfied, and when the institutions fit its needs. A highly dynamic society is rarely content with static institutions, and with a permanent status for each class of its members. Our present world, at least among western peoples, is highly dynamic; in fact some think it is charged with dynamite and likely to blow up. Revolutions have served a useful purpose in destroying outworn systems and régimes; rarely is a revolutionary movement directly constructive.

The new type of family is likely to be unified, democratic, and adaptable. How much permanence is necessary to secure unity will be a practical question for the future rather than an academic one for the present. How much freedom the members may possess within the home and outside depends less upon the independence they use than upon the interdependence they accept. America is fortunate above other countries in having little first-hand experience with traditional modes of family organization, which are being completely reorganized. Already well on the way toward an improved

Conclusion

family type, Americans should help to give the world a really modernized family, progressive, true to human nature and conforming to the requirements of the Twentieth-Century Renaissance.

Possibly our conservatism in changing the family is representative of the Missouri trait of wanting to be shown something better. Probably our apparently unintelligent retention of past molds is due to fear that we cannot invent and reorganize wisely. Undoubtedly we fail to realize the strength of the grip, or the devastating effect, of the past. *If it took five or six millennia to abandon the primitive hand-method of making goods, how can we expect in a century or two to reorganize society's most important human institution?*

XVII

TRENDS AND TENDENCIES IN EDUCATION

The individual re-learns the accumulated experience of the
race. Education may, therefore, present an epitome of past
achievements worth knowing, understanding, and using.
Without education in the broader sense, civilization would
continue with difficulty from generation to generation. The
social heritage is based on effecting a continuous stream of
accomplishment. The torch is taken up by successive groups,
presumably bearing the light higher unless accident or calamity prevent. This double function of education should count
more than it does in the re-training of modern youth. Society
is almost exclusively concerned with passing on the *mores*.
Education pretends to train for the future, but in ninety-nine
cases out of one hundred that future is of the individual not
of society. The preparation, if there be preparation, is for a
place in a society such as that which has been transmitted.
Schools have been concerned with glorifying the past and
training students to attain the ideals represented by past
achievements. In static societies this is unobjectionable, in
dynamic groups it is fatal. Knowledge of the changes which
are occurring today command relatively little attention. Our
respect for the negative side of education looms very large,
the positive dwindles until we echo James Harvey Robinson's
oft repeated statement that there is too much teaching and
too little learning in our schools and colleges.

In past dynamic periods, such as those represented by the
Renaissance or Reformation or by the French Revolution and
the new democracy, education usually was reorganized. A
new type was sought and, in time, developed. Today American and European schools are seeking to keep abreast of
rapid developments in business and in general life. More

education has been deemed a necessity. The nineteenth century accepted with reluctance public high-school education, but many states and some foreign countries now require completion of the secondary school to meet the new standards of democracy in the Machine Age. Educators are reaching out to find subjects, courses, and methods of training better than the past has provided. It is doubtful whether one generation will "arrive." In its first century the Industrial Revolution had made relatively little progress. It yet remains to be seen whether our apparent advance is simply a reaction against those old educational products which were least worth while. Pessimists are content if the best of the old is saved from the innovations of extravagant politicians or schoolmen who want something different. Optimists ask the schools of tomorrow to aid and promote modern changes which will give us a better and finer civilization.

Democracy in Education

Why education is free, public and compulsory   Modern education is free, public, compulsory mass training. It is a commonplace that democracy is impossible without an educated citizenry. The political excuse is inadequate as an explanation for general education in a democracy. If countries which call themselves democratic were truly self-governing, more thorough and fairly intensive preparation would be inevitable. The individual as a person, as well as a citizen, needs a training which examines and develops his capacities. Preparation for life is more than preparation for the future holding of office or political coöperation. Citizenship is social rather than political. It involves and includes multifold relationships, some distinctly personal but economic, some preëminently civic, but others social and of many types. The democratic state must accept its obligation of making the most of the group as well as of the individual; this cannot be done without education far more universal and successful than any we have had.

To secure a comprehension of our social environment, to find better the place which the citizen may and must occupy in it, to improve relationships in which each finds himself or which it is desirable for him to establish: these are among the primary purposes of public education, at least above the elementary and grammar school level. The name *social orientation* is well applied to this task and objective of modern education at secondary and upper levels. As we have discovered in the course of these pages, this task is not so simple as it might appear on the surface, partly because it is not easy to discover the social heritage and its influence upon the associations and institutions of today, partly because those organizations which are both political and economic, or economic and social and incidentally public, can be studied rather easily in *form* but not so readily in fact. There is great danger that information in regard to the structure of our institutions and systems and present economic and social order may pass for knowledge. It may underlie the necessary knowledge, and thorough knowledge may be essential to understanding and comprehension of our present world and the American scene. From the public point of view the great essential of public education for a democratic society in this changing world is better school organization and learning opportunities, in order that educational leaders shall not face too great a task in combating tradition, ignorance and prejudice among the masses.

Very few in America or in Europe now believe that free, compulsory, public education is undesirable. It is *free* because ability among students does not coincide with parental wealth; and opportunity must be offered to all. It is free because the public accepts its obligation of providing a knowledge of the social inheritance, to which every child in its midst is entitled. It is free because democracy wishes to give every member information regarding the duties of citizenship and the opportunities for earning a living which are furnished by society. It is free because a little education is a dangerous thing when much is required to discover present trends and anticipate future development.

Education is *public* because the public is disinterested yet much concerned with proper training for children and youth. It is public because of the growing solidarity of society of which we are members. It is public because the whole community, the whole nation must accept the responsibility for the right preparation of all, in many ways and for many future possibilities,[1] including those considered in this chapter. These are days of propaganda, but propaganda is not alone characteristic of the twentieth century. It is found in every age and clime and in every group, secular or religious. Human nature is not fundamentally judicial; it is tempermentally prejudiced. Unconsciously we take sides, and the side is usually the one we were brought up to understand and like. If we dislike the things we are taught, then we are prejudiced in favor of the opposite. Balanced judgment is almost as rare as the vacuum which nature is supposed to abhor. To avoid propaganda of locality, or sect, or special associations, the public pays the instructors of youth. In turn it instructs them not to proclaim special creeds, business slogans, and local prejudices, unless demanded by law or desired by local boards of education.

The larger though unreasoned ideas and ideals of the whole people can thus be presented clearly and effectively. If patriotism were little different from prejudice, if national ideals and international standards were still provincial, teacher and pupil would be obliged to accept them. They are the best the group has and they are the social patterns according to which the group acts. If perchance these norms are the standards of the preceding generation, of an outgrown culture, of a partisan dictator, civilization pays a high price for public control of youth training.

Education is *compulsory* because foundations must be laid in immaturity, when the need and the purposes are not apparent to the pupil. It is compulsory not only in attendance but in a minimum of acquisition because the younger members must discover why modern man is the heir of all the ages. It is compulsory because society owes an obligation to itself as well as to its youth to prepare for something better than what exists. The individual and society cannot escape the demand of the times for a preparation without which the

[1] See pp. 296–299.

future will fail. In all ages society has accepted institutions and ideas as among its most precious possessions. From the days of Theodosius the Great to the early nineteenth century the state church was such an institution. It is difficult for us to think of heresy as being in the same category with treason; but that was inevitable when religion as well as politics was an essential of the state. Just as formerly each adult was compelled to enroll in a church and now each mature citizen must accept civic obligations especially in time of war, so each child must gain preparation for adulthood.

The problem of compulsory education presents many interesting questions and furnishes a most suggestive analogy. If education is to be made compulsory, how long shall students be compelled to remain in the public school? Will the limit be the same for those of rather low ability as for the average? If a school system has not changed an old type of education intended for rather selected students, how wise is compulsory study of semi-academic or other general courses which the students of lower mentality cannot possibly learn or use? If education is compulsory, is there not special reason for giving equal opportunities everywhere rather than having one county give twice as much, or furnish twice as good schools, as its neighbors? Should one state have poorer school opportunities over a shorter school year, than a neighboring state can and does afford? If students are compelled to remain in school long after their interest has departed and far beyond any real gain in skills, training or knowledge, how wise is compulsory education, for example, through high school, as a public policy? [2]

[2] The problem of *compulsory education* is analogous to a social problem of *compulsory work opportunities*. One reason we have compulsory education at all is the nature of our society and the fact that training for life, and life work, in it is essential. It has been absurd to deny children under fourteen the right to work where no educational opportunities were offered to boys and girls twelve and thirteen years of age. That, however, is not the main problem of the present day. It is this. If opportunities for work are rather limited, although everyone must live either through his own efforts or through public help of some kind, *does it not become a matter of compulsion to our economic organization that it provide necessary and possible work for adults, just as our schools must provide necessary and valuable training for children and youth?*
Possibly the analogy should not be carried too far. But after all, *the*

If education is free and public, what of its aims and purposes? What should it include? Democracy seems new and modern, but among the Greeks there was well developed, at least by the leaders, the idea of education in and for the state. As Plato declares in the *Republic:* the end of the state is the virtue and happiness of the citizens, a result achieved through education. Education is, therefore, a primary function of the state. Aristotle in his *Politics* realized the need of adapting the educational system to the ends desired by the public: "The educational system must always be relative to the particular polity . . . *e.g.,* the democratic character of a democracy, an oligarchical of an oligarchy and so on, and, the higher this character of the citizens, the higher is the policy it produces." [3] Again, "as the end proposed to the state as the whole is one, it is clear that the education of all the citizens must be one and the same, and the superintendence of it a public affair rather than in private hands." [4] As our economic and social system is larger and more complicated than that of the Greek city states, it calls for a more complete and a better training to cope with pressing problems, individual or collective.

From past
to present

Possibly the reason that we have so little democracy in government is the result of so little education in our old democracy and so little democracy in our former education. A few years ago less than half of those who entered the first grade finished the fifth, and only one in four entered high school. Of the latter, less than one-fourth finally graduated. How can we expect to be governed intelligently by men and women who have had no better preparation than that? Today the majority of those who begin school complete most of the grammar work as well as that given in the primary grades.

fundamental reasons for compulsory education at public expense are very much like the public reasons for compulsory work opportunities. Shall we say also at public expense? Let us hope that the schools are a true part of the general system, doing their part successfully in preparation, since the economic organization has its responsibility to keep all employables employed. The school, therefore, must try to reduce the percentage of those unemployable. Somehow business should be able to increase the percentage of those employed.

[3] Aristotle, *Politics,* Book V, ch. I (pp. 222–23, Welldon Ed.).
[4] *Ibid.*

How much better educated are they? They can read, but do they? When they read, what do they read, how intelligently do they understand?

Assuming careful mastery of the subjects offered, how much has the grammar school graduate been prepared for citizenship or life? The learning of a generation ago certainly did not fit the needs or requirements of any individual. It was too distinctly intellectual; too little personal, emotional, or social. The academic mind might be well sharpened on the grind-stone of the classics and pure mathematics. But was intelligence tested? Were the mental capacities enlarged? Did the student understand himself better or know how to live with his fellows?

The methods of literal memorizing prevalent everywhere in the mid-nineteenth century gave place to a saner procedure in learning materials rather than words. Then examinations counted more than the daily preparation; because facts that were not remembered were of little value. The sponge needed only to absorb; but the pedant had to squeeze out the erudition. The danger of a little learning was avoided, but accumulators of great masses of information, walking encyclopedias, paraded as valedictorians. Frequently they surprised the critics by almost as marked success after commencement as they had reached before. Although I. Q.'s had not been discovered, this training sometimes discovered intelligence and set it upon new paths in which mental ability really counted. The psychologist might declaim that there is no transfer of learning. Usually there is not with a conglomeration of facts; but frequently the trained mind of a Michelson or a Millikan made its successes in new fields of research, wonderfully equipped by the severe discipline of the classroom.

Discipline has yielded to interest, academic learning to socialized curricula, the teaching of subjects to the training of the individual. How much better are we educated? How much more successfully are we prepared to take our places in a democracy? How much more democratic are our educational systems? Textbook learning may be well on the wane, but are we getting better results from diagnostic tests together with specific, factual, and objective checks? In so far as work has been made real, interesting, and vital, the gain has been great. If the interest is in education, and not in everything else, there should be more self-development under the new plan than was possible under the old. If the pupils share in making decisions of courses they are to take, or voluntarily prepare work formerly accepted with reluctance, if rules are made but not enforced because pupil cooperation makes enforcement unnecessary, then we should have more education for democracy and more democracy in education.

Some changed plans and objectives

In our discussion of public education as an evidence of socialization [5] we noted the organization in the mid-nineteenth century of elementary schools almost everywhere. We noted especially, but almost entirely in the last half century, the development of free public high-school education. We did not note the movement starting early in the nineteenth century for the creation of state universities, in which practically no tuition is charged except for special courses. Nor did we take into account the establishment of local public colleges which give only the work for the first two years of college, usually known as junior colleges. As we discovered, the students in these advanced institutions who are receiving collegiate education without cost, or much cost, for tuition number not very much less than a quarter million.

The eight-year primary and grammar school arrangement, introduced probably from Germany, although a continuation of the post-Renaissance English schools, remains the normal type found throughout the United States. However, in a large number of cities an average of three or four *junior high schools* per community has been established to take care of the work formerly presented in grades seven, eight and nine. The importance of the junior high schools is not in the fact that they reach a million students, but that they present a totally different type of work and opportunity for students of those years. Instead of giving more of the same thing that

[5] Pp. 291–294.

has been presented in the elementary and lower grammar grades, these schools are distinguished by introduction of new exploratory, combined, or fusion courses, a totally new attitude and atmosphere of student relationship to school and fellow students and by departmental or semi-departmental organization, with specialization of teaching staff. It would be difficult to appraise any special feature of the junior high school as representing a change from the old type of education more important than any other because so many of them are distinctively new, progressive, and forward-looking.

Not only in the *junior high school*, but to a very large extent in the kindergarten and primary grades of many school systems, has *the type of instruction and student participation been changed radically*. Memorizing even of a selective type has yielded first place to student participation in group projects and activities in which the student has a real part. By this participation new interest is aroused and new attitudes are created. The junior high may be somewhat more formal in its organization and techniques than is the elementary system in which the student activity programs have been developed most. In junior high, however, opportunity is offered for *student organization, guidance in home room,* and *forms of student participation in which the students get actual experience* working with their fellows under the guidance, only, of their teachers. Of what value is it to have education made compulsory above the sixth grade if the student's reaction to it is like that of a generation ago, so well characterized by Mr. Dooley when he declared that it doesn't matter what we teach the boy, provided he doesn't like it. Fortunately interest really has supplanted discipline. Frequently it is as hard in this generation to keep the student away from the school as it was in those earlier years to make him attend.

In the opinion of most observers, the old *high school,* a four-year institution which is still the prevalent type in the United States, has yielded less to the onslaught of the new age than any other part of the whole educational set-up, except possibly the more conservative four-year old type college. Yet here, as in the junior high schools, we find a marked shift in the type

of course that is offered and taken, especially in the shift from
academic toward practical or technical courses. A considerable
change in methods of instruction has been made, new objectives are used, new student attitudes sought. The classics
have yielded most, but mathematics has suffered sharply, and
to some extent modern foreign languages. These subjects, of
course, are more traditional, more disciplinary, more scholastic
than the new age seems to demand. The social sciences have
come in for quite a considerable share of attention, but, curiously enough, history, which is frequently regarded as a social
science, reached its peak before the World War and has declined rather sharply in the last decade. In fact, the protest
against the old type of semi-factual history has made the progress of the newer, interpretative type rather difficult. The demand for fusion of history with other social studies or of
history with English, or with other subjects more or less related, has gone on apace in progressive school systems, but
chiefly in the junior high schools.

Newer even than the junior high school is the *junior college,*
an institution which carries secondary education two years beyond its former limit. The junior college is preëminently the
opportunity of the student who is not yet sufficiently trained
for making a living in our present world, highly competitive
from the worker point of view. Most junior colleges offer also
to the students who cannot attend an institution except in their
own locality the first two years of a regular college curriculum.
The junior college, although compelled usually to conform
with the requirements of state universities for its regular college students, especially in academic courses, has real freedom
in organizing and improving new types of *terminal courses*
for students who wish to go beyond the high school and for
whom high school training was really inadequate. A former
United States Commissioner of Education urged that communities having a four-year junior high school should have it
followed by a four-year junior college. The experience with
this type of school organization in and around Chicago and in
Pasadena and other western communities shows the opportu-

nity which a six-four-four plan has in modernizing the whole system at this upper high school and lower college level.

The colleges and universities have changed in giving much more varied and enriched curricula than was formerly the case. Outwardly the four-year college has changed relatively little, but if one were to take a census of the students enrolled in different courses a shift is noticeable from decade to decade and from generation to generation. Even as late as the World War a course of this type would not be found within the classic walls of any collegiate institution. The purpose of a college education has changed in ways too numerous for examination.

THE PROBLEM OF MASS EDUCATION IN THE MACHINE AGE

Technical education is the chief response to preparation for life in an age of machines and power. The classics are passé for life, and higher mathematics is too hard and meaningless for the practical-minded captain of industry or student. If it is true that our affairs are directed in part by those who never could work out difficult problems in Algebra or pass a standardized test in English, something is wrong either with our preparation or with the character of that leadership, possibly with both. The substitution for mental discipline of hand-training techniques leaves us in an embarrassing position. Mechanical experience seldom gives insight to other than the manipulation of certain machines, the capacity to do a definite thing. Skills rather than abilities are thus acquired. Trade schools, a minor part of present-day education, can never be justified as being the desired public education in a democracy, Machine Age or no Machine Age. Fortunately technical education has made great advance in secondary school and beyond. The excellent series of articles published under the editorship of Charles A. Beard and entitled *Toward Civilization* justifies faith in that type of training and its possible solutions of present difficulties. *The technological age has been more useful in destroying old school systems than in creating new.* It has helped us get rid of medieval courses and norms, establishing in their place useful subjects and more practical meth-

Results of mass education

ods. To make our education utilitarian might modernize it but probably would not improve it.

Criticisms of our schools usually simmer down to one of three things: we are turning out students who are too much alike; our graduates are not educated; our schools are too expensive. There is a conflict between the first of these and the other two. Handmade goods cannot compete in price with those produced by machines. There is a regularity and a symmetry, but very little individuality, to machine products whether of factory or school. Give more individuality, allow more attention of teacher to pupil, and the cost will be greater. Extensive studies have been made which have proved to those who made them and to administrators who use them that education in large groups is just as satisfactory if not more complete than training with small numbers. Comparisons by standardized tests show that the students who have had this bulk experience stand quite as high as those who have been coddled in smaller groups. Why not? Machine-made articles measure higher on norms of uniformity and possibly of symmetry than do goods made in other ways. First-class books can be turned out on our large high-powered rotary presses superior to those which could be produced on the old-fashioned double-page hand press. If we were dealing with inanimate materials instead of with human beings, the superiority of mass production would be expected, judged by usual methods of tests and measurements. Do standardized tests, however, measure even the knowledge, not to mention the comprehension or gain in power, we wish the students to possess? Mass education is inevitable and *sometimes* highly desirable. Is it not far better to place five hundred college students under the lecture leadership of the best man in that field, especially if he is an experienced and magnetic speaker, than to expose them in small groups to poorly paid, inexperienced graduate instructors?

In education as in business we frequently get no more than we pay for. Look up the reports of the National Bureau of Economic Research. Compare the pay of teachers with that given to clergymen, locomotive engineers, or some of the newer learned professions.[6] Notice that in 1934 more than thirty per cent of all teachers in America were receiving an annual income lower than the 1933 code requirements for the poorest class of unskilled labor. Is it any wonder if our normal schools, in spite of bright, interesting girls who teach until they marry, or our schools of education, fail to attract in large numbers those whose interests are intellectual? Undoubtedly the teaching profession is thronged with those who "love to teach," who are sufficiently public spirited to sacrifice pay to service, or whose social-mindedness holds them in a profession often lauded but more often "damned with faint praise." Or is the praise omitted?

If we must have mass education and if the masses must become larger and more nearly average, how shall we give the superior students the education to which they are entitled by their capacities, and by their intellectual drive? If we are to emerge happily from the Twentieth-Century Renaissance we must have more and better leadership. Leaders may be born not trained; but only a short-sighted public would overlook the danger from unpreparedness. Who shall estimate the loss from a universal education that sacrifices the capacity of the able student? Democracy has always overpaid its routine workers and underpaid those who formulate its policies and direct its affairs. This is a heritage from our eighteenth-century standards and ideals of equality. Leadership among those who teach and special instruction for those who are trained as leaders does not mean an aristocracy of knowledge which is inconsistent with true democracy.[7] From the standpoint of student and public the chief fault of mass education is this willingness to accept the same levels for all which characterized the old individualist democracy, already well on its way to the scrapheap.

To the taxpayer the problem is not one of what we shall teach, or how we shall learn, but "how much does it cost?" Overburdened as he is, the mounting expenditures for education make him rail at our spend-thrift schools. Expenditures

School finance and the world of business

[6] Leven, *Income in the Various States*, pp. 101, 103.
[7] *Cf.* pp. 365–371.

for schools are high. In 1926 the total exceeded two billion dollars, whereas a half century ago the amount was only seventy-eight millions. That remarkable increase represents to some extent the change from the old régime of rural life and individualism to the Machine Age. As recently as 1920 American schools cost only a billion dollars. What opportunities for wastes and fads, if not for graft, is represented by the present cost! Possibly the increase has been due to our realization that democracy must be made safe for the world; possibly it represents more preparation for the world problems we are facing. Possibly we are responding to the public demand that we end the amazing illiteracy and ignorance revealed by the World War examinations. Possibly more public education due to new laws and new higher levels of training has made this difference. Possibly we look upon good education as the best of investments!

Although most school expenditures are for teachers' salaries, many will be amazed to learn that it was not until 1920 that the average American teacher received an annual income of as much as a thousand dollars. It did not take the depression long to bring the average back to three figures, either, for school expenses were reduced twenty per cent between 1930 and 1934. How much shall we reduce that stipend for those to whom we have given the responsibility of training our young people? Even if our schools give ten or twelve years of training—and that unfortunately is still far more than most have—it does so three times out of four at *a cost considerably below a thousand dollars per pupil, for a training and service that must be the foundation of the whole life.* That is little more than the original cost of a five-year car; and below the total cost of the automobile to its owner.

When we compare the increased cost of schools with the increase in the cost of all government and the increase of national income, we find that the *percentage* of all taxes spent for schools was slightly lower in 1926 than in 1913; we discover that, in the eight years from 1921 to 1929, teachers' salaries did not increase as rapidly as did the wages of all American artisans. Our schools, therefore, are not the spendthrifts

that we may have thought them; rather are they spending too
little, although they are costing the taxpayer too much. What
would you think of the family which spends on its children in
the home as small a percentage of its income as our nation
spends upon them in our schools? Of the eighty billion dollars of annual national income before 1929, less than two and
one-half were devoted to formal education. Of all government
expenses after 1929 none except "capital outlay" was cut so
much as education. There are many luxuries, including liquor,
for which we probably spend as much as we do for the schools.

One reason our schools seem expensive is the inexcusable
dependence upon that tax bequeathed us by nineteenth-century
agricultural America—the general property tax. To meet the
vital needs of America at present we need a reallocation of
public funds. Since the World War Uncle Sam has had far
more than his share from what should be the chief source of
all taxes—income. On the contrary, the schools are financed
by realty, a form of wealth, including the small home of the
worker and farm land which does not yield two per cent net
on its value. If the schools could command the rates on the
net profits of modern business which Congress has been able to
command, and were Congress dependent upon a land tax, we
should have more schools and fewer battleships. Should we
not prefer Minerva to Mars? Of course we need good roads,
but should our chief item of state and local expenditure be
the highways? Do you recall Will Roger's quip, while the depression was going from bad to worse, that when we went to
the poorhouse, at least we should have good roads clear to
the door?

The age of science, machines, and power calls for more and
better education. A machine civilization, with its accumulated
wealth, makes possible longer and fuller school years, and increases the age at which workers begin earning a living. If
society refuses necessary funds for schools, business will suffer
from the lack of training for the worker, the leader, and the
enterpriser. Big business might acquire a new attitude if not a
conscience. If it fights education, education in turn might
show up the faults and defects, the selfishness and greed

which has always marked profit-making but which are more conspicuous the larger business grows. Education is an essential of a progressive, self-directing society; the present age will fail if it either throttles academic freedom or pulls tight the purse strings of the schools.

WHAT EDUCATION FACES

New standards and methods

The problem which education faces is really too educational for a new world. This new education must be modern and socialized; possibly it must be mechanized to fit a machine civilization; and it must be democratic. If we allow the suggestion of Everett Dean Martin that we are known by the dilemmas we keep, what choice shall we make of this dilemma? We must prepare for the solution of difficult personal and public problems, but we must also work with material much of which cannot be prepared properly or adequately. If mass education means universal educational preparation, we shall not rise much above the level of the achievement attainable by the average. That means that we are placing a premium upon mediocrity. Again citing Martin, "In the supremacy of man as mass the mediocre man, he who in all things corresponds to type, and is reducible to average, is King."[8]

There must be adaptation of the type of training and development to the capacities and the interest of the person who is educated. The subjects taught should be offered at the level of the students instructed. Some of our instruction now is above that level, much of it below. College presidents may complain about inexcusable waste in expending five thousand dollars on the education of a fifty dollar boy. They may urge that three-quarters of the students in college should be doing something else. In the formative years the classroom is not necessarily the only source of education; and it may not be the best. If a man spends his life on more or less routine things day after day, how helpful is intensive study of some literary or scientific theme? Are student activities a good preparation for treadmill toil by the slave of a machine? If the classroom robs a person of the opportunity to begin out-

[8] Martin, E. D., *The Meaning of a Liberal Education*, p. 155.

side work which he can do better at fifteen than he can at twenty, are those five years well spent?

When the whole of regular training comes at the beginning of life, whereas the need of helpful suggestions continues throughout the years, it seems odd to carry school education to Commencement and never expect courses beyond that point. We are just beginning to realize how wisely "Commencement" is named. Many a student is never aroused to the importance of study, to the ways in which it will help in his work or his life, until schoolroom doors have closed behind him with the finality of fate. Formerly we believed that adults learn slowly or not at all. Apparently when our minds and thoughts are engrossed with practical problems, we lose habits of study. Thorndike's investigations seem to offer real proof that adult learners are not handicapped by age, that in our later years the mind is plastic and that we are just as teachable as in youth, even if adult fixations make us slower to change.

Will not society help us integrate our lives from the educational, social, and business points of view? What an achievement that would be! Would it mean a lower age as the end of intensive school training and an earlier period as the beginning of life tasks outside of school? Would that involve a combination of business and education, not of the Cincinnati or Antioch type, because it might include most occupations except the learned professions? If business needs shorter hours of work, especially when most women as well as most men become wage-earners, we shall need not only to educate for leisure but we shall also need to work out a healthful and practical educational program for those who continue to learn as they proceed with work.

May not the greatest educational need in dynamic America be the continued training of adults and their constantly improved understanding of the changing world? May not the greatest educational contribution of society to modern civilization be this education for mature citizens? It cannot be compulsory, as well as free and public; for any element of coercion would destroy the very thing we need and are trying to do. It cannot be formal or scholastic or severe and accomplish its real purpose. The new education has therefore substituted for old methods and characteristics many which adult education should probably have. Can it work out courses or arrange discussion groups or perfect plans that will arouse interest, stimulate investigation, open closing minds and motivate abilities? If the world of tomorrow threatens more and more unemployment, unless loads are spread, leisure will be adequate for more "study" in the later years. Can an educational program and procedure be devised and put over which will find the average adult "Barkis is willin'," which will make the transitions of a dynamic civilization easier for individuals and for society?

To be humanly helpful, twentieth-century educational re-adaptation must, first of all, be constructive. The elimination of old social patterns is particularly valuable when outgrown privileges, attitudes, or institutions must be discarded or modified. In a dynamic civilization the carry-over from one generation to another must represent as little as possible those social habits which do not fit into the new life. When the old order changes, the reorganization should modify contradictions, should reduce conflicts, and should work out new adaptations. Maladjustments, whether of institution to need, of individual to his surroundings, of groups to new situations, call for true comprehension of present changes, real leadership in making effectual the readjustment to a different environment. It is the task of the teacher to understand, to explain, to prepare, and to prevent. If civilization as well as business is adrift, his is the responsibility to diagnose, to prescribe, possibly to cure. Too often he is satisfied with tactics, when what is needed is strategy. He must be forward-looking, anticipating inevitable shifts in institutions and in systems, planning for adjustments, personal and social, that may be necessary in the future. The centrifugal tendencies of a twentieth-century renaissance must be studied from many angles, that the underlying trends and tendencies of present reorganization should be apparent, even if they do not stand out sharply and clearly. Somehow the study must be unified and integrated, to give comprehension of the world that is in preparation, for a future that will be successful, if we are trained to make it so.

In recent years the reorganization of education has been a major project of a multitude of education experts, one of the ablest and the most influential of whom is John Dewey, whose educational philosophy has dominated much of the new plans in education. Schools of education have sprung up everywhere. Some of these have maintained laboratories in which the voluminous materials of many subjects have been analyzed and classified. From science, education has borrowed careful and extensive, sometimes intensive, experimentation on particular problems. Business has been copied, in that conferences have been held without end in order to compare notes and work out the best procedure. New techniques have been devised continually. The school profession has been pelted with questionnaires, frequently so numerous and so full as to interfere with the work of the classroom and necessary study by the instructor. Some of this investigation has been done by those who have had little contact or experience with classes or students. Naturally these educationists and teachers have found more points of difference than of agreement. This result has been inevitable if each formulates his own hypothesis or educational theory with which the materials are expected to conform.

The new education [9] has changed from subject, matter, to

Character-istics of the new educa-tion

[9] Several years ago the new aims of education were summarized by William H. Kilpatrick:

"In the first place, we wish an education which does enter the child's life now to remake it.

"In the second place, while the new experiences are being added, we wish the child's personality to be made more and more a well integrated affair.

"In the third place, if we wish an education which enters the child's life now to remake it; if we wish that as new experiences enter the child's life the child's personality will be more and more an integrated affair, education will mean the progressive integration of the meanings of life and experience.

"In the fourth place, we wish to get the progressive integration of meanings in such a way that intelligent self-direction is included; that the self becomes more and more able to get the meanings of a situation, and more and more disposed to obey those meanings.

"In the fifth place, we wish to manage things so as to give the greatest promise that the learner will keep on growing in the ways just described. It can be done. We can build habits so as to keep alive what plasticity exists.

subject, person. Subjects as such are rapidly being discredited because they represent watertight compartments of knowledge, artificial in character and untrue in fact as the old faculties with which the former psychologist endowed human nature. The curriculum has been enriched, not only in the addition of delightful courses but in the quality of personal appeals. If the enrichment were chiefly characteristic of prosperity, the opposite frequently became a public demand in depression. Use is made of an educational psychology, utilizing real knowledge of laws of learning. To discover those laws, as little dependence as possible is placed upon introspective thinking, much upon outward, objective tests and measurements. The science of educational statistics sometimes rivals in intricacy and technical terminology some of the most advanced engineering sciences. We owe a big debt to this earnest groping toward the light of a better day. Fact searchers for truth may give us a fund of information upon which may be built a solid, satisfactory educational system neither antiquated, mechanized, nor standardized. The materials of our present civilization are too vast, the study of child nature and ever-changing youth is too intricate, to make simple the problem of understanding the present and its tendencies. The difficulties are not insurmountable, but intriguing. Kilpatrick, Dewey, and others have stressed the interdependence of a new education and a changing social order.

"It was implied in our introductory survey of the social demands made upon education to-day that the democratic way of life is that in which the identity of interest of the individual and the social is best realized. . . . It is now seen that the positive side of the principle needs attention: namely, the extension of democracy to the creation of the kind of institutions that will effectively and constructively serve the development of *all* individuals. It is at once obvious that this extension affects economic, as well as legal and political, institutions.

"Social arrangements are to be judged ultimately by their

"These are the characteristics of a desirable education.
"This is the vision—let us follow it."

educative effect, by what they do in the way of liberating, organizing, integrating the capacities of men and women, boys and girls. These capacities include esthetic factors, those which lie at the basis of music, literature, painting, architecture in both production and appreciation; intellectual and scientific power and taste; capacities for friendship; and capacities for appropriation and control of natural materials and energies. It is the function of education to see to it that individuals are so trained as to be capable of entering into the heritage of these values which already exist, trained also in sensitiveness to the defects of what already exists and in ability to recreate and improve. But neither of these ends can be adequately accomplished unless people are trained to grasp and be concerned about the effect of social institutions upon individual capacities, and this not just in general but in discriminating detail." [10] "Education must itself assume an increasing responsibility for participation in projecting ideas of social change and taking part in their execution in order to be educative. The great problem of American education is the discovery of methods and techniques by which this more direct and vital participation may be brought about. We have conceived that the office of a philosophy of education at the present time is to indicate this pressing need and to sketch the lines on which alone, in our conception, it can be met. The method of experimental intelligence as the method of action cannot be established as a constant and operative habit of mind and character apart from education. But it cannot be established *within* education except as the activities of the latter are founded on a clear idea of the active social forces of the day, of what they are doing, of their effect, for good and harm, upon values, and except as this idea and ideal are acted upon to direct experimentation in the currents of social life that run outside the school and that condition the effect and determine the educational meaning of whatever the school does." [11]

[10] W. H. Kilpatrick, *et al., The Educational Frontier,* D. Appleton-Century Co., pp. 292–293.
[11] *The Educational Frontier,* p. 319.

In seeking to develop for ourselves and our descendents a juster, better, and more modern social order we probably will not attempt to reach the goal so sharply stressed by Glenn Frank, that education should enable us to *create, comprehend and control a new social order.* "Western education . . . has tragically failed to fit him [the western man] for realistic statesmanship in the ground plan and goverance of his social order."[12]

A dynamic civilization demands a new education.

Capitalizing the emotions and the spirit　The new education is stressing and apparently capitalizing emotion, for the first time making emotion an asset rather than a liability in preparation for life. The scholar will not be needed less in the Republic because the layman has learned to control his impulses and to redirect his drives. More attention is also being given to character education. By ingenious and effective means character is not only measured but developed. Business men will be aided if the schools can train in honesty and in dependability as they have encouraged regularity, industry, and, in former days, thoroughness. Education must be of mind, may be of emotion, should be of character. The ultimate goal may well be what Alexander Meiklejohn calls "the unitary life of the spirit."

Three ideas seem to appear as traits of modern business, of modern government, and modern education. The first of these is *effectiveness.* Of what use business unless profits are secured? Of what use government unless order is maintained and the good of society protected and promoted? Of what use education unless it develops, trains and prepares the members of society?

The second of these ideas is *voluntary coöperation.* We work in organized groups and we do best when the work is of us as well as by us. Business efficiency is not a matter of chance but of organization, system, planning, and coöperation. Government is successful in the degree that it meets needs and secures support. Notice the 1933 N. R. A. campaign and the Blue Eagle. Modern schools get results when administration, teachers, and pupils work together for a common cause.

[12] Frank, Glenn, *Thunder and Dawn,* The Macmillan Co., p. 207.

A third standard by which society will judge itself in the future, undoubtedly, is the idea of *responsibility*. Students are becoming more responsible for their own work and are learning self-direction. Somehow schools and society can help our governments to accept responsibility. "Invisible government" must go. Business must become responsible publicly and socially as well as economically. It will do so to insure its own future. "To refuse to face the task of creating a vision of a future America immeasurably more just and noble and beautiful than the America of today is to evade the most crucial, difficult, and important educational task."[13]   In a growing consciousness of *public* responsibility we find possibly the most distinctive trait of the new social order contrasted with the old.

The Twentieth-Century Renaissance is capitalizing these new contributions of government—the new spirit of solidarity growing out of voluntary coöperation; of business—efficiency as means and effectiveness as end; and of the schools—responsibility for action that thus becomes right.   Our dynamic civilization is already bringing reorganization in each of these three fields, and in each of these three respects.   In relation to internal problems the future of civilization may well depend on the extent to which each field develops and uses all three characteristics.   Without reflection upon the contributions of home or church, possibly civilization's success may well be determined by the completeness of the integration secured by these three working together.   The problem of understanding what is needed and of comprehending how the result may be attained challenges the education of the future.

[13] Counts, George S., *Dare the School Build a New Social Order?* The John Day Co., p. 55.

XVIII

RELIGION IN A NEW WORLD

Religion would not be religion if it were not an integral part of life. If the individual is different and society is different, when the old order changes as life is transformed, religion must change. If it failed to do that, it would cease to be most truly and successfully religious, because it would be much better adapted to an outgrown civilization than to the one that is in process of re-formation.

These conclusions might seem to indicate that religion does not possess the permanence, unchanging authority, and constant ethical values which we expect of it. Religion, is, after all, a human thing. As Abba Hillel Silver declares, "Religion is, in a sense, a summary of the basic spiritual interests and needs of all ages. It is concerned with what is timeless and fundamental in human experience." [1] Yet, because religion deals with the eternal verities is no reason why religion as a human characteristic does not change for us with the years— as youth ages. The religion of the child should not be that of the youth, nor that of youth the religion of maturity, if the years offer experience and bring growth. What is true for the individual probably is true for the race.

Religion, ethics, and civilization are interrelated; each changes with the other. "Both as a means to a moral end and as an end in itself for which the moral life is the means, the future of religion is involved in the ethical reconstruction of modern society.[2] "The fact is that more men in our modern era are irreligious because *religion has failed to make civilization ethical* than because it has failed to maintain its intellec-

[1] Silver, *Religion in a Changing World,* Harper and Brothers, p. 19.
[2] Niebuhr, Reinhold, *Does Civilization Need Religion?*, The Macmillan Co., p. 17.

tual respectability. For every person who disavows religion because some ancient and unrevised dogma outrages his intelligence, several become irreligious because the social impotence of religion outrages their conscience." [3]

The religious situation today can probably be analyzed and explained best in relation to our changing civilization but we may be well repaid if we examine religious changes in their historical setting. In this study a comparison can be made between our times and some outstanding period somewhat similar to our own. With the examination of the problems and conditions to which adaptation of a religious character must be made, there is a remote possibility that some light may be thrown either on the causes of present unrest and irreligion or on ways in which our present religious institutions may be readapted to meet present needs better.

RELIGION AND THE CHURCH IN DYNAMIC SOCIETIES

The development of humanity has been marked greatly by the limitation of that field of personal or group experience which we call religious.[4] Owing to the difficulty of deciding what is religion and what is not, it is impossible to state the real extent to which religion is a part of the life of each generation, society, or race. Nevertheless, *human history has witnessed a great increase of the secular field.* This has been actual through the remarkable advance in scientific or mechanical achievements but relative also in the lessened time devoted to church meetings and work. Even in the short history of America established churches have been discontinued, the final disestablishment being preceded by a movement toward religious freedom, that in turn being dependent upon actual experience with religious toleration.

Extension of the secular field

Going one step farther back we discover that medieval Europe left a very large part of all *social activities* and many *political controls* to ecclesiastical authorities. In the Feudal Age there was little schooling except as preparation for cleri-

---

[3] *Ibid.*, p. 12.
[4] Wieman, H. N., *Religious Experience and Scientific Method*, Part III, especially pp. 368–369.

cal duties. Most of the learning was the possession of the priests. Business was frequently managed in monasteries or by the regular clergy. The church of the Middle Ages formulated the rules under which business should be done, fair prices should be charged, and money should be lent, usually without interest. *The church was a government as well as an ecclesiastical organization.*

It may well be questioned, however, whether the medieval church played so large a part in the life of the people as did religion and religious organizations in early historic times. In ancient Egypt and Babylonia most knowledge was a priestly prerogative. A fair percentage of the land was owned by the priesthood and much of the business was done by religious orders.

In prehistoric times, if we are to judge from our slight knowledge of primitive people in recent times, religion was associated with commonplace things of everyday life. Taboo made distinct the work of man and woman, and carried religious sanction. The planting of the fields or the harvesting of crops, the undertaking of a voyage, even the beginning of distinctly routine tasks of the day involved ritual and, if sufficiently important, festivals. Not alone in the burial of the dead but in the preservation of the living was something called religion an essential without which the whole would fail. An underlying purpose of this ceremonial seems to have been pacification, motivated by fear and steeped in what later generations usually named superstition.

Evolution of religion in early times

The upward progress of humanity, from the religious point of view, has been marked by numerous changes, only three of which need be considered in this brief summary. The first of these has been suggested: the *separation of religion from different fields of human activity:* economic, social, or political; personal, community or national. A second transformation has been the radical *change in the concept of Deity* and the attitude of the individual toward God. A third phase of this development deals with *changing religious mores* which, in successive centuries and millennia, have been worked out as the *social response of their time* to the religious impulse. This has usually been a modfication of the social heritage and it usually has represented the religious attitudes and actions accepted as standards by that particular race and generation.

Alfred North Whitehead refers to four factors represented in the external expression of religion in human history. These are "ritual, emotion, belief, rationalization." "All these four factors are not of equal influence throughout all historical epochs. The religious idea emerged gradually into human life, at first barely disengaged from some other human interests. The order of the emergence of these factors was in the inverse order of the depth of their religious importance: first ritual, then emotion, then belief, then rationalization." [5]

Probably the most distinct advance in religious thought and response has come in periods of abrupt economic or social reorganization. A new order of society might be created out of demand for a different religion. It seems far more probable that *religious reorganization has itself been an adjustment* to a new way of living, to new internal relationships within the tribe or nation, or to different bonds or conflicts with other similar societies.

There are no exact records to show us the revolutionary change in religion which must have accompanied the transition from the hunting stage of prehistoric existence to the pastoral and agricultural form of life in the mid-neolithic period. Many authorities believe that a large part of our ritual and many of our religious beliefs and acts are but slightly changed from those prepared to meet the new occupation and life of the first agriculturalists. *Some students contend that the religious problem of the present day grows primarily out of the displacement of rural life by urban,* of an agricultural system by an industrial one. Undoubtedly these contentions carry an element of truth and embody an idea which must not be overlooked by the clergy, social worker, or moralist of the present day.

Records are available in practically every household (the Old Testament) by which one can trace the transition from pastoral to more settled life in the history of the Hebrew na-

[5] Whitehead, *Religion in the Making,* The Macmillan Company, pp. 18–19.

tion. The religious thought of the free shepherd life on the hills of Palestine was developed into a superior form of religion totally different from that held by the city dwellers of Canaan. Before the time of Amos and Isaiah the Hebrew people who had kept themselves free from heathen idolatry were concerned almost solely with ritual. Religion was little more than the series of formulae to be carried through that Jahweh should be propitiated. *The eighth-century prophets, followed by the heretic Jeremiah, gave a moral as well as an emotional character to what was a new Hebrew belief.* The trials and problems in Judea and Israel, but particularly the Babylonian Captivity, created an integrated religion, spiritual, ethical and national. In the history of humanity few revolutions are comparable to this reorganization. A new concept of Deity emerged, a new type of worship, a new understanding of individual responsibility in relation to the Creator.

Out of this background, both ethical and spiritual, Jesus of Nazareth came with His Gospel. In simple language without reference to creed or dogma He proclaimed eternal principles. They were not adapted to any particular social condition nor did they deal with the distinctive problems of His race and time. The older Hebrew concept of God took on new meaning and, therefore, assumed new dignity; *spiritual communion with God was linked up as never before with service to men.* This teaching, carefully systematized in a theology by Paul, found opportunity in the unity of the Roman world and became the basis of a new religion and a new civilization throughout the West.

Religious transformations in modern times

Several centuries ago there occurred a re-formation and a re-organization of life analogous to that through which we are passing. Invention and discovery played some part but with fifteenth-century Renaissance folk, as with us, the primary need was the sloughing off of outworn, outgrown ways of making a living and of living. Feudalism was dead but did not know it; business was throwing off the shackles of provincialism; governments were emerging on a national scale; society was breaking out of the shell of medievalism. In a similar way the modern world may be emerging from nationalism,

from supposed absolute sovereignty to a new internationalism; business, already transformed from small-scale hand
work into colossal machine-driven corporations is facing a future of further reorganization; society has broken the bonds
of caste and class for what it hopes may be a new freedom.
In a sense the most important development of the great
Renaissance was the necessary transformation of the medieval
church, stripped of forms, functions, and powers which in that
new age were considered secular rather than religious. In the
present period no corresponding change is likely to occur in
the religion of the nineteenth century. Any alteration affecting it will probably come from within the church because of
any older attitudes, beliefs, and work which do not represent
the religious needs of our own time. One should not underestimate the influence upon the Protestant Reformation of
the New Learning, of new ideas regarding the world, of different concepts of the individual in relation to God. Possibly each of these may find its counterpart in the religious
development of the twentieth century.

Outwardly sixteenth-century religion showed its greatest
difference from that of the fifteenth in the creation of large
numbers of sects—a great diversity replacing former unity. A
splendid example of the way in which a religious sanction
persists even when its followers are in revolt against the old
form was shown in the field of *authority*. Medievalism had
built its religion upon the infallibility of Mother Church. The
protest of the Reformation was very sharp against the uniformity of belief and doctrines prescribed by an ecclesiastical
hierarchy. Protestantism, however, although split into many
parts, after blind groping found its way back to authority as
the basis of its religion. *Orthodoxy* was determined by *Scripture* instead of by *Pope and Council*. *National state churches*
supplanted a *universal religious empire*. The whole power of
a state church, combining both clerical and political groups,
treated heresy as it did treason—an offense against king and
state.

The analogy between the great fifteenth-century Renaissance and our own must not be carried too far, because each

age has its own readjustments to make to a civilization environment peculiar to itself. These experiences of the Renaissance illustrate rather clearly, however, the type of readaptation inevitable in this present age of change. Before the World War we might complacently have believed that *the concept of Deity held by Christian nations* was worthy of God and of Christ. Evidently we are still bound with the chains of tribal thought. The Anglo-Saxon God whom many of us worship has His first thought, some hope, for the business prosperity of His adherents. The German Deity differs less in character than in constituency. There seems to be a close resemblance between the call of David upon Jahweh to smite his enemies and the Prussian attitude in 1914 toward Gott who was the divine guardian of Kultur. Possibly the irreligion and the materialism, the mechanistic ideas of cosmos, which have pervaded much of modern thought, have been a reaction against the narrow, selfish, un-Christlike interpretation of God as the special guardian and protector of those who have sought to become His beneficiaries by enrolling under the standard of Jesus.

A second characteristic of nineteenth-century religion was its bourgeois character. When agriculture was king and most families in America or France owned land, or in England and Germany lived close to the soil, religion as represented by church attendance and service was a natural part of the weekly routine of the majority. The Industrial Revolution, by creating a proletariat, has left without religious care great masses of workers. Ritual and service based upon the needs and desires of an agricultural people seem to find little place or response in the lives of urban workmen. Protestantism has been losing its hold on the masses because of its burgess interests and its failure to provide a place for daily needs. Far more wisely the Catholic organization paternally has watched over all its people, particularly those who have little of this world's goods and has given opportunity for daily communion and worship. It may not have discovered the real demands of the present; but it has kept a hold upon those whose families are associated with it.

In both the old Renaissance and the new there has been a problem of readjusting old religion to new science. The revival of Greek science gave first aid to Erasmus and others who ridiculed the follies of a tradition-ridden church oligarchy. Not until after Luther and Calvin, however, did Copernicus and Galileo create a new science in which the earth was no longer the center and in which medieval ideas of cosmography generally yielded to a new knowledge of our solar system and the universe. With natural reluctance the churches, Catholic and Protestant, refused to adapt their doctrines and beliefs to astronomical facts which contradicted ideas closely interwoven with their old religion. Few today insist upon a flat earth, which has no existence, or think themselves irreligious because they accept without question the scientific discoveries of three or four centuries ago. Unfortunately, *a similar battle is being waged today because new revelations in science do not seem to fit old revelations in religion.*

Problems of Adaptation of Religion to Changes of the Present Day

There is a problem of a conservative church in a changing world. Mankind is conservative. We may say that we love change; but under all most of us think the old ways are best. Fortunately each new generation puts a new dress upon the old, even though it may not alter the substance of that which is clothed. In the field of religion we are inescapably more conservative than in almost any other. The social heritage which we consider religious takes on a sacredness possessed by nothing else in our possession or experience. Unfortunately, instead of seeing life whole and religion as eternal truth, we probably accept as religion that which the preceding generation thought was religion.

It might be safe to assert that the majority who find themselves sharply out of sympathy with present-day religion do so for one of three reasons. The first is their inability to accept the creed which they were taught when childish imagination and intelligence could not grasp truth clearly. A sec-

The problem of the conservative

ond reason is that the standards placed before us as religious interfere with those business activities or personal pleasures which may have become the chief end of existence. A third group may be irreligious because they have never had real contact with any organization which represents present-day religion.

Finding itself confronted by a transition from an agricultural to an industrial society and by each of these three problems, *the ultra-conservative church withdraws within itself.* The more faith is questioned, the more loudly its claims are presented. The conservative church stresses the divine authority upon which it acts. The old ritual may have lost meaning to many; but it now becomes one of the most precious possessions of the few, those conservative enough to understand its ancient significance and its present value to the devout. Doubt is not recognized as an inevitable but probably short-lived experience of youth. Hence *questioning becomes sacrilege, and inability to accept the old faith in its entirety, heresy.* The result is the withdrawal not only of the church within itself but also of the doubters from the church body.

Some knowledge of history and a little more information in regard to human nature might help the church in this crisis of change. It is not enough to idolize the past or prepare for the future. Rather do we need an understanding of the present and a better presentation of God in the world today. There was bound to be a revulsion of feeling, a protest against Puritanism and Victorianism, including both religion and morals. For a world which was natural and human the standards set by Calvinist and Victorian were too artificial and severe. Any return to Christ would inevitably have discarded many of the meaningless restraints of blue laws or self-repression. The conservative who has wished to be religious in a changing world should be rather successful if his conservatism takes him back to the religion of Jesus, to the Master's understanding of the human heart,[6] to His insight into

---

[6] The psychology of religion must modify a philosophy of dogma because religion must be a capitalization of human emotion and aspirations. The whole super-structure based upon a policy of fear, upon a system of rewards and punishments, fitted illy with Christ's statement that the kingdom of heaven is within us.

the eternal laws of living, and to the meaning of love and service.

Compared with the conservative who builds upon tradi- The problem of the liberal tion and commands all the prestige and authority of past successes, the liberal is at a disadvantage. He must establish the very foundations of his new faith. His ideas change as he matures or learns or as his social environment changes. It is impossible that there should be *agreement among religious leaders* who seek to adapt their faith and works to the new needs. Most of them are in *different stages* of departure from conservatism. Even more difficult is the attainment of agreement among their followers. Intense is the travail in the birth of a better religious system for a new age.

Liberalism may involve doctrine but is more likely to be concerned chiefly with practice. Most successful, undoubtedly, has been the church which seeks to reach the daily need of its members and others. The *institutional church* is not a Sabbath-day place solely for formal service. It seeks to become *a church home whose doors are rarely closed* to the seeker for truth or the learner whose needs are physical and emotional as well as spiritual. The new type of church service is often marked by lecture rather than by sermon. Real progress has been made by organizations like the Y's that do not bear the name of church but carry the name of Christ or the idea of service.

Corresponding to this broadening of function and attempted humanizing of action which many modern religious institutions have undertaken is the unification of groups that have heretofore been divided. In the days before the Eighteenth Amendment it was said that in a small community the Devil preferred several churches to an equal number of saloons. Now small, struggling, competing, critical congregations all working in the name of the same Master have frequently formed *union churches* with results at least outwardly happy, harmonious, and helpful. Much as the foreign field has been divided wisely between the different denominations, this policy of unification has given fairly aggressive strong churches under permanent guidance instead of weak, struggling, unsuccessful organizations under intermittent pastors. The union of local groups has set an excellent example to the combination of national bodies, some of which have formed a nominal union while retaining their own spiritual standards and their own peculiar internal organization. Creed, once thought the essence of religion, is seldom made the criterion for membership. Salvation is not chiefly a matter of future salvation but of individual rebirth and social service.

Liberal gains are likely to be individual rather than general. For the liberal, science may open the door to new truths or make old truths more real and spiritual. He finds a new conception of creation because he sees miracles in the cell and reaches out to the great bounds of our own universe and what seems infinity of the greater universes beyond. His religion is probably not so deep, possibly not so vital, as that of him who unquestionably has faith and because of faith gains love. The one who has seen a new light in regard to what he thinks religion is, the one who has a fairly definite if passing idea of the relation of religion to science, prides himself that he is not as other men who cling to doctrines of a bygone day.

The extremists are always in a minority, far more today than we realize because the vast majority is silent. Is that silence the result of indifference? If so, *indifference may be a truer characteristic of present religion—and a greater problem—than any dispute between fundamendalist and radical.* When the extremists are interested in controversy rather than religion, and when they can control law and education, the Devil takes more than the hindmost. Time is wasted in religious conflict that should be spent on the extraordinarily difficult problem of understanding needs of our changing civilization and necessary adjustments to make religion the best of that civilization.

Religion in an indifferent world

To many observers religion seems to be on a decline. Interest in affairs that are religious seems driven out by things secular; an overwhelming majority do not attend church. To what extent is this indifference apparent or real? Is our day and generation less religious than those preceding it? Is the twentieth century so much concerned with the making of dollars or the enjoyment of material advantages that the spirit is starved because the body is overfed? The answer to this question takes us back again to the definition of religion. If we identify religion with nineteenth-century church attitudes, with interest in ritual or service, with a study of Scripture, the answer must be a positive one— religion is on the decline. Few young people know their Bibles as did the older generation. Piety and piosity fare rather leanly in the strenuous atmosphere of modern life. Ritual never has had the significance for a Protestant that it has for a Catholic because the Protestant service stresses simplicity and directness. Symbols may play less part in the present presentation of truth than was necessary in a less skeptical and less literal age. *If religion seems to be on the decline,* it is due in part to dissatisfaction with church services and standards which have lost appeal, in part to a mad enthusiasm for secular entertainment, and in part to disapproval of the ethical failures of a church which unconsciously protects the classes against the masses.

Our generation has escaped the crudities of nineteenth-century appeal and criticism. Modern high-pressure salesmanship takes a back seat compared with old-time emotional evangelism. The difference between the purchaser of goods on installment and the camp-meeting convert shows itself clearly in the period after persuasion. The buyer continues to pay or forfeits his purchase. Those who have held to emotionalism in the high-pitched excitement of revival seldom gain that spiritual regeneration which underlies a complete conversion. In consequence, there is probably a reversion to lifelong habits based upon a carnal experience rather than new reactions leading to a spiritual goal. On the contrary, critics of the atheist type or their agnostic successors were worthy of little consideration. Ingersoll could go up to the beginnings of Hebrew development and ask if the nineteenth-century Christian believed in the God of cruelty which the Old Testament shows us was the idea of these people emerging from barbarism. The agnostic could unconvert by appealing to ignorance as effectively as the evangelist could turn the sinner temporarily from evil ways. The one disregarded the obvious historical fact that, in the experience of the individual and the race, religion is a growth. The other ignored the equally obvious truth that faith and reason are supplementary. The chief purpose of faith, hope and love as needs of the human heart was overlooked.

The gospel for an age of doubt has given way to a new gospel of worship and service for an age of indifference. It was a mistake to divorce religion from esthetics, almost as harmful as the attempt now is to separate religion from social obligation and human helpfulness. Instead of barnlike tabernacles, beautiful buildings appeal to the eye and to the senses. Attractive auditoriums charmingly lighted, no longer provided with benches of penance for the bored worshipper, attract men and women if not children. A real message is brought by deep-toned organs and thoughtful sermons rather than studies of Hebrew antiquities. Nineteenth-century appeal to fear, and ancient invective against sin, find their modern counterpart in a message of love and a demand for action. The old religion sought through discipline to harden men and women that they might resist the devil; the new risks the danger of being soft, when it belittles temptation and evil. The old asked a man to be good to escape eternal punishment; the new urges him to be good for something because humanity needs help. To those prejudiced against "religion" the new religion will seem more a combination of philosophy, ethics, and humanitarian effort than it does of theology, discipline, and ineffective piety.

New Defining of Religion in Terms of Modern Life

Science and religion

The great scientist is almost invariably religious; the great religious teacher is never unscientific.

Controversy between religion and science is largely academic and beside the point. The two are complementary. Science deals with an impartial, objective and impersonal field. Religion is inevitably subjective, introspective, and teleological. Science observes, compares, and generalizes but de-

sires and sees no purpose. Religion seeks personal help,
reaches out and makes practical the things it believes. Both
show faith. Religion postulates hypotheses that, in the nature of things, it is impossible to prove. Science formulates
hypotheses which are the basis of experiment, but its conclusions are not necessarily proved as mathematics is subject
to proof. Pure science is theory. We have heard electrons
but we have not seen one. How can a real line be drawn
with a deposit of material? How can the laboratory, hampered by the limitation of material objects, prove that which
underlies objective things?

However little conflict there may be between true science
and true religion, there is a real controversy between the
present-day champions of both. Both William Jennings
Bryan and his opponents would agree upon his aphorism:
"Truth is truth and must prevail;" but when applied to "evolution" they arrived at diametrically opposite conclusions. To
the religionist who must check all his science by traditional
views of science furnished by the religion of the past, many
distinctive achievements of modern science will be unac-
ceptable. History may not repeat itself; but our adjustment
is similar in kind, although not in degree, to that of three
centuries ago. Our religious ancestors were obliged to adjust
their ideas of both science and religion to the Copernican concept of the sun, not the earth, as the center of the solar system. We are asked to adjust ours on the one hand to a
biological theory that all life is one and to an astronomical
concept that our vaunted solar system is a tiny speck in a
creation of vast dimensions.

In the whole history of man's religious experience there is
a constant discarding of old ideas and an assimilation of new
knowledge to man's real needs. The revelations of Isaiah and
Jeremiah were sacrilege to the orthodox Jew of their day.
The Hebrews would have none of Jesus. The medieval church
attempted to spurn the religious Renaissance. In each case
there was a readjustment of the old, not always the best, to
the new. Instead of destroying religion there often came with
each advance a better knowledge of God, a truer understand-

ing of creation, a greater willingness of man to make religion outward and effective instead of simply a means of personal gain.

George Hall Ashley gives an excellent summary of common aims and purposes in science and religion. "Modern scientists and modern religionists agree: (1) That, as revealed by evolution, nature is progressive and purposeful; (2) That man is a stage in the unfolding of that purpose; (3) That that purpose is as yet unrealized and challenges man to carry on toward its realization; (4) That behind that purpose is something akin to mind, or to the power behind growth or evolution, which they agree to call God; (5) That the relation of God is not typified by the potter and his clay, but by father and son; (6) That as the power and pattern of growth appear to be *in* the growing thing, so in man is the power and pattern —God if you will—that will drive man on to fulfillment; (7) That it is this power and pattern in man that inspires him to seek truth, to create beauty, to be and do good; (8) That the upward progress of man demands, biologically, the building up of a broad human platform or pyramid, and therefore demands of man not only that he seek to raise himself through a knowledge of truth, but that he share this truth and its benefits with his fellow men; (9) That human success is measured by human progress toward the goal of a complete knowledge of truth, the complete application of that knowledge to human welfare and advancement, and in the realization of the beauty that will result from that application; (10) That if a man believes life is purposeful and desires to fulfill that purpose or if he believes that living is an art and desires to live beautifully, he will find in the words and ways of Jesus of Nazareth the best demonstration known to modern man of how to live beautifully." [7]

New needs of religion   From the standpoint of religion, like that of the family, the chief problem of civilization today is a better adaptation of an old system to the new age. The American family in frontier conditions easily lost many distinctive characteristics of patriarchal family organization. On the contrary, the re-

[7] An unpublished manuscript.

ligious experience of the American colonists carried them
backward quite as much as forward. Seeking religious freedom they found their justification in the reëstablishment of
many pre-Christian ideals and standards. They did not free
themselves from the state church, although they do deserve
credit for exercising a large degree of religious toleration and
finally of taking the epoch-making step forward of gaining
religious freedom. They, therefore, freed religion from the
bonds of politics although they threw it back into the bondage
of pre-Grecian thought.

Religious freedom, protected by constitutional safeguards
from the return of political interference, was a first and important step in the separation of religion from some of the
secular forms in which it had been molded. The most that
the last generation or two has been doing, unconsciously to
it and with objection from conservatives, has been the further
purging of religious gold from the dross it has contained.
Our generation cannot be expected to discover and discredit all
the surviving elements of paganism and materialism which
have become highly interrelated with "religion" as we know it.
Probably no logical analysis could distinguish between those
elements which belong to religion and those which are foreign to it, because *religion is a human achievement fitting a
certain part of human nature and meeting a need which no
material civilization can satisfy.* Human nature changes little,
but human aspirations change with new situations and opportunities, especially in a dynamic age. Deity we used to think
changed not at all. If modern science is correct, creation may
not have ceased and the Creator, being eternal and omnipotent,
may well be dynamic rather than static, as the older religion
seemed to teach.

It is very difficult to attempt a separation of things religious
from things secular. If psychologists cannot agree upon the
character of human nature and the proper sphere for their
interesting but growing subject, if Benjamin Anderson a few
years ago could find 117 definitions of "social value," it is
improbable that there would be an agreement among church
leaders and certainly not among captains of industry or

statesmen regarding the nature of religion and its place in modern life.

Of several things we may be certain. *Religion will continue to represent a large element of conservatism.* The gains of the past are more notable in the fields of religion than in the fields of invention and scientific discovery. Why lose them? In its search for truth the human heart may well have been less hampered in the simple ages of the past and in the solitary places of the world than in the strenuous market place or the complicated struggle for existence which marks the present day. There may be little truth in the old feeling that poverty produces character and makes for religious insight. If possession of this world's goods is a bar to heaven, it might easily keep heaven from entering into the personality of its owner.

Religious
possibilities
of the
new age

What are some of the religious possibilities in the new era? "Religion can be healthy and vital only if a certain tension is maintained between it and the civilization in which it functions."[8] "The future of religion and the future of civilization are thus hung in the same balance."[9] "An unethical civilization will inevitably destroy the vitality of the religion of the victims and the sincerity and moral prestige of the religion of the beneficiaries of its unethical inequalities."[10] The interdependence of religion, business, politics, and civilization is stressed very effectively by L. P. Jacks.[11] The ethical concepts and solutions of a simple age are inadequate to explain new, involved, but apparently unethical, problems and relationships of a complex civilization. In spite of the fact that *each epoch seeks to remake tradition in its own image,* in the new scheme of things inherited ideals and standards may be unadaptable to the need of either religious or non-religious persons.

The separation of religion from subjects formerly its own should stimulate rather than discourage. In an age of specialization, limitation of field makes new successes possible. Neu-

[8] Niebuhr, *Does Civilization Need Religion*, p. 69.
[9] *Ibid.*, p. 17.   [10] *Ibid.*, pp. 16–17.
[11] P. 419.

rology and psychology may show that mind is dependent upon brain, and soul upon mind. However, they do not explain personality in terms of neurons, aspirations as by-products of the endocrines, or social achievements as bio-chemical products. Personality is more than a combined series of reflexes integrated at their best. Lloyd Morgan's *Emergent Evolution* is not the final explanation; but personality and character are as much more than the physiological elements out of which they emerge as a drop of water is different from two parts of hydrogen and one of oxygen. Instead of bringing us materialism, the wealth and consequent leisure of machine industry and modern invention should give time for thought on what is worth while, on the real values of life. Scientific research and explanation of the tiniest and largest of nature's accomplishments naturally broaden our vision of life and should not dull its meaning or its purpose.

If religion is diverted from inspection of the human soul to problems of human need, who shall say it represents backsliding or regression? If today we pay less attention to preparation for future happiness than to a capitalization of human capacities, are we less religious than our ancestors? Because the mysteries of tree and stream and atmosphere no longer seem supernatural, is there nothing within us that does not carry us beyond discovering what we shall eat or wherewith we shall be clothed? Does scientific understanding of the chemical composition of the drop of water or the combination of two cells for a new life make any less miraculous the change which nature is providing? Does one get a higher concept from the phrase "he made the stars also" in the sixteenth verse of the first chapter of Genesis than he finds in the writings of George Ellery Hale on the new universe?

The *brotherhood of man* has long been taken as the corollary of religious dependence on God the Father. In no century before the twentieth has there been equal realization of the humanitarian need or the religious significance of this concept. From the negative Ten Commandments to the positive requests of the Sermon on the Mount was a great stride forward in human experience. The embodiment of Christ's ideas in the law and custom of all nations would represent almost as sharp and notable an advance in human progress.

Is this age irreligious? Is the twentieth century irreligious or is it groping its way toward different and eventually higher levels? Check its progress by the standards set by the Master and it rates higher than it does by the church requirements of most denominations. *What constitutes religion and religious standards?* Take for example the attitude toward the Deity and self. Have we faith and is our faith impaired by wealth, by materialism, by knowledge? The first two of these rather modern products would never have been possible without faith which literally has removed mountains; the last undermines faith only when its information and learning are neither knowledge nor wisdom. If understanding be a requirement, how do earlier centuries compare with ours for opportunities to know the truth and become free? Reverence rarely characterizes youth. America is an adolescent nation. The transformations of a new renaissance are impossible without an irreverence for that which must go. Otherwise, how replace the ideas and institutions bound, or that should be bound, for oblivion? Steadfastness is a virtue only when it anchors its faith to worthwhile systems. Critics of religion are often critical chiefly because the church and the clergy have staked their lives and the salvation of their followers on a maintenance of the *status quo.*

How does the twentieth century stand the acid test of qualities which might determine religion? Our age is less artificial than many which preceded it. But sincerity is religious, and those who despair of modern youth overlook the salvation-value of this trait. How much of old-fashioned holiness was piosity, the kind of semi- or real hypocrisy which brought down on the Pharisees unqualified denunciation? If holiness is whole-ness, does the twentieth century yield to the nineteenth, or for that matter to the first, in the era of our Lord? If righteousness is less self-righteousness than right-ness, will the genuiness of modern life be classed as irreligious? Open diplomacy is certainly an advance upon secret intrigue. The exchange of diplomatic discourtesies, the evil intent concealed by graceful terms, has not yet disappeared. No observing or thoughtful person can contend that either modern business or international affairs represent Christianity. Truth is certainly as rampant in the twentieth century as it ever was. Lawlessness and immorality are on the increase. The behavior of our Mr. Hydes has opportunity for expression denied in small communities before the age of science. But do our Dr. Jekylls more often lose their battles with their evil selves?

If we pass to proofs of religious character, is it true that the new age is more selfish or is its selfishness more conspicuous? A comparison of politics in the heroic period of American national beginnings with the unheroic era of the World War shows just as much forward-looking, disinterested effort on the part of Wilson as of Washington. Love is certainly more prominent today than ever before, particularly in the sermons of modern clergy, but possibly also in the thought and lives of the rank and file. Those who know human nature as an animal product, those who have followed the rise from the era of tooth and claw to that of musket and machine, marvel at the kindliness with which we work together in harmony and even settle our world-wide international differences!

Spiritual growth has always been too much an end, not enough a means of achieving. Sought for itself as it was in the older religion, how could it embody the actual development, ethical and religious, which comes from normal growth? Too much have we lost sight of the truth that he who seeks to save his life has difficulty in keeping it. The measurement of growth is not to be determined by itself, but by its products: possibly by this one token alone—service. Shall self-development be measured by the same negative standards of conduct that prevailed in an age of discipline? Attempted self-direction may lead to much irresponsible behavior. If so, shall we call the present generation immoral and irreligious? The spirit of the servant in the house may not pervade modern life, but it enters into social relations as never before in the history of the world. For those who can master only simple things, *complex civilization* has its faults and its difficulties.

Its opportunities are multifold, meeting every need and taste, appealing to every interest; but possibly it *may strain the capability and the self-control of most of us.*

New Religious Unity and New Ethical Standards

There is no renaissance without religious revolution because the need of reorganization and revaluation pervades every major field.

The Gloomy Dean states rather effectively one of the important shifts of recent years which has been in the making. "The center of gravity in morals, as in theology, is changing from authority to rational motive and the conscience of the individual. We can hardly overestimate the importance of this emancipation of the conscience and reason. New ethical demands arise from the new knowledge and from the new circumstances. These demands are very easily silenced by authoritative tradition . . . the victory of moral autonomy is not yet secure." [12]

Important in this whole scheme of reorganization is that series of readjustments to remove inconsistencies or contradictions in ideas and attitudes, if not services and systems, that have been due to rapid changes. Of equal importance is the whole series of adaptations to the dynamic world itself. We are too close to ourselves "to see oursel's as ithers see us." This is as true for nations and for generations as for individuals. Impossible it is to separate from our inheritance the things we need and the elements we should preserve. Equally unattainable is the unification and integration of the new with the old, of one part with another. The attempt to reconcile industrial capitalism with political democracy is simplicity itself compared with this ordeal. The usage that we want to keep, the custom we wish to discard, are interwoven in almost inseparable threads in the social and religious fabric. If we attempt this task with minds saturated with prejudice, with an attitude of fundamentalist or radical scientist, with the unquenchable reforming spirit of liberalist, how shall we dis-

---

[12] Inge, *Christian Ethics and Moral Problems*, G. P. Putnam's Sons, p. 216.

tinguish the dark gray of the obsolete from the light gray of the dawning?

Religious unity does not necessarily involve consolidations of congregations; there will be fewer mergers of churches than of factories. New standards may not at first seem to belong to the field of ethics. They are if they represent juster relations between ruler and subject, between employer and employe, between husband and wife. They may stand for better democracy because of more voluntary coöperation with groups or between groups. They may become religious because they are ethical and accepted as standards by large numbers. *Vox populi vox Dei* may then represent the choice of the people because God wills it.

Somehow *the new knowledge, the new freedom, the new social responsibility for which modern life is notable must make more real the fatherhood of God and the brotherhood of man.* To get knowledge does not necessarily mean wisdom; but if we can know the truth, the truth will make us free. "All God's chillun got wings." Paul's contrast between the carnal man and the spiritual man should take on new meaning. The world, the flesh, and the Devil cannot keep man from climbing the heights of spiritual growth.

Undoubtedly, there will be *new means of harmonizing on higher levels the relations of individual and society.* To many brought up to fear and heed the warnings of conscience, there seems sacrilege in the thought that the individual conscience chiefly reflects that of the race. If it were not so, why do many of those most conscientious in each generation magnify the errors of their day? It well may be that the renaissance and religious re-formation of the twentieth century will find their main distinction from those of the fifteenth and sixteenth centuries in stressing not individualism as an escape from medieval collectivism, but social solidarity as an escape from the disrupting forces of modern disintegration.

XIX

SCIENCE AND CIVILIZATION

We began with machines; we end with science. They are not separate; rather are they interrelated and interdependent. Contemporaneous civilization is largely the product of these two. Machines have increased the quantity of material goods on which we depend; applied science has multiplied their variety and character. Applications of science, with the technology of the machine, have enabled us to penetrate the depths of the sea, to overcome gravitation, to annihilate space, to make nature our servant in countless other ways. The ideas which have enriched our thought and changed our outlook are by-products of science. Future civilization, contrasted with that of the present, may depend upon a reorganized industrial capitalism or an integrated public substitute for it; but will keep step with scientific advance. Not a mechanical key but a scientific one will probably unlock the doors of future progress. Upon science to a very great extent will depend the technical development and the cultural character of the Twentieth-Century Renaissance.

DEVELOPMENT OF MODERN SCIENCE

Science before the nineteenth century

In a real sense modern science is the creation of the last two or three generations. Its influence in the present age and the extent to which it makes our civilization dynamic can best be understood by some idea of its development as well as a brief survey of its revolutionary advance in recent years.

The ancients had sufficient knowledge of the solar system to determine rather accurately the length of the solar year. This was done by the Egyptians and Babylonians and independently and more accurately by the Maya Indians of southern

548

Mexico and Central America. The Greeks increased greatly the scientific knowledge of mankind. Before Aristotle the sphericity of the earth was explained, and later Eratosthenes computed its size with fair accuracy. More remarkable than their attainments were their conjectures. Democritus and others made the guess that all matter is divided into infinitely small molecules called atoms. These are identical in chemical quality and are endowed with perpetual motion as a necessity of their existence. These atoms, by combining according to certain affinities, give us different substances.

Copernicus was in a real sense the first of the modern scientists. By showing that the sun rather than the earth is the center of our solar system and that the earth and other planets revolve around the sun, he laid a new foundation for cosmography. Galileo laid the foundation of modern experimental science. By the use of the first practical telescope he was able by observation as well as by computation to prove the Copernican theory and to establish many of the new principles upon which modern astronomy rests. When we realize that Galileo was able to observe only six or seven thousand stars, we can see how limited was the knowledge upon which he based his epoch-making discoveries. We think of Newton chiefly in connection with the establishment of the idea of gravitation, but that idea was understood before his day. Newton's real contribution was rather in the formulation of the laws of motion and the establishment of different types of mathematical calculations to determine astronomical facts.

The completion of our knowledge of our solar system was a triumph of computation rather than of observation. As early as 1772 Bode had worked out a law to determine the approximate position of each of the planets within the solar system. Herschel the elder accidently discovered Uranus soon after, and two mathematical astronomers independently located Neptune a half century later.

In the nineteenth century scientific progress was so rapid that even a summary of discoveries or of distinguished scientists would be voluminous and boring. Sir Charles Lyell laid

Gains of a century

the foundations of the study of modern geology, greatly influencing Charles Darwin's *The Origin of Species,* a real beginning of the new biology. Michael Faraday, with a perspicacity unfortunately not equaled by his mathematical training, more than a century ago predicted the probable interchange of different forms of energy. A generation later, however, so distinguished a scholar as von Helmholtz confused force and energy. It was not until well into the century that scientists were convinced of those two fundamental ideas and principles of physics and chemistry—the conservation of matter and the conservation of energy. It was not until the very last of the nineteenth century that Sir J. J. Thompson established the nature of the atom, the component element of all matter. Somewhat earlier mankind had gained some knowledge of the cell, the constituent basis of all living matter. Following close in time upon the researches of Thompson, August Weismann gave us more complete knowledge of the structure of the cell and formulated his theory of the continuity of the germ plasm.

Meanwhile astronomers had been working on theories of the origin of universes and had been proving the comparative identity of the materials of the different parts of our universe and probably of others.

The advance in pure science has been accompanied throughout by applications of scientific knowledge in technology and in many utilitarian ways.[1] In some cases practical knowledge preceded theoretical. Watt's steam engine had been in use many years before scientists understood the reason for the extraordinary energy created by expanding steam. Usually, however, knowledge of pure science predetermined successful uses of applied science. Electricity as a "power" and as a source of light has done much to modernize the present world. Many factories and many non-industrial businesses maintain elaborate science laboratories in which research proceeds apace. Invention or discovery in one field may not only revolutionize production or use valuable materials; it may offer

[1] See pp. 91–92, 558–561.

suggestion and stimulate research along allied lines. It is frequently true that no great discovery or invention is isolated, and many illustrations of that might be given.[2] We have cited the almost simultaneous discovery of Neptune by Adams and Leverrier, the interesting coincidence in the biological researches of Darwin and Wallace, the complications over the disputed invention of the telephone.

BIOLOGICAL SCIENCE AND CHANGED CONCEPTS OF LIFE

Machine civilization makes less use of biology than of physics and chemistry; an improved social order as much of biology and psychology as of physical science. The new renaissance is greatly affected by our new understanding of ourselves, our minds, and our place in the world of living things.

At least since the time of Aristotle we have had classified knowledge of similarities and differences among animals and plants. Our knowledge of the structure of animate organisms does not take us back a century. There have been numerous experiments in which scientists maintained that they have created life. For a long time investigators have been able to make a synthesis of organic products. The time undoubtedly will come when the aphorism "all life comes from life" may not be literally true.

How life has been changed by the new biology

Living organisms consist of protoplasm, but the protoplasm takes many varied forms, dependent upon the function which it is supposed to perform. If we contrast brain and brawn, we intentionally make a distinction between man at his highest and just ordinary man. When we speak of gray matter, we select out that part of the brain which represents the most active, most adaptable, and, therefore, most intelligent combination of protoplasmic cells of the human body. C. Judson Herrick compares the brains of rats and men, basing the study largely upon the small amount of cortex or gray matter possessed by the rodents. If we think the comparison odious, we might stop to consider that all protoplasm possesses the power of reaction and, in a sense, of intelligent adaptation.

[2] See p. 28.

A quarter of a century ago, H. S. Jennings startled the world by claiming real intelligence for the humble peromoecium.

Although we know so little about ourselves, our knowledge is vast compared with that of a half century ago. The future gain may well be more remarkable and humanly more helpful than that of the recent past. Our dawning comprehension of heredity is practically a twentieth-century product. Gregor Mendel's main research took place before 1865; but it was not until 1900 that the results of his investigations were rediscovered. Mendel's law deals with the character and proportion of the inheritance from two unlike parents. His main proposition might be stated briefly as follows. If the parents are dissimilar, a quarter of the offspring are exactly like one parent, another quarter are exactly like the other parent; but the other half seem like one parent, the dominant one, though they are really mixed. Mixing offspring, if combined with mixed offspring, will give one quarter like one grandparent and one quarter like the other grandparent. Weismann showed clearly that we inherit through our parents but from our ancestors. The inheritance comes through germ plasm, the germ plasm being separated at the beginning from the somatic or body cells. The stream of germ plasm is continuous from generation to generation. Modern investigators have shown that the germ cells are by no means homogeneous, three parts possibly being more important than others; the nucleus, the cytoplasm, and the chromosomes. The chromosomes consist of a large number of parts, each of which carries an ancestral characteristic for a particular part of the body of the offspring. For much of our modern knowledge of heredity we are indebted to Thomas Hunt Morgan.

From the sociological viewpoint it is interesting that we have gained a knowledge of the significance of family in inheritance at a time when "family" has ceased to dominate the making of new marital unions. It is just possible that this understanding of the part played by remote ancestry in predetermining physical characters and mental ability may be of the highest value to the family of tomorrow. This new and significant knowledge makes possible a real science of genetics upon which the future may base its plan for a society that shall be superior to the present, biologically, sociologically, and intellectually.

That science is one, although studied from different angles and therefore called by different names, is well illustrated in the field which we know as bio-chemistry. Until recent years little was known about the human body from the chemical point of view. Even now only a beginning has been attempted. Scarcely a half-century has elapsed, for example, since attention was drawn to the importance of the different ductless glands, which separately and together might predetermine much of human personality and success. Naturally the ductless glands are only a small part of the chemical equipment of the human body, for digestion in all of its phases involves some chemistry. The circulatory system touches upon it continually. The whole functioning of the nervous system, including the central cerebro-spinal system, is conditioned by it, for nerve action must be more closely allied to a chemical process than to the transmission of an electrical current. Human hygiene, including mental hygiene, depends for its success upon the knowledge and application of the best principles of bio-chemistry, and after all, possibly human organization and social action may be predetermined in large part by the body chemistry of the individual members.

The unity of mankind is now accepted by all students of the subject, because Neanderthal man and still more primitive predecessors apparently have disappeared from the face of the earth. All of us are of the genus "homo" and the species "sapiens." But what's in a name! Whether one accepts a theory of evolution or not, modern anatomy brings out numerous similarities in body structure of men and of the higher animals. Bio-chemistry shows the practical identity of special chemical extracts of human and animal bodies. If we depend upon the adrenalin or thyroxin of sheep or cattle to supply a deficiency of those necessities in our own systems, it ill becomes us to deny some kinship, distant though it may be, with these lowly animals. Pride may struggle, therefore, with knowledge, because of these poor relations of ours in the animal world. Man, as lord of creation and the controller of his environment, may well humble himself before the Creator and His creation. Especially is this true if a mechanical man can accomplish quickly tasks that even the trained scholar covers slowly. If robots learn to think as well as to work, will man achieve greater mastery of himself and his environment? Or will this Frankenstein reduce him rather literally to the level of a slave in a machine world?

The human value of applied biological science But two groups of illustrations need be given to show the human value of applied science in the field of living things. One of these is connected with the food supply; the other with the conquest of disease.

Soil chemistry depends for its success greatly upon nitrogen supplied by the nodules of leguminous plants. It does this by the "simple" process of taking this inert element, unwilling to remain long in chemical combination, from the air, where it is not needed, to the soil, where it helps free desired soil elements. The laboratory studies soils and finds the needs of plants. By experimentation as well as by the application of scientific knowledge lands considered worthless are made fertile and desirable agricultural fields. Crops that paid a bare living give a good margin of profit. Plants imported from other regions, like alfalfa or the naval orange, become real sources of wealth.

Human life has been prolonged. The chief gain has been in the reduction of the death rate in infancy and childhood, particularly in cities. Science therefore permits longer periods of training, better health in all years, and, through technology, shorter work days and years. More than once humanity has suffered a decline of civilization because of devastating epidemics, no longer common and in some instances now impossible. The "Dark Ages" after the "Fall of Rome" might not have been nearly so dark if terrible epidemics had not destroyed vast numbers of people throughout Europe, and with the people the possibilities of continuing the old culture at a decent level. If this invasion could be traced to Attila the Hun, it dwarfs the terrors of his military onslaught. The Black Death put an end to the thirteenth-century Renaissance, postponing for a century or two Europe's emergence from the feudal period of its existence.

The conquest of disease is as unnecessary to detail as it is impossible. Lower death rates tell in definite figures a small part of the story. Small-pox, still a scourge in the Far East, which almost defeated the American armies in the Revolutionary War, rarely breaks out even in American slums or seaports exposed to Asiatic commerce. Diphtheria and scarlet-fever no longer take their heavy annual toll. Tuberculosis is far less deadly. Pernicious anemia and Bright's disease yield to well-directed attacks of modern research. Bio-chemistry constantly increases our knowledge of our wonderful human machine; and the foods or drinks most helpful or most to be avoided. Balanced diets may not be individually the greatest essential; but undoubtedly the best diet for each will eventually increase greatly both human happiness and human efficiency.

Knowing his past, and mankind is learning slowly the history of his experience on the earth, he may easily have a very optimistic view regarding himself, his possibilities, and the future of some species of "homo." There is great promise in the upward progress, long and slow though it has been, which pre-history and history reveal. What man has done is simply a mild fore-runner of what he may attain. "Homo sapiens" may be the climax of creation so far, but the idea of a superman may not be simply a literary phrase or an optimistic forecast. It may be a possibility of future development though remote in time as we count the years and centuries. Without change of body or brain structure, man's grasp of mechanical devices has lengthened his reach, and his growing knowledge has unrolled the scroll of hidden mysteries. These gains, with the controls which enable men to live and work together in large groups may increase the sphere of human activities as the telescope has widened our knowledge of the universe.

NON-BIOLOGICAL SCIENCE

Interrela-
tions of the
inorganic
sciences

The new age is what it is largely because of our new knowledge and our many practical uses of physics, chemistry, geology, and astronomy, four sciences predominantly inorganic, and closely interrelated. In each and all of these fields we are striding forward with seven-league boots. When the writer was in college, the age of the earth was placed by the geologists at eighty to ninety million years, although astronomers contended that seventeen million years was the extreme limit of time since the earth began to form. Now geologists have concluded rather definitely that a half billion years, probably a billion and possibly two billion, have elapsed since the birth of this world of ours. Our knowledge of the atom and of radium and radioactivity have changed absolutely the chemists' and astronomers' ideas regarding the earth's beginnings and its age. The chemist rather than the geologist can compute for us with very great accuracy the antiquity of any particular stratum of rock in which certain minerals are found. Uranium gives off electrons, not gradually but at intervals. In this process uranium gradually is transformed into lead. If a geological deposit is found in which uranium and lead occur, it seems safe to decide the age of that deposit by noting the proportion in which uranium and lead are found together. It is estimated that after a billion years the substance which started as uranium has been turning to lead and is found in the proportion of eight parts of uranium to one of lead. After two billion years the proportions have changed to two parts of lead for seven of uranium. As Sir James Jeans tells us: "A small amount of uranium provides a perfect clock, provided we are able to measure the amount of lead it has formed, and also the amount of uranium still surviving." [3]

All matter, organic or inorganic, is made up of molecules, which are in constant motion. If a molecule seeks to elbow its way against its neighbor, this is more successful if the molecules are in a gaseous state than it would be with less elbow room. If the molecules are reduced to a liquid form,

[3] Jeans, *The Universe Around Us,* The Macmillan Co., p. 148.

there is comparatively little opportunity for movement. When the substance forms a solid, the molecules are usually compounds made up of a combination of two or more elements in different proportions. For example, water is frequently called by its chemical formula H_2O, a compound, made up of two atoms of hydrogen to one of oxygen.

The elements seem to be ninety-two in number, and the various atoms of which each is composed vary in weight from one to ninety-two. Let us examine a tiny microscopic atom of hydrogen, the lightest of all the elements. It is like a solar system of its own. At the center is a relatively stable charge of positive electricity known as a proton. Whirling about this, at a speed greater than that of earth or sun or stars, is a single charge of negative electricity known as an electron. All electrons are of equal weight, but the other elements have greater weight than hydrogen because instead of having one proton and one electron they have many light electrons and many much heavier protons. Some of these atoms, as uranium, are exceedingly complex. Uranium "seems to have (1) a core of 238 hydrogen nuclei or protons; and (2) along with these, 146 inner electrons; and (3) outside these again, 92 outer electrons." [4] As already indicated in the infinitely slow transformation of uranium into lead, at intervals the atoms give up electrons. When this occurs, one element is transformed into a different element, heat and energy being created in the process. But heat and energy are a continuous product of the constant and extraordinarily rapid motion of molecule, atom, and electron. Is it necessary that we should capture this potential energy and harness it to a modern power house, in order to show its importance in the new renaissance?

In our studies into the smallest of the things that go to make up matter, we find a marvelous simplicity. This is the basis of a still more marvelous complexity of compounds, especially in the cells of living organisms. In the world about us our knowledge of ourselves and the universe comes not only from the submicroscopic studies of physics and chemis-

[4] Sir J. Arthur Thomson, *Modern Science*, G. P. Putnam's Sons, p. 94.

try but from the photo-telescopic researches of different astronomical observatories. Scientists have mapped but a small part of the heavens, but we find the stars of our own universe, according to the estimate of Frederick Hanley Seares, nearly five million times as numerous as those which Galileo was able to observe, although other estimates exceed his, some being five times as large. This includes only our own universe or galactic system. Outside this we have a large number of nebulae, of which two million are made visible on the photographic plate by the one-hundred-inch reflector at the Mt. Wilson Observatory. If each of these universes averages as large as our own, and if a larger number will be revealed by the new two-hundred-inch reflector of the Rockefeller Observatory, our imaginations will be staggered still more by any attempt to grasp the magnitude of the creation. If Walter S. Adams and Albert Einstein are right, these universes occupy a finite rather than an unlimited area. Already astronomical observation and experimentation are giving us a real understanding of the composition of celestial bodies, of the origin of universes, and of materials necessary to a better comprehension of other sciences.

This knowledge may not be essential to life, but it gives us some relative knowledge if not knowledge of relativity. Light, according to the last and rather satisfactory studies of Michelson, travels at the rate of 186,285 miles per second. Our own universe is probably from 250 to 350 thousand light years in length, possibly one third as wide, although very much thinner. A few years ago we had penetrated one hundred forty million light years into space; now we have more than doubled that distance; soon that distance will be dwarfed. More important than distance is the knowledge we have gained of gases, of solids, and of processes that took place when the star light which we see now was being emitted.

Applied physical science

The physical sciences are used daily in the life of all civilized people. The uses of chemistry in business are multifold. Without electricity, itself a transformation, the Industrial Revolution would have stopped far short of its present reach and level. In the household we are continually using these

conveniences, some of which turn darkness into light, as for
example an electric bulb, purchased for a few cents and worth
several dozen of great grandmother's candles, besides the convenience and saving of costs. Woman's emancipation has been
promoted greatly by conveniences which are applications of
science. The friction match reduced for our grandfathers and
grandmothers the work and the bother of using tapers or
keeping fires alive. Gas or electric stoves contribute their
share. Vacuum cleaners save attention at rush hours or do a
much better job with very much less work. The home is
furnished with numerous synthetic and rather inexpensive articles. Lenses are not simply convenient for elders and a great
many younger people in reading, but without them we should
still be geocentric and provincial in our ideas, not knowing
any worlds but our own. Without science there would be no
inexpensive fuel for the family automobile, and no automobiles within the purse of the average family.

Science has upset many old businesses by the creation of
products which nature does not provide lavishly. Elsewhere
we have considered the economic influence of these products
upon business. From the standpoint of culture these results
are not negligible. Unemployment or shift of occupation has
frequently resulted from new inventions or applications of
science which have thrown out of work those employed in the
older process. The amount of unemployment caused in this
way is probably little, for the new demand may be greater
than the old. That does not always solve the problem of the
displaced worker or of the country, which now must seek
other fields, not for conquest but for export and trade advantage. Artificial indigo, more uniform and cheaper than
the natural product, practically drove out of existence the
plantations formerly devoted to that commodity. Synthetic
nitrates are responsible, it is said, for four revolutions in western South America. Yet on high authority it is stated that
the world's commerce was promoted rather than retarded by
the substitution of these compounds for natural commodities.
The making of artificial ammonia has upset the businesses
which formerly provided the trade with that article. The

point to be noted here is not the effect upon business, but the improved level and raised standard of living which has resulted from cheap factory production of goods formerly produced by nature in small quantities and within limited areas. It is impossible to detail the numerous means by which science has made life easier, more comfortable, and more worthwhile.

The peace of the world should be promoted by scientists, who are natural internationalists. They belong to no country, and their achievements to no definite time, after the work has been begun. War interferes with the exchange of ideas and achievements in different sciences. Yet war itself has been made so destructive by science that unless science can conquer war, war will destroy both science and civilization. Before the end of the World War science laboratories in America, in Britain, France and Germany had developed gases so deadly that their use would have ended that war. Those gases and others even more inimical should make impossible any thought of another war among civilized peoples. Science should create a socio-political philosophy which will not tolerate barbaric or military struggles over petty or major difficulties of nations or groups of nations. The philosophy of today, used not by a statesman or a social leader, but by the research student or the academic scholar is a philosophy of science rather than a philosophy of inherited ideas. Modern philosophy not only adopts principles accepted as true in scientific study and checked by comparison with scientific data; but it develops new concepts and standards suggested by science.

Humanity in general may not have gained and may never gain universally any true conception of matter, of life, of mind, and of creation. Nevertheless, modern science and modern scientific methods have changed for us absolutely the world of which we are as well as the world in which we live. From our viewpoint our ancestors had about themselves and their work and their surroundings a very limited conception; to us their ideas seem provincial. We must readjust our thought to realities of what is literally a new heaven and a new earth. In this improved environment do we voluntarily remain provincial? The transformations of applied science cause amazement, whether we are dealing with every-day affairs like the telephone or an incandescent light or with new marvels such as television. The internal combustion engine and electricity, by reducing space and time, are helping to make the whole world kin. The accomplishments of Aladdin's genii were not more marvelous than are the wonders conjured by the Wizard of Menlo Park or by the research magicians of Manhattan or of Leipzig.

SCIENCE AND SOCIETY

Science gave us the Machine-Power Age, the Technological Age. Without science the economy of scarcity would never have started to become an economy of plenty. Aside from the marvellous changes in our material civilization, how much has science made us different, affected our thought, improved our culture? The wands that we wave reduce distance, people our world with mechanical slaves to do our bidding, multiply the "reach" of arm, foot, eye, and tongue. Have the aids to the senses stimulated more brain action? If so, has a quickened cortex made us more cognizant of our capacities, more responsive to human needs, and more adaptable to social demands? If so, why does Guy Stanton Ford remark: "The newest in science is accepted without question, while the most timid suggestions of social and political readjustment and the most evident parallels from history are rejected without hesitation, [—these differences] are a challenging comment on science and civilization." [5]

Limits of science in practical affairs

Science and the scientific method probably have not transformed human thinking greatly, especially mass thinking. Scholars and some leaders, reasoning from fact to conclusion, understand well the underlying facts of life and modern society, and apply this knowledge to practical affairs. In some slight degree, science has been able to overcome the vagaries of men's minds, substitute reasonable actions for superstition or other inherited ways of doing things, and redirect social

[5] *Science and Civilization*, Number One, The Day and Hour Series, University of Minnesota, 1933, p. 9.

thought or re-motivate emotion. In their laboratories captains of industry have paid high-geared scientists low-priced salaries to invent or perfect labor-saving technics. In managing big business or dominating public affairs, economic and political leaders seldom have been bothered about gaining scientific knowledge or understanding scientific principles about the fields in which they were leading followers equally blind—or uninformed.[6]

Poverty of thought in leadership is not blamable on science but may be due to a lack of understanding and to the unscientific use of observed facts. Scientists themselves have usually been unable to apply their methods to human problems or to discover important principles involved in a study of society. Does the human equation upset calculations? Are dynamic situations too difficult for analysis by scientific methods usually applied to static or theoretical conditions? The scientist of society is far behind his fellow biologist or chemist. The research scientist is not much better, or not so good, if when dealing with human problems he argues from a major premise that is not even social fact, only a supposition or an analogy.

Difficulties
in developing
a science of
society

Evidently we need to bridge the gap between pure science and science as applied to society. Again quoting from Dean Ford, "The object of science is neither to destroy nor to defend. It recognizes no ancient authority whether creedal or moral, esthetic, economic, or political. Armed only with a question mark it challenges man and nature and forces mankind in the end to build the fortress of civilization upon firmer and higher ground." [7]

"If we turn now to ask what is the most characteristic social result of science and invention, the answer can be put briefly. The result of science is to illustrate, emphasize, and increase

---

[6] Pages of recent history are replete with proofs that either these leaders have not been more than "exposed" to science or that there has been no "carry over" of scientific knowledge into affairs of society. A splendid example of needed information and understanding is furnished in Beard's *America Faces the Future*. André Maurois cites the comments of more than a score of business leaders made in the fall of 1929 on the events of that trying period.

[7] *Science and Civilization*, p. 6.

the interdependence of men and nations. This revelation through science of interdependence and unity arises from the very nature of science itself. Science is not interested in individuals. There is no science possible if only a single thing is investigated. If what was observed by the scientist applied to one thing alone and to no other thing or series of related things wherever they may be found in nature, it would not be science. Science seeks the laws that bind phenomena together and then goes on to find higher and more universal laws under which wider and wider reaches of the apparently unlike must be rearranged in bondage to their basic common likenesses. There is no science of single things. Every scientific law that is discovered is a new revelation of unity and draws nature into a new community life while it makes the world about us smaller as each new likeness is revealed." [8]

It would not be fair to ask how much science is responsible for the most serious of our present dilemmas. If it were, we should probably be unable either to trace that connection and determine that responsibility or to discover ways in which science could dissolve any dilemma of its creation. Its impersonal character, without thought of purpose or result, humanly speaking, makes it an instrument of change but not a formula for relief. In itself it is therefore neither social or anti-social. When it places in the hands of those whose motives are also neither social or anti-social, though thoroughly selfish, if only selfishly ambitious, it ceases to have socially the impartial, disinterested character which makes it science, which distinguishes the real scientist.

Much as bio-chemistry links the physical and the biological sciences, so psychology may some day link the nature sciences with those which are more distinctively human or social. Biology in some form is necessarily the foundation for all society, and therefore underlies any type of human organization, and in the end, human civilization. Psychology formerly was treated as a physiological science and necessarily has a physiological and neurological basis. *Possibly psychology, especially social psychology, might be a means of bringing to*

Science and the social sciences

[8] *Ibid.*, p. 14.

the social sciences some of the special gains of science which we have not yet been able to capture and make our servants in the special fields of human relations and experience. The chemist and the engineer make nature the servant of man and raise man's standard of living. Can the social psychologist and the human engineer make mankind a better servant of humanity to raise the standards of life and of thought?

The ways of the research scientist and of the engineer probably will not be the ways of the human engineer. But the one who is trying to use the gains of science directly or indirectly in social relations, and for human betterment, may well take some leaves out of the book of the scientist. First of all it probably will be helpful never to lose sight of the close connection between pure science and applied,[9] in distinctively human relations as well as in those primarily industrial. Secondly, if advances in science are gained through constant experiments under semi-theoretical conditions, that method of study should not be overlooked by the human scientist. We must keep in mind, however, the fact that the scientist works usually with non-living materials and can study his specimens and their reactions without the limitations which the social scientist finds in dealing with living persons who must be studied under living conditions. It is practically impossible to isolate an individual or a human group and experiment on him or it without limitation or regard for results.

Scientific methods as such can probably not be carried over into these laboratories of human experimentation. It may be necessary to revamp *scientific attitudes* as well. The worker with human beings may seek only the truth; but he cannot cut his way ruthlessly through to that goal. To reach it he cannot sacrifice a human life. He may not cripple one of his controls. He should not leave the group with which he works less capable and less free to face the future. To an impersonal and objective point of view he must add a willingness to find human betterment, if he can, because that may be, socially, more important than truth. Consequently, most social workers see the goal and retain only those discoveries which will carry

---

[9] See pp. 91–92, 558–563.

them toward it. As the editor of a study on many types of psychology remarks, a disinterested psychological observer, impartial though he tries to make himself, almost always will bolster up his theory by facts discovered by even the most careful laboratory investigations.[10]

If seekers of truth in the fields of social science attack too big a field, they will do what pseudo-scientists have done when they attempt the same. Yet for them much more than for the scientist a vision of the whole is rather essential. A scientist, absolutely without bias in making investigations in his own work, may be absolutely unable to discuss politics or religion or personalities without being dominated by emotion and showing the most violent prejudices and even irrational methods of thinking. If the objective scientist is thus handicapped, how shall the social scientist escape the emotional twists of his preferences and possibly prejudices, and avoid the pitfalls in reasoning which his early training, or lack of training, or emotional immaturity would place before him?

To discover the gains of science, and apply them not as applied science but as remedial human science, is one of the great needs of the present age. Until we can do that, there will always be the danger, if not a threat, that we shall lose the best that science should have given us for several reasons. First, scientific contributions outside the field of science might easily be chiefly in the field of material "culture." Secondly, science, the chief creator of modern civilization, may increase many human and cultural lags, when the greatest social need is a reduction of those lags. Thirdly, only through the discovery of human gains, comparable with those of science, if not corresponding with those gains, can human civilization in this dynamic age become safe for humanity.

If science itself cannot close, or bridge, the gap between its advance and the lag of correlated institutions, can it help us find a substitute which will really bridge the gap? Science has helped to destroy individualism, for the gains of science are of value only when widely used. Science did not do this directly, for too much individuals kept not the use but the

[10] Murchison, Carl, *Psychologies of 1925*, Preface.

profits of scientific progress, until the slowing down of the use caused protest and led to general extension of the invention or idea. In general education and in government science has made a beginning by showing the value of facts and of careful, accurate study of those facts. Even the minor investigations of Senate committees and the Federal Trade Commission provide material on public problems which show much that is wrong with our politico-economic system. These have barely scratched the surface of the whole field of socio-public conditions, relations and problems. Scientific investigations of politics or comparative government and the political trend would throw at least a few beams of light on what is wrong with our present system. Apparently one of the greatest present needs is a greater ability to use science for the good of society.

XX

CONCLUSION

To lift the veil of the future would be a vain if profitable task. How many in February 1929 looked forward to the conditions of February 1932, and how many in February 1933 anticipated the sharp changes of the following spring or summer and the possible, or probable, changes of the years just ahead? Careful studies of recent social changes define the very uneven progress humanity makes in different fields. It is impossible for law and religion to keep up with science and invention, except by rashly artificial stimulus or revolutionary readjustment. The rank and file follow rather intelligently— at least such is our boast in America—provided it is their material interest to do so.

Quo vadis?
Whither America?

Will the dilemmas of capitalism and of industrialism disappear as we advance? Can we look for any greater concentration of power in guiding investment, directing industry, and controlling consumption than was possessed potentially by the great clique of dominant American financiers of the "New Era"? What a lost opportunity was theirs! *The integration of almost all important business and close coördination of government and business was within their grasp.* What a mess for which they sold their opportunity; possibly because the birthright was not theirs but society's! Can any other group, in the name of the public, or of humanity, or of civilization, in the near future, gain equal authority? Will their successors in control avoid their mistakes, provide clear-visioned leadership and make American civilization safe for America?

WESTERN CIVILIZATION—AN OVERVIEW

To describe western civilization before this present renaissance as conservative, traditional, or semi-static may be mean-

General

567

ingless. Yet in contrast the new seems radical, breaks with tradition, and is dynamic. Certain it is that whatever may be the outcome of the present reorganization it will depend upon the same human nature as the old and will reach back in more ways than one to the accomplishments of our prehistoric ancestors. There is likely to be more difference in size than in character between international organization of the near future and that of kingdoms, formed out of tribes before the dawn of history. The principles according to which the group regulated business and social relations, as revealed by the Sumerian code of very early historic times, differ very little from the principles upon which economic relationships and social obligations are being reëstablished. The family of the early agricultural period still has a real resemblance to the present family; and its norms may continue with relatively little change. The reorganized family probably will meet well both the needs of human nature and the requirements of society in the later machine age.

Material "culture"

The clock of time can not be turned backward from industrialism to agriculturalism any more than the neolithic period could return from agriculture to hunting as its main source of living. Since machines can not supply directly the most important human necessity, food, the development of adequate supplies is making radical changes in food production and distribution. One of these is the utilization of the scientific knowledge, procedure, and technics which we have been gaining, although time-honored methods rather than a scientific agriculture still dominates the production of most foods in most civilized countries. The Russian agricultural experiment is an attempt to wipe out an old system, much more antiquated than that of the United States, substituting for it a huge mass type, possibly neither scientific nor modern.

In the actual changes from preceding centuries to the present the most conspicuous differences are noted in industrial capitalism and science. In assessing gains of today over yesterday we should be unfair as well as misinformed did we belittle or undervalue the astounding productivity of a machine-power industry. Because economic organization may be primary, new forms of power, new, more effective methods of production, and a vast new surplus wealth have made changes inevitable in society and government as well as business. Since before the dawn of history man has lived in groups and the groups have been directed by an individual leader or a set of rulers. These leaders may not have been the most wealthy, but their power has usually been based upon business as well as exercised through government. The new age has accentuated sharply the power of captains of industry. They may or may not control governments—usually they do—but they dominate occupations and persons including possibly the preparation and the daily lives of those who earn their living or furnish the supplies under the aegis of the money power.

Industrial capitalism may not be the ultimate form of modern economic organization but it certainly is the controlling element of our twentieth-century civilization. The successes of industrial capitalism, and its concentrated authority, evils though they may appear to socialist or communist, after all give promise of necessary and successful reorganization. *Because wealth is concentrated it can be made responsible.* It can be held accountable not only for the wise and satisfactory administration of any government which it may control, but for desirable improvements and developments in the political reorganization necessary in the twentieth century. Capitalism in the new age will not stand or fall on its successes or failures in government, nor will it prove itself by its successes or non-successes as a money-making institution. *Industrial capitalism is too much the heart of our present order, social and economic, to be excused on the ground that it is business and only business.* If anyone thinks that its concern can be solely the making of profit, notice the number of ways in which it permeates every part of our social structure, not only business and government. Before any new order worthy of the name can be created, it is therefore necessary to face the dilemmas of both industrialism and financialism. If neither can go forward easily or go back at all, in what direction can we proceed?

One of the most difficult economic readjustments from the

old order to the new has been caused by the survival of old rules conferring privileges and rights which have become most unsatisfactory from the social viewpoint and most *inadequate as a means of protecting the public.* Prominent among these is the use by the giant corporation—a legal creature wisely created to accomplish what natural persons could not do— of the rights and immunities of persons. This economic leviathan has made itself great by arrogating to itself legal rights which enabled it to pool wealth, and exploit natural resources of a public character, without accepting the corresponding obligations.

Social and public relations   *The problem of government reorganization is almost as much economic as political.* In domestic affairs there is need for a political system which shall be efficient, though not managed like a business, in relation to business and public. If it hopes for success, this public reorganization must fit a reconstructed industrial capitalism and be properly coördinated with it. In international affairs the new political world is more than national; and it is international largely because business has led the way and is setting the pace. Nationalism is not a spent force, but self-sufficing nations, like kings, may have had their day. *Only by the acceptance of international limitations analogous to the constitutional bounds placed upon despots a century or two ago can nations hope to survive.*

Democracy, which seemed in the ascendent during the World War and in eclipse following that conflict, is coming more and more into its own. Its spirit is pervading every phase of human life. The individual is becoming more self-directing, if not in the earning of a living at least in his education, in his thought, and in the use of his own time. The present family is distinguished from that of the past largely by being democratic in character; but the new family is likely to be organized upon democratic principles far more than the present realizes.

The family is already well on its way toward reorganization. One cannot agree with some writers that the worst is past and the main lines of reorganization are already determined.

That seems improbable. The traditional family, often designated as patriarchal, has little place in a really modern world.
"Family disorganization must of course be seen as a natural
and inevitable consequence of a changing social order. It is
as desirable as it is inevitable."[1] A carry-over from the individualism of the great Renaissance and the individualism
of eighteenth-century democracy is leaving, within the family,
temporarily much more to individual tastes and interests than
the past permitted, and possibly more than the future is likely
to consider wise.

One of the most certain although possibly little conspicuous trends of the present age is *socialization that regards
the individual highly.* This is not yet sharply noticeable in public life; but it is coming more and more to the fore
in business; and it may influence our whole social organization as the years pass. Recent human experience has given
us a consciousness of the individual and of his right to self-
direction denied him in all civilized history. Our new social
democracy is permeated with these ideas. There is every
reason to believe that the new family will give both woman
and child an independence, a self-determination under social
control, which no past age has granted. Far more than land
predetermines the agricultural problem of the new age, family
relations are predetermined by sex and by social interests and
responsibilities second only to the necessity of securing a general supply of food.

The present world is different from the past and the new
age will be different from the present because more attention
is being paid to individual and group preparation for the
future. Three needs are paramount: a public understanding
of what education should be, more preparation for leadership,
and a better directed development of individual and group
training for the new age.

Religion of the old type is on the decline. Religion is doing
what is has done for ages—abandoning to secular interest
many fields which formerly were deemed religious. By ceasing
to be extensive there is promise that religion, becoming more

[1] Reuter and Runner, *The Family,* p. 478.

intensive, will get a clearer idea of itself, a better concept of Deity, and a clearer realization of the service by which religion should be measured in the future.

General
summary

Humanity may not advance by leaps and bounds, but it does make progress by rebounds. The Great Renaissance was not chiefly a reaction against medieval civilization. Its name indicates a rebirth of old civilization and culture; but the ideas surviving from medievalism, or revived in spite of it, were cast into molds that really were new. The monarchies of the early modern period might be more or less absolute, but they were built on racial unity, upon patriotic support and upon groups with like-mindedness that never existed in ancient or feudal times. *The individualism of the Great Renaissance* represented a *goal* rather than an *achievement*, for it was not easy to change society at once or very much. That individualism which started in bud several centuries ago tried to blossom in the fields cultivated by the individualist farmers of the American frontier, in the factories of American and European manufacturers, especially in the nineteenth century. A hundred years ago progressive peoples, whether they were emerging from post-feudalism in central Europe or from frontierism in America, tried to get, in organization and in practice, the companion ideas of that day—nationality and democracy.

In Europe the dead hand of the past worked through custom or fixed institution or sanctions; consequently in Europe social reconstruction was slow and the final product was imperfect. The English, possibly the most democratic of modern peoples, still have titles of nobility; they reverence aristocracy, whatever they may say "to the contrary notwithstanding." Germany has hardly begun to escape from the *social prison houses* which held her people in bondage for so many centuries.

America had cut the Gordian knots of tradition, but the fragments she found quite inadequate for binding together her people to meet their needs well. In the first place, America was too large. In the second place, America, at least along the sea coast, was provincial. In the third place, the

American frequently could not trace his ancestry back to other generations on this continent. Melting pots may require the almost fiery heat of revolution to destroy old or different *mores,* ideas, prejudices, or ambitions.

Our solution for the problem of size, at least our political solution, *was a system of federalism.* A real union was cemented out of a group of semi-sovereign states, each of which became an integral part of the Union, though retaining its own autonomy and separate character and self-direction. This solution was begun in the eighteenth century and accomplished in the nineteenth. Politically, however, it is proving itself rather out-worn in the twentieth. The separateness of the parts interfere with the unity of the whole. State boundary lines, significant in the day of ox-carts, cease to be important in days of railroads and automobiles, especially disappear with the flight or over-view of the airplane and are invisible in the sphere of radio. State systems of law are inadequate for those who travel to Reno, who purchase materials in Michigan or fuels in Texas, and who sell their products in every state, even in all the ports bordering on the Seven Seas. Federalism as a political system may need to be modified, but *federalism as a pattern for social organization and action has hardly sprung into imagination, let alone thought or action.* Consider how the principle of unity with diversity may become a satisfactory type of organization, a social pattern, in almost every field, or group of contacts, in a complex modern society.

The American people have gone a long way toward creating a new civilization built upon the principles of social federalism, democratically directed. The materialism of large-scale mass-production has not sufficed to bury the possibilities of this new epoch-making idea and organization. The class distinctions arising out of capitalism—and in the last analysis historical classes have been created by separating those who have from those who have not—has only blurred the picture of a highly integrated society in which each individual or small coöperating group has its place and share. As society solves the dilemma of industrialism and capitalism, there is no good reason why necessary and desirable economic changes and the co-related political readjustments should not give new impetus to this movement of creating something new, socially. Will society, at least the American people, answer this social responsibility? Will it fail of its opportunity? Can it realize or even approximate its ideal?

OUR GREAT NEED IN THE NEW AGE

Is humanity growing up?

Human experience has been far more accidental than planned. Intelligent direction of humanity's affairs is occasional rather than persistent, in very limited or narrow areas, not even attempted in the whole field of either economic or political reorganization. The social order, as distinct from that of business or government, is a residue of social heritage plus a by-product of the existing régime. Rarely can any conscious effort remake the social structure. Dents in some offensive, projecting surface of the social structure by reformers, by disgruntled onlookers or by oppressed, revolting victims may temporarily make some social monstrosity less odious, may relieve some inner social pressure. But as a substitute for intelligent, scientific reorganization most social reform is absurd in theory and a failure in practice.

A program of "recovery" is simple compared with a philosophy of civilization, on which reorganization must be based. What a pity that we have so little understanding of social psychology! It might throw a flood of light upon humanity's possible further advance. But, the past makes us optimistic. If creation is not static, and men, with kinship to the animal kingdom, have reached their present relatively high level by working together, with a common purpose and for common ends, *present coöperation can develop endlessly.* The self-seeking of business, the narrowness of culture, the envious strife of nations: these are incidents of immaturity, to be sluffed off as the years pass and their unwisdom becomes apparent. *The stature of manhood, for the whole human race, is not for us or of our day.* Yet is it too much to ask that we put away as childish things those toys, like armies, and fears, as the dread of others different from ourselves, and complexes such as progress by pulling down rivals, with which the child-hood of humanity has been obsessed? So far as we fail to make necessary adaptations to new conditions, do we fail because we still are children, refusing to face our problems, unwilling to grow up?

As we mature, and most of us hope we are escaping infancy, if we make the most of our changing civilization, it is inevitable that we apply different standards than the past approved and found necessary. In an age of scarcity industry had a different meaning from that essential in an age of abundance. "Blessed be drudgery" may still be true in working out individual salvation; but drudgery as the basis of worldly success yields to intelligent industry at worth-while tasks. If the California Institute of Technology experts spend years watching a drip process to find the elements of the atom, the patience required of the research scientist may be duplicated in other constructive work. When the skilled artisan advances his adjustments from $\frac{1}{500}$ of an inch to $\frac{1}{5000}$, accuracy and carefulness are better measures of the new order than of the old. For the new Mt. Palomar telescopic mirror the variation from accurate curve is nowhere more than $\frac{1}{1000}$ of $\frac{1}{1000}$ inch.

Some new standards (margin note)

Speaking of the new ethical standards a well known educationist referred to honesty as an outworn attribute, no longer a virtue. The writer did not ask him what he meant; he simply disagreed. Honesty may not have seemed the best policy before Cervantes' time; but it was a professed business policy of one of our unscrupulous post-Civil War speculators. "Caveat emptor" was excuse for all kinds of chicanery and swindle, during an age of individualism. Even among good church members David Harum's iron rule was honored above the golden rule in practice. "Do unto the other fellow what he would do to you, only do it fust." In those days patent medicine, even more than now, was taken at the risk of the consumer. If the buyer was able to bargain without hindrance, why have a government interfere? It was his business if he bought sand with his sugar, balky horses for racers or dry oil wells. A change of heart, socially, is not due simply to the difficulty a consumer today has in discovering the quality of goods, therefore "caveat vendor." Nor is it the result of new public preference for paternalism. It arises out of a growing consciousness of public responsibility.

The old honesty was chiefly a matter of dollars. Is the new? How many men's word is as good as their bond? Yet in Wall Street a second's decision to buy or sell must be kept at all hazards; the dishonesty or overreaching must occur in some other way. Or does Wall Street, and do most of us, have one standard for friends and associates, another for outsiders? If there is more frankness than formerly, is there less mental dishonesty? As a wife becomes less subservient to one formerly "lord and master," is she tempted so often to petty deceit? Youth that is no longer under a rule of iron, with greater self-direction and more responsibility, tends to become more, or less, honest, do you think? If there is more cheating in examinations than once was true, is it due to the substitution of honor schemes for strictly supervised contests; or is it the fault of the "new type" test, in which cheating is easier? Reverting to business again, if a man has control of most of a supply and charges accordingly, does a socialized society countenance his asking much more than his articles are worth? Will society provide for him the "conscience" that does not permit the charging of three prices; and see that he uses it?

New standards for old *The substitution of social responsibility or public control for individual initiative or personal bargaining might seem to show a lowering of the ethical standards of the individual.* If humanity is growing up, are the individual members less able to take care of themselves? Is self-control less necessary because the public limits the danger of injury? Is personal responsibility for training lowered by a lengthened period of education? Will socialization reduce chances for individual growth? In short have we reduced standards of individual attainment in the transition from individualism to socialization? Before answering, consider whether coöperation requires less self-development than does self-help. The need of intelligent personal and group responsibility is certainly greater in a complex, integrated society than in one little organized and with few contacts and interrelations for the members. A democratic government asks of the voters more intelligence, better understanding, more constant coöperation than any other. What about a *society* that represents perfected group organization of all kinds, each group perfected from within?

New standards for old are probably a necessary part of a transition from an agricultural civilization to one that is industrial. Health and hygiene requirements are higher, partly because there are more dangers in congested cities and more risk that disease may spread. Personal preferences must frequently be subordinated to public need. One great gain of the present is the releasing of many unmoral inhibitions. Badly as crime is defined, for our laws on "stealing" and other offenses are very inconsistent, it seems not to be on the increase, at least from 1900 to 1930, much as we hear of the spread of lawlessness. Delinquency and personal immorality are different from that of the past, partly because youth's code does not always agree with that of the elders. Unquestionably temptation is very much greater; and the movie and the automobile do not help. It is doubtful whether the bootlegger and the racketeer have misled the present generation as much as the successful buccaneer did that of a half century ago. Certainly our captains of industry and the new masters of capital have much higher ethical standards than those operating before 1900. In public life we do not tolerate the personal lapses of the heroic days or the open corruption of the older democracy. Our ethical balance sheet, compared with that of our ancestors, shows some losses but many gains.

Possibly humanity's greatest necessity is a re-creation of social and ethical standards. The individual or the group has deemed itself moral and religious if it conformed to the criteria borrowed from its ancestors, and accepted practically without thought from generation to generation. The disintegrating character of any renaissance or revolutionary movement is most marked in the abandonment of accepted rules which do not appeal to wish or apply to reason in the new age. Slowly and painfully society discovers new and it believes *more rational bases* upon which proper conduct shall be determined.

Whether an action is individually or socially right or wrong will not then be left haphazard or to chance. In a materialist age little time and thought can be spared for a study, a formulation and a restatement of these necessary standards, many of which must reverse ideas represented by the old system. So the war between tradition and change goes on. The conservative clings to what it has both because it is old and because it has seemed good. The modern demands a set of new social action patterns which shall involve up-to-date principles and reasonable ideas and standards. It asks for norms which shall correspond with human nature and meet the needs of the new age. Time will tell whether we are moving in circles or whether *humanity is marching rather steadily uphill.*

Needed: A New Philosophy of Civilization

Values and proportions

Maturity and wisdom, even a gentle measure of each, bring changing *concepts of value.* In some ways it was a useless venture for long past generations to figure out the items on which time, effort or wealth should be expended. The choices were too few; the possibilities of change too limited and too hampered by usage or by scarcity. Our generation is among the first, blessed or cursed with potential plenty,[2] to face the problem of possible, intelligent, planned reorganization. Fortunately fate drives us forward and divine discontent forces where wisdom fails. We may not stand still or use only socially approved standards. Isolation and provincialism are almost obsolete for communities that are alive. We may not choose between coöperation, or its opposite, with our fellows. We can only choose, perhaps a Hobson's choice, within very narrow limits, among the types of those forced upon us, and the duration of their use.

The rebuilding of a civilization is not hopeless, but we must change the standards by which we evaluate; and we must actually revaluate. Because we have put too many of our eggs in an industrial basket, we had too much omelet in the depression. There are not eggs enough left for music, educa-

---

[2] The potential plenty is found in only a very, very few phases of our whole work and life together.

tion, voluntary leisure and religion. Too highly we prize the creation of wealth, and, sadly enough the created wealth must be personal—the corporation being a person by the way—not general. Otherwise we would not voluntarily reduce our product to produce profit or hoard a surplus which involves poverty for others. Too often we judge values by the price-mark on the article. In recent years there have been several instances of great musicians standing on street corners offering freely to hurrying and unheeding throngs selections that soon after commanded five dollars a seat from the community's best known patrons of art. Jenny Lind had an interesting experience. Caught in an out-of-the-way village in which she was not known, she was allowed to take part in a local song contest. To her surprise she polled only one vote, from an old fellow who had told her that she might compete—and felt sorry for the stranger.

Often we deem law the ultimate standard, and measure all things in terms of legality; but law is a laggard, never quite up-to-date at its best, and at its worst the quintessence of tyranny. Often it may be the dead hand of the past. What price legality at the cost of either justice or progress! The challenge of a new day cannot be satisfied by material reconstruction alone. Ethical revaluations must be based on spiritual standards as well. Sacrifice and service must find a place with self-interest, lest the new like the old fail because of our short-vision. No lesson of the past is clearer than this: selfishness and dishonesty are anti-social and correspondingly self-destructive in a social world.

Present-day civilization would be better were it better balanced. *Values determine proportions*, but with us, as with the heathen in their blindness, tradition outbalances readjustment and materialism obscures culture. Production is everything, consumption nothing. Individualism has had more than its share, as shown in the survival of rural democracy.

Like the ingredients of a cake *the elements of a civilization must be properly proportioned*. What could we think of a farmer who combined 100 acres of land, the hand labor of one man, without power machines, a sack of fertilizer and five bushels of seed wheat? Possibly the ideal combination is denied any society because some thing is always too abundant and some other thing always too scarce. The right proportions of a civilization cannot be decided in advance or for all time. They vary with circumstance. They certainly would change radically from a society in which capital was scarce to one surfeited with wealth. *Every important invention, each new social demand, all national or international departures from tradition cause a resifting of the materials to be combined, and a reshifting of proportions in combination.* From the cultivated field to the huge industrial plant, from the governing of a village to the management of the public affairs in a great country, if the best results are to be obtained, there must not be too much or too little of any one factor or element of which the whole is made. It is not enough to get the exact proportions for production or international trade alone, for consumption must have its share and national business only its allotted part of the well-balanced scheme of things. We need therefore more than good proportions according to wise human evaluation; but *we need better proportions for the whole system,* as well as its many parts.

Coördination and integration

Trial and error is a universal method of learning, but none would laud it as a wise use of gray matter. What happens when a world that calls itself civilized depends on a social system—and a non-social order—built largely upon trial and error, but in which even further use of these blind agents is *verboten* by custom, law, or vested interests? We have done better than that in our rather stupid civilization, at least in our business development. A real case can be made out for big business because it has been adaptable and progressive. Competition had a high historical value, if it has low survival utility. It stimulated initiative, enterprise, and efficient organization. It kept the competitors on their toes, for the struggle was never over and the victory was to the swift and to the persistent. Competition's mistakes and limitations were so self-evident that they compelled *coöperation.* Too often the survival of the fittest was the elimination of the more worthy and the fair dealing. Our way out is not unselfishness, for that may have too low standards of efficiency and of progress. But, in the interest of success, the short-sighted selfishness, the unfair trade practices and the anti-social methods of the past should not again be permitted. They are too destructive of business as well as society. They would bring chaos where a little sensible coöperation would establish order. Self-interest need not be abandoned. All it needs is a little redirection and a better articulation with social advance —a simple lesson but one we continually relearn and are as constantly forgetting.

No one would think of driving an automobile with the carburetor, the timer, and the valves working at cross purposes. If he did, he would take it out in thinking; he would not even get the thing started. Without proper *correlation* of its parts, business proceeds haltingly and a social order wonders what is wrong with itself. The best part of America's political machine is the brakes, for in the eighteenth century individualism's dread of despotism gave us *a remarkable system of checks and balances.* The bourgeoisie made a tremendous improvement over the privileged class order of the ancient régime; but where is the sturdy middle class which was the chief pride of the late nineteenth century? If most Americans become identified with it by inheritance or by education —that is no longer possible by occupation—perhaps they can furnish a social nucleus around which a highly *coördinated group organization* may be developed.

What Bach did in music, Newton in science, Adam Smith in the old economics, needs redoing in religion, social relations and public economics in our day. Any old Stradivarius is sufficient for the master, as the heritage of the race is adequate for the re-builder of the future. Only a true leader and a great psychologist can overcome "the immobility of men's minds" in remaking our civilization. Fiat reconstruction has inherent limitations, being a vestigial by-product of political and social absolutism. Rulers can tell us the process of bringing the social equine to water, but only business and the public can make him drink. It's up to the social engineers to figure out the best ways to get better *integration* of the finely inter-related parts of our whole social order; it's up to us to make the system work. Upon our experience and our capacities the changing world makes this appalling demand. We need fear its challenge far less than we distrust our own ignorance.

Conclusion   As American democracy, socialized and vitalized, may give us the clue to better coöperation and coördination, American federalism may furnish the idea of probable future integration. Unity in the past has been too much arbitrary centralization, too greatly undifferentiated social solidity. The mass may have had unity, but what else had it? There was lacking all the finer adjustments and the desirable automony of the member groups or parts of the mass. Federalism is unity with diversity. Apply the principles to the relations of citizen and state, of nation to the "civilized" world, of a factory to the whole of that industry, of the family to the community. *Self-direction of the individual member or group combined with social organization and development would result in an integrated society and might help to make humanity safe for humanity.* Much that is best in individualism could thus be harmonized, even coördinated, with what is usable in socialism. All things will never be made new and there will be great danger that, time and again, like Omar Khayyám, we shall go out the same door by which we came in. Nevertheless, if humanity is to continue its upward climb, we must let our leaders discover and formulate, and mankind by experiment and growth must redetermine, *the principles of a new philosophy of civilization.* Then where shall we be? How many of us will see the task to be done; how many will be able or willing to do it?

SELECTED BOOKS FOR READING

The following titles have been selected from a very much larger number as especially usable with the different chapters of the book. For some of the others, consult the *Study Guide,* the Manual to accompany this text, in which fairly specific references are given to each topic in each chapter. No periodical references are included. The books of special usefulness are indicated by an asterisk. Titles for main sections of chapters are grouped together and separated by blank lines.

GENERAL INTRODUCTION

Randall, J. H., *Our Changing Civilization,* 1929
Recent Social Trends, 1932 (used with almost all chapters)
Encyclopedia of the Social Sciences, 1930–35 (numerous articles, especially on V and XII)
Spengler, Oswald, *The Hour of Decision,* 1934

Hobhouse, L. T., *Elements of Social Justice,* 1922
*Taylor (ed.), *Contemporary Problems in the United States,* 1935
Davis, Jerome, *Capitalism and its Culture,* 1935
*Hubbard, J. B. (ed.), *Current Economic Policies,* 1934
Adams, J. T., *Our Business Civilization,* 1929
Counts, G. S. and Others, *Social Foundations of Education,* 1934
Frank, Glenn, *Thunder and Dawn,* 1932
Thomas, C. W. (ed.), *Essays in Contemporary Civilization,* 1931
Veblen, Thorstein, *Essays in Our Changing Order,* 1934

Chase, Stuart, *Men and Machines,* 1929
Robinson, J. H., *The Mind in the Making,* 1929
Dewey, John, *Human Nature and Conduct,* 1922
Siegfried, André, *America Comes of Age,* 1927
Fosdick, R. B., *The Old Savage in the New Civilization,* 1928

I ESSENTIALS IN OUR OLDER SOCIAL HERITAGE

*Chapin, F. S., *Cultural Change,* 1928 (also II)
Ellwood, C. A., *Cultural Evolution,* 1927

Thorndike, Lynn, *A Short History of Civilization,* 1926
Hedger, G. A. (ed.), *Introduction to Western Civilization,* 1933
Dorsey, G. A., *Man's Own Show, Civilization,* 1931
Usher, A. P., *History of Mechanical Inventions,* 1929

II The Industrial and Political Revolutions

Ogg, F. A. and Sharp, W. R., *The Economic Development of Modern Europe,* 1926
*Hobson, J. A., *The Evolution of Modern Capitalism,* 1926 (also IV)
Mumford, Lewis, *Technics and Civilization,* 1934
Nussbaum, F. L., *A History of the Economic Institutions of Modern Europe,* 1933
Beard, C. A. (ed.), *A Century of Progress,* 1933
Ogg, F. A., *Social Progress in Contemporary Europe,* 1912

Barnes, H. E., *World Politics in Modern Civilization,* 1930
Hayes, C. J. H., *Essays on Nationalism,* 1926
Robinson, J. H. and Beard, C. A., *The Development of Modern Europe,* 2 vols., 1929

III The World War as an Epitome of Contemporaneous Civilization

*Barnes, H. E. and Schmitt, B. E., *Recent Disclosures Concerning the Origins of the World War,* 1926
Fay, S. B., *Origins of the World War,* 1928
Renouvin, Pierre, *Immediate Origins of the War,* 1928
Cooke, W. H., *Readings in European International Relations since 1879,* 1931

Benns, C. E., *Europe since 1914,* 1935
Patterson, E. M., *The World's Economic Dilemma,* 1930 (also VII)
Bogart, E. L., *Direct and Indirect Costs of the Great World War,* 1919
Langsam, W. C., *The World since 1914,* 1933

IV Civilization in Transition—Agricultural Civilization and the Present World

*Ogburn, W. F., *Social Change,* 1922 (also X)
MacIver, R. M., *Society: Its Structure and Changes,* 1931 (also X)

Barnes, H. E., *Living in the Twentieth Century*, 1928
Wallace, H. A., *New Frontiers*, 1934 (also VIII and IX)
Beard, C. A. (ed.), *Toward Civilization*, 1930 (also V)
Hacker, L. M. and Kendrick, B. B., *The United States since 1865*, 1935
Zimmermann, E. W., *World Resources and Trade*, 1933

V THE DILEMMA OF INDUSTRIALISM

*Marshall, L. C. (ed.), *Production in the Modern Order*, 1929 (also II)
*Henderson, Fred, *Economic Consequences of Power Production*, 1933
Hamilton, W. H. (ed.), *Current Economic Problems*, 1925
*Berle, A. A. and Means, G. C., *The Modern Corporation and Private Property*, 1933
Mitchell, W. C., *Business Cycles*, 1927
Recent Economic Changes in the United States, 1929 (also IV)
Frankel, O. K. and Brandeis, L. D., *The Curse of Bigness*, 1934
Hamlin, Scoville (ed.), *The Menace of Over-Production*, 1930
Nourse, E. G. and Others, *America's Capacity to Produce*, 1934
Polakov, W. N., *The Power Age*, 1933
Rugg, Harold, *The Great Technology*, 1933
Todd, A. J., *Industry and Society*, 1933
Watkins, M. W., *Industrial Combinations and Public Policy*, 1927

VI THE DILEMMA OF FINANCIALISM

*Slichter, S. H., *Modern Economic Society*, 1931
Keynes, J. M., *Treatise on Money*, 2 vols., 1930
*Dennis, Lawrence, *Is Capitalism Doomed?*, 1932
*King, W. I., *The National Income and Its Purchasing Power*, 1930 (also XIV)
Clark, Evans and Galloway, G. B. (eds.), *The Internal Debts of the United States*, 1933
Corey, Lewis, *The House of Morgan*, 1934
Doane, R. R., *The Measurement of American Wealth*, 1933
Rogers, J. H., *America Weighs Her Gold*, 1931
Warren, G. F. and Pearson, F. A., *Prices*, 1933
Willis, H. P., Chapman, J. M., and Robey, R. W., *Contemporary Banking*, 1933

VII International Forces Affecting Industrial Capitalism

*Patterson, E. M., *The World's Economic Dilemma*, 1930 (also III)

Fraser, H. F., *Foreign Trade and World Politics*, 1926

Leith, C. K., *World Minerals and World Politics*, 1931

Beard, C. A. and Smith, G. H. E., *The Idea of National Interest*, 1934 (also XV)

*Salter, Sir Arthur, *Recovery, the Second Effort*, 1932

Feis, Herbert, *Europe, the World's Banker, 1870–1914*, 1930

Miller, F. P. and Hill, H. D., *The Giant of the Western World*, 1930

Winkler, Max, *Investments of United States Capital in Latin America*, 1929

VIII Needs, Purposes, and Means of Economic Reorganization

Ostrolenk, Bernhard, *The Surplus Farmer*, 1932

Royal Institute of International Affairs, *World Agriculture*, 1932

Gee, Wilson, *Social Economics of Agriculture*, 1932

Willcox, O. W., *Reshaping Agriculture*, 1934

*Douglas, P. H., *Real Wages in the United States, 1890–1926*, 1930 (also XIV, B)

Patterson, S. H., *Social Aspects of Industry*, 1935

*Douglas, P. H. and Director, Aaron, *The Problem of Unemployment*, 1931

Wright, P. Q. (ed.), *Unemployment as a World Problem*, 1932

Perkins, Frances, *People at Work*, 1934

Thomas, Norman, *Human Exploitation in the United States*, 1934

*Nystrom, P. H., *Economic Principles of Consumption*, 1929

Hoyt, E. E., *The Consumption of Wealth*, 1928

*Leven, Maurice and Others, *America's Capacity to Consume*, 1934 (also XIV)

Clark, Evans, *Financing the Consumer*, 1930

Hobson, J. A., *Poverty in Plenty*, 1931

Kyrk, Hazel, *Economic Problems of the Family*, 1933

Roosevelt, F. D., *Looking Forward*, 1933
Beard, C. A. and Smith, G. H. E., *The Future Comes*, 1933
Wilcox, Clair and Others, *America's Recovery Program*, 1934
Ayres, L. P., *The Economics of Recovery*, 1933
Buck, N. S. (ed.), *Survey of Contemporary Economics*, 1934
Elliott, W. Y., *The Need for Constitutional Reform*, 1935
Hoover, Herbert, *The Challenge to Liberty*, 1934

IX   A New Public Economics of Plenty

*MacIver, R. M. (ch.), *Economic Reconstruction*, 1934
Beard, C. A. (ed.), *America Faces the Future*, 1932
Soule, George, *A Planned Society*, 1932
Chase, Stuart, *A New Deal*, 1932
Hansen, A. H., *Economic Stabilization in an Unbalanced World*, 1932
Frederick, J. G. (ed.), *A Philosophy of Production*, 1930
Smith, Adam, *The Wealth of Nations*, 1776
Foster, W. T. and Catchings, Waddill, *The Road to Plenty*, 1928
Slichter, S. H., *Towards Stability*, 1934
Tugwell, R. G., *Industry's Coming of Age*, 1927

X   Old and New in Transition

*Overstreet, H. A., *We Move in New Directions* (also **XX**)
Dewey, John, *Individualism, Old and New*, 1930
Wallas, Graham, *Our Social Heritage*, 1921 (also I)
Coe, G. A., *The Motives of Men*, 1928
Cooley, C. H., *Social Organization*, 1909
Robertson, H. M., *Aspects of the Rise of Economic Individualism*, 1933

XI   Interrelations of Political and Economic Organization and Possible Effect on Dilemma

*Clark, J. M., *Social Control of Business*, 1926
Delaisi, Francis, *Political Myths and Economic Realities*, 1927 (also III)
Beard, C. A. and Beard, William, *The American Leviathan*, 1930
Merriam, C. E., *Political Power*, 1934
Beard, C. A. and Smith, G. H. E., *The Open Door at Home*, 1934

Holcombe, A. N., *Government in a Planned Democracy*, 1935

Jones, Eliot and Bigham, T. C., *Principles of Public Utilities*, 1932

Keezer, D. M. and May, Stacy, *The Public Control of Business*, 1930

MacIver, R. M., *The Modern State*, 1926

Prendergast, W. A., *The Public Utilities and the People*, 1933

XII POLITICAL DEMOCRACY AND SUBSTITUTES

*Bryce, James, *Modern Democracies*, 2 vols., 1921

Sait, E. M., *Democracy*, 1929

Laski, H. J., *Democracy in Crisis*, 1933 (also XI)

Holcombe, A. N., *Foundations of the Modern Commonwealth*, 1923

Buell, R. L. (ed.), *New Governments in Europe*, 1934

Adams, Mary (ed.), *The Modern State*, 1933

Cole, G. D. H. and Cole, M. I., *A Guide to Modern Politics*, 1934

Corwin, E. S., *The Twilight of the Supreme Court*, 1934

Haines, C. G. and Haines, B. M., *Principles and Problems of Government*, 1934

Munro, W. B., *The Governments of Europe*, 1931

Parmelee, Maurice, *Bolshevism, Fascism, and the Liberal-Democratic State*, 1934

Robinson, E. E., *Evolution of American Political Parties*, 1924

XIII SOME ESSENTIALS OF MODERN DEMOCRACY

*Graves, W. B., *Readings in Public Opinion*, 1928

*Holcombe, A. N., *The New Party Politics*, 1933

Lowell, A. L., *Public Opinion and Popular Government*, 1913

Lippmann, Walter, *Public Opinion*, 1922

*Merriam, C. E., *New Aspects of Politics*, 1925

*Mill, J. S., *On Liberty*, 1859

Bogardus, E. S., *Leaders and Leadership*, 1934

*Bryce, James, *The American Commonwealth*, Vol. II, 1911

Pound, Roscoe, *Criminal Justice in America*, 1930

Burgess, J. W., *Reconciliation of Government with Liberty*, 1915

Kent, F. R., *The Great Game of Politics*, 1923

Laski, H. J., *Liberty in the Modern State*, 1930

Moley, Raymond, *Our Criminal Courts*, 1930

XIV Welfare as a Public Responsibility

*Rubinow, I. M., *The Quest for Security*, 1934
Epstein, Abraham, *Insecurity, a Challenge to America*, 1933
Armstrong, B. N., *Insuring the Essentials*, 1932

Wood, Edith Elmer, *Recent Trends in American Housing*, 1931
National Industrial Conference Board, *The Cost of Living in the United States, 1914–1930*, 1931
Wolman, Leo in *Recent Economic Changes in the United States*, 1929
Kirkpatrick, E. L., *The Farmer's Standard of Living*, 1929
Gries, J. M. and Ford, James (eds.), *President's Conference on Home Building and Home Ownership*, 2 vols., 1933
Lynd, R. S. and Lynd, H. M., *Middletown*, 1929 (also XVI)

XV Nationalism versus Internationalism

*Schumann, F. L., *International Politics*, 1933 (also XI)
Moon, P. T., *Imperialism and World Politics*, 1926 (also III)
Buell, R. L., *International Relations*, 1929
Viallate, Achille, *Economic Imperialism and International Relations during the Last Fifty Years*, 1923 (also III)
Hayes, C. J. H., *The Historical Evolution of Modern Nationalism*, 1931
League of Nations Secretariat, *Ten Years of World Coöperation*, 1930
Shotwell, J. T., *International Problems and Relations*, 1926
Foreman, Clark, *The New Internationalism*, 1934
Hudson, M. O., *The Permanent Court of International Justice*, 1925
Stratton, G. M., *Social Psychology of International Conduct*, 1929

XVI The Changing Family

*Groves, E. R. and Ogburn, W. F., *American Marriage and Family Relationships*, 1928
Mowrer, E. R., *The Family: Its Organization and Disorganization*, 1932
Reuter, E. R. and Runner, J. R. (eds.), *The Family*, 1931
Groves, E. R., *The American Family*, 1934

Spaulding, C. A. (ed.), *Twenty-Four Views of Marriage,* 1930
Beard, Mary, *On Understanding Women,* 1931
Breckinridge, S. P., *Women in the Twentieth Century,* 1933
Folsom, J. K., *The Family,* 1934
Lichtenberger, J. P., *Divorce,* 1931

XVII Trends and Tendencies in Education

*Dewey, John, *Democracy and Education,* 1916
Meiklejohn, Alexander, *The Liberal College,* 1920
*Ogburn, W. F. and Goldenweiser, Alexander (eds.), *The Social
    Sciences and Their Interrelations,* 1927
*Kilpatrick, W. H. and Others, *The Educational Frontier,* 1933
Thorndike, E. L. and Others, *Fundamentals of Learning,* 1932
Bennett, M. E., *College and Life,* 1933
Briggs, T. H., *Secondary Education,* 1933
Eells, W. C., *The Junior College,* 1931
Flexner, Abraham, *Universities: American, English, German,*
    1930
Kilpatrick, W. H., *Education and the Social Crisis,* 1932
Thorndike, E. L. and Others, *Adult Learning,* 1928

XVIII Religion in a New World

*Niebuhr, Reinhold, *Does Civilization Need Religion?,* 1927
Rauschenbusch, H. S., *Christianity and the Social Crisis,* 1920
Whitehead, A. N., *Religion in the Making,* 1926
Hobhouse, L. T., *Morals in Evolution,* 1925
Tufts, J. H., *America's Social Morality,* 1933
Jacks, L. P., *Responsibility and Culture,* 1924 (also XX)
Lippman, Walter, *A Preface to Morals,* 1929
Mathews, Shailer, *Christianity and Social Process,* 1934

XIX Science and Civilization

Ford, G. S., *Science and Civilization,* 1933
Jeans, Sir James, *The Universe Around Us,* 1931
Thomson, J. A., *Modern Science,* 1930
Eddington, A. S., *The Nature of the Physical World,* 1928
Millikan, R. A., *Science and the New Civilization,* 1930
Morgan, T. H., *The Theory of the Gene,* 1926

XX CONCLUSION

Dewey, John, *Human Nature and Conduct,* 1922
Mumford, Lewis, *Sticks and Stones,* 1924
Whitehead, A. N., *Adventures of Ideas,* 1933
Bouglé, C. C. A., *The Evolution of Values,* 1926
Dewey, John, *Reconstruction in Philosophy,* 1920
Merriam, C. E., *Civic Education in the United States,* 1934 (also
    XVII)

INDEX

A

Academic education, 507–510, 512

Adams, W. S., 91

Adaptation of education to social needs, 521–524

Adjustment as a social process, 81–90, 167–169

Adler, Alfred, 405

Administration:

American problem of, 264;

governmental, 148–151, 206–207, 228, 237–243, 259–260, 265, 320–325, 351–352, 388–392, 393–396

Adult education, 519–520

Advertising:

229, 231–232, 416;

and the consumer, 230–232

Africa, 176–177

Aged, care of, 412–413

Agnostics, religious, 537–538

Agricultural Adjustment Administration, 206–207, 237–238

Agricultural civilization and the present world, ch. IV

Agriculturalism and industrial capitalism, 43–44

Agriculture:

early, 15;

medieval, 21–22;

problems of, 201–211;

products of, 202–204

Alphabet, 18

America:

contradictory characteristics of, 7–8;

cultural problems of, Pt. IV;

economic problems of, Pt. II;

international problems of, chs. VII, XV;

the new internationalism and, 455–457;

political problems of, chs. XI–XIII;

problem of in dynamic world, 7–9;

self-contained, 458–465;

World War and, ch. III

American courts, procedure in, 89–90

American doctrine of judicial supremacy, 348, 353

American Medical Association, 229

American Telephone and Telegraph Co., 119, 121, 122

Anderson, B. M., Jr., 190–191, 541

Antioch plan, 519

Anti-trust laws, 321, 322–323

Applied science, 28–31, 91–92, 548, 550, 553–555, 558–561, 562–566; *see also* technology

Appointments, political, 352

Arabian civilization, 6

Aristotle, 508, 551

Armies, European, 49, 50

Ashley, G. H., 540

Ashley, R. L., 288, 389

Asia, 177–178; *see also* Orientalism

Assembly, League, 448

Associations, *see* organization

Assyria, 17

Astronomers and business, 91–92

Astronomy, 558

Athens, 17, 154; *see also* Greece

Atkins, W. E., *et al.*, 231–232

Atoms, 557

Attitudes:

changing, general, *see* individualism and public;

changing, personal (individual and group), 295–296, 298–299;

changing, toward family, 495–497;

scientific, 562, 564–565

Austria, 58, 59, 60, 449

"Authority," decline of, 74–81, 299–300, 531

Autocracy: as cause of war, 62–63; to-day, 361–365

Autocratic government since World War, 65

593